D0772661

FLORA'S
ORCHIDS

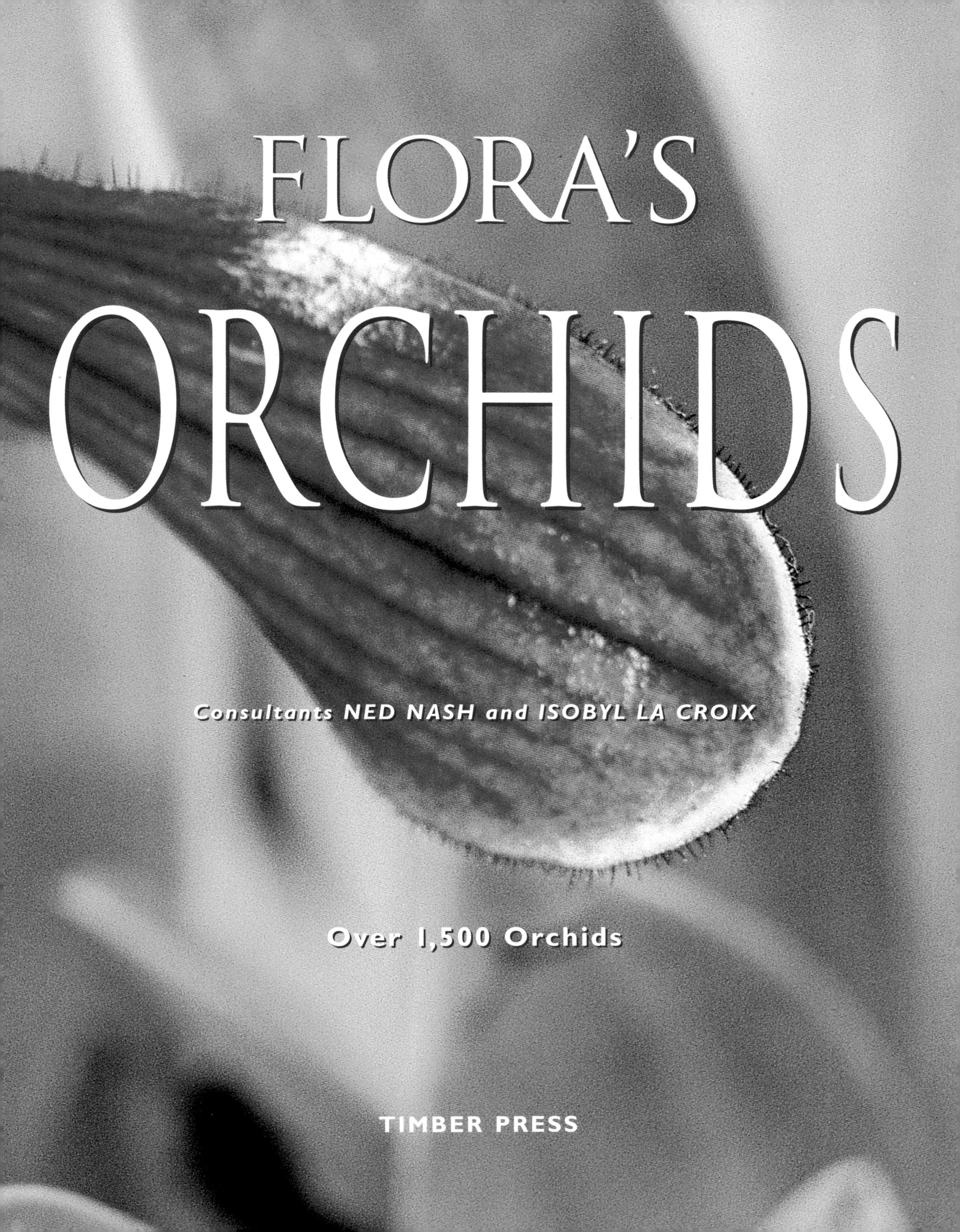

FLORA'S
ORCHIDS

Consultants *NED NASH* and *ISOBYL LA CROIX*

Over 1,500 Orchids

TIMBER PRESS

This edition published in 2005 by Timber Press
133 SW 2nd Ave., Ste. 450, Portland, Oregon 97204, USA
Website: www.timberpress.com

For contact information for editorial, marketing, sales, and distribution in the United Kingdom, see www.timberpress.com/uk.

Produced by Global Book Publishing Pty Ltd
Unit 1, 181 High Street, Willoughby, NSW 2068, Australia
Ph 612 9967 3100   Fax 612 9967 5891
Email rightsmanager@globalpub.com.au

All rights reserved. No part of this publication may be reproduced,
stored in a retrieval system, or transmitted in any form or by any
means, electronic, mechanical, photocopying, recording, or otherwise, without the prior written permission of the Publisher.

This publication and arrangement
© Global Book Publishing Pty Ltd 2005
Photographs © Global Book Publishing Photo Library
(except where credited otherwise on page 368)
Text © Global Book Publishing Pty Ltd 2005

The moral rights of all contributors have been asserted.

ISBN 0-88192-721-X

Catalog records for this book are available from the Library of
Congress and the British Library.

Printed in Hong Kong by Sing Cheong Printing Co. Ltd

Publisher	Gordon Cheers
Associate publisher	Margaret Olds
Art director	Stan Lamond
Project manager	Dannielle Doggett
Consultants	Ned Nash Isobyl la Croix
Principal writer	David P. Banks
Editors	Kate Etherington Janet Parker
Picture research	Gordon Cheers
Photo library	Alan Edwards
Cover design	Stan Lamond
Index	Loretta Barnard
Production	Bernard Roberts
Foreign rights	Dee Rogers

Photographers: The publisher would be pleased to hear from
photographers interested in supplying photographs that could
be included in new editions of *Flora's Orchids*.
Email: photoeditor@globalpub.com.au

Suggestions: The editors would be pleased to hear from plant
nurseries, general gardeners, and specialty groups about any plants
they feel should be added to future editions of *Flora's Orchids*.
Email: editor@globalpub.com.au

Captions for preliminary pages and openers
Page 1: *Zygopetalum mackayi*
Pages 2–3: *Paphiopedilum* species with frog
Pages 4–5: *Dendrobium speciosum*
Pages 6–7: *Vanda* (Gordon Dillon × Robert Fuchs)
Pages 8–9: Mixed orchids and ferns
Pages 10–11: *Epidendrum anceps*
Pages 56–57: *Polystachya pubescens* 'Gleneyrie'

Contents

The World of Orchids 10

What is an Orchid? 12

Orchid Taxonomy and Classification 22

Hybrids and Hybridization 24

History of Orchid Cultivation 26

Cultivating Orchids 36

Propagating Orchids 48

Orchid Pests and Diseases 52

Conserving Orchids in the Wild 54

A–Z of Orchids 56

Glossary 321

Cultivation Table 324

Index 356

Contributors

David P. Banks has been growing orchids for over 30 years, and owns the specialist nursery Hills District Orchids in Sydney, Australia. Since 1980, David has had over 200 papers relating to orchids published internationally, and is a sought-after lecturer throughout Australia and overseas on a wide range of orchidaceous topics. He has been the Editor of the *Australian Orchid Review* since 1999, and is the author of four books, including the critically acclaimed *Orchids of Australia*, co-authored with botanical illustrator John Riley. David's award-winning photographs have been published in numerous domestic and international journals, as well as in a number of orchid books.

Geoff Bryant is a New Zealand-based horticultural writer and photographer and was a plant propagator and nurseryman for some 10 years. He has written 11 books, including several widely sold plant propagation handbooks, as well as numerous magazine articles illustrated with his own photographs. He has been a technical editor, writer, and/or photographic contributor to many major plant and gardening titles. Geoff's photographs are represented internationally by several stock photo libraries, and he has recently launched an internet site featuring his writing and photography.

Colin Jennings is a retired chemistry teacher who has a keen interest in horticulture, especially orchids. He was appointed as an Australian Orchid Council Judge in 1974, and was elected Registrar General of Judging in 1993. In 2003, he was awarded a Fellowship of the AOC and appointed AOC Publications Director. Colin is a Life Member of the Orchid Club of South Australia, was President for three years, Registrar of Judges for nearly ten years, and is currently an active member. He has attended National and World Orchid Conferences, judging and presenting lectures.

Steve Johnson is an Associate Professor of Botany at the University of KwaZulu-Natal in Pietermaritzburg, South Africa. He has a particular interest in the pollination biology and systematics of orchids and has published more than 70 scientific papers and numerous popular science articles on these topics. He enjoys doing fieldwork in remote localities, especially when this involves climbing mountains. He is also a keen photographer and has published images in many of the world's leading natural history magazines. He co-wrote and illustrated the award-winning book *Table Mountain: A Natural History*, which was published in 1999.

David Jones, a Research Scientist at the Centre for Plant Biodiversity Research in Canberra, Australia, has been studying Australian native orchids for more than 40 years. This research has taken him to most orchidaceous areas of Australia, and more than 300 new species have been recognized as a result of these studies. He has also made research trips to New Zealand, New Caledonia, and Papua New Guinea to study relationships between the orchid floras of these countries and Australia. The most recent and highly successful study involved elucidating the taxonomy of Tasmanian orchids in collaboration with Tasmanian colleagues and resulted in the publication of volume 3 of *Australian Orchid Research*, followed by the book *Orchids of Tasmania*.

Dr. Folko Kullmann was born and raised in Stuttgart, Germany. His passion for orchids started in 1989, and his interest in plants led him to study horticulture in Munich during the 1990s. He undertook work experience at the Royal Botanical Gardens, Kew, during his studies, and he obtained a PhD for his research on mycorrhizal fungi. Folko has a special interest in South American orchid species, and he has made numerous field trips to habitats in Europe, South Africa, eastern Asia, and Australia. He is currently working in Stuttgart as an editor, author, and photographer for a range of garden books and magazines.

Isobyl la Croix studied Botany at Edinburgh University. She has always been interested in orchids, so when her husband's work took him to Malawi, she spent much of her time orchid hunting. This culminated in the production of *Orchids of Malawi*. On her return to Britain, she wrote the two-volume account for the Flora Zambesiaca of the orchids of Malawi, Mozambique, Zambia, Zimbabwe, and Botswana. Since then she has also written the FZ accounts of Colchicaceae and Dracaenaceae and has written up many orchid genera for the *RHS Dictionary of Gardening*. In 1997, *African Orchids in the Wild and in Cultivation* was published by Timber Press. She now lives with her family in northwest Scotland, where she grows African orchids and works as Editor of *The Orchid Review*.

Marilyn S. Light received her post-secondary education at McGill University, Montreal, Canada. She is the author of numerous orchid-related articles, books, and scientific papers including *Growing Orchids in the Caribbean* (Macmillan Education). She has registered 20 of her own orchid hybrids, is a past president of the Canadian Orchid Congress, and moderates a monthly internet discussion group on orchid topics at www.orchidsafari.org. Marilyn is a member of the Botanical Society of America, the Garden Writers of America, and the American Orchid Society. In 2000, she received the Silver Medal Award from the Ontario Horticultural Association.

Ned Nash received a BA in Botany from the University of California at Santa Barbara in 1975. He has been involved in the orchid business for most of his professional life, writing extensively for journals around the world. In 1995, Ned accepted a position as Director of Education and Conservation at the American Orchid Society (AOS), which he held until 2003. This followed on the heels of a career-long involvement on the volunteer side of the AOS as a judge, committee member, and chair, as well as a Trustee for two terms. He has recently retired from judging after over 20 years as an accredited judge. Ned has countless orchid articles and a well-received book to his credit.

Ron Parsons has been interested in and growing orchids for over 30 years, as well as photographing them for almost 25 years. He has many photographs of orchids published in books, magazines, brochures, and advertisements, and has recently co-authored a book on *Masdevallia* orchids published by Timber Press. Ron gives lectures in the United States and abroad on a variety of orchid-related topics. As well as orchids, Ron is also interested in California wildflowers, cacti and succulents, insectivorous plants, bulbous plants, bromeliads, and Gesneriads, and he lectures on some of these plant groups as well.

Andrew Perkins was born in Sydney, Australia, in 1973 and raised on a small rural property near Windsor, 25 miles (40 km) northwest of Sydney. From the age of three he attended orchid meetings and grew a variety of orchids with his parents. In 1994, he graduated from the University of Sydney with a BSc, after studying orchid–fungal associations during the Honors year of the degree. He graduated in 2001 with a PhD from the University of Sydney, after conducting research into the evolutionary relationships of the Australian orchid genus *Calochilus*. Since 2002, he has worked on research projects at the National Herbarium of New South Wales, the Royal Botanic Gardens in Sydney, and the University of Sydney.

Dr. Yoshitaka Tanaka was born in Kobe, Japan, in 1948. He started cultivating orchids from the age of 14, and his daughter's name is Ran (which is Japanese for "orchid"). Dr. Tanaka is a specialist in plant breeding and tropical agricultural development, and he is the Executive Director of the Foundation of Agricultural Development and Education in Thailand. He has published a number of books on orchids and other plants of Asia, including *Wild Orchids in Myanmar; Tropical Fruits in Southeast Asia; Vegetables, Herbs, Spices and Mushrooms in Vietnam; Indigenous Plant Genetic Resources Used By Ethnic Minorities in Vietnam;* and *An Illustrated Flora in Vietnam.*

The World of Orchids

What is an Orchid?

If a simple explanation sufficed, orchids just would not be orchids. The popular conception of an orchid, whether of a frilly purple cattleya, a white moth orchid, a pastel cymbidium, or a goblin-like *Mormodes*, is only a small part of what constitutes the glamor and mystique of this unique group of plants. The history, the mystery, and the sheer differences between orchids and any other plants renders them immediate and obvious subjects for the obsessive-compulsive collectors of the world. Without the mystique, the cachet, carried by the simple word "orchid," you probably wouldn't be reading this book. Nor would some of the famous and popular "urban legends" about this wonderful family have arisen. And, unlike so many other objects of desire and devotion, orchids actually have sound value

The very form, the very scent,
not heavy, not sensuous,
but perilous perilous
of orchids, piled in a great sheath.
HILDA DOOLITTLE (1886–1961),
"At Baia"

behind them. No other horticultural subject has the same beauty, the same long-lasting floral display, the same near-assurance of reblooming given reasonable care. For it is not just the exquisite beauty or distinction of the orchid flower that renders these plants among the most sought-after and expensive of all horticultural subjects. If they were accessible, if they all looked alike, if they were inexpensive, if they were all easy to grow, if they didn't offer an almost endless palette of color and shape and size, they would not command the attention they do. Nevertheless, many orchids make excellent horticultural subjects: many are easy and fast to grow, relatively easy to control, available through existing marketing venues, and wonderful value for consumers. It is no wonder that orchids are

Below: Named for its propagator, Francisco d'Aquino, Cattleya intermedia var. aquinii features ruffled magenta-streaked petals. Due to these markings, this plant is known as a "splash-petalled" cattleya.

the fastest-growing segment of the world floriculture industry. Indeed, since 1995, when wholesale figures were first tracked in the United States, orchid sales have grown to over $121 million (in 2002) to make orchids the second-largest selling potted flowering plant, exceeded only by the winter-blooming poinsettia. The booming market is leading to a profound shift in the public perception of the orchid, not only due to a rapidly increasing supply of affordable plants, but also due to their presence in just about every conceivable marketplace. How will this affect the alluring mystique that has surrounded orchids since time immemorial? Will they remain the apple of the collector's eye? Only time will tell. But, for the time being, we can revel in all that makes them the premier horticultural group in the world, and, hopefully, remind old growers as well as inform new converts about why they ought to be excited about the world of orchids!

A RAINBOW OF COLORS

Orchids are available in a wide variety of flower colors, from white and lemon to the deepest shade of purple, and the petals can be marked with stripes, spots, or blotches in a similar or contrasting color. Polystachya pubescens *'Gleneyrie' (above) has delicate yellow flowers, with the upper petals striped brown. The orange color of the* Ascocenda *Pramote blooms (left) is due to the influence of one of its parents,* Ascocentrum curvifolium. Cymbidium *hybrids (middle left) range in color, but many of the most popular plants have flowers in shades of pink with spotting or blotching in a similar hue on the lip. As suggested by its species name, which comes from the Latin word for "blood,"* Broughtonia sanguinea *(below left) has deep pink to reddish purple flowers.*

FLORA'S ORCHIDS SYMBOLS

Each species entry in this book features symbols that provide at-a-glance information about the species.

 FLORA AWARD—the plant is recommended by our consultants as outstanding in its group

 SPREAD—the width of the mature plant in cultivation

 HEIGHT—the height of the mature plant in cultivation

 EPIPHYTE—the plant grows naturally on the trunks or branches of trees

 LITHOPHYTE—the plant grows naturally on rocks

 TERRESTRIAL—the plant grows naturally in the soil

 FULL SUN—the plant thrives in sunny conditions

 HALF SUN—the plant thrives in dappled sunlight or part-shade

 SHADE—the plant thrives in shady conditions

 WARM-GROWING—the plant copes with a minimum winter temperature of 60°F (16°C)

 INTERMEDIATE-GROWING—the plant copes with a minimum winter temperature of 50°F (10°C)

 COOL-GROWING—the plant copes with a minimum winter temperature of 39°F (4°C)

 FROST TOLERANCE—the plant tolerates moderate levels of frost

 SHOWY FLOWERS—the plant produces large, colorful, and/or numerous flowers

 POT-GROWN—the plant is best cultivated in a pot

 MOUNT-GROWN—the plant is best cultivated on a mount

Left: Dendrobium subclausum is naturally found in New Guinea, at many different elevations. Due to the shape of its blooms, it is sometimes called the almost-closed flower dendrobium.

Orchid Distribution Around the World

Perhaps no other family of plants is more widely distributed, in more diverse climates, from sea level to above the tree line. There are few places in the world where, if you know when and where to look, you won't find orchids (except, of course, at the bottom of the sea!). From near the Arctic Circle to the Antarctic Circle, orchids occupy niches of opportunity. The ability of orchids to effectively evolve to meet changing conditions has led to their fantastic diversity and subsequent incredible number of species. The orchid family is one of the three largest families of flowering plants (along with daisies and grasses) and comprises—depending on which taxonomist you ask—from 25,000 to 35,000 naturally occurring species. Certainly, the public generally considers orchids to be "hot-house flowers," plants of the steaming tropics, and this is true—to some extent—of many of the most widely cultivated types. However, orchids also grow in temperate, more seasonally governed zones as well. Where freezing temperatures or periods of drought might affect the plants, a terrestrial habit is imperative to allow for a protected dormancy. Where conditions are more favorable, as in the tropics and subtropics, and competition consequently more fierce, many

Right: Registered in 1996, the red-flowered hybrid Phragmipedium Jason Fischer has P. Memoria Dick Clements and P. besseae as its parents. P. besseae has orange to bright red flowers and is native to Ecuador and Peru.

orchids have "taken to the trees" as epiphytes in an effort to gain an advantage in light quality and quantity.

In their evolution, orchids have had, like most plants, centers of diversity and population radiation. For orchids, two of the most important have been the New World tropics, particularly around Ecuador, Colombia, and Panama; and the Old World tropics centered on the larger island archipelagos of the South Pacific, as well as Malaysia and Thailand. Terrestrial temperate-zone orchids have been especially plentiful and diverse in Central Europe and mainland China. Where conditions are favorable, actively evolving groups like orchids can diversify into available niches with astonishing rapidity. An excellent example of this facility is seen in the New World genus *Masdevallia*, many members of which inhabit medium- to high-elevation habitats where cool and moist conditions prevail. These higher elevation habitats are often quite steep and discontinuous, rent by deep canyons and high ridges. Each canyon, effectively cut off from its neighbor and subject to unique pollinators, can host its own species, closely related to those in the next canyon over, but distinct as a population, though only a mile or two distant.

Today, orchid distribution is too often as much a result of human intervention as it is of historical and evolutionary factors. Unfortunately, as larger and larger areas of the tropics in particular are opened up to exploration and settlement, people change the environment to suit their needs—to

the detriment of the biological diversity found in such areas. Indeed, soil quality in many tropical rainforests is so poor and nutrient-deficient, that a terrestrial habit may be nearly impossible. This is the chief reason why the "slash and burn" subsistence agriculture now razing the remaining rainforests is basically so unsound: the soil gained will only support crops for a few years before the farmers have to move on to fresh ground. The previous rainforest vegetation will almost certainly never come back, diminishing further the pool of genetic diversity upon which our planet ultimately depends. While we in the developed world would like to slow or curtail such activities, it is a fact of life that as populations grow, food and fuel needs dictate that habitats will change, often irreversibly, and for the worse.

On the other hand, many orchid species are opportunistic, and they are among the first plants to spread into disturbed habitats. Indeed, it is just this facility that ensures that we will always have orchids. Zygopetalums have been known to grow in road verges in Brazil, their leaves regularly chopped off by road crews, flower stems rising above the remains

Above: Vandas are found from Sri Lanka and India, across Southeast Asia to New Guinea and north-eastern Australia, and thousands of vanda hybrids have been bred.

of the foliage. In Colombian road cuts, in the cloud-forest zone, swaths of tiny *Phragmipedium* seedlings often grow in the heavy clay soil, obviously rained down from a mature plant somewhere above the cleared area. Nevertheless, the best places to look for orchids are almost always the furthest away from human intervention, or where such intervention is impossible due to terrain or elevation. In such areas, many orchids are known as "locally abundant." That is, profuse where conditions are, for whatever reason, right. This leads to unparalleled sights of fields of blooming terrestrial orchids, or tree branches dripping with festoons of lovely scented blooms.

Above: An epiphyte from the cloud forests of montane regions in Costa Rica, Panama, Colombia, and Ecuador, Masdevallia nidifica is just one of almost 500 species found in this New World genus.

which can grow up in the canopy and take advantage of detritus, bird droppings, and so on have quite an advantage over those plants "stuck" on the ground in the very poor soil.)

Within these more general guidelines are the more specific "needs" or "preferences" of each species. It is actually a combination of luck and opportunity that governs where any particular orchid plant grows. Luck in where the seed lands and opportunity in the plant getting started in growth, establishing itself in the location where it has adapted to do well. Often this lucky chance means more than just one plant of a given species in an area, as an adult plant's many progeny fall around its base and take advantage of the same opportunities. Here is also where microclimates come into play. What are the very specific environmental factors that make one area favorable for a certain species and not for another? Higher or lower elevation? North, south,

Above: Found from north Queensland to southern New South Wales in Australia, Dockrillia linguiformis *grows epiphytically or lithophytically. Its fleshy leaves store water, allowing the plant to grow on rocks exposed to the drying heat of the sun.*

Orchid Habitats, Climates, and Microclimates

Orchids, as herbaceous perennials with relatively low nutrient requirements, do not generally occupy niches where they are forced to compete with their neighbors. Rather, orchids are opportunistic, growing where competition is less, in what for other plants would be considered marginal habitats. It helps to remember what the environment must provide for a plant's well-being: light, moisture, and nutrients. Whichever of these components is in shortest supply can be thought of as the critical factor. This is also the factor that is most likely to be influential in any competitive situation. For a non-orchid example, in a desert-like habitat, moisture or nutrients (or both) may be the limiting critical factor. In such cases, the plants are liable to be spaced in a way that allows each plant to obtain the critical moisture or nutrients necessary for its survival. Competition prevents any other plants from growing between each chief competitor. In other cases, it may be that nutrients are in generally low supply, due to environmental factors such as pH, and plants that tolerate lower nutrient levels essentially prevent other plants from gaining a foothold. Or, light may be the limiting factor, as in tropical rainforests, where very little light actually reaches the forest floor, and only those plants that have adapted to an epiphytic lifestyle closer to or actually in the forest canopy can flourish. (It needs to be said that nutrients are also quite limited in rainforests, as most of the available nutrients are tied up in the biomass of the forest. Therefore, those plants

Right: Depending on the species, epiphytic orchids either grow better when attached to the main trunk of the tree, where they receive more protection and nutrients from fallen leaves, or they flourish on the outer branches, where light and air circulation is more prevalent.

east, or west exposure? Shaded behind a rock, or in front of a rock that can act as a solar collector? Higher or lower in the tree? In the crook of the branch, where more nourishing detritus can collect and moisture is higher, or out swinging on the branch tip, where air circulation is highest and most drying? On top of the hill, where the desiccating winds blow relentlessly, or in the protected lee of the hill, where moisture can accumulate? These and many other elements enter into the success or failure of any individual plant. This is not to say that each plant has to be in the perfect location—far from it. However, plants in too much shade to flower well, or so much sun that heat stress prevents them from ever reaching mature size, are essentially dead ends, unable to flower and reproduce their unique genetic makeup.

THE IMPORTANCE OF MICROCLIMATES

The concept of microclimates has profound implications for the grower hoping to maximize the growth potential and flowering of their orchid plants. Just like any habitat, a growing area has many different microclimates, determined by distance from the ceiling; proximity to heaters, coolers, vents, or fans; shading from neighboring plants; and other, seemingly inconsequential factors that when added together make one spot much better than another for a certain plant. In the same way field biologists must observe all environmental aspects in nature that may potentially affect why a plant grows where it grows, savvy orchid growers know their growing area and its peculiarities. They constantly monitor their plants' reactions and compare against other locations in the growing area. The distance of only a few inches can sometimes make all the difference.

A human being isn't an orchid, he must draw something from the soil he grows in.
SARA JEANNETTE DUNCAN (1861–1922)

Most orchids in common cultivation originate from the tropics or subtropics, where they grow at varying elevations as epiphytes. An important fact to remember is that a rise in elevation is analogous to moving away from the Equator. In other words, a higher elevation is generally cooler than a lower elevation. A significantly greater diversity of orchid species can be found at mid- to high elevations in the tropic zones than at sea level. The steamy hot habitat imagined by gardeners in the Victorian era and emulated in their greenhouse "stoves" is simply not conducive to growing many of the most popular orchid types. Rather, it would help to visualize a fresh spring day, with moderate temperatures, a light cooling breeze, and dappled sunshine. This much more closely approximates the environment where so many of the most popular orchids are found. Interestingly, if one were to visit a prime orchid habitat and see what grew alongside orchids up in the trees, it would make the culture of orchids far less intimidating to the uninitiated. Ferns, cacti, begonias, peperomias, bromeliads, aroids (philodendron types), gesneriads (African violet relatives), and other plants long popular as "house plants" grow side by side with orchids.

Above: Native to forests in the highland areas of New Guinea, Mediocalcar decoratum *is a miniature mat-forming epiphyte that bears yellow-tipped orange flowers in autumn–winter.*

Top: Dyakia hendersoniana *is an epiphyte from Borneo that grows naturally at an elevation of around 2,620 ft (800 m). Up to 30 fragrant rose to magenta flowers appear on each raceme.*

Below: Rhizanthella slateri *from eastern Australia is a saprophytic orchid. It grows mostly underground, with the flowerheads sometimes breaking through the surface of the soil.*

Orchid Types

As opportunists, orchids have adapted to a broad variety of habitats with a vast array of growth habits. Epiphytic, hemi-epiphytic, lithophytic, saprophytic, terrestrial, subterranean … the list goes on. And growth habits have evolved due to particular habitat issues, such as drought, high or low light levels, nutrient paucity, high or low acidity, and so on. Despite the great differences in the many ecological niches occupied by orchids, their basic growth habits can be classified in one of two ways: sympodial (growing laterally and producing leafy growths along a rhizome; like an iris or bamboo) or monopodial (growing upward from a single, occasionally branched, stem producing flower stems and leaves along that stem).

From these two basic growth patterns have radiated the range of plant appearances in the family as a whole.

Orchid plants can range from extraordinarily tiny—under ½ in (12 mm) tall in some bulbophyllums and pleurothallids—to huge—over 20 ft (6 m) in extreme cases such as dendrobiums, grammatophyllums, sobralias, or vining types like the vanillas. Orchids' ability to quickly and effectively adapt to a changing environment is intimately tied to the wide range of plant forms they exhibit. There really is no common thread by which orchid plants may be distinguished while not in flower. However, experienced orchidists are able to identify an out-of-flower plant as an orchid by a certain aspect of the plant.

TERRESTRIAL ORCHIDS

The temperate zones are home to many of the truly terrestrial orchids (those that grow in the soil), if only because the protected, often tuberous, roots allow for a deciduous habit and protection from weather extremes. Whether exposed to heat, cold, or drought, terrestrial orchids are able to survive otherwise untenable climatic situations by dormancy. Often, the terrestrial orchids' physiology is adapted in such a way that without an enforced dormant season, the plant simply does not survive. This feature, tied to the complex relationship most terrestrial orchids have with the living ecosystem of the substrate in which they grow, has restricted the cultivation of temperate-zone terrestrials to the hands of experts. There are two ground-dwelling growth habits that will essentially never be seen in cultivation: subterranean and

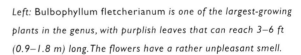

Left: Bulbophyllum fletcherianum *is one of the largest-growing plants in the genus, with purplish leaves that can reach 3–6 ft (0.9–1.8 m) long. The flowers have a rather unpleasant smell.*

Below: A terrestrial from eastern Australia and northern New Zealand, Thelymitra matthewsii *has delicately spiraling leaves. The single rose purple flower with purple veining blooms in spring.*

saprophytic. Subterranean orchids grow underground with only emergent flowerheads (the Australian orchid, *Rhizanthella gardneri*, being the best known). Saprophytic orchids (*Corallorrhiza* is one) grow by the utilization of the by-products of plant decay, not by their own photosynthetic products. These are most often seen growing in rich forest humus, where their bizarre flower stems poke through the humus layer to attract pollinators. No chlorophyll is present, so the colors are pale and unearthly.

As one travels toward the Equator, the climate becomes more favorable for the year-round growth of herbaceous perennials (like orchids). Orchids that come from areas where pronounced dry seasons exist, particularly in monsoonal regions, tend to have a deciduous habit, though often coupled with a water-storage capacity of some sort, whether swollen stems (pseudobulbs), heavy leaves, or fleshy roots, or some combination. Niches where the substrate is evenly moist as a result of heavy shade, high compost content, even precipitation throughout the year, will have orchids with softer foliage and less obvious, if any, water-storage organs. Ground-dwelling plants in these habitats are often hemi-epiphytes, the term given to plants that don't grow "in" the soil, but rather in the layer of humus that collects on the forest floor. Good examples of this type are paphiopedilums, cymbidiums, and jewel orchids such as *Anoectochilus* and *Ludisia*.

EPIPHYTIC ORCHIDS

The hemi-epiphytes mark the transition of orchids from terrestrial to a truly epiphytic habit. Note that epiphytic orchids are not parasitic; they derive no nutrients directly from the host plant's metabolism, only support and a substrate upon which to grow. As the forests become denser, with a more complete canopy of foliage that is often in several layers, the epiphytic habit offers several distinct advantages. It gets the orchid up into the canopy where light is more plentiful, useful for plants that prefer strong, often dappled, light. Secondly, it allows the fleshy velamen-covered orchid roots to ramble freely and to gather nutrients from bird droppings, leaf detritus, and other organic products, nutrients that are often lacking nearer the forest floor. Epiphytic orchids are the ones we see most often in cultivation, so matching the airy, evenly moist environment of the forest is the challenge faced by orchid growers.

LITHOPHYTIC ORCHIDS

Orchids' need to inhabit marginal areas has led to a further adaptation in growth habit: lithophytic orchids literally "grow on rocks." While many laelias, cyrtopodiums, and other orchid genera have evolved this unique habit, it is clear that these plants were at first epiphytes, and have secondarily adapted to growing on—not in—the ground. The lithophytic habit offers its own set of challenges, not the least of which is the often-low level of organic nutrients available in rocky areas. Moisture is also limited, though this type of orchid has by necessity become expert both in efficiently obtaining and storing precious water resources. The roots of lithophytes will travel and accumulate along the rock fissures, sometimes forming an almost solid mass of water-retentive tissue. When occasional precipitation occurs, the water can be efficiently gathered and stored for later use. Another difficulty faced by lithophytes can be the blazing sun. This is dealt with by producing hard, upright foliage that minimizes exposure to the burning rays, as well as heavy red pigmentation to shield the more delicate green chlorophyll.

Above: Dendrobiums are mostly epiphytes, although some will also grow lithophytically. They are widely distributed from India and Sri Lanka to Southeast Asia, Australia, and the Pacific Islands.

Left: Growing either as a terrestrial or a lithophyte, Paphiopedilum concolor is often found in limestone soils on steep slopes or in leaf detritus on limestone rocks, and is always in shady locations.

Left: As well as having attractive flowers, Cymbidium canaliculatum *is drought tolerant. Its stiff leathery leaves channel what little moisture it receives down to the pseudobulb, which stores the water.*

Orchid Physiology

There are a few important aspects to orchid physiology that, when combined together, define what makes orchids "different" from "other" plants. As noted earlier, many orchids have evolved some degree of drought tolerance. The ability to tolerate periodic dryness—whether diurnal or seasonal—can be anatomical (heavy leaves with a waxy cuticle, fleshy stems or pseudobulbs, thick tuberous roots) or metabolic. It is the metabolic feature that concerns us here. Many drought-tolerant plants utilize a CAM-4 (or similar) metabolic system. The plants produce

In the marsh pink orchid's faces
With their coy and dainty graces,
Lure us to their hiding places—
Laugh, O murmuring Spring!

SARAH FOSTER DAVIS,
"Summer Song"

one step in the photosynthetic pathway during daylight hours when they have their stomata closed to conserve moisture— this portion of the process requires light energy but no gas exchange. They "finish" the portion of the process requiring gas exchange (CO_2) at night, when cooler and moister conditions allow the stomata to be open. Many orchids utilize this method to conserve moisture.

The structure of orchid seeds is another rather specialized feature. Unlike the seeds of many other flowering plants, which contain endosperm— a starchy material used to provide nourishment until the seedling's photosynthetic pathways can kick into gear— orchid seeds are essentially devoid of this valuable starter. The seeds are consequently very fine and dust like, and produced in vast quantities (to say millions is not an understatement). In nature, these seeds are wind-distributed and can be blown some distance from the parent plant, or fall directly under, depending on circumstances. The few seeds, or single seed, which happen to land in just the right place, will enter into a symbiotic relationship with a mycorrhizal fungus (part of what constitutes "just the right place" is the presence of the fungus appropriate to the orchid). The fungus will invade the orchid seed through a specially adapted thin area in the seed coat, and the by-products of the fungal metabolism will allow the orchid seed to germinate and begin its life. It is easy to see what a puzzlement this must have been to early horticulturists, who

ORCHID LEAF VARIETY *Orchids boast a wide range of leaf shapes and colors.* Paphiopedilum insigne *(far left) usually has green leaves, but an unusual variegated form is sometimes seen.* P. tonsum *(top left) has a tesellated pattern on the upper surface of its leaves, which are reddish underneath.* Dendrochilum tenellum *(below left) is sometimes mistaken for a grass when not in flower.*

found only after much experimentation that the seed would often germinate only on the pot of the parent plant or another well-established plant. Why? Because the mycorrhizae had been imported with the plant and enabled the orchid seed to germinate. However, even in the best of circumstances, germination was chancy and too sparse to be commercially meaningful. Early in the twentieth century, thanks to the pioneering work of Bernard and Knudson, Lewis Knudson discovered the relationship between the fungus and the orchid seed. By adding the same nutrients provided by the fungal metabolism to a sterile media, profuse and reliable germination of orchid seeds was first accomplished, leading to the establishment of the orchid industry we know today.

Many orchid seedlings outgrow their dependence on the mycorrhizae or the nutrients provided in the culture media. Clearly, few cultivated plants have had any contact with mycorrhizal fungi and so must be growing independent of their influence. However, there are a significant number of terrestrial orchids that grow in a complex relationship with the flora and fauna of their substrate, and will simply not grow in cultivation, at least for any length of time. Some of these are showy and worthy of further cultivation, presenting a unique challenge to orchid growers. Today, the real frontier of orchid cultivation is the forwarding of cultural methods for these recalcitrant subjects and their entry into more common cultivation. For example, 20 years ago it was common knowledge that the pot culture of cypripediums (lady's slippers) was impossible. For the past few years, magnificent potted specimens have begun to be displayed, proving that "impossible" is just a goad to a certain type of orchid grower.

THE PARTS OF AN ORCHID FLOWER

Orchids are members of one of the two main divisions of the flowering plants, the Monocot group (Dicots being the other). This group shares many characteristics, such as parallel venation of leaves and tripartite floral structure. It is in the floral structure that orchids are set apart not only from all other flowering plants, but even from their closest relatives, the lilies. Orchid flowers are formed from two whorls of three parts. The outer whorl forms the sepals and the inner whorl the petals, with one of the petals usually modified into a structure known as the lip (or labellum), which attracts pollinators. The color or size of the lip serves to attract pollinators who

dorsal sepal — petals — column — lip — lateral sepals

THE FLOWER AND ITS PARTS
Epigeneium triflorum *var. orientale (left)* has a classic orchid flower shape, and the sepals, petals, column, and lip can be clearly seen. Blooming in late summer, this plant has up to 17 flowers per spike.

Right: After the flower has finished blooming and dropped off, the ovary that is usually behind the Paphiopedilum malipoense *flower is visible.*

interact with the orchid's uniquely joined sexual structure: the column. The male part (the anther) is joined in the same structure with the female organ (the stigma). The male structures are almost always positioned so that the pollinator does not pick up the particular flower's pollinia until after it has deposited previously attached pollinia on the stigmatic surface, which is most often positioned behind the anther (toward the ovary). This is not to say that self-pollination does not sometimes occur, or even that it may not be the principal method of pollination in some species, because it is. However, much more often, species will not self-pollinate due to physiological barriers and so must be outcrossed—crossed with another distinct member of the same species.

Right: Thelymitra *species are terrestrials that rely on a mycorrhizal fungus for survival, so they have proven very difficult to maintain in cultivation. The best species to try to grow is* Thelymitra ixioides, *as it is robust.*

Orchid Taxonomy and Classification

The need to categorize the organisms around us has lead to systems of naming (nomenclature) and categorization (classification or taxonomy) used for both plants and animals. The science of plant classification has a long history, and in its early stages was intimately associated with herbalism. Gradually, a botanical terminology was established and some plants began to be described in detail. The most significant change occurred in 1753 when the Swedish botanist Carl von Linné, usually known as Linnaeus, produced the first edition of *Species Plantarum*. This work contained botanical descriptions of a range of plants, including orchids, and each plant was given a two-part (binomial) name and assigned to a system of classification based on the number and position of the stamens and pistils. This system provides the basis for modern plant classification.

Orchids, because of the tremendous range of morphological and vegetative variation they display, are a difficult group to classify. However, as a group they have been studied in detail by many botanists over the last two centuries and a classification system is now well established. It must be emphasized at this stage, however, that competent botanists can hold significantly different viewpoints on aspects of orchid classification and this conflict can cause major confusion with amateur enthusiasts and orchid growers.

The basic unit of classification is the species. There are various definitions for this entity but the simplest is "a group of organisms with a common set of features that sets them apart from another group with a different set of features." This definition is useful but subjective because it relies on interpreting morphological differences and can lead to conflicting views between botanists. Biologically speaking, species can be defined as "populations which can interbreed but are reproductively isolated from each other." This definition has the advantage that reproductive isolation can be proven by modern techniques such as DNA analyses, and the measurable data obtained can help support the morphological features. Whatever definition

MORPHOLOGICAL VARIATION *Early botanists found orchids difficult to classify due to their wide-ranging forms.* Brassia verrucosa *(top left) has large spidery flowers, while* Miltoniopsis *Jean Carlson (top right) has pansy-like blooms with broad petals and sepals.* Zygopetalum crinitum *(left) has 3 in (8 cm) flowers that feature a large, veined, hairy lip.*

is used, a group of similar or closely related species makes up a genus.

Orchid Nomenclature

The binomial system of naming becomes clear when examples are considered. Two well-known generic names in orchids are *Dendrobium* and *Phalaenopsis*. There are many species in each of these genera, two examples in *Dendrobium* being *D. moschatum* and *D. moniliforme*, and in *Phalaenopsis*, *P. amabilis* and *P. schilleriana*. In taxonomy, there is a hierarchy of names used to classify plants.

Categories below the rank of species, namely subspecies and variety, are used by some botanists to account for minor variations resulting from isolation or adaptation to specific microclimates or habitats. At a higher ranking, genera are grouped together into aggregations known as families. Orchids are grouped into the family Orchidaceae, one of the largest families of flowering plants, with recent estimates suggesting that it comprises 750–900 genera and 25,000–35,000 species.

Plant nomenclature is the naming of plants according to a system of rules. The naming and description of a species is based on a specimen known as a type that is lodged in a recognized botanical institution. Two important rules that can have significant impacts on the names growers use for their orchid plants concern priority of publication. When two or more validly published names are applied to a species, then the name that was first published takes precedence over the other. Also, if the same name is used for two different species in a genus, then the second use of that name is incorrect.

Orchid Taxonomy

Botanical taxonomy is the study of plant classification. Modern taxonomic classifications are based on studies that involve a range of factors including floral morphology, vegetative features, anatomy, ecological and environmental factors, pollination systems, fungal

relationships, chromosomes, and chemical constituents of the plant organs. In recent years, molecular studies have made significant contributions to taxonomy and in some cases have resulted in major re-thinking of evolutionary patterns and changes in relationships within and between major orchid groups and genera.

A notable example is the genus *Dendrobium* that has traditionally been treated as a large conglomeration of more than 1,000 species. Recent DNA studies have shown that the genus splits neatly into two major groups, one group mainly of Asian origin and the other from Australasia and the Pacific Islands. The former group contains *Dendrobium moniliforme*, the type plant of the genus *Dendrobium*, and the latter group includes the well-known genera *Cadetia*, *Diplocaulobium*, and *Flickingeria*, which some botanists have suggested should be included in *Dendrobium*. The recent molecular results mean that the traditional classification treating *Dendrobium* as one large conglomerate genus is scientifically untenable and genera such as *Cadetia*, *Diplocaulobium*, and *Flickingeria* must be recognized as distinct entities. Numerous additional name changes at generic rank have resulted from these studies and more are forecast. Indeed, it is probable that *Dendrobium* itself will end up being a small readily definable genus of only 50–60 species.

Above: Dockrillia *was once part of* Dendrobium. *In 1981, it was suggested that "terete-leafed" dendrobiums from Australia and New Guinea be moved into their own genus, as they differed from true dendrobiums in their lack of pseudobulbs and their leaf and flower form.*

Left: Epidendrum porpax *is a classic example of a plant with many different botanical names, some of which may still be in common usage even though they are not the validly published name for the plant. Synonyms include* Nanodes mathewsii *and* Neolehmannia porpax.

Hybrids and Hybridization

Left: Cattleya × guatemalensis *is a natural interspecific hybrid between* C. skinneri *and* C. aurantiaca, *and is named for its place of origin, Guatemala. It blooms during the spring months.*

on the task of correlating all hybrid orchid names to that point and keeping the records from that time on. The Royal Horticultural Society (RHS) took over this job in the mid-twentieth century. No other major horticultural group of plants has such an enviable system, nor, as a result, the completeness of information as a heritage to breeders present and future.

Hybrid Naming System

The unprecedented ability of orchids to successfully breed across both species and generic lines has given rise to a range of hybrids, and attempting to understand the hybrid naming conventions is often daunting to the newcomer. In a nutshell, intrageneric (interspecific) hybrids are given a grex name by the originator of the hybrid, defined as the person actually making and flowering the first of a hybrid between any two distinct species (a "primary" hybrid) or between two distinct gregi (plural for grex, a "complex" hybrid). The best analogy for this is to think of your family: the genus name is analogous to the specific name for people, *Homo sapiens*. The grex name is analogous to your family name, for example, Jones. So, your family is *Homo sapiens* Jones. Within any grex are even more specific entities called cultivars, which are the individuals resulting from the particular hybrid. They can be compared to your personal name, for example, Bill. So, *Homo sapiens* Jones 'Bill' is the human equivalent of, say, *Cattleya* Bow Bells 'Virgin,' denoting one specific individual from the *Cattleya* hybrid named Bow Bells.

HYBRID NAMES *The officially registered name for the hybrid* Phalaenopsis Haifang's Queen × P. Saluspot × P. Baby Angel *is* P. Sogo Fireworm *(below left).* 'Tipmalee' *(below middle) is a cultivar of* Brassolaeliocattleya Alma Kee. *The genus name of* Sophrolaeliocattleya Trizac *(below right) is derived from the names of the parents involved in the intergeneric cross—Sophronitis, Laelia, and Cattleya.*

The main fact that makes orchids "special" when it comes to hybridizing is that physiological barriers have not developed against interspecific (between different species of the same genus) or intergeneric (between different but related genera) hybrids. This has led to nearly countless man-made hybrids—over 120,000 registered since the inception of record keeping in the middle of the nineteenth century—of overwhelming complexity. For example, in the cattleyas, there are intergeneric hybrids that can be traced back over 12 generations to the species parents, and there are currently nonageneric (nine genera) intergeneric hybrids. A corollary of the complexity of the hybridizing that has been of immeasurable value is the unbroken system of record keeping that has existed in orchid breeding from nearly the beginning. Late in the nineteenth century, Sander's & Sons of St. Albans in England took

Intergeneric hybrids (with two or more genera in their makeup) have an additional convention. When two or, occasionally, three genera are involved, the intergeneric name is a combination of the generic names involved in the cross. For example, *Laelia* × *Cattleya = Laeliocattleya*. This could obviously get unwieldy with three, four, or more genera, so a further convention dictates that these more complex artificial genera are named for the originator, or their designate, and end in –ara. For example, *Laelia* × *Brassavola* × *Cattleya* × *Sophronitis = Potinara; Odontoglossum* × *Cochlioda* × *Oncidium = Wilsonara.* The list could go on and on, and it does.

The advantage to this system is uniformity; all hybrids are registered by a central authority and retain a "paper trail" throughout their life and beyond. The disadvantage is that no record is kept of what particular cultivar was used to make any particular hybrid, and this obviously can lead to wildly differing results from what, on paper, would appear to be the same hybrid. As hybrids grow increasingly complex, this problem is amplified. Another problem that is difficult to address is the changing taxonomy of the orchid family, as it has come to be better understood over the last 150 years. What was once an *Oncidium* may have become an *Odontoglossum*, then may have been moved to *Lemboglossum.* How to account for this in the necessarily conservative registration system has

yet to be satisfactorily addressed. A corollary of this problem is the mystery surrounding many of the early hybrids made and used for further breeding. Because early record keeping was less than accurate in some cases, the method of growing seedlings in the early years lent itself to confusion, and the arcane nature of the process itself led some to conceal which two parents were actually used (if they knew in the first place), mistakes are perpetuated through the system. Nevertheless, it is basically a good system.

When two friends understand each other totally, the words are soft and strong like an orchid's perfume.

UNKNOWN

The last drawback in trying to interpret anything from hybrid records is the fallacy that parentage, particularly generic affinities, tells you anything about the growing conditions for the plant. "It's got *Laelia* in it, it will be cold-tolerant…. It is an *Odontoglossum*, it has to be grown very cool…. All vandas need full sun." Nothing could be further from the truth. And the truth is that the plants will grow how they grow, within certain general parameters. Your best source of knowledge, vanishing too rapidly, is your professional orchid grower. Sadly, so few orchid nurseries can afford to produce what they sell, or have it on hand long enough to know its cultural vagaries, that you may have trouble getting the sort of local knowledge that used to be commonplace.

Above: Potinara *is a complex genus that comprises* Laelia × Brassavola × Cattleya × Sophronitis. Potinara *Burana Beauty, seen here, is a brightly colored hybrid in the genus.*

Top: Before it was transferred to Odontoglossum, O. wyattianum *was originally known as* Oncidium wyattianum. *The taxonomy of orchids is constantly changing, as botanists learn more about this unique plant group.*

History of Orchid Cultivation

Right: In parts of India, rheumatism is relieved by applying cloths that have been dipped in hot water in which the Spathoglottis plicata plant has been boiled.

Man has known about and used orchid plants and flowers for longer than recorded history. The history of orchid cultivation, and the influence these exquisite plants have had on societies and cultures all over the world, is fascinating both for orchid enthusiasts and those just discovering the beauty of orchids.

Indigenous Uses— Medicinal and Culinary

Confucius, over 2,000 years ago in ancient China, described the graceful foliage and delicate fragrance of cymbidium orchids, giving them the Chinese name for orchids—*lan*— that signifies perfume and beauty. The Greeks also knew about orchids. The word "orchid" is derived from the Greek word for testicles, *orchis*, which the tubers of certain terrestrial orchid species resemble. The plants were thought to grow where animals had spilled their semen. The Classical Age had the Doctrine of Signatures, which dictated that plant and animal parts act upon the portions of the human body they resemble. Therefore, the resemblance of the tubers of *Orchis* species to testicles was thought to give them the power to confer virility when eaten. Orchids did not form a significant part of the Western garden palette much before the late eighteenth century. A part of the pharmacopeia, certainly, but the garden, no.

Above: Indigenous people from pre-Columbian Central America have been known to use the seed pods of the summer-blooming Trichocentrum cebolleta as a type of hallucinogen.

Top: Cymbidium tracyanum is an epiphytic orchid species found from Thailand to China. It has highly fragrant flowers.

Left: An extract from the pseudobulb of Pholidota chinensis is used in India to alleviate the pain of a toothache. A tincture made from the plant is utilized to treat asthma, dysentery, and tuberculosis.

Tropical cultures had uses for their indigenous orchids that would have surprised Western practitioners of medicine had they but known of them. For example, it has only recently been discovered that the seed pods of *Trichocentrum cebolleta* (syn. *Oncidium cebolleta*) have potent psychotropic powers. The bulbs of other orchids were used to make glue due to their mucilaginous properties. And, of course, there is vanilla, which has been cultivated for its fragrant and flavorful seed pods for centuries, if not millennia. It is interesting to speculate on how the often-bizarre uses for some orchids were discovered. For example, the pollinator for vanilla does not exist in most of the places where the plant is cultivated. It took orchid growers some time to discover how to pollinate an orchid, and the hand-pollination of vanilla is crucial to bean production. What is perhaps more to the point, however, is how relatively few practical uses have been discovered for orchids, especially considering their nearly ubiquitous and showy nature. Modern science continues to search among folk remedies for replicable results and active ingredients. Hopefully, one day we will find the bonanza of practical orchid use we seek.

Even more astounding, considering the broad range of things that people will eat, is the very few culinary uses for orchids. We are all familiar with vanilla. The only other widespread use of orchids as a food product is in eastern Europe and the Middle East, where the tubers of various terrestrial orchids are ground for their starchy content and used in ice cream and other similar dishes. Known as salep, the production of this substance consumes literally millions of orchid plants each year. Salep production has only recently shown up on the radar of conservation groups, who have begun to seriously study the effects of tuber harvest on the long-term survival of the affected species. How this will play out and how it will affect the livelihood of those involved in the harvest and sale of this product remains to be seen.

Orchids in Literature and Folklore

Any group of plants as obvious in their beauty and, sometimes, strangeness is sure to be the subject of attention in the stories told around the campfire or in literature. The fantastic nature of orchids lends them an aura of mystery that feeds any imagined powers that may be ascribed to them. They are used

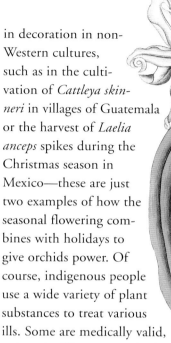

Right: There are around 100 species in the genus Vanilla. *Most of the world's vanilla is derived from the seed pods of just one species, V. planifolia, which has been cultivated for centuries.*

in decoration in non-Western cultures, such as in the cultivation of *Cattleya skinneri* in villages of Guatemala or the harvest of *Laelia anceps* spikes during the Christmas season in Mexico—these are just two examples of how the seasonal flowering combines with holidays to give orchids power. Of course, indigenous people use a wide variety of plant substances to treat various ills. Some are medically valid, at least by Western standards, and some are anecdotal at best. These uses are passed along in the oral history of the culture.

Western culture, though, has embraced orchids as symbols of the strange and wonderful. Orchids were imbedded in Classical and European pharmacopeias long before they were cultivated for their flowers. In more recent times, many writers have used orchids in their plot lines. H. G. Wells, arguably the first science fiction writer, wrote about an exotic orchid whose fragrance lured and then killed its victims in a Victorian-era greenhouse. Perhaps the best-known use of orchids to further a story is in the Nero Wolfe mysteries, where the amateur detective, Wolfe, obsessively tends his orchid collection housed in a rooftop greenhouse. More recently, orchids have been featured in several popular novels, the best of which was Eric Hansen's *Orchid Fever*, an account of the many ways orchid lovers find to express their fanaticism, and *The Orchid Thief* by Susan Orlean, based on the true story of plant dealer John Laroche.

> *The leaves were blackish green and the flower itself was glossy yellow, the yellow of a newly waxed taxi, and it was spattered with hundreds and hundreds of burgundy flecks.... Staring at the pattern of the flecks was dizzying. Staring at it for a long time was hypnotizing.*
>
> SUSAN ORLEAN, *The Orchid Thief*

Below: A New York Times *bestseller,* The Orchid Thief *by Susan Orlean was the inspiration for the film* Adaptation *(2002). Interestingly, the orchid image on the cover shown below is upside down.*

Right: George Forrest (1873–1932) was a plant hunter and botanist. Named for him to honor his important work, Pleione forrestii was just one of the many orchids and other plants he collected from China.

Plant Hunters and their Prey

The earliest tropical orchid to flower in England (1731) arrived as a "dried" herbarium specimen and sprouted from what seemed like a lifeless bulb. When potted up, it grew and flowered. We now know this plant as *Bletia verrucunda*. This was the beginning of a growing mania for the plants of the diverse Orchidaceae. It was the "Bachelor Duke" of Devonshire, William Spencer Cavendish, whose passion for *Psychopsis papilio* (syn. *Oncidium papilio*) raised orchid collecting from a mere sideline obsession of Victorian England to the hobby of kings it became. The Duke's obsessive interest in this new class of plants, his willingness to send collectors to the tropics specifically to find new and more beautiful plants, and his patronage of Joseph Paxton as his gardener, led his peers to compete with him to accumulate and display the very best of these exotic plants. It was the rare combination of desire and talent that enabled this group of plants to become better known in Western culture. Desire for the new and exotic, and talent in the form of Joseph Paxton, whose pioneering efforts in admitting fresh air to the stifling "stoves" or orchid greenhouses of the day and his subsequent success in these methods, led to an explosion in the public knowledge of orchids as flowers of the rich and famous.

Above: An illustration of Bollea coelestis appeared in the 1882 edition of Paxton's Flower Garden, which was illustrated by Constans and Prevost.

We know now that our most commonly cultivated orchids come from areas where they have access to strong dappled light; continual air movement; moderate, but not stifling, humidity; and periods of wet and dry conditions, with passing showers. Too, many of these same orchids come from areas of seasonal dryness and cooler temperatures, often from higher elevations in the foothills of tropical areas. Such conditions were the antithesis of the Victoria "stove," which was kept hot, humid, and shady. Nor were early collectors eager to dispel the myth of stovehouse culture, either, as it would

Right: The sixth Duke of Devonshire, William Spencer Cavendish (1790–1858), delighted in the unusual nature of Psychopsis papilio, and funded many expeditions to the tropics in search of other orchid species.

have served both to unlock the secrets of the plants' true habitats, and, if fewer plants died in these miserable conditions, reduce their potential future market. Nevertheless, as questions were answered by the combination of experience and thoughtful observation, more unknowns came to the forefront. These questions arose as scientifically oriented explorers and expeditions ranged farther and farther afield, in search of not just orchids and other botanical novelties, but knowledge of the wide world they found. Botanical curiosities were in great demand by the scientifically oriented aristocracy, as they or the scientists they patronized investigated the pharmacology and other economic uses of these startling new finds.

Today, with the almost complete globalization of our world, where we can be nearly anywhere we please, usually with our luggage, within 24 hours, it is difficult to conceive of a time when such travel was not the norm, when only the most driven and ambitious pioneers could entertain the notion of such rough-and-tumble adventure. Sailing ships—and later, steamships— mules, and travel by foot were the rule. Tropical diseases and unfriendly natives were the dangers. And once the elusive prize was found, it was an equally arduous journey back to Europe. Today, our only knowledge of some of these men is the species names that honor them. While the great nurseries of the day— Loddiges, Veitch, Sander's, and others—sent out collectors to supply their auctions, and the wealthy sent their own explorers out to improve their collections, still others were driven by simple greed or wanderlust. More than a few lost their lives in the pursuit. Even more inconceivable than the difficulties posed by travel to and within the newly discovered lands were the sheer volume of plants stripped from their habitats. "Sustainable yield" was not a viable concept. Rather, all the plants of a desirable species that could be

It seemed as if the breezes brought him, It seemed as if the sparrows taught him, As if by secret sign he knew Where in far fields the orchids grew.

RALPH WALDO EMERSON (1803–1882), "Thoreau"

found in an area were removed, and often the trees were chopped down in the process. Thus, not only were there few or no remnants left to replenish the population, there was no habitat for the population to inhabit, and, most importantly, no further plants for rivals to collect, even if the rival could unravel the web of lies constructed around the true habitat of any given species. Judging by the auction lists of the period, where quantities of thousands, tens of thousands, or merely "tons" were not uncommon, and taking into account the hardships imposed by travel difficulties, the sheer volume of collected plants must have been staggering.

Above right: Habenaria species are naturally found throughout the tropical and subtropical areas of the world. H. rhodocheila *is native to Indochina and southern regions of China.*

Right: Named in honor of Cardinal Haynald of Kaloesa, Hungary, Paphiopedilum haynaldianum *was discovered by Gustav Wallis close to Manila, the Philippines, in the mid-1800s.*

Below: In the 1870s, Carl Roebelin was exploring an island of the Philippines when an earthquake hit. He found a plant in the rubble, later named Vanda sanderiana. *Below is a form of the species.*

Influential Plant Breeders and Nurseries

An inevitable side effect of the desires of the rich is the creation of a class to serve those desires. So were the first orchid nurseries formed, and so did the rich drive the early orchid breeders. The earliest orchid nurseries were extensions of firms founded by growers trained at the estates of the wealthy. These firms began by growing the various novelties entering cultivation from the newly explored areas of the world, orchids being just one facet of their product line. One of the earliest nurseries was Loddiges and Sons, remembered by the many species names given in their honor, such as *Cattleya loddigesii* and *Cycnoches loddigesii*. Young men were apprenticed to wealthy estates, and the most ambitious went on to be nurserymen. (This pattern emerges more than once in the history of modern orchid growing.)

Early progress in orchid cultivation, once Joseph Paxton had elucidated the proper techniques, remained largely in the collections of the landed rich, such as the Duke of Devonshire and his peers. As the demand for new orchids grew, firms like Veitch, Sander's,

Right: Cattleya loddigesii *was named for nurseryman Conrad Loddiges, who opened London's first orchid nursery in Hackney in 1812. There are a number of pink-flowered hybrids of* C. loddigesii.

Charlesworth's, and "hybrids" like Alexander began to take the lead. (H. G. Alexander's firm was a prime example of a wealthy individual's, in this case Sir George Holford, grower successfully striking out on his own, thereby creating a "hybrid" of a wealthy hobbyist's collection and a commercial firm.)

PROBLEMS WITH ORCHID BREEDING

Two great impediments stood in the way of orchid hybridization: pollinization and seed culture. Until the middle of the nineteenth century, no one was even sure how seed pods formed on orchids. Certainly, plants were imported with seed pods already formed, and, occasionally by chance, seedlings resulted. But what went where and why was a mystery. The prudish attitude of Victorians toward sex did not help matters. That the male (pollinia) and female (stigmatic surface) features of the orchid flower were contained in the one organ was doubly confusing. But when John Dominy, an employee of the Veitch nursery, placed the pollinia of one flower onto the stigmatic surface of another, resulting in a seed pod, our modern world of orchid hybrids was born. The first days of orchid

Above: The attractive hybrid Vanda Robert's Delight *has a heavy* V. sanderiana *influence. This particular species was named for Frederick Sander, an avid orchid collector and renowned nurseryman.*

Left: Masdevallia veitchiana *was named for horticulturist and nurseryman James Veitch, who first imported, grew, and bloomed this species in England. Veitch employed many men to collect orchids from tropical regions.*

Right: The immature seed pods of *Jumellea sagittata* stay on the plant for 4–8 months. In the early days of orchid cultivation, not much was known about how seed pods formed on orchid species.

hybridization were heady indeed, with the flowering of the first hybrid, a *Calanthe*, making news not only in the horticultural world but in the general press as well. People were amazed. One prominent scholar went so far as to say "You will drive the botanists mad!" Thankfully, by the time the artificial production of orchid seed pods was possible, growers discovered that seeds germinated relatively well if sown around the base of the parent plant or another well-established plant. Still, only a few, or a few dozen at best, plants resulted—hardly commercial quantities. It remained for scientists to trace the role of the mycorrhizal fungi in seed germination and apply the knowledge to large-scale commercial culture, later in the early twentieth century.

Another obstacle to successful orchid hybridization little considered today is the complete lack of any genetic information on orchids (or any other plants, for that matter). The work of Mendel had been lost before it had even been discovered, and only anecdotal success- (or failure-) based methods remained. Most practitioners had a pretty good idea of how to breed a good hog or horse, but an orchid? No one really even knew which were closely related, and the orchids' ability to hybridize freely even between genera was not yet on the horizon. Lots of trial and error, combined with astute observation, would be needed before a hybridizing "plan" could be put into action. So, at first, it was simply cross everything with everything else and see what happens. Slowly, genetic affinities began to appear. The first intergeneric hybrid, a *Laeliocattleya*, flowered. Not only were hybrids produced, but also sibling crosses between fine forms of popular species began to result in vastly superior forms

Fly forward, O my heart,
from the Foreland to the Start—
We're steaming all-too slow,
And it's twenty thousand mile
to our little lazy isle
Where the trumpet-orchids blow!
RUDYARD KIPLING (1865–1936),
"L'Envoi"

unseen in wild-collected plants. This development was an eagerly awaited one, because, even in those far-off days, the dwindling (by their standards at least) supplies of good quality species was being noticed. Even today, we have yet to surpass the line-bred *Odontoglossum crispum* created by Joseph Charlesworth nearly 100 years ago.

THE FIRST SUCCESSFUL ORCHID BREEDERS

Then, as now, the potential orchid breeders with the keenest sense of observation coupled with a superlative memory had the most success. We remember these men (and a few notable women like Eileen Low) as heroes, not just for their accomplishments, but because we understand that they were able to make so much from so little. If one breeder were to epitomize the new nurseryman/hybridizer, it would be H. G. Alexander. His achievements have been so far-reaching and so profound that without his work, we would

Above: The first intergeneric hybrid that was bred successfully was a cross between *Laelia* and *Cattleya*—a *Laeliocattleya*. Since then, many highly variable hybrids have been created, featuring a wide variety of flower colors.

Left: Laeliocattleya (*Pittiana* × Cattleya leopoldii) × L. *Interglossa* is an example of one of the many Laeliocattleya hybrids made possible because of the pioneering work of the first orchid breeders.

But it is not just the results of his orchid hybridizing that guarantee H. G. Alexander a place in the pantheon of orchid greats. He was instrumental, directly and indirectly, in the training of the men who would carry on the tradition of excellence in orchid hybridizing well into the next generation. His best-known pupil was certainly B. O. Bracey, who, through his long tenure at Armacost & Royston in the middle of the twentieth century, and into his own nursery after World War II, used both Alexander's stud plants and his training to further cattleyas and other select genera into a form recognizable to us today. Bracey's influence was particularly important as he had the opportunity to use Knudson's breakthrough orchid culture media to grow literally tens of thousands of his hybrid seedlings on to flowering and thereby select the best for further breeding. Not only was Bracey able to advance Armacost's breeding in this way, but the wide distribution of seedlings made possible by this first instance of mass-produced orchids gave others access to breeding that they might otherwise have missed. And, like Alexander, Bracey—abrasive as he has often been portrayed— was a superb judge and trainer of men. So many influential orchid growers received their training at Armacost & Royston during Bracey's days that it would take a whole book just to contain their achievements: Leo Holguin, Ernest Hetherington, Herb Hager, and Joe Ozzella are just a few of those who went on with the Bracey legacy.

Above: In the early 1900s, Cymbidium erythrostylum became one of the three species of that genus from Myanmar and Indochina (along with C. parishii and C. insigne) that were available to orchid breeders.

have a far different, and probably much poorer, range of hybrids today. He is perhaps best known for his introduction of *Cymbidium* Alexanderi 'Westonbirt' FCC/RHS, the most influential cymbidium parent of all time, and the vanguard of polyploidy breeding that we know today. But his significant creations do not stop at just the one. *Laeliocattleya* Lustre 'Westonbirt' has had nearly the same influence in lavender cattleyas as Alexanderi had in pastel cymbidiums. It was later discovered to be a tetraploid, as well. Alexander once said about *Paphiopedilum* Hellas 'Westonbirt' FCC/RHS that it would prove to be as important as *Cymbidium* Alexanderi. History has proven him perhaps less than completely right, but no one who really knows paphiopedilums would omit Hellas from a list of the most important parents of all time. The best red cattleya for many years in the mid-twentieth century was *Sophrolaeliocattleya* Falcon, its fame only lessened perhaps because it proved to be a poor parent, and almost entirely virused, which ruined its chance to be an important potted plant.

The Judge's money brings
architects to make his mansion fair;
The Hales have seven gardeners
to make their roses grow;
The Judge can get his trees from Spain
and France and everywhere,
And raise his orchids under glass
in the midst of all the snow.

JOYCE KILMER (1886–1918),
"The Snowman in the Yard"

PLANT BREEDERS AFTER WORLD WAR II

The years between the two World Wars and after, well into the 1970s, were the glory years of orchid nurseries and hybridizing. So many famous nurseries were founded, prospered, and, sadly, faltered, that it would be impossible to treat them all fairly. English nurseries such as Charlesworth's, Alexander's, Black & Flory, Armstrong & Brown, and Mansell & Hatcher flew the Union Jack to great effect around the world. Unfortunately, World War II and its resulting fuel and currency shortage led to these collections and others being sent overseas for "safe keeping," with the remaining plants often in great jeopardy. English nurseries never really recovered from this disaster, and American nurseries began to come to the fore. Armacost & Royston, H. E. Patterson, Rivermont, the McDades, and others led the field into the immediate post-war years.

However, it was during the 1950s and 1960s, with the rapidly expanding economy and disposable income of the middle class, that the number and variety of American nurseries began to flourish. Men trained by Armacost, before World War II, and their peers branched out across the United States, creating their own nurseries, or running those of wealthy men who were trying to justify their hobby. Many had their own breeding programs. Most of these nurseries were vertically integrated, breeding and growing what they ultimately sold. These were exciting times for the orchid hobby, with nurseries like Fred A. Stewart Orchids, Jones & Scully, Rod McLellan Company, Carter & Holmes, and numerous others providing a wonderful selection of great hybrids in colorful catalogs, tempting growers to order just one more seedling.

The resulting excitement led to the rapid rise of both national and local orchid societies. The American Orchid Society (AOS) grew from a few hundred members to over 20,000 during this period, while becoming the premier judging system in the world. Sadly, a combination of economic and market factors have seen this wonderful time end. Since the 1990s, smaller orchid growers have found it nearly impossible to compete utilizing their own production and have shifted more and more to the product of mass growers. This is leading to a homogenization of the available product that will have a profound effect on the type of person attracted to the hobby. Whether there will be fewer or more people attracted remains to be seen.

Below: Phragmipedium Eric Young was one of the first phragmipedium hybrids originated by the Eric Young Foundation, situated on the island of Jersey in the English Channel. It is a hybrid between P. besseae and P. longifolium, registered in 1991.

Below: In 1962, Sophrolaeliocattleya Jewel Box was registered. As well as being very easy to cultivate, it has proven to be an outstanding parent of many compact-growing gregi, including S. Mine Gold 'Orchid Centre', seen here.

Left: Phalaenopsis *hybrids are widely available from nurseries as either seedlings or more mature plants—but it may take some research to find a particular hybrid, such as Sogo Yukidian (seen here).*

ORCHID WEBSITES

Orchid enthusiasts can visit the following websites to discover more about orchids, or to find an orchid society in their area. This is only a sample of the hundreds of websites devoted to orchids.

NORTH AMERICA

American Orchid Society—http://www.aos.org
Canadian Orchid Congress—http://www.CanadianOrchidCongress.ca/
Native Orchid Conservation (Manitoba, Canada)—http://www.nativeorchid.com/
Orchid Specialist Group—http://go.to/orchid-specialist-group
Cymbidium Society of America—http://www.cymbidium.org/
Encyclia Enthusiasts—http://www.encyclias.org/
The *Odontoglossum* Alliance—http://www.odontoglossumalliance.org/
International *Phalaenopsis* Alliance—http://www.phal.org/
The Pleurothallid Alliance—
http://www.pleurothallids.com/The_Pleurothallid_Alliance.htm
The Slipper Orchid Alliance—http://www.slipperorchid.org/

EUROPE

International Orchid Register (RHS)—
http://www.rhs.org.uk/plants/registration_orchids.asp
British Orchid Council—http://www.british-orchid-council.info/
Orchid Society of Great Britain—http://www.orchid-society-gb.org.uk/
The North of England Orchid Society—http://www.orchid.org.uk/intro.htm
The Hardy Orchid Society—http://www.hardyorchidsociety.org.uk/
British *Paphiopedilum* Society—http://www.paphiopedilum.org.uk/
The Pleurothallid Alliance UK—http://www.pleuro.co.uk/
Vereinigung deutscher Orchideenfreunde (Germany)—http://www.orchideen-journal.de/

ASIA-PACIFIC

The Orchid Society of South-East Asia—http://www.ossea.org.sg/
Australian Orchid Council—http://www.orchidsaustralia.com/
Australasian Native Orchid Society—http://www.anos.org.au/
Orchid Council of New Zealand—http://www.orchidcouncil.co.nz/
New Zealand Native Orchid Group—
http://www.anos.org.au/groups/newzealand/nznogframe.html

AFRICA

South African Orchid Council—http://www.saoc.co.za/
Cape Orchid Society—http://capeorchids.itgo.com/
Witwatersrand Orchid Society—http://www.saoc.co.za/tos.htm
Disa Orchid Society of South Africa—http://www.saoc.co.za/dosa.htm

Modern Trends in Orchid Cultivation

The single most important trend in modern orchid culture is the stratification of the industry. Formerly, most orchid nurseries would grow what they sold and were thus intimately familiar with their product. Today, the global nature of the orchid industry has led to each stage of the life of an orchid being handled by a distinct segment, often in a different country. Breeding units may be just about anywhere, and produce the hybrid seedlings or the meristem mother plants. However, for those segments of the industry still reliant on seedlings, like phalaenopsis, the producers are generally in warmer areas where labor is inexpensive. The young plants are grown in warmer lower-cost areas, before being shipped off to finishing nurseries close to the final markets. This is all cost-driven. When pennies can make the difference, the cheapest (whether by efficiency, intrinsically lower labor costs, or some combination of these factors) method will be the winner. This has led to an unprecedented availability of inexpensive, generally high-quality plants on the mass market. People are exposed to orchids who might never have considered them a viable purchase.

Sadly, many traditional orchid nurseries are no longer able to compete in this arena. Proponents of the mass market will note that perhaps these nurseries were founded on unrealistic expectations. They may also point to the many cultural advances pioneered by the mass-market nurseries that have enabled them to compete more effectively and grow plants in a fraction of the time once thought necessary. The traditionalists will point to the lack of diversity in the products on today's market, as well as the almost complete lack of knowledge on the part of many, if not all, vendors. Yes, it is a good thing to be able to get a phalaenopsis from seed to flowering in well under 36 months, and, yes, it is an even better thing if the flower quality matches that of awards from ten years ago, especially at the low price point often seen. But when it comes at the expense of the type of business upon which the basis of the hobby was founded, it is certainly open to debate.

ORCHIDS ON THE WORLD WIDE WEB

It is safe to say that no other phenomenon has had a more profound affect on the availability of orchid-related information. Where in the past—until the

Right: Orchid growers can find out the parentage and originator of gregi like Epidendrum Orange Glow, *as well as other useful information, from the International Orchid Register on the RHS website.*

last ten years or so—hobbyists had to rely on local experts, local nurserymen, their local or national orchid society, or books for knowledge on how to grow their plants, today information is just a mouse-click away. Membership in national societies was *de rigueur* if one wanted to receive the best of all information sources, the society's journal. Both the Royal Horticultural Society's *Orchid Review* and the American Orchid Society's *Orchids* magazine (formerly the *AOS Bulletin*) are prime examples of the traditional method of information dissemination. Not only were the articles and columns written by the best and most knowledgeable of available sources, but in addition the advertising section alone was often worth the price of the magazine. Where else could one evaluate and, if desired, obtain examples of the very latest trends in orchid availability than in the month ads brought to them in their society's publications? And, of course, local knowledge was served by membership in the local or regional orchid society, often affiliated with the national group. Here, beginning growers could get the most up-to-date information on which orchids grew best in the particular area, what "tricks" were known to work, and who the most reliable sources in the area might be. Often, reputations were made based on writing skill in various hobby-oriented publications. Sadly, writing skill and orchid skill were not always linked, as more than one instance of "snake-oil" type self-promotion can be cited.

The rise of the World Wide Web has proven to be both a boon and a bane to orchid growers. In some ways, it has sounded a wake-up call to national societies, who find their publications' relevance called into question by declining membership numbers. In other ways, it has served to create an entire new class of orchid expert, by giving "publication" space to just about anyone with a keyboard and a little time. Unfortunately, people are still prone to believe just about anything they see in print, and to believe that having your print appear in public somehow qualifies you as something other than a typist. Nonetheless, the World Wide Web is, on balance, a great boon to the average orchid hobbyist. It provides instant access to good

quality information, especially if one knows where to look and exercises a modicum of good sense in accepting what one reads. The Web provides a venue for dozens of on-line forums, where hobbyists can, in real time, discuss their problems and successes with other orchid growers literally around the world. Commercial growers can quickly distribute offerings of what is seasonally appropriate, allowing consumers, for really the first time, access to their own personal nurseryman, someone who can tell them "what's good" right now. Photographs, hints, warnings, politics, indeed all aspects of the orchid hobby are available through any search engine in widespread use.

Above: The American Orchid Society website has a wealth of information on cultivating and propagating orchids, orchid shows, AOS awards, pests and diseases, and a whole lot more.

Left: Orchid enthusiasts looking to find out about the genus Pleurothallis *or species like P. marthae can visit the websites of the Pleurothallid Alliance in either the USA or UK.*

Cultivating Orchids

Above: Like all members of this genus, Stanhopea nigroviolacea *should be cultivated in a basket to allow its pendent spikes to spear through the medium and burst into bloom.*

Above: This healthy Brassia arcuigera *plant is quite at home on its weldmesh bench, as warm moist air is easily able to circulate around it.*

There are many important considerations when cultivating orchids, from where to keep the plants to the choice between pots and mounts. Other variables include temperature requirements, watering needs, and fertilization.

Growing Orchids in a Shadehouse

A shadehouse is a well-ventilated structure that provides shade and maintains higher humidity than outside. It is also a few degrees cooler in summer than the outside temperature, while in winter it provides some protection from mild frosts. When selecting a site for the shadehouse, choose a place that receives maximum winter sun, as it's a lot easier to apply shade than to increase light. It is courteous to let the neighbors know what you are building, and you may also need approval from your local council. Most shadehouses are constructed from water pipes or similar, which are connected by metal clips designed for this type of construction. Treated timbers can also be used. Plan on having a high roof to allow for a greater volume of air in the shadehouse and more hanging room.

There are various types of shadecloth available today, the most popular being the knitted types in the traditional dark green color. A grade of 70 percent shade is recommended. In a larger shadehouse, you can have two or three different grades, and bench the plants accordingly. In exposed or very hot situations, you may wish to add another layer of shadecloth during summer.

Weldmesh should be used to create the benches. This does not deteriorate, and it allows for greater air circulation around the plants. It is purchased in sheets and can be cut with bolt cutters or an angle grinder. It is often recommended to have benches at "hip height", so you don't have to bend down to attend to your plants. Setting up the benches slightly lower than this can be an advantage, as there is more humidity closer to the floor, it is often slightly cooler in summer at this level, and it allows more room to hang plants above the benches,

often two or three layers of them. If you intend to grow a lot of mounted plants, you may wish to install an "A" frame (again, made out of weldmesh) in the middle of your shadehouse.

Some growers like to have concrete, pavers, or blue metal on the floor of their orchid houses. Earth floors add more humidity to the shadehouse and, if the conditions are right, ferns will grow under the benches. Sawdust and wood shavings may also be used in thick layers. Pavers or a generous layer of blue metal are recommended for the walkways.

A misting system provides the finishing touch to the shadehouse. While it doesn't replace watering by hand, it is effective in maintaining a consistent level of humidity throughout the year and cooling the plants on warm summer evenings.

Growing Orchids in a Greenhouse

The installation of a greenhouse will markedly increase the range of orchid genera that can be successfully grown and enjoyed. If you live in an area that experiences a lot of frosts and sub-zero temperatures, you may have to invest in a greenhouse to grow your orchids. They are not only used to heat plants in

Right: Orchid greenhouses can be built to any size, depending on the size of the yard and the number of plants that will be grown.

winter, but are just as effective in keeping cool-growing orchids comfortable in summer. It does not have to be made of glass either, as fiberglass panels and sheets of laserlite are increasing in popularity. The house may also be lined with clear or bubble plastic to assist insulation. There are many pre-fabricated greenhouse models available, in a range of styles and sizes. Most of these do not have a high enough roof. To overcome this, a sturdy brick and concrete base can be built up, with the greenhouse supports bolted into this. You could also excavate what will be the floor of the greenhouse to increase the functional height and volume of air. Check with your local council for height and building restrictions.

The positioning of the greenhouse will depend on what you intend to grow. Select a bright sunny aspect if you intend concentrating on lowland tropical orchids, such as "hardcane" dendrobiums, cattleyas, and vandaceous genera. A shadier position would be preferable for masdevallias, paphiopedilums, *Phalaenopsis*, and most montane species. If you are not sure, go for the sunny site, as you can always increase the shading.

While shadecloth may be draped directly over the greenhouse, it is preferable to build or modify a frame around the greenhouse for this purpose, with a gap of around 12 in (30 cm) from the roof. This allows airflow between the shading and the house. If you cover this frame with a layer of chicken wire before attaching the shadecloth, you will also have more protection against hailstones and other debris. A spare layer of shadecloth may be useful in summer; it can be removed once the threat of very high temperatures has passed.

Left: To grow "hardcane" dendrobiums like Thai Pinky in a greenhouse, ensure that the building is situated in a sunny location as these plants prefer warmer conditions.

Left: Modern greenhouses are usually constructed of translucent sheets of laserlite or fiberglass that have been riveted or bolted onto a wooden or metal frame. A small "window" lets fresh air into the greenhouse.

Below left: A greenhouse in a shady location, either under trees or protected by a large hedge, is suitable for plants from tropical rainforests, such as Phalaenopsis parishii.

Far left: Benches in orchid shadehouses can be set up at different heights to accommodate the growth habits of a variety of orchids, and leave plenty of room for hanging baskets.

Above: Myrmecophila tibicinus *plants tend to take up a lot of room in the orchid greenhouse, a factor that needs to be taken into account if the greenhouse is small.*

Above right: Dracula velutina *is a cool- to intermediate-growing species from Colombia. It can be cultivated in a greenhouse that has an adequate cooling system installed.*

Right: The temperature in orchid greenhouses can successfully be monitored by using a specially designed thermometer. Many measure temperature in both Fahrenheit and Celsius.

Many growers and nurseries are installing under-bench misting systems to maintain or increase humidity and reduce the temperature during warm days without wetting the orchids. Ensure there is plenty of air movement. Ceiling fans or oscillating fans strategically placed will keep your orchids happy. An exhaust fan is also useful for extracting hot air during the warmer months. The combination of electricity and water can be fatal. Make sure you have waterproof fittings and switches installed by a qualified electrician, and be vigilant when watering.

There is a range of greenhouse heaters available. For a small house, a domestic fan heater (with internal thermostat) will often suffice for a few winters before burning out. Many nurseries have had success with oil heaters, hot water systems, and professional glasshouse heaters (that blow hot air or use radiant heat). Some are more energy efficient than others. The main suppliers advertise in horticultural magazines.

Some tropical orchids, from near the equator, can be difficult subjects to bloom (or even grow) when moved away from their native home, even when their optimum temperature requirements are provided. This is because we cannot replicate the uniform day lengths experienced by equatorial plants. By the time they are getting enough light so that their

growth or flowering has commenced, the days shorten and flowering is often aborted. They produce their new growths (which may take two years to mature) in response to 12 hours of sunlight. Plants grown in heated greenhouses in temperate climates are always a few months behind. During winter, when the days are "shorter," they just stop growing (which they don't do in the wild), and are most susceptible to rot.

Remember that greenhouses are not just used to heat plants in winter. They may also be cooled with the installation of an evaporative cooler or air conditioner. This modifies the atmosphere to make it conducive to the culture of cool-climate genera that dislike high summer temperatures. These conditions would be ideal for genera including *Odontoglossum, Masdevallia, Dracula*, plus many of the high altitude (and often colorful) *Dendrobium* species from New Guinea.

Growing Orchids in the Home

Orchids certainly can brighten up the home when in bloom, but not all types can be grown year-round in a similar way to other "house plants." In most cases, orchids thrive in areas with high humidity. In the home, the humidity is significantly less than experienced outside. The bathroom is considered high in humidity, but this is not a great choice, as often the bathroom is at the "shady" end of the house and the only time the humidity is high is when someone is having a shower.

Over recent years, *Phalaenopsis* hybrids have been marketed as flowering pot plants. *Phalaenopsis*, or "moth orchids" as florists know them, are one of the most majestic flowers on the planet, and, if you don't have a greenhouse, they are the best orchids to try to grow indoors. Select a room that receives light for most of the day. Don't place the plant on the windowsill, as they dislike direct light. Sit the pot on a large saucer of pebbles, which will hold about ¾ in (18 mm) of water. This will help create more humidity around the plant, but don't sit the pot itself in the water. Every couple of weeks, give the plant a thorough watering outside and also wash any dust off the leaves. Keep an atomizer next to the plant (preferably with some dilute foliar fertilizer mixed with the water) and mist the plant every time you walk past it. It will reward you for this attention!

South American slipper orchids (*Phragmipedium* species and hybrids) also make excellent indoor plants, and these are even easier to care for than *Phalaenopsis*. For many years these orchids were considered difficult to grow well, because most orchid enthusiasts tended to give them the same growing conditions as the Asiatic slipper orchids from the genus *Paphiopedilum*. However, phragmipediums prefer higher light than most paphiopedilums and definitely more water. The roots systems on *Phragmipedium* plants are generally more extensive and finer than the few very thick roots that occur in *Paphiopedilum*. A number of orchid growers started experimenting with growing phragmipediums in the home in the early 1990s. Many of these chose bright windowsills, that didn't receive full, direct sunlight (which would burn the leaves). But the big cultivation breakthrough was to place the tall pots into containers that held about 2 in (5 cm) of water. The phragmipediums flourished and bloomed throughout the year.

Miniature orchid species can be grown in modified glass fish tanks, using cool lighting tubes designed for plant growth that are connected to a timer to control the amount of light the plants receive. Generally a "day" period of 14 hours is best employed for most genera. A layer of pebbles or gravel is placed on the bottom of the tank, to a depth of about 2 in (5 cm), with a water level kept at about 1 in (25 mm). The potted plants then sit on top of the gravel, which allows water to be kept in the tank without the bases of the pots sitting in water, which could lead to rot problems. Small mounted orchids can also be housed on the back and side walls of your new growing chamber.

Left: Phalaenopsis *hybrids like Hakugin are a popular choice for indoor cultivation. They are compact, will grow in a variety of light conditions (but not direct light), and prefer a temperature that people find comfortable.*

Right: Phragmipedium pearcei *is an ideal house plant, as long as the pot is allowed to sit in a shallow saucer of water that doesn't dry out. This ensures that the plant receives enough moisture to thrive.*

Potting Material

There are many different media that may be used for the cultivation of orchids in pots or baskets. Some may be used exclusively, while others are mixed in various ratios.

POTTING MATERIAL

Pine bark derived from Pinus radiata trees (top) is most often used in either medium or fine grades when potting up orchids. Sphagnum moss (above) is getting harder and harder to come by, as supplies of this species dwindle. If it is available, ensure that the sphagnum moss has been soaked for five minutes before use. Perlite (right) is a light-weight vitreous rock, which is been expanded by heat. It is added to orchid potting mixes for its ability to hold water.

PINE BARK

Pine bark is readily available in various grades, from very fine (¼ in, or 6 mm) to fairly coarse (1¼ in, or 30 mm). The best (hardest) bark comes from mature trees that grow above the snow line. Suitable for most orchid genera, composted or treated pine bark (to remove most tannins, while impregnating the bark with small amounts of fertilizer) is increasing in popularity. Pine bark generally lasts for up to five years.

CHARCOAL

The use of charcoal is declining in popularity. Only a good-quality chunky grade, from hardwood trees, should be considered. It should be washed before use to remove dust. This is a suitable medium to improve drainage of the mix. It should only be used for seedlings or plants that are repotted every couple of years, as charcoal absorbs salts—which will burn the roots. Most growers that use charcoal employ it in combination with other materials, with the charcoal component rarely exceeding 20 percent.

TREEFERN FIBER

The use of *Osmunda* fiber and treefern fiber was common in orchid culture a few decades ago. Generally, treefern is getting harder to obtain, as most species are now protected plants. It has been used for its moisture-holding capabilities, but can quickly become sour if kept wet in warm weather.

GRAVEL

The use of river gravel or blue metal adds weight to the mix and also assists drainage. Particle size is usually ¼–½ in (6–12 mm), and it is commonly combined with bark, to about 20 percent of the mix.

SPHAGNUM MOSS

Sphagnum moss has a very high water-holding capacity and was traditionally used for plants in quarantine. Today, it is a popular medium for mountainous plants that enjoy cooler conditions and year-round moisture. It is an excellent choice for the cultivation of many "difficult" species and for establishing smaller divisions. Best results are obtained by repotting into fresh moss annually.

PEAT MOSS

Peat moss varies in quality, but they all have high water-retentive qualities. It provides little nutritional value to the plant, but is still an important element of *Cymbidium* composts.

PERLITE

This is useful as an additive to orchid composts. It is an inert material that "lightens" the mix, while also retaining moisture. It is often used as 10 percent of the overall potting mixture.

SAND

Coarse gritty sand affords excellent drainage, but dries out quickly after watering and has low water-holding capacity. Quartz sands are among the best. Sand is a good additive to terrestrial orchid mixes and is popular with *Cymbidium* growers. The ratio of its usage can be up to 25 percent of the mix.

Left: All odontiodas, like Odontioda Bugle Boy, grow well in sphagnum moss or in a potting mix that includes fine-grade bark and perlite. They need to be kept well-watered in a humid yet cool area of the greenhouse or shadehouse.

Growing Orchids on Mounts

In the wild, many orchid species spend their lives as epiphytes, growing on the trunks, branches, or outer twigs of trees. So it comes as no surprise that many orchids prefer to spend their lives on "slabs" or "mounts" in preference to the confines of pot culture. In fact, there are some orchid species that hate to have their roots covered at all and need to have them exposed to the air.

Once you have decided to "slab-up" a plant, you need to choose what sort of medium to use. The most popular choices include treefern slabs, cork, and weathered hardwood (such as old fence palings). When using treefern slabs, ensure that the fibers are running vertically. The use of various tree branches is popular with some growers—it should be a long-lasting timber, with a bark that will not peel off. Pine bark chunks may also be used for smaller epiphytes. Other substrates that have been used with varying degrees of success include inverted terracotta pots, rubber plaques (made from recycled tires), and oases (moisture-retentive materials used in floral art).

Use plastic-coated wire to secure the plants tightly to the host (but be careful that you don't sever either the rhizome or the roots). Nylon fishing line or strips of old pantyhose may also be used. If the plant to be mounted has few roots (or is a moisture-loving species), include a pad of sphagnum moss around the base of the plant. This helps to re-establish many orchid plants with a truncated root system.

Mounted orchids have traditionally been displayed in a vertical manner on the walls of the orchid house or on "A" frames within the structure. While this is still very popular, there is now a shift toward growing many species on horizontal slabs. These can be placed directly on the bench with your potted plants or suspended from the roof of the structure with a wire hook through the centre of the mount. Remember that plants grown on slabs require fairly high humidity, ample fresh air circulation, and quite bright light. Low humidity and a watering regime more suited to cacti are the main reasons for the failure of mounted orchids to thrive.

Above: Commonly known as the pineapple orchid, Bulbophyllum elisae *from eastern Australia has been successfully cultivated on mounts made from cork.*

Top left: Of all the members of the genus, Brassavola cucullata *is perhaps the best species to grow on a mount, as it has an appealing pendent growth habit.*

Right: Encyclia polybulbum *thrives on a horizontal slab, while hanging underneath is* Neolauchea pulchella *on a more traditional vertical mount.*

Above: Small compact-growing cattleyas are perfect specimens for slab culture, as they often grow epiphytically in the wild. These plants are also suitable for pots, as long as they have unimpeded drainage.

Above: Dendrobium cuthbertsonii is a miniature species with extraordinarily large flowers for its size. Sphagnum moss is often used to keep these plants moist when grown in pots.

Below: Plastic pots in an organic color like green are highly suitable for use with orchid plants, as they blend in with the color of the foliage and allow the flower hue to dazzle.

Growing Orchids in Pots

Most orchids are grown in pots for convenience and practicality. All terrestrial and most epiphytic orchids are grown in pots that accommodate the plant's root system while also retaining moisture. Pots are easily acquired, transported, and displayed, and are relatively inexpensive. Another bonus is that they are reusable after cleaning in a mild bleach solution.

There is a wide range of pots available. It is most important that the pots be sturdy and have generous drainage holes. Today, plastic pots are most frequently used, coming in a variety of sizes, styles, colors, and depths. There are now businesses that specialize in the production of orchid pots made from a durable black plastic that does not deteriorate in sunlight. Many orchid growers in North America use clear pots with great success. This way the root system can be monitored without disturbing the plants. Care must be taken not to subject the side of these pots to direct sunlight, to avoid cooking the roots. Algae can also become a problem on the sides of the pot.

If possible, try to keep plants with the same pot size together on the bench. No only does it look tidier, but the pots should dry out at the same time (if in the same mix), so they can safely be watered in a block.

TERRACOTTA POTS

Traditional terracotta pots were the nursery standard decades ago, before the invention of suitable plastic containers. They were deep pots that required "crocking" (filling up to a third of the height of the pot with broken pieces of terracotta to assist drainage). Today, there would be few orchid growers that "crock" their pots. Terracotta pots are expensive, heavy, and invariably have poor drainage holes that need enlarging. Another disadvantage is that many orchids with thick roots (such as cattleyas and vandaceous orchids) cling tightly to the inside and outside of the pot, and the roots are invariably damaged when removed. Drying out the plant and its potting medium over a few days, so that the roots and mix slightly contract, makes the job of getting the plant out much easier, minimizing damage to the root system.

However, there are still a lot of orchids that enjoy life in terracotta pots. It must be remembered that orchids in terracotta pots will dry out much faster than their counterparts in plastic containers. Some of the squat designs, coupled with round drainage holes on the sides of the pot, have proved popular with most medium-sized monopodial orchids, many of the rock-growing *Laelia* species, and "hardcane" dendrobiums. You will find the roots will run all over both surfaces of the pot and obviously through the drainage holes. Many orchids are happy to spend their lives undisturbed, simply clambering over the container. That is fine, until the mix deteriorates. If this occurs, either tip the plant upside down and use your fingers to dislodge any stray compost, or use a jet of water to wash away the old material (without dislodging or damaging the roots). Then fill the cavity with new potting medium (generally bark). This is best done while the plant is in active growth. You will find orchids treated this way will respond with renewed vigor.

STANDARD PLASTIC POTS

There are many different orchids (some terrestrial or semi-terrestrial) that have an extensive or deep root system that prefers standard-sized pots. The large-flowered or "standard" cymbidiums, plus many of the "intermediate" types, certainly prefer the deeper pots. Many of the evergreen terrestrials, including *Calanthe triplicata, Neobenthamia gracilis, Phaius tankervilleae, Sobralia,* and *Thunia,* enjoy the extra room for their roots. Some of the very tall-growing dendrobiums (such as *Dendrobium fimbriatum* and *D. pulchellum*) also perform with enhanced vigor. Many growers add a handful of large pebbles to the bottom of the pots of tall-growing plants, to boost the pot's weight and stability.

> *When the emotions are strong one should paint bamboo; in a light mood one should paint the orchid.*
>
> CHUEH YIN

SQUAT PLASTIC POTS

These are arguably the most popular pots used for the cultivation of most orchids. Generally they are about two-thirds the height of standard pots and their diameter exceeds their depth. The advent of squat pots has made redundant the old practice of "crocking" pots. Most growers and nurseries are using the squat-style pots for "miniature" cymbidiums and some of the less vigorous "intermediates."

When to Repot

In the main, orchids love being repotted into fresh mix. They seem to get a new lease of life, coupled with a burst of leaf and root growth if the conditions are conducive. It is often recommended that repotting of late winter- or spring-flowering orchids should only take place after flowering. While this is true in many cases, there are orchids which can be potted-on (carefully moving the plant and potting mix into a larger pot, then adding additional potting media)

REPOTTING Clump-forming orchids like Dendrochilum cobbianum often need repotting every few years as they outgrow their containers. Squeeze the pot to loosen the plant, then carefully pull it out of the pot. Use your fingers to gently tease out the roots. Place the plant in a large pot that allows for at least two years of growth, then fill the pot with fresh potting mix. You could also divide the plant before repotting it, to increase the number of new bulbs that are formed.

or divided at most times of the year. Mid-winter and mid-summer are the traditional exceptions, unless you provide your plants with the ideal conditions that will not put them under stress during these times.

The best time to repot plants is when they are in active growth, when new growths appear that are quickly followed by fresh root activity. You will find that most orchids in cultivation like to be repotted in spring. There are many cooler-climate orchids that have their main growth spurt after the heat of summer, in autumn and winter. So these plants need to be tended to after the hot weather has passed.

Quite simply, orchids need to be repotted when they have outgrown their pots, or the potting mix has deteriorated. Orchids in sphagnum moss should be repotted at least every two years, even though annually is preferable. Adult cymbidiums like to be repotted every two to three years, with younger plants (seedlings and propagations from back-bulbs) moved annually or even biannually. Plants in a bark-based mix can be happy for up to five years. Sick plants should be repotted into fresh mix or sphagnum moss regardless of the time of year.

Above: Black plastic pots come in a wide range of shapes and sizes. Some have larger holes in the bottom to accommodate the orchid species that need excellent drainage.

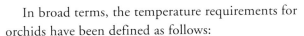

Left: Cochleanthes amazonica *is an epiphyte found from Brazil to Colombia. It is a fine example of a warm- to intermediate-growing orchid species.*

Temperature Requirements

When we read or talk about the temperature ranges of orchids, emphasis tends to be placed on their minimum winter requirements, with not much said about the summer temperatures. While it is true that there are lowland tropical orchids that will suffer or even die if the temperature drops below a certain point for an extended length of time, there are also montane species that dislike high temperatures during summer. In mountainous regions near the equator, where most of the world's tropical epiphytic orchids grow, the plants only experience a narrow corridor of temperature variation. Generally, the temperature rarely falls much below 50°F (10°C) or gets above 78°F (26°C). Obviously these are ideal conditions for the species that make their homes in these parts. In cultivation, we tend to grow lots of vastly different types of orchids in a handful of microclimates in the orchid house. Thankfully, most orchids are adaptable and are able to take cooler or warmer temperatures than they would experience in the wild.

In broad terms, the temperature requirements for orchids have been defined as follows:

- **Cool-growing**—with a winter nighttime minimum of 39°F (4°C); aim to keep these plants cooler in summer.
- **Intermediate-growing**—with a winter nighttime minimum of 50°F (10°C); these can take cooler temperatures for short lengths of time.
- **Warm-growing**—with a winter nighttime minimum of 60°F (16°C); very unforgiving if temperatures drop below 50°F (10°C), these can take high temperatures as long as the humidity is high.

WINTER COLD

There are very few epiphytic or lithophytic orchids that can handle temperatures at or below freezing for longer than a few hours. Even though there are orchids that may be dusted in snow in winter, such as *Dockrillia striolata* and *Dendrobium speciosum*, the plants certainly do not enjoy it. Frost is an enemy of orchids and can kill plants if they have been kept moist. It is important for the plants to have an increase in temperature during the day, hopefully in conjunction with clear skies. Ideally, only water orchids in the morning on sunny days, preferably when there are prevailing winds, as the plants must dry out before sundown.

Many deciduous terrestrial orchids from temperate climates have adapted to cold winter temperatures, when they grow and flower, and actually go dormant underground (as tubers) during the hot and often dry summers experienced in those regions.

Above: With a bounty of delightful pink flowers, Disa Watsonii *is a cool-growing hybrid between South Africa's famous* Disa uniflora *and the hybrid* Disa Kewensis.

Right: An unusual back view of the Dockrillia striolata *flower. These plants tolerate cold, and in the wild may endure snow cover during winter.*

Right: Anguloa uniflora *is native to mountainous regions of Venezuela, Peru, Colombia, Ecuador, and Bolivia. It dislikes high heat levels and can wilt easily if the roots dry out.*

SUMMER HEAT

Many high-altitude or montane species from 4,920 ft (1,500 m) above sea level and higher never experience high temperatures in the wild. Anything above 86°F (30°C) is uncommon. In cultivation, leaf burn and leaf drop are the main side effects of high summer temperatures. The main genera that suffer include *Anguloa*, montane *Bulbophyllum* and *Dendrobium*, *Disa*, *Dracula*, *Masdevallia*, *Mediocalcar*, *Pleurothallis*, and *Thunia*. It is imperative during heat waves to keep humidity high in the orchid-growing area, keep the floor damp, and only water plants once the sun is off them. Adding an extra layer of shadecloth can also help to lower the temperature and prevent scorching.

Watering Your Orchids

Watering is the most basic task for gardeners. However, when related to orchids, it always seems to provide many novices with problems and hesitation. Sometimes it gets to the point where many are "scared" to water their orchids, for fear of killing them with kindness! In general, most growers don't water their orchids enough. It is imperative that the plant's root system is allowed to drain freely and quickly and that there is constant movement of fresh air. Watering is a science that can only be mastered

with practice. Basically, plants in active growth need more water than when they are in a dormant state. Ensure the plants get a "deep" watering, with excess water flowing liberally out of the drainage holes, as opposed to a splash with the hose. Common sense also tells us that almost all plants require more moisture in summer than in winter. It should be remembered that there are many orchids that require a dry period as part of their annual growth cycle. Generally this occurs in the cooler months, and this dormancy needs to be respected.

Plants grown in the garden or under shadecloth have the advantage of receiving natural rainwater. They enjoy the heavy rain of a thunderstorm, which has additional nitrogen due to a chemical reaction caused by lightning. The downsides are the strong winds and hailstones that can often accompany severe storms. A few days after such a downpour, have a good look at the root systems of your plants. You will find that they have longer green root-tips and the foliage has added luster. Another positive is that you will find many of the "one-day wonders" (orchids that have blooms which generally last for less than 24 hours) will initiate inflorescences and bloom in about nine or ten days' time. Orchids that respond in this manner include *Dendrobium* (Section *Rhopalanthe*, which includes the dove orchid, *D. crumenatum*), *Diplocaulobium*, some *Eria*, *Flickingeria*, and *Grastidium*. It is not uncommon to have a whole suite of different species in bloom on the same day, a week or so after a storm.

Above: Watering orchids by hand is the best way to ensure that each plant obtains the necessary moisture for survival. An adjustable rose nozzle allows the orchid grower to control the strength of the water flow.

Left: Naturally found in the forests of New Guinea, Mediocalcar decoratum detests hot dry conditions and must be kept moist and partly shaded.

Left: All coelogynes, such as the deliciously named Coelogyne flaccida *'Caramel', enjoy humid growing conditions and regular watering throughout the year.*

Ideally, nothing can compare to hand-watering, where you also get the opportunity to personally inspect your plants, and can take necessary action if you spot a problem. A rose nozzle delivers a gentle shower of water to your plants without blasting them away. There are also extension wands that are ideal for watering hanging pots and baskets as well as mounted plants that are hung up high in the orchid house. Some hose attachments deliver an ultra-fine mist, which is most useful for dampening the foliage and quenching mounted orchids.

Above: Like many orchids, lycastes require a reasonable level of water when in active growth and reduced watering when they are dormant. Hand-watering gives you this control.

Right: Zygopetalum crinitum *and other members of this genus will respond to frequent feeding, and prefer increased fertilizing in spring–autumn when they are in active growth.*

It is also efficient to channel rainwater off the roof of the family home, garage, and orchid houses with a solid roof, into a water tank. This is particularly important in areas where the town water supply is questionable. Many local supplies have high concentrations of chlorine, which can be poisonous to sensitive plants, and will quickly kill growing sphagnum moss. If practical, store this water for at least 24 hours in an open vessel before using it on your orchids, so that the chlorine has dissipated.

Misting systems can also be installed in the orchid house. Basic systems (which include plastic tubing, nozzles, and hose attachments) are relatively inexpensive and easily installed. You can even have its operation computer-controlled or on a timer that snaps onto the tap. Misters are primarily used to increase the level of humidity and cool the temperature around the plants. Regardless of how many nozzles you install, there will always be dry patches, particularly if the foliage of one plant shields another. There is more chance of uniform coverage if there is a swirling breeze. Depending on the area to be covered (and the size of the collection), it may be wise to install a number of runs, with the number of nozzles governed by your water pressure.

Fertilizing Your Orchids

There are many brands of fertilizer on the market, with most promising amazing results. There are two main types: organic (natural) and inorganic (chemical). Organic fertilizers can sometimes vary in quality due to the raw materials and the time of year produced. Chemical fertilizers are more consistent, as their contents can be measured exactly.

The primary elements for plant growth are nitrogen (N), phosphorus (P), and potassium (K); these three components are defined as the NPK of the mixture. Secondary elements such as calcium, magnesium, and sulfur are also important for plant growth. Other trace elements—including boron, manganese, zinc,

copper, and iron—are only required in minute quantities. The outer packaging of fertilizers provides the chemical breakdown and ratio of its ingredients. A high-nitrogen (N) fertilizer is used from late spring to early autumn, when most orchids are in active growth. The nitrogen helps the growth of the plant and gives it a greener luster, during this period of higher temperatures and stronger light. For a mixed collection, a suitable fertilizer would have an NPK ratio of 22:8:12 or similar. From mid-autumn to spring, a fertilizer that promotes healthy roots, boosts the quality of the flowers, and strengthens the plant should be used. This has a lower nitrogen content, as most orchid genera have slowed their growth rate considerably and are now concentrating on flowering. A suitable fertilizer would have a higher potassium (K) component and an NPK ratio of 12:12:20 or similar. Of course, there are many variations available, and you will quickly learn what works best for your conditions and collection. It is imperative that the manufacturer's application instructions are adhered to. Higher than recommended concentrations of fertilizer will not make the plants grow faster—in fact, you run the risk of burning the roots and foliage. Many growers feed their plants lower than the manufacturer's recommended rate, but apply it more frequently.

For a small collection, a watering can with a rose nozzle is perfect for fertilizing your plants. This way you also know exactly how much food you are giving your plants. Make sure the ingredients are fully dissolved before applying; adding a dash of hot water will accelerate the process. Many garden centers now sell plant feeders (with a screw-on jar to hold the fertilizer), complete with rose nozzle, which snaps into the end of the

> *There dumbly like a worm*
> *all day the still white orchid feeds;*
> *But never an echo of your daughters' laughter*
> *Is there, nor any sign of you at all*
>
> EDNA ST. VINCENT MILLAY (1892–1950),
> "Ode to Silence"

hose. Water mixes with the contents and will dispense fertilizer for about 15 minutes, very handy if you are only doing a small section. For a larger collection of plants, a fertilizer proportioner can be attached to the hose at the tap.

Because orchids don't grow as fast as annuals and most foliage plants, the fertilizing rate may be reduced to half of the manufacturer's recommendation. It is always best to lean on the side of not enough fertilizer than too much. There are some vigorous orchids that can be safely fertilized at full strength during their active growing period. These "heavy feeders" include cymbidiums, "softcane" dendrobiums, *Phalaenopsis*, and thunias. Manure pellets and slow-release inorganic fertilizers (with the chemicals inside tiny balls) can be applied during the growing season. These release their nutrients over a few months. Organic fertilizers can be applied to the surface of the mix, while it is best to slightly cover the tiny beads of the inorganic fertilizers, as they have a tendency to deteriorate quickly when exposed to sunlight, and release their contents at once.

Below: Feeding orchids like Ascocenda Carolaine 'Kathleen' during the growth period not only helps to maintain the plant's vigor, but may also lead to an increase in flower production.

Right: Dendrobium Stardust is just one of the many "softcane" dendrobiums that are vigorous enough to have full-strength fertilizer applied during the growing season.

Propagating Orchids

Above: Regardless of the method you use to propagate your orchids, it is always a good idea to clearly label the plants with important information like their name and the date they were propagated.

There are several different methods of propagating orchids, some more difficult than others. Specific propagating methods are more suitable for particular species or growth forms, so each genus entry in the A–Z section of this book suggests an optimum method for that group of plants.

Division

The most common and simplest method of reproducing orchids, this should only be done with larger plants and preferably at a time coinciding with the start of the plants' main growth cycle. With most orchids this is early spring.

In most cases when dividing plants, you don't want to have any divisions with less than four growths. These smaller pieces will take longer to re-establish and may not bloom the following season. With paphiopedilums and phragmipediums, it is best not to "cut" the plants to make divisions. They grow and flower better as larger plants. Only separate these if natural divisions fall apart while repotting.

Take the plant out of the pot, and remove the old mix and any dead roots. Look at the growth of the plant and decide where the divisions will take place. If you are not sure at this stage, it may be best to simply put the plant into a slightly larger pot with fresh mix. If you have decided that you are going to divide the plant, make a vertical cut through the rhizome halfway between the pseudobulbs. The cut areas may be dusted with sulfur powder, or may be simply dried for about an hour before potting.

Always use sharp secateurs that have been sterilized in a saturated sugar soap solution for at least five minutes, or heated to almost glowing point. This is done to help prevent the spread of viruses and diseases. Remember to sterilize your secateurs before moving on to another plant. Finally, don't forget to label your plants. Apart from its name, include the month and year of repotting and any interesting history about the plant (who it came from, price, country of origin or collection data, date of acquisition, and blooming season). UV-stabilized tags only seem to last for a few

DIVISION Coelogyne Memoria W. Micholitz is an excellent subject for division, as it has outgrown its pot. Locate the natural division between the pseudobulbs and cut the rhizome vertically. Gently pull the two sections of the plant apart. Place some potting mix in the bottom of the pot before positioning the plant, to stop the roots of the plant from escaping out of the holes in the base of the pot. Place the plant in the pot and fill the pot with potting mix. Lastly, water the plant until the water runs clear—this removes the fines from the potting mix.

BACK-CUTTING Laelia anceps *has plenty of exposed roots, and can easily be propagated by back-cutting. Vertically cut between the pseudobulbs, ensuring that there are at least three pseudobulbs in the new section. A second section can be cut off if there are enough pseudo-bulbs. When potting up the section, place the back of the plant at the back of the pot, as laelias grow forward. In a short time, a new shoot should emerge from the dormant eye.*

years, so it is best to push them right into the pot, or tie them behind the mount. Fine permanent black felt markers are good, but tend to fade with age. The good old lead pencil is not as esthetically appealing, but it is more permanent.

Back-cutting

This is a great way to develop specimen plants of the sympodial growth types. It works best with genera that have an exposed rhizome and non-clustering pseudo-bulbs. Simply make a full vertical cut halfway between the pseudobulbs, about every three or four growths. This will activate dormant eyes into new growth, often within weeks. This process is best done in late winter or early spring, and works particularly well with members of the *Cattleya* alliance, *Coelogyne*, *Dendrobium*, *Encyclia*, and *Miltonia*. Again, remember to sterilize your secateurs before moving on to another plant.

Back-bulbs

Whole potfuls of cymbidiums with dried and leafless back-bulbs look fairly ordinary, even when they are in bloom. These back-bulbs are the "insurance policy," in case something happens to the main growing section. When dividing your cymbidiums (trying to keep divisions to at least three pseudobulbs), cut away the back-bulbs (do them individually), remove the dried husks on the bulb, and cut off all the roots. Each of these bulbs should have a dormant "eye," which will shoot if it is healthy, and may be planted in a community pot, or separately, in standard cymbidium mixture or fine bark. Sphagnum moss may also be used, as long as you make sure it doesn't stay wet. It is best to bury them to about a third of the length of the

bulb. Then just treat them as per your other plants, with perhaps a bit more shade. Keep an eye out for any rot (these bulbs will obviously need to be removed and discarded), and all being well you should see a new shoot emerge in three to six months' time. It generally takes three or four years for these plants to flower, but it is worth the wait for choice cultivars.

Of course, it is not just cymbidiums that provide back-bulbs with which to start new plants. Many other orchids can be grown from back-bulbs, as long as the dormant eyes have not expired. Genera that can be grown from single back-bulbs include *Calanthe*, *Catasetum*, *Coelia*, *Phaius*, and *Zygopetalum*.

There are other genera that will only "strike" if there is a cluster of two or three bulbs. Use the same potting medium as you would for adult plants. Included in this category are *Ada*, *Anguloa*, *Ansellia*, *Brassia*, *Bulbophyllum*, *Cattleya*, *Coelogyne*, *Coryanthes*, *Cuitlauzina*, *Dendrobium*, *Dendrochilum*, *Encyclia*, *Laelia*, *Lycaste*, *Maxillaria*, *Miltonia*, *Odontoglossum*, *Oncidium*, *Osmoglossum*, *Pholidota*, and *Stanhopea*.

Below: Dendrochilum cobbianum *can be propagated by potting up back-bulbs taken from the adult plant. For this species, there must be a group of two or three back-bulbs potted together, otherwise the dormant eyes will not send out shoots.*

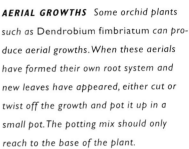

Bottom right: A classic "reed-stem" or "crucifix" type of Epidendrum, E. ibaguense is most often propagated by division. It may also produce aerial growths over time.

Below: Many members of the genus Restrepia, such as R. antennifera, can be propagated by removing the juvenile plants that have formed in the leaf axils of older plants.

AERIAL GROWTHS *Some orchid plants such as* Dendrobium fimbriatum *can produce aerial growths. When these aerials have formed their own root system and new leaves have appeared, either cut or twist off the growth and pot it up in a small pot. The potting mix should only reach to the base of the plant.*

Aerial Growths

The production of aerial growths is an excellent means of propagation. These are growths produced randomly along sections of pseudobulbs, generally the leafless older ones. Leave these aerials (or "keikis," as they are sometimes known) on the adult plant for at least 12 months. The leaves should have lost their "glossy" appearance and should have their own root system. Often it is best to wait until the aerial produces its first new growth before removal. There is rarely a need to cut them off, as most will easily twist off in your hand. These young plants, once they have matured, establish very quickly when potted or mounted. Genera with representatives that frequently produce aerial growths include *Dendrobium*, *Epidendrum*, *Grastidium*, and *Neobenthamia*. Many *Restrepia* and *Pleurothallis* will also produce young plants from the axis of older leaves.

Stem Cuttings

This is a productive method to multiply the terrestrial genus *Thunia*. Cut off the previous season's leafless cane, about 2½ in (6 cm) from the base of the plant (don't touch the current leafy growth). Leave the cut piece for a couple of days to seal the wound, then drop it into a tall pot with about 2 in (5 cm) of sphagnum moss at the bottom. New plants will form over the next couple of months. Other variations of this method involve cutting the stem into sections, or laying the stem down.

A similar method works well for "softcane" dendrobiums (hybrids derived from the species *Dendrobium nobile* and its relatives). These produce nodes along the pseudobulbs that, if the growing conditions are correct, will produce blooms in late spring. If the plants are very shaded, receive too much nitrogen fertilizer, or the roots have been damaged, the plant will naturally transform these nodes into young plants at the expense of flowers. You can use this knowledge to your advantage. In late spring (when the plants are in bloom), select canes that

are at least three years old. It is best to leave three connected growths intact on the main plant (the current growth, the flowering growth, and the previous year's growth). Cut off the old pseudobulbs (three years and older) at the base of the plant. The key here is to find sections of the stem that did not flower, and look for a slight bump on the bulb. This will only work on nodes that have not bloomed. Slice into sections halfway between the nodes, leaving two or three nodes between each cut. Discard any of the sections where all the nodes have expired (if they have bloomed, they will not re-shoot). Half bury the remaining "stem cuttings" in pots of fine bark, and keep shaded and only just moist. They will start shooting in about three to six months' time, and will take about three or four years to bloom. If you are really keen to multiply a particular clone, you can sacrifice the leading mature growth (that has not flowered), remove the leaves, and follow the above method.

Seeds

Orchids produce very fine seeds, in very large numbers, that rely on specific fungi or nutrients for germination. Specialist laboratories undertake commercial seed raising. The seed is firstly germinated in a sterile agar jelly with a range of nutrients. Upon germination, and when the seeds have transformed into manageable young plants, they are transferred into a special growth medium for another 12 months or so.

While this is out of the scope of many backyard orchidists, you may have some success with fresh

A Ram's Horn orchid
seedpod for a woodchuck
Sounds something like.
Better than farmer's beans
To a discriminating appetite…

ROBERT FROST (1874–1963),
"The Self-Seeker"

seeds sprinkled on the top of healthy plants, preferably of the same genus. Potted plants with some active root growth around the surface are ideal. With luck, and if the conditions are conducive, you may end up with a few plants. A couple of the best types of orchids to try growing from seed are *Epidendrum radicans* and its hybrids, and many of the Australian temperate dendrobiums, such as *Dendrobium speciosum* and *D. kingianum*.

Tissue Culture

Plants reproduced by mericloning or tissue culture are genetically identical to the parent plant. However, sometimes there may be mutations from this process that will be slightly different to the original. This is a complex process generally undertaken in laboratories, where small sections of the meristematic tissue are extracted and multiplied on a medium to proliferate the cells. These are divided and replated into flasks containing an agar growth medium. The benefit of mericloning has been the production of large numbers of superior cultivars, which are within the budget of most orchid growers. This has been commercially utilized mainly with hybrid cymbidiums, the *Cattleya* alliance, the *Oncidium* alliance, "cut-flower" *Dendrobium* hybrids, and some vandaceous orchids. At this stage the ever-popular genera *Paphiopedilum* and *Phragmipedium* have not been able to be tissue cultured or mericloned in great quantities, which accounts for the high price of divisions of particular cultivars.

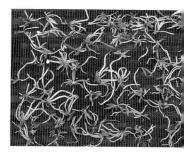

Above: The easiest way to start an orchid collection is to purchase young plants. Once the plants are large enough, stem cuttings or divisions can be made to increase the number of plants.

Top: Spent seed pods should be removed from the orchid plant as part of the maintenance process. The seeds from the pods are so fine that they are difficult to collect, and they need the right growing conditions to germinate.

CUTTINGS Papilionanthe *Mundyi* is a good candidate for propagation by cuttings. As the second image shows, new growth on the plant has been encouraged by a previous cutting. Using a clean pair of secateurs, make the cut so that the piece of plant has a number of roots attached, then pot up the section.

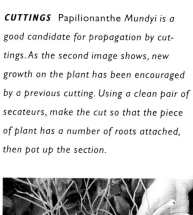

Orchid Pests and Diseases

With proper hygiene, healthy orchids are generally free of pests and diseases. Not all insects in the orchid house are "bad." Many, such as praying mantids, ladybugs, and spiders are quite useful in controlling pests. So don't kill every creature that you see! There are many pests to test the patience of the orchid enthusiast. Caterpillars can make a meal of buds, flowers, and tender new growths if left unchecked. Grasshoppers and crickets can do a lot of damage in a short space of time. *Dendrobium* beetles strip flowers and destroy new growths. Neglected plants can often provide homes for sucking insects such as mealybugs and various species of scale. In fact, scale and mealybugs

appear to be the most universal pest with regard to orchid cultivation. If plants are often kept very dry, red spider mites could become a problem, especially with cymbidiums. Frequent hosing under the foliage will help. Aphids can be a nuisance and cause the developing growths and inflorescences to become stunted. Commercial snail pellets can be laid in damp weather to combat slugs and snails, but make sure they are not accessible to young children or the family pet. These pellets can be sprinkled on the floor of the orchid house and/or scattered over the plants. "Torch visits" of an evening can reap rewards by catching many nocturnal creatures, such as grasshoppers,

Below: The putrid smell of the Bulbophyllum echinolabium *flower may be unpleasant to human noses, but it attracts the species of fly that this plant relies on for pollination.*

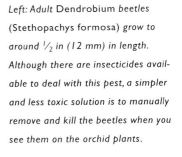

Left: Adult Dendrobium *beetles* (Stethopachys formosa) *grow to around ½ in (12 mm) in length. Although there are insecticides available to deal with this pest, a simpler and less toxic solution is to manually remove and kill the beetles when you see them on the orchid plants.*

Left: Dendrobium *beetles lay their soft clusters of whitish eggs in the developing growths or buds of rock orchids. When the eggs hatch, the larvae bury themselves in the nearby shoots, eating the fleshy inside part. This damages the orchid canes but does not usually kill the plant.*

Left: There are over 20 species of scale, and most are difficult to detect. The first sign is usually the damage caused to the underside of orchid leaves by the scale insects, which suck the sap from the plants. Scale-affected plants can be treated with insecticides, rubbing alcohol, mineral oil, or soapy water.

Left: The rich yellow flowers of Laelia Canariensis *are marred by small dark spots caused by the botrytis fungus. This type of infection is often seen during times of wet weather, when orchid flowers remain damp. Remove affected flowers, and ensure there is adequate air movement in the orchid house.*

crickets, slugs, and snails, which can do a lot of damage if left unchecked. Baits may need to be set if mice and rats are a problem. Again, make sure these baits are not accessible to the family pet.

Most people today do not like using insecticides (for health reasons and because they often kill "good" insects), and only employ them as a last resort. Instead of spraying the whole collection, "spot-spray" for the specific problem, using a small atomizer. A couple of such atomizers filled with a long-lasting pyrethrum mix are handy to keep in the orchid house for localized application. Check with your local garden center or orchid nursery for advice on what products are registered, recommended, and available for the specific pests in your area. If you have to use pesticides, make sure you comply with the manufacturer's instructions, wear protective clothing (and a mask), and have a shower immediately afterward. Beware of "spray drift," and only apply in still conditions—preferably first thing in the morning or at sundown.

There are increasing numbers of orchid growers who are growing some of the Southeast Asian tropical pitcher plants (*Nepenthes* species) as a natural way of combating many flying and crawling pests. The term "tropical" is a bit of a misnomer, as many of these (like the orchids) come from montane regions and are often found growing adjacent to orchids. These carnivorous plants grow into vines and enjoy the same conditions as orchids. They need high humidity for pitcher production. Some of the warm-growing "lowland" species include *N. ampullaria*, *N. mirabilis*, *N. rafflesiana*, and *N. truncata*. The cooler-growing "highland" species and their hybrids will take brief periods of frost, as long as there is a significant increase in the daytime temperature. Recommended species include *N. alata*, *N. maxima*, *N. sanguinea*, *N. tobaica*, and *N. ventricosa*.

Fungicides may be used in times of prolonged damp and still conditions, to prevent or reduce outbreaks of rot. The best defense against such problems is to have your plants well spaced, meticulously remove dead leaves and husks off older back-bulbs, and ensure the plants receive plenty of air circulation.

Warm, humid, and still conditions are the ideal breeding grounds for fungi.

Viruses are arguably the biggest enemy to orchid growers, and they can affect most popular genera. They weaken the plant so that it produces malformed flowers, sometimes with color breaks. Unfortunately, there is no cure for infected plants, which should be destroyed. Keeping the plants "isolated" within a mixed collection is not an option, and may facilitate the rapid spread of a virus throughout the neighboring plants. There are many strains of virus that are spread by mites, scale, aphids, and other sucking or chewing insects. However, the worst culprits are the orchid growers themselves. Using unsterilized cutting implements is the fastest way of spreading many types of virus—such as *Cymbidium* mosaic; *Odontoglossum* ring-spot; and orchid fleck virus, a type of rhabdovirus—throughout the orchid collection. Remember, even harvesting your flowers or spent spikes by hand or cutters could spread a virus. Sterilize your cutting implements by heating them in a fire until they glow, or (after rinsing in water) drenching in bleach or a saturated solution of trisodium phosphate (sugar soap) for at least five minutes.

... diadems
Of brown bee-studded orchids
which were meant
For Cytheraea's brows are hidden here
Unknown to Cytheraea, and by
yonder pasturing steer
OSCAR WILDE (1854–1900),
"The Burden Of Itys"

Above: Nepenthes alata *is an ideal companion plant for cool-growing orchids. The sweet nectar around the rim of the pitchers attracts insects, which slip down the waxy insides into the digestive liquid at the pitchers' base, where they quickly drown.*

Top: Cattleyas are susceptible to Cymbidium *mosaic virus. However,* Cattleya intermedia 'Do Hector', *shown here, is a healthy specimen, without the spotting or streaking on the petals or leaves associated with the virus.*

Conserving Orchids in the Wild

No other subject will get more discussion, usually with less hard information, than orchid conservation, particularly "conserving orchids in the wild." The simple fact is that so little hard research has been done on orchid habitats that no one really knows what constitutes a perfect orchid habitat (for any given species), what the true population status of any given species really is, and what factors are adversely affecting that status. There are few, if any, documented orchid extinctions, but this is not to imply that orchid collection for sale does not affect wild orchid populations, because it can and does. Even when a particular species is common in cultivation, with a long history of seed propagation, the discovery of a long-lost habitat will lead to a frenzy of collecting for greedy dealers and eager hobbyists, without a thought as to the overall effect this has on the long-term survival of the species.

However, it is generally believed that what endangers orchids most in the wild is people—too many people. Habitat degradation is a given in undeveloped countries, where it is necessary to supply farmland for food and fuel production needs for a population growing at an alarming rate. But what about habitat degradation that occurs to further the needs of the developed world, such as the forests that are cut to provide pulp for hamburger wrappers, or to open up grazing for the cattle that make the hamburgers? You can do your part in supporting the various agencies that deal in obtaining and setting aside land for plant conservation. There are so many things we can do to be less greedy and more thoughtful when it comes to either the direct or indirect habitat loss that we may cause.

The loss of tropical orchid habitats is not the only loss that is going on. Small patches of woods and other pockets of wilderness in suburbia may contain native orchids that are threatened by the dumping of rubbish or the harvesting of wild

Left: Bulbophyllum fletcherianum *is naturally found in New Guinea, where it grows on rock faces in riverine forests. Removing the plant from the wild could endanger the delicate balance of the forest ecosystem.*

Right: A Nidema ottonis *plant in Costa Rica's Jardín Botánico Lankester. Botanical gardens play an important role in orchid conservation, with research aimed at discovering more about these plants.*

plants to grace the home. Wildflowers never look better than in their own habitat, so rationalizing that the population, even if it is adversely affected by collecting, can always rebound is false thinking. This is not to say that limited numbers of wild-collected plants should not be permitted into cultivation, because brood stock is always needed. The smaller commercial firms that specialize in providing these more esoteric plants should not be cut off from their livelihood. Propagation by seed and division has to be supported. But when the hobbyist circumvents his local nursery by importing his own orchid plants or by patronizing international vendors from range countries, and then wonders why the local guy falters, it is clear that there is a disconnect. Of course, the advantage of using a range country vendor is that, presumably, the nursery workers from the country of origin are helping to support sustainable orchid harvest from existing forests, thereby enhancing the forests' value to the indigenous peoples and preventing the locals from so cavalierly cutting the forests down. The answer here may be well-considered shopping. The cheapest plants aren't necessarily the best value. Your local nursery will have stabilized the plants and will be taking the losses. This is built into the price you pay. However, there is no way they can stock some of each and every species that the range state vendor can provide. There is room to support more than one grower, and by spreading the support around, the survival of a vital orchid supply network, and its continued support of orchid conservation, can be better assured.

Are there any simple answers? No, unfortunately. However, that does not mean we should not approach the many controversial issues that surround the subject of conserving orchids in the wild. It is contingent on every orchid grower to develop their own sense of the facts and fallacies about orchid conservation, so they can arrive at an independent conclusion. The information is out there. Make use of it.

CITES

CITES stands for the Convention on International Trade in Endangered Species. It is a voluntary agreement between member countries that regulates the international trade of threatened flora and fauna, thus conserving endangered species for generations to come. The majority of orchids are approved to be traded internationally, as long as the plants have the necessary documentation from the country of origin. However, the following species may not be traded between countries (except under very specific circumstances): *Aerangis ellisii, Dendrobium cruentum, Laelia jongheana, Laelia lobata, Paphiopedilum* species, *Peristeria elata, Phragmipedium* species, and *Renanthera imschootiana*.

Above: Cyrtopodium punctatum *is native to the region stretching from Florida in the USA to French Guiana. It is endangered in its native habitats in Florida.*

Above left: Laelia jongheana *is a montane species from Brazil. As it is highly rare in the wild, it is protected from international trade by CITES.*

Left: Habitat destruction is just one reason why Renanthera imschootiana *is endangered. It was fully protected by CITES in 1979.*

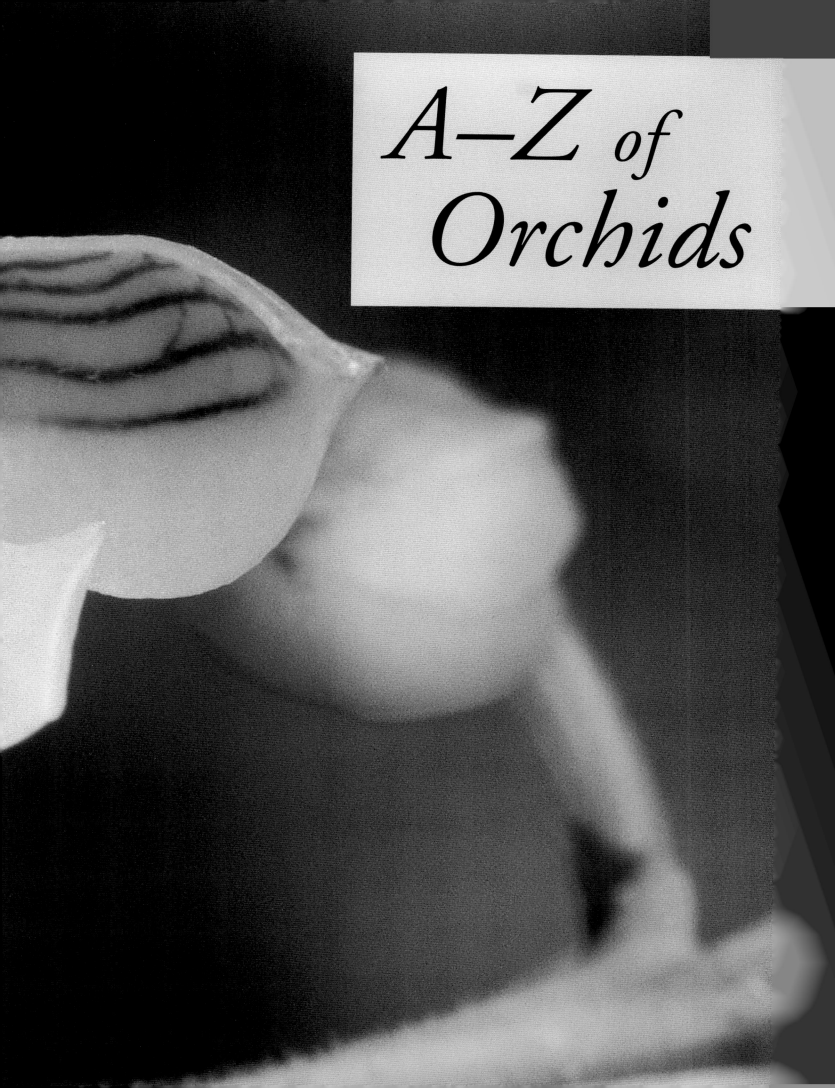

A–Z of Orchids

A

ACACALLIS

This genus contains between 2 and 4 species, of which 1 is common in culture. They grow epiphytically in lowland forest and seasonally flooded forest in Colombia, French Guiana, Guyana, Venezuela, and the Amazon Basin of Brazil. The pseudobulbs are slender, egg-shaped, and bear 1 to 3 leaves. They grow on a sympodial, creeping, sometimes climbing rhizome. The arching inflorescence appears at the base of the new shoot and bears a few large and showy flowers.
CULTIVATION: *Acacallis* grows best under warm and humid conditions throughout the year. During the day, temperatures may rise up to 86°F

(30°C) and should not fall below 65°F (18°C) at night. Avoid direct sun; light should be diffused. Without strong air movement, the leaves are susceptible to fungal disease. The plants prefer high humidity (80 percent and above) during most of the year; it can be a little lower during winter, but no resting period is needed. Due to the climbing rhizome, the plants grow best on cork slabs with a layer of moss or on tree fern. When grown in pots, the coarse organic substrate should be left to dry out between watering. Propagation is by dividing larger sections of the rhizome, ideally with 4 to 5 pseudobulbs per section.

Acacallis cyanea

syns *Acacallis coerulea, A. fimbriata, A. hoehnei, A. oliveriana*

↔ 8–12 in (20–30 cm) ↑ 6–12 in (15–30 cm)
🪴 ☼/☀ ◆ 🗑/🔧

From Colombia, Venezuela, and Brazil. Leaves oblong to lance-shaped, to 8 in (20 cm) long. Arching inflorescence arises from base of new pseudobulb, with 5 to 10 flowers in spring–late summer. Blooms pale lavender to blue, lip reddish brown to purple. Also a very rare white-flowered variety.

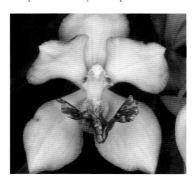

Acacallis cyanea

Acampe rigida

ACAMPE

This is a small monopodial genus of about a dozen epiphytic or lithophytic species with a wide distribution, from eastern Africa through Southeast Asia to Indonesia. They are essentially tropical lowland plants that grow in very brightly lit situations. The deeply channeled leaves are quite thick, rigid, and succulent. The roots can also be very robust and fleshy, and branched in older specimens. In general, the

blooms of the various species are quite small in relation to the plant size. The flowers are produced on short and often-branched inflorescences, with the individual blooms in tight bunches.
CULTIVATION: These orchids require warm humid conditions year round. Seed-raised plants are generally slow growing until they reach maturity, after which they become reliable bloomers throughout the warmer months, provided they are given strong light. They can be grown on cork or tree-fern rafts, but perform best in wooden slatted baskets in a coarse bark medium, allowing for perfect drainage.

Acampe ochracea

syn. *Acampe dentata*

↔ 16–24 in (40–60 cm) ↑ 16–24 in (40–60 cm) 🪴 ☼ ◆/◆ 🗑

From India; robust species with stout roots. Stems woody, to 24 in (60 cm) long. Leaves thick, recurved. Branched inflorescence to 12 in (30 cm) long, with many blooms in summer. Flowers scented, pale yellow blotched with brown, lip white with purple marks.

Acampe papillosa

↔ 12–24 in (30–60 cm) ↑ 24–36 in (60–90 cm) 🪴 ☼ ◆/◆ 🗑

Large species found from Nepal to Thailand. Stem long, branched, climbing. Leaves 3–6 in (8–15 cm) long, oblong. Short inflorescence, with many flowers in autumn. Flowers scented, about ½ in (12 mm) across; sepals and petals yellow spotted with brown, lip white with purplish spots at base.

Acampe rigida

syn. *Acampe multiflora*

↔ 12–24 in (30–60 cm) ↑ 8–60 in (20–150 cm) 🪴 ☼ ◆/◆ 🗑

From mainland Africa and Madagascar, to Southeast Asia, China, and Malaysia. Little variation between

Acanthephippium mantinianum

populations despite enormous range in distribution. Large species from Asia, often forming large clumps. Stiff strap-shaped leaves, 6–18 in (15–45 cm) long. Inflorescence 2–8 in (5–20 cm) long, with many flowers in summer. Flowers fleshy, scented, about ½ in (12 mm) across; sepals and petals yellow, barred with red-brown; lip white, spotted with red.

ACANTHEPHIPPIUM

This genus of terrestrial orchids includes about 15 species occurring in tropical Asia, as far east as Fiji. They have large ovoid pseudobulbs, usually with 3 large pleated leaves at the apex. The inflorescences are unbranched and bear few flowers. The flowers are showy, waxy, and urn-shaped, with the sepals joined into a tube enclosing the petals and lip. The petals are free, the lip has 3 lobes. The genus name is derived from Greek, *akantha* meaning thorn and *ephippion* meaning saddle, referring to the saddle-shaped lip.
CULTIVATION: These plants should be grown in pots in a well-drained terrestrial compost and watered and fertilized freely while in growth. While resting, they should be kept drier and cooler. Plants should only be repotted when absolutely necessary as they are said to dislike disturbance. Propagate by division.

Acanthephippium mantinianum
↔ 12–24 in (30–60 cm) ↑ 24–30 in (60–75 cm) ❁ ☀ ◆ ❋ ☐

From the Philippines. Pseudobulbs conical, to 6 in (15 cm) high. Leaves

Aceras anthropophorum

Acianthus confusus

to 24 in (60 cm) long, thin-textured. Inflorescence erect, to 6 in (15 cm) long, with up to 6 flowers in summer. Yellow flowers, striped with red, about 1 in (25 mm) across.

ACERAS
MAN ORCHID

This is a monotypic genus, found from England and western and central Europe to North Africa. The sole member is a deciduous terrestrial, which is closely related to the genus *Orchis*, and has a clear preference for alkaline soils. These orchids grow in full sun in grasslands, and in many locations would be covered by snow during their winter dormant period, where they retreat underground to a simple fleshy tuber.
CULTIVATION: These orchids are rarely seen in cultivation and are suitable only for cool-temperate climates. Specialist growers have reported some success by growing plants in a well-drained potting mix with the addition of dolomite. The dormant tubers must be kept dry in winter, and do not like temperatures above 82°F (28°C) during their growing and blooming seasons of late spring and summer. Propagation is from seed.

Aceras anthropophorum
↔ 4–12 in (10–30 cm) ↑ 4–24 in (10–60 cm) ❁ ☀ ◇ ☐

Leafy species. Loose rosette of up to 10 oblong to lance-shaped leaves. Upright crowded inflorescences; mature plants can bear up to 40 blooms in summer. Blooms 1¼ in (30 mm) long,

Acianthus exsertus

colored from pale yellow to brownish green. Species name refers to "human-like" appearance of blooms.

ACIANTHUS
GNAT ORCHID, MOSQUITO ORCHID

A genus of about 30 terrestrial species found in Australia, New Caledonia, New Guinea, New Zealand, and the Solomon Islands. The tuberous deciduous plants grow singly or in colonies in humid litter in open forest. There is a single heart-shaped leaf, sometimes located part-way up the stem. Above this leaf rises a slender inflorescence with several flowers. The flowering period is from autumn to early spring depending upon the species. After flowering, the plants die back when the mature tuber rests for about 4 months before resuming growth.
CULTIVATION: While some species are easy to grow in cultivation, others are difficult to keep alive for more than a few seasons. Plant dormant tubers in a perfectly drained gritty mix of coarse sand and leaf mold. Mulch with dry pine needles. Once plants emerge, place the pot in a shady spot with good air movement and humidity. Keep

moist. Allow the plants to dry off after blooming. Propagate from extra tubers that may form or from seed.

Acianthus confusus
syn. *Acianthella confusa*
MOSQUITO ORCHID
↔ 1 in (25 mm) ↑ 2½–4 in (6–10 cm) ❁ ☀ ◆ ☐

Only found in New Caledonia, in sheltered spots in moist open forest in litter. Heart-shaped leaf, 1 in (25 mm) long, red underside. Several pinkish green flowers with broad lip. Winter-blooming. Difficult to cultivate.

Acianthus exsertus
LARGE MOSQUITO ORCHID
↔ ½–1½ in (12–35 mm) ↑ 2–4 in (5–10 cm) ❁ ☼/☀ ◆/◇ ☐

From eastern Australia, found in various habitats, from dry to moist forest to more open areas near streams. Leaf reddish green, red beneath, heart-shaped, ½–1½ in (12–35 mm) long. Several flowers, variable, greenish pink to reddish purple, dorsal sepal green, lip darker red to purple, in autumn–late winter. Easy to cultivate. Often confused with the smaller *A. pusillus*.

Ada keiliana

Ada aurantiaca

ADA

This genus has 13 or 14 species, and now includes some species that were formerly placed in *Brassia*. They are mostly encountered as epiphytes on moss-covered branches, but sometimes also growing lithophytically on steep embankments. They thrive in wet Andean cloud forests, occurring in mountainous forests in Colombia, Peru, Ecuador, Venezuela, and Central America at altitudes of 1,310–8,200 ft (400–2,500 m) above sea level. The egg-shaped flattened pseudobulbs grow sympodially and very closely

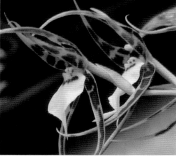

Ada glumacea

packed, forming dense clumps. Flower color, which varies with the species, ranges from red to yellow to brown. *Ada aurantiaca* is used in hybridization with both *Odontoglossum* and *Oncidium* for its vivid orange to red color, which is inherited.

CULTIVATION: The members of this genus are among the easier species to cultivate under cool to intermediate conditions, depending on the distribution and the altitude at which the species occurs. Temperature should drop at night. They grow best in pots in a standard organic substrate for epiphytes. Use the smallest size possible for the plant to fit in. High humidity and strong air movement are essential. Never expose to direct sunlight as this will lead to leaf damage. The plants rest during winter, when watering should be reduced to a minimum. Propagation is by division, when the plant grows over the rim of the pot.

Ada aurantiaca
syn. *Ada lehmanni*

↔ 8–16 in (20–40 cm) ↕ 10–16 in (25–40 cm) ♀/⋀ ☀/☀ ◇ ⊟

From the central Andes of Colombia and Venezuela, at altitudes of 7,550–8,200 ft (2,300–3,500 m). Flattened pseudobulbs; single leaf, 14 in (35 cm) long; several smaller leaves around pseudobulb. Arching inflorescence, to 14 in (35 cm) long, carries 7 to 12 flowers in spring. Bright orange to red flowers, to 1¼ in (30 mm) long, opening only at tip; lip faces upward.

Ada glumacea
syn. *Brassia glumacea*

↔ 8–16 in (20–40 cm) ↕ 8–12 in (20–30 cm) ♀/⋀ ☀ ◇ ⊟

Cool-growing species from Venezuela and Colombia. Can produce 2 inflor-

escences per pseudobulb in winter. Glossy flowers, to 5 in (12 cm) tall; sepals and petals greenish with brown markings, lemon yellow lip.

Ada keiliana
syn. *Brassia keiliana*
DR. KEIL'S ADA

↔ 8–16 in (20–40 cm) ↕ 6–12 in (15–30 cm) ♀ ☀/☀ ◇ ✱ ⊟

Native to Ecuador, Venezuela, and Colombia. Pear-shaped pseudobulbs; single narrow leaf. Short stems bear up to 14 fragrant flowers in early spring. Spidery flowers 4–6 in (10–15 cm) wide; sepals and petals orange and red to brown with white to parchment-colored lip. 'Our Tropics', intensely colored flowers.

AERANGIS

This genus consists of some 60-odd miniature-growing epiphytes and lithophytes from Madagascar and tropical Africa. The plants have flattish channeled leaves in 2 rows and short to long inflorescences of disproportionately large white to cream flowers. These monopodial plants are related to *Angraecum* and are one of the genera known as angraecoids. Various species bloom throughout the year, with the greatest concentration in the warmer months. The flowers, with long nectar-filled spurs, are highly fragrant in the evening and are pollinated by moths.

CULTIVATION: *Aerangis* species are best grown on cork or tree-fern slabs (either vertical or horizontal), as few like their roots covered. They need to be kept moist all year round. Larger specimens can be grown in small baskets. They enjoy semi-shade to strong light and are best suited to greenhouse culture in all but tropical climates. They require warm conditions throughout the year, disliking temperatures that drop below 50°F (10°C). Propagate from cuttings.

Aerangis citrata

Aerangis biloba

↔ 4–16 in (10–40 cm) ↑ 5–8 in (12–20 cm)
♀ ☀ ◆/◇ ❈ ⧚

Found in forest and woodland in western Africa. Leaves to 7 in (18 cm) long, bilobed at apex, dark green with black dots. Racemes spreading, 4–16 in (10–40 cm) long, with up to 10 blooms in autumn–winter. Flowers white, 1½–2 in (3.5–5 cm) across; spur pinkish, 2 in (5 cm) long.

Aerangis citrata

↔ 5–12 in (12–30 cm) ↑ 2½–5 in (6–12 cm)
♀ ☀ ◆/◇ ❈ ⎁/⧚

From Madagascar. Leaves glossy, dark green, to 5 in (12 cm) long. Up to 30 blooms, neatly arranged in 2 rows, on pendent sprays to 10 in (25 cm) long, in winter. Flowers ¾ in (18 mm) across, pale yellow to creamy white.

Aerangis cryptodon

↔ 6–15 in (15–38 cm) ↑ 6–15 in (15–38 cm)
♀ ☼ ◆/◇ ❈ ⎁/⧚

From Madagascar. Leaves dark green, to 6 in (15 cm) long. Flowers resemble white birds in flight. Upright sprays of up to 16 white blooms, 2 in (5 cm) wide, in 2 ranks, in autumn.

Aerangis distincta

↔ 5–10 in (12–25 cm) ↑ 6–8 in (15–20 cm)
♀ ☀ ◇ ❈ ⧚

From riverine forest in Malawi. Leaves triangular, deeply bilobed at apex. Pendent or spreading racemes, to 10 in (25 cm) long, with 2 to 5 flowers in summer or autumn. White flowers, tinged with pink, 2–2½ in (5–6 cm) across; spur pink, straight, 6–10 in (15–25 cm) long.

Aerangis ellisii

syns *Aerangis alata, A. caulescens, A. platyphylla*

↔ 8–16 in (20–40 cm) ↑ 16–32 in (40–80 cm) ♀/⋀ ☀ ◇ ❈ ⎁/⧚

Robust plants from Madagascar. Stems woody, up to 32 in (80 cm) long, becoming pendent. Leaves oblong, light green, slightly fleshy, to 6 in (15 cm) long, in 2 rows. Spreading to pendent raceme, to 16 in (40 cm) long, with 12 to 18 blooms. Flowers white, sometimes tinged with salmon, sepals often winged on back; sepals and petals reflexed; spur to 6 in (15 cm) long. Autumn-blooming.

Aerangis kotschyana

↔ 6–18 in (15–45 cm) ↑ 4–8 in (10–20 cm)
♀ ☀ ◆/◇ ❈ ⧚

Found in woodland in tropical Africa. Roots stout. Leaves to 8 in (20 cm) long, often with wavy edges, apex unequally bilobed. Pendent or arching raceme, to 18 in (45 cm) long, with up to 20 blooms in autumn–winter. Flowers white, pinkish in center, about 2 in (5 cm) across; lip fiddle-shaped; spur pinkish, 5–10 in (12–25 cm) long, with a corkscrew twist.

Aerangis rhodosticta

syn. *Aerangis luteoalba* var. *rhodosticta*
↔ 4–10 in (10–25 cm) ↑ 2½–7 in (6–18 cm)
♀ ☼ ◆/◇ ❈ ⧚

From Central Africa; one of the most attractive and distinctive members of the genus. Arching inflorescences of up to 20 blooms in 2 ranks in spring–autumn. Flat 1¼ in (30 mm) wide flowers, cream to white, with unique bright red column. Can be difficult to maintain in cultivation.

AERANTHES

syn. *Aeranthus*

About 30 species from Madagascar, the Comoros and Mascarene Islands, and mainland Africa are known in this genus. Most species grow as epiphytes or lithophytes in hot rainforests and humid montane forests at altitudes of 3,280–4,920 ft (1,000–1,500 m), with 2 species found growing at elevations of up to 6,560 ft (2,000 m). They are monopodial plants with a short stem and leaves arranged in 2 rows. The inflorescence is hanging and carries one or more somewhat transparent flowers.

CULTIVATION: Despite their montane origin, most *Aeranthes* species grow better under warm conditions in humid shade. Regular watering all year round is essential. Because of their thick aerial roots, they grow best in a coarse organic substrate in baskets or mounted. The inflorescence grows very slowly and can reflower the following season, so do not cut it off after the flowers have wilted. Propagation is by seed.

Aeranthes grandiflora

Aeranthes caudata

syn. *Aeranthes imerinensis*
↔ 12–16 in (30–40 cm) ↑ 32–48 in (80–120 cm) ♀ ☀ ◆ ⎁

From Madagascar and the Comoros Islands. Stem short, to 6 in (15 cm) long, covered with old leaf bases. Several leaves, 10–12 in (25–30 cm) long, strap-shaped, edges slightly wavy. Inflorescences pendent, 20–40 in (50–100 cm) long, with 3 to 8 flowers in summer–autumn. Flowers 3–4 in (8–10 cm) across, green. Sepals 4–5 in (10–12 cm) long; petals similar but smaller; lip 2 in (5 cm) long, with a short slender spur.

Aeranthes grandiflora

syns *Aeranthes brachycentron, Angraecum grandiflorum*

↔ 12–16 in (30–40 cm) ↑ 6–12 in (15–30 cm) ♀ ☀ ◆ ⎁/⧚

Found in Madagascar in hot humid forests from the coast to the central plateau at altitudes of up to 3,940 ft (1,200 m). Leaves to 8 in (20 cm) long. Hanging, thin, almost thread-like inflorescence to 20 in (50 cm) long, with 1 or 2 greenish white, fragrant, long-lasting flowers with tapered sepals and petals. Flowers any time of year, but mostly in summer.

Aerangis rhodosticta

Aerangis cryptodon

A

AERIDES

The name *Aerides* literally means air-plant, which is appropriate for these monopodial epiphytes that cling onto their host by only a few thick roots, with the remainder aerial. Some grow on rocks as lithophytes. Many of the 20 recognized species are sturdy plants that are found in the warm lowlands of Southeast Asia, however there are species from the mountains as well, from northern India to Indochina and China. Many of the species have similar blooms, although differing in the structure of the lip. All species have strappy leaves and arching to pendulous racemes of flowers, mostly blooming in spring and summer. There have been many hybrids made between *Aerides* and other members of what is loosely termed the "vandaceous" family. Such combinations include *Aeridocentrum* (× *Ascocentrum*), *Aeridopsis* (× *Phalaenopsis*), *Rhynchorides* (× *Rhynchostylis*), and *Aeridovanda* (× *Vanda*). Many of these hybrids come in a wide range of colors due to the high degree of genetic diversity.

CULTIVATION: *Aerides* are easy to grow and have highly perfumed long-lived flowers, which have made them popular in horticulture. They grow and display well in wooden slatted baskets, with some chunks of pine bark initially supporting the plant. *Aerides* species are frequently cultivated in gardens in warm climates, attached to the trunks of suitable trees that do not shed their bark. In optimum conditions, the thick white roots will attach firmly to the host and ramble quite a distance from the plant. They enjoy intermediate to warm conditions throughout the year, with high humidity and bright light.

Aerides crassifolia
↔ 8–16 in (20–40 cm) ↕ 8–20 in (20–50 cm)
♀ ◐/☼ ◆/◈ ❄ ⛁/≋

From Thailand and Myanmar. Rigid fleshy plant. Small arching to pendulous clusters of blooms in spring–summer. Large flowers, around 1½ in (35 mm) wide, fragrant, bright purple. Does well mounted on cork or in a wooden basket.

Aerides crassifolia

Aerides falcata
↔ 8–20 in (20–50 cm) ↕ 8–40 in (20–100 cm) ♀ ◐/☼ ◆/◈ ❄ ⛁/≋

Species found from northern India to Indochina. Up to 20 flowers, 1½ in (35 mm) across, lilac and cream, highly fragrant, in summer. Blooms are long lasting if kept dry.

Aerides houlletiana
↔ 8–20 in (20–50 cm) ↕ 8–24 in (20–60 cm) ♀ ◐/☼ ◆/◈ ❄ ⛁/≋

From Thailand and Vietnam. Very similar to *A. falcata* but with yellow, white, and purple blooms and less robust. Some taxonomists regard this as a color form of *A. falcata*.

Aerides krabiensis
↔ 6–10 in (16–25 cm) ↕ 8–24 in (20–60 cm) ♀ ◐/☼ ◆ ❄ ⛁/≋

Species from Peninsular Malaysia and Thailand; forms colonies on vertical rock faces in full sun at low elevations. Arching inflorescence with up to 16 blooms, each around ¾ in (18 mm) wide in spring–summer.

Aerides lawrenciae
↔ 12–27 in (30–70 cm) ↕ 12–48 in (30–120 cm) ♀ ◐/☼ ◆ ❄ ⛁/≋

Endemic to the island of Mindanao in the Philippines. Arguably the most spectacular member of the genus, and at times thought to be a giant form of the closely related species, *A. odorata*. Strongly arching inflorescences with up to 36 blooms in spring–summer. Large flowers, 1½ in (35 mm) across, highly fragrant, white with deep amethyst to purple markings on tips of floral segments. Also albino (white) forms of the species.

Aerides leeana
↔ 12–20 in (30–50 cm) ↕ 8–16 in (20–40 cm) ♀ ☼ ◆/◈ ❄ ⛁/≋

From the Philippines. Lacks pseudobulbs; leathery strap-like leaves. Short pendulous racemes densely arranged with many blooms in winter. Flowers small, fragrant, purple-pink, spurred.

Aerides multiflora
↔ 8–24 in (20–60 cm) ↕ 8–36 in (20–90 cm) ♀ ◐/☼ ◆ ❄ ⛁/≋

Found from northern India to Indochina. Numerous strap-shaped leaves. Arching inflorescence crowded with rose-purple flowers in spring–summer. Flowers to 1½ in (35 mm) across, fragrant, waxy. More cold tolerant than most members of genus.

Aerides odorata
↔ 8–40 in (20–100 cm) ↕ 8–72 in (20–180 cm) ♀ ◐/☼ ◆/◈ ❄ ⛁/≋

Widely distributed throughout Southeast Asia; most commonly seen species of genus. Fleshy strap-shaped leaves to 12 in (30 cm) long. Inflorescences arching, with up to 40 blooms in spring–summer. Flowers 1 in (25 mm) wide, variable in color, ranging from deep pink to pure white, very sweetly fragrant. White-flowered forms are highly prized by collectors. Adaptable species, thriving out of doors in most frost-free climates.

Aerides lawrenciae

Aerides houlletiana

Aerides krabiensis

Aerides leeana

Aerides odorata

Aerides quinquevulnera

↔ 8–16 in (20–40 cm) ↕ 8–40 in (20–100 cm) ♀ ☼/☀ ◆/◇ ❄ ⛏/⚶

Species from the Philippines and New Guinea. Narrow strappy leaves to 8 in (20 cm) long. Arching stems with sprays of up to 40 waxy pink flowers, spotted to deep purple, 1 in (25 mm) wide, in spring–summer. Flowers can last for over a month.

Aerides rosea

syn. *Aerides fieldingii*

↔ 8–24 in (20–60 cm) ↕ 8–36 in (20–90 cm) ♀ ☼/☀ ◇ ❄ ⛏/⚶

Found from India to Indochina; long been popular in cultivation. Long pendent inflorescences of numerous,

1 in (25 mm) wide, lolly-pink flowers, with some darker spotting on petals, produced as foxtail of blooms in spring–summer.

AMESIELLA

This genus is endemic to the Philippines. The miniature monopodial plants grow as epiphytes in mountain forest at altitudes of up to 3,280 ft (1,000 m). The contrast between the small size of the plant and its large and striking flowers makes it a favorite with many orchid growers. It was formerly placed in *Angraecum* but later separated in a genus of its own. The genus was considered to be monotypic until 2 new species were described in 1998 and 1999, 1 only known from the type specimen.

CULTIVATION: Best grown in small pots in coarse organic substrates or on a slab under temperate to warm conditions, never below 60°F (15°C). In summer, temperatures up to 82°F (28°C) are tolerated. The humidity should not fall below 60 percent. A resting period is not required. Keep out of direct sun. Repot only when roots are growing, best time is spring. Propagation is by seed.

Amesiella monticola

↔ 4–6 in (10–15 cm) ↕ 2–4 in (5–10 cm) ♀ ☼/☀ ◆ ❄ ⛏/⚶

Discovered in 1995, described in 1998; native to rainforests on the Philippines. Narrow leathery leaves, to a little under 4 in (10 cm) long. Short stems carry up to 5 pure white flowers, to 2½ in (6 cm) wide, in winter–spring. Requires cool conditions but will not tolerate frost or extreme summer heat.

Amesiella philippinensis

syn. *Angraecum philippinensis*

↔ 2–4 in (5–10 cm) ↕ 1¼–2 in (3–5 cm) ♀ ☼/☀ ◆ ❄ ⛏/⚶

Native to the Philippines; found growing at lower elevations than *A. monticola*. Leaves fleshy, dark green, to 4 in (10 cm) long. Flowers fragrant, white, showy, and large for size of plant, to around 2 in (5 cm) in diameter, on short racemes; long slender spur. Blooms in winter.

Amesiella monticola

Anacamptis pyramidalis

ANACAMPTIS

PYRAMIDAL ORCHID

Until recently, this genus was considered monotypic, but now includes several species formerly in *Orchis*. They are found in Europe, North Africa, Turkey, the Caucasus, and Syria, where they grow terrestrially in grasslands, among shrubs, and in meadows, at altitudes up to 7,870 ft (2,400 m). The plants grow leafy shoots from subterranean tubers, with a terminal inflorescence. CULTIVATION: These species do not adapt well to artificial cultivation and are not easily grown. They grow in symbiosis with mycorrhizal fungi. Try a free-draining substrate or grow planted out in the garden on limy, nutrient-poor soil. Propagate most species from offsets.

Anacamptis pyramidalis

syn. *Anacamptis urvilleana*

PYRAMIDAL ORCHID

↔ 4–10 in (10–25 cm) ↕ 8–32 in (20–80 cm)

Orchid from Europe and North Africa; found growing on chalky soil or lime-

stone in grasslands. Clumps of 4 to 10 leaves, each 3–10 in (8–25 cm) long. Inflorescence to 32 in (80 cm) tall, bearing many small flowers on a pyramidal raceme, from early spring to mid-summer. Flowers light rose to dark purple. Difficult to propagate, as they grow from seed in symbiosis with special fungi.

ANCISTROCHILUS

This genus of 2 species is from Africa. They are semi-terrestrials or epiphytes, growing in the forests of Nigeria and Cameroon to Uganda and Tanzania at altitudes of 1,640–4,600 ft (500–1,400 m). The small onion-shaped pseudobulbs resemble those of *Pleione* and are connected through a thin rhizome. They bear 2 deciduous leaves. The showy flowers appear in autumn and the plant is dormant in winter. CULTIVATION: Grow under temperate conditions, never below 60°F (15°C). After flowering, reduce watering until new shoots appear in spring. They are very sensitive to over-watering. Humidity should be kept as high as possible, especially during the growing season. Grow on slabs or in small baskets in a free-draining organic substrate. Repot only when new growth appears. Propagate by division.

Ancistrochilus rothschildianus

syn. *Ancistrochilus hirsutissimus*

↔ 6–10 in (15–25 cm) ↕ 4–14 in (10–35 cm)

From the tropics of western Africa. Leaves to 12 in (30 cm) long, in pairs on a small onion-shaped pseudobulb. Usually 1, or rarely 2, inflorescences with 2 to 5 flowers in late autumn when the leaves begin to shed. Showy flowers, to 3 in (8 cm) wide; sepals and petals rose-colored, darker lip.

ANGRAECUM

COMET ORCHID

This large genus has more than 140 species, ranging from warm- to cool-growing, large to miniature plants, and neat clump-forming to rambling species. In the wild, they often grow on rocks and trees, exposed to drying winds and strong light. These monopodials have leathery, channeled, dark

green leaves in 2 rows and short to long inflorescences. Most species have large, perfumed, white and green flowers, with a long nectar-filled spur. The majority are highly fragrant at night, to attract the moths that pollinate them in their native Madagascar and Africa. The famous naturalist Charles Darwin accurately predicted the pollination of *A. sesquipedale* by a giant hawk moth, found some fifty years after his death. CULTIVATION: These are epiphytic plants for the greenhouse or conservatory, as few species will survive temperatures down to frost level. Most prefer a temperature range of 50–86°F (10–30°C). Larger-growing species need plenty of room to grow, and like to be grown in pots in a well-drained, open, bark-based medium or can be incorporated into gardens in tropical climates. Propagate from offsets.

Angraecum calceolus

↔ 12–15 in (30–38 cm) ↕ 10–12 in (25–30 cm)

Short-stemmed plants from Madagascar, the Mascarene Islands, and Mozambique, forming clumps. Leaves numerous, about 8 in (20 cm) long, strap-shaped. Inflorescence 6–10 in (15–25 cm) long, branched in older plants, with several flowers from summer to winter. Pale yellow-green starry flowers, ½–¾ in (12–18 mm) wide; spur about ½ in (12 mm) long, slightly swollen at tip.

Angraecum didieri

↔ 4–6 in (10–15 cm) ↕ 4–6 in (10–15 cm)

From Madagascar. Thick, warty, silvery white roots. Often hidden, white blooms, 2½ in (6 cm) wide, on very short single-flowered inflorescences in summer. Prefers to be kept cooler and slightly drier in winter.

Angraecum distichum

↔ 6–8 in (15–20 cm) ↕ 6–10 in (15–25 cm)

Found in rainforest in western and central Africa. Branched stems, rather sprawling, 6–10 in (15–25 cm) long, leafy along their length. Leaves ½ in (12 mm) long, fleshy, bilaterally flattened, oblong. Inflorescence has single, small, white flower; sepals and petals spreading; spur straight. Flowers sporadically throughout year.

Angraecum eburneum

↔ 20–40 in (50–100 cm) ↕ 12–30 in (30–75 cm)

Robust plants, occurring in eastern Africa, Madagascar, the Comoros and

Ancistrochilus rothschildianus

Mascarene Islands, and the Seychelles. Robust plants, forming large clumps. Numerous leaves, stiff, strap-shaped, to 20 in (50 cm) long, arranged in 2 rows. Erect inflorescences, 12–30 in (30–75 cm) long, with up to 20 blooms in winter. Flowers to 3 in (8 cm) wide; sepals and petals greenish-white; lip white, shell-shaped, held uppermost; spur 2–3 in (5–8 cm) long. Four subspecies recognized, differing in proportions of flower. *A. e.* **subsp.** *eburneum* from Madagascar, the Mascarene and Comoros Islands, and the Seychelles; *A. e.* **subsp.** *giryamae* from eastern Africa; *A. e.* **subsp.** *superbum* from Madagascar, and *A. e.* **subsp.** *superbum* **var.** *longicalcar*, spur 14–16 in (35–40 cm) long; and *A. e.* **subsp.** *xerophilum* from Madagascar.

Angraecum firthii
↔ 4–6 in (10–15 cm) ↕ 3–4 ft (0.9–1.2 m)
♀ ☀/◉ ◆ ❀ ▯/🖊

Found in Cameroon, Uganda, and Kenya. Vine with conspicuous aerial roots opposite the axils of the short, leathery, bright green leaves. Small yellowish flowers borne singly on short stems that often appear at base of aerial roots. Autumn-flowering.

Angraecum infundibulare
↔ 6–8 in (15–20 cm) ↕ 3–10 ft (0.9–3 m)
♀ ☀ ◆ ❀ ▯

Scrambling plant from western and central Africa. Long leafy stems. Leaves 4–6 in (10–15 cm) long, elliptic. Inflorescence 6–8 in (15–20 cm) long, with a single flower in autumn–winter. Greenish white flowers, about 5 in (12 cm) wide, scented; lip white; spur to 9 in (23 cm) long.

Angraecum Lemforde White Beauty
↔ 8–12 in (20–30 cm) ↕ 8–12 in (20–30 cm)
♀ ☀/◉ ◆ ❀ ▯

Hybrid between *A. magdalenae* and *A. sesquipedale,* registered in 1984. Leaves narrow, to 12 in (30 cm) long. Pure white flowers that are large for an *Angraecum,* over 4 in (10 cm) wide, very fragrant at night. Several cultivars, such as '**Mr. Wonderful**', tinted pale green; '**Max**', especially large flowers.

Angraecum scottianum
↔ 3–6 in (8–15 cm) ↕ 3–12 in (8–30 cm)
♀ ☀ ◆/◇ ❀ ▯/🖊

Slender plant from Madagascar. Thin stems; semi-cylindrical leaves. White flowers, 2 in (5 cm) wide, in spring–autumn. Seedlings quick to mature and will tolerate quite shaded and moist conditions.

Angraecum sesquipedale
↔ 12–24 in (30–60 cm) ↕ 8–36 in (20–90 cm) ♀ ☀ ◆/◆ ❀ ▯

From Madagascar. Largest and most spectacular flowers in the genus. Dark green leaves to 12 in (30 cm) long. Racemes of up to 4 blooms in winter. Flowers, to 8 in (20 cm) wide, open greenish, turning pure white after a couple of days; spur to 12 in (30 cm) long. Mature plants enjoy warm moist conditions and strong light.

Angraecum Veitchii
↔ 12–24 in (30–60 cm) ↕ 8–40 in (20–100 cm) ♀/\ ☀ ◆/◆ ❀ ▯

Primary hybrid between *A. sesquipedale* and *A. eburneum.* Popular and robust plant. Leaves pleated, to 12 in (30 cm) long. Racemes of up to 8 flowers in winter. Flowers 4 in (10 cm) wide, open greenish, turning pure white after a couple of days.

ANGULOA
TULIP ORCHID

The 10 species in this genus are epiphytes or terrestrials from mountainous regions of Colombia, Ecuador, Peru, Bolivia, and Venezuela, and are closely related to *Lycaste*, with fat pseudobulbs and large, thin, pleated leaves. The waxy tulip-shaped flowers do not open fully and are borne singly on erect stalks from the base of the pseudobulb in spring and summer, coinciding with new growth.
CULTIVATION: These plants require a cool to intermediate growing environment. Because their roots must not dry out during the growing season, they are best suited to containers. Water well when in active growth. Propagation is by division.

Anguloa clowesii
↔ 12–24 in (30–60 cm) ↕ 16–24 in (40–60 cm) ✵ ☀ ◆/◇ ❀ ▯

Native to Colombia and Venezuela; arguably the most popular species in cultivation. Leaves lance-shaped, pleated. Flowers bright lemon to golden yellow, highly perfumed, in spring–summer.

Anguloa uniflora

Anguloa hohenlohii
↔ 12–24 in (30–60 cm) ↕ 16–24 in (40–60 cm) ✵ ☀ ◆/◇ ❀ ▯

From Venezuela. Large leaves, thin, pleated. Erect stalk bears solitary flower in spring–summer. Flowers deep bronze-red on inside and pale greenish brown on outside. Often seen incorrectly labelled in collections as *A. ruckeri.*

Anguloa uniflora
↔ 12–24 in (30–60 cm) ↕ 16–24 in (40–60 cm) ✵ ☀ ◆/◇ ❀ ▯

From Venezuela, Colombia, Ecuador, Peru, and Bolivia. Flowers somewhat variable in color, with white to creamy base, finely to coarsely spotted in pink, in summer–autumn. Some clones appear dark pink. Often confused with the closely related *A. virginalis.*

Angraecum Veitchii

Angraecum didieri

Angraecum firthii

Angraecum scottianum

A

ANGULOCASTE

This hybrid genus is a cross between the sympodial genera *Anguloa* and *Lycaste*. These hybrids have fat pseudobulbs and large, thin, pleated leaves. The waxy flowers are borne singly on erect stalks from the base of the pseudobulb and appear in spring and summer, coinciding with new growth. The color and shape of the blooms can vary considerably, depending on the genetic makeup of the hybrid.

CULTIVATION: These hybrids are cool-to intermediate-growing epiphytes or semi-terrestrials best grown in pots, as roots must not dry out in the growing season. Heavy feeders when in active growth, they need copious watering. Propagate by division.

Angulocaste Jupiter × *Anguloa hohenlohii*

↔ 24–36 in (60–90 cm) ↕ 16–24 in (40–60 cm) ⚲/❀ ☀ ◆/◇ ❈ ⬓

Unregistered hybrid, shows heavy *Anguloa* influence with its upward-facing tulip-shaped blooms.

Angulocaste Rosemary

↔ 24–36 in (60–90 cm) ↕ 16–24 in (40–60 cm) ⚲/❀ ☀ ◆/◇ ❈ ⬓

Hybrid between *A.* Sanderae and *Lycaste* Balliae. Strong *L. skinneri* influence, with *L. macrophylla* and *Anguloa clowesii* also in its ancestry.

ANOECTOCHILUS

This genus has around 25 species of small mainly terrestrial orchids with creeping rhizomes. They occur in warm-temperate to tropical Asia and the western Pacific. Some form small rosettes, others have ascending stems with alternate pairs of leaves. Often known as jewel orchids, they are cultivated more for their foliage than their

Anoectochilus sp.

flowers. The leaves are velvet-textured, frequently deeply colored, and often conspicuously veined. The flowers are small, usually white, and are borne on erect or semi-pendulous stems. Several species have medicinal potential and *Anoectochilus formosus* extracts are used to treat liver disorders.

CULTIVATION: These plants are frequently sold as house plants, requiring no special care other than a free-draining soil mix. Some species will tolerate cool conditions, but most can be grown outdoors only in the subtropics and tropics. Most make excellent terrarium plants, thriving in high humidity. Fairly bright conditions are required to maintain the foliage color, but full sun may burn. Propagation is by division of well-established clumps.

Anoectochilus koshunensis

↔ 8–12 in (20–30 cm) ↕ 2–6 in (5–15 cm) ❀ ☀ ◆ ❈ ⬓

Species from Taiwan. Leaves to over 3 in (8 cm) long, gold-veined, dark green, downy. Upright spikes with widely spaced downward-facing flowers, mainly white, dorsal sepal pinkish red. Dorsal sepal and petals form hood, base of lip with fringed edge. Vigorous large plants flower for most of year. Species in great demand for medical research.

ANSELLIA

AFRICAN TIGER ORCHID, LEOPARD ORCHID

The sole species of this genus occurs in subtropical and tropical areas of Africa south to northern Namibia, Botswana, and South Africa. The preferred habi-tat is hot dry river valleys. A sought-after plant for cultivation in tropical and subtropical gardens, this orchid will also even survive short periods of mild frost. The root tips grow upward to form a basket to collect leaves and debris. The plants form huge clumps in trees and specimens weighing more than 2,240 lb (1,015 kg) have been recorded. The arching inflorescence appears in spring and early summer. As the plants are very variable in growth and coloring, numerous varieties and species have been described, which all can be attributed to a single species.

CULTIVATION: Best grown in bright light on a slab or in shallow pots in a very coarse substrate mixture. They do not like to be disturbed, so do not repot for several years. They can grow into impressive specimen plants. Keep drier in winter to induce flowering. Propagate by division.

Ansellia africana

syns *Ansellia confusa, A. congoensis, A. gigantea, A. humilis, A. nilotica*

↔ 16–60 in (40–150 cm) ↕ 16–40 in (40–100 cm) ⚲ ❁ ◆ ❈ ❈ ⬓/▨

Tall cane-like pseudobulbs form dense clumps, with frond of leaves at tip. Arching inflorescence produced near end of bulb, with many scented flowers in early spring. Flowers variable in color, from plain yellow to densely spotted with chocolate brown. '**Alba**', pale greenish flowers, bright yellow lip; '**Kruger Rand**', greenish flowers, heavily spotted with brown; '**Tinonee**', pale greenish flowers, heavily blotched with maroon, yellow lip.

Angulocaste Rosemary

Angulocaste Jupiter × *Anguloa hohenlohii*

Ansellia africana 'Kruger Rand'

Ansellia africana 'Tinonee'

Ansellia africana

Ansellia africana 'Alba'

ARACHNIS
syn. *Arachnanthe*

SCORPION ORCHID, SPIDER ORCHID

This genus has about 7 species, found from Southeast Asia, Indonesia, and the Philippines to New Guinea and the Solomon Islands. They grow epiphytically or as lithophytes in warm, humid, lowland rainforest at altitudes of up to 3,280 ft (1,000 m). The leaves are thick, fleshy, and strap-shaped and grow in 2 alternating rows.
CULTIVATION: *Arachnis* species require high humidity, high temperatures, and bright light, even full sun to thrive. No resting period is required. Their long stems make them unsuitable for pot culture, so try growing them on a long slab or piece of cork or hanging free without any substrate attached. Some species reach an impressive size, too

large for a small greenhouse. Propagate by division or from root stem cuttings.

Arachnis flos-aeris
syn. *Arachnis moschifera*

↔ 20–32 in (50–80 cm) ↑3–15 ft (0.9–4.5 m) ♀/↑ ☼ ◆ ❄ ᛉ

Found from Malaysia through Sumatra to Java, Indonesia. Tall species with climbing stem. Branched inflorescence to 4 ft (1.2 m) long. Flowers musky, yellowish green with irregular dark brown spots and striations. Usually blooms twice a year, in spring–early summer and again in early winter.

Arachnis hookeriana
syns *Arachnanthe alba*, *Arachnis alba*

WHITE SCORPION ORCHID, WHITE SPIDER ORCHID

↔ 12–20 in (30–50 cm) ↑3–15 ft (0.9–4.5 m) ♀/↑ ☼ ◆ ❄ ᛉ

From Vietnam, Borneo, Malaysia, and Singapore; grows in sandy soil and among shrubs in coastal areas. Inflorescence seldom branched. White to creamy flowers, finely spotted with purple, mainly in autumn.

ARANDA
Crossing *Arachnis* and *Vanda* has produced this hybrid genus of monopodial epiphytic orchids with excellent potential as cut flowers. They have sturdy stems with aerial roots at the base and many opposite pairs of dark green, narrow, leathery leaves that are cylindrical in cross-section. Branching upright sprays of small flowers, usually in shades of pink, orange, or red, appear at the stem tips.

CULTIVATION: Grow in a bright position that receives a few hours sun. Although they require bright light, this should be tempered with high humidity. Propagation is usually by stem cuttings or tissue culture.

Aranda Noorah Alsagoff
↔ 12–20 in (30–50 cm) ↑16–24 in (40–60 cm) ♀ ☼ ◆ ❄ ▯/ᛉ

Widely cultivated in Singapore; several forms grown. Pink or blue flowers produced over a long season; mature plants flower for most of year.

ARANTHERA
Aranthera is a man-made hybrid combination between *Arachnis* and *Renanthera*. They are scrambling to upright monopodial epiphytes, with leathery

leaves produced in 2 ranks. Erect inflorescences carry up to 20 flowers that can be somewhat spidery to shapely, and are long lasting, coming in a range of colors. Mature plants can grow quite tall. They are important plants for the cut-flower industry in Singapore, Thailand, and the Philippines.
CULTIVATION: These hybrids demand strong light to full sun and hot humid conditions for them to successfully grow and bloom. Propagation is by division or from seed.

Aranthera Beatrice Ng
↔ 12–24 in (30–60 cm) ↑16–84 in (40–200 cm) ♀ ☼ ◆ ❄ ᛉ

Hybrid between *Renanthera storiei* and *Arachnis* Ishbel. Yellow blooms can be produced throughout year.

Aranda Noorah Alsagoff

Aranthera Beatrice Ng

Arpophyllum giganteum

Arpophyllum giganteum

ARPOPHYLLUM
CANDLE ORCHID

The 5 species of this small sympodial genus are found throughout Central America, Jamaica, and Colombia. The pseudobulbs are reduced to thickened stems. The plants have long-lasting, strong, leathery, upright to arching leaves, and erect candles of tightly packed pink to purple flowers.
CULTIVATION: They perform best if given high light levels and intermediate to warm growing conditions. Shallow pots or saucers filled with a bark-based orchid medium have provided the greatest success. Plants flower best if somewhat potbound, and should only be divided when absolutely necessary.

Arpophyllum giganteum
↔ 12–36 in (30–90 cm) ↑ 16–32 in (40–80 cm) ⚲ ☀ ◆/◈ ❄ ▽

From Central America. Widespread species, the most frequently seen in

cultivation. Inflorescences erect, cylindrical, 1¼ in (30 mm) wide and 8 in (20 cm) tall, tightly packed with numerous, upside-down, purple-pink flowers. Spring-flowering. Often confused with the closely related, but less robust, *A. spicatum.*

Arpophyllum spicatum
SICKLE-LEAFED ARPOPHYLLUM
↔ 12–20 in (30–50 cm) ↑ 32–48 in (80–120 cm) ⚲/⋀/⭳ ☀ ◆/◈ ❄ ▽

Tall species found throughout the range of the genus. Single fleshy leaf. Inflorescences 6 in (15 cm) long, tightly packed with numerous, small, pink flowers, around ¾ in (18 mm) wide, in winter.

ARUNDINA
BAMBOO ORCHID

This small genus of about 8 terrestrial species has a wide natural distribution extending from northern India across Asia to the Pacific Islands. Its reed-like stems give it a bamboo-like appearance. The leaves are narrow and grass-like. The flowers are produced in shades of purple and white, and they each only last a day or two, however, they are in such numbers that large plants are always in bloom. *Arundina graminifolia* has become a weed in Hawaii, colonizing old lava flows to the extent that many consider it an indigenous plant.
CULTIVATION: All *Arundina* species will do well in the garden in warm climates. If grown in the greenhouse, select a large pot to accommodate the extensive root system and use a well-drained medium such as *Cymbidium* compost. Plants can be propagated from aerial growths produced along the upper nodes of the bamboo-like pseudobulbs, and do well sitting in trays of water to 2 in (5 cm) deep.

Arundina graminifolia
↔ 12–36 in (30–90 cm) ↑ 16–84 in (40–200 cm) ⭳ ☀ ◆ ❄ ▽

Southeast Asian species. Narrow grass-like leaves. Erect inflorescences bear attractive blooms that resemble a small *Cattleya.* Flower color ranges from white to deepest purple, often with contrasting shades on lip. Blooms throughout the year.

ASCOCENDA

This is arguably one of the most popular of the orchid genera. The plants of this genus are man-made hybrids between the natural genera *Ascocentrum* and *Vanda.* Erect-growing to about 48 in (120 cm) high, these epiphytes have thick cord-like roots, strap-like channeled leaves, and long-lasting flowers. In tropical climates they bloom year round; elsewhere mainly during spring and summer. The colorful showy blooms are long lived. The influence of *Ascocentrum* has greatly reduced the plant size, injected a range of vibrant colors, and given the blooms a rounder shape.
CULTIVATION: These popular hybrids are ideal plants for bark-filled wooden baskets, enjoying warm conditions and high light levels. The thick roots will often venture outside the pot or basket, and this culture should be encouraged, as the roots need unimpeded air circu-

lation and must dry out quickly after watering. Propagation is by division of rooted basal shoots.

Ascocenda Hybrids
↔ 12–24 in (30–60 cm) ↑ 16–48 in (40–120 cm) ⚲ ☀ ◆ ❄ ▽

Ascocenda hybrids include **Carolaine 'Kathleen'**, pink flowers, heavily spotted with darker pink to red, 5 *Vanda* species and *Ascocentrum curvifolium* in its parentage; **Fuchs Gold**, one of the fine hybrids developed by Robert Fuchs of R. F. Orchids, Florida, USA; **Fuchs Serval**, unusual hybrid with bold spotting and mustard-colored background; **Guo Chia Long**, yellow-orange blooms with maroon spotting; **Kwa Geok Choo**, hybrid made by the Singapore Botanic Gardens, created using the albino (green and white) form of *Vanda sanderiana;* **Pramote**, orange blooms (an influence from *Ascocentrum curvifolium*) that last equally well on the plant or as a cut flower, and mature plants will bloom a number of times during the warmer months; **'Pranam'**, clusters of apricot flowers; **Princess Mikasa**, with flower shape and color a legacy from *Vanda coerulea;* **Udomchai Beauty**, 4 different *Vanda* species and *Ascocentrum curvifolium* in its makeup; **Wichot**, primary hybrid between *Vanda bensonii* and *Ascocentrum ampullaceum.*

Arundina graminifolia

Ascocenda (Vanda Pimsai*) × (Vanda* Keeree × Prackypetch*)* (hybrid)

Ascocenda Fuchs Serval (hybrid)

Ascocenda Princess Mikasa 'Pink' (hybrid)

Ascocenda Carolaine 'Kathleen' (hybrid)

Ascocenda Yip Sum Wah × *Vanda* Bitty Hearthrob 'Pink' (hybrid)

Ascocenda Pramote (hybrid)

Ascocenda Kwa Geok Choo (hybrid)

Ascocenda Udomchai Beauty (hybrid)

Ascocenda Wichot (hybrid)

ASCOCENTRUM

This monopodial genus contains about 8 small compact epiphytic species from Southeast Asia. They are erect growing, with short strap-like channeled leaves in 2 ranks. Larger plants may branch at the base, and have numerous, very thick, cord-like roots. The inflorescences appear from the stem at the base of the leaf. They are mostly spring- and summer-flowering, but in the tropics the larger plants can bloom throughout the year. *Ascocentrum* has been bred with members of *Vanda* to create the hybrid genus *Ascocenda*. CULTIVATION: Best suited to container or basket culture, these species require warm conditions and high light levels. Water and feed well during active growth and throughout the flowering season. Roots need to dry out quickly after watering and do best if allowed to grow beyond the confines of the container. Propagate by division of mature basal shoots.

Ascocentrum ampullaceum

↔ 8–12 in (20–30 cm) ↑ 6–10 in (15–25 cm)
♀ ☼/☀ ◆/◇ ❄ ☐

Species found in the Himalayas and Myanmar. Strap-like fleshy leaves to just under 6 in (15 cm) long. Wild species typically has deep red-pink flowers, ¾ in (18 mm) wide, borne on racemes in spring–summer; white-, mauve-, and pink-flowered forms are common in cultivation.

Ascocentrum ampullaceum

Ascocentrum aurantiacum subsp. *philippinense*

↔ 8–12 in (20–30 cm) ↑ 4–16 in (10–40 cm)
♀ ☼ ◆/◇ ❄ ☐/⟋

Endemic to the Philippines; larger than *A. aurantiacum*, which is not known in cultivation. Upright inflorescences with up to 40 flowers in summer. Bright orange blooms almost ½ in (12 mm) wide, with a darker colored lip.

Ascocentrum aurantiacum subsp. *philippinense*

Ascocentrum christensonianum

↔ 8–12 in (20–30 cm) ↑ 4–8 in (10–20 cm)
♀ ☼/☀ ◆ ❄ ☐

Native to Vietnam. In bright light the strap-like leaves often have purple-red undersides; color continues into the small flowers, which are white to pale pink flushed with magenta, darker at center. Inflorescence to 6 in (15 cm) long, in spring–summer.

Ascocentrum christensonianum

Ascocentrum garayi

↔ 5–10 in (12–25 cm) ↑ 5–12 in (12–30 cm)
♀ ☼ ◆ ☐

From Thailand. Strap-like leaves. Bright orange spring flowers ensured its popularity in cultivation. Nurseries have selected horticulturally superior forms and propagated these in large numbers from seed. Often confused with *A. miniatum,* a close relative.

Ascocentrum ampullaceum

ASCOGLOSSUM

Only 2 monopodial species are known, from Indonesia and the Philippines to New Guinea and the Solomon Islands. They are medium to very large epiphytes, growing in tropical lowland forests, and they produce long aerial roots that hold them in place on the branches. The succulent leathery leaves grow in 2 rows. The many-flowered inflorescence is often branched, and longer than the leaves, and the flowers are notable for their vivid coloring.

CULTIVATION: Requires bright light, high temperatures, and high humidity to thrive. No resting period is required. Best suited to cultivation on a long slab, because of the climbing habit. Propagation is by division or seed.

Ascoglossum calopterum

↔ 8–16 in (20–40 cm) ↕ 12–20 in (30–50 cm) ♀ ☼ ◆ ⟋

From the Moluccas in Indonesia, the Philippines, and New Guinea east to the Solomon Islands; found growing on branches high in the canopy, from sea level to about 1,970 ft (600 m). Only patchily distributed, and needs protection. Leaves succulent, leathery, narrow, arranged in 2 rows. Branched inflorescence arises near base of leaves from stem, with about 30 small purple flowers in spring–early summer.

Ascoglossum purpureum

syn. *Saccolabium purpureum*
↔ 8–16 in (20–40 cm) ↕ 12–20 in (30–50 cm) ♀ ☼ ◆ ⟋

Found on the Indonesian island of Ambon; very similar to *A. calopterum*

Ascocentrum garayi

in all aspects and even considered a synonym by some taxonomists.

ASCORACHNIS

This is a man-made, bigeneric, vandaceous hybrid created between the natural genera *Ascocentrum* and *Arachnis*. *Ascocentrum* has been used to dwarf the excessive rambling and climbing habit of *Arachnis*, which are known as scorpion orchids. They are upright-growing monopodial plants with leaves in 2 ranks. The colorful showy blooms are long lived. As at 2005, there are only 2 registered hybrids in this genus. These types of hybrids are primarily raised for the cut-flower trade.

CULTIVATION: These monopodial orchids enjoy high light levels and warm conditions throughout the year.

Ascorachnis Shah Alam City

↔ 8–20 in (20–50 cm) ↕ 8–40 in (20–100 cm) ♀ ☼/☀ ◆ ❄ ☐/⟋

Hybrid between *Ascocentrum* Mona Church (a primary hybrid between orange-flowered *Ascocentrum miniatum* and the purple-flowered *Ascocentrum ampullaceum*) and *Arachnis hookeriana*. Summer-blooming; can bloom throughout the year in the tropics.

ASPASIA

This tropical American genus contains 8 to 10 species of epiphytic orchids with ovoid pseudobulbs to over 4 in (10 cm) long, each with 2 narrow lance-shaped leaves to over 12 in (30 cm) long. The flowers can be very large and have narrow brown-marked or barred sepals and petals contrasting with a pastel-toned lip, sometimes reminiscent of *Zygopetalum*. Most species flower in summer, producing long-lasting blooms that are very heat tolerant. *Aspasia* species are sometimes crossed with *Odontoglossum crispum* to produce *Odontoglossum*-like hybrids that are better able to cope with summer heat.

Aspasia psittacina

They are ideal plants for wooden baskets. In tropical climates they can be incorporated into the garden, either on trees or within well-drained rockeries. Propagate by division of mature basal shoots or from seed.

CULTIVATION: Plant these orchids in a small pot with very free-draining mix in a bright but not too sunny position. They are easy to grow but must have fairly warm night temperatures and should be kept near-dry in winter. Feed and resume watering when new growth appears. Simple propagation is by dividing the clustered pseudobulbs in late winter.

Aspasia lunata

↔ 8–12 in (20–30 cm) ↕ 10–16 in (25–40 cm) ♀ ☀ ◆ ☐

Species from the Brazilian rainforests. Narrow lance-shaped leaves to 6 in (15 cm) long. Flowers 3 in (8 cm) wide, usually borne singly, in spring–autumn. Narrow green sepals, petals spotted or barred red-brown, lip white with central magenta area.

Aspasia psittacina

↔ 8–12 in (20–30 cm) ↕ 10–16 in (25–40 cm) ♀ ☼/☀ ◆ ☐

Found in northern South America, in forests that are seasonally dry but moistened by frequent fogs. Narrow lance-shaped leaves to 6 in (15 cm) long. Spicily scented flowers from mid-spring to summer. Green sepals and petals with broad brown bars, lip white to pink. Sepals angled sharply upward, petals point downward; flower shape resembles a stick figure with raised arms.

Ascorachnis Shah Alam City

B

Barkeria lindleyana, in Jardín Botánico Lankester, Costa Rica

Barkeria scandens

BARBOSELLA

This genus, containing about 20 species, is found from Central America in the north to southern Brazil and northern Argentina in the south. The small sympodial epiphytes grow creeping or in dense tufts on branches and trunks in mountain forests. They are characterized by single flowers on long inflorescences. The flowers are relatively large for the size of the plant and have a lip that works like a ball and socket. The genus was named in honor of Barbosa Rodriguez, a well-known Brazilian botanist. They are easy to cultivate and favorites with many collectors of miniature orchids.

Barkeria melanocaulon

CULTIVATION: They do best in intermediate or cool growing conditions. They will tolerate somewhat higher temperatures during the day, when the humidity is high. Keep relative humidity around 80–90 percent throughout the year. They thrive in small shallow pots in a fine organic substrate or on slabs with a layer of living moss. Propagate by division of large tufts of plants, but do not disturb the plants too often.

Barbosella cucullata
↔ 2–4 in (5–10 cm) ↑ 3–6 in (8–15 cm)
♀ ☀ ◆/◇ ▣/⬚

From Venezuela through Colombia and Bolivia; found in dense mountainous forests at altitudes of 4,600–11,160 ft (1,400–3,400 m). Single, erect, rough-textured leaf with small stem. Inflorescence to 6 in (15 cm)

long, with a single flower, about 2 in (5 cm) long, mainly in winter. Flowers range from yellow to blue. 'Hillside', grass-green sepals and petals.

BARKERIA
This genus from Mexico and Central America contains about 15 sympodial epiphytes or lithophytes that are allied to *Epidendrum*. Flower colors range from pale to vivid pink through to a deep magenta; however, there are some species with almost white blooms.
CULTIVATION: These orchids must be kept dry during winter (when most species defoliate, then bloom), so many growers cultivate these plants on cork slabs to ensure that the thick roots dry out quickly. Propagate by division.

Barkeria lindleyana
↔ 16–32 in (40–80 cm) ↑ 16–24 in (40–60 cm) ♀ ☼/☀ ◆/◇ ❄ ▣/⬚

Found from Mexico to Costa Rica. Pseudobulbs to 6 in (15 cm) long; narrow leaves 6 in (15 cm) long, can be flushed purple-red. Long racemes with many blooms in winter. Flowers white, mauve, or purple, to 3 in (8 cm) wide; large lip, often with white center.

Barkeria melanocaulon
↔ 6–8 in (15–20 cm) ↑ 12–16 in (30–40 cm) ⋀ ☼/☀ ◆/◇ ❄ ▣/⬚

Mexican species with very restricted natural distribution in Oaxaca State.

Small clustered pseudobulbs. Dark flower stems with up to 25 flowers, produced in late winter or with arrival of seasonal rain. Flowers soft pink, 1¼ in (30 mm) wide, with distinctive large columns.

Barkeria scandens
↔ 4–8 in (10–20 cm) ↑ 5–16 in (12–40 cm) ♀/⋀ ☼/☀ ◆/◇ ❄ ▣/⬚

From Mexico; grows in strong light in open forests. Upright inflorescence carries up to 12 flowers in spring–summer. Flowers intense magenta-red, 1¼ in (30 mm) wide; lip broad, round, with small white disc at center. Closely related to *B. lindleyana*.

Barbosella cucullata 'Hillside'

Bartholina etheliae

BARLIA

Of the 2 species of terrestrial orchid in this genus, one comes from the Mediterranean region, while the other is endemic to the Canary Islands. The rootstock is tuberous, with 2 large unlobed tubers. The stem is stout, with large basal leaves grading into bracts further up the stem. The inflorescence is cylindrical, densely many-flowered, with leafy bracts that are longer than the flowers. The dorsal sepal and petals form a hood, the lateral sepals are spreading; the lip is spurred. The genus was named in honor of French botanist J. B. Barla (1817–1896). CULTIVATION: Plants should be grown in a freely drained terrestrial compost with added lime. They should be watered well while in growth but kept dry while they are dormant. Propagate from seed.

Barlia robertiana

GIANT ORCHID

↔ 10–12 in (25–30 cm) ↕ 12–32 in (30–80 cm) ✢ ☀ ◇ ⊓

Robust plants from the Mediterranean region; found growing in grass and scrub. Round or ovoid tubers; shiny light green leaves to 12 in (30 cm) long. Short cylindrical spike, to 6 in (15 cm) in height, densely covered with many flowers and with prominent floral bracts. Fragrant flowers to almost 2 in (5 cm) long, purple or greenish; sepals and petals forming hood, lip 3-lobed, spur conical. Summer-flowering.

BARTHOLINA

This genus contains just 2 deciduous terrestrial species, which are both endemic to South Africa. They produce a single, round, ground-hugging leaf that is followed on mature plants by a solitary bloom. It has been noted that plants bloom exceedingly well after heathland fires the year before. The flowers are quite bizarre, with the highly divided lip being the outstanding feature. Blooming from

Beallara Marfitch 'Howard's Dream'

late spring to summer, they revert to dormant tubers in winter. CULTIVATION: Members of this genus are not known in cultivation and are best left in their natural habitat.

Bartholina etheliae

↔ 2½–4 in (6–10 cm) ↕ 8–12 in (20-30 cm)

✢ ☀ ◆/◇ ❈ ⊓

Species from South Africa. Small underground tubers; single leaf. Erect inflorescence to 4 in (10 cm) long, with a single flower in late spring–summer. Flowers predominantly white to pale green, with highly developed lip that radiates to about 20 points, complete with a small bulge at end of each point. Some clones with purple coloration in center of bloom.

BEALLARA

This complex generic orchid hybrid is a combination of *Brassia, Cochlioda, Miltonia,* and *Odontoglossum.* Generally, the crossing of *Miltassia (Miltonia × Brassia)* with *Odontodia (Odontoglossum × Cochlioda)* is the path used by hybridists to create these members of the *Odontoglossum* alliance. These sympodial hybrids are more tolerant of higher temperatures than most pure odontoglossums, will grow in a wide range of conditions, and have long-lasting blooms that are often fragrant.

Beallara Tahoma Glacier

CULTIVATION: These orchids should be potted in sphagnum moss or a fine bark mix. Beallaras have a fine root system, and do not like to dry out throughout the warmer months of the year. They require a drier rest period during winter when they should be watered only sparingly. They require abundant water during the remainder of the year. They are suitable for cool to intermediate growing conditions, but should be grown in a semi-shaded position. Propagate by division of established clumps in spring.

Beallara Marfitch 'Howard's Dream'

↔ 12 in (30 cm) ↕ 30 in (75 cm)

♀ ☀ ◆ ❈ ⊓

Strong color inherited from *Miltonia spectabilis.* Upright inflorescence with up to 10 flowers, in spring.

Beallara Tahoma Glacier ★

↔ 8–12 in (20–30 cm) ↕ 8–30 in (20–75 cm)

♀ ☀ ◆/◇ ⊓

Heavily influenced in color and shape by *Odontoglossum crispum, Miltonia spectabilis,* and *Brassia verrucosa.* Flowers in spring and summer.

Bifrenaria harrisoniae

BIFRENARIA

This is primarily a Brazilian genus of about 20 species of sympodial epiphytes or lithophytes related to *Lycaste* and *Maxillaria*. Some taxonomists still include the quite distinct multifloral and smaller-bloomed *Stenocoryne* within *Bifrenaria*. Most bifrenarias have robust pseudobulbs with a single leathery leaf. They bloom in spring and summer, with many species producing large showy flowers that are fragrant and long lasting.

CULTIVATION: Bifrenarias are adaptable to a wide range of temperatures and quickly grow into specimen plants if conditions are suitable. They will take quite bright light and in fact may not bloom if grown in shade. They prefer to be potted in a coarse bark-based mix and perform best when slightly pot-bound. Propagate by divisions of at least 3 pseudobulbs.

Bifrenaria harrisoniae

↔ 8–24 in (20–60 cm)   ↕ 8–12 in (20–30 cm)

Variable species from Brazil; popular in cultivation. Off-white to yellowish cream blooms, almost 4 in (10 cm) across, with purple lip covered in fine silky hairs, in late spring. Albino form with pure white blooms and yellow at base of lip rarer but easier to flower.

BLETIA

This genus of about 30 to 40 species, is found from Florida in the USA to southern Brazil. They grow as terrestrials in grassland, found on hills and embankments, from sea level to altitudes of about 8,860 ft (2,700 m). Sometimes they are also found as lithophytes on rocks. *Bletia* species are easily recognized by the corm near the surface and the veined thin leaves. The flowers are very showy and appear on a basal inflorescence that arises at the side of the corm.

CULTIVATION: These orchids should be grown in well-drained soil. During the growing period, the plants require abundant water and fertilizer. Watering should be reduced in autumn and plants should be kept rather dry during winter. Propagation is by separating the corms and planting them in individual pots. Propagation by seed is also possible.

Bletia purpurea

PINEPINK

↔ 16–24 in (40–60 cm)   ↕ 20–60 in (50–150 cm)

Very variable species, widespread from Florida in the USA, to Brazil. Subterranean radish-shaped pseudobulbs;

with 2 deciduous pleated leaves that resemble palm fronds. Very long erect racemes, to 5 ft (1.5 m) long, bear flowers in spring–early summer. Flowers to 2 in (5 cm) wide, range from various shades of pink to white.

BLETILLA

CHINESE GROUND ORCHID

This genus contains about 10 species of deciduous sympodial terrestrial orchids from temperate regions of China, Taiwan, and Japan. They have corm-like pseudobulbs, from which 3 to 4 lance-shaped pleated leaves arise. The inflorescence is a terminal raceme and carries up to 12 flowers. They are dormant in autumn and winter, blooming with the flush of new growth in early spring.

CULTIVATION: These orchids require a well-drained but rich potting mixture that retains moisture, or can also be grown in the garden. They can be grown in semi-shade to full sun, and appreciate regular watering in spring and summer. Caterpillars can often disfigure the leaves, particularly the young shoots after their dormant period. They will withstand cold winters, however, the new growth needs to be protected from any late heavy frosts. Propagate by division.

Bletilla striata

↔ 12–48 in (30–120 cm)   ↕ 12–24 in (30–60 cm)

Hardy species, frequently grown as garden plant, often without the owner knowing it is an orchid! Leaves lance-

Bletilla striata

shaped, to 18 in (45 cm) long. Up to 8 blooms, each 2 in (5 cm) wide, pale pink to rose-purple (rarely white), resembling a small *Cattleya* flower. Also form with variegated leaf. Blooms in early spring–summer.

BOLLEA

This genus has 11 species from the Andean mountains of Colombia, Ecuador, and Brazil, found growing as epiphytes in very wet cloud forests at altitudes of 3,280–5,900 ft (1,000–1,800 m). They have short stems on a sympodial rhizome, which bear sheaths to form a fan-shaped growth of leaves. The arching or pendent inflorescence carries a single, showy, long-lasting flower that is waxy in substance. Species are known for their deep "orchid blue" (violet) flowers.

CULTIVATION: Grow these plants under intermediate to warm conditions with cooler nights. Humidity should be very high throughout the year and the plants should never be allowed to dry out completely. They thrive best in pots or baskets in a medium-draining organic substrate such as sphagnum that retains the moisture. Propagation is by division of sufficiently large specimens.

Bollea coelestis

↔ 10–20 in (25–50 cm)   ↕ 10–20 in (25–50 cm)

From Colombia; found on the southwestern slopes of the Andes. Strap-shaped leaves, each to 12 in (30 cm) long. Waxy flowers 3–4 in (8–10 cm) wide; sepals and petals blue to violet, tipped white. Blooms in summer. Quite tolerant concerning temperature range, but humidity is more easily maintained at higher levels in the intermediate to cool range.

Bollea coelestis

B

BONATEA

About 10 to 12 terrestrial species are known from the eastern half of Africa from eastern South Africa to Ethiopia, and the southern Arabian Peninsula. They grow in coastal bush, deciduous woodland, and open forests, from sea level up to about 3,940 ft (1,200 m). The plants are characterized by very fleshy tuberous roots, which have a covering of fine hair, and green and white flowers with a hood-like dorsal sepal. The leaves often start to wilt when the flowers appear. The genus is named after M. Bonat, a botanist from Padua, Italy.

CULTIVATION: Grow under dry bright conditions in a sandy soil or substrate. When growing, the plants need regular watering and fertilization. Reduce watering when the leaves start to die off. After flowering, the plants must be kept completely dry, otherwise the tuberous roots will rot. Start watering when new growths have reached 1 in (25 mm) in size. Propagate from seed.

Brassavola cucullata

Brassavola flagellaris

Bonatea polypodantha

↔ 6–10 in (15–25 cm) ↕ 10–14 in (25–35 cm) ✲ ☼/☀ ◆/◇ ☐

South African species; closely related to *B. pulchella*. Erect inflorescences of up to 8 flowers arranged loosely on the spike. Flowers pale green and white, to almost 2 in (5 cm) across. Blooms from late summer to autumn.

Bonatea speciosa

syn. *Habenaria bonatea*
SPIDER ORCHID

↔ 8–12 in (20–30 cm) ↕ 16–24 in (40–60 cm) ✲ ☼/☀ ◇ ☐

From southeastern Africa. Leafy stems; lanceolate to ovate leaves. Terminal inflorescence of up to 60 flowers mostly during autumn or winter, although flowering time varies. Flowers to 2 in (5 cm) wide, green with white lip. Some populations grow in winter rainfall regions and will tolerate more humidity. '**Green Egret**', dark green and white flowers.

BRASSAVOLA

LADY OF THE NIGHT ORCHID

This genus contains about 25 sympodial epiphytes or lithophytes from Central and South America. Each of the very small pseudobulbs has a single cylindrical leaf. The plants are often pendent and produce impressive displays of long-lasting white to pale green flowers in clusters. The flowers are highly fragrant in the evening. Members of this genus have been used in a number of hybrids with related genera in the *Cattleya* alliance. The "brassavola" most usually involved in the well-known *Brassocattleya* and *Brassolaeliocattleya* hybrids is now reclassified in the genus *Rhyncholaelia*.

CULTIVATION: Brassavolas grow well in small pots, baskets, or on slabs, as long as they dry out between waterings. They enjoy high light, intermediate to warm temperatures, and can take cool temperatures in winter if kept dry. Propagate by division.

Brassavola cucullata

↔ 24 in (60 cm) ↕ 12 in (30 cm)
☙ ☼/☀ ◆/◆ ❋ ☒

From Central America. Pendulous growth habit; ideal for slab culture. Small pseudobulbs; fleshy dark green leaves to 10 in (25 cm) long. Individual flowers quite large, up to 7 in (18 cm) tall, lax, with yellowish green sepals and petals and partially serrated white lip. Summer-flowering.

Brassavola flagellaris

↔ 8–12 in (20–30 cm) ↕ 8–24 in (20–60 cm)
☙/∧ ☼/☀ ◆/◆ ❋ ☐/☒

Endemic to eastern Brazil; closely related to both *B. perrinii* and *B. tuberculata*. Interesting plant even out of bloom. Cylindrical leaves to 18 in (45 cm) long. Short inflorescences of up to 12 flowers in summer. Flowers 2½ in (6 cm) wide, pale yellowish-green; white lip.

Brassavola nodosa

↔ 8–12 in (20–30 cm) ↕ 12–18 in (30–45 cm) ☙/∧ ☼ ◆ ❋ ☐/☒

Species from the West Indies and Central America. Stems slender, to 6 in (15 cm) long; leaves to 12 in (30 cm) long, fleshy, curved. Spike to 8 in (20 cm) long, with 3 to 5 blooms. Large long-lasting flowers to 3 in (8 cm) across, cream or pale green with a white heart-shaped lip, strongly scented at night. Blooms throughout the year.

Bonatea speciosa 'Green Egret'

Bonatea polypodantha

B

Brassia arcuigera, in Jardín Botánico Lankester, Costa Rica

Brassavola subulifolia

syn. *Brassavola cordata*

↔ 8–12 in (20–30 cm) ↕ 6–8 in (15–20 cm)
♀ ☀ ◆ ❀ ⬚/☌

From the West Indies and Brazil.
Stems to 3 in (8 cm) long; leaves erect
or arching, 5–6 in (12–15 cm) long,
narrowly cylindrical. Racemes carry
a few blooms in summer. Green or
cream flowers, 2 in (5 cm) across,
lip white; vanilla-scented at night.

BRASSIA

SPIDER ORCHID

This genus of about 20 epiphytic
sympodial orchids from tropical

America is popular in cultivation due
to their large, often strongly perfumed, spidery blooms. The arching
inflorescences carry up to 12 blooms,
which can reach over 12 in (30 cm)
wide. These plants are very amenable
to cultivation over a wide range of
climatic conditions. *Brassia* has also
been used in hybrids with related
genera such as *Miltonia, Odontoglossum,* and *Oncidium.*
CULTIVATION: Many of these species
are from the lowlands and like warm,
moist, and bright conditions. They
grow well in pots in a bark-based
medium. Larger plants look good

Brassia gireoudiana

in hanging baskets. In frost-free climates they can also be attached to
garden trees that do not shed their
bark. Propagate by striking back-
bulbs or by division.

Brassia arcuigera

syn. *Brassia longissima*

↔ 8–16 in (20–40 cm) ↕ 12–24 in
(30–60 cm) ♀ ☀ ◆/◈ ❀ ⬚/☌

Found from Costa Rica to Ecuador.
Flowers among largest in genus, to
10 in (25 cm) tall, with narrow yellow
petals and sepals, heavily marked with
rustic brown, giving an overall bronze
cast. Blooms in spring–summer.

Brassia gireoudiana

↔ 16–20 in (40–50 cm) ↕ 12–16 in
(30–40 cm) ♀ ☀/☀ ◆/◈ ❀ ⬚/☌

Native to Costa Rica and Panama.
Large laterally flattened pseudobulbs
with pair of narrow strappy leaves, to
20 in (50 cm) long. Long arching inflorescence carries up to 15 blooms

in spring and autumn. Flowers with
very narrow sepals up to 6 in (15 cm)
long. Sepals and petals pale yellow-
green with deep brown markings, lip
white to pale green with brown spots.

Brassia lawrenceana

↔ 12–20 in (30–50 cm) ↕ 12–16 in
(30–40 cm) ♀ ☀/☀ ◆/◈ ❀ ⬚/☌

Species from tropical northern South
America. Narrow ovoid pseudobulbs,
slightly flattened. Leaves to 4 in
(10 cm) long. Inflorescence 12–16 in
(30–40 cm) long, carries up to 11
flowers in spring. Petals and sepals
pale green to soft yellow-brown with
reddish spots at base; lip white or pale
green to parchment-colored; petals
cross over at tips.

Brassia maculata

↔ 12–16 in (30–40 cm) ↕ 10–14 in
(25–35 cm) ♀ ☀/☀ ◆/◈ ❀ ⬚/☌

Native of the West Indies and Central
America. Compressed ovoid pseudobulbs; leaves to 4 in (10 cm) long.
Fragrant flowers, 6 in (15 cm) wide,
with long narrow sepals and inward-
curving petals that touch at tips.
Sepals and petals green with brown
markings at base; lip similarly colored,
though lighter.

Brassia verrucosa

syn. *Brassia brachiata*

↔ 8–24 in (20–60 cm) ↕ 8–12 in (20–30 cm)
♀ ☀/☀ ◆ ❀ ⬚/☌

Found from Mexico to Venezuela;
very popular species in cultivation
and reliable late-spring bloomer.
Narrow ovoid pseudobulbs; leaves
to 18 in (45 cm) long, lance-shaped.
Large fragrant flowers, 8 in (20 cm)
wide, spidery, pale green to yellowish,
with fine dark spotting at base. Performs well in shadehouse conditions
in frost-free climates.

Brassia lawrenceana

Brassia verrucosa

B

Brassia Edvah Loo (hybrid)

Brassia Rex 'Christine' (hybrid)

Brassia Spider's Gold (hybrid)

Brassia Memoria Fritz Boedeker (hybrid)

Brassia Chieftain (hybrid)

Brassia Chieftain × *B.* Rex (hybrid)

Brassia Spider's Feast (hybrid)

Brassia Rising Star (hybrid)

Brassia Hybrids

↔ 24 in (60 cm)   ↑ 12 in (30 cm)
♀ ☼ ◆/◇ ❊ ⛁/⤳

These hybrids are particularly vigorous and worth cultivating. They bloom best when grown as large, somewhat crowded specimens. Most have large, highly fragrant, spider-like blooms appearing in spring and summer. **Chieftain**, maroon and yellow petals and sepals with maroon-spotted lemon yellow lip; **Chieftain** × *B.* **Rex**, lemon yellow flowers with red-brown spotting; **Edvah Loo**, primary hybrid between *B. arcuigera* and *B. gireoudiana*, both large-flowered species; **Memoria Fritz Boedeker**, yellow-green petals and sepals, creamy lip, all with red-brown markings; **Rex 'Christine' ★**, arguably most popular *Brassia* hybrid in cultivation, primary hybrid between *B. gireoudiana* and *B. verrucosa*, blooms at full potential when grown into a large plant; **Rising Star**, yellow-green petals and sepals, creamy lip, all with very dark spotting; **Spider's Feast**, impressive hybrid between *B.* Chieftain and *B. verrucosa*, which has all its blooms out at once and well presented on the flower spike; **Spider's Gold**, hybrid between *B.* Arania Verde and the large-flowered *B. arcuigera*.

BRASSIDIUM

This man-made bigeneric sympodial genus is a hybrid between *Brassia* and *Oncidium*. The long, upright, sometimes branched inflorescences bear numerous long-lasting flowers. The somewhat spidery blooms are a legacy from the *Brassia* parent.

CULTIVATION: These vigorous hybrids enjoy warm bright conditions. They grow well in pots in a bark-based medium and need frequent watering when in active growth. While they have the potential to bloom at any

Brassidium Fly Away 'Taida'

time, the flowers are more frequently produced in the warmer months. Propagate by division.

Brassidium Fly Away 'Taida'

↔ 8–24 in (20–60 cm)   ↑ 8–12 in (20–30 cm)
♀ ☼ ◆/◇ ❊ ⛁

Hybrid with 3 species in its background: *Brassia arcuigera*, *Oncidium wentworthianum*, and *Oncidium maculatum*. Spidery blooms, green sepals and petals, white lip; all floral segments with brown markings. Flowers from winter–summer.

Brassidium Shooting Star × *Brassia* Rex

↔ 8–20 in (20–50 cm)   ↑ 8–20 in (20–50 cm)
♀ ☼/☼ ◆ ❊ ⛁

Unregistered hybrid with 3 *Brassia* species in its background, (*B. gireoudiana*, *B. longissima*, and *B. verrucosa*), as well as an injection of *Oncidium wentworthianum*. Spidery blooms; sepals and petals olive green, lip paler; all floral segments with brown markings. Summer-flowering.

Brassidium Shooting Star × *Brassia* Rex

Brassidium Wild Warrior 'Santa Barbara'

Brassidium Wild Warrior 'Santa Barbara'

↔ 8–24 in (20–60 cm)   ↑ 8–12 in (20–30 cm)
♀ ☼ ◆/◇ ❊ ⛁

Hybrid between *Oncidium leucochilum* and the large-flowered hybrid *Brassia* Stardust (*B. gireoudiana* × *B. maculata*).

BRASSOCATTLEYA

This man-made bigeneric sympodial genus is a hybrid between *Brassavola* and *Cattleya*. In most cases such hybrids have *Rhyncholaelia digbyana* (previously known as *Brassavola digby-*

ana) as one of the parents. Hybrids created using this species, which has predominantly green and white blooms, result in the other parent of the hybrid having a strong influence on the resulting flower shape. The showy blooms are often produced in large numbers and can be fragrant.

CULTIVATION: These orchids have a compact habit and grow well in small terracotta or plastic pots, baskets, or on slabs, but they must be allowed to dry out fully between waterings. They enjoy high light, intermediate to warm temperatures, and can take cool temperatures in winter if kept dry. Propagate by division.

Brassocattleya Hybrids

↔ 12 in (30 cm)   ↑ 10 in (25 cm)
♀ ☼/☼ ◆/◇/◊ ❊ ⛁/⤳

Large numbers of showy blooms, often pleasantly fragrant, in spring or autumn. **Binosa ★**, hybrid between *Brassavola nodosa* and *Cattleya bicolor*, long-lasting flowers; **Island Charm 'Carmela'**, with *Cattleya intermedia* as

Brassocattleya Island Charm 'Carmela' (hybrid)

Brassocattleya Binosa (hybrid)

one of its parents, clusters of blooms in spring; **Maikai**, large plant, spectacular in bloom, floriferous primary hybrid between *Brassavola nodosa* and *Cattleya bowringiana*; **November Bride 'Santa Clara'**, large flowers ranging from pink to white; and **Sunny Delight**, primary hybrid between *Brassavola perrinii* and *Cattleya aurantiaca*, with yellow to orange flowers.

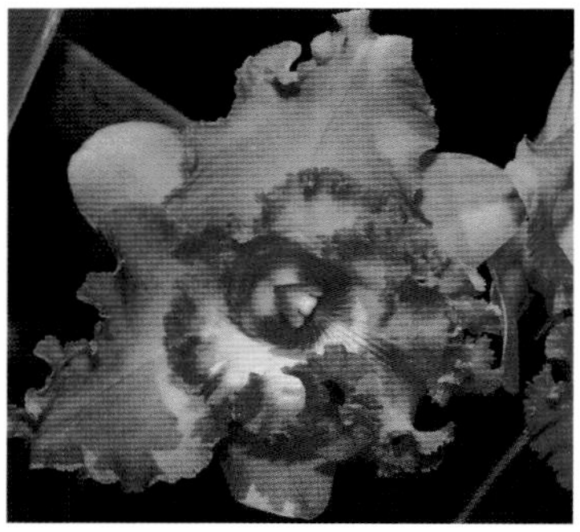

Brassocattleya November Bride 'Santa Clara' (hybrid)

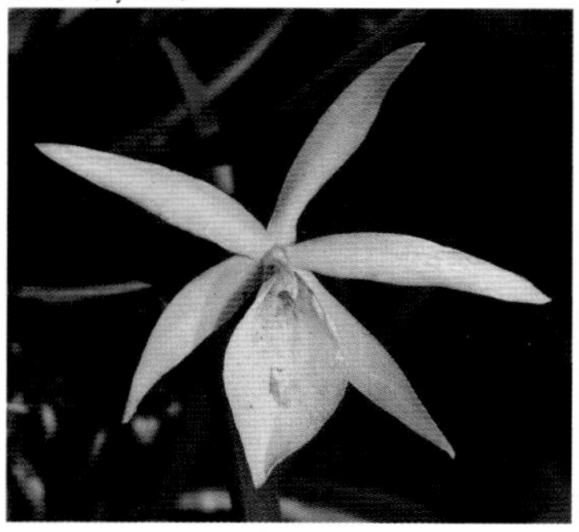

Brassocattleya Sunny Delight (hybrid)

BRASSOLAELIOCATTLEYA

Most of the "cattleya orchids" with large single or twin flowers seen at florists and orchid shows are actually members of the hybrid genus *Brassolaeliocattleya*, which is a man-made combination between the sympodial epiphytic orchid genera *Brassavola, Laelia*, and *Cattleya*. But many of the registered intergeneric hybrids listed as involving *Brassavola* have *Rhyncholaelia digbyana*, previously known as *Brassavola digbyana*, as one of the parents. This species imparts not only fragrance, but also a large fringed lip that is a distinctive feature of many of the hybrids. Many of the larger-flowering types are grown commercially for cut-flower production. CULTIVATION: These hybrids require semi-shade to strong light, but will burn if exposed to direct sunlight. They grow best in pots incorporating a coarse bark-based medium to ensure unimpeded drainage. Healthy plants will develop an extensive system of thick white roots, which are long-lived and branch freely. The plants require additional warmth on winter evenings, but will tolerate cooler winter temperatures for short periods if kept dry while dormant. The attractive flowers are long lasting and the whole plant can be brought indoors to be enjoyed when in bloom. Propagation is by division.

Brassolaeliocattleya Hybrids

↔ 8–24 in (20–60 cm) ↑ 8–24 in (20–60 cm)

Durable plants with long-lasting blooms. **Alma Kee 'Tipmalee'**, large genetic influence from the warm-growing species, *Cattleya dowiana* var. *aurea*; bright yellow petals and sepals, bright red lip; **Ann Cleo 'Hallona'**, distinctively colored hybrid with more than a dozen different orchid species in its makeup; **Bingham Vick**, salmon pink flowers, ruffled red lip, with orange veining at throat; **Dundas 'Olga'**, vivid cerise flowers, ruffled lip, orange at throat; **Erin Kobayashi × *Cattleya walkeriana***, unregistered hybrid back-crossed onto the small-growing Brazilian *Cattleya* species to create a more compact-growing plant; **Gold Bug**, pink-tinged cream petals and sepals, orange and pink lip; **Golden Tang**, deep yellow petals and sepals, orange lip peppered with reddish spots; **Hawaiian Satisfaction 'Romantic'**, cultivar propagated using tissue culture to produce large numbers of genetically identical plants—it is rare for seedling orchids to flower with such unusual color combinations; **Lucky 'Golden Ring'**, huge, highly fragrant, long-lasting flowers; large flared lip with velvet-like texture, distinctly lined and blotched with rich color; (**Memoria Benigno Aquino × Golden Embers**), unregistered hybrid with gold petals and sepals, dark red lip; **Memoria Julia Piferrer**, heavily influenced by infusions of *Cattleya dowiana* and *Rhyncholaelia digbyana*, from which it inherits the fringed lip; **Rosemary Hayden 'Paradise'**, a fine example of one of the traditional colored "cattleyas," autumn-flowering hybrid with 9 different species in its background; **Samba Splendor**, cerise flowers, ruffled lip golden orange and red at throat; (**Shades of Jade × Waikiki Gold**), "splash-petalled" hybrid—flower gives the impression of having 3 lips; actually lip color has been generically transposed onto the petals; **Sunstate's Easter Parade**, cerise flowers with ruffled edges, velvety purple-red lip; **Toshi Aoki 'Blumen Insel'**, bright yellow petals and sepals, bright red lip; genetic influence from *Cattleya dowiana* var. *aurea*; **Toshi Aoki 'Pokai'** ★, one of the most popular and highly awarded yellow hybrids, bred in Hawaii; **Waianae Leopard**, cluster-type hybrid, heavily influenced by the spotted *Cattleya guttata*; **Williette Wong**, spectacular orchid, named for a respected member of the Honolulu Orchid Society, Hawaii; eye-catching plant that gets its distinctive color from *Cattleya dowiana* var. *aurea*.

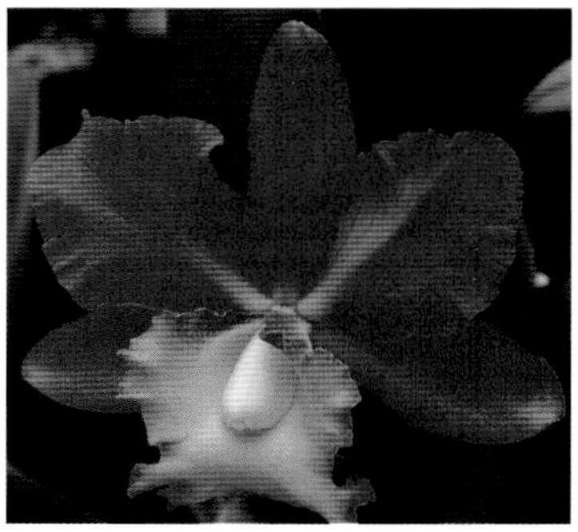

Brassolaeliocattleya Erin Kobayashi × *Cattleya walkeriana* (hybrid)

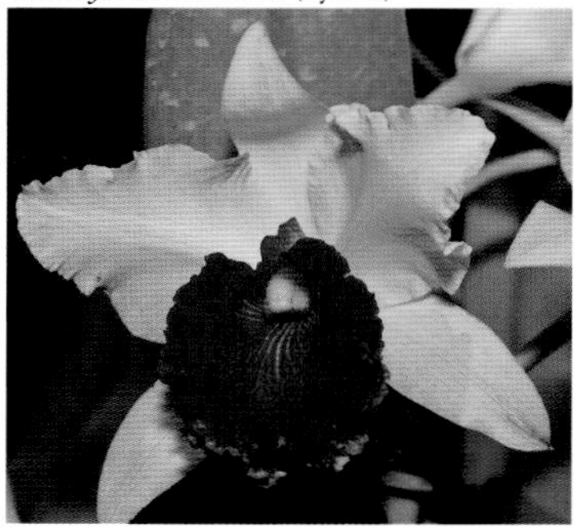

Blc. Alma Kee 'Tipmalee' (hybrid)

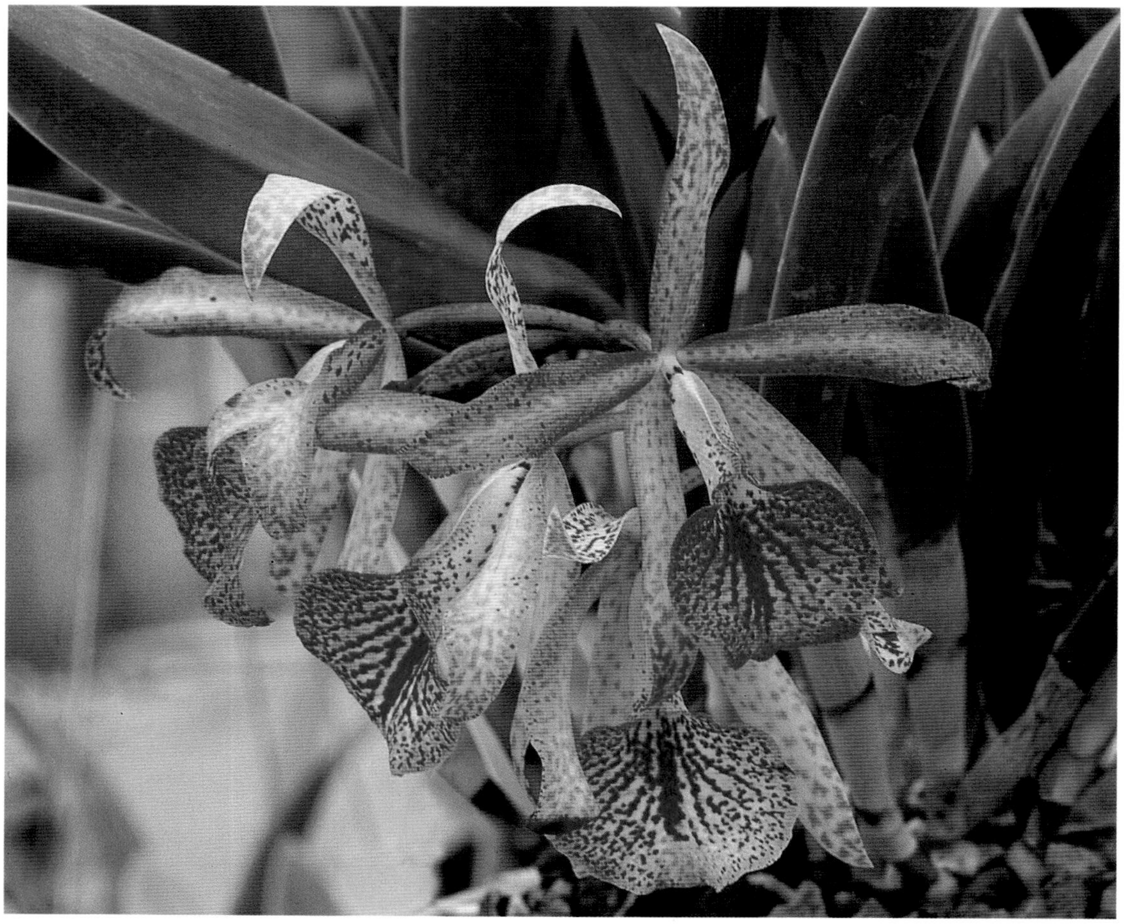

Brassocattleya Maikai (hybrid)

Brassolaeliocattleya Hawaiian Satisfaction 'Romantic' (hybrid)

Brassolaeliocattleya Gold Bug (hybrid)

Brassolaeliocattleya Sunstate's Easter Parade (hybrid)

Brassolaeliocattleya Memoria Julia Piferrer (hybrid)

Brassolaeliocattleya Toshi Aoki 'Pokai' (hybrid)

Brassolaeliocattleya Ann Cleo 'Hallona' (hybrid)

Brassolaeliocattleya Bingham Vick (hybrid)

B

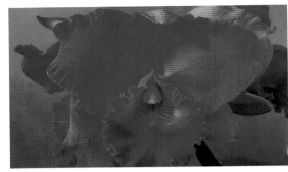

Brassolaeliocattleya Dundas 'Olga' (hybrid)

Brassolaeliocattleya (Memoria Benigno Aquino × Golden Embers) (hybrid)

Brassolaeliocattleya Mem. Helen Brown × *Laeliocattleya* Tokyo Magic (hybrid)

Brassolaeliocattleya Rosemary Hayden 'Paradise' (hybrid)

Brassolaeliocattleya Lucky 'Golden Ring' (hybrid)

Brassolaeliocattleya George King × *Laeliocattleya* Janet (hybrid)

Brassolaeliocattleya Golden Tang (hybrid)

Brassolaeliocattleya Toshi Aoki 'Blumen Insel' (hybrid)

Brassolaeliocattleya Waianae Leopard (hybrid)

Brassolaeliocattleya Williette Wong
(hybrid)

BROUGHTONIA

The 2 species in this genus are found
in Jamaica, where they grow as epiphytes in hot lowland forests, sometimes quite low in the trees. They have
globular, somewhat flattened pseudobulbs in clusters, about 2 in (5 cm)
in height and 1½ in (35 mm) wide.
These bear 1 to 4 leaves with smooth
edges. The inflorescence is about
8–12 in (20–30 cm) tall. *Broughtonia
sanguinea* is often used in breeding for
its shape and color and also to en-
hance the substance of flowers.
CULTIVATION: Grow under warm
conditions with high humidity and
very bright light. Either pot them in
small baskets in a free-draining substrate or grow epiphytically on a cork
slab. Water generously when growing;
reduce watering when shoots mature.
Do not cut off old inflorescences as
they may produce new buds from the
apex. Propagate by division.

Broughtonia negrilensis
↔ 8–16 in (20–40 cm) ↑ 8–27 in (20–70 cm)

Compact-growing plant, endemic to
Jamaica. Clusters of ovoid pseudobulbs; up to 3 leathery leaves. Long
inflorescences, to 27 in (70 cm) high,
produce up to 14 blooms in spring–
summer. Pink to lavender flowers,
about 2 in (5 cm) across, not widely
opening, tubular-shaped lip finely
and intricately veined.

Brassolaeliocattleya (Shades of Jade × Waikiki Gold) (hybrid)

Broughtonia negrilensis

Broughtonia sanguinea

Broughtonia sanguinea

↔ 6–8 in (15–20 cm) ↑ 8–24 in (20–60 cm)
♀ ☀ ◆ ⛺/🎒

Attractive species from Jamaica. Clustered pseudobulbs; leathery leaves to 7 in (18 cm) long. Simple or branched inflorescences, to 20 in (50 cm) long, can be erect or pendent, with 5 to 12 flowers in late spring–early summer. Flowers typically about 2 in (5 cm) wide, deep pink to reddish purple. Yellow, white, and semi-alba varieties are also found.

BROWNLEEA

This is primarily a South African genus of deciduous terrestrials, with outlying species recorded from Kenya and Cameroon and extending to Madagascar. There are 7 described species. Most of the species have upright inflorescences of white blooms with varying degrees of mauve and purple in the lip. They bloom from late summer to autumn, and revert to dormant tubers in the winter.
CULTIVATION: *Brownleea* species are rarely seen in cultivation, however there has been some success with plants grown in a well-drained potting medium that incorporates peat moss and coarse sand in the mix. Propagation is from seed.

Brownleea parviflora

Brownleea parviflora

↔ 8–16 in (20–40 cm) ↑ 8–24 in (20–60 cm)
♀ ☀/◐ ◆/◇ ⛺

Type species of genus. From South Africa; grows in damp grassland and montane heathland at altitudes from around sea level to 9,840 ft (3,000 m). Slender upright inflorescences of 20 to 60 white blooms in late summer–autumn. Flowers almost ½ in (12 mm) tall (*parviflora* means small-flowered).

BULBOPHYLLUM

This is a huge genus, with more than 1,500 named species, and many more still being discovered. In this cosmopolitan genus, there are plants with flowers in all shapes, sizes, and colors. These sympodial orchids grow as epiphytes and lithophytes. The majority of species produce a cylindrical pseudobulb with a single leaf, which develops along a creeping rhizome. However, there are numerous species, particularly from Africa and Mada-

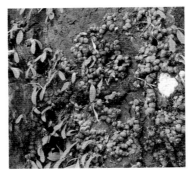

Bulbophyllum sp.

gascar, that are 2-leafed. *Bulbophyllum* includes some of the world's smallest orchids, plus others that form massive plants. The flowers are unlike most orchids, and are highly specialized to attract specific pollinators. Most species have very mobile lips.
CULTIVATION: Most bulbophyllums are creeping plants that have only a short root system, which rarely branches. They grow well on tree-fern slabs and rafts, while the larger species may be grown in pots, baskets, or shallow saucers. In general, they

Bulbophyllum ambrosia

prefer shaded conditions and constant moisture around the roots. Some species of *Bulbophyllum* only flower in response to wet and dry seasons, while others flower throughout the year. Propagate by division.

Bulbophyllum absconditum

syn. *Bulbophyllum neocaledonicum*
↔ 4–6 in (10–15 cm) ↑ 1–2 in (2.5–5 cm)
♀ ☀ ◆ 🎒

From the islands of Java, Bali, and Sumatra, in Indonesia. Pendent rhizomes. Pseudobulbs narrow; about

Bulbophyllum absconditum

B

Bulbophyllum appendiculatum

Bulbophyllum carunculatum

Bulbophyllum corolliferum

½ in (12 mm) long; single narrow leaf, about 1 in (25 mm) long. Short inflorescences with a single translucent white or greenish flower, very small, almost hidden in sheaths of rhizome.

Bulbophyllum ambrosia

↔ 4–6 in (10–15 cm) ↕ 6–8 in (15–20 cm)
♀ ☀/☀ ♦/◆ ❋ ▽/⍀

From southern China. Orange-yellow elliptical pseudobulb; single leathery leaf. Fragrant flowers, 1¼ in (30 mm) wide, borne singly, with reduced petals and white to pale pink or green sepals with fine magenta to red-brown longitudinal stripes; lip similarly colored but with fine spotting rather than stripes. Winter-blooming. Mount on cork or tree fern or grow in a small pot, repotting often.

Bulbophyllum appendiculatum

syn. *Bulbophyllum putidum*
↔ 8–14 in (20–35 cm) ↕ 2–4 in (5–10 cm)
♀ ☀/☀ ♦/◆ ❋ ▽/⍀

From Myanmar, Thailand, Vietnam and Laos. Clustered pseudobulbs each with a single short leathery leaf. Inflorescence to 4 in (10 cm) high, with a single flower, mainly in late summer–autumn; can flower any time under favorable conditions. Pendulous green and purplish flowers; lower sepals fused, petals and apical sepal fringed with filaments.

Bulbophyllum carunculatum

↔ 10 in (25 cm) ↕ 24 in (60 cm)
♀ ☀ ♦ ⍀

Species from Sulawesi and the Philippines. Upright inflorescence produces up to 5 impressive flowers. Blooms 5 in (12 cm) long, yellowish green, widely opening. Summer-blooming. Probably pollinated by flies attracted by its robust odor.

Bulbophyllum contortisepalum

↔ 6–8 in (15–20 cm) ↕ 6–8 in (15–20 cm)
♀ ☀/☀ ♦ ⍀

Found in New Guinea. Slender inflorescence produces a single flower; can bloom any time of year. Flower about 2 in (5 cm) long, distinctive for its deep purple-red, sometimes white-spotted sepals that are fused together to form one structure: a heart-shaped flower with a long twisted tail.

Bulbophyllum corolliferum

↔ 6–8 in (15–20 cm) ↕ 4–6 in (10–15 cm)
☀/☀ ♦/◆ ❋ ▽/⍀

Species found from Thailand to Borneo and Sumatra in Indonesia; member of the *Cirrhopetalum* section of *Bulbophyllum*. Ovoid pseudobulbs. Umbels of up to 12 blooms in winter. Flowers deep purple-red, about 1 in (25mm) long. Lateral sepals exude a sugary substance that helps to attract potential pollinators.

Bulbophyllum Daisy Chain

syn. *Cirrhopetalum* Daisy Chain
↔ 12 in (30 cm) ↕ 5 in (12 cm)
♀ ☀ ♦ ❋ ▽/⍀

Primary hybrid between *B. makoyanum* and *B. amesianum*. Flowers presented like spokes of wheel. Blooms in autumn–winter.

Bulbophyllum dearei

↔ 5–6 in (12–15 cm) ↕ 6–8 in (15–20 cm)
♀ ☀ ♦ ❋ ▽/⍀

From the Philippines, Borneo, and Malaysia. Conical pseudobulbs to 1½ in (35 mm) tall; single leaf, to 7 in (18 cm) long. Inflorescence 3–6 in (8–15 cm) long, with a single flower in summer–autumn. Large showy flowers, to about 3 in (8 cm) across, sometimes scented, yellow, veined with orange and purple.

Bulbophyllum exiguum

syn. *Dendrobium exiguum*
AUTUMN BULBOPHYLLUM
↔ 8–16 in (20–40 cm) ↕ ¾–2 in (1.8–5 cm)
♀/⋀ ☀/☀ ♦/◇ ⍀

Found mainly in rainforests and sclerophyll forests of southeastern Queensland to southeastern New South Wales, Australia. Leaf elliptic to lance-shaped or narrowly oval. Racemes of greenish yellow or white flowers, to ½ in (12 mm) across, in autumn.

Bulbophyllum Daisy Chain

B

Bulbophyllum fletcherianum

Bulbophyllum falcatum

Bulbophyllum falcatum

syn. *Megaclinium falcatum*

↔ 8–24 in (20–60 cm) ↑ 5–12 in (12–30 cm)

♀ ☀ ◆/◈ ▽/➤

From western Africa; one of the 2-leafed bulbophyllums. Bizarre and elongated inflorescence with the blooms arranged on either side of the flattened rachis in summer. Variable species with a number of different color forms, both in blooms and flower spike. Blooms less than ½ in (12 mm) across.

Bulbophyllum fletcherianum

↔ 10–24 in (25–60 cm) ↑ 12–40 in (30–100 cm) ⋀ ☀ ◆ ❉ ➤

From New Guinea. One of the largest-growing plants in the genus. Pseudo-bulbs often larger than tennis balls. Pendulous, purple-stained, leathery wide leaves up to 36 in (90 cm) long. Clusters of up to 20 smooth, fleshy, claret-colored blooms that do not open fully. Most unpleasant aroma. Flowers from summer to autumn.

Bulbophyllum globuliforme

↔ 1¼–4 in (3–10 cm) ↑ ½–¾ in (12–18 mm) ♀/⋀ ☀/☀ ◆/◇ ➤

Australian species, found in montane areas around the New South Wales–Queensland border where it grows on branches in the upper canopy of hoop pines. At one stage, this species featured in editions of the *Guinness Book of World Records* as the "smallest orchid in the world"—now considered second or third on the list. Pseudobulbs only about 3 mm wide, with translucent yellowish green blooms only marginally larger. Flowers in spring. Recently reclassified as *Oncophyllum globuliforme*, but this has yet to receive widespread acceptance.

Bulbophyllum graveolens

↔ 24 in (60 cm) ↑ 20 in (50 cm)

♀ ☀ ◆ ❉ ▽/➤

Robust species from New Guinea. Loose umbel of up to 12 flowers, each 3 in (8 cm) long, in autumn–spring. Petals and sepals pale green to light orange, sometimes finely spotted in

Bulbophyllum graveolens

Bulbophyllum lingulatum (seed capsules)

dark purple; bright red mobile lip. Rather unpleasant fetid smell.

Bulbophyllum guttulatum ★

↔ 10 in (25 cm)　↑ 10 in (25 cm)

From India and Nepal. Small upright inflorescence of up to 8 flowers in late winter. Cream, yellow, or greenish flowers, finely spotted with purple; lip white with deep pink spots.

Bulbophyllum levatii

↔ 6–8 in (15–20 cm)　↑ 6–8 in (15–20 cm)

Native to New Guinea and Vanuatu. Cream flowers with faint purple-red markings, in spring. Rare in cultivation but not too difficult to grow.

Bulbophyllum lingulatum

↔ 3–4 in (8–10 cm)　↑ 1½–2 in (3.5–5 cm)

Small creeping species from New Caledonia. Pseudobulbs very small, set up to ½ in (12 mm) apart, each with a single leaf, to 1½ in (35 mm) long. Inflorescence about 1½ in (35 mm) tall, with 2 flowers from autumn to spring. Flowers minute, white or pale yellow flowers.

Bulbophyllum longissimum

↔ 6–12 in (15–30 cm)　↑ 6–12 in (15–30 cm)

Very distinctive species found in Borneo and Malaysia. Ovoid pseudobulb; single leathery leaf. Produces up to 4 flowers on a pendent inflorescence in autumn–winter. Individual blooms very long, to 12 in (30 cm), white.

Bulbophyllum Louis Sander

↔ 8–12 in (20–30 cm)　↑ 6–8 in (15–20 cm)

Distinctive vigorous-growing hybrid between *B. longissimum* and *B. appendiculatum*. Thick leathery leaves held almost horizontally. Wiry stems bear heads of flesh pink flowers, of which all parts are fused into a petal-like structure. Blooms arranged in semi-circle, resembling half a daisy flower-head. Autumn-flowering.

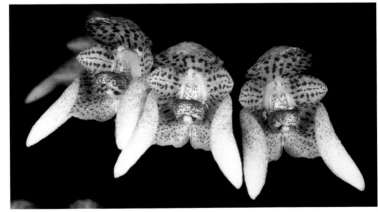

Bulbophyllum guttulatum

Bulbophyllum levatii

Bulbophyllum macrobulbum

↔ 10–24 in (25–60 cm)　↑ 12–40 in (30–100 cm)

From New Guinea. Pendulous, long, leathery leaves. Large blooms, in small groups, from summer–autumn.

Bulbophyllum longissimum

Bulbophyllum macrobulbum

Bulbophyllum ngoyense

Bulbophyllum nymphopolitanum

Bulbophyllum patella

Bulbophyllum rothschildianum

Bulbophyllum morphologorum

↔ 6–8 in (15–20 cm) ↕ 6–8 in (15–20 cm)
♀ ☼/☀ ◆ ⬚

From Thailand and Vietnam. Large, ovoid, bright green pseudobulbs, each with a thick, fleshy, apical leaf. Very unusual inflorescence: masses of tiny flowers clustered together on short spikes that first open down near pseudobulbs. Flowers purple-brown and yellow, sepals fused to form a pouch. Autumn-flowering.

Bulbophyllum ngoyense

↔ 4–12 in (10–30 cm) ↕ 1–2 in (2.5–5 cm)
♀ ☀ ◆/◈ ⬚

From New Caledonia; found growing in shaded forests. Mat-forming species; can form sizable clumps in right conditions. Single-flowered inflorescence produces tiny blooms in spring; color varies from yellow to red and purple. Plant should be kept moist; avoid direct sunlight.

Bulbophyllum nymphopolitanum

syn. *Bulbophyllum levanae*
↔ 8–10 in (20–25 cm) ↕ 4–8 in (10–20 cm)
♀ ☀ ◆ ⬚

From the Philippines. Ovoid pseudobulbs; leathery dark green leaves. Red elongated lower sepals; petals and apical sepal golden yellow to orange, flushed with red. Winter-flowering.

Bulbophyllum patella

↔ 2½–4 in (6–10 cm) ↕ 2–2½ in (5–6 cm)
♀ ☼/☀ ◆/◇ ⬚/⬚

Relatively new species, endemic to montane regions of New Guinea; found on moss-laden trees. Conical pseudobulbs; single spoon-shaped leaf. Flowers about ½ in (12 mm) wide, bright yellow with red on lip, one per inflorescence, at any time of year. Flowers close somewhat at night.

Bulbophyllum pectenveneris

syn. *Bulbophyllum flaviflorum*
↔ 16 in (40 cm) ↕ 3–6 in (8–15 cm)
♀ ☼ ◆ ⬚

From China, Vietnam, Laos, and Thailand. Up to 10 short sprays of blooms. Individual blooms 1¼ in (30 mm) long, majority of flower comprised of bright yellow fused lateral sepals; tiny purplish petals and lip.

Bulbophyllum picturatum

↔ 6–12 in (15–30 cm) ↕ 10–12 in (20–30 cm) ♀ ☀ ◆ ❀ ⬚/⬚

From the Himalayan foothills, Vietnam, and Thailand. Ovoid pseudobulbs; linear leaves to 6 in (15 cm) long. Erect inflorescence with several yellowish blooms overlaid with crimson to maroon flecking, in autumn–spring. Flowers arranged in semi-circle with points of the fused lateral sepals radiating outward.

Bulbophyllum pulchellum

↔ 4–8 in (10–20 cm) ↕ 6–10 in (15–25 cm)
♀ ☼/☀ ◆ ❀ ⬚

Species from Malaysia. Clusters of pseudobulbs, each of which produces an umbel-like inflorescence on a wiry flower stem with a head of up to 12 tiny flowers in late summer. Pouch-like flowers, flesh pink deepening to red at base.

Bulbophyllum rothschildianum ★

syn. *Bulbophyllum ornatissimum*
↔ 24 in (60 cm) ↕ 10 in (25 cm)
♀ ☼ ◆/◈/◇ ❀ ⬚

From India. Member of the *Cirrhopetalum* section of *Bulbophyllum*, generally characterized by having flowers in an umbel, lower sepals fused, and filaments and appendages on upper sepal and petals. These "flags" move in the slightest breeze and help attract potential pollinators. Single leaf to 6 in (15 cm) long. Inflorescence to 6 in (15 cm) long, arises from base of mature pseudobulbs, bears around 3 unpleasantly scented flowers in autumn. Green and crimson flowers to 4 in (10 cm) long, mostly made up of fused lower sepals.

Bulbophyllum rufinum

RED FOX BULBOPHYLLUM
↔ 12–20 in (30–50 cm) ↕ 4–8 in (10–20 cm)
♀ ☼/☀ ◆/◈ ❀ ⬚/⬚

From India and the Himalayan foothills. Elongated pseudobulbs; single leaf to 10 in (25 cm) long; downward-curving flower stem, 6–16 in (15–40 cm) long. Numerous small flowers, less than ½ in (12 mm) in size, yellow green with fine purple-red stripes. Main flowering season is late summer–autumn, can flower any time under favorable conditions.

Bulbophyllum pectenveneris

Bulbophyllum picturatum

Bulbophyllum rufinum

Bulbophyllum schillerianum

Bulbophyllum speciosum

Bulbophyllum sulawesii

Bulbophyllum tridentatum

Bulbophyllum unitubum

Bulbophyllum wendlandianum

Bulbophyllum schillerianum

↔ 3–6 in (8–15 cm) ↕ 2½–8 in (6–20 cm)

Pendent miniature species from Australia. Succulent leaves. Masses of flowers along rhizome. Orange blooms only ¼ in (6 mm) tall, but a well-flowered plant can put on quite a show. Flowers from spring to autumn.

Bulbophyllum speciosum

syn. *Hapalochilus speciosus*

↔ 4–10 in (10–25 cm) ↕ 3–8 in (8–20 cm)

Compact plant from New Guinea. Relatively large blooms are borne in spring–summer; unlike many bulbophyllums, flower features fixed lip. Keep moist; grows well in small pots of sphagnum moss.

Bulbophyllum sulawesii

↔ 16–20 in (40–50 cm) ↕ 10–16 in (25–40 cm)

Found on Sulawesi, Indonesia. Wiry stem, to 24 in (60 cm) long, with up to 5 unpleasantly scented flowers opening in succession in spring–summer. Flowers to 8 in (20 cm) long, golden to orange, apical sepal light green to pale gold. Twisted and greatly elongated lower sepals, petals reduced.

Bulbophyllum tridentatum

↔ 12 in (30 cm) ↕ 10 in (25 cm)

Rambling species from Thailand. Single leathery leaf connected by a rhizome to a round pseudobulb covered in papery scales. Small sprays of unpleasantly scented flowers.

Bulbophyllum unitubum

↔ 8 in (20 cm) ↕ 5–8 in (12–20 cm)

Impressive species from New Guinea; only recently entered general cultivation. Large flowers, in shades of yellow and orange, short-lived. Reblooms several times throughout year.

Bulbophyllum wendlandianum ★

syn. *Bulbophyllum collettii*

↔ 4–12 in (10–30 cm) ↕ 8–12 in (20–30 cm)

From Thailand and Myanmar. Spreading clump of rhizomes; short leathery leaves. Inflorescences emerge from new growths in late spring–early summer. Heads of up to 6 flowers, closely clustered to look like a single large bloom. Flowers yellow-green to orange, heavily suffused and striped red to brown to purple. Lower sepals much elongated and rolled together, apical sepal edged with red filaments.

Cadetia taylori

CADETIA

This genus of about 60 small epiphytic orchids has its greatest representation in New Guinea, with other species found in neighboring countries, including 4 in northern Australia. They are related to *Dendrobium* and have a slender pseudobulb with a single leaf. The flowers appear singly from a sheath at the top of the bulb, from which they can rebloom a number of times; they are generally white, but some species bear pale pink blooms. Plants flower randomly throughout the warmer months of the year.
CULTIVATION: These miniature orchids form small tight clumps and look best when grown as specimens. Most species prefer to grow on cork or tree-fern slabs, with regular watering throughout the year. Some taller-growing species can also be grown in small pots of sphagnum moss or a fine bark mixture. Propagate by division.

Cadetia taylori

↔ 4–8 in (10–20 cm) ↕ 4–6 in (10–15 cm)
◷/⋀ ☼ ◆ ▽/☂

From northeastern Queensland; grows on trees and rocks in rainforests and mangroves. Single white blooms, ½ in (12 mm) in size; lip color can vary between individuals from palest yellow through orange to purple. Flowers sporadically in summer–autumn.

CALADENIA

SPIDER ORCHID
This is a large genus of about 200 terrestrial orchid species. The plants are primarily Australian with some smaller populations found in New Zealand and New Caledonia. They produce a single, often hairy, leaf and either a single bloom or a small inflorescence with a number of flowers from winter to late spring. The plants are dormant throughout the hot dry Australian summers, when they retreat to underground tubers. The unusual flowers are pollinated by various species of native bees and wasps. There has recently been an upheaval with the naming of many of these orchids, with some

botanists splitting the group into a number of smaller genera, although it is too early to tell if this reclassification will receive general acceptance.
CULTIVATION: These spider orchids rely on a mycorrhizal fungus for their survival and have proved very difficult to maintain in cultivation, with the plants annually declining in vigor. Specialist growers of terrestrial orchids have had some success by growing some species in a free-draining sandy mixture containing a small amount of organic matter. Propagate by division.

Caladenia arenicola

↔ 6–10 in (15–25 cm) ↕ 12–24 in (30–60 cm) ⚑ ❀ ◆/◇ ❋ ▽

From southwestern Australia, found in a restricted area north of Perth, in open sandy heathland in full sun. Single hairy leaf; upright inflorescence of up to 3 narrow, segmented, pink to purple blooms, 4 in (10 cm) tall, in late spring. Recently reclassified as *Arachnorchis arenicola*, but this has received limited acceptance amongst orchid specialists.

Caladenia chapmanii

↔ 4–8 in (10–20 cm) ↕ 6–18 in (15–45 cm)
⚑ ❀ ◇ ❋ ▽

Only known from southwestern Western Australia. Unusual deep pink flowers appear in spring. Recently transferred to new genus *Arachnorchis*, though this new classification is yet to gain wide acceptance.

Caladenia flava

COWSLIP ORCHID
↔ 4–10 in (10–25 cm) ↕ 8–12 in (20–30 cm)
⚑ ❀/❀ ◆/◇ ❋ ▽

Found in natural woodlands and older pine plantations of Western Australia, growing in sandy soils. Single basal hairy leaf, somewhat broad, lanceolate, to 10 in (25 cm) long. Slender hairy stem, 12 in (30 cm) long, bears up to 4 highly variable star-shaped flowers, golden-yellow, often with red spotting or lines on dorsal sepal and petals, in spring. Hybridizes with *C. latifolia* in nature.

Caladenia chapmanii

Caladenia arenicola

Caladenia flava

Caladenia longicauda

Caladenia latifolia

PINK FAIRIES

↔ 4–10 in (10–25 cm)   ↕ 8–18 in (20–45cm)
❦ ☼/☀ ◆/◇ ❈ ⊟

Found in well-drained soils of open
areas, dunes, and coastal regions of
Western Australia and southern
Australia, including Tasmania. Single
basal, hairy, lanceolate leaf, to 10 in
(25 cm) long. Bears up to 4 flowers,
bright pink to white, somewhat hairy;
lip white. Blooms in spring, a little
earlier than *C. flava*.

Caladenia longicauda

↔ 7–10 in (18–25 cm)   ↕ 14–24 in
(35–60 cm)   ❦ ☼ ◆/◇ ❈ ⊟

Large-flowered spider orchid from
southwestern Australia; widespread in
southwestern corner of Western Australia. Closely related to *C. patersonii*.
White flowers, 6 in (15 cm) in size,
in late spring. Recently reclassified as
Arachnorchis longicauda, but this has
received limited acceptance.

Caladenia nana

↔ 2–4 in (5–10 cm)   ↕ 2–6 in (5–15 cm)
❦ ☼/☀ ◆/◇ ❈ ⊟

From southwestern Australia; flowers
profusely in forested areas that have
been burnt the previous summer.
Colony-forming species; mature
clumps can consist of over a dozen
plants. Produces pink blooms, ¾ in
(18 mm) in size, in spring.

CALANTHE

This large genus of 120 to 150 species
is mainly terrestrial, rarely epiphytic,
occurring throughout the tropics but
with most in Asia. They have large or
small pseudobulbs, each with two to
several pleated leaves, and can be evergreen or deciduous. The flowers are
showy, white, pink, lilac, purple, or
yellow, the sepals and petals similar,
usually spreading, the lip 3-lobed and
spurred. The genus name derives from
Greek, *anthos* meaning flower and *kalos*
meaning beautiful. *Calanthe* Dominyi
was the first recorded man-made
orchid hybrid to flower, in 1856. In
the late nineteenth century, deciduous

Caladenia harringtoniae

↔ 6–10 in (15–25 cm)   ↕ 8–16 in (20–40 cm)
❦ ☼ ◆/◇ ❈ ⊟

Species from southwestern Australia;
blooming stimulated by forest fires
of the previous summer. One of the
smallest-flowered of the spider orchids;
produces up to 3 musk pink blooms,
each 3 in (8 cm) in size, in late spring.
Recently reclassified as *Arachnorchis
harringtoniae*, but this has received
lukewarm acceptance.

Caladenia nana

Caladenia harringtoniae

Caladenia latifolia

hybrid calanthes were widely grown, then fell out of favor, but more recently have regained popularity. CULTIVATION: Pseudobulbs of the deciduous *Calanthe* species should be kept dry in a cool—minimum 50°F (10°C)—but bright place after the leaves have died back. In spring, the new pseudobulbs should be cleaned and potted up singly in a fairly rich terrestrial compost. They should be watered and fertilized freely once the new growth has started to develop. When the flower spikes appear in autumn, the leaves start to die back, and, after flowering, the plants are dried off again. Evergreen species must not be allowed to dry out completely, although they should be kept drier while they are resting. Propagation is by division.

Calanthe discolor

↔ 8–12 in (20–30 cm) ↑16–20 in (40–50 cm) ✤ ✱ ◇ ✿ ▔

Evergreen orchid from forests in Japan, including the outlying Ryukyu Islands. Small pseudobulbs; leaves to 10 in (25 cm) long. Inflorescence to 20 in (50 cm) tall, bears 10 to 15 flowers in spring. Flowers 1½–2 in (3.5–5 cm) across; sepals and petals purplish or bronze; lip pale pink, 3-lobed, midlobe notched at apex.

Calanthe Rose Georgene

↔ 8–20 in (20–50 cm) ↑12–24 in (30–60 cm) ✤ ✱/✱ ◆/◇ ✿ ▔

Brightly colored hybrid, inheriting its dark color from *C. rosea*. As with most of this style of "deciduous" *Calanthe*, this hybrid blooms in autumn. Keep blooms dry to help prolong life of flowers.

Calanthe rosea

↔ 10–20 in (25–50 cm) ↑12–20 in (30–50 cm) ✤ ✱ ◆/◇ ✿ ▔

Deciduous species from Myanmar; Hourglass-shaped pseudobulbs; lance-shaped pleated leaves. Flowers pale pink, lip even paler, turning white. Autumn- to winter-flowering.

Calanthe striata

syns *Calanthe discolor* var. *flava*, *C. sieboldii*

↔ 16–18 in (40–45 cm) ↑12–20 in (30–50 cm) ✤ ✱ ◇ ✿ ▔

Evergreen species from Japan. Leaves 12–18 in (30–45 cm) long, elliptic to lance-shaped, pleated. Inflorescence to 20 in (50 cm) tall, with up to 20 blooms in spring. Flowers 2–2½ in (5–6 cm) wide, yellow or yellow and brown; sepals and petals spreading, lip 3-lobed, spur slender.

Calanthe Rose Georgene

Calanthe sylvatica

syns *Calanthe masuca*, *C. natalensis*, *C. volkensii*

↔ 12–20 in (30–50 cm) ↑20–30 in (50–75 cm) ✤ ✱ ◆ ✿ ▔

From Africa, Madagascar, and the Mascarene Islands. Evergreen leaves to 14 in (35 cm) long, in basal tuft. Inflorescence 20–30 in (50–75 cm) tall, densely-flowered in summer. White or purple flowers, 1–2 in (2.5–5 cm) wide, orange at throat.

Calanthe triplicata

syn. *Calanthe veratrifolia*

↔ 20–40 in (50–100 cm) ↑32–40 in (80–100 cm) ✤ ✱ ◇ ✿ ▔

Robust evergreen orchid species found from India through Southeast Asia to Australia. Leaves 18–24 in (45–60 cm) long, dark green. Inflorescence to 40 in (100 cm) tall, densely covered in flowers in summer. Flowers white, pale green at tips, with yellow or orange mark on lip.

Calanthe vestita

↔ 16–30 in (40–75 cm) ↑24–36 in (60–90 cm) ✤ ✱ ◆/◇ ✿ ▔

Deciduous plants from Southeast Asia to Sulawesi, Indonesia. Large oblong pseudobulbs, 3–5 in (8–12 cm) long; leaves 18–24 in (45–60 cm) long. Inflorescences arching, to 36 in (90 cm) high, densely covered in blooms in winter. Flowers white to pink, 2–3 in (5–8 cm) across, yellow blotch on lip.

Calanthe striata

Calanthe sylvatica

C

Calochilus paludosus

Calopogon tuberosus

Calypso bulbosa

CALOCHILUS

BEARD ORCHID

About 12 species are known in this genus, which are distributed in Asia, Australia, and New Zealand. They are terrestrial orchids with subterranean tuberoids, found in open forest, along ridges and slopes, and in grasslands. They range from tropical areas to temperate regions in the south. They have a solitary, deciduous, and erect leaf and a tall slender inflorescence between 12 in (30 cm) and 40 in (100 cm) high. The inflorescence carries between 2 and 20 flowers. A characteristic feature of the genus is the bearded lip, which is covered in dense "hairs."

CULTIVATION: These plants are very difficult to cultivate because they need special mycorrhizal fungi to survive. They are not recommended for cultivation. Propagate by division.

Calochilus campestris

COPPER BEARD ORCHID

↔ 2–4 in (5–10 cm) ↑ 16–24 in (40–60 cm)
☙ ☼ ◆/◇ ❋ ☐

Found from eastern Australia to New Zealand. Tall inflorescence to 24 in (60 cm) high bears 5 to 15 flowers, each about 1 in (25 mm) in size, from late summer till winter.

Calochilus paludosus

RED BEARD ORCHID

↔ 2–3 in (5–8 cm) ↑ 10–14 in (25–35 cm)
☙ ☼/☀ ◆/◇ ❋ ☐

Slender orchid from Australia and New Zealand; listed as an "At Risk" species in New Zealand. Single leaf, to 7 in (18 cm) long, ribbed, triangular in cross-section. Inflorescence to 14 in (35 cm) tall, with 2 to 9 flowers in autumn–winter. Flowers scented, not opening wide, about 3 in (8 cm) wide, green to bronze-red, lip covered with dark glossy purple to red hairs.

CALOPOGON

This genus contains 4 species of terrestrial orchids, which are found from southern Canada to the southeastern states of the USA, chiefly growing in bogs and wet swamps with very acidic soil. The grass-like leaves are quite tall, appearing from a subterranean corm or tuberoid. The showy flowers have a hinged lip that snaps down when inexperienced bees land on it, stamping the pollinia on their backs.

CULTIVATION: Quite easy to cultivate. Grow in a substrate of acidic peat or sphagnum moss mixed with gravel, and keep cool during winter. Propagation is by dividing larger colonies of tuberoids or from seed.

Calopogon tuberosus

syn. *Calopogon pulchellus*

GRASS PINK

↔ 2–4 in (5–10 cm) ↑ 12–16 in (30–40 cm)
☙ ☼ ◇ ❋ ☐

Most widespread of the genus, found from Canada to southeastern USA. Leaves grass-like, ribbed, and triangular in cross-section. Long inflorescence bears up to 25 showy pink flowers, to 1 in (25 mm) in diameter, with a prominent lip. Flowers from spring in the south till summer in the north.

CALYPSO

This monotypic genus has a distribution range all over the Northern Hemisphere. Its sole representative is a dwarf terrestrial, growing from sea level up to 9,840 ft (3,000 m) in damp mossy areas, bogs, and in coniferous forest in temperate climates. The genus name is derived from Greek mythology, named for one of the water nymphs in Homer's *Odyssey*.

CULTIVATION: Very difficult to keep alive over longer periods. Try to grow in a shallow pot or pan under cool to cold conditions. Use an acidic mixture of leaf mold, peat, or sphagnum as a substrate and keep drier during spring and summer. It needs a distinct resting period in winter and is susceptible to slug damage. Propagation is by dividing larger colonies of tuberoids.

Calypso bulbosa

syns *Calypso borealis, C. japonica, C. occidentalis*

CALYPSO, FAIRY SLIPPER

↔ 1–2 in (2.5–5 cm) ↑ 6-8 in (15–20 cm)
☙ ☀ ◇ ❊ ❋ ☐

Underground corm; single leaf, ovate to elliptic, dark green. Inflorescence pinkish, with single, fragrant, nodding flower, about 1½ in (35 mm) wide, in spring–summer. Dark pink sepals and petals, lip with yellow or white tuft of "hairs" in center. There are 3 distinct populations: *C. b.* **var.** *americana*, found in North America, yellow tuft on lip; *C. b.* **var.** *bulbosa*, found in Asia and Scandinavian Europe, white tuft on lip; and *C. b.* **var.** *occidentalis*, found in Japan, white tuft on lip.

CANNAEORCHIS

This is a recently (1997) described genus of unusual terrestrials (sometimes epiphytes) that were previously treated within *Dendrobium*. All of the 12 or so named species are endemic to New Caledonia and its offshore islands, growing on the margins of stunted rainforest. *Cannaeorchis* means "caned orchid," which is most appropriate for these bizarre orchids, whose foliage and pseudobulb arrangement, which can be either simple or branched, is reminiscent of some bamboos. The flowers are produced off nodes opposite the leaves and are carried singly, in pairs, or in small bunches. There appears to be no main flowering time for these orchids, with large specimens often having blooms in some stage of development. This genus is primarily of botanical interest.

CULTIVATION: These orchids are very rare in cultivation and are seldom encountered, apart from within specialist collections and botanical institutions. They have had some success growing plants in large pots with a high percentage of ultrabasic soil and crushed rock incorporated into the potting medium. Propagation would be by careful division of large clumps (these orchids resent disturbance) or seed.

Cannaeorchis verruciferum

syn. *Dendrobium verruciferum*

↔ 8–20 in (20–50 cm) ↑ 16–48 in (40–120 cm) ♀/☙ ☼/☀ ◆/◆ ❋ ☐

From New Caledonia; arguably most common species in genus, particularly widespread on southern end of island. Solitary (rarely in pairs) flowers, 2 in (5 cm) tall, range from rustic tones through yellowish-green to green.

Cannaeorchis verruciferum

CATASETUM

This genus of about 50 species occurs in tropical Central and South America and the West Indies. Most species are epiphytic, but they may be lithophytic or terrestrial. The plants have fleshy, ovoid, conical, or spindle-shaped pseudobulbs covered in leaf sheaths when young. The large pleated leaves are deciduous. Inflorescences arise from the base of the pseudobulbs and may be erect, arching, or pendent. The flowers are showy and almost always unisexual; the male and female flowers are different in appearance and may occur on the same inflorescence or on separate ones. In both, the sepals and petals are free and spread, and the lip is pouch-like. The genus name comes from the Greek *kata* meaning down, and the Latin *seta* meaning a bristle, referring to two appendages at the base of the column in the male flowers.
CULTIVATION: These plants may be potted but are more usually grown in baskets in a coarse bark-based compost. They like bright, humid, well-ventilated conditions but not direct sunlight. Female flowers are more likely to be produced when plants are stressed, for example when it is too bright and dry. After the leaves have fallen, plants should be kept cooler and drier. Propagate by division.

Catasetum saccatum

↔ 12–16 in (30–40 cm)   ↑ 12–24 in (30–60 cm)   ♀ ☼ ◆ ❋ ☐

Large plants from Brazil, Guyana, and Peru. Pseudobulbs 3–8 in (8–20cm) long; leaves 8–16 in (20–40 cm) long, erect or spreading. Inflorescence erect or arching, to 16 in (40 cm) long, loosely arranged with several flowers. Male flowers to 4 in (10 cm) across,

greenish, marked with purple-brown; female flowers smaller, yellow-green with red-brown dots. Flowers in summer–winter.

Catasetum tenebrosum

↔ 12–16 in (30–40 cm)   ↑ 12–18 in (30–45 cm)   ♀ ☼/☀ ◆/◆ ❋ ☐

Robust plant from Ecuador and Peru. Pseudobulbs to 6 in (15 cm) long; pleated leaves 8–12 in (20–30 cm) long. Inflorescences to 10 in (25 cm) long, densely arranged with few to many flowers, in spring–autumn. Male flowers around 2 in (5 cm) wide, showy, maroon to brownish-red, lip yellow. Female flowers yellow-green.

CATTLEYA

This tropical American genus is one of the most popular groups of orchids in cultivation, with over 50 species and literally thousands of hybrids. These sympodial rock- and tree-dwellers have showy, colorful, long-lasting, and often highly fragrant flowers produced on stout plants with club-shaped to cylindrical pseudobulbs. They are topped with 1 (unifoliate) or 2 (bifoliate) dull green leathery leaves. There have been thousands of hybrids made within the genus and related members of the *Cattleya* alliance or family, especially *Laelia*, *Rhyncholaelia* (often credited in hybrid lists under *Brassavola*), and *Sophronitis*, with many of the larger-flowering types grown commercially for cut-flower production.
CULTIVATION: Cattleyas enjoy high light and intermediate to warm temperatures, with some taking cooler conditions in winter. Most species require warmth in winter, but the Brazilian bifoliate autumn-flowering types will stand cooler winter temperatures for short periods, if kept dry while dormant. They must all have unimpeded drainage and a coarse bark-based medium. Most grow best in plastic or terracotta pots and must dry out between waterings. Healthy plants will develop an extensive system of thick white roots, which are long-lived and branch freely. Propagate by division.

Cattleya aclandiae

↔ 4–12 in (10–30 cm)   ↑ 3–6 in (8–15 cm)   ♀ ☼ ◆/◆ ❋ ☐/☀

Small-growing bifoliate species, endemic to Brazil. Leathery leaves to 4 in (10 cm) long. Blooms 3 in (8 cm) in diameter, usually solitary, olive green, heavily blotched with dark maroon; flared lip, cream at base, graduating to deep rose-lavender.

Flowers in autumn–winter. Performs well in small wooden baskets, or on slabs of cork.

Cattleya amethystoglossa

↔ 12–20 in (30–50 cm)   ↑ 30–50 in (75–130 cm)   ♀/⋀ ☼ ◆ ❋ ☐/☀

Brazilian species. Cylindrical pseudobulbs, 20–40 in (50–100 cm) long, 2-leafed at apex. Spreading leaves, oblong, 6–10 in (15–25 cm) long. Inflorescence with 5 to 10 flowers, each 2–4 in (5–10 cm) across; sepals and petals white or pale pink, spotted with deep purple; lip with white side lobes and magenta mid-lobe. Blooms in summer. *C. a.* var. *coerulea*, off-white sepals and petals highlighted with lavender blue dots, lip with lavender to magenta mid-lobe.

Cattleya amethystoglossa var. *coerulea*

Cattleya aclandiae

Cattleya aurantiaca 'Golden Dew'

Cattleya aurantiaca 'Marigold'

Cattleya aurantiaca 'Red'

Cattleya aurantiaca

↔ 6–24 in (15–60 cm) ↕ 5–24 in (12–60 cm)
♀ ☼/☀ ◆/◈ ⊡

Central American species; smallest
flowers of genus, with up to 12 glossy
flowers, 2 in (5 cm) wide, ranging
from yellow through shades of orange
(the most common color) to deep red,
occasionally white, in summer. In
some clones the flowers do not open
fully, while inferior forms are self-
pollinating. '**Golden Dew**', golden
flowers, splash of red at throat, early
blooming; '**Marigold**', vivid orange
flowers, with darker dappling at throat;
'**Red**', bright vermilion flowers.

Cattleya bicolor

↔ 8–24 in (20–60 cm) ↕ 8–48 in
(20–120 cm) ♀/∧ ☼/☀ ◆/◈ ❈ ⊡
Bifoliate species from Brazil. Cylindrical pseudobulbs; leathery leaves
to 4 in (10 cm) long. Up to 8 flowers,
3 in (8 cm) wide, apple or olive green,
sometimes with a coppery cast, and
a contrasting purple lip. Blooms in
autumn. *C. b.* **var. *braziliensis***, significantly larger but fewer blooms,

which often have a stronger color.
C. b. '**Golden Gate**', yellow-green
flowers with contrasting crimson lip.

Cattleya bowringiana

↔ 4–24 in (10–60 cm) ↕ 6–36 in (15–90 cm)
∧ ☼/☀ ◆/◈ ❈ ⊡

Strong, easily grown, popular species
from Guatemala and Belize, found
on rocky cliffs, in bright humid conditions. Forms large clusters of up to
20 rose-purple blooms, each 3 in
(8 cm) wide, in autumn.

Cattleya gaskelliana

↔ 8–20 in (20–50 cm) ↕ 8–16 in (20–40 cm)
♀ ☀ ◆/◈ ⊡

From Venezuela; species has one of
the largest flowers in the genus. Up
to 5 pale pink to lavender highly
fragrant blooms, to 7 in (18 cm)
across the petals, in summer. *C. g.*
var. *alba*, an albino form, has pure
white flowers.

Cattleya × guatemalensis

↔ 12–16 in (30–40 cm) ↕ 12–14 in
(30–35 cm) ♀ ☼/☀ ◆ ❈ ⊡

Natural hybrid between *C. skinneri* and
C. aurantiaca; native to Guatemala.
Inflorescence to 6 in (15 cm) long, bears
few to many flowers, each 2 in (5 cm)
wide, ranging in color from white to
purple and red. Spring-blooming.

Cattleya intermedia

↔ 4–12 in (10–30 cm) ↕ 6–16 in (15–40 cm)
♀ ☀ ◆/◈ ❈ ⊡

Variable species from Brazil; comes in
a range of shapes, sizes, and colors—
from pure white through shades of

Cattleya bicolor 'Golden Gate'

Cattleya gaskelliana

Cattleya × guatemalensis

Cattleya intermedia var. *alba*

Cattleya intermedia var. *amethystina*

pink to deep purple. Up to 5 blooms, 3½ in (9 cm) wide, borne in spring. *C. i.* var. *alba*, fragrant white flowers; 'Breckinridge Snow', long-lasting pure white flowers. *C. i.* var. *amethystina*, white flowers, pink or lavender at lip; *C. i.* var. *aquinii*, attractive splash-petalled form; *C. i.* 'Do Hector', pinkish sepals and petals, lip deepening in color at tip; ('Do Hector' × var. *alba gigantea*), similar to 'Do Hector', but with paler sepals and petals; and 'Irrorata', ivory flowers, tip of lip tinged with magenta.

Cattleya intermedia 'Irrorata'

Cattleya intermedia var. *aquinii*

Cattleya intermedia

Cattleya intermedia 'Do Hector'

C

Cattleya loddigesii

Cattleya loddigesii 'Bella Vista'

Cattleya loddigesii 'Blue Sky'

Cattleya loddigesii

↔ 4–12 in (10–30 cm)   ↑ 6–24 in (15–60 cm)

From Brazil and Argentina. Pseudo-bulbs cylindrical; leaves leathery. Up to 8 flowers, 4 in (10 cm) wide, in autumn. Pale pink to purple (rarely white) petals and sepals, sometimes finely speckled with darker purple, lip white, yellow, and purple. Color intensity of blooms can be improved if they are given strong light when in bud. These plants are very similar to, and often confused with, *C. harrisoniana*. 'Bella Vista', rich pink flowers, pink and lemon yellow lip; 'Blue Sky', pale lavender-blue flowers, white and yellow lip; and 'Impassionata', purple-pink flowers, lip white, yellow, and purple; ('Pink Spots' × 'Dark Pink') and ('Pink Spots' × 'Monty'), both with pink flowers with yellow and pink lip; and ('Shorty' × 'Sweetheart'), rose pink-purple blooms, lip tipped with pink and lemon.

Cattleya loddigesii ('Pink Spots' × 'Dark Pink')

Cattleya loddigesii ('Pink Spots' × 'Monty')

Cattleya loddigesii ('Shorty' × 'Sweetheart')

Cattleya lueddemanniana

syn. *Cattleya speciosissima*

↔ 4–12 in (10–30 cm)   ↕ 6–20 in (15–50 cm)

/\ ☼ ◆/◇ ❄ ⊔

Unifoliate species from Venezuela. Will grow on rocks in quite exposed positions in the wild. Bears shapely white and orchid pink to purple blooms, to 8 in (20 cm) wide, with as many as 4 on each stalk, in winter.

Cattleya mendelii

syn. *Cattleya labiata* var. *mendelii*

MENDEL'S CATTLEYA

↔ 16–18 in (40–45 cm)   ↕ 16–18 in (40–45 cm)   ♀/\ ☼ ◆ ❄ ⊔

Colombian species. Cylindrical pseudobulb; 1 large leathery leaf. Bears 2 to 5 fragrant pink flowers, 7–8 in (18–20 cm) in size, with a dark purple and yellow lip, from late spring–early summer. Albino and semi-albino color forms also occur.

Cattleya nobilior

NOBLE CATTLEYA

↔ 7–12 in (18–30 cm)   ↕ 5–8 in (12–20 cm)

♀/\ ☼/☼ ◆ ❄ ⊔

From Brazil, typically found in very hot and sunny conditions that often undergo severe drought. Similar to *C. walkeriana* in blooming from separate growth off rhizome but differs in 2 leaves per pseudobulb and lip structure of flower. Usually 1 or 2 flowers, 4 in (10 cm) wide, fragrant, pink with white or yellow on lip, in spring.

Cattleya schilleriana

↔ 4–12 in (10–30 cm)   ↕ 4–6 in (10–15 cm)

♀ ☼ ◆/◇ ❄ ⊔/☇

Bifoliate species, endemic to Brazil; closely related to *C. aclandiae*. Cylindrical pseudobulbs; leathery leaves. Generally produces flowers either singly or in pairs, olive-green to bronze, heavily spotted in red-brown, 3 in (8 cm) wide, in spring. Petals particularly wavy at edges, lip with network of purple stripes.

Cattleya schofieldiana

↔ 8–20 in (20–50 cm)   ↕ 12–40 in (30–100 cm)   ♀ ☼ ◆/◇ ❄ ⊔

From Brazil; closely related to *C. granulosa*, but larger in all its parts, and much taller. Produces from 2 to 5 flowers, mustard yellow, densely spotted with maroon, up to 4 in (10 cm) across, in summer.

Cattleya schroderae

SCHRODER'S CATTLEYA

↔ 16–18 in (40–45 cm)   ↕ 16–18 in (40–45 cm)   ♀ ☼ ◆ ❄ ⊔

Colombian species, usually found on older trees near moving water. Single large leathery leaf per pseudobulb. Light pink to white flowers, bright orange disk on lip. Blooms in autumn–winter. Very similar to *C. trianaei*, sometimes considered a form of that species. Differs in the very crisp lip and petals, orange coloration on lip, and very intense fragrance.

Cattleya mendelii

Cattleya schilleriana

Cattleya lueddemanniana

Cattleya species

Cattleya schofieldiana

C

Cattleya skinneri var. *alba* 'Rebemic'

Cattleya skinneri var. *coerulescens*

Cattleya skinneri
SKINNER'S CATTLEYA

↔ 12–16 in (30–40 cm) ↕ 12–14 in (30–35 cm) ♀ ☀ ◆ ❀ ⛩

Found in humid forests of Guatemala south to Costa Rica. Bifoliate plant; pseudobulbs very narrow at base, thickening near apex. Usually carries 5 to 14 purple to pink flowers, white to yellow at throat of tubular lip, in spring. Several color forms naturally occur. *C. s.* **var.** *alba* '**Rebemic**', albino form of species, lacking pigments, with white flowers. *C. s.* **var.** *coerulescens* lacks red pigment of typical forms, giving flowers a bluish cast. *C. s.* '**Casa Luna**', attractive cultivar.

Cattleya walkeriana

↔ 4–10 in (10–25 cm) ↕ 3–6 in (8–15 cm) ♀ ☀ ◆ ❀ ⛩

Brazilian species. Unique flowering style—short specialized spike emerges from rhizome near base of previous growth, bearing 1 or 2 flat rather than cup-shaped 4 in (10 cm) blooms that are generally lilac-pink to purple. *C. w.* **var.** *alba*, one of numerous albino forms bearing flowers of the purest white. Many of these "superior white forms," that have allegedly been "line bred" (and often curiously flower from top of pseudobulb), may, in fact, be hybrids. *C. w.* **var.** *alba* '**Pendentive**' is one of the popular cultivars.

Cattleya skinneri 'Casa Luna'

Cattleya skinneri

Cattleya Hybrids

↔ 8–24 in (20–60 cm) ↕ 8–32 in (20–80 cm)

A selection of some popular cultivars and recent seedlings shows the variety of color available. Most of these hybrids bloom in spring or autumn. **C. Bow Bells 'July'**, white flowers, golden yellow at throat; **Bowgata**, magenta-pink flowers; (**Browniae** × ***loddigesii***) can be grown over a range of climates; protect plants from frosts; **Earl 'Imperialis'**, bred from albino forms of *C. trianaei*, *C. gaskelliana*, and *C. mossiae*, large white blooms; **Eclipse**, primary hybrid between *C. maxima* and *C. skinneri*, clusters of large magenta flowers in spring; **Frasquita**, a tall-growing primary hybrid between *C. bicolor* and *C. velutina*, clusters of glossy brown flowers with bright purple lip; **Hawaiian Comfort**, compact growing hybrid with crisp pure white to cream blooms that are excellent as cut flowers and for use in corsages; **Humming Bird Hybrids**, sprays of up to 8 flowers, often called "cluster cattleyas;" **Luteous Forb**, a primary hybrid between *C. luteola* and *C. forbesii*, clusters of apple green and yellow flowers; **Miyuki 'Abe'**, rich pink flowers with ruffled yellow lip, floriferous hybrid ideal as a specimen plant; **Penny Kuroda 'Spots'**, popular hybrid used as a parent in many new crosses, pink flowers with darker lip, distinctive spotting is derived from *C. guttata*.

Cattleya Bow Bells 'July' (hybrid)

Cattleya Bowgata (hybrid)

Cattleya (Browniae × *loddigesii*) (hybrid)

Cattleya walkeriana var. *alba*

Cattleya walkeriana var. *alba* 'Pendentive'

Cattleya walkeriana

C

Cattleya Earl 'Imperialis' (hybrid)

Cattleya Eclipse (hybrid)

Cattleya Hawaiian Comfort (hybrid)

Cattleya Humming Bird (hybrid)

Cattleya Miyuki 'Abe' (hybrid)

Cattleya Penny Kuroda 'Spots' (hybrid)

Cattleya Frasquita (hybrid)

Cattleya Luteous Forb (hybrid)

Cephalanthera austiniae

CATTLEYOPSIS

This genus contains 3 xerophytic (drought-tolerant) epiphytes from the lowland forests of Cuba and the Bahamas. They often grow in full sun under hot and rather dry conditions. The small egg-shaped pseudobulbs form dense clusters. The leaves are succulent and have rough sharp edges. The very showy flowers resemble those of *Cattleya*, with long sepals and a tube-shaped lip, however, they differ in having 8 pollinia, not 4 as in *Cattleya*, which appear at the end on a long pendent raceme.
CULTIVATION: *Cattleyopsis* are rather difficult to keep in good condition over longer periods. Grow intermediate to warm, with bright light and high humidity during the growing season. These plants need a distinct resting period, otherwise flowering will be inhibited. They are sensitive to root rotting when kept too wet. Propagation is by division, but it is not advisable to disturb an established specimen. These orchids are not suitable for windowsill cultivation.

Cattleyopsis lindenii
syn. *Laeliopsis lindenii*
↔ 4–6 in (10–15 cm) ↕ 4–6 in (10–15 cm)
♀ ☼ ◆ ❈ ☐

From Cuba and the Bahamas. Pseudobulbs cylindrical, to 3 in (8 cm) high; 1 to 3 slender, very leathery leaves. Inflorescence emerges from base of pseudobulb, mainly in late spring–late summer. Clusters of 3 to 6 flowers appear at end of inflorescence. Light pink sepals and petals, to 2 in (5 cm) long, lip even larger, whitish pink, yellow in center and dark violet striations on mid-lobe.

CATTLEYTONIA

Cattleytonia is a genus created by combining members of the sympodial genera *Cattleya* with *Broughtonia*. Generally, the West Indian species *Broughtonia sanguinea* is dominant in their backgrounds. These are often highly colored hybrids with flowers produced on tall, thin, but sturdy inflorescences off compact plants.
CULTIVATION: These hybrids grow well in small pots of a coarse bark-based medium, wooden baskets, or cork or tree-fern slabs, as long as they dry out between waterings. They enjoy high light and intermediate to warm temperatures throughout the year.

Cattleytonia Maui Maid
↔ 4–12 in (10–30 cm) ↕ 4–20 in (10–50 cm)
♀ ☼/☀ ◆/◈ ❈ ☐/☒

Delightful hybrid created using the white-flowered form of *Broughtonia sanguinea*. Flowers last for over 6 weeks in fine conditions.

Cattleytonia Starrlyn
↔ 4–12 in (10–30 cm) ↕ 4–20 in (10–50 cm)
♀ ☼/☀ ◆/◈ ❈ ☐/☒

Registered in 1996. Flowers of pinkish red, with yellow throat. Four species in its make-up—*Broughtonia sanguinea*, *Cattleya aurantiaca*, *C. bicolor*, and *C. intermedia*. Blooms in autumn.

CAULARTHRON
syn. *Diacrium*
Caularthron, which means "jointed stem," is a genus of 2 or 3 species. They are found growing as epiphytes and lithophytes in the tropical lowland forests of the southern Caribbean islands and northern South America to Amazonas, Brazil, often growing in full sun. The plants have spindle-shaped pseudobulbs, with 2 to 4 leaves at the apex of the bulbs. At least one of the species has hollow pseudobulbs, which in nature are inhabited by ants. The elongate inflorescences carry several flowers, typically white, which turn pinkish orange as they age or are pollinated. There is a tendency toward cleistagamous (self-pollinating) flowers. These plants have been used in hybrids with other members of the *Cattleya* group.
CULTIVATION: These plants are easy to grow with the right conditions. They are warm-growing, requiring a minimum of 61–64°F (16–18°C), and they should be grown in bright light. They appreciate being watered freely and fertilized while growing, but they require a distinct dry rest after flowering. Hanging pots, baskets, and mounts are ideal for giving them bright light, and when potted, medium-grade bark suits them well. Propagation is by division.

Caularthron bicornutum
VIRGIN ORCHID
↔ 14–18 in (35–45 cm) ↕ 18–24 in (45–60 cm) ♀/☊ ☼ ◆ ☐/☒

Widespread species from islands in the south Caribbean to northern South America, south to Amazonas in Brazil, often found on coast. Spindle-shaped pseudobulbs, 2 to 4 leaves near apex. Elongate spike with several fragrant white flowers; lip 3-lobed with yellow disk and purple spotting. Usually spring-blooming.

CEPHALANTHERA
HELLEBORINE
A genus of 12 to 15 terrestrial species, distributed throughout Europe, North Africa, and Asia, with 1 species native to western USA and southwestern Canada. They are found in variety of habitats, from moist to dry areas in light woodland and mountainous areas from sea level up to 8,200 ft (2,500 m) in the Moroccan mountains. The rhizome has hairy roots and grows 4–5 in (10–12 cm) below the surface. Each shoot usually has 2 to 6 ovate to lanceolate leaves and is topped by an inflorescence that usually bears few large white to pink flowers.
CULTIVATION: As all species grow in symbiosis with special mycorrhizal fungi, it is not possible to keep the plants alive in cultivation for long periods. Propagation is by division.

Cephalanthera austiniae
PHANTOM ORCHID, SNOW ORCHID
↔ 3–4 in (8–10 cm) ↕ 20–26 in (50–65 cm)
❦ ☼ ◇ ❈ ❈ ☐

From western USA. Stem white, lacking leaves. Up to 20 white flowers, not opening wide, sepals about ¾ in (18 mm) long, loosely arranged on inflorescence in summer–autumn.

Cephalanthera damasonium
syns *Cephalanthera alba*, *C. grandiflora*
WHITE HELLEBORINE
↔ 4–8 in (10–20 cm) ↕ 8–24 in (20–60 cm)
❦ ☼ ◇ ❈ ❈ ☐

From temperate regions of Europe to northern Iran, Bhutan, and Yunnan, China. Stem to 6 in (15 cm) long; 2 to 4 stiff leaves, at right angle to stem. From 4 to 12 flowers at end of stem, white to yellowish, open only partially.

Cephalanthera longifolia
SWORD-LEAFED HELLEBORINE
↔ 3–4 in (8–10 cm) ↕ 6–24 in (15–60 cm)
❦ ☼ ◇ ❈ ☐

From Europe, North Africa, and the Middle East. Several leaves, to 7 in (18 cm) long. Inflorescence with 10 to 20 blooms in spring–summer. Flowers white with an orange-yellow patch on lip, not opening wide, rather small.

Cephalanthera rubra
syn. *Epipactis atropurpurea*
RED HELLEBORINE
↔ 4–8 in (10–20 cm) ↕ 4–24 in (10–60 cm) ❦ ☼ ◇ ❈ ❈ ☐

From Europe, North Africa, and central Asia. Erect stem; 3 to 6 lanceolate leaves. Inflorescence to 8 in (20 cm) long, with 4 to 15 pink flowers that open only partially, in summer.

Cattleytonia Maui Maid

Cattleytonia Starrlyn

Ceratostylis incognita

Ceratostylis retisquama

Chiloglottis formicifera

CERATOSTYLIS

This genus contains about 100 species, distributed from the Himalayas and Indochina through Malaysia, Indonesia, and the Philippines to New Guinea and the Solomon Islands, as far east as some Polynesian islands. They grow as epiphytes in forests at various altitudes, from sea level up to 6,560 ft (2,000 m). They have simple or branched tufted stems and long fibrous roots. There are 3 main growing habits: short, many branched rhizomes with short stems and thin leaves; long creeping sympodial rhizomes with long stems topped by large leaves; and sympodially branched upright or hanging stems. Most species only have small flowers, colored from white to salmon pink.
CULTIVATION: Grow under hot and very humid conditions, in hanging baskets or on a slab. Water well during growing season and less after the new growth has matured, but never leave to dry out completely. Depending on the species, keep in bright to rather shady light conditions. Propagate by division.

Ceratostylis incognita
↔ 4–8 in (10–20 cm) ↕ 3–7 in (8–18 cm)
Endemic to the Philippines; semi-pendulous. Cylindrical leaves. solitary flowers, less than ¾ in (18mm) in size, white, sometimes with minor red edging on segments; bright yellow lip.

Winter-flowering. Recently described, previously misinterpreted as *C. loheri*.

Ceratostylis retisquama
↔ 4–6 in (10–15 cm) ↕ 8–16 in (20–40 cm)
Restricted to the Philippines, found on islands of Luzon and Mindanao. Long hanging stems; leaves to 5 in (12 cm) long, thin, fleshy. Orange flowers produced several times during year.

CHILOGLOTTIS
BIRD ORCHID

The 30-odd terrestrial species in this genus come from Australia and New Zealand, where they grow in the moist litter of native forests or pine plantations. They usually have 2 basal leaves and a single dull flower borne on a short stalk that elongates after pollination. Blooms appear in spring to autumn depending upon the species. Each species features a lip with a particular pattern of glandular protrusions called a callus, which mimics both the appearance and scent of a female wasp, each species mimicking a different wasp species. Male thynnine wasps are attracted to and deceived by the odor and shape. During a wasp's attempts to copulate, pollen is deposited or removed. After seed release, plants enter a resting stage for 4 to 6 months before resuming growth.
CULTIVATION: *Chiloglottis* species can be maintained in cultivation, where most grow vigorously. Plant tubers in

a moist well-drained mix of sand and leaf mold topped with a mulch of chopped pine needles. Propagate from seeds or from additional tubers, which may form freely in some species.

Chiloglottis formicifera
ANT ORCHID
↔ 3–6 in (8–15 cm) ↕ 4–12 in (10–30 cm)
Vigorous orchid from eastern Australia. Two oval leaves, to 3 in (8 cm) long, with wavy edges. Single flower, ½–¾ in (12–18 mm) wide, greenish brown with reflexed petals clasping the ovary, in spring. Lip broad with a callus of shiny, black, stalked globules resembling an ant.

Chiloglottis gunnii
COMMON BIRD ORCHID, LARGE BIRD ORCHID, TALL BIRD ORCHID
↔ 3–8 in (8–20 cm) ↕ 3–12 in (8–30 cm)
Robust species from eastern Australia; can form dense groups in shady damp forests and plantations. Two shiny oval leaves to 4 in (10 cm) long. Single flower, brownish purple, beak-like yellow anther cap, shiny black callus on lip. Flowers in spring–summer.

CHILOSCHISTA

A genus of about 15 species found from Sri Lanka through India and the whole of the Australasian region. They grow as epiphytes in bare branches in low to medium altitude forests, from sea level up to 3,280 ft (1,000 m). Almost all the species are completely lacking leaves—the roots have taken over photosynthesis. The stem is very compressed and the plants look like a bundle of roots. The inflorescence, sometimes hairy, appears at the base of the stem between the roots and carries between 4 and 20 flowers.
CULTIVATION: Grow these plants on a slab or piece of rough bark. Keep warm and humid during summer and water regularly. During winter they can be kept somewhat drier and cooler. A sign of successful culture is a vigorous root system with flattened roots. Propagate from seed.

Chiloschista lunifera
↔ 2½–8 in (6–20 cm) ↕ 1–5 in (2.5–12 cm)
Leafless species found from India to Thailand. Pendent flower spikes of up to 20 blooms appear from the growing point in spring. Green to yellowish shapely flowers, less than ½ in (12 mm) wide, quite showy. Plants appreciate frequent misting of the root system.

Chiloglottis gunnii

Chiloschista lunifera

Chiloschista parishii
↔ 2–3 in (5–8 cm) ↑ 2–4 in (5–10 cm)
☿ ☼ ◆ ⚐

From Himalayan Nepal, Myanmar, Thailand, and China (Yunnan); found growing in lowland forests. Flowers about ½ in (12 mm) wide; sepals and petals faint yellow, green, cream, or brighter yellow with brownish spots and markings, lip white with maroon striations. Some flowers lack markings. Flowering mostly in early summer.

CHYSIS
The cooler temperate forests found from Mexico to Peru are the origin of the 5 to 6 species of this genus. They grow as epiphytes on moss-covered branches at altitudes of 3,600–4,920 ft (1,100–1,500 m). They have somewhat slender pseudobulbs, crowned by 3 to 5 leaves, which often hang downward on the branches. The flowers appear on a pendent raceme, are often self-pollinating, and sometimes even do not open at all.
CULTIVATION: Grow under temperate or better cool-temperate conditions on a moss-covered slab or in small baskets in a fibrous substrate. The pseudobulbs can become heavy, so secure them to prevent plant from tipping over. After the leaves are shed, the plants go through a distinct resting period and must be kept rather dry and temperatures should not exceed 59°F (15°C) during the night. However, relative humidity should always be in the region of 75–80 percent. Propagation is by division.

Chysis aurea
syns *Chysis limminghei, C. maculata*
↔ 8–10 in (20–25 cm) ↑ 8–24 in (20–60 cm)
☿ ☼ ◆ ❄ ⚐

Found from Venezuela to Mexico. Pseudobulbs slender, to 8–24 in (20–60 cm) high; 3 to 5 leaves, each

Chiloschista parishii

6 in (15 cm) long. A record plant from Costa Rica had 4 ft (1.2 m) long pseudobulbs. Leaves are shed after pseudobulbs have matured. Arching inflorescence bears 8 to 15 blooms in late spring–early summer. Flowers 2–2½ in (5–6 cm) wide, rich yellow; lip lighter yellow, almost whitish toward base, with red striations.

Chysis bractescens
↔ 6–8 in (15–20 cm) ↑ 6–10 in (15–25 cm) ☿ ☼ ◆ ❄ ⚐

From Mexico. Similar to *C. aurea*, but pseudobulbs shorter, more compact. Inflorescence pendent; flowers larger, to 3 in (8 cm) across, ivory colored, lip light yellow on inside, with reddish markings. Summer-flowering.

CIRRHAEA
syns *Sarcoglossum, Scleropteris*
This genus of about 4 species is distributed in coastal forests of southeastern Brazil, where they are found as epiphytes. The egg-shaped pseudobulbs are grouped densely together, are ribbed, and bear a single, narrow, and pleated leaf on a short stem, reminiscent of those of the genus *Gongora*. The hanging inflorescence appears at the base of the pseudobulb and bears many flowers. They are very variable, which resulted in the description of at least 17 species (and a long list of synonyms) that can be grouped together to 3 or 4 species.
CULTIVATION: Grow under half-shade and intermediate temperatures, as for cattleyas and *Gongora*. Humidity should be high all year round, and watering should be reduced during the resting period in winter. Because of the hanging inflorescence, plants are best grown in baskets with a fibrous substrate or on a slab with moss cover. Propagation is by division.

Cirrhaea dependens
syns *Cirrhaea hoffmanseggii, C. nasuta, C. tristis, C. viridipurpurea, C. warreana*
↔ 8–12 in (20–30 cm) ↑ 10–14 in (25–35 cm) ☿ ☼ ◆ ⚐

From southeastern Brazil, found in the States of Rio de Janeiro, Sao Paulo,

Paraná, and Santa Catarina. Ovoid pseudobulbs, each with single pleated leaf. Up to 20 bizarre-looking waxy flowers, each about 2 in (5 cm) in diameter, appear on a hanging spike in summer. Flower color varies from green, rusty banded to deep wine colored types. Flower morphology is also variable with differently shaped flowers found on the same inflorescence.

CLEISOSTOMA
This genus contains about 90 monopodial epiphytic species, which are found throughout Southeast Asia; in the wild, a few species can be found growing as lithophytes. Most species are small and of botanical interest. Most have fleshy succulent leaves in 2 ranks along an erect or arching to pendent stem. The flowers are small, but often produced in numbers along a simple or branched inflorescence.
CULTIVATION: *Cleisostoma* species grow well in small pots, baskets, or slabs. They enjoy humid conditions combined with high light levels and intermediate to warm temperatures, and appreciate regular waterings throughout the year. Propagation is by division or from seed.

Chysis bractescens

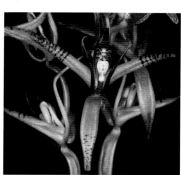

Cirrhaea dependens

Cleisostoma racemiferum

Cleisostoma racemiferum
↔ 20–27 in (50–70 cm) ↑ 10–20 in (25–50 cm) ☿ ☼ ◆ ⚐

From India and Nepal to Southeast Asia. Roots stout; leaves strap-shaped, to 14 in (35 cm) long, leathery. Inflorescence much branched, bears many flowers in spring. Flowers small, yellow and chestnut brown.

Cleisostoma recurvum
syn. *Cleisostoma rostratum*
↔ 8–18 in (20–45 cm) ↑ 8–18 in (20–45 cm) ☿ ☼ ◆ ⚐

From China, Laos, Vietnam, and Thailand. Stem leafy, 8–18 in (20–45 cm) long, sometimes branched. Leaves 4–6 in (10–15 cm) long. Racemes loosely arranged with many blooms in summer. Flowers small; sepals and petals yellowish with two brown stripes, lip purplish-pink, 3-lobed.

Cleisostoma weberi
↔ 4–8 in (10–20 cm) ↑ 6–18 in (15–45 cm) ☿ ☼ ◆ ⚐

From the Philippines. Small-growing species; upright habit; rounded cylindrical leaves. Short inflorescence carries up to 12 small blooms, brown, white, and purple, in summer.

Cleisostoma recurvum

Cleisostoma weberi

CLOWESIA

This genus contains 6 species found from Mexico to Venezuela, Suriname, Amazonian Brazil and Ecuador, where they grow as epiphytes in lowland forests. The pseudobulbs are pear-shaped with few soft and deciduous leaves, arranged in 2 rows. The pendent raceme appears at the lower part of the pseudobulb and the rather large flowers have the lip pointing upward. They were separated from the closely related genus *Catasetum* because the flowers are bisexual and not dioecious. One species, *Clowesia warscewiczii*, is unique among orchids for its pollinating mechanism, called "bees-knees-pollination:" male *Eulaema* bees stick their front legs into a special lip cavity, rub them together and loosen the pollinia—these then stick to the leg (knee) of the bee.

CULTIVATION: Grow under warm to intermediate conditions in bright light with shading during hottest part of the day. Water regularly when in growth and keep dry during the resting period after the new shoot is fully developed. Propagation is by division.

Clowesia rosea

syn. *Catasetum roseum*

↔ 8–12 in (20–30 cm) ↕ 12–20 in (30–50 cm) ♀ ☼ ◆ ☐

From the States of Oaxaca and Michoacan in Mexico, often found growing on oak trees in bright sunny locations. Type species of genus; pseudobulbs up to 4 in (10 cm) long, topped by 6 or more leaves, each 6–16 in (15–40 cm) long. Bears 6 or 7 cinnamon-scented flowers, borne on

Clowesia warscewiczii

Cochleanthes amazonica

Cochlioda rosea

a hanging raceme, in spring. Light pink flowers; lip with longer fringing, petals with very short fine fringing.

Clowesia warscewiczii

↔ 6–10 in (15–25 cm) ↕ 8–20 in (20–50 cm) ♀ ☼ ◆/◆ ✿ ☐

Species from Costa Rica, Panama, Colombia, and Venezuela. Pendulous inflorescences with up to 12 blooms in summer–autumn. Blooms to 1½ in (35 mm) across, cream tinged with green, pleasantly fragrant.

COCHLEANTHES

This is a genus of about 16 sympodial epiphytic species, found in parts of Central and South America. They lack true pseudobulbs and have thin bright green leaves arranged like a fan. The flowers are produced singly on short spikes from between the leaf axils, and generally range from white through various pinks to purple.

CULTIVATION: These orchids need high humidity and freely circulating air to avoid fungal spots on the soft leaves. They grow best in small pots in sphagnum moss or a fine bark mix, as they must be kept moist. They like more shade than most orchids and must not be exposed to direct light. They require intermediate to warm temperatures. Propagation is best done from seed, or by division of large established plants.

Cochlioda vulcanica

Cochleanthes amazonica

↔ 4–10 in (10–25 cm) ↕ 4–20 in (10–50 cm) ♀ ☼ ◆/◆ ☐

Species found from Brazil to Colombia; forms fan-like clumps. Large white blooms, 4 in (10 cm) in size, produced infrequently at base of plant. Flowers bruise easily; keep dry to avoid marking.

Cochleanthes discolor

↔ 6–8 in (15–20 cm) ↕ 4–8 in (10–20 cm) ♀ ☼ ◆ ☐

Short-stemmed plants from Central America, Cuba, and Venezuela. Leaves 3 to 5, each 6–8 in (15–20 cm) long, forming a fan. Inflorescence erect, to 4 in (10 cm) long, single-flowered. Flowers to 2 in (5 cm) across; sepals and petals green, petals violet-tinged; lip funnel-shaped, deep violet with darker veins, paler at edges. Flowers off and on through year.

COCHLIODA

This genus contains 6 species from the mountainous cloud forests of Peru, Ecuador, Bolivia, and the State of Amazonas in Brazil, where they grow as epiphytes, rarely on rocks or thick moss layers on the ground, at altitudes of 5,580–9,840 ft (1,700–3,000 m). They grow in dense clusters with close-

packed, flattened egg- or pear-shaped pseudobulbs that bear 1 large leaf, surrounded by 2 smaller leaf sheaths. The upright or arching unbranched inflorescence appears at the base of the upper sheath and bears few to many flowers, each 1–2 in (2.5–5 cm) wide. They are very intensely colored—from bright pink to deep orange-red. Pink-flowered *Cochlioda rosea* and the orange-red *C. noezliana* were used to produce the colorful hybrids in the *Odontoglossum-Oncidium-Miltonia* complex. The resulting crosses are *Burrageara* (*Cochlioda* × *Miltonia* × *Odontoglossum* × *Oncidium*), *Odontioda* (*Odontoglossum* × *Cochlioda*), *Wilsonara* (*Odontoglossum* × *Oncidium* × *Cochlioda*), and the famous *Vuylstekeara* (*Odontoglossum* × *Miltonia* × *Cochlioda*).

CULTIVATION: Similar cultivation requirements to *Odontoglossum*, but somewhat warmer, less humid, and brighter. Keep under shade during hot summer days, and water regularly during the growth season. They grow equally well in pots in a free-draining organic substrate as on a slab with a moisture-retaining layer of moss or sphagnum. Propagation is by division, but the plants do not like to be disturbed too often.

Cochlioda noezliana

↔ 6–8 in (15–20 cm) ↕ 8–14 in (20–35 cm) ♀ ☼ ◆ ☐/▨

From Bolivia and Peru, may be also found in Ecuador. Type species of the genus; important in hybridization. Pseudobulbs to 2 in (5 cm) high, leaf to 10 in (25 cm) long. Inflorescence to 14 in (35 cm) long, with many bright orange-red flowers, 1½ in (35 mm) wide, in summer–autumn.

Cochlioda rosea

↔ 5–6 in (12–15 cm) ↕ 12–18 in (30–45 cm) ♀ ☼ ◆/◇ ☐/▨

From Ecuador and Peru. Pseudobulbs 2–3 in (5–8 cm) tall, ovoid, 1-leafed.

Coelia bella

C

Leaves 6–8 in (15–20 cm) long, strap-shaped. Inflorescence to 18 in (45 cm) long, arching. Flowers about 1½ in (35 mm) across, deep pink to crimson; sepals and petals spreading, lip 3-lobed. Flowers late spring–summer.

Cochlioda vulcanica
↔ 5–6 in (12–15 cm) ↕ 8–14 in (20–35 cm)
☉ ◇/◊ ▽/≋

From Peru and Bolivia. Leaves around 8 in (20 cm) long; inflorescence arching, 8–14 in (20–35 cm) long, bears 6 to 12 flowers in late spring or in autumn. Flowers around 1 in (25 mm) wide, deep rose pink; sepals and petals spreading, lip 3-lobed.

COELIA
Formerly considered monotypic, this genus from Mexico, Central America, Cuba, and Jamaica now includes 4 former members of the genus *Bothriochilus*. They grow as epiphytes, terrestrials, or lithophytes from sea level up to 9,840 ft (3,000 m) in lowland and cloud forests with high rainfall. They are immediately recognized by their globular pseudobulbs, each about 2 in (5 cm) across, topped by 3 to 5 very thin grass-like leaves that grow up to 3 ft (0.9 m) long. The bulbs are connected through short rhizomes, from which the flower stalk also emerges. These plants display very vigorous growth.
CULTIVATION: Keep these plants under intermediate to cool conditions in high humidity and grow in pots in a free-draining organic substrate. When grown on a slab or piece of vine, choose a large one because of the size of the plant. They are easy to cultivate and thrive in half-sun to bright conditions. Do not disturb too often and try to leave them to grow in their pot for several years. They can easily be divided into several specimens when repotting.

Coelia bella
syn. *Bothriochilus bellus*
↔ 6–20 in (15–50 cm) ↕ 16–32 in (40–80 cm) ☿ ☼/◑/☀ ◆ ✿ ▽/≋

From Mexico and Guatemala; a most spectacular and eye-catching member of the genus. Upright inflorescence bears up to 8 blooms in spring. Pink-tipped white flowers, 2 in (5 cm) wide, fragrant; bright yellow lip.

COELOGYNE
This large diverse group of sympodial orchids from Asia contains about 100 species. *Coelogyne* species form distinct pseudobulbs that are linked by woody rhizomes. Depending on the species,

Coelogyne chloroptera

Coelogyne corymbosa

from 1 to 3 leaves are produced from the top of each pseudobulb. Most members of this showy genus of epiphytes and lithophytes have white or green flowers, with contrasting lips displaying profuse brown markings. Flowering often occurs from the developing new growths, or from specialized points at the base of the previous year's pseudobulb. Some species have fragrant blooms.
CULTIVATION: Generally from mountainous regions, about 80 percent of *Coelogyne* species are suitable for cultivating in cool to intermediate conditions. However, there are also species from the monsoonal tropical lowlands. They are generally easy to grow and will rapidly build into specimen plants if conditions are favorable. Most are grown in pots in a bark-based growing medium, but those species with pendulous flower spikes, or with long rhizomes, do best when grown in baskets. They enjoy humid conditions and regular watering all year-round. Propagate by division.

Coelogyne Burfordiense

Coelogyne Burfordiense
↔ 8–32 in (20–80 cm) ↕ 10–36 in (25–90 cm) ☿ ☼ ◆ ✿ ▽

Large-growing hybrid between the tropical species *C. asperata* and *C. pandurata*; often confused with the latter. Large, 4 in (10 cm) wide, green flowers, lip almost black in color, on long arching inflorescences of about 12 blooms, in spring or summer.

Coelogyne chloroptera
↔ 6–12 in (15–30 cm) ↕ 6–12 in (15–30 cm) ☿ ☼ ◆ ✿ ▽

Endemic to the Philippines; often mistaken for the closely related, but rare, *C. confusa*. Upright to arching inflorescences carry up to 14 blooms in spring. Flowers translucent green, each up to 1½ in (35 mm) across.

Coelogyne corymbosa
↔ 4–8 in (10–20 cm) ↕ 5–10 in (12–25 cm) ☿ ☼ ◇/◊ ▽

From the Himalayas. Arching inflorescence carries a number of white flowers in early summer. Requires

cool summer evening temperatures to thrive. Best grown in small pots of sphagnum moss.

Coelogyne cristata
↔ 12–16 in (30–40 cm) ↕ 8–12 in (20–30 cm) ☿ ☼ ◇/◊ ✿ ▽

From the Himalayas. Oblong to globose pseudobulbs, to 3 in (8 cm); 2 lanceolate leaves, 6–8 in (15–20 cm) long. Inflorescences arching to pendent, 6–12 in (15–30 cm) long, with 3 to 10 flowers in spring. Flowers to 3 in (8 cm) across, scented, pure white, lip with yellow or orange crest.

Coelogyne flaccida
↔ 4–27 in (10–70 cm) ↕ 5–15 in (12–38 cm) ☿ ☼ ◇/◊ ✿ ▽

Variable, fragrant, spring-blooming species found from Nepal to China. Most clones have pendulous spikes of up to 14 cream to light bronze flowers. Reliable bloomer, very fast-growing. 'Caramel', sepals and petals caramel colored, contrasting lip; 'Dark', popular cultivar with ocher flowers.

Coelogyne flaccida

Coelogyne flaccida 'Caramel'

Coelogyne flaccida 'Dark'

C

Coelogyne lawrenceana

Coelogyne huettneriana

Coelogyne speciosa

Coelogyne tomentosa

Coelogyne nitida

Coelogyne Memoria W. Micholitz

Coelogyne huettneriana

↔ 6–12 in (15–30 cm) ↕ 4–8 in (10–20 cm)
♀ ☀/☀ ◆/◇ ❀ ⊡

From Myanmar and Thailand. Ovoid pseudobulbs, 2-leafed. Leaves to 12 in (30 cm) long, narrowly lance-shaped. Arching inflorescence, to 6 in (15 cm) long, with up to 8 white to cream flowers, approximately 2 in (5 cm) across, lip marked brown and yellow. Blooms in spring–summer.

Coelogyne lawrenceana

↔ 12–18 in (30–45 cm) ↕ 10–12 in (25–30 cm) ♀ ☀ ◆/◇ ❀ ⊡

From Vietnam. Ovoid pseudobulbs 2–5 in (5–12 cm) long; 2-leafed. Leaves 8–16 in (20–40 cm) long, lance-shaped. Inflorescence erect at first then arching, to 12 in (30 cm) long, with 1 to 3 blooms in summer.

Flowers 4–5 in (10–12 cm) across, scented, greenish-yellow, lip with brown and yellow markings.

Coelogyne Memoria W. Micholitz

↔ 8–20 in (20–50 cm) ↕ 8–27 in (20–70 cm)
♀ ☀ ◆/◇ ❀ ⊡

Primary hybrid between C. lawrenceana and the large white-flowered C. mooreana. Flowers appear at various times throughout the year, primarily in summer.

Coelogyne nitida

syn. Coelogyne ochracea

↔ 6–12 in (15–30 cm) ↕ 6–10 in (15–25 cm)
♀ ☀/☀ ◆/◇ ❀ ⊡

Species occurring from India to Myanmar and Laos. Oblong pseudobulbs; 2 lance-shaped leaves to 10 in (25 cm) long. Upright inflorescences grow from axil of new growth, with up to 9 blooms in spring. Fragrant white flowers, 1½ in (35 mm) wide, white lip with bright yellow to orange crest.

Coelogyne ovalis

↔ 6–12 in (15–30 cm) ↕ 3–4 in (8–10 cm)
♀ ☀ ◆/◇ ⊡

Creeping plants occurring from India and Nepal across to Thailand. Pseudobulbs 1–2 in (2.5–5 cm) tall, oblong, 2-leafed. Leaves 4–6 in (10–15 cm) long, elliptic. Erect inflorescence, 2–3 in (5–8 cm) long, carries 2 to 3 flowers, to 1 in (25 mm) across, buff yellow; fringed lip, with purple-brown blotch. Blooms produced off and on throughout year.

Coelogyne pandurata

↔ 8–48 in (20–120 cm) ↕ 8–24 in (20–60 cm) ♀ ☀ ◆ ❀ ⊡

Robust species from Borneo, the Philippines, and Indonesia. Oblong to spherical pseudobulbs. Long arching inflorescences of up to 12 blooms, in spring or summer. Large flowers, 4 in (10 cm) wide, fragrant, green, with an almost black lip.

Coelogyne speciosa

↔ 15–20 in (38–50 cm) ↕ 10–27 in (25–70 cm) ♀ ☀ ◆/◆ ❀ ⊡

Creeping plants from southeastern Indonesia. Pseudobulbs ovoid, set close together, to 4 in (10 cm) long, single-leafed. Leaves 8–15 in (20–38 cm) long, elliptic or lance-shaped. Erect or pendent inflorescence, to 27 in (70 cm) long, bears several flowers in spring–summer. Flowers 2–3 in (5–8 cm) across, pale green to yellow-green, lip cream to brown.

Coelogyne tomentosa

syn. Coelogyne massangeana

↔ 10–12 in (25–30 cm) ↕ 40–50 in (100–130 cm) ♀ ☀ ◆/◇ ❀ ⊡

From Peninsular Malaysia, and Java and Sumatra, Indonesia. Pseudobulbs ovoid, 2–6 in (5–15 cm) long, 1- to 2-leafed. Leaves 5–27 in (12–70 cm) long, with long stalk. Inflorescence pendent, 12–20 in (30–50 cm) long, bears 10 to 30 flowers, mainly in summer. Flowers about 2 in (5 cm) across, pale yellow or brownish yellow, veined with brown.

Colmanara Wildcat 'Exile' (hybrid)

Colmanara Wildcat 'Gemma Webb' (hybrid)

Colmanara Wildcat 'Carmela' (hybrid)

COLMANARA

Colmanara is a trigeneric hybrid, with the parents being *Miltonia*, *Odontoglossum*, and *Oncidium*. Many of these hybrids have blooms with rich colors and striking patterns on tall inflorescences. There can be great variation within seedlings derived from the same crossing or seed capsule. The most vigorous and outstanding cultivars have been multiplied through modern tissue culture techniques to satisfy the growing demand for these easily grown plants.

CULTIVATION: Colmanaras do not like their roots to dry out, so they should be planted in sphagnum moss or a fine bark mix. They are suitable for cool humid growing conditions, and require abundant water throughout the year and a position in part-shade. Propagation is by division.

Colmanara Hybrids

↔ 8–12 in (20–30 cm) ↕ 8–30 in (20–75 cm)

These hybrids range in color from yellow and brown tones through to deep red-maroon clones, mostly with contrasting lip colors. Segments often spotted and blotched with darker color. **Wildcat 'Carmela'** ★, very vigorous, wide range of colors; **Wildcat 'Exile'**, orange blooms heavily overlaid with maroon blotching and contrasting white and maroon marked lip; **Wildcat 'Gemma Webb'**, spectacular deep blood-red variety; **Wildcat 'Hildos'**, golden-yellow blooms, heavily overlaid with maroon.

Colmanara Wildcat 'Hildos' (hybrid)

COMPARETTIA

A genus of 7 to 9 species, found from Mexico to Peru and Bolivia, where they grow as epiphytes in subtropical forests at altitudes of 2,300–5,250 ft (700–1,600 m) above sea level. The small flattened pseudobulbs grow in dense clusters and bear a single leaf, about 4 in (10 cm) long. The arching inflorescence bears up to 10 showy flowers, each about 1–2 in (2.5–5 cm) wide, with a long spur. The genus is closely related to *Rodriguezia*.

CULTIVATION: Grow under intermediate conditions in bright light. Keep humidity high all year round. Reduce watering in winter, when the plants are not growing, but do not allow the fine roots to dry out completely. Because of the hanging growth and the arching inflorescences, the plants thrive best in small hanging baskets or on a slab or cork branch. Propagation is by division.

Comparettia falcata

syn. *Comparettia rosea*

↔ 3–5 in (8–12 cm)　↑ 4–6 in (10–15 cm)
♀ ☀ ◆ ❋ ▢/▨

Found from Mexico to Bolivia and in the Caribbean. Often found in cultivated land and plantations of *Citrus* or guavas, at altitudes of 2,300–4,920 ft (700–1,500 m). Flowers up to ¾ in (18 mm) across, rose-pink with darker veins; end of lip is deeply cut. Flowers in autumn–winter.

Comparettia speciosa

↔ 3–5 in (8–12 cm)　↑ 4–6 in (10–15 cm)
♀ ☀ ◆ ❋ ▢/▨

From forests in Ecuador, Bolivia, and Peru, at altitudes of 4,600–4,920 ft (1,400–1,500 m). Flowers to just over 1½ in (35 mm) across, golden yellow to orange, petals and sepals have 3 to 5 darker stripes; lip is only dented at tip. Blooms in autumn–winter.

Comparettia speciosa

COMPERIA

This genus contains one terrestrial species found in the Aegean Islands and the Middle East, where it grows in dry, wooded, upland areas. The rootstock is tuberous, with two unlobed oblong or ellipsoid tubers. The stem is erect with a few leaves arranged along its length. The sepals and petals form a hood; the lip is the most prominent part of the flower. The genus is named in honor of French botanist and landowner, D. Compère, who collected the type specimen.

CULTIVATION: Plants should be grown in a free-draining terrestrial compost with added lime. Water with care while plants are growing and keep them dry during the resting period. Propagation is from seed.

Comperia comperiana

KOMPER'S ORCHID

↔ 6–8 in (15–20 cm)　↑ 10–24 in (25–60 cm)
�><> ☀ ◇ ▢

From some Aegean Islands and the Middle East; found in open woodland. Tubers 2, ovoid. Leaves 2 to 4, erect, to 6 in (15 cm) long. Cylindrical spike bears up to 30 blooms in summer. Flowers greenish tinged with lilac with lilac lip, or brownish-purple with pink lip. Sepals and petals joined, forming hood. Lip 3-lobed, mid-lobe divided into two, all lobes drawn into threadlike processes 1–3 in (2.5–8 cm) long. Spur short, curving down.

CONDYLAGO

This monotypic genus was discovered in 1975 in northwestern Colombia, near the border with Panama, growing epiphytically in a localized area of wet virgin forest; it was described in 1982. The plants lack pseudobulbs, with the leaves growing on thin stem-like ramicauls. The leaves grow in clumps, on a branched rhizome. Inflorescences grow from the base of the leaves, are flexuous (zig-zag), and bloom sequentially for many months. This genus features flowers with a hinged lip.

CULTIVATION: These plants are generally easy to grow in a collection of cool-growing species. They like bright shade and high humidity with good air movement. They will grow well potted, in baskets, or mounted, with moss. They should be kept moist using good quality water. Temperatures should be kept between highs of 75–79°F (24–26°C) to a minimum of 55–59°F (13–15°C). Propagate by division or from seed. Division of plants should be carried out when they have many leaves; each division should have at least 8 to 10 leaves.

Condylago rodrigoi

Condylago rodrigoi

↔ 3 in (8 cm)　↑ 10 in (25 cm)
♀ ☀ ◆/◇ ▢/▨

Found in moist montane forests in Colombia. Tufted, with narrow oblong leaves; lacks a pseudobulb. Flowers, bloom sequentially from a zig-zag spike that eventually grows to 10 in (25 cm) long. Flowers ½ in (12mm) tall, dark red, silvery hairs along sepals; unusual hinged lip, triggered by insect pollinators. Nearly ever-blooming.

CORALLORRHIZA

CORAL ROOT

The 14 terrestrial species in this genus are mostly from Central America, from Mexico and the southernmost States of the USA to Guatemala, with 7 species in Mexico, and 1 species found throughout the Northern Hemisphere. The inflorescence, which grows from a coral-shaped rhizome, lacks any chlorophyll.

CULTIVATION: Plants live in symbiosis with mycorrhizal fungi and obtain their nutrients from decaying detritus, which is broken down by the fungus. Due to this complicated symbiosis, it is not possible to cultivate the species of this genus successfully.

Corallorrhiza striata

↔ 3–4 in (8–10 cm)　↑ 12–20 in (30–50 cm)
✕ ☀ ◇ ❄ ▢

Leafless species from USA and Canada. Stem purplish, almost covered with tubular sheaths. Inflorescence loosely arranged with many blooms in spring–summer. Flowers yellowish pink with purple veining, rather bell-shaped; sepals around ½ in (12 mm) long.

Corallorrhiza trifida

syn. *Corallorrhiza innata*

EARLY CORAL ROOT, NORTHERN CORAL ROOT

↔ ¾–1¼ in (18–30 mm)　↑ 5–8 in (12–20 cm)　✕ ☀/◐ ◇ ❄ ▢

Found in temperate forests in the Northern Hemisphere in cool humid

Corallorrhiza striata

forests up to 6,560 ft (2,000 m) and above. They are equally found in beech forests as well as in coniferous forests, and are often found growing in dense groups. Leafless plants bear up to 10 flowers; sepals greenish-yellow, lip white with red spots at base. Early to late summer-flowering.

CORYANTHES

There are about 40 epiphytic species in this neotropical genus, found from Mexico in the north to Brazil and Bolivia in the south in warm to hot very humid rainforests from sea level up to 3,940 ft (1,200 m). *Coryanthes* are extraordinary orchids. The clustered bulbs carry 2 large pleated leaves. They live in a peculiar symbiosis with biting ants, providing them with nectar from extrafloral nectaries and a base for their nest with their roots. In exchange, the plants are defended against pests and herbivores and fertilized by the feces of the ants. This allows a very rapid growth rate; the plants reach flowering size in the wild in 2 to 3 years, compared to 5 to 20 years in other orchids. Propagation is enhanced by the massive number of seeds produced—a single seed capsule may contain up to 600,000 seeds. *C. bruchmuelleri* holds the record for the heaviest orchid flower—a single flower weighs up to 3½ oz (100 g). The flowers are the most complex of all orchids and are pollinated by male *Euglossa* bees. On entering the flower, the bee falls into a liquid-filled bucket in the lip and the only escape is by the stigma and the pollinarium. As the bee remembers the unpleasant visit for a while, it does not return to the same flower, and thus self-pollination is prevented. Each species has its own fragrance, attracting different bee species, thus preventing hybridization. CULTIVATION: Grow under warm and humid conditions in semi-shade to shade in a free-draining substrate in hanging baskets or mounted. Repot yearly. The plants mature and age quickly and should be propagated by seed in time. To minimize stress, some inflorescences should be clipped as the process of flowering is very exhausting for the plants. Propagate by division or from seed.

Coryanthes macrantha

↔ 24–30 in (60–75 cm) ↕ 30–40 in (75–100 cm) ♀ ☀ ◆/◇ ✽ ☐/⋔

From Guyana, Peru, Venezuela, and Trinidad. Pseudobulbs clustered, ovoid, 4–5 in (10–12 cm) long, 2-leafed. Leaves to 18 in (45 cm) long. Pendent inflorescences, 5–7 in (12–18 cm) long, arise from base of pseudobulbs, with 1 to 3 flowers in summer. Large flowers, variable in color, buff yellow to orange or red, purple-red spotted.

Coryanthes speciosa

↔ 24–30 in (60–75 cm) ↕ 30–40 in (75–100 cm) ♀ ☀ ◆/◇ ✽ ☐/⋔

Found from Guatemala to Peru. Flowers fairly large, lateral sepals and lip to 2 in (5 cm) long; variable in color, most often light bronze densely speckled with maroon, cream lip, flushed with maroon, in summer.

CORYBAS

HELMET ORCHID

This genus consists of about 100 temperate species, found from Southeast Asia to Australia, the Pacific Islands, and New Zealand. Many of the Australian representatives are known as helmet orchids, and are pollinated by fungus gnats. Most of these deciduous, small-flowered, single-leafed species occur in heavily shaded moist areas in mountain forests, often in association with sphagnum moss. Borne mostly in autumn and winter, the solitary flowers are sensitive to minor variations in humidity, and will quickly collapse if the air becomes too dry. CULTIVATION: There are a number of colony-forming *Corybas* species that are relatively easy to cultivate, bring into flower, and multiply, as long as their basic requirements are met. Two of the most important aspects are high humidity and cool temperatures. They are best grown in a well-drained mix containing a high proportion of peat moss (for moisture) and coarse sand (for drainage). They become dormant in summer and revert to small, white, pea-sized tubers; at this time the pots should be allowed to dry out. They are best repotted every year or two, with the dormant tubers repositioned 1¼ in (30 mm) below the soil surface. Some *Corybas* species can be grown in terrariums. Propagation may be achieved through the production of extra tubers during active growth, or from seed.

Corybas barbarae

↔ ¾–1½ in (18–35 mm) ↕ ½–2 in (12–50 mm) ⚍ ☀ ◆/◇ ☐

Found in moist gullies in parts of eastern Australia. Ground-hugging, single, round leaf. Flower hooded, predominantly white, ½ in (12 mm) in size; resembles developing white toadstool.

Corybas diemenicus

PURPLE HELMET, STATELY HELMET, VEINED HELMET ORCHID

↔ 1–1½ in (12–35 mm) ↕ 1–4 in (25–100 mm) ⚍ ☀ ◆/◇ ☐

From forests of eastern Australia; forms extensive colonies in deep shade. Single rounded leaf to 1½ in (35 mm) long with pale undersurface. Solitary flower ½ in (12 mm) in size, dark reddish purple, veined, helmet-like dorsal

sepal, lip purple with white center and toothed edge. Spring-flowering.

Corybas montanus

↔ ¾–1½ in (18–35 mm) ↕ ½–2 in (12–50 mm) ⚍ ☀ ◆/◇ ☐

From Australia, found in moist gullies in mountainous parts of southeastern Queensland. Round ground-hugging, leaf. Single, hooded, deep maroon flower, less than ¾ in (18 mm) in size.

Corybas pruinosus

↔ 1–1¼ in (25–30 mm) ↕ ½–1½ in (12–35 mm) ⚍ ☀ ◆/◇ ☐

From coastal New South Wales, Australia. Flowers with dark red markings. Blooms in winter only a few weeks after the ground-hugging leaf emerges from dormancy.

Corybas diemenicus

Corybas barbarae

Corybas montanus

Corybas pruinosus

Cycnoches barthiorum

CRYPTOPUS

This is a small genus of 3 species of monopodial epiphytic orchids from Madagascar and the Mascarene Islands. They produce long slender stems, with leathery leaves that are produced in 2 ranks along their length. Roots are produced off nodes opposite the leaves and may travel some distance from the plant for both support and for increasing the overall surface area of the root system for it to collect moisture from the fogs in the natural habitat as well as from rain. All species have white blooms that are reminiscent of some of the *Angraecum* species, to which they are related.

CULTIVATION: Essentially, these twig epiphytes are best grown on generous slender slabs of cork or hard tree fern, allowing ample room for the developing roots system, which will branch on healthy specimens. They should be kept warm in a moist environment, as they will suffer in low humidity and quickly decline if temperatures drop below 54°F (12°C). These plants need constant watering year-round, as they do not have a dormant period. Propagation is by seed germinated in specialist laboratories or from cuttings of healthy mature specimens that have at least 4 active roots.

Cryptopus elatus

↔ 6–12 in (15–30 cm) ↑ 20–40 in (50–100 cm) ♀/⋀ ☀ ◆ ☐/⧉

From the Mascarene Islands; most common species in cultivation. Erect leafy stems, 20–40 in (50–100 cm) long. Leaves 1–3 in (2.5–8 cm) long. Erect or spreading inflorescences, to 24 in (60 cm) long, in summer. Flowers to 2 in (5 cm) across, white to greenish yellow, marked orange or red on lip; petals 4-lobed, lip 3-lobed.

CUITLAUZINA

syn. *Lichterfeldia*

A monotypic genus that was formerly included in *Odontoglossum*. It grows as an epiphyte in bright light in oak forest on the Pacific coast of Mexico from Najarit to Oaxaca, at altitudes of 4,600–7,550 ft (1,400–2,300 m). The pseudobulbs are packed very closely, forming dense clumps. *Cuitlauzina* was separated from *Odontoglossum* due to the very different habitat, hard pseudobulbs, and the pendulous inflorescence that appears with the new shoot.

CULTIVATION: Grow under cool conditions, with temperatures between 46°F (8°C) and 68°F (20°C) and a temperature drop at night. Bright light is necessary, even full sun when temperatures can be kept low. During the growing season, keep humidity high, but let the roots dry off between waterings. These plants are sensitive to root rotting, so are best cultivated on a cork slab. Keep rather dry in winter and spring until the flowers open in mid-summer. Start watering after the flowers are gone. This means no water (but high humidity) for almost 6 months! Propagation is by division.

Cuitlauzina pendula

syns *Odontoglossum citrosmum*, *O. pendulum*

↔ 8–14 in (20–35 cm) ↑ 6–12 in (15–30 cm) ♀ ☀/☀ ◇ ⧉

Mexican species. Pseudobulbs oval, 2½ in (6 cm) high, becoming wrinkled with age; 2 grayish green, lance-shaped, leathery leaves. Pendent inflorescences up to 12 in (30 cm) long, with up to 15 flowers from late spring to mid-summer. White flowers with yellow center, to 2 in (5 cm) wide, sweetly scented. 'Shin Soon', white flowers, tinged with lavender-pink.

CYCNOCHES

SWAN ORCHID

This genus contains about 12 species of epiphytic or lithophytic orchids from Central and South America with long pseudobulbs and thin-textured pleated leaves. The inflorescences are erect, arching, or pendent, with few to many flowers. The flowers are often large and showy and are unisexual, with the male and female flowers differing in appearance. Male flowers tend to be produced at lower light levels and so are more common in cultivation; they have reflexed sepals and petals and a long arched column, which gives rise to the common name.

CULTIVATION: Plants can be potted, but tend to be more successful in baskets, which should be hung up in a well-ventilated humid position that is bright but not in full sun. When the plants are resting, they should be kept dry and given as much light as possible. Propagate by division.

Cycnoches barthiorum

↔ 14–20 in (35–50 cm) ↑ 14–20 in (35–50 cm) ♀ ☀ ◆ ❉ ⧉

Colombian species. Pseudobulbs to 7 in (18 cm) tall; several leaves each to 8 in (20 cm) long, almost 2 in (5 cm) wide. Inflorescence pendent, to 7 in (18 cm) long, densely arranged with up to 15 flowers in winter. Male flowers about 2 in (5 cm) across, pale olive-green, flushed and spotted with maroon; lip white with purple spots, with 4 pairs of lobes. Female flowers not known.

Cycnoches ventricosum

↔ 12–27 in (30–70 cm) ↑ 12–26 in (30–65 cm) ♀ ☀ ◆ ❉ ⧉

From Central America. Pseudobulbs to 12 in (30 cm) long, cylindrical but slightly compressed, with several leaves, each to 14 in (35 cm) long. Inflorescences arising from upper leaf axils, 6–12 in (15–30 cm) long, with several flowers in summer–autumn. Male flowers 4–5 in (10–12 cm) in diameter, scented, green, the lip white with a black callus; female flowers rather similar but slightly smaller.

CYMBIDIELLA

syn. *Caloglossum*

This genus contains 3 species from Madagascar. They grow as epiphytes and terrestrially in hot humid forests. They are very specialized in their habits, *Cymbidiella pardalina* grows only on staghorn fern (*Platycerium madagascariensis*), which itself grows only on the tree *Albizia fastigiata*; *C. falcifera* is an epiphyte on the palm *Raphia ruffia*; and *C. flabellata* grows terrestrially in sphagnum moss. The epiphytic species have slender pseudobulbs, topped by long, narrow, grass-like leaves. The terrestrial species has thin pseudobulbs spaced widely apart on a creeping rhizome. The upright inflorescence can reach up to 36 in (90 cm) in length.

CULTIVATION: The epiphytic species should be grown in baskets with the natural host; *C. flabellata* can be grown like *Phaius*. Keep constantly under hot conditions with copious water, but watch for clogging. The leaves must not be exposed to full sun, as this will burn them. Propagation is by division.

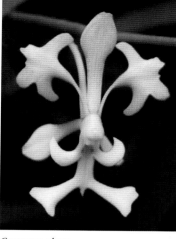

Cryptopus elatus

Cymbidiella flabellata

↔ 12–32 in (30–80 cm) ↑ 12–27 in (30–70 cm) ✹ ☀/☀ ◆/◇ ❉ ⧉/⧉

Endemic to Madagascar. Pseudobulbs widely spaced; long linear leaves. Up to 12 blooms, 2½ in (6 cm) in size, yellow-green with red pepper spotting on base of petals, distinctive and very dark maroon-black lip. Flowers borne in spring–summer.

Cymbidiella pardalina

syns *Cymbidiella rhodocheila*, *Grammangis pardalina*

↔ 16–60 in (40–150 cm) ↑ 16–40 in (40–100 cm) ♀ ☀ ◆ ❉ ⧉

From Madagascar, found growing in mountainous forests at altitudes of 1,970–2,620 ft (600–800 m). Resembles *Cymbidium*; long upright inflorescence bears up to 20 flowers in late spring. Flowers 3–4 in (8–10 cm) wide; greenish sepals and petals, the latter with fine black spots. Mid-lobe of lip deep red and crinkled, side lobes same color as sepals.

Cuitlauzina pendula 'Shin Soon'

Cymbidiella flabellata

Cymbidiella pardalina

C

Cymbidium canaliculatum

Cymbidium canaliculatum var. *sparkesii*

CYMBIDIUM

This genus has 50 or so species, which are distributed throughout southern and eastern Asia and into Australia. Most of the sympodial species from the mountains are terrestrial, with upright to arching flower spikes, bearing blooms in many colors. They produce a fleshy pseudobulb with many long, durable, strap-like leaves. In the lowlands, most cymbidiums grow epiphytically, in high light. Many species have long pendent inflorescences and thick leathery leaves. Over the past century tens of thousands of hybrids have been created, which are often loosely categorized by their flower size: miniature, under 2½ in (6 cm); intermediate, 2½–3½ in (6–9 cm); and standard, over 3½ in (9 cm). These hybrids form the basis of an important pot-plant and cut-flower industry in temperate climates. Traditionally, the main flowering season has been winter to spring, but selective breeding is continually extending this. These orchids have been cultivated for centuries in China and Japan, where they are also valued for spiritual and medicinal purposes. Variegated-leafed and unusual flower forms are also highly prized.

CULTIVATION: Most hybrid species are grown in commercially available "orchid composts," which are usually free-draining but retain some moisture. *Cymbidium* species are remarkably hardy. Epiphytic species prefer a mix incorporating a high percentage of coarse bark. They should be kept moist year-round, increasing watering and fertilizing from spring to autumn while they are actively growing. Most cool-growing species and complex hybrids need a night-time drop in temperature of at least 18°F (10°C) during summer evenings, to help initiate flowering for the following season. This can be manipulated by giving the plants a regular light misting of water at sunset during the warmer months. Propagation is by division.

Cymbidium bicolor
↔ 18–24 in (45–60 cm) ↕ 16–26 in (40–65 cm) ♀ ☼/☀ ◆ ❄ ⊟

Widespread in tropical Asia, from the Philippines west through to India and Sri Lanka, often in seasonally dry forests. There are 3 subspecies. Several stiff, strap-like, succulent leaves per pseudobulb; makes large clusters. Arching to pendulous inflorescences produce several to many flowers in spring–summer. Flowers to just under 2 in (5 cm) in size, maroon with whitish edging. Lip cream with maroon markings. Lightly scented.

Cymbidium canaliculatum
↔ 18–24 in (45–60 cm) ↕ 16–26 in (40–65 cm) ♀ ☼ ◆/◆/◇ ❄ ⊟

From Australia, found from tropical Queensland south to northern New South Wales; very drought tolerant. Several very stiff leathery leaves on either side of elongate pseudobulbs. Arching to descending spikes crowded with 20 to 50 small blooms in spring. Flowers greenish or yellowish with dark red spotting to nearly solid dark maroon. *C. c.* **var.** *sparkesii*, very dark maroon, nearly black flowers.

Cymbidium erythrostylum ★
↔ 8–24 in (20–60 cm) ↕ 12–27 in (30–70 cm) ♀ ☼/☀ ◇ ❄ ⊟

Species from Vietnam. Ovoid pseudobulbs. Erect inflorescences carry up to 10 blooms in autumn. Flowers white, 2½ in (6 cm) in size; yellow and white lip netted with thick red-orange veins. Petals usually do not open fully, and tend to embrace the column and lip.

Cymbidium insigne
↔ 24–36 in (60–90 cm) ↕ 27–32 in (70–80 cm) ♥ ☼ ◇ ❄ ⊟

Beautiful species from northern Thailand, Vietnam, and Hainan Island, China; used heavily in hybridization. Round pseudobulbs; very long narrow leaves. Very tall and erect spike with several to many flowers clustered near apex in autumn–winter. Flowers are 2½–4 in (6–10 cm) wide, white,

Cymbidium lancifolium

Cymbidium erythrostylum

Cymbidium lowianum

variable lip coloration. Well-known
clone, '**Mrs. Carl Holmes**' is now
thought to be a hybrid of *C. insigne*.

Cymbidium lancifolium
syns *Cymbidium aspidistrifolium,*
C. bambusifolium

↔ 4–18 in (10–45 cm)   ↑ 4–20 in (10–50 cm)

Extremely variable species due to its
distribution throughout much of tropical Asia; usually grows in deep shade.
Upright spindle-shaped pseudobulbs;
dark green leaves, narrowly to broadly
oval, distinct leaf stalk. Each stem
carries 2 to several flowers, 1½–2 in
(3.5–8 cm) across, white to green
sepals and petals, often with a red line
down mid-vein. Lip white with red
spotting. Blooms spring–summer.

Cymbidium lowianum

↔ 8–36 in (20–90 cm)   ↑ 12–48 in
(30–120 cm)

Hardy species, found from Thailand
to China. Up to 30 very long arching
spikes, bearing olive green flowers,
3 in (8 cm) long, with contrasting
cream and red lip, in spring. *C. l.*
var. *concolor*, bright green sepals
and petals, yellow and gold lip.

Cymbidium lowianum var. *concolor*

Cymbidium suave

Cymbidium parishii

↔ 12–16 in (30–40 cm) ↑ 12–16 in (30–40 cm) ♀/♥ ☼ ♦/◇ ❋ ⊟

From Myanmar. Pseudobulbs about 5 in (12 cm) long, spindle-shaped. Leaves arranged in 2 rows, to 20 in (50 cm) long. Upright inflorescence, about 10 in (25 cm) long, with 2 to 3 flowers in summer. Flowers scented, not opening wide, around 3 in (8 cm) across, white, lip with yellow marks on mid-lobe and purple streaks on side lobes.

Cymbidium sanderae

syn. *Cymbidium parishii* var. *sanderae*

↔ 20–27 in (50–70 cm) ↑ 20–30 in (50–75 cm) ♀ ☼ ◇ ❋ ⊟

Beautiful species, endemic to Vietnam, found in montane forest; used extensively in hybridization. Pseudobulbs 3–4 in (8–10 cm) tall; several, narrow, arching leaves. Arching spike, about 20–24 in (50–60 cm) long, with 3 to 15 flowers in spring. Flowers

pinkish-white, to 3 in (8 cm) wide, maroon spotting on lip with two yellow calli. Often confused with *C. parishii* because flowers are quite similar, but growth habit differs greatly.

Cymbidium sinense

syn. *Cymbidium hoosai*

↔ 20–24 in (50–60 cm) ↑ 20–30 in (50–75 cm) ♀/♥ ☽/☀ ♦/◇ ❋ ⊟

From open to dense montane forests in India, Thailand, Myanmar, southern China, and Taiwan. Round pseudobulbs; upright stiff leaves, shiny, dark green. Upright spike bears several flowers, 1½–2 in (35–50 mm) wide, usually dark maroon, cream lip spotted red, in spring. Cultivated in Asia for centuries, for fragrance and plant forms. 'Red Star', flowers deep pinkish red, cream lip spotted with deep red.

Cymbidium suave

↔ 8–32 in (20–80 cm) ↑ 12–48 in (30–120 cm) ♀ ☽/☀ ♦/◇ ❋ ⊟

Australian species. Grass-like leaves; thickened stem. Pendent sprays of up to 50 apple green to pale yellow-brown flowers, 1 in (25 mm) long, fragrant. Late spring- to summer-flowering, tolerant of a wide temperature range but not of frost.

Cymbidium tracyanum

↔ 8–36 in (20–90 cm) ↑ 12–48 in (30–120 cm) ♀ ☽/☀ ◇ ✼ ❋ ⊟

Large species, found from Thailand to China. Flowers strongly fragrant, 6 in

(15 cm) long, light green, heavily marked, and striped with red-brown, giving blooms an overall deep bronze appearance. Autumn-flowering.

Cymbidium Hybrids

↔ 8–36 in (20–90 cm) ↑ 12–48 in (30–120 cm) ♥ ☽/☀ ♦/◇ ❋ ⊟

Thousands of *Cymbidium* hybrids have been registered, varying widely in shape and color. Many have been mericloned or tissue cultured to increase numbers to satisfy demand. **African Adventure 'Sahara Gold'**, sunset tones, some new colors are being developed; **Anita 'Pymble'**, green flowers on tall arching spikes; **Astronaut 'Raja'**, buttery yellow flowers flushed with red, lip spotted with deep maroon; **Bulbarrow 'Friar Tuck'** ★, intermediate-style, distinctive color combination from *C. devonianum*; **Castle of Mey 'Pinkie'**, miniature, with up to 25 pinkish white cascading blooms on each stem; **Dilly 'Del Mar'**, yellow flowers, late-blooming; **Fanfare 'Spring'**, flowers vary from yellow green to deep apple green; **Ice Ranch**, dusky pink and cream flowers, yellow and maroon lip; **John Woden**, large salmon pink blooms, deep maroon spotted lip, on tall spikes; **Lady McAlpine 'Jersey'**, white flowers, lip white, maroon, and lemon; **Little Bighorn 'Prairie'** ★, intermediate hybrid, many upright inflorescences of mainly green blooms with white lips with maroon spots; **Mavourneen 'Jester'** ★, unusual standard hybrid with lip colors transposed onto petals; **Mini Verd 'Captain Cook'**, dense, bright yellow and green flowers, maroon and yellow lip; **Orchid Conference 'Green Light'**, bronze flowers, red lip; **Pontac 'Trinity'**, purplish red flowers; **Sumatra 'Astrid'**, sprays of dark pink flowers, yellow lip with purple markings; **Sunshine Falls 'Green Fantasy'**, miniature-flowered, highly fragrant and floriferous, from *C. madidum* heritage; **Sylvia Miller 'Gold Cup'**, miniature, golden flowers, rosy tones on lip; **Tinsel 'Harriet'**, pink flowers on slender spike; **Valley Legend 'Gee Wizz'**, chartreuse flowers, lip yellow and deep red.

Cymbidium madidum

Cymbidium madidum

syn. *Cymbidium leroyi*

↔ 24–36 in (60–90 cm) ↑ 20–32 in (50–80 cm) ♀ ☼ ♦ ❋ ⊟

From New South Wales and Queensland in eastern Australia; can form huge masses in the wild. Large pseudobulbs; strap-shaped leaves. Long pendulous infloresences with many ¾–1 in (18–25 mm) yellowish-green flowers, in spring. Yellow and brownish-red lip. Used in hybridization to impart a pendent spike and higher flower count.

Cymbidium tracyanum

Cymbidium hybrid

Cymbidium Alexfrida 'The Queen' (hybrid)

Cymbidium Alegria 'Saint Lita' (hybrid)

Cymbidium African Adventure 'Sahara Gold' (hybrid)

Cymbidium Aunty MacKovich (hybrid)

Cymbidium Australian Midnight (hybrid)

Cymbidium Astronaut 'Raja' (hybrid)

Cymbidium (Atalanta × Gottianum) (hybrid)

Cymbidium Baldoyle 'Melbury' (hybrid)

Cymbidium Anita 'Pymble' (hybrid)

C

Cymbidium Blazing Fury 'Fatboy' (hybrid)

Cymbidium Belle Park 'Orange Gleam'
(hybrid)

Cymbidium Bisou Bisou 'Geyserland'
(hybrid)

Cymbidium Cape Crystal (hybrid)

Cymbidium Black Forest 'Just Desserts'
(hybrid)

Cymbidium Bolton Grange (hybrid)

Cymbidium Castle of Mey 'Pinkie' (hybrid)

Cymbidium Champagne Robin (hybrid)

Cymbidium Bulbarrow 'Friar Tuck' (hybrid)

Cymbidium Dilly 'Del Mar' (hybrid)

Cymbidium Dolly 'Featherhill' (hybrid)

Cymbidium Clauboda 'Sydney Rothwell'
(hybrid)

Cymbidium Colina 'Ember' (hybrid)

Cymbidium Cranbourne 'Chase' (hybrid)

Cymbidium Desirée 'Elizabeth A. Logan'
(hybrid)

Cymbidium (Disney Girl × Robin) (hybrid)

Cymbidium (Dolly × Kimberley Szabo) 'Royale' (hybrid)

C

Cymbidium (Dream Temple × Pure Ice) (hybrid)

Cymbidium Esmeralda (hybrid)

Cymbidium Fair Delight 'Highfields' (hybrid)

Cymbidium Finetta 'Glendessary' (hybrid)

Cymbidium (Eastern Star × Sleeping Nymph) (hybrid)

Cymbidium Emerald Glory 'Valerie' (hybrid)

Cymbidium Electric Ladyland 'Peats Ridge' (hybrid)

Cymbidium Fanfare 'Spring' (hybrid)

Cymbidium Fare Wand 'Numan' (hybrid)

Cymbidium Highland Advent (hybrid)

Cymbidium Ice Ranch (hybrid)

Cymbidium Gibson Girl 'Mephisto Waltz' (hybrid)

Cymbidium (Globetrotter × Minniken)
(hybrid)

Cymbidium Highland Lassie 'Jersey' (hybrid)

Cymbidium Gripper 'Royale' (hybrid)

Cymbidium Highland Glen 'Cooksbridge'
(hybrid)

Cymbidium 'James Tee Kirk 81' (hybrid)

C

Cymbidium Jeanette 'Enid Haupt' (hybrid)

Cymbidium (Katy Shaw × Southborough) (hybrid)

Cymbidium Joker 'Foul Play' (hybrid)

Cymbidium John Woden (hybrid)

Cymbidium Paul Robeson (hybrid)

Cymbidium Joker 'Irish Mist' (hybrid)

Cymbidium Kabuki Moon 'Alice' (hybrid)

Cymbidium James Toya 'Royale' (hybrid)

Cymbidium Kiku Ono (hybrid)

Cymbidium Levis Duke 'Bella Vista' (hybrid)

Cymbidium Kiri te Kanawa (hybrid)

Cymbidium Lady McAlpine 'Jersey' (hybrid)

Cymbidium (Khyber Pass × Dolly) (hybrid)

Cymbidium Little Bighorn 'Prairie' (hybrid)   *Cymbidium* Lancashire Rose 'Maureen' (hybrid)

Cymbidium Little Bighorn 'Calga' (hybrid)

Cymbidium (Lustrous Damsell × Alvin Bryant) (hybrid)

Cymbidium Mary Smith 'Lucy' (hybrid)

Cymbidium Lynette Artemis (hybrid)

Cymbidium Marie Bashir (hybrid)

Cymbidium Marilyn Sharp 'Curvaceous' (hybrid)

Cymbidium (Melinga × Pharaoh's Gold) × Dural (hybrid)

Cymbidium (Mighty Mouse × Beach Girl) 'Carly' (hybrid)

Cymbidium Mavourneen 'Jester' (hybrid)

Cymbidium Mighty Margaret (hybrid)

Cymbidium Orange Crush (hybrid)

Cymbidium Orchid Conference 'Green Light' (hybrid)

Cymbidium Mighty Tracey 'Royale' (hybrid)

Cymbidium Mini Goddess 'Apricot' (hybrid)

Cymbidium (Paul Robeson × Mighty Mouse) 'It's Nice' (hybrid)

Cymbidium Mini Verd 'Captain Cook' (hybrid)

Cymbidium Iris Cooper 'Drama Queen' (hybrid)

Cymbidium Pontac 'Trinity' (hybrid)

Cymbidium Pywacket 'Royale' (hybrid)

Cymbidium 'Royale Jester' (unusual sport) (hybrid)

Cymbidium Rumours 'Desiree' (hybrid)

Cymbidium (Red Beauty × Cronulla)
(hybrid)

Cymbidium Red Idol 'Royale' (hybrid)

Cymbidium Rievaulx (hybrid)

Cymbidium San Francisco (hybrid)

Cymbidium Sleeping Nymph 'Glacier'
(hybrid)

Cymbidium (So Bold × Rajah's Ruby)
(hybrid)

Cymbidium Spotted Leopard 'Showtime' (hybrid)

Cymbidium Saint Aubins Bay (hybrid)

Cymbidium Sleeping Nymph 'Perfection' (hybrid)

Cymbidium Spanish Lullaby 'Douce Josephine' (hybrid)

Cymbidium Sunshine Falls 'Green Fantasy' (hybrid)

Cymbidium Surman's Rose 'Gosford Gold' (hybrid)

Cymbidium Sylvia Miller 'Gold Cup' (hybrid)

Cymbidium Valley Legend 'Gee Wizz' (hybrid)

Cymbidium Wallacia 'Burnt Gold' (hybrid)

Cymbidium Sumatra 'Astrid' (hybrid)

Cymbidium Tinsel 'Harriet' (hybrid)

Cymbidium Tea Time 'Afternoon Delight' (hybrid)

Cymbidium Wesley Davidson 'Geyserland' (hybrid)

Cymbidium Wesley Davidson 'Netty' (hybrid)

Cymbidium (Wallara × Huckleberry Mountain) 'Royal Jewels' (hybrid)

Cymbidium Yowie Rose 'Cabernet' (hybrid)

CYPRIPEDIUM

LADY'S SLIPPER

This deciduous genus consists of about 50 sympodial species found in North and Central America, Europe, and Asia. These plants are characterized by a short rhizome, with up to 4 basal leaves, which are often pleated. The slender inflorescences carry up to 12 showy flowers, which appear from late spring and into summer, come in a range of colors, and feature an impressive, often contrasting, slipper-like lip. One of the rarest of terrestrial genera, they are protected, and should not be removed from the wild under any circumstances.

CULTIVATION: In cool to temperate climates, these plants can be grown in pots or in the garden, in soils rich in decayed leaf matter. They will not grow in subtropical or tropical climates. Propagate by division.

Cypripedium acaule

MOCCASIN FLOWER, PINK LADY'S SLIPPER

↔ 6–8 in (15–20 cm) ↕ 8–18 in (20–45 cm)
✹ ☀ ◇ ❄ ❀ ⛉

From eastern USA and Canada. Leaves 2, elliptic, pleated, 4–12 in (10–30 cm) long. Inflorescence erect, to 16 in (40 cm) tall, singly flowered (rarely with two). Flowers nodding, 2½ in (6 cm) across, sepals and petals yellow-green to maroon, lip pink, rarely white. Flowers spring–summer.

Cypripedium calceolus

LADY'S SLIPPER ORCHID

↔ 10–12 in (25–30 cm) ↕ 8–24 in
(20–60 cm) ✹ ☀ ◇ ❄ ❀ ⛉

From northern and central Europe and Asia as far east as central China. Leaves 3 to 4, spread up stem, pleated, broadly elliptic, to 7 in (18 cm) long. Inflorescence usually single-flowered, sometimes with 2 or 3 flowers, from late spring to mid-summer. Flowers showy, sepals and petals maroon-brown, about 2 in (5 cm) long, the petals twisted; lip bright yellow.

Cypripedium californicum

↔ 4–6 in (10–15 cm) ↕ 20–48 cm
(50–120 cm) ✹ ☀ ◇ ❄ ❀ ⛉

Clump-forming species from Oregon and California, USA. Leaves 5 to 10, 2–6 in (5–15 cm) long. Raceme laxly arranged with 4 to 12 flowers, which all open at once. Small flowers, 1½ in (35 mm) across, scented, nodding; sepals and petals pale yellow-green, lip white, yellow at base, with brownish marks inside. Blooms from mid-spring to mid-summer.

Cypripedium formosanum

↔ 4–12 in (10–30 cm) ↕ 4–10 in (10–25 cm)
✹ ☀ ◇ ❀ ⛉

Mountain-dwelling species from Taiwan. Pair of attractive, fan-like, wavy leaves. Single pale pink flower, to 3 in (8 cm) wide, with darker

Cypripedium acaule

markings and large inflated lip. Dislikes warm temperatures; easy to grow in cool climates.

Cypripedium montanum

MOUNTAIN LADY'S-SLIPPER

↔ 6–8 in (15–20 cm) ↕ 8–16 in (20–40 cm)
✹ ✺/☀ ◇/◇ ❄ ❀ ⛉

From forested mountains of western Canada and USA, where it grows on well-drained slopes. Leafy stem, leaves oval, pointed, pleated, to 4 in (10 cm) long. Terminal inflorescence, to 6 in long, usually with 2 flowers, can bear 1 to 4 flowers, in early summer. Blooms slightly fragrant, sepals and petals maroon, white lip marked maroon within.

Cypripedium parviflorum

syn. *Cypripedium calceolus* var. *parviflorum*

YELLOW LADY'S-SLIPPER

↔ 4–10 in (10–25 cm) ↕ 6–20 in (15–50 cm)
✹ ✺/☀ ◇ ❄ ❀ ⛉

From forests and marshes of eastern North America to the eastern Rocky Mountains. Leafy stem, leaves 3 to 4, oval, pointed, to 6 in (15 cm) long. Highly variable flowers, 1 or 2, sweetly fragrant, lip yellow, red spotting within, petals and sepals spirally twisted to flat, yellow green to maroon, on 6 in (15 cm) long terminal inflorescence, in spring. *C. p.* var. *pubescens* (syn. *C. pubescens*), large flowers, to 4 in (10 cm) long, prefers a drier habitat.

Cypripedium reginae

QUEEN'S LADY'S-SLIPPER, SHOWY LADY'S-SLIPPER

↔ 8–12 in (20–30 cm) ↕ 16–32 in
(40–80 cm) ✹ ✺/☀ ◇ ❄ ❀ ⛉

From calcareous wetlands of eastern North America, often in large colonies. Leafy stem, hairy; 5 to 8 leaves, hairy, oval, pointed, to 10 in (25 cm) long. Flowers 1 or 2, rarely to 4, white, with rose pink to carmine red, rarely white, lip, in summer. Sensitized persons may develop a rash after handling plant.

CYRTOCHILUM

This large genus of some 150 species of medium- to large-sized epiphytic or lithophytic orchids comes from tropical Central and South America. They have large pseudobulbs, which are leafy at the apex. The long, erect or arching inflorescences arise from the base of the pseudobulb and may be simple or branched, and rather loosely arranged with many flowers. The sepals and petals are spreading, with the petals usually being slightly smaller; the lip is fleshy, smaller than the sepals and petals, entire or 3-lobed, with a basal ridged callus.

Cypripedium formosanum

Cypripedium parviflorum

The name is derived from Greek, *kyrtos* meaning curved and *chilus* lip.
CULTIVATION: Grow in pots of standard epiphyte compost and water plants throughout the year, though less after growth is complete. The long inflorescences need to be staked or trained. Propagate by division.

Cyrtochilum falcipetalum
syn. *Oncidium falcipetalum*
↔ 32–48 in (80–120 cm) ↑ 10–20 ft (3–6 m)
♀/⋀ ☀ ◇ ❉ ▽

Large plants from Colombia, Ecuador, Peru, and Venezuela; scrambling habit. Pseudobulbs to 6 in (15 cm) long, 1- to 2-leafed, set 8–10 in (20–25 cm) apart on rhizome. Leaves to 24 in (60 cm) long. Inflorescence branched, to 20 ft (6 m) long. Flowers 2–3 in (5–8 cm) across, sepals dark brown with yellow apex, petals yellow and brown, lip greenish-brown.

Cyrtochilum microxiphium
syn. *Oncidium microxiphium*
↔ 8–24 in (20–60 cm) ↑ 12–60 in (30–150 cm) ♀ ☀/☀ ◆/◇ ❉ ▽

From Peru and Ecuador, often grows among grasses and mosses in high rainfall areas, also grows around the ruins of Machu Picchu. Numerous blooms carried on very long inflorescences at intervals along the rachis, throughout the year. Flowers 2½ in (6 cm) in size; brown sepals, white and purple petals.

Cyrtochilum species

Cyrtochilum microxiphium

C

CYRTOPODIUM
syn. *Tylochilus*
CIGAR ORCHID

This genus contains some 30 species of medium- to large-sized orchids. They are found from southern Florida, USA, through Central America to Argentina and Paraguay in the south, with a concentration of species on southeastern Brazil. They grow as epiphytes, lithophytes, or terrestrials in dry shrub or forest. The long cigar-shaped pseudobulbs carry alternating, thin, deciduous leaves and reach 3 ft (0.9 m) or more in some species. The long branching inflorescence carries numerous long-lasting flowers that have undulated flower segments.

CULTIVATION: *Cyrtopodium* species make magnificent specimen plants, some too large for the average greenhouse.The terrestrial species are cultivated similar to *Eulophia*, in a mineral substrate. Epiphytic species are similar to deciduous *Catasetum* and do better if grown mounted, to accommodate their nest-like root system. All species need a very distinct cool and dry resting period when not in growth. Propagation is by division.

Cyrtopodium holstii
↔ 20–40 in (50–100 cm) ↕ 32–40 in (80–100 cm) ✿ ◆ ▽

Found in coastal regions of northern Brazil in the state of Bahia, where it grows in hot arid regions. Clustered pseudobulbs grow from a sympodial rhizome. Inflorescence carries many small flowers, each about 1 in (25 mm) wide, in summer. Yellow sepals with lots of reddish markings, petals and lip are clearer yellow.

Cyrtopodium punctatum
syns *Cyrtopodium gigas, C. tigrinum, Epidendrum punctatum*

BEE SWARM ORCHID, CIGAR ORCHID

↔ 3–4 ft (0.9–1.2 m) ↕ 3–5 ft (0.9–1.5 m) ✿ ◆ ▽

Found from Florida, USA, to French Guiana, growing in arid shrub at elevations of 330–3,940 ft (100–1,200 m). Pseudobulbs to 3 ft (0.9 m) high, from a sympodial rhizome, covered in clump of white roots. Leaves, in 2 rows, add another 2 ft (0.6 m) to size of plant. Basal inflorescence, to 5 ft (1.5 m) high, with a mass of 2 in (5 cm) wide, large, greenish yellow flowers with brownish spots, in spring–summer.

Cyrtorchis arcuata

CYRTORCHIS
A genus of 16 species, which are found only in Africa. They are found as epiphytes, and sometimes as lithophytes, in woodlands and riverine forests, at elevations of 1,970–8,200 ft (600–2,500 m). The monopodial stems are leafless in their lower parts and pendulous with age, which is quite characteristic for the genus. They are easily recognized by their star-shaped, creamy white to greenish flowers, which have a long spur and a pleasant smell during the night. When wilting, they turn to dark yellow or yellowish brown. The species were formerly treated as *Angraecum* or *Mystacidium*, from which they are readily distinguishable.

CULTIVATION: Despite the subtropical provenance of most species, they thrive best in a warm house with bright light and high humidity. The robust roots need a lot of fresh air; a slab or basket is better suited than a pot. Propagate by division, but do not disturb the plant too frequently.

Cyrtorchis arcuata
syns *Angraecum sedeni, Cyrtorchis sedeni, C. whitei*

↔ 16–20 in (40–50 cm) ↕ 12–20 in (30–50 cm) ✿ ◆/◇ ▨

Widespread in southern Africa. Long stem, covered in brown sheaths of dead leaves and 6 to 12, fleshy, robust, bilobed leaves. Very prominent, robust, white roots. Arching inflorescence, to 8 in (20 cm) long, carries 10 to 14 waxy star-shaped flowers, in summer.

CYRTOSTYLIS
GNAT ORCHID

This genus of diminutive, deciduous, terrestrial orchids consists of 6 species, with 4 species found in southern Australia and 2 species endemic to New Zealand. Closely related to *Acianthus*, this group of gnat orchids produces a

Cyrtostylis reniformis

single leaf and an upright inflorescence of botanical insect-like blooms. The species form extensive colonies, growing in moist humus-rich sites among ferns, shrubs, and grasses. They reproduce by seed and by vegetative proliferation via the formation of new tubers at the end of long slender roots.

CULTIVATION: Specialist growers of deciduous terrestrial orchids have had success in cultivating these unusual plants by growing them in a well-drained potting medium with the addition of humus, peat moss, and coarse sand. Under good culture, the plants multiply annually and are best repotted into fresh medium in summer while the plants have reverted to dormant tubers. Unfortunately blooming has proved to be unreliable in many instances, however, experiments with "smokewater" have been encouraging.

Cyrtostylis reniformis
syn. *Acianthus reniformis*

↔ ¾–2 in (18–50 mm) ↕ 1¼–5 in (3–12 cm) ✿/✿ ◆/◇ ▽

Species from southeastern Australia, with many plants in the wild not blooming. Optimum blooming is achieved the year after a bushfire, when almost all plants flower. Leaves kidney-shaped. Up to 5 greenish yellow to reddish brown blooms, ½ in (12 mm) in size, with narrow segments, in winter–spring.

Cyrtopodium punctatum

DACTYLORHIZA

MARSH ORCHID

This deciduous terrestrial genus consists of about 35 sympodial species native to Europe, the Mediterranean region, northern and western Asia, and North America. They are orchids of the grasslands, frequently found growing in moist situations in bogs and drainage patterns. Most of the variable species have green leaves that are heavily spotted with maroon, and long 2-pronged tubers from which the plant grows. The genus name comes from *dactylos,* the Greek word for finger, referring to these finger-like tubers. Flower color is mostly confined to a range of pink tones, with finer and darker spotting.
CULTIVATION: In cool to temperate climates these herbaceous perennials can be grown in pots or in the garden in soils that are rich in decayed leaf matter. Although the members of this genus are quite frost hardy, they do appreciate protection from the most severe frosts. Constant moisture is required throughout the warmer months, but the plants must be kept drier in winter. They will not grow in subtropical or tropical climates. Propagation is by division.

Dactylorhiza elata
syn. *Orchis elata*
ROBUST MARSH ORCHID
↔ 6 in (15 cm) ↑ 24 in (60 cm)

European native. Plain, unspotted, green leaves. Spikes crowded with large deep violet flowers in summer.

Dactylorhiza foliosa
MADEIRAN ORCHID
↔ 4–10 in (10–25 cm) ↑ 12–27 in (30–70 cm)

European species, also prolific on the Portuguese island of Madeira; forms large colonies when well cultivated. Unspotted leaves. Densely covered with pink to purple flowers in spring–summer.

Dactylorhiza fuchsii
syn. *Orchis fuchsii*
COMMON SPOTTED ORCHID
↔ 4–10 in (10–25 cm) ↑ 8–24 in (20–60 cm)

European species; likes slightly alkaline limestone soils. Spotted leaves. Flowers pale pink to white. Summer-flowering species, often confused with the closely related *D. maculata.* 'Cruickshank', mauve to purple flowers; 'Rachel', white flowers.

Dactylorhiza foliosa

Dactylorhiza fuchsii

Dactylorhiza fuchsii 'Cruickshank'

Dactylorhiza fuchsii 'Rachel'

D

Dactylorhiza urvilleana

Dactylorhiza incarnata

Dactylorhiza incarnata

syn. *Orchis incarnata*

EARLY MARSH ORCHID

↔ 4–10 in (10–25 cm) ↕ 8–24 in (20–60 cm)

Widespread European species; bears smaller flowers than many in genus. Erect sword-shaped leaves. Spike cylindrical, to 24 in (60 cm) tall, densely arranged with up to 40 flowers in spring–summer. Pale pink to mid-pink flowers, ¾ in (18 mm) tall; lip sometimes 3-lobed.

Dactylorhiza majalis

syn. *Dactylorhiza latifolia*

BROAD-LEAFED MARSH ORCHID

↔ 5–12 in (12–30 cm) ↕ 8–30 in (20–75 cm)

Variable plants from Europe, as far west as western Russia. From 4 to 8 leaves, to 6 in (15 cm) long, usually with maroon spots on uppersurface. Spike ovoid or cylindrical, densely arranged with many flowers, bracts sometimes longer than flowers. Lilac to magenta-purple flowers; lip paler in throat with darker streaks and whorls, 3-lobed, side lobes broader than mid-lobe; spur curving downward. Blooms from late spring to mid-summer.

Dactylorhiza praetermissa

syn. *Dactylorhiza majalis*
subsp. *praetermissa*

SOUTHERN MARSH ORCHID

↔ 8–12 in (20–60 cm) ↕ 8–27 in (20–70 cm)

Species from western Europe. From 4 to 9 leaves, suberect, to 10 in (25 cm) long, may be spotted or unspotted. Spike cylindrical, densely arranged with many flowers in summer. Flowers pinkish purple to red-purple in color; lip spotted, with 3 shallow equal lobes. Spur conical, curving downward.

Dactylorhiza romana

syns *Dactylorhiza sulphurea*,
D. sulphurea subsp. *pseudosambucina*

↔ 8–12 in (20–30 cm) ↕ 6–14 in (15–35 cm)

From southern Europe. Basal rosette of 3 to 7 leaves, unspotted, to 6 in (15 cm) long. Spike shortly cylindrical, densely arranged with many flowers in spring–summer, bracts longer than flowers. Individual flowers yellow, cream, flesh-colored, or violet-red; lip 3-lobed; spur upturned.

Dactylorhiza sambucina

ELDERFLOWER ORCHID

↔ 6–8 in (15–20 cm) ↕ 4–12 in (10–30 cm)

Rather widespread in Europe. From 3 to 7 leaves, sometimes in a basal rosette, unspotted, to 10 in (25 cm) long. Spike cylindrical, with many flowers from spring to mid-summer. Flowers yellow or magenta, rarely bicolored; lip with 3 shallow lobes, marked with dots in horseshoe pattern.

Dactylorhiza urvilleana

↔ 4–10 in (10–25 cm) ↕ 10–32 in
(25–80 cm)

From Europe. Slender plant, with about 4 or 5 stem-clasping leaves produced along inflorescence that bears up to 90 lilac to purple blooms on robust specimens, in spring–summer.

DARWINARA

This multigeneric orchid genus was named for naturalist Charles Darwin, and combines 4 monopodial genera— *Ascocentrum*, *Neofinetia*, *Rhynchostylis*, and *Vanda*. They are erect-growing epiphytes, with strap-like channeled leaves, in 2 ranks. The colorful showy blooms are long lived. Larger plants may branch at the base, and have numerous, very thick, cord-like roots. CULTIVATION: They prefer intermediate to warm conditions and high light levels. Thick roots often venture outside the confines of the pot or basket, and this should be encouraged, as the roots require unimpeded air circulation and must dry out quickly after watering. Propagate by division.

Darwinara Pretty Girl

↔ 8–15 in (20–38 cm) ↕ 8–24 in (20–60 cm)

Cool-growing, miniature, Japanese species *Neofinetia falcata* is one of the parents, making this hybrid adaptable to a range of climatic conditions and temperatures. White to deep purple flowers are borne throughout the warmer months, and year-round in the tropics.

Darwinara Pretty Girl

Degarmoara Winter Wonderland
'White Fairy'

DEGARMOARA

This trigeneric orchid genus is a combination of *Brassia*, *Miltonia*, and *Odontoglossum*. These essentially spidery sympodial hybrids are more tolerant of higher temperatures than most pure odontoglossums, due to the *Brassia* parent. They grow in wideranging conditions and have longlasting often fragrant flowers, making them popular flowering pot plants.
CULTIVATION: These hybrids have a fine root system, and do not like to dry out during warmer months of the year. They require a drier rest in winter when they should only be watered sparingly. Pot the plants in sphagnum moss or a fine bark mix. They are suitable for cool to intermediate conditions, and require abundant humidity throughout the year and to be grown in semi-shade. Propagate by division.

Degarmoara Skywalker 'Red Star'

↔ 8–16 in (20–40 cm) ↕ 8–32 in (20–80 cm)
♀ ☀ ◆/◇ ✳ ▽

Upright inflorescence carries up to 6 starry flowers in spring. Flowers a rich strong color, darker overlay of spotting, contrasting lip.

Degarmoara Starshot 'Fashion'

↔ 8–16 in (20–40 cm) ↕ 8–32 in (20–80 cm)
♀ ☀ ◆/◇ ✳ ▽

Has over 10 different species in its genetic background, with influence of *Brassia verrucosa* prominent. Flowers in spring–early summer.

Degarmoara Winter Wonderland 'White Fairy'

↔ 8–16 in (20–40 cm) ↕ 8–32 in (20–80 cm)
♀ ☀ ◆/◇ ✳ ▽

Popular cultivar; mass propagated for its introduction as a pot plant. Can bloom more than once a year; individual flowers can last about 6 weeks.

Degarmoara Skywalker 'Red Star'

Degarmoara Starshot 'Fashion'

D

Dendrobium aduncum

Dendrobium alexandrae

Dendrobium albosanguineum

Dendrobium amethystoglossum

Dendrobium anosmum

DENDROBIUM

The genus *Dendrobium* has always been popular with orchid growers. It enjoys a wide distribution, from India and Sri Lanka, through Southeast Asia to southern China, New Guinea, Australia, and the Pacific Islands. They are almost exclusively epiphytes or lithophytes, with a sympodial growth habit. There is an amazing diversity of plant habit, flower form, and color in this large genus, which contains around 900 species. Almost all colors and combinations are represented in the flowers. Some species' individual blooms last for only a few hours, while others can persist for up to 9 months in pristine condition.

Many hybrids have been developed; for both orchid enthusiasts and the important cut-flower industry in tropical countries. The majority of flowers marketed as "Singapore orchids" are actually *Dendrobium* hybrids, which last well as cut flowers. *D. nobile* and related species have been used to create the thousands of colorful and long-lasting "softcane" *Dendrobium* hybrids. Over the past couple of decades, there have been many new Australian native *Dendrobium* hybrids. These are very popular and relatively fast growing, incorporating species such as *D. kingianum*, *D. speciosum*, and *D. tetragonum*.

CULTIVATION: Being such a large and varied genus, dendrobiums also have a range of diverse cultural requirements. Quite a number of species and hybrids produce new plants off the older pseudobulbs. These plants are called aerials or "keikis," a Hawaiian word meaning baby. Once these growths have hardened off and produced roots, they can be removed and grown as a new plant. In the dry season, the "softcane" types shed their leaves and are dormant. Once the rains come, the plants burst into flower and produce next season's growth. This deciduous feature is common with many of the *Dendrobium* species, which have evolved to adapt to distinct wet and dry seasons. Most dendrobiums can be grown in a bark-based medium with some types performing well on tree-fern or cork slabs. Some of the smaller-growing species from mountainous regions grow well in sphagnum moss that is kept damp. Propagate by division.

Dendrobium aduncum
↔ 18–24 in (45–60 cm) ↕ 12–24 in (30–60 cm) ♀ ☀ ◆/◈ ❋ ⊔

From Vietnam, southern China, Myanmar, Thailand, Nepal, Bhutan, and eastern India; found growing in open forests that are seasonally dry. Cane-like pseudobulbs; few to several thin deciduous leaves. Small clusters of blooms are borne along bare canes in spring–autumn. Pink to white flowers, 1–1½ in (25–35 mm) wide; pointed cup-like lip. Closely related to *D. hercoglossum*.

Dendrobium aemulum
IRONBARK ORCHID, WHITE FEATHER ORCHID
↔ 8 in (20 cm) ↕ 4–6 in (10–15 cm)
♀ ☀ ◇ ❋ ➴

From rainforests and sclerophyll forests of Queensland and north coast of New South Wales, Australia. Leaves light to mid-green, alternate, oval. Flowers to 1½ in (35 mm) wide, off-white ageing to pink, reddish purple markings on lip, carried on racemes, in late winter–spring.

Dendrobium albosanguineum
↔ 14–16 in (35–40 cm) ↕ 14–16 in (35–40 cm) ♀ ☀ ◈ ❋ ⊔

From montane regions of Myanmar and Thailand; partial to tall tree tops; habitat is under serious threat from deforestation. Cane-like pseudobulbs; 7 to 10 deciduous leaves. Long-lasting flowers, around 2–3 in (5–8 cm) wide, creamy white, large crimson blotch on either side of lip toward base. Spring-blooming.

Dendrobium alexandrae
↔ 8–20 in (20–50 cm) ↕ 8–27 in (20–70 cm)
♀ ☀ ◆/◈ ❋ ⊔

Uncommon species from New Guinea; only recently entered general cultivation. Inflorescences carry up to 8 blooms that can last for a number of weeks. Yellow to green flowers, often purple spotted, with purple-marked lip. Spring-blooming.

Dendrobium atroviolaceum

Dendrobium amethystoglossum

↔ 18–27 in (45–70 cm) ↑ 34–38 in (85–95 cm)

Endemic to northwestern Luzon Island in the Philippines; found in moist montane forests that have dry-winter climates. Tall upright canes; several oval, pointed, deciduous leaves. Plants usually bloom when canes are bare, with 15 to 20 fragrant flowers on downward-arching inflorescences, in spring. Flowers 1–1¼ in (25–30 mm) wide, fragrant, white; lip pink and white.

Dendrobium anosmum

syn. *Dendrobium superbum*

↔ 8–16 in (20–40 cm) ↑ 8–48 in (20–120 cm)

Found from Vietnam and Laos to the Philippines and New Guinea; very popular in cultivation. Pendulous habit; slender pseudobulbs produce pairs of blooms along their length once leaves have shed. Flowers to 4 in (10 cm) in size, vary from dark pink to pure white; strong, pleasant, berry-like fragrance.

Dendrobium antennatum

↔ 4–12 in (10–30 cm) ↑ 8–24 in (20–60 cm)

From northeastern Australia, New Guinea, and the Solomon Islands; grows in warm, humid, tropical, lowland forests; one of the summer-flowering "antelope orchids." Stiff upright inflorescences of up to 12 long-lasting blooms, predominantly white, greenish yellow tips to spiralled petals and sepals; white lip with heavy purple veining.

Dendrobium atroviolaceum

↔ 8–24 in (20–60 cm) ↑ 8–20 in (20–50 cm)

From New Guinea. Small clusters of long-lasting, nodding, white to greenish yellow blooms, 2 in (5 cm) in size, finely spotted with maroon, appear throughout the warmer months, and year-round in the tropics.

Dendrobium bigibbum

COOKTOWN ORCHID

↔ 8–24 in (20–60 cm) ↑ 4–24 in (10–60 cm)

From Australia, common in the Cape York Peninsula. Spectacular purple blooms, on sprays of up to 20 flowers, in autumn. Must be kept dry in winter when dormant. *D. b.* subsp. *phalaenopsis*, large purple flowers; *D. b.* var. *compactum* ★, small-growing form to 5 in (12 cm) tall, with chunky pseudobulbs.

Dendrobium bulbophylloides

Dendrobium bracteosum

↔ 5–15 in (12–38 cm) ↑ 6–14 in (15–35 cm)

Native of New Guinea. Long-lasting blooms form in tight clusters, generally off older leafless pseudobulbs, all through warmer months, year-round in tropics. Flower color varies from white through various shades of pink to deep red-purple.

Dendrobium bulbophylloides

↔ 2–8 in (5–20 cm) ↑ ½–1¼ in (12–30 mm)

From New Guinea. Miniature creeping species that hugs its host. Yellow-orange to red-brown blooms, quite large considering size of plant, in winter–spring. Does best when grown on a tree fern that is kept damp, so mosses can also grow on the mount.

Dendrobium bullenianum

syn. *Dendrobium topaziacum*

↔ 8–16 in (20–40 cm) ↑ 8–40 in (20–100 cm)

From the Philippines; lowland species. Pseudobulbs initially grow in an erect manner, becoming pendulous as they mature. Dense clusters of up to 30 blooms, less than ¾ in (18 mm) in size, bright orange overlaid by red striping. Spring-flowering. Stake potted plants upright along their length to keep tidy, or grow on slabs to give a more natural look.

Dendrobium bigibbum var. *compactum*

Dendrobium bracteosum

Dendrobium canaliculatum

Dendrobium capituliflorum

Dendrobium cacatua

↔ 4–12 in (10–30 cm) ↕ 4–12 in (10–30 cm)
🝙 ☀ ◈/◇ ❈ ⬚

Shade- and moisture-loving species from northeastern Australia. Semi-pendulous habit with 4-sided pseudo-bulbs. Small clusters of starry apple green to yellowish blooms, 4 in (10 cm) in size, with a contrasting pure white lip. Spring-flowering. Previously incorrectly known as *D. tetragonum* var. *hayesianum*—this epithet is reserved for the albino form of the true *D. tetragonum*.

Dendrobium canaliculatum

ONION ORCHID

↔ 4–16 in (10–40 cm) ↕ 4–16 in (10–40 cm)
🝙 ☀ ◆ ❈ ⬚

From northern Queensland, Australia. Often found growing on paperbark (*Melaleuca*) trees. Unique scaly pseudobulbs give it its common name. Several racemes with up to 40 blooms in spring. Narrow and twisted flowers, white with yellow to brown tips, white and purple lip. Likes warmth and bright light, with a dry rest in winter.

Dendrobium capitisyork

syn. *Dendrobium tetragonum* var. *giganteum*

CAPE YORK SPIDER ORCHID

↔ 4–20 in (10–50 cm) ↕ 6–24 in (15–60 cm)
🝙 ☀ ◆ ❈ ⬚

From northeastern Australia; rainforest species, range of sizes and colors. Semi-pendulous pseudobulbs. Spidery blooms, 2½–6 in (6–15 cm) tall, cream to yellow-green, with dark purple to brown blotches; white lip marked with brown to purple spots or streaks. Winter- and spring-blooming.

Dendrobium capituliflorum

↔ 8–12 in (20–30 cm) ↕ 6–12 in (15–30 cm)
🝙/⋀ ☀ ◆ ⬚/⬚

From New Guinea and Solomon Islands region; variable in habitat, grows in mangrove, savannah, and coastal rainforest. Thickened, short, cane-like pseudobulbs; dark green leaves, purple on underside, seasonally deciduous. Clusters of up to 50 blooms along bare canes in spring. Small flowers, about ¼ in (6 mm) wide, greenish-white with green tips.

Dendrobium ceraula

syn. *Dendrobium gonzalesii*

↔ 4–10 in (10–25 cm) ↕ 6–16 in (15–40 cm)
🝙 ☀ ◈/◇ ❈ ⬚

From mountainous forests in the Philippines; prefers cool, moist, shady conditions. Flowers vary from blue-mauve through pink to white, with flat purple-striped lip. Blooms in winter–spring.

Dendrobium chameleon

↔ 4–8 in (10–20 cm) ↕ 5–24 in (12–60 cm)
🝙 ☀ ◆ ❈ ⬚

Pendulous species from the Philippines; requires moist shady conditions. Flowers ivory white and creamy yellow to brown, in autumn and winter.

Dendrobium ceraula

Dendrobium cacatua

Dendrobium chittimae

↔ 4–10 in (10–25 cm) ↕ 4–12 in (10–30 cm)

Uncommon and recently (in 1997) described species from Laos and Thailand. Rambling growth habit, often producing aerial growths along pseudobulbs. Shapely blooms, 1 in (25 mm) in size, produced either singly or in pairs, in spring.

Dendrobium chrysocrepis

↔ 4–6 in (10–15 cm) ↕ 8–12 in (20–30 cm)

Small robust orchid from Myanmar. Extremely flattened pseudobulbs, leaves 1½–2 in (35–50 cm) long. Inflorescence with 1 flower borne at tip of pseudobulbs. Fragrant flowers, 2 in (5 cm) across, yellow, with unique spherical golden lip, in early summer rainy season.

Dendrobium chrysotoxum

↔ 8–24 in (20–60 cm) ↕ 8–16 in (20–40 cm)

Robust plant found from India to southern China. Swollen pseudobulbs produce sprays of up to 25 golden yellow to orange waxy flowers in late spring. **D. c. var. suavissimum** differs in having a dark reddish orange blotch on lip.

Dendrobium crumenatum

DOVE ORCHID, PIGEON ORCHID

↔ 8–24 in (20–60 cm) ↕ 8–24 in (20–60 cm)

From India, Southeast Asia. Needs a sudden drop in temperature, of about 18°F (10°C), to induce flowering—such an event takes place during tropical storms. Exactly 9 days later the plant, plus any others in the district, will profusely burst into bloom. producing blooms that last only one day. Short inflorescence with several fragrant white flowers just over 1½ in (35 mm) wide.

Dendrobium cucullatum

syns *Dendrobium aphyllum, D. pierardii*

↔ 10–16 in (25–40cm) ↕ 27–36 in (70–90cm)

Very widespread species from tropical Southeast Asia; often in mangrove habitat. Pendent cane-like pseudobulbs, thin in structure; narrow, thin, deciduous leaves. Many fragrant thin-textured flowers, 18–22 in (45–55 cm), soft pink to blush-white, light to bright yellow spot on lip. Blooms throughout year. Grows well on slabs or in baskets.

Dendrobium curvicaule

syn. *Dendrobium speciosum* subsp. *curvicale*

↔ 12–48 in (30–120 cm) ↕ 8–36 in (20–90 cm)

Robust species from northeastern Australia; ideal as garden plant in frost-free climates. Arching inflorescences with numerous highly fragrant blooms, 1½–3 in (3.5–8 cm) in size, predominantly cream, white lip stained with maroon markings, in spring. '**Bee Creek**', attractive golden yellow blooms.

Dendrobium curvicaule 'Bee Creek'

Dendrobium chameleon

Dendrobium curvicaule

Dendrobium chittimae

Dendrobium chrysotoxum

Dendrobium cucullatum

Dendrobium cuthbertsonii ★

↔ 2–8 in (5–20 cm) ↕ 1–3 in (2.5–8 cm)
♀ ☀ ◆/◇ ❄ ⛶/⬈

From New Guinea; miniature plant with disproportionately large blooms. Flowers throughout year, individual blooms can last up to 9 months under favorable conditions. Comes in range of bright colors, including red, orange, yellow, pink, white, plus bicolor forms. Plants must be kept moist; sphagnum moss is often used for potted plants.

Dendrobium × *delicatum* 'Pretty Good'

Dendrobium × delicatum

syn. *Dendrobium kesteveni*

↔ 16–20 in (40–50 cm) ↕ 12–20 in (30–50 cm) ♀/⋀ ☼/☀ ◆/◇ ❄ ⛶

From eastern-central New South Wales north to Queensland, in Australia; found growing on rocks and cliff faces, often in full sun. Natural hybrid of *D. kingianum* and *D. tarberi*. Pseudobulbs wider at base, tapering toward apex; persistent oval leaves. Clusters of flowers from bulb apex, white to pink, favoring *D. kingianum* in appearance. Spring-blooming. Quite easy to cultivate. '**Pretty Good**', deep pink blooms.

Dendrobium densiflorum

syns *Dendrobium guibertii*, *D. schroderi* Hort.

↔ 16–20 in (40–50 cm) ↕ 12–18 in (30–45 cm) ♀ ☀ ◆ ❄ ⛶

Widespread species from India, Nepal, Myanmar, Laos, and southwestern China; grows on moss-covered trees in montane forests that have a long seasonal dry period. Club-like narrow pseudobulbs; 3 to 5 leaves near apex. Pendent spikes carry bright yellow flowers, about 2 in (5 cm) in size, orange-yellow lip. Spring-blooming.

Dendrobium densiflorum

Dendrobium dichaeoides

↔ 2½–8 in (6–20 cm) ↕ 2–3 in (5–8 cm)
♀/⋀ ☀ ◆/◇ ❄ ⛶/⬈

Endemic to New Guinea; found growing on moss-covered branches and rocks. Very variable in habit, some plants upright, others crawling; possibly more than 1 species involved. Small canes; many small opposite leaves. Clusters of small flowers, less than ¼ in (6 mm) in size, bright pink, sometimes with red. Flowers bloom sporadically throughout year.

Dendrobium discolor

↔ 1–4 ft (0.3–1.2 m) ↕ 1–6 ft (0.3–1.8 m)
♀/⋀ ☼ ◆ ❄ ⛶

Tall-growing variable species from Australia and New Guinea. Large spikes of undulating brown and yellow flowers, most of year. Coastal species; enjoys strong light and does best when given a lot of room.

Dendrobium dixanthum

↔ 6–12 in (15–30 cm) ↕ 8–30 in (20–75 cm)
♀ ☼/☀ ◆/◆ ❄ ⛶

Slender-growing species from Myanmar, Thailand, and Laos. Up to 3 bright buttercup yellow flowers, 1¼ in (30 mm), disc-shaped predominantly golden lip, in spring. Blooming occurs off previous season's naked pseudobulbs that shed their leaves some 3 months beforehand.

Dendrobium engae

↔ 8–20 in (20–50 cm) ↕ 8–27 in (20–70 cm)
♀ ☀ ◆ ❄ ⛶

Robust species from the mountains of Enga Province, Papua New Guinea. Up to 12 large, greenish cream,

Dendrobium cuthbertsonii

Dendrobium dichaeoides

Dendrobium engae

Dendrobium findleyanum

fragrant flowers to 2½ in (6 cm) wide in late spring–summer. Blooms can last for up to 4 months.

Dendrobium farmeri
↔ 12–18 in (30–45 cm) ↕ 12–18 in (30–45 cm) ♀ ☼ ◆ ❀ ⛶/🗻

Widespread species from northeastern India, Bhutan, Nepal, Thailand, Myanmar, Laos, and Malaysia; grows in forests with cool dry winters. Narrow 4-sided pseudobulbs: 2 to 4 evergreen leaves at apex. Pendent inflorescences, with up to 30 fragrant blooms in spring. Flowers around 1½ in (35 mm) wide, pink to white; roundish golden lip. *D. f.* **var.** *alboflorum*, white flowers, yellow on lip, often sold as *D. palpebrae.*

Dendrobium fimbriatum
↔ 1–4 ft (0.3–1.2 m) ↕ 1–7 ft (0.3–2 m) ♀ ☼/◑ ◆/◇ ❀ ⛶

From Southeast Asia. Pure yellow to orange flowers, on small spikes, in late spring. *D. f.* **var.** *oculatum*, more often cultivated, orange flowers, deep maroon blotch on lip.

Dendrobium findleyanum
↔ 16–24 in (40–60 cm) ↕ 14–24 in (35–60 cm) ♀ ☼/◑ ◆ ❀ ⛶

Occurs in Myanmar and Thailand. Cane-like pseudobulbs, very swollen along joints; several deciduous leaves. Fragrant flowers, around 3 in (8 cm) in size, bloom along bare canes in spring. Flowers white with purple tips, large yellow disk on lip.

Dendrobium fimbriatum var. *oculatum*

Dendrobium discolor

Dendrobium dixanthum

Dendrobium farmeri var. *alboflorum*

D

Dendrobium goldschmidtianum

Dendrobium flaviflorum

Dendrobium gibsonii

Dendrobium harveyanum

Dendrobium flaviflorum

↔ 8–16 in (20–40 cm) ↕ 8–20 in (20–50 cm)
♀ ☀/☀ ◆/◇ ❖ ☖

From Taiwan. Very dense arrangement of very slender pseudobulbs. Short sprays of rounded bright dark yellow blooms, around 2 in (5 cm) in size, slightly darker lip, in summer. Can bloom off the same pseudobulb for many years.

Dendrobium formosum

↔ 14–18 in (35–45 cm) ↕ 16–18 in (40–45 cm) ♀/⋀ ☀/☀ ◆ ❖ ☖

Beautiful species from mountainous areas of India, Bhutan, Nepal,

Thailand, Myanmar, and Vietnam. Cane-like pseudobulbs: shiny leaves, 4–5 in (10–12 cm) long, dusted with fine black hairs. Large white flowers, 2–3 in (5–8 cm) wide, golden yellow on lip. Blooms from spring to autumn in cultivation, late spring in the wild.

Dendrobium gibsonii

↔ 12–24 in (30–60 cm) ↕ 12–48 in (30–120 cm) ♀ ☀/☀ ◆ ❖ ☖

Uncommon species, found from Nepal to China. Glossy golden blooms, 2 distinctive deep maroon blotches on lip. Summer- to autumn-flowering.

Dendrobium goldschmidtianum

syn. *Dendrobium miyakei*

↔ 8–24 in (20–60 cm) ↕ 8–36 in (20–90 cm)
♀ ☀/☀ ◆/◆ ❖ ☖/⩘

Showy species from Taiwan. Clusters of up to 20 bright purple blooms, produced off leafless pseudobulbs, from late winter to summer.

Dendrobium gracilicaule

↔ 8–36 in (20–90 cm) ↕ 8–24 in (20–60 cm)
♀/⋀ ☀/☀ ◆/◇ ☖/⩘

Australian species. Slender pseudobulbs. Small arching spikes of fragrant flowers, yellowish green, heavily blotched with red-brown on back of segments. Flowers in early spring.

Dendrobium × gracillimum

↔ 24–30 in (60–75 cm) ↕ 18–24 in (45–60 cm) ♀ ☀/☀ ◆/◇ ☖

Occurs in New South Wales and Queensland in eastern Australia; typically found in open sclerophyll forests. Natural hybrid between *D. gracilicaule* and *D. tarberi*. Cane-like pseudobulbs. Small creamy yellow flowers, in clusters near apex, in spring.

Dendrobium harveyanum

↔ 8–16 in (20–40 cm) ↕ 8–16 in (20–40 cm)
♀ ☀ ◆ ❖ ☖

Native to Thailand and Vietnam; unique among genus because of its

highly fringed petals and lip, which are both bright canary yellow. Up to 5 blooms are produced on short inflorescences from near top of pseudobulb in spring. Grows slowly and particularly resents disturbance.

Dendrobium hercoglossum

↔ 8–24 in (20–60 cm) ↕ 6–16 in (15–40 cm)
♀ ☀/☀ ◆/◆/◇ ❖ ☖/⩘

From Thailand and Indochina; closely related to *D. aduncum* and *D. linguella*. Slender pseudobulbs. Pale to dark pink flowers in late spring–summer. Amenable to a range of climates.

Dendrobium jenkinsii

syn. *Dendrobium aggregatum*
var. *jenkinsii*

↔ 4–5 in (10–12 cm) ↕ 2½–4 in (6–10 cm)
♀ ☀ ◆ ⩘

Found from mountain forests of China and Southeast Asia to India. Hard ribbed pseudobulbs; single stiff leaf, to 2 in (5 cm) long. Erect inflorescence with up to 3 blooms, in spring. Flowers fragrant, golden yellow, 1¼ in (30 mm) wide. Grow mounted. Provide bright, humid, warmer conditions when in active growth. A cooler dry environment in winter is needed to have flowers the following season.

Dendrobium formosum

Dendrobium johnsoniae

↔ 8–20 in (20–50 cm) ↕ 8–20 in (20–50 cm)

From New Guinea; grows at elevations of 1,640–3,940 ft (500–1,200 m). Pseudobulbs spindle-shaped, with 4 to 5 leaves. Clusters of attractive, long-lasting, fragrant blooms, on short upright spikes, throughout warmer months of year. Flowers to 5 in (12 cm) wide, pure white, lip striped with purple, disproportionately large for size of the plant.

Dendrobium keithii

↔ 6–16 in (15–40 cm) ↕ 4–16 in (10–40 cm)

From Thailand. Greenish yellow blooms, to 1 in (25 mm) across. Peak flowering in early spring, flushes of blooms may occur any time of year.

Dendrobium kingianum ★

↔ 4–48 in (10–120 cm) ↕ 2–36 in (5–90 cm)

Popular and highly variable species found in Australia. Cone-shaped pseudobulbs. Up to 12 fragrant flowers off compact plants. Colors vary from pure white through most shades of pink to deep beetroot purple. White lip, sometimes blotched and splashed with lilac, through to solid deep purple. Spring-flowering. *D. k.* var. *album*, pure white flowers, yellow splotched lip. *D. k.* 'Steve', pale pink with darker tinges, dark lip. Many superior cultivars have been developed through selective line breeding of desirable forms.

Dendrobium jenkinsii

Dendrobium keithii

Dendrobium kingianum 'Steve'

Dendrobium kingianum

Dendrobium johnsoniae

Dendrobium kingianum var. *album*

Dendrobium macrophyllum

Dendrobium macrophyllum, seed pod

Dendrobium laevifolium

↔ 2½–8 in (6–20 cm) ↕ 2½–6 in (6–15 cm)

Miniature species from New Guinea. Blooms off leafless pseudobulbs in summer. Vibrant purple flowers last for up to 8 weeks. Keep moist all year.

Dendrobium lawesii

↔ 4–12 in (10–30 cm) ↕ 6–20 in (15–50 cm)

From New Guinea. Semi-pendent leafy habit, attractive even when not in bloom. Bright tubular flowers, upturned tip to lip, probably bird-pollinated. Flower color most variable, with red, orange, yellow, pink, purple, and bicolored forms. Flowers throughout year, mainly in spring.

Dendrobium lichenastrum

syn. *Dendrobium prenticei*

↔ 4–6 in (10–15 cm) ↕ ½–¾ in (12–18 mm)

From northeastern Australia; grows in moist rainforests and open forests. Lacks a pseudobulb, arises directly from creeping rhizome; small, succulent, leathery leaves. Small flowers, about ¼ in (6 mm), whitish pink with thin dark striping; lip yellow to orange. Blooms sporadically throughout year. Some taxonomists have recently transferred this into the new genus *Davejonesia* as *D. lichenastra.*

Dendrobium lindleyi

syn. *Dendrobium aggregatum*

↔ 8–16 in (20–40 cm) ↕ 8–16 in (20–40 cm)

Found from India to China. Pendent sprays of up to 20 lemon yellow to golden flowers, quite large considering its compact growth habit. Blooms in spring–summer.

Dendrobium lituiflorum

syn. *Dendrobium hanburyanum*

↔ 18–27 in (45–70 cm) ↕ 24–27 in (60–70 cm)

Tree-top orchid of seasonally dry forests, widespread from northeastern India, Thailand, Myanmar, Laos, and southwestern China. Clustered pendent cane-like pseudobulbs; thin deciduous leaves, 3–5 in (8–12 cm) long. Racemes with 1 to 5 flowers in spring. Fragrant flowers, 1–1½ in (25–35 mm) wide, light purple to white; lip with darker base and white or yellow surrounds.

Dendrobium laevifolium

Dendrobium lawesii

Dendrobium lituiflorum

Dendrobium lichenastrum

Dendrobium monophyllum

Dendrobium moniliforme

Dendrobium macrophyllum

↔ 8–24 in (20–60 cm) ↕ 8–27 in (20–70 cm)

Robust species from Malaysia to New Guinea and across to some Pacific Islands; often forms huge clumps in the wild. Clustered pseudobulbs with 3 to 7 leaves. Up to 30 long-lasting blooms per inflorescence, during the warmer months. Flowers greenish cream, contrasting highly detailed lip with distinctive fine maroon veining; backs of sepals and ovary covered in dense green hairs.

Dendrobium masarangense

↔ 2–5 in (5–12 cm) ↕ 1–2 in (2.5–5 cm)

Compact-growing, tufted, miniature species found in New Guinea. Long-lasting greenish cream blooms, bright orange-red blotch on lip, in winter–spring. Dislikes continual warm temperatures, must be kept moist in cultivation.

Dendrobium melaleucaphilum

Dendrobium melaleucaphilum

syn. *Dendrobium tetragonum* var. *melaleucaphilum*

↔ 8–20 in (20–50 cm) ↕ 8–24 in (20–60 cm)

Species from eastern Australia. Semi-pendulous, with 4-sided pseudobulbs. Clusters of up to 10 blooms in spring. Flowers each 4 in (10 cm) in size, greenish yellow bordered with band of dark reddish brown; flared white lip with purple and brown markings. Previously known as the "mid-north coast form" of *D. tetragonum*.

Dendrobium moniliforme

↔ 8–24 in (20–60 cm) ↕ 4–10 in (10–25 cm)

From Japan and China. Compact and variable plant; type species of genus. Fragrant white to pink blooms, in spring. Also variegated leafed forms.

Dendrobium monophyllum

↔ 8–12 in (20–30 cm) ↕ 2½–8 in (6–20 cm)

Eastern Australian species, found from Cape York Peninsula in Queensland to northeastern New South Wales; grows in bright situtations. Yellowish pseudobulbs; 1 to 2 leaves at apex. Erect to arching spike with several nodding, yellow, fragrant flowers, about ¼ in (6 mm) in size. Flowers intermittently from spring to autumn. Recently classified as an *Australorchis* species, but it is too early to tell if this will receive universal acceptance.

Dendrobium masarangense

Dendrobium nobile

Dendrobium nobile var. *virginale*

Dendrobium mutabile

↔ 16–60 in (40–150 cm) ↕ 8–36 in (20–90 cm) ♀/\ ☀/☀ ◆/◇ ❄ ▽

From seasonally dry forests of Java and Sumatra in Indonesia. Thin, cane-like, branching pseudobulbs; persistent leaves, 3–5 in (8–12 cm) long. Flowers bloom along canes in small groups in spring–summer. Flowers to 1½ in (35 mm) wide, white to light pink, small orange spot on lip below column.

Dendrobium nobile

↔ 8–24 in (20–60 cm) ↕ 8–24 in (20–60 cm) ♀ ☀/☀ ◆/◆/◇ ❄ ▽

Found from India to China. Highly variable species, one of the "softcanes;" great beginner's orchid. Deep purple to pure white flowers, with many shades and bicolored combinations, in spring. *D. n.* **var.** *cooksonianum*, unusual, with lip coloring in petals;

D. n. **var.** *nobilius,* large, deep purple flowers; *D. n.* **var.** *virginale*, pure white flowers.

Dendrobium pandanicola

↔ 4–16 in (10–40 cm) ↕ 4–24 in (10–60 cm) ♀ ☀ ◆/◇ ❄ ▽/≋

From the mountains of New Guinea. Closely related to *D. subclausum*. Small clusters of long-lasting, bright yellow, bell-shaped blooms, under 1 in (25 mm) in size, appear on older leafless pseudobulbs in autumn.

Dendrobium peguanum

↔ 2½–3 in (6–8 cm) ↕ 1½–3 in (3.5–8 cm) ♀ ☀ ◆ ▽

From India and Myanmar; grows in forests with an annual long dry period. Stubby cane-like pseudobulbs; narrow deciduous leaves. Flowers about ½ in (12 mm) wide, fragrant, in clusters, whitish with dark purple

lip with pink edge. Blooms in winter–spring. Can be difficult in cultivation.

Dendrobium phalaenopsis

syn. *Dendrobium bigibbum* var. *superbum*
COOKTOWN ORCHID

↔ 4–12 in (10–30 cm) ↕ 8–32 in (20–80 cm) ♀ ☀/☀ ◆ ❄ ▽/≋

From northeastern Australia; the floral emblem of Queensland. Spectacular purple blooms, about 1½ in (35 mm) in size, on sprays of up to 20 flowers, in autumn. Backbone of *Phalaenanthe*-style *Dendrobium* breeding. Must be kept dry in winter when dormant.

Dendrobium primulinum

↔ 12–20 in (30–50 cm) ↕ 16–32 in (40–80 cm) ♀ ☀ ◆/◇ ❄ ▽/≋

Robust medium-sized species from India, Myanmar, Thailand, Vietnam, Malaya, and Southern China; grows in mountain rainforests. Pendent cane-like pseudobulbs; several leathery deciduous leaves. Fragrant flower produced from each node in spring. Blooms 2–2½ in (5–6 cm) across, light purple to near white, large pale yellow tubular lip. Best grown on mounts or in baskets.

Dendrobium pseudoglomeratum

↔ 8–20 in (20–50 cm) ↕ 8–27 in (20–70 cm) ♀ ☀ ◆/◇ ▽

From New Guinea. Heads of up to 16 blooms, an unusual and striking color

combination of hot pink and orange, off leafless pseudobulbs, in spring.

Dendrobium pulchellum

↔ 1–3 ft (0.3–0.9 m) ↕ 1–7 ft (0.3–2 m) ♀ ☀/☀ ◆ ❄ ▽

Found from Nepal to China. Can produce very long cane-like pseudobulbs. Up to 12, cream to apricot, fragrant flowers, with dark maroon blotches on lip, on pendent spikes off older leafless stems, in summer.

Dendrobium rex

syn. *Dendrobium speciosum* var. *grandiflorum*

↔ 12–60 in (30–150 cm) ↕ 12–48 in (30–120 cm) ♀/\ ☀/☀ ◆/◆/◇ ❄ ▽

Very robust species from southern Queensland, eastern Australia; ideal as garden plant in frost-free climates. Long arching to pendent inflorescences with up to 200 pale yellow to deep gold fragrant blooms, each less than ½ in (12 mm) in size; white lip stained with maroon markings, in spring.

Dendrobium roseipes

↔ 18–24 in (45–60 cm) ↕ 14–24 in (35–60 cm) ♀ ☀ ◆ ▽

From New Guinea; found growing on moss-covered trees. Cane-like pseudobulbs, upright to pendent; many leaves, which are deciduous before blooming. Bare canes have clusters of pink and white tubular flowers that bloom along nodes. Blooms sporadically throughout year. Grows best in baskets, using moss.

Dendrobium rupestre

↔ 2–4 in (5–10 cm) ↕ 1–2 in (2.5–5 cm) ♀ ☀ ◆/◇ ▽

Miniature species from New Guinea. Reddish purple blooms in winter–spring. Dislikes continual warm temperatures, must be kept moist in cultivation.

Dendrobium mutabile

Dendrobium pandanicola

Dendrobium rex

Dendrobium peguanum

Dendrobium roseipes, in bud

Dendrobium pseudoglomeratum

Dendrobium roseipes

Dendrobium rupestre

Dendrobium primulinum

Dendrobium sanderae

↔ 20–24 in (50–60 cm) ↑ 27–36 in
(70–90 cm) ♀ ☀ ◆/◇ ❀ ▽

Endemic to Philippine Islands; grows
on rainforest trees; beautiful species
that occurs in several regional varieties. Upright cane-like pseudobulb
with numerous evergreen leaves, both
covered in fine black hairs. Canes will
bloom for several years, with clusters
of 3 to 12 flowers in spring–summer.
Flowers white, 3–4 in (8–10 cm) in
size; white lip with reddish purple
side lobes. *D. s.* var. *luzonicum*,
smaller plant, flowers with longer
spur; *D. s.* var. *major*, larger plant
and flowers; *D. s.* var. *milleri*, lip with
purple throat; *D. s.* var. *parviflorum*,
smaller flowers; *D. s.* var. *surigaense*,
pink-striped side lobes to lip.

Dendrobium scabrilingue

syns *Dendrobium galactanthum*,
D. hedyosmum

↔ 12–18 in (30–45 cm) ↑ 10–14 in
(25–35 cm) ♀ ☀ ◆/◇ ❀ ▽

From Myanmar, Thailand, and Laos;
grows in humid forests. Cane-like
pseudobulbs and persistent leaves
covered with fine black hairs. Fragrant
flowers, 1½–2 in (35–50 mm) wide,
in spring–summer. Petals and sepals
greenish-white, lip yellow and green.

Dendrobium schildhaueri

syn. *Dendrobium virgineum*

↔ 14–18 in (35–45 cm) ↑ 12–16 in
(30–40 cm) ♀ ☼/☀ ◆/◇ ❀ ▽

From Myanmar, Thailand, Laos, and
Vietnam; occurs in seasonally dry
forests. Cane-like pseudobulbs and

evergreen leaves covered in fine-black
hairs. White flowers, about 2½ in
(6 cm) wide; orange lip, large upturned spur. Can bloom anytime
from spring to autumn.

Dendrobium secundum

↔ 12–24 in (30–60 cm) ↑ 40 in (100 cm)
♀ ☀ ◆/◇ ▽

Widespread in tropical Asia, from
lowlands of Myanmar, Thailand,
Peninsular Malaysia, Vietnam, and
Indonesia to Philippines. Thick cane-
like pseudobulbs; deciduous leaves.
Flowers on bare canes, usually toward
apex, in clusters of dozens of small
flowers, under ½ in (12 mm), which
all face one direction and can appear
any time of year. Blooms usually
brilliant pink, with bright orange

or yellow, rarely white, lip. '**White**',
white flowers with bright yellow lip.

Dendrobium smillieae

BOTTLEBRUSH ORCHID

↔ 8–27 in (20–70 cm) ↑ 8–48 in
(20–120 cm) ♀ ☼/☀ ◆ ❀ ▽

Native to Australia and New Guinea.
Densely packed clusters of blooms
from white to pinkish green, with a
dark bottle green lip, throughout the
warmer months, year-round in tropics.

Dendrobium speciosum

KING ORCHID, ROCK LILY

↔ 1–10 ft (0.3–3 m) ↑ 4–48 in (10–120 cm)
♀/⋀ ☼/☀ ◆/◇ ❀ ▽/🌧

Variable orchid from New South
Wales, Australia; has sister species
recognized at specific level as *D.
curvicaule*, *D. pedunculatum*, *D. rex*,
and *D. tarberi*. Popular garden plant,
thrives in frost-free climates, where it
blooms from late winter to spring.
Particularly large inflorescences
crowded with white to yellow, highly
fragrant flowers. A most robust plant.

Dendrobium spectabile

↔ 8–24 in (20–60 cm) ↑ 8–32 in (20–80 cm)
♀ ☼/☀ ◆ ❀ ▽

From New Guinea. Unique species
with twisted and somewhat distorted
floral segments, on inflorescences of
up to 20 blooms, in spring–summer.
Blooms can last for some weeks.

Dendrobium subclausum

↔ 4–12 in (10–30 cm) ↑ 6–20 in (15–50 cm)
♀ ☀ ◆/◇ ❀ ▽

From New Guinea. Thin upright to
flaccid pseudobulbs that frequently
branch and produce aerial growths.
Bright flowers from red to yellow, also
bicolored forms. Blooms year-round.

Dendrobium sulphureum

↔ 2–5 in (5–12 cm) ↑ 1–2 in (2.5–5 cm)
♀ ☀ ◆/◇ ❀ ▽

Miniature from New Guinea. Long-
lasting greenish yellow blooms, bright
red blotch on apex of lip, Flowers all
year. Dislikes continual warm temperatures, must always be kept moist.

Dendrobium secundum 'White'

Dendrobium schildhaueri

Dendrobium spectabile

Dendrobium sanderae var. *surigaense*

Dendrobium scabrilingue

Dendrobium subclausum in the wild, New Guinea

Dendrobium subclausum

Dendrobium sulphureum

Dendrobium smillieae

D

Dendrobium tarberi, in the wild, Lamington National Park, Australia

Dendrobium tapiniense

Dendrobium tetragonum

Dendrobium tetragonum 'Black Boy'

Dendrobium tortile

Dendrobium wentianum

Dendrobium thyrsiflorum

Dendrobium trilamellatum

Dendrobium wardianum

Dendrobium williamsonii

Dendrobium tapiniense

↔ 8–24 in (20–60 cm) ↑ 8–32 in (20–80 cm)
🌱 ☀/◐ ◆/◇ ❄ ⊤

Robust species from New Guinea. Spikes carry up to a dozen blooms that are very thick, in spring–summer. Blooms can last up to 3 months. Appreciates warm days and cool nights in cultivation.

Dendrobium tarberi

syn. *Dendrobium speciosum* subsp. *hillii*
↔ 12–60 in (30–150 cm) ↑ 8–44 in (20–110 cm) 🌱/⋀ ☀/◐ ◆/◇/◇ ❄ ⊤

Robust species from eastern Australia; ideal as a garden plant in frost-free climates. Long thin pseudobulbs. Long arching to pendent inflorescences produce up to 200 slender blooms, each 1–2 in (25–50 mm) in size, highly fragrant, white to cream, lip white stained with maroon markings. Spring-flowering.

Dendrobium tetragonum

↔ 4–20 in (10–50 cm) ↑ 4–27 in (10–70 cm)
🌱 ☀ ◆/◇ ❄ ⊤/⩘

Australian species; highly variable; 3 distinct geographical populations have been recognized at species level: *D. cacatua*, *D. capitisyork*, and *D. melaleucaphilum*. Semi-pendulous pseudobulbs, distinctly 4-angled in cross-section. Spidery blooms, cream to yellow-green, often with dark purple to brown blotches and borders on floral segments. Lip can be white or marked with brown to purple spots or striations. Blooms in spring–summer. 'Black Boy', attractive cultivar.

Dendrobium thyrsiflorum

↔ 8–36 in (20–90 cm) ↑ 8–24 in (20–60 cm)
🌱 ☀ ◆/◆ ❄ ⊤

Found from India to China; easily grown species. Clustered upright pseudobulbs. Short-lived pendent clusters of flowers in late spring. Floral segments white, sometimes with faint pink flush, lip bright yellow, resemble a bunch of grapes.

Dendrobium tortile

syn. *Dendrobium dartoisianum*
↔ 20–24 in (50–60 cm) ↑ 16–20 in (40–50 cm) 🌱/⋀/⩗ ☀/◐ ◆/◆ ❄ ⊤

Species from deciduous forests in northeastern India, Thailand, Myanmar, Laos, Vietnam, and Peninsular Malaysia. Thin cane-like pseudobulbs, erect to pendent; few, thin, deciduous leaves. Flowers bloom on bare canes from spring to autumn. Very fragrant flowers, 3–4 in (6–8 cm) wide, twisted segments, lilac to white, cream-colored tubular lip.

Dendrobium trilamellatum

syn. *Dendrobium semifuscum*
↔ 16–24 in (40–60 cm) ↑ 18–24 in (45–60 cm) 🌱 ☀/◐ ◆/◆ ❄ ⊤/⩘

Found from northern Queensland in Australia (where it is often found growing in paperbark woods) to southern New Guinea and nearby islands. Upright cane-like pseudobulbs; several leaves. Flower spikes with up to 15 fragrant blooms in late winter–spring. Floral segments yellowish to brown, yellow lip with darker markings.

Dendrobium vexillarius

↔ 2–5 in (5–12 cm) ↑ 1–5 in (2.5–12 cm)
🌱 ☀ ◆/◇ ❄ ⊤

Miniature species from New Guinea. Egg-shaped to cylindrical pseudobulbs with up to 10 leaves. Racemes of up to 5 flowers all year. Bright red, very long-lasting flowers; also wild populations with very wide range of other colors present, including orange, yellow, cream, to unusual bluish gray tones. Dislikes continual warm temperatures, must be kept moist in cultivation.

Dendrobium victoriae-reginae ★

↔ 8–20 in (20–50 cm) ↑ 8–24 in (20–60 cm)
🌱 ☀ ◆/◇ ❄ ⊤

From the Philippines; one of the few "blue" orchids. Up to 4 flowers, lilac to dark bluish purple and white, on short sprays, from nodes along branching pseudobulbs, throughout year. Prefers cool moist conditions.

Dendrobium wardianum

↔ 8–16 in (20–40 cm) ↑ 8–27 in (20–70 cm)
🌱 ☀/◐ ◆/◆ ❄ ⊤

One of the softcane species found from India to China. Waxy, fragrant, tri-colored blooms borne on short racemes in late spring, off leafless pseudobulbs.

Dendrobium wentianum

syn. *Dendrobium obtusisepalum*
↔ 4–12 in (10–30 cm) ↑ 8–32 in (20–80 cm)
🌱 ☀ ◆ ❄ ⊤

Stunning species from New Guinea. Pendulous growth habit. Bright orange blooms, waxy texture, in spring. Enjoys cool, moist, humid conditions.

Dendrobium vexillarius

Dendrobium williamsonii

↔ 8–12 in (20–30 cm) ↑ 8–16 in (20–40 cm)
🌱 ☀ ◆/◆ ⊤

Found from India to Thailand. Fine, short, black hairs along pseudobulb. Mature cane has 1 or 2 waxy, cream to pale yellow flowers, red blotch on lip, in spring–summer. Needs to dry out between watering.

Dendrobium Hybrids

The numbers of *Dendrobium* hybrids have greatly increased in recent decades, particularly "hardcane" hybrids for the cut-flower market.

Dendrobium victoriae-reginae

D

AUSTRALIAN HYBRIDS

↔ 8–30 in (20–75 cm) ↑ 4–24 in (10–60 cm)

This is a selection of some Australian hybrids, bred from indigenous species, such as *D. kingianum*, *D. speciosum*, and *D. tetragonum*. Most of these bloom in winter and spring, and will bloom off the same pseudobulbs for a number of seasons. They are compact plants that will often produce masses of highly fragrant blooms. **Bardo Rose**, popular early primary hybrid; **Barry Simpson**, mauve and white flowers; **Bellingen**, orange-red and yellow flowers; **Biddy**, yellow flowers with orange-red edges; **Brinawa Sunset**, hybrid between *D. Peewee* and *D. falcorostrum*; **Burgundy Cream**, orange-yellow petals and sepals, yellow lip; **Elegant Heart**, hybrid between *D. Peewee* and *D. speciosum*, developed in the 1980s by Walter Upton; **Hilda Poxon ★**, very popular primary hybrid between *D. speciosum* and *D. tetragonum*, blooms a number of times during year; **Jonathan's Glory**, one of the newer hybrids, similar to an improved *D. kingianum*; **Kayla**, slow-growing, with strong *D. speciosum* influence; **Kim**, white flowers, faintly edged with mauve; **Lorikeet**, white flowers with magenta markings, especially on lip; **Maroon Star**, bright yellow spider-like flowers, edged with maroon; **Memoria Kevin Conroy**, deep pink flowers; **Our Reg**, deep crimson and cream flowers; **Ronnie Gee**, white flowers edged with deep crimson, especially on lip; **Warrior**, yellow-green petals and sepals, crimson and white lip; **Wonga**, creamy yellow flowers with deep red markings on lip; **Yondi Brolga**, superb hybrid made by the late Sid Batchelor; **Zeus**, starry purple flowers produced numerous times throughout year.

Dendrobium Elegant Heart
(Australian hybrid)

Dendrobium Bardo Rose (Australian hybrid)

Dendrobium Hilda Poxon
(Australian hybrid)

Dendrobium (Angellene × Ellen Glow) (Australian hybrid)

Dendrobium Barry Simpson (Australian hybrid)

Dendrobium Biddy (Australian hybrid)

Dendrobium Burgundy Cream (Australian hybrid)

Dendrobium Bellingen (Australian hybrid)

Dendrobium (fleckeri × discolor) (Australian hybrid)

Dendrobium Golden Dorn (Australian hybrid)

Dendrobium Brinawa Sunset (Australian hybrid)

Dendrobium Jonathan's Glory (Australian hybrid)

Dendrobium Our Reg (Australian hybrid)

Dendrobium Kayla (Australian hybrid)

Dendrobium Zeus (Australian hybrid)

Dendrobium Memoria Kevin Conroy (Australian hybrid)

Dendrobium Lorikeet (Australian hybrid)

Dendrobium Warrior (Australian hybrid)

Dendrobium Kim (Australian hybrid)

Dendrobium Maroon Star (Australian hybrid)

Dendrobium Wonga (Australian hybrid)

Dendrobium Yondi Brolga (Australian hybrid)

Dendrobium Ronnie Gee (Australian hybrid)

"HARDCANE" HYBRIDS
↔ 8–32 in (20–80 cm) ↕ 8–40 in
(20–100 cm) ⚲ ❉/☀ ◆ ❄ ▽

These hybrids have been derived
from many of the lowland tropical
Dendrobium species such as *D.
bigibbum*, *D. discolor*, and *D.
phalaenopsis*. Blooms are produced
throughout the year. **Chao Praya
Rose,** magenta blooms that are very
long-lived, both on plant and as a cut
flower; **Floralia,** white sepals and
petals, rich yellow lip; **Nagasaki,**
white flowers, edges tinged with pink,
lip with maroon base; **Nora Tokunaga,**
white flowers with purple speckling,
heavy purple stripes on lip; **Pua'ala,**
triploid hybrid of *D. bigibbum, D.
macrophyllum,* and *D. spectabile,* deep
red flowers with white edges; **Sedona,**
white sepals and petals, magenta lip;
Suzanne Neil, deep pink-purple
flowers; **Thai Pinky,** important horticultural plant for florist trade;
Thanaid Stripes, heavily veined
magenta blooms; and **White Fairy,**
white flowers tinged with yellow.

Dendrobium Chao Praya Rose (hardcane hybrid)

Dendrobium Pua'ala (hardcane hybrid)

Dendrobium Suzanne Neil (hardcane hybrid)

Dendrobium Thanaid Stripes (hardcane hybrid)

Dendrobium hybrid (hardcane hybrid)

Dendrobium Nagasaki (hardcane hybrid)

Dendrobium Thai Pinky (hardcane hybrid)

Dendrobium Andree Millar
(hardcane hybrid)

Dendrobium Floralia (hardcane hybrid)

Dendrobium White Fairy (hardcane hybrid)

Dendrobium Sedona (hardcane hybrid)

D

Dendrobium Colorado Springs (softcane hybrid)

Dendrobium Hanafubuki (softcane hybrid)

"NIGROHIRSUTE" OR BLACK-HAIRED STYLE HYBRIDS

↔ 8–16 in (20–40 cm)   ↕ 8–16 in (20–40 cm)
♀ ☼/☀ ◆/◇ ❋ ☐

These dendrobiums have short black hairs on the pseudobulbs and usually have white to cream blooms with contrasting colors on the lip. **Frosty Dawn**, a hybrid between *D.* Dawn Maree and *D.* Lime Frost, produces flowers in spring–summer, with blooms lasting about 8 weeks.

"SOFTCANE" HYBRIDS

↔ 6–16 in (15–40 cm)   ↕ 8–24 in (20–60 cm)
♀ ☼/☀ ◆/◇ ❋ ☐

Hybrids derived from *D. nobile*, or closely related species. Short-lived leaves are shed from pseudobulbs before flowers appear in spring–early summer. Up to 5 flowers from each node along naked pseudobulb, with potential for many long-lived blooms along length of swollen stems. **Akatuki Queen**, bright mauve flowers, lip with dark blotch surrounded by white ring; **Bohemian Rhapsody**, primary hybrid between *D. cucullatum* and *D. loddigesii*; **Christmas Chime 'Azuka'**, white flowers, petals with white tips, lip with dark blotch surrounded by white ring; **Colorado Springs**, white flowers, tinged mauve at tips, lip with yellow blotch; **Gatton Monarch**, mauve and white flowers, lip with dark blotch; **Golden Blossom 'Kogane'**, yellow flowers, crimson blotched lip; **Golden Blossom 'Venus'**, pale yellow flowers; **Hanafubuki**, white flowers, yellow-blotched lip; **Honey Leen**, mauve-pink and white petals and sepals, lip with dark blotch; **Kay Lynette**, white flowers, pink at tips, dark blotch and yellow markings on lip; **Lilac Frost**, magenta flowers, lip marked with dark blotch; **Lovely Virgin 'Angel'**, magenta and white flowers, large yellow blotch on lip; **Maihime 'Beauty'**, deep pink and white flowers, lip with yellow throat; **Oriental Paradise 'Aurora'**, white flowers marked with deep pink, lip with dark blotch; **Sagamusmi**, white flowers, lip faintly yellow; **Sailor Boy**, pastel colors most popularly white with yellow center, with pale pink tips; **Sailor Boy 'Pinkie'**, white flowers, tipped with mauve, lip with yellow blotch; **Stardust**, yellow flowers, lip with darker markings; **Super Star 'Dandy'**, magenta flowers, lip with yellow and white markings; and **Yukidaruma 'King'** ★, arguably the most popular softcane hybrid.

Dendrobium Bohemian Rhapsody (softcane hybrid)

Dendrobium Gatton Monarch (softcane hybrid)

Dendrobium Christmas Chime 'Azuka' (softcane hybrid)

Dendrobium Golden Blossom 'Kogane'
(softcane hybrid)

Dendrobium Akatuki Queen (softcane hyb.)   *Dendrobium* Kay Lynette (softcane hybrid)

D

Dendrobium Stardust (softcane hybrid)

Dendrobium Sagamusmi (softcane hybrid)

Dendrobium Lilac Frost (softcane hybrid)

Dendrobium Yukidaruma 'King' (softcane hybrid)

Dendrobium Golden Blossom 'Venus'
(softcane hybrid)

Dendrobium Sailor Boy 'Pinkie'
(softcane hybrid)

Dendrobium Lovely Virgin 'Angel'
(softcane hybrid)

Dendrobium Sailor Boy (softcane hybrid)

Dendrobium Honey Leen (softcane hybrid)

Dendrobium Maihime 'Beauty' (softcane hybrid)

Dendrobium Oriental Paradise 'Aurora' (softcane hybrid)

Dendrobium Super Star 'Dandy' (softcane hybrid)

Dendrochilum species in the wild, Sabah
Kinabalu National Park, Borneo, Malaysia

Dendrochilum cobbianum

DENDROCHILUM

CHAIN ORCHID

Members of this large genus of over
200 sympodial botanicals produce
a single leaf per pseudobulb and are
related to *Coelogyne*. Most are epiphytes that grow in mossy cloud
forests in mountainous regions, where
there are rarely significant temperature
extremes. Only a few make their
homes in the tropical lowlands. The
main center of distribution for the
genus is the Philippines, with numerous species found in Borneo and
Sumatra, Indonesia. They bloom
once a year, with the developing
new growth, and their small but often
colorful flowers are arranged in 2 rows
and alternately along an inflorescence
that is spiralled in some species.
CULTIVATION: Easy to grow, with
most being clump-forming and well
suited to pot culture. Sphagnum moss
may be used solely as a medium for
the miniature growers and any plants
up to 4 in (10 cm) pot size. Larger
plants grow well in a bark-based mix,
with a small proportion of gravel, perlite, and chopped moss added. Fresh
air and constant high humidity is
important and these plants happily
bloom in shaded conditions. They
also like to be kept constantly moist.
Try to keep these plants as cool as
possible during hot summer months
and protect them from the chill in
winter. Propagation is by division.

Dendrochilum arachnites

↔ 8–12 in (20–30cm) ↑ 6–8 in (15–20 cm)
♀ ☼/☀ ◆ ❀ ▭

Rather untidy orchid from the
Philippines. Ovoid pseudobulbs to
2 in (5 cm) tall; leaves to 6 in (15 cm)
long. Arching inflorescences bear
about 30 blooms in winter. Thinly

segmented, pale yellowish green
flowers, about ¾ in (18 mm) across,
probably the largest in the genus.

Dendrochilum cobbianum ★

↔ 8–20 in (20–50 cm) ↑ 6–20 in (15–50 cm)
♀ ☼ ◆/◇ ❀ ▭

From the Philippines; arguably the
most frequently seen member of the
genus in cultivation. Pseudobulbs
clustered, 2½–3 in (6–8 cm) tall,
narrowly conical; single leaf, 2–14 in
(5–35 cm) long, narrowly oblong,
mid-rib prominent. Inflorescence
erect at first then drooping, to 32 in
(80 cm) long, densely arranged with
many flowers, papery bracts. Flowers
white to yellow and green, lip can be
contrasting color; nectar gland in
center of lip is a distinctive feature.
Spring- to autumn-flowering.

Dendrochilum filiforme

↔ 14–18 in (35–45 cm) ↑ 14–18 in
(35–45 cm) ♀ ☀ ◆/◇ ❀ ▭

From the Philippines. Pseudobulbs
to 1 in (25 mm) long; erect, narrowly
strap-shaped leaves. Inflorescence
very slender, pendent, 14–18 in
(35–45 cm) long, densely arranged
with many flowers in spring–summer.
Flowers small, scented, pale yellow,
lip often golden yellow.

Dendrochilum glumaceum

HAY-SCENTED ORCHID

↔ 8–24 in (20–60 cm) ↑ 8–16 in (20–40 cm)
♀ ☼ ◆/◇ ❀ ▭

From the Philippines. Egg-shaped
pseudobulbs with 1 leaf. Up to 60
flowers form on inflorescence in
winter–early spring. Flowers with very
pointed sepals and petals, white to
cream, with a wide color range in lip,
which may be orange, yellow, green,
or brown.

Dendrochilum latifolium

Dendrochilum arachnites

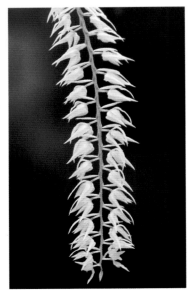

Dendrochilum glumaceum

Dendrochilum latifolium

↔ 8–20 in (20–50 cm) ↕ 6–20 in (15–50 cm)
♀ ☼ ◆/◇ ❀ ☖

From the Philippines; one of the
larger species. Single leaf, to 16 in
(40 cm) long; inflorescence longer
than leaves, with up to 60 flowers in
summer. Flowers scented, creamish
green with brown lip.

Dendrochilum niveum

↔ 6–8 in (15–20 cm) ↕ 6–8 in (15–20 cm)
♀ ☀ ◆ ❀ ☖

From the Philippines. Pseudobulbs to
1¼ in (30 mm) tall, ovoid; single leaf,
to 7 in (18 cm) long, mid-vein prominent on underside. Inflorescences
appear with new growth, longer than
new leaves, with about 30 flowers in
winter. Flowers very small, scented,
pure white with a pale yellow lip.

Dendrochilum saccolabium

↔ 8–24 in (20–60 cm) ↕ 8–16 in (20–40 cm)
♀ ☼ ◆ ❀ ☖

Spectacular and horticulturally attractive species from the Philippines.

Arching inflorescences with up to
40 glossy, round, dull to bright red
flowers, in winter.

Dendrochilum simile

syn. *Acoridium simile*

↔ 20–30 in (50–75 cm) ↕ 20–30 in
(50–75 cm) ♀ ☀ ◆ ❀ ☖

From Peninsular Malaysia, and
Sumatra and Java in Indonesia. Single
leaf to 14 in (35 cm) long. Inflorescences erect at first then drooping,
about 16 in (40 cm) long, with many
flowers in winter–spring. Small
flowers, greenish-yellow with brown
marking on lip.

Dendrochilum tenellum

↔ 8–32 in (20–80 cm) ↕ 8–16 in (20–40 cm)
♀ ☼ ◆ ❀ ☖

From the Philippines; forms large
clumps on moss-covered rainforest
trees. One of the most "unorchid-like"
species in foliage, with very fine,
cylindrical, grass-like leaves. Tiny
white to cream flowers in late winter–
early spring.

Dendrochilum niveum

Dendrochilum simile

Dendrochilum tenellum

D

Dimorphorchis lowii

Dichaea sodiroi

Dichaea glauca

DIAPHANANTHE

syn. *Sarcorhynchus*

This genus of about 20 small to medium-sized monopodial epiphytes is confined to mainland Africa and the islands in the Gulf of Guinea. Many species that were previously included in *Diaphananthe* are now placed in *Rhipidoglossum*. Plants have long or short stems, numerous roots often with white streaks noticeable when wet, and small or large leaves. Inflorescences are racemose, with small or medium-sized translucent flowers, which are white, green, yellow, or straw-colored. The name is derived from the Greek *diaphanos*, meaning transparent, and *anthos*, meaning flower, referring to the translucent quality of the flowers.

CULTIVATION: Short-stemmed species can be grown in pots in a medium bark-based compost, but those with long stems and numerous roots do better mounted on bark. Almost all require intermediate to warm conditions with fairly heavy shade and high humidity. When not actively growing, they should be kept drier but not allowed to dry out completely. Propagate from seed.

Diaphananthe fragrantissima

↔ 10–12 in (25–30 cm)   ↑ 20–30 in (50–75 cm)   ♀ ☀ ◆/◇ ❀ ▱

Robust species from eastern tropical Africa and South Africa. Stems pendent, to 20 in (50 cm) long; leaves narrow, pendent, fleshy, dull green, 4–16 in (10–40 cm) long. Inflorescences pendent, 8–24 in (20–60 cm) long, densely arranged with many flowers, mainly in spring. Flowers translucent cream or yellow-green, scented, about 1 in (25 mm) wide.

DICHAEA

This is a genus of over 120 species of epiphytes and lithophytes from Central America and the northern half of South America. They live in mist forests, growing on trees co-existing with abundant mosses. Some species have pendent growth habit; others are erect. These plants lack pseudobulbs, but have thickened stems that may branch, with closely arranged short leaves in 2 ranks. The plants tend to hug the host and rarely venture into mid-air. The spent leaves are persistent. The somewhat cup-shaped but colorful blooms are produced singly from nodes at the base of the leaves. Many species have highly fragrant blooms that are pollinated by native bees. This is a poorly studied genus in need of taxonomic revision.

CULTIVATION: These moisture-loving species are best grown in shade. Pendent species do best on tree-fern mounts, and the erect species in pots. The plants should not be exposed to direct sunlight or allowed to become dry for an extended period. Propagate by division of large plants.

Dichaea glauca

↔ 6–8 in (15–20 cm)   ↑ 16–24 in (40–60 cm)   ♀ ☀ ◆ ❀ ▱/↘

From the West Indies and Central America. Stems leafy, erect or pendent.

Leaves overlapping, to 3 in (8 cm) long, oblong, gray-green. Single-flowered inflorescences, to 1 in (25 mm) long, borne near top of stems. Flowers scented, about ¾ in (18 mm) across, off white with mauve or lavender marks. Spring-flowering.

Dichaea muricata

↔ 4–5 in (10–12 cm) ↕ 12–18 in (30–45 cm) ♀ ☀ ◆ ▽

From Jamaica and Hispaniola; has been confused with other species in the past. Stems erect, somewhat flattened, covered with leaves and leaf sheaths; leaves overlapping, oblong, to around 1½ in (35 mm) long. Inflorescence to 1 in (25 mm) long, with a single flower in winter. Flowers scented, whitish, about 1 in (25 mm) in diameter.

Dichaea pendula

↔ 12–20 in (30–50 cm) ↕ 16–24 in (40–60 cm) ♀ ☀ ◆ ▨

From the West Indies and Central America. Pendent leafy stems; overlapping leaves, to 2 in (5 cm) long. Flowers about 1 in (25 mm) across, yellowish with lilac markings; lip lilac. Spring-flowering.

Dichaea sodiroi

↔ 4–8 in (10–20 cm) ↕ 3–20 in (8–50 cm) ♀ ☀ ◆/◇ ❀ ▨

Pendulous orchid from Ecuador and Peru. Individual blooms, less than ¾ in (18 mm), borne throughout the year. Flower color is a montage of translucent greens, purples, and white.

DIMORPHORCHIS

A truly magnificent genus containing 2 species. They are found in Borneo, in Sarawak, where they grow in hot, humid, coastal forests on trunks and branches over rivers, and in neighboring Sabah, where they favor mountainous areas up to 1,970 ft (600 m). These orchids grow to a huge size and the enormous inflorescence bears 2 different types of flowers, hence the name, from the Greek *di-*, two, and *morphe*, shape. They became famous when a 7 ft (2 m) specimen in the collection of Lord Rothschild flowered in June 1887 with 16 inflorescences and 650 flowers! CULTIVATION: Grow in large containers, filled with chunks of charcoal, bricks, or other coarse material. During the growing season, the plants need warmth and frequent watering. A resting period with much reduced watering is essential for the induction of flowering. Only mature plants flower. Propagation is by division.

Dimorphorchis lowii

syns *Arachnanthe lowii, Vanda lowii, Vandopsis lowii*

↔ 40–60 in (100–150 cm) ↕ 60–80 in (150–200 cm) ♀ ❉ ◆ ❀ ▽

From Borneo. Huge stems to 7 ft (2 m) long; multiple branches from base. Leaves to 27 in (70 cm) long. Mature plants develop multiple inflorescences, each to 10 ft (3 m) long, with up to 40 flowers, in summer. Flowers on lower part of raceme are yellowish with small purple spots and do not open; upper flowers open fully, and are deeply spotted with chocolate brown.

DIPLOCAULOBIUM

This genus contains around 100 species of small to medium-sized epiphytic or sometimes lithophytic plants related to *Dendrobium*, occurring in Malaysia, New Guinea, the Pacific Islands, and northeastern Australia. The single-leafed pseudobulbs are either swollen at the base and cylindrical above, set closely on the rhizome, or rather flattened and set apart. The inflorescence is axillary and has 1 flower. The flowers are small to medium-sized, dull-colored or showy, but last for only one day. The sepals and petals are somewhat similar, the lip may be 3-lobed. CULTIVATION: Most species of *Diplocaulobium* are fairly compact and can be grown in pots or baskets in a standard bark mixture, or mounted. Although they need plenty of water while growing actively, good drainage is essential. Propagate by division.

Diplocaulobium aratriferum

↔ 5–6 in (12–15 cm) ↕ 5–6 in (12–15 cm) ♀ ❉ ◆/◇ ▽/▨

Compact plants from New Guinea. Flowers about 4 in (10 cm) across, spidery looking with narrow lateral sepals about 3 in (8 cm) long, white or cream, lip marked with yellow and maroon. Flowers off and on throughout year.

DIPTERANTHUS

This is a South American genus of about a dozen small-growing, sympodial, epiphytic species, from the fringes of montane forests. They generally produce short inflorescences of primarily yellow insect-like blooms. They have tiny pseudobulbs and fans of bright green flattened leaves. Some members of the genus have been placed in the genus *Zygostates* by some taxonomists. CULTIVATION: These twig epiphytes enjoy intermediate and humid conditions and must have good air circulation. They are best grown on small cork or tree-fern slabs in bright shady conditions. Direct sunlight is to be avoided. They appreciate copious watering, and should not be allowed

Dipteranthus estradae

to dry out for an extended period of time. Propagate by division of mature multigrowth plants.

Dipteranthus estradae

↔ 1½–4 in (3.5–10 cm) ↕ ¾–3 in (1.8–8 cm) ♀ ☀ ◆ ❀ ▨

From Ecuador. Arching to pendulous inflorescences of up to 16 bright yellow blooms, less than ½ in (12 mm) tall. Flowers in winter–early spring. Blooms bear a superficial similarity to the unrelated *Oncidium cheirophorum*.

Diplocaulobium aratriferum

DISA

Primarily a South African terrestrial orchid genus with over 100 species. While the famous *D. uniflora*, known colloquially as "The Pride of Table Mountain," is well known to orchid growers, the majority of the species are only of botanical interest and few of these are in cultivation. In the wild, they are often seen growing on the fringes of marshlands or on the banks of flowing streams, in substrates that generally are low in nitrogen content, and they often grow in association with sphagnum moss. There have been numerous attractive hybrids bred, particularly over the past decade. Many of these have a high percentage of *D. uniflora* in their pedigree, and generally exhibit hybrid vigor. The color range is also expanding, with whites, lemons, and pinks now supplementing the reds and oranges.

CULTIVATION: Live sphagnum moss has proved the best medium for cultivated plants. They are very particular about water quality, and rainwater is best. The plants should be kept moist all year. Do not sit them in trays of water for extended periods. Some growers have had success with "waterwell" containers. Mature specimens may produce daughter plants at the edge of the pot (or at times through the drainage holes!). These can be potted separately when they are large enough to handle. Repot the plants annually into fresh moss a few months after the main summer flowering period. They enjoy cool to intermediate conditions. Propagate by division.

Disa uniflora

Disa lugens

Diuris maculata

Disa aurata

syn. *Disa tripetaloides var. aurata*
↔ 8–12 in (20–30 cm)   ↕ 4–24 (10–60 cm)
¥ ☼ ◇ ❈ ▽

Evergreen species from the provinces of Western Cape, Eastern Cape, Northern Cape, and the western half of North-West, South Africa. Leaves in basal rosette, to 6 in (15 cm) long. Flowers in summer. Very similar to *D. tripetaloides* but flowers bright yellow and slightly larger.

Disa cardinalis

↔ 4–8 in (10–20 cm)   ↕ 12–27 in (30–70 cm)
¥ ☼ ◇ ❈ ▽

From the provinces of Western Cape, Eastern Cape, Northern Cape, and the western half of North-West, South Africa; evergreen species, sometimes spreading by stolons. Leaves in basal rosette, 2–4 in (5–10 cm) long. Raceme fairly densely arranged with up to 25 flowers in spring–summer. Flowers bright red, about 2 in (5 cm) across, dorsal sepal forming a hood with a conical spur.

Disa lugens

↔ 1½–4 in (3.5–10 cm)   ↕ 18–40 in (45–100 cm)   ¥ ☼/☽ ◇ ❈ ▽

Endemic to South Africa; becoming rare in the wild. Upright to arching inflorescences of up to 20 blooms, in late spring. Flowers 1¼ in (30 mm) tall, blue to lilac, lip with distinctive yellow beard. This species has proved difficult to maintain in cultivation.

Disa racemosa

↔ 3–5 in (8–12 cm)   ↕ 3–40 in (8–100 cm)
¥ ☼ ◇ ❈ ▽

Evergreen species, Found in the same areas in South Africa as *D. aurata*. Leaves to 4 in (10 cm) long, in basal rosette. Raceme loosely or densely arranged with 2 to 12 flowers in summer. Flowers small, white or mauve. Can be difficult in cultivation.

Disa tripetaloides

↔ 8–12 in (20–30 cm)   ↕ 4–20 in (10–50 cm)
¥ ☼ ◇ ❈ ▽

From the provinces of Western Cape, Eastern Cape, Northern Cape, the western half of North-West, and KwaZulu-Natal, South Africa; evergreen plants, spreading by stolons. Leaves in basal rosette, each to 6 in (15 cm) long. Raceme carries up to 25 flowers, each to 1 in (25 mm) across, white, fading to pink. Plants from KwaZulu-Natal flower in winter, remainder flower in summer.

Disa uniflora ★

↔ 4–10 in (10–25 cm)   ↕ 6–32 in (15–80 cm)
¥ ☼/☽ ◇ ❈ ▽

Magnificent species from South Africa. Despite its specific name, it can produce up to 6 flowers on an erect inflorescence during summer. Large flowers, color varies from brilliant scarlet-red through various shades of orange, to rare yellow (lutea) forms.

Disa Hybrids

↔ 4–10 in (10–25 cm)   ↕ 8–32 in (20–80 cm)
¥ ☼/☽ ◇ ❈ ▽

The following hybrids have been primarily bred from the popular and award-winning *D. uniflora*, developed to improve flower count and quality, as well as to expand the range of colors. Summer-flowering. **Diores**, hybrid between *D. uniflora* and *D. Veitchii*, long-lasting flowers, popular for cutting; **Kewbett**, hybrid between *D. Betty's Bay* and *D. Kewensis*; **Kewensis**, hybrid of *D. uniflora* and *D. tripetaloides*; and **Watsonii**, hybrid of *D. uniflora* and *D. Kewensis*.

DIURIS

DONKEY ORCHIDS, DOUBLETAILS

A genus of Australian deciduous terrestrial orchids with close to 100 species. They generally grow during autumn and winter, then bloom in spring, reverting to dormant tubers during the hot dry summers. They produce only a few grass-like leaves, and upright scapes of up to a dozen flowers, depending on the species. Blooms are generally yellow, with other combinations of colors, including browns, purples, and reds. There are also pink- and white-flowered species. Most are pollinated, in the wild, by native bees, which mistake the blooms for superficially similar (but unrelated) pea-flowers. CULTIVATION: Grow in a well-drained terrestrial mix, up to 50 percent of coarse gritty sand. They enjoy bright light and detest stagnant conditions. Repot the dormant tubers in summer. These are orchids for specialist collectors. Propagate from seed.

Diuris maculata

↔ 4–8 in (10–20 cm) ↕ 4–16 in (10–40 cm)

Variable species from Australia. Leaves to 10 in (25 cm) long. Up to 8 blooms produced on an erect inflorescence in early spring. Yellow to orange and brown blooms, heavily spotted, dark brown on outer surface of petals.

Disa Diores

Disa Watsonii

Disa Kewbett

Disa Kewensis

DOCKRILLIA

PENCIL ORCHID

Dockrillia is essentially an Australian and New Guinean genus consisting of about 30 sympodial orchids, with outlying populations throughout parts of the Pacific Islands. This genus, only recently recognized, loosely accommodates the previously so-called "terete-leafed" *Dendrobium* species. The principal characteristics that separate *Dockrillia* from *Dendrobium* include a lack of pseudobulbs, succulent leaves (which are often terete and circular in cross-section), and flowers that are generally nonresupinate (not upside down), with the lip uppermost, making it easy to distinguish between the 2 genera. The genus name commemorates the well-known Australian orchidologist, Alick Dockrill.

CULTIVATION: *Dockrillia* species are among the easiest of orchids to cultivate, and may be treated in many ways. The larger-growing pendent species grow well on generous slabs of tree fern or cork, where they will be happy for many years and will even tolerate a degree of neglect. Some of the species that clump at the base may be grown in small pots or wooden baskets, in a bark-based medium.

They have a vigorous root system, which prefers not to be disturbed. They grow and bloom in quite strong light, and tolerate a wide range of temperatures. However, some of the mountain species will not thrive (and will rarely bloom) in tropical lowland conditions. Propagation is by division.

Dockrillia cucumerina

syn. *Dendrobium cucumerinum*
CUCUMBER ORCHID, GHERKIN ORCHID
↔ 6–10 in (15–25 cm) ↕ 1½–2 in (3.5–5 cm)
♀ ☀ ◆/◇ ⋙

Unusual species from New South Wales and Queensland in eastern Australia. Dark green, bumpy, succulent leaves that look like gherkins. Flowers up to 1 in (25 mm) wide, in clusters of up to 12, cream with maroon near base of segments and on undulate lip. Blooms anytime from late spring to summer. Can be difficult in cultivation.

Dockrillia linguiformis

syn. *Dendrobium linguiforme*
THUMBNAIL ORCHID, TONGUE ORCHID
↔ 4–24 in (10–60 cm) ↕ 1–5 in (2.5–12 cm)
♀/∧ ☼/☀ ◆/◇ ❈ ⋙

Variable Australian orchid; type species for the genus. Great creeping foliage plant. Fleshy leaves to just over ½ in (35 mm) long. Bears short sprays of feathery blooms, opening greenish yellow, ageing to white within a few days, in spring. Larger but narrower blooms than the related and rough-leafed *D. nugentii*.

Dockrillia schoenina

syn. *Dendrobium beckleri*
↔ 4–20 in (10–50 cm) ↕ 4–32 in (10–80 cm)
♀ ☼/☀ ◆/◇ ❈ ⋙

From eastern Australia; untidy growth habit, with each new cylindrical leaf smaller than the previous. Fragrant, cream to green, striated blooms, 1¼ in (30 mm), produced either singly or in pairs, in spring. Purple, green, and white lip, with ruffled fringe.

Dockrillia striolata ★

syn. *Dendrobium striolatum*
↔ 4–20 in (10–50 cm) ↕ 4–30 in (10–75 cm)
∧ ☼/☀ ◇ ❈ ❈ ⊡/⋙

Variable clump-forming orchid from southeastern Australia, mainly found growing in mountain regions. Pendulous leaves turn deep purple in full sun. Flowers greenish yellow to mushroom pink, darker striations on back of blooms, contrasting pure white lip with frilled edges. Blooms in late spring. Cold tolerant, plants in some locations periodically dusted with snow. Easy to grow, but difficult to flower in subtropical and tropical climates.

Dockrillia teretifolia

syn. *Dendrobium teretifolium*
BRIDAL VEIL ORCHID
↔ 1–3 ft (0.3–0.9 m) ↕ 1–10 ft (0.3–3 m)
♀ ☼/☀ ◆/◇ ❈ ⊡/⋙

Species from eastern Australia; arguably most outstanding species in genus. Pendulous leaves to 24 in (60 cm) long. Masses of fragrant, white to greenish cream, slender, feathery blooms, in late winter–early spring. Does best in position with good air circulation.

Dockrillia wassellii

syn. *Dendrobium wassellii*
↔ 2½–8 in (6–20 cm) ↕ 2½–6 in (6–15 cm)
♀ ☼/☀ ◆/◆ ❈ ⋙

Adaptable species from far northern Queensland, Australia; can be grown in a range of climatic conditions. Attractive, succulent, erect leaves. Up to 50 densely crowded, slender, white blooms with yellow lip, on upright inflorescences. Blooms spasmodically during warmer months.

Dockrillia linguiformis

D

Dockrillia striolata, in the wild, Victoria, Australia

Dockrillia wassellii

Dockrillia cucumerina, leaves

Dockrillia schoenina

Dracula chimaera

Dracula gigas 'Mamie'

Dracula polyphemus

Dracula Quasimodo

DRACULA

These are cool-growing sympodial orchids related to *Masdevallia*, and previously placed within this large diverse genus. Most of the 100 or so species live in the moist high cloud forests of western Colombia and Ecuador. Being close to the equator, there are no seasons, so plants experience the same weather conditions and day length all year. The plant habit is very similar for most of the species, with a single, somewhat fleshy,

upright leaf that may be paddle-shaped. Blooms are outstanding; you can see "faces" in many flowers, with the tiny petals becoming the "eyes." Increasing numbers of *Dracula* hybrids are being produced, which are easier to grow. Combinations with *Masdevallia* have created the genus *Dracuvallia*.

CULTIVATION: These orchids need cool conditions, and will deteriorate quickly if conditions do not suit them. They do not like daytime

temperatures rising above 79°F (26°C), and prefer a nighttime minimum of 54°F (12°C). This very narrow range must be observed if cultivated plants are to thrive. They also demand constant air movement and high humidity. Most successful growers cultivate plants in live sphagnum moss. Because many species have a descending inflorescence, suspended baskets or mesh pots are used. Seventy percent shade suits most species; they will not take bright sunlight, particularly in combination with high temperatures. Growers often modify or create new growing enclosures just to house this genus, because of their large, spectacular, bizarre flowers. Blooms collapse in high temperatures but can be rehydrated by misting with cold water. Propagate by division.

Dracula bella
syn. *Masdevallia bella*
↔ 10–12 in (25–30 cm) ↕ 7–12 in (18–30 cm)

From shady, moist, montane forests of Colombia. Lacks pseudobulbs; erect, thin, narrowly oblong leaves, in tufts. Descending spikes with triangular flowers, 5–7 in (12–18 cm) wide, yellowish overlaid with red; long sepal tails, very small petals, large, white, hinged, mushroom-like lip. Blooms sporadically throughout year. Best grown under cool conditions in baskets with moss.

Dracula Cafe Mocha
↔ 8–16 in (20–40 cm) ↕ 8–14 in (20–35 cm)

Hybrid between *D.* Quasimodo and *D. tubeana*. Yellow blooms with red speckling, borne in winter–spring. Draculas must not be allowed to dry out, and they detest direct sunlight.

Dracula chimaera
syn. *Masdevallia chimaera*
↔ 12–16 in (30–40 cm) ↕ 7–18 in (18–45 cm)

Endemic to Colombia; grows in moist, shady, mountainous forests; may have largest flowers in the genus. Lacks pseudobulbs; thin erect leaves in tufts. Flowers large to very large, 12–18 in (30–45 cm) long including sepal tails; very variable color but usually light to dark brown with yellow mottling, covered in bristly hairs. Tiny petals, lip white to pink, one of few draculas with unhinged lip. Blooms sporadically throughout year. Best cultivated in baskets due to spike habit.

Dracula gigas
syn. *Masdevallia gigas*
↔ 10–14 in (25–35 cm) ↕ 14–18 in (35–45 cm)

From Colombia and Ecuador; grows in cool mountain forests. Thin narrow leaves in tufts. Semi-erect spike has a few sequential flowers that face down and bloom sporadically throughout year. Flowers 6–8 in (15–20 cm) in size, pinkish-brown, darker sepal tails, hinged white lip. Grows well in baskets with cool moist conditions. 'Mamie', yellowish brown flowers.

Dracula polyphemus
syn. *Masdevallia polyphemus*
↔ 12–16 in (30–40 cm) ↕ 20–24 in (50–60 cm)

Endemic to Ecuador; grows in cool, moist, montane forests. Narrow oblong leaves, thin in texture, growing in tufts. Spikes horizontal to pendent with several sequential blooms. Flowers large, 8–12 in (20–30 cm) long, reddish with white markings in center; long tails triangular and are very flat. Nearly ever-blooming.

Dracula Cafe Mocha

Dracula Quasimodo

↔ 8–16 in (20–40 cm) ↕ 8–14 in (20–35 cm)
♀ ☀ ◆/◇ ❄ ▽

Primary hybrid between *D. gigas* and *D. bella*. Flowers pale yellow with red speckling borne in winter–spring. Net basket culture is required to allow the thin pendulous spikes to penetrate to produce these bizarre blooms.

Dracula tubeana

↔ 4–16 in (10–40 cm) ↕ 4–16 in (10–40 cm)
♀ ☀ ◆ ❄ ▽

Species from Ecuador. Medium-sized, creamy white blooms, with distinct red-brown border and white lip; sepals with fine hairs on edges. Spring-blooming.

Dracula vampira

syn. *Masdevallia vampira*

↔ 12–16 in (30–40 cm) ↕ 20–24 in (50–60 cm) ♀ ☀ ◆/◇ ❄ ▽

Spectacular species from Ecuador; found growing in moist mountainous forests. Thin narrowly oblong leaves in tufts. Spike horizontal to descending, with several sequential blooms. Flowers large, 10–14 in (25–35 cm) in size, with blackish and white stripes on sepals, tiny petals, pinkish lip. Almost always in bloom. **'Bela Lugosi'**, highly awarded clone, very large full-shaped flowers.

Dracula velutina

↔ 4–16 in (10–40 cm) ↕ 4–16 in (10–40 cm)
♀ ☀ ◆/◇ ❄ ▽

From Colombia; smaller-flowered species. Narrow leaves. White blooms with dark purple tails attached to sepals. Blooms produced sequentially in spring–summer.

DRAKAEA

HAMMER ORCHID

This genus of deciduous terrestrial orchids consists of about 10 species

Drakaea glyptodon

that are endemic to southwestern Western Australia. Most species are found in open heathland and clearings in deep sand. They are known as hammer orchids on account of their predominant, hinged, insect-like lips that deceive their pollinators, who attempt to mate with the flower—this is known as pseudocopulation. The thynnid wasp attempts to carry off the lip, which it thinks is a potential mate, and in doing so is thrust into the reproductive parts of the bloom. The lip is not only wasp-like in appearance, but also gives off a similar scent as the insect. The rest of the bloom is most insignificant, and from a distance gives the impression that the lip is airborne. These orchids often feature on documentaries on specialist flower pollination. CULTIVATION: Despite many and various attempts at cultivating these species, the general response is for these specialist and highly evolved plants to fade away after a couple of seasons. They are best observed and left in their native habitat.

Drakaea glyptodon

↔ ½–1½ in (12–35 mm) ↕ 4–14 in (10–35 cm) ⚲ ☼/☀ ◆/◇ ❄ ▽

From southwestern Australia; the most common and well-known of the spring-flowering hammer orchids. Tiny ground-hugging leaf; long inflorescence bears a single bizarre bloom, 1¼ in (30 mm) in size, with a lip that mimics its wasp pollinator.

Dracula velutina

Dracula tubeana

DRYADELLA

syn. *Trigonanthe*

About 30 species of *Masdevallia* were separated to form this genus. They are found from Guatemala to Brazil, where they grow epiphytically in large clumps in moist cloud forests at altitudes of 1,330–8,200 ft (400–2,500 m). The creeping rhizome bears single leaves with each shoot and small flowers, which are often hidden in the foliage.

Dryadella zebrina

CULTIVATION: Keep moist and humid all year round without any resting period. Does equally well in shallow pots in a fine organic substrate or on a slab with a layer of living moss. Propagation is by division of larger clumps.

Dryadella edwallii

syns *Masdevallia edwallii*, *Trigonanthe edwallii*

↔ 1–2 in (2.5–5 cm) ↑ 1–2 in (2.5–5 cm)

Miniature species found in moist forests in Brazil. Dark green leathery leaves to 3 in (8 cm) in length. Yellowish flowers, spotted with purplish brown, about 1 in (25 mm) across, mostly in summer and occasionally at other times of year.

Dryadella pusiola

syns *Dryadella albicans*, *Masdevallia albicans*

↔ 2–3 in (5–8 cm) ↑ 2½–3 in (6–8 cm)

Diminutive species from Ecuador; found in moist forests. Lacks pseudobulbs; tufts of linear thickened leaves. Spikes shorter than leaves. Flowers small, under ¾ in (18 mm) in size, triangular, white, with short sepal tails. Blooms randomly throughout year. Grows well potted or mounted, with moss.

Dryadella zebrina

syn. *Masdevallia zebrina*

↔ 1½–2 in (3.5–5 cm) ↑ 2–2½ in (5–6 cm)

Miniature species from southeast Brazil; found in shaded humid forests. Tufts of linear leaves, sometimes with purple pigment. Small flowers, less than ½ in (12 mm) in size, very triangular with short sepal tails, greenish-yellow, striped and spotted with reddish brown. Blooms randomly. Grows well potted or mounted.

DYAKIA

This monotypic monopodial orchid genus from Borneo was previously included within *Ascocentrum*. It differs in its floral structure, as well as in its leaves, which are broad and flat, rather than the strongly channeled leaves of *Ascocentrum* species. Fragrant flowers are borne on erect racemes.

CULTIVATION: These epiphytes are quite compact and need warm to hot, moist conditions throughout the year. They grow best either in small pots or on cork mounts. Propagate by division.

Dyakia hendersoniana

Dyakia hendersoniana ★

syn. *Ascocentrum hendersoniana*

↔ 2½–6 in (6–15 cm) ↑ 3–8 in (8–20 cm)

From Borneo. Upright, densely packed spikes bear vivid rose to magenta flowers with a contrasting white lip. Blooms in warmer months, year-round in tropics.

Dryadella pusiola

ELYTHRANTHERA
ENAMEL ORCHIDS

This is a genus of 2 species of deciduous terrestrial orchids that are closely related to the genera *Glossodia* and *Caladenia*. They are endemic to the southwestern corner of Western Australia, growing in coastal heath and *Banksia* woodland. They have a single green leaf that is up to 3 in (8 cm) long in both species, and is often stained purple on the underside. They produce up to 4 flowers on an upright slender inflorescence. Blooming is markedly more profuse following summer fires.

CULTIVATION: Unfortunately these orchids have been extremely difficult to maintain in cultivation and should be left in their natural habitat.

Elythranthera brunonis
PURPLE ENAMEL ORCHID

↔ 1–3 in (2.5–8 cm) ↕ 6–12 in (15–30 cm)
❦ ☼/☀ ◆/◇ ❄ ⛉

From southwestern Australia; one of Western Australia's most recognizable and popular wildflowers. Very glossy purple blooms, to 1¼ in (30 mm) across, in spring.

ENCYCLIA

This complex genus contains over 200 sympodial orchids from Mexico, and Central and South America, most of which are intermediate- to warm-growing species. This genus was once included within the related *Epidendrum*. Often clumping plants with a distinct pseudobulb, they are usually topped with 2 or 3 leaves. Recently, sections of *Encyclia* have been transferred to separate genera. In 1998 a large group of the "cockleshell" *Encyclia* species was moved into the genus *Prosthechea*. This met with some resistance, even though they are easily recognized by their "upside down" flowers and lip that displays varying degrees of dark purple striation. Most species flower in summer and are also highly fragrant.

CULTIVATION: *Encyclia* species are readily grown, on cork slabs or potted in a well-drained bark-based medium. Most species have a dormant period from late autumn to early spring. The majority enjoy bright light conditions. Propagate by division.

Encyclia alata

↔ 8–20 in (20–50 cm) ↕ 8–36 in (20–90 cm)
♀ ☼/☀ ◆/◇ ❄ ⛉/⛰

From Central America. Numerous forms, varying widely in number of blooms and size. Conical pseudobulbs. Light brown flowers with a white and yellow lip with deep purple striations, on tall inflorescences, in summer. *E. a.* subsp. *virella* (syn. *E. belizensis*), up to 16 fragrant long-lived flowers, mustard yellow with a brown overlay, 1½ in (35 mm) across.

Encyclia hanburyi

↔ 8–20 in (20–50 cm) ↕ 8–27 in (20–70 cm)
♀ ☼/☀ ◆/◇ ❄ ⛉/⛰

From Mexico. Clusters of conical pseudobulbs; leaves to 10 in (25 cm) long. Upright spikes of brown flowers, 1½ in (35 mm) wide, contrasting rosy purple lip, in spring–summer.

Encyclia randii

↔ 12–24 in (30–60 cm) ↕ 12–24 in (30–60 cm) ♀ ☀ ◆/◇ ❄ ⛉/⛰

From Brazil and Colombia. Onion-shaped pseudobulbs, 2 or 3 long-lived leathery leaves at apex. Up to 12 blooms are produced in spring–summer. Flowers 1½ in (35 mm) in size; chocolate brown petals and sepals, pure white lip stained purple.

Elythranthera brunonis

Encyclia alata subsp. *virella*

Encyclia randii

Encyclia hanburyi

E

EPIBLASTUS

This is a small group of about 15 cool- to intermediate-growing, somewhat succulent, sympodial orchids. They come from higher areas of Sulawesi in Indonesia, New Guinea, and parts of the Pacific Islands. They have branching rhizomes and in the wild they produce clusters of brightly colored blooms throughout the cooler months of the year. In cultivation most species bloom from autumn to early spring.
CULTIVATION: These uncommon species perform best in pots of sphagnum moss; larger plants can be grown on tree-fern rafts, as long as the substrate is kept moist. These plants dislike hot dry conditions and must be kept moist in a buoyant atmosphere. Propagation is by division.

Epicattleya Siam Jade

Epiblastus basalis
↔ 4–12 in (10–30 cm)   ↕ 4–12 in (10–30 cm)
🌱/🌿 ☀ ◆ ❄ ▢/🗻

Native of New Guinea; the species most frequently seen in cultivation. Small clusters of waxy bright red blooms, just over ½ in (12 mm) in diameter, in spring.

EPICATTLEYA

This artificial bigeneric sympodial hybrid between *Epidendrum* and *Cattleya* has produced a range of novelty hybrids that are often vigorous and free flowering. Many of the registered combinations involve members of the genus *Encyclia*, previously included within *Epidendrum*. *Epicattleya* hybrids are compact-growing orchids. The showy blooms are often produced in large numbers and are frequently pleasantly fragrant.
CULTIVATION: These orchids grow well in small terracotta or plastic pots, in baskets, or on slabs, but must dry out fully between waterings. They enjoy high light and intermediate to warm temperatures, and can take cool temperatures in winter if kept dry. Propagate by division.

Epicattleya Purple Glory 'Moir's Pride'
↔ –6–16 in (15–40 cm)   ↕ 8–20 in (20–50 cm)   ♀ ☀ ◆/◈ ❄ ▢/🗻

Primary hybrid between *Encyclia adenocaula* (previously known as *Epidendrum nemorale*) and *Cattleya violacea*. Produces upright inflorescences of up to 6 attractive pink to purple blooms that are 4 in (10 cm) across the petals.

Epicattleya Siam Jade
↔ 4–16 in (10–40 cm)   ↕ 8–16 in (20–40 cm)   ♀ ☀/☀ ◆/◈/◇ ❄ ▢/🗻

Popular hybrid resulting from the combination of 7 different orchid species; most prominent species are the albino form of *Cattleya guttata* and the green and white *Euchile mariae* (previously well-known as *Encyclia mariae*). Bears green and white flowers in spring.

Epiblastus basalis

Epicattleya Purple Glory 'Moir's Pride'

Epidendrum species

Epidendrum barbeyanum

Epidendrum anceps

EPIDENDRUM

This is a large sympodial orchid genus from southern USA, Mexico, and Central and South America, with more than 1,000 recognized species. Many gardeners are familiar with "crucifix" orchids, which are actually "reed-stem" *Epidendrum* species and their hybrids. While most species have thin reed-like stems, some have thickened stems that form functional pseudobulbs. Many of these species grow as terrestrials among grasses in bright positions, frequently in full sun. The majority of the species, however, occur as lithophytes or epiphytes. *Epidendrum* belongs to the same group of genera as *Brassavola*, *Cattleya*, *Encyclia*, *Laelia*, *Rhyncholaelia*, and *Sophronitis*.

CULTIVATION: As the various species come from a range of altitudes, there would be some to suit most frost-free climates, but most enjoy bright and warm conditions. The "reed-stem" or "crucifix" types may be grown in the ground in frost-free climates. Some species have a dormancy period, while many are in continual growth. Many species may be grown in a free-draining bark-based medium or tied onto slabs of cork or tree fern. Propagation is by division.

Epidendrum anceps

↔ 16–20 in (40–50 cm) ↑ 24–36 in (60–90 cm) ♀/⋀ ☀ ◆/◇ ❄ ▭/≋

Species found in wet forests of the American tropics, from south Florida in the USA, and Mexico, south to

Brazil and Peru. Cane-like pseudobulbs, and about 4 green to purple leaves. Branched inflorescences produce flowers in spring–summer for several years. Flowers less than ¾ in (18 mm) each, in clusters, and very variable in color, usually greenish or yellowish brown to purple.

Epidendrum barbeyanum

↔ 4–10 in (10–25 cm) ↑ 4–10 in (10–25 cm) ♀ ☀ ◆/◇ ❄ ▭/≋

Native of Central America. Produces succulent growths that bear small showy heads of apple green flowers, 2 in (5 cm) across, with broad lips, in spring–summer. In cultivation, this orchid prefers moist conditions throughout the year.

Epidendrum ciliare

↔ 8–36 in (20–90 cm) ↑ 8–24 in (20–60 cm) ♀ ☼/☀ ◆/◇ ❄ ▭/≋

From Central America; variable species. Resembles a cattleya in growth habit, but without the telltale floral sheath. Can produce inflorescences of up to 8 flowers in summer and autumn. Blooms spidery, green, 4 in (10 cm) in size; white lip. Needs strong light and a dry winter rest to bloom.

Epidendrum ibaguense

↔ 8–48 in (20–120 cm) ↑ 8–48 in (20–120 cm) ♀/⋎ ☼/☀ ◆/◇/◇ ❄ ▭

From Central and South America. Common and widespread species; the classic "reed-stem" or "crucifix" orchid that is popular in horticulture.

Spherical heads of red to orange blooms, 1¼ in (30 mm) across; modified yellowish lip. Requires strong light; will continue to bloom throughout the year in favorable conditions.

Epidendrum ilense ★

↔ 8–24 in (20–60 cm) ↑ 8–48 in (20–120 cm) ♀ ☀ ◆ ❄ ▭/≋

Amazing species from Ecuador. Small bunches of bizarre flowers, 1½ in (35 mm) in size, hang down from tall pseudobulbs. Somewhat bland pinkish green petals and sepals, with a highly specialized white lip fringed with long fine hairs. Requires consistently warm moist conditions; large plants may flower constantly, as they re-bloom from the same stem for many years.

Epidendrum ciliare

Epidendrum ibaguense

Epidendrum ilense

Epidendrum lacustre

↔ 12–24 in (30–60 cm) ↑ 12–44 in (30–110 cm) ✿ ☼/◑ ◆/◇ ❀ ☂

From Venezuela; "reed-stem" orchid, often grows in grasslands and disturbed sites. Leafy pseudobulbs; upright inflorescence emerges from top of pseudobulb, and bears clusters of up to 10 flowers in summer. Blooms 1½ in (35 mm) wide, bright green, with predominantly white lip.

Epidendrum medusae

syn. *Nanodes medusae*

↔ 4–16 in (10–40 cm) ↑ 4–12 in (10–30 cm) ♀ ☼ ◆/◇ ❀ ☂

Rare species from the Andes region of Ecuador. Clustered stems; fleshy bluish green leaves, twisted at base. Large, waxy, green to deep maroon flowers, deeply fringed lip, in spring. Prefers cool, shaded, and humid conditions, in pots or baskets of sphagnum moss.

Epidendrum × obrienianum

↔ 30–50 in (75–130 cm) ↑ 6–30 ft (1.8–9 m) ✿ ☼ ◆ ❀ ☂

Hybrid orchid between *E. ibaguense* and *E. secundum*, first created by Veitch in England in 1888, now naturalized in several parts of the world, e.g. Hawaii. Branched cane-like stems, scrambling or erect, to 30 ft (9 m) in height. Leaves, 2–5 in (5–12 cm) long, oblong, in 2 rows. Terminal inflorescences produce numerous red, orange, yellow, or magenta flowers, about 1½ in (35 mm) wide; lip sometimes held uppermost, sepals and petals spreading, lip 3-lobed, lobes with fringed edges. Flowers produced throughout the year.

Epidendrum parkinsonianum ★

↔ 8–24 in (20–60 cm) ↑ 1–7 ft (0.3–2 m) ♀ ☼/◑ ◆/◇ ❀ ☂/☈

Central American species. Pendulous habit; succulent purple-stained foliage. Up to 4 large greenish flowers, 5 in (12 cm) across, white lip, in spring. Grow on large slabs of cork or tree fern, or in small wooden baskets.

Epidendrum porpax

syns *Nanodes mathewsii*, *Neolehmannia porpax*

BEETLE ORCHID

↔ 2–12 in (5–30 cm) ↑ 1–2½ in (2.5–6 cm) ♀ ☼ ◆/◇ ❀ ☂/☈

Vigorous, creeping, and branching species; found from Mexico to Peru; several flower forms. Green beetle-like flowers, 1 in (25 mm) in size, glossy purple lip; other forms with purple-green petals and sepals. Also an albino form, with apple green flowers, from Costa Rica, prefers warmer temperatures. Grows well in shallow saucers or mounted on large cork or tree-fern plaques. Flowers in winter–spring.

Epidendrum pseudepidendrum

↔ 4–16 in (10–40 cm) ↑ 8–40 in (20–100 cm) ♀ ☼ ◆ ❀ ☂

Tall "reed-stem" orchid from Costa Rica and Panama. Glossy flowers, among the most spectacular in genus, 3 in (8 cm) tall; sepals and petals apple green; broad, protruding, bright orange to red lip; green, orange, and pink column. Summer-flowering.

Epidendrum secundum

syn. *Epidendrum elongatum*

↔ 8–48 in (20–120 cm) ↑ 8–36 in (20–90 cm) ✿ ☼/◑ ◆/◇ ❀ ☂

"Reed-stem" epidendrum from Central America. Common species, in a range of colors. Spherical heads of blooms, ¾ in (18 mm) in size, borne throughout year. 'Clark', rich pink flowers, lip pink, white, and gold.

Epidendrum stanfordianum

↔ 8–30 in (20–75 cm) ↑ 10–20 in (25–50 cm) ♀ ☼/◑ ◆/◇ ❀ ☂

From Central America, Venezuela, and Colombia; very popular in cultivation. Unusual flowering habit—branched inflorescence originates directly from rhizome between the distinct oval pseudobulbs; 2 to 4 leathery leaves. Individual blooms, 1½ in (35 mm) in size, are attractive and come in a number of color forms. In the typical form, flowers are yellowish-brown, overlaid with darker maroon pepper spotting, lip white to pink. There are also pink forms and albino clones with apple green tepals and a pure white lip. Winter- to spring-flowering. 'Tabitha Davis', greenish flowers.

Epidendrum medusae

Epidendrum porpax

Epidendrum lacustre

Epidendrum parkinsonianum

Epidendrum Hybrids

↔ 8–48 in (20–120 cm) ↕ 8–48 in (20–120 cm) ▽ ☀/☀ ◆/◈/◇ ❄ ⬓

Most common types in cultivation are the "reed-stem" or "crucifix" orchids, which come in a range of colors, with deep reds predominating. Globular heads of blooms can rebloom off the same flowering stem many times, and at any time of year. While many older hybrids can grow up to 48 in (120 cm) tall, there are also more recent hybrids that are more compact growing, to 24 in (60 cm) tall, with larger and more brightly colored flowers. **Cosmo Dream Color 'Momo 1'**, bright pink flowers, fringed lip, with a splash of golden yellow at throat; **Hokulea**, orange-red blooms, lip golden yellow and bright orange; **Hokulea 'Santa Barbara'** ★, compact growing habit, boldly colored blooms; **Joseph Glow 'Seto Raspberry'**, orange-red flowers, lip orange and golden yellow with red spotting; **Joseph Lii 'Reiddy'**, crimson blooms, yellow at throat; **Orange Glow**, apricot-orange flowers, lip lemon and gold at center, deepening to orange hues toward fringed edges; **Pacific Ember**, vivid orange flowers, fringed lip apricot at center, deepening in color toward edge; **Pacific Girl**, bright orange blooms, lip bright yellow at center; **Pom Pom**, orange-red blooms; **Venus Valley 'Lemon'**, yellow flowers. White-flowering forms have also been developed.

Epidendrum pseudepidendrum

Epidendrum secundum

Epidendrum secundum 'Clark'

Epidendrum Hokulea 'Santa Barbara' (hybrid)

Epidendrum stanfordianum 'Tabitha Davis'

Epidendrum Hokulea (hybrid)

Epidendrum Cosmo Dream Color 'Momo 1' (hybrid)

Epidendrum Joseph Glow 'Seto Raspberry' (hybrid)

Epidendrum Pacific Vista (hybrid)

Epidendrum Pacific Vista (hybrid)

Epidendrum Orange Glow (hybrid)

Epidendrum Pacific Ember (hybrid)

Epidendrum Joseph Lii 'Reiddy' (hybrid)

Epidendrum Pacific Girl (hybrid)

Epidendrum Pom Pom (hybrid)

Epidendrum 'Salmon Sunset' (hybrid cultivar)

Epidendrum Pretty Princess (hybrid)

Epidendrum Venus Valley 'Lemon' (hybrid)

Epidendrum 'Tiny Red' (hybrid cultivar)

Epidendrum 'Tokyo Snow' (hybrid cultivar)

Epipactis gigantea

Epipactis helleborine

EPIGENEIUM

This is a genus of about 35 species of small to medium-sized epiphytic or lithophytic plants found from India and Nepal across Asia to the Philippines. The 2-leafed ovoid or conical pseudobulbs are set well apart on a creeping rhizome. Borne terminally on the pseudobulb, the inflorescence is racemose, and produces up to 20 blooms. The medium to large, often showy flowers are usually white, greenish-white, or bronze flushed with pink, often striped or spotted with red. The sepals and petals are spreading, the lip is 3-lobed and motile.
CULTIVATION: Because of their creeping habit, *Epigeneium* species are best grown in shallow baskets in a bark compost or on rafts of bark or tree fern. They like high humidity while in growth and should be kept drier while resting, but the pseudobulbs should not be allowed to shrivel. Propagation is by division.

Epigeneium triflorum
syn. *Dendrobium triflorum*
↔ 8–16 in (20–40 cm) ↕ 5–12 in (12–30 cm)
♀ ☼/☀ ◆/◈ ❄ ☷/☈

Creeping species endemic to Java, Indonesia, found growing in forested mountain regions. Ovate pseudobulbs; 1 to 2 linear leaves. White to creamy yellow flowers, 6 to 17 per spike from apex of bulb; lip white, yellow, and reddish. Blooms in late summer. *E. t.* var. *orientale* is larger, with up to 17 flowers per spike.

EPIPACTIS

SWAMP ROOT ORCHID
This genus of about 35 species occurs mainly in temperate areas of Europe, Asia, and North America, with 3 species found in tropical Africa. They

are terrestrial plants with a creeping rhizome, fleshy roots, and erect leafy stems. The terminal inflorescence has few to many usually green or greenish purple flowers, often with prominent leafy bracts. The sepals and petals are free, spreading or curving forward; the lip is concave at the base.

CULTIVATION: Many species are frost hardy and can be grown in shady spots in gardens in temperate areas, where they may spread to form colonies; a few of the hardier species can tolerate full sun. Easily cultivated in sandy soil or in a mixture of loam, peat, sphagnum, and sand. Propagation is by division of larger colonies of plants.

Epipactis gigantea
syn. *Epipactis americana*
GIANT HELLEBORINE, STREAM ORCHID
↔ 8–16 in (20–40 cm) ↕ 24–40 in (60–100 cm) ❈ ❂ ◇ ❈ ❈ ⬜

Found in Canada, the USA, and south to Mexico along rivers, near springs, and in seepage banks, at altitudes of 500–1,640 ft (150–500 m). From 4 to 12 ovate leaves, up to 8 in (20 cm) long. Very large flowers, can reach over 3 in (8cm) across; yellowish green sepals, pinkish petals, dark red veined lip. Blooms in spring–summer.

Epipactis helleborine
BROAD-LEAFED HELLEBORINE
↔ 4–12 in (10–30 cm) ↕ 8–40 in (20–100 cm) ❈ ☀ ◇ ❈ ❈ ⬜

Widespread in Europe; has become naturalized in parts of North America. Stem erect, leafy; 4 to 10 ovate leaves, 2–6 in (5–15 cm) long, spirally arranged up stem. Inflorescence loosely

Epiphronitis Veitchii

or densely arranged with smallish flowers in summer. Flowers all face one way, greenish to dull purple.

Epipactis palustris
MARSH HELLEBORINE
↔ 4–6 in (10–15 cm) ↕ 12–16 in (30–40 cm) ❈ ❂ ◇ ❈ ❈ ⬜

From Europe, Eurasia, and northern Africa; found from sea level to 5,250 ft (1,600 m) in marshy spots, on seeping banks, and moist forest clearings. Up to 15 flowers, to 1 in (25 mm) across, in summer at tip of growth. Greenish sepals, creamy petals flushed with reddish hues and tipped with white; lip white with reddish veins.

Epipactis viridiflora
syn. *Epipactis purpurata*
VIOLET HELLEBORINE
↔ 4–8 in (10–20 cm) ↕ 8–36 in (20–90 cm) ❈ ☀ ◇ ❈ ❈ ⬜

Species from northwestern and central Europe; sometimes forms clumps. Leaves 4 to 10, to 4 in (10 cm) long, ovate, gray-green with purplish tinge, spirally arranged up stem. Spike densely packed with many flowers in

Eria aporoides

late summer–early autumn; stalk with dense short hairs. Sepals and petals greenish-white, often violet-tinged, lip white or pale pink.

EPIPHRONITIS
A primary intergeneric hybrid between *Epidendrum* and *Sophronitis*. There are about 15 crosses registered, a majority of which use *Sophronitis coccinea* as a parent, which influences flower color, size, and shape. These hybrids have flat, somewhat rounded, flowers, in shades of blood red to cerise. *Sophronitis* tends to dominate the flower characteristics. The plant habit of the *Epidendrum* parent dominates the plant form. Hybrids using a "reed-stem" *Epidendrum* retain the "reed-stem" habit, whereas a pseudobulbous *Epidendrum* parent leads to compact pseudobulbous hybrids.
CULTIVATION: Grow "reed-stem" types in pots of free-draining mix, and pseudobulbous types mounted or in clay pots. *Epiphronitis* thrives under intermediate to warm conditions in bright filtered light. Provide high humidity and good air movement. Apply dilute fertilizer weekly when plants are in active growth. Allow roots to dry between waterings. Propagate by division. "Reed-stem" types produce aerial offsets (keikis), which can be removed to separate pots after roots have formed.

Epiphronitis Veitchii
↔ 2–6 in (5–15 cm) ↕ 4–20 in (10–50cm) ❈/❈ ☀ ◆/◇ ❈ ⬜/≋

Hybrid between *Epidendrum radicans* and *Sophronitis coccinea*; compact reed-stem habit. Leaves oval, fleshy, to 2 in (5 cm) long. Flat scarlet flowers, 1½ in (35 mm) wide, broad lip with central yellow marking that fades with age. Blooms open successively from a terminal inflorescence, in spring–autumn.

ERIA
The diverse sympodial genus *Eria* is widespread through tropical Asia, New Guinea, Australia, and Polynesia. Despite having several hundred representatives, only a small percentage are in cultivation. Many species have pseudobulbs, while others lack pseudobulbs, possessing reed-like stems or thickened rhizomes. Individual flowers last for less than a week, but plants often bloom a number of times during the year. Some species are quite spectacular when in flower, and make up for the small size of their blooms by the large numbers they produce. They generally occur as epiphytes, but some are lithophytes, and there are a number of distinct plant forms.
CULTIVATION: Most *Eria* species are easy to cultivate as long as their moisture and temperature requirements are met. They like to grow in dappled light, but many will take strong light for part of the day. Some smaller-growing species perform best in pots; grow in a bark-based medium and keep moist while plants are in active growth. The lowland species require year-round warm conditions, while those from the mountainous regions appreciate cooler temperatures. Propagation is by division.

Eria aporoides
↔ 4–10 in (10–25 cm) ↕ 4–10 in (10–25 cm) ❈ ❂/❈ ◆/◇ ⬜

Endemic to the Philippines; produces blooms 9 days after thunderstorms. It is thought that the sudden change in barometric pressure triggers all plants in the same area to synchronize their flowering for a specific day. Blooms are produced singly from nodes between the shark-tooth-like fleshy foliage in summer. Small flowers, less than ½ in (12 mm) in size, pure white, each lasting only a single day.

Epigeneium triflorum var. *orientale*

Eria gigantea

Eria gigantea

↔ 8–24 in (20–60 cm) ↕ 8–36 in (20–90 cm)

Native to the Philippines. Produces a number of spikes from top of matured pseudobulb. Flowers ½ in (12 mm) across, pale yellow, peppered with very small purple spots, produced sequentially over a couple of months.

Eria mysorensis

syns *Eria flava, E. pubescens*

↔ 4–24 in (10–60 cm) ↕ 4–16 in (10–40 cm)

Found from Nepal to Indochina. Blooms 1¼ in (30 mm) wide, mustard yellow to green reddish purple lip. Backs of flowers and inflorescence have white woolly hairs, giving them a felt-like texture. Autumn-flowering.

Eria spicata

↔ 6–20 in (15–50 cm) ↕ 4–14 in (10–35 cm)

Species from Nepal, northern India, China, Myanmar, and Thailand. Clustered cylindrical pseudobulbs to 6 in (15 cm) long; 2 to 4 leaves, 2–9 in (5–22 cm) long, narrowly elliptical. Inflorescences 2–3 in (5–8 cm) long, ovoid, densely covered with blooms in summer–autumn. Flowers small, white or straw yellow, brown marks on lip.

Eria stricta

↔ 4–10 in (10–25 cm) ↕ 4–10 in (10–25 cm)

Small tufted plant from India and Nepal. Upright spikes of small creamy white flowers, less than ¼ in (6 mm) in size, that all face the same way. Backs of flowers distinctly woolly. Summer-flowering.

Eria xanthocheila

↔ 4–16 in (10–40 cm) ↕ 6–16 in (15–40 cm)

From Thailand, Malaysia, Indonesia, and the Philippines. Slender pseudobulbs, up to 4 leaves. Inflorescences arise from near top of pseudobulbs and carry up to 20 yellowish green blooms, less than ¾ in (18 mm) in size, with a bright yellow lip. Also an extremely rare variegated-leafed form from the Philippines.

ERIOPSIS

From Costa Rica, Panama, Colombia, Ecuador, Peru, Bolivia, Venezuela, Guyana, and Brazil, this genus contains 5 to 6 epiphytic, lithophytic, or terrestrial species. The variable plants have conical to elongate, nearly cylindrical pseudobulbs, usually topped by 2 to 4 leaves that are leathery and flexible to stiff in posture. The upright, sometimes quite long, inflorescences originate from the base of the bulbs. Flowering is synchronized, with several to many flowers per spike. The flowers of the various species are generally brownish with densely spotted lips. The genus name means "*Eria*-like" for some similarity to an unrelated genus of orchids.

CULTIVATION: These plants love humidity and like to be well watered and fertilized while growing, needing less when growths have matured. Depending on the species, some like half-sun, others nearly full sun. Some species can handle quite cold temperatures, but generally the minimum should be 50–55°F (10–13°C). Plants probably do their best when potted. *Eriopsis* is not known for its ease of culture, some plants only doing well for a few years. Propagate by division.

Eriopsis biloba

syn. *Eriopsis rutidobulbon*

↔ 16–20 in (40–50 cm) ↕ 18–40 in (45–100 cm)

Variable plants from Costa Rica, Panama, Colombia, Venezuela, Guyana, and Peru. Pseudobulbs usually blackish, furrowed, conical; usually 2 to 4 large leathery leaves; Inflorescence 16–40 in (40–100 cm) tall, with up to 35 flowers, 1–1¼ in (2.5–3 cm) wide, in autumn–winter. Petals and sepals yellowish-brown, white lip spotted brown and maroon. Can be difficult to bloom in cultivation.

ERYCINA

There are only 2 species in this genus. Both species come from Mexico, where one is a lowland coastal species, and the other from the highlands, each from seasonally dry forests. Plants of both species are quite similar, basically with compressed ovoid pseudobulbs and thin deciduous leaves. Once the leaves have fallen, the bracts around the bulb become dry and papery. Like most plants related to *Oncidium*, the inflorescences originate from the sides of the bulbs, but in this genus they can also grow occasionally from the apex of the bulb. Flowers of both species are very similar, with very reduced petals and sepals, but the large lips differ in shape.

CULTIVATION: Culture is basically the same for both species except for temperatures. The plants do best when grown mounted, but can also be potted in an open mix, kept well-watered and fertilized while in active growth. Once the pseudobulbs have matured and the leaves drop, it is best to reduce water and give them brighter light. Keep them a bit cooler and much drier during winter. Propagation is by divisions of 3 or more pseudobulbs when plant is in growth (not dormant), or from seed.

Erycina echinata

syn. *Oncidium echinatum*

↔ 5–8 in (12–20 cm) ↕ 4–8 in (10–20 cm)

Species from coastal west Mexico, found growing at elevations of up to 330 ft (100 m), often found on scrub or dead trees. Small compressed pseudobulbs; 2 leaves, often striped reddish, deciduous. Inflorescences to 8 in (20 cm) tall, usually arise from base of bulb, but sometimes apically. Flowers small, less than 1 in (25 mm) in diameter, with reduced brown or green segments, disproportionately large yellow lip. Spring-flowering. Best grown mounted. Water freely while growing.

ESMERALDA

This small genus, related to *Vanda*, contains 2 large scandent species. They come from the Himalayas and Southeast Asia, and may be epiphytic, lithophytic, or terrestrial. The leaves are leathery, in two rows, twisted at the base to face one way. The showy flowers are yellow, marked with brown. The sepals and petals are spreading; the lip is 3-lobed and has no spur. The name comes from the Greek *smaragdus*, meaning emerald green, and is thought to refer either to the beauty of the flowers or to the rich green foliage.

CULTIVATION: Plants should be grown in heavy pots or in baskets in a very coarse bark-based compost, with canes or wires to support the scrambling stems. They need plenty of water and as much light as possible. Propagate from seed.

Esmeralda clarkei

Eriopsis biloba

Esmeralda cathcartii

↔ 16–24 in (40–60 cm) ↕ 40–80 in (100–200 cm)

Large plants from eastern Himalayas. Stems usually pendent. Leaves to 6 in (15 cm) long, oblong. Inflorescence to 14 in (35 cm) long, with 3 to 5 flowers in spring–summer. Flowers 2–3 in (5–8 cm) across; sepals and petals yellow with dense, horizontal, brown stripes; lip white in center with 2 red stripes and a broad yellow edge.

Esmeralda clarkei

↔ 8–20 in (20–50 cm) ↕ 8–40 in (20–100 cm)

Monopodial species from Nepal; closely related to *Vanda*. Produces short inflorescences of up to 4 blooms in autumn–winter. Flowers up to 3 in (8 cm) across, with yellow to mustard background overlaid with distinctive dark brown bands, giving the flower a distinctive concentric pattern.

Eria xanthocheila

E

EUCHILE

This genus contains 2 species, formerly included in several other genera, that are found in Mexico, growing as epiphytes in dry oak and pine forests. The leaves have a distinct blue-gray appearance, and the plants appear almost gray from a distance. Both species have very showy flowers.

CULTIVATION: Among the more difficult orchids to cultivate, *Euchile* species need cool to intermediate conditions, bright light, and high humidity at night. During the resting period, keep drier and the temperature should drop to 46–50°F (8–10°C) at night for *Euchile citrina*. This species should be grown only on cork slabs. *E. mariae* may also be grown in pots in a coarse free-draining substrate. Propagation is by division.

Euchile mariae

syns *Encyclia mariae, Epidendrum mariae, Hormidium mariae*
↔ 4–6 in (10–15 cm) ↕ 6–10 in (15–25 cm)
♀ ☀ ◆ ❄ ▽/🖉

From Mexico, found at lower altitudes than *E. citrina*, at 3,280–3,940 ft (1,000–1,200 m)—reflected in its tolerance of higher temperatures in cultivation. More upright and less hanging

Eulophia clavicornis

than *E. citrina*. Upright flower stalk, to 8 in (20 cm) long; 1 to 3 flowers, in late winter–spring. Sepals and petals green, lip large, showy, white with greenish center.

EULOPHIA

This large genus of some 250 terrestrial species, is distributed throughout the tropics and some warm-temperate regions, with the majority occurring in Africa, followed by Asia and the Americas. The leaves are long, narrow to pleated, and deciduous, retiring to fleshy underground rhizomes when dormant. Tall erect spikes produce numerous flowers that are highly variable in shape and color.

CULTIVATION: These orchids should be potted in a well-drained terrestrial mix and appreciate a high proportion of coarse sand with some organic matter. They require bright light to induce flowering and like to be kept moist when in active growth. The potting medium should be allowed to dry out during the dormant period. Propagate by division.

Eulophia clavicornis

↔ 4–16 in (10–40 cm) ↕ 4–36 in (10–90 cm)
🌠 ☀/🌣 ◆/◇ ❄ ▽

Deciduous species from South Africa; grows in grassland. Upright inflorescences carry up to 30 blooms in spring–summer. Flowers brown to pink, to 1½ in (35 mm) across.

Eulophia ovalis

↔ 4–16 in (10–40 cm) ↕ 6–27 in (15–70 cm)
🌠 ☀/🌣 ◆/◇ ❄ ▽

Uncommon deciduous species from the eastern half of South Africa; found growing in open grassland. Up to 16 blooms are produced on upright inflorescences in summer. Individual

flowers to 2½ in (6 cm) across; brownish green sepals, white petals and lip.

Eulophia spectabilis

syns *Eulophia nuda, E. squalida*
↔ 8–12 in (20–30 cm) ↕ 18–40 in (45–100 cm) 🌠 ☀/🌣 ◆ ❄ ▽

Widespread in tropical Asia. Subterranean pseudobulbs, almost round, 2- to 3-leafed. Pleated leaves 8–20 in (20–50 cm) long. Inflorescence to 40 in (100 cm) tall, unbranched, rather loosely arranged with several flowers in spring. Flowers about 1 in (25 mm) across, not opening wide, pinkish, red-brown to purple-red, lip with yellow crests.

Eulophia welwitschii

↔ 4–16 in (10–40 cm) ↕ 10–36 in (25–90 cm) 🌠 ☀/🌣 ◆/◇ ▽

Deciduous species from the eastern half of South Africa; grows in dry to marshy grasslands. One of the most attractive and distinctive species in the genus. Short, dense, upright inflorescences carry up to 20 blooms in summer. Flowers bright yellow to greenish yellow, to 3 in (8 cm) across.

EULOPHIELLA

The 4 species in this genus are found in Madagascar, where they grow as epiphytes or more rarely terrestrially. They have slender pseudobulbs that grow wide apart on a robust rhizome, and long grass-like leaves. They grow only on various species of palms (*Vomitra* species), tree ferns, and screw pines (*Pandanus*), and are among the showiest and most desirable of all orchids of Madagascar.

CULTIVATION: Found very rarely in cultivation and little is known of their requirements. Try to grow these plants under warm conditions in half-shade

Eurychone rothschildiana

mounted on a long slab. Keep moist in spring and summer and reduce watering in winter. Do not keep under 59°F (15°C). Propagation is by division.

Eulophiella elisabethae

syn. *Eulophiella perrieri*
↔ 16–20 in (40–50 cm) ↕ 24–36 in (60–90 cm) ♀ 🌣 ◆ ❄ 🖉

Found in eastern Madagascar, growing in rainforest. Spindle-shaped pseudobulbs; bulbs reach 6 in (15 cm) high; grass-like leaves to 32 in (80 cm) long. Overhanging inflorescence, 16–32 in (40–80 cm) long, with 15 to 30 flowers in winter. Flowers each just over 1½ in (35 mm) across, waxy, white, flushed with rose; lip yellow.

EURYCHONE

This genus contains 2 epiphytic species, which are found in equatorial Africa. The plants have short monopodial stems with dark green leaves, the edges of which are slightly wavy. They grow in the dark shady understory of tropical rainforests. They are closely related to *Angraecum*, but can easily be separated from that genus by their thicker columns in the flower.

CULTIVATION: Grow under shady, very warm conditions, similar to the warmest-growing *Phalaenopsis*. As the inflorescences are pendent, they are best grown mounted on a slab with a small layer of moisture-retaining moss. Temperatures should not fall below 64°F (18°C). Propagation is from seed only, as the plants do not produce lateral offshoots.

Eurychone rothschildiana

syn. *Angraecum rothschildianum*
↔ 8–12 in (20–30 cm) ↕ 4–6 in (10–15 cm)
♀ ☀ ◆ ❄ 🖉

From equatorial Africa, found in rainforests from Guinea to Nigeria, the Democratic Republic of the Congo (formerly Zaire), and Uganda. Leaves about 6 in (15 cm) long, with wavy edges. Usually 2 inflorescences appear, each with 2 to 10 flowers, mostly in spring or autumn. Greenish white flowers to 2 in (5 cm) in diameter, with tubular lip.

Eulophia ovalis

Eulophia welwitschii

FERNANDEZIA

This is a group of striking miniature monopodial species, without pseudobulbs, distributed from Venezuela to Peru. The 10 or so species rank among the most spectacular of orchids with their tiny plants, proportionally large flowers, and brilliant floral colors, in pink, orange, and red. They are twig epiphytes of the high cloud forests, which experience very cool to cold temperatures. Individual blooms are produced from the leaf axils of the upper leaves.

CULTIVATION: These orchids are extremely difficult to maintain in cultivation, as it is almost impossible to replicate their natural environment. They will only tolerate a very narrow temperature range, which must not be allowed to drop below 43°F (6°C), yet they will quickly defoliate and die if temperatures exceed 75°F (24°C). Excessive heat, coupled with low humidity, can kill plants within days. Specialist growers of montane plants have had some success with these orchids, in carefully controlled greenhouses that maintain high humidity, and good air circulation in the temperature range mentioned above. They are also grown on moss-covered pieces of tree-fern that are never allowed to fully dry out. For these reasons, the plants are seldom seen in cultivation.

Fernandezia subbiflora

↔ 1¼–4 in (3–10 cm) ↑ 1¼–5 in (3–12 cm)
♀ ☀ ◇ ❀ ⧆

From Ecuador and Colombia; grows in cloud forests that are always moist, windy, and quite cold. Bright fire engine red flowers, with yellow band at end of column. Individual blooms to just over ½ in (12 mm) tall, disproportionally large lip.

Fernandezia subbiflora

GALEANDRA

This genus contains about 25 species found in Florida, USA, and from Mexico through Central America and the Caribbean to Brazil and Paraguay. They grow as epiphytes, rarely terrestrial, in forests. The pseudobulbs are similar to those of *Catasetum*, but more slender; the pleated leaves are deciduous. The terminal inflorescence carries several showy flowers with a tubular lip that has a prominent spur.
CULTIVATION: Keep under shady and temperate conditions while growing, and bright and cooler during the resting period after flowering. Just mist to keep the pseudobulbs from shrinking

Galeandra baueri

during that time. They grow more vigorously in pots, but epiphytic culture is possible as well. Propagation is by division.

Galeandra baueri

syn. *Galeandra cristata*
↔ 8–12 in (20–30 cm) ↑ 12–16 in
(30–40 cm) ♀ ☀ ◆ ⧆

Type species of genus; from Mexico to Panama, found growing in pine forests and on palms at elevations of 2,630–3,940 ft (800–1,200 m). Pseudobulbs reach 10 in (25 cm) high, topped by 8 in (20 cm) long leaves. Arching inflorescence, often branched, bears a few fragrant and long-lasting flowers in spring–early summer. Yellowish brown to greenish brown sepals and petals, whitish to violet-purple lip.

GASTROCHILUS

The 20-odd species in this genus are monopodial epiphytes, found from India to eastern Asia and Malaysia, growing in different kinds of forests, and they are similar in appearance to *Aerides*. The rough leaves grow from a short to elongated stem, and the fleshy flowers are closely packed together.
CULTIVATION: Grow under intermediate to warm conditions. Moderate shade and high humidity are essential. They thrive in small baskets or on a cork slab or wood mount. Water the plants well during the growing season and slightly less after blooming. Propagation is by seed.

Fernandezia subbiflora

Gastrochilus calceolaris

syns *Aerides calceolare, Saccolabium calceolaris*

↔ 6–8 in (15–20 cm) ↑ 4–6 in (10–15 cm)
♀ ☀ ◆ ❀ ⧆/⧆

Type species of genus, found in cool to hot forests from the Himalayas to Vietnam, Malaysia, Java in Indonesia, and the Philippines. Leathery leaves arranged alternately along stem. Very short peduncle bears 2 in (5 cm) wide flowers, downy, light green with purplish spots, in autumn.

Gastrochilus formosanus

syns *Gastrochilus nebulosus, G. quercetorum, Saccolabium nebulosum*

↔ 1–2 in (2.5–5 cm) ↑ 3–4 in (8–10 cm)
♀ ☀ ◆ ❀ ⧆/⧆

Miniature species from Taiwan. Arching and rambling stems; leaves small, pressed flat to stem. Flower spikes with clusters of bright yellow flowers, lip white, spotted red all over. Blooms in spring–summer.

Gastrochilus japonicus

Gastrochilus suavis

Gastrochilus japonicus

syn. *Gastrochilus somai*

↔ 4–12 in (10–30 cm) ↑ 2–6 in (5–15 cm)

From Japan and Taiwan. Short spikes of up to 8 bright yellow blooms, just over ¾ in (18 mm) in size, in autumn. Grows well on small slabs of cork bark.

Gastrochilus obliquus

↔ 4–14 in (10–35 cm) ↑ 2–6 in (5–15 cm)

Found from India to Indochina. Short inflorescences of up to 8 blooms in autumn. Flowers yellow to ochre-colored, just over ¾ in (18 mm) in size; specialized lip white with purple and orange-brown spotting.

Gastrochilus suavis

↔ 4–12 in (10–30 cm) ↑ 2–6 in (5–15 cm)

From Thailand; named in 1988. Blooms just over ¾ in (18 mm) in size, greenish yellow, lip predominantly white. Flowers in autumn–winter. Recently reclassified as *G. obliquus* var. *suavis* by some authorities.

GASTRORCHIS

Each of the 7 or 8 species in this genus are from Madagascar, except for one from the Mascarene Islands. Beautiful and horticulturally desirable, they are quite closely related to *Phaius*, with which they are often synonymized, but are highly distinctive in appearance. They are typically terrestrial with round to spindle-shaped pseudobulbs clustered or spread along the rhizome, which itself is horizontal to ascending. The leaves of most species are long, but vary from grass-like to quite broad and pleated. Arising from the newest matured bulb, the erect inflorescences bear few to several flowers that vary in size from 1½–2½ in (3.5–6 cm). The flowers are usually sequential, with a few blooms open at a time, and are somewhat long-lasting.

CULTIVATION: All species should be grown in an open terrestrial mix, and usually perform best in pots. They also like to have plenty of good quality water while growing, but require a cooler and drier rest in winter, with a general minimum of 55°F (13°C).

Gastrochilus obliquus

Grow in medium to bright shade. Propagation is from seed, or by division of plants, with 3 or more pseudobulbs per division.

Gastrorchis pulcher

↔ 20–24 in (50–60 cm) ↑ 24–30 in (60–75 cm)

From Madagascar, found in shady humid forests. Small rounded pseudobulbs spaced along rhizome, long grass-like leaves. Inflorescence can reach 20–30 in (50–75 cm) tall, with several white flowers, each 2–2½ in (5–6 cm) in size, in spring. Rose, pink, or white lip with yellow callus. *G. p.* var. *alba*, pure white flowers except for yellow callus on lip.

Gastrorchis steinhardtiana

↔ 8–16 in (20–40 cm) ↑ 8–20 in (20–50 cm)

Evergreen species, endemic to Madagascar; grows in montane forest. Rare, recently discovered, only described in 1997. Upright inflorescences of up to 6 shapely white blooms, 2½ in (6 cm) in size; lolly pink lip with a ridge of bright yellow calli. Summer-flowering.

GEORGEBLACKARA

This is a multigeneric hybrid merging 4 different epiphytic genera in the *Oncidium* alliance: *Comparettia*, *Leochilus*, *Oncidium*, and *Rodriguezia*. They are usually neat compact plants with brightly colored blooms.

CULTIVATION: These intermediate- to warm-growing hybrids perform best in small terracotta or clay pots utilizing a very well-drained bark-based medium. They may also be mounted on small

Gastrorchis steinhardtiana

pieces of tree fern or cork. Ensure that plants drain and dry out rapidly after watering. Do not allow water to collect in the leaf axils, as this could lead to leaf rot and put the plant under undue stress.

Georgeblackara Tribute

↔ 3–6 in (8–15 cm) ↑ 3–10 in (8–25 cm)

Hybrid between the bright orange- to red-flowered *Comparettia speciosa* and *Howeara* Mini-Primi (*Rodrocidium* Primi [*Oncidium sarcodes* × *Rodriguezia lanceolata*] × *Leochilus oncidioides*).

GLOSSODIA

WAX-LIP ORCHID

A small terrestrial genus of 2 species from southern and eastern Australia including Tasmania, that can be found growing in open forest, grasslands, heathlands, and disturbed open areas including dunes. These tuber-forming orchids have a single, basal, hairy, narrow, stalked leaf. Slender racemes carry 1 to several showy, somewhat glossy, blue-mauve to white, sweet-smelling, short-lived flowers in winter or spring.

CULTIVATION: Glossodias are challenging to raise in cultivation. They prefer full sun to part-shade and well-drained, acidic, sandy soil with some added humus. Water with care while in active growth, as tubers are prone to rot. Maintain humidity during the flowering period. Permit foliage to die back naturally after blooming, when the next season's tuber will rest for 4 to 6 months before resuming growth. Propagate from seed.

Glossodia major

LARGE WAX-LIP ORCHID

↔ 2–4 in (5–10 cm) ↑ 4–14 in (10–35 cm)

From open woodland and heathland of Australia, including Tasmania.

Gastrorchis pulcher var. *alba*

Leaves lance-shaped, to 4 in (10 cm) long. Stems to 14 in (35 cm) tall, with a single flower in spring. Blue-mauve to white flowers, sweetly fragrant; lip mauve, upper part white with prominent yellow callus.

GOMESA

This genus of about 12 species is found only in southeastern Brazil and adjacent Paraguay and Argentina. They are small epiphytes, and the pseudobulbs form dense clusters on branches in forests at various altitudes. Only 2 species have an elongated rhizome between the pseudobulbs. The flattened pseudobulbs bear 2 leaves and are covered in sheaths. They are easily recognized by their flower aspect, but to identify the species can be tricky. CULTIVATION: Grow these plants under intermediate to cool conditions and rather shady light. Water well when in growth, and reduce watering after the flowers have wilted just to keep the pseudobulbs from shrinking. They thrive equally well in pots or mounted on a slab or piece of bark. Propagation is by division.

Gomesa crispa

syns *Gomesa polymorpha*, *G. undulata*
↔ 6–8 in (15–20 cm) ↕ 6–8 in (15–20 cm)
♀ ☀ ◇ ❄ ⛉/⚡

From southeastern Brazil. Densely clustered pseudobulbs, 2 thin leaves. Inflorescence to 8 in (20 cm) long, densely flowered in summer–autumn. Fragrant green flowers, yellowish lip.

GONGORA

The sympodial genus *Gongora* contains 80 or so species, and is distributed from Mexico to Peru and Brazil. The flowers are relatively short-lived, rarely lasting for more than a week; most species flower from spring to summer; the flowers rarely wither on the spike like most orchids—they drop their blooms when they have had enough. The blooms are fairly similar in shape, but the range of colors is significant.

Gomesa crispa

CULTIVATION: Most gongoras like warm humid conditions with plenty of air circulation. They are best grown in hanging baskets, or in pots that are suspended by hangers, due to the long pendulous inflorescences that are a feature of most species. They can be grown in a bark-based mix or in sphagnum moss. These plants enjoy being kept moist and relatively shaded, as direct sunlight will scorch the broad thin leaves. Propagate by division.

Gongora histrionica

↔ 27 in (70 cm) ↕ 36 in (90 cm)
♀ ☀ ◆/◈ ❄ ⛉

Found from Costa Rica to Colombia. Long hanging spike with up to 25 blooms, each 2 in (5 cm) wide, golden yellow, heavily blotched and spotted with dark reddish brown. Flowers in spring–summer.

Gongora nigropunctata

↔ 20–24 in (50–60 cm) ↕ 20–27 in (50–70 cm) ♀ ☀/☀ ◆/◈ ❄ ⛉

Endemic to Peru; grows in montane wet forests. Ovoid ribbed pseudobulbs, 2 to 3 broad pleated leaves. Arching to descending inflorescences, to 26 in (65 cm) long, with 25 to 30 fragrant flowers produced sporadically through year. Blooms under 2 in (5 cm) in size, red-purple and yellow with blackish-red spots, lip yellow and red-purple.

Gongora pleiochroma

↔ 8–24 in (20–60 cm) ↕ 8–20 in (20–50 cm)
♀ ☀ ◆/◈ ❄ ⛉

From Colombia, Ecuador, and Peru. Arching to pendulous inflorescences of up to 30 blooms in summer–autumn. Individual flowers, 3 in (8 cm) in size, vary in color from yellow overlaid with red speckling to tan and dark red.

GOODYERA

JEWEL ORCHID, RATTLESNAKE ORCHID, RATTLESNAKE PLANTAIN

This genus of about 40 species of terrestrial orchids is known from tropical and temperate regions of the world, except Africa. They inhabit forests from sea level to about 6,560 ft (2,000 m). Grown primarily for their decorative foliage, the plants have attractive, somewhat fleshy leaves, which are retained for several growing seasons, and often feature net veining or checkered patterning. Creeping fleshy stolons with thick roots give rise to leafy stems that can form compact rosettes or become more elongated. Mature stems flower once only before producing offsets. The inflorescence is an erect terminal raceme of few to many white to salmon pink flowers.

Georgeblackara Tribute

CULTIVATION: Raise specimens in shallow pots of well-drained compost. Keep evenly moist and humid. Fertilize lightly only when in active growth. Grow cool to warm depending upon origin, with a cooler period after blooming for those species from high altitude or temperate regions. Provide enough light to maintain color and form. Propagate by division of the stolon or from seeds.

Goodyera biflora

LARGE-FLOWERED GOODYERA
↔ 2½–3 in (6–8 cm) ↕ 2–6 in (5–15 cm)
🌿 ☀/☀ ◆/◇ ⛉

From humid pine, oak, and rhododendron forests in China, India, Japan, Korea, and Nepal. Erect stems with

Glossodia major

4 to 5 oval pointed leaves, to 1½ in (35 mm) long, green with white net veining. Up to 4 large elongate flowers, white tinged pink, to ¾ in (18 mm) long, at the end of a short terminal inflorescence in early summer.

Goodyera tesselata

TESSELLATED RATTLESNAKE-PLANTAIN
↔ 2½–4 in (6–10 cm) ↕ 4–10 in (10–25 cm)
🌿 ☀/☀ ◆/◇ ⛉

From coniferous to mixed deciduous forests of eastern North America. Rosettes of about 5 gray-green leaves, white to silver tessellations, oval, to 1½ in (35 mm) long. From 6 to 30 flowers on a somewhat 1-sided spike in summer. Flowers white, lip cupped and within sepals, slightly spicy scent.

Gongora histrionica

Gongora nigropunctata

Gongora pleiochroma

Grammangis ellisii

Grammatophyllum elegans

GRAMMANGIS

This genus includes 2 species of large, sympodial, epiphytic orchid from Madagascar. They have large pseudobulbs with 3 to 5 flat fleshy leaves at the apex. The inflorescences are racemose and arise from the base of a new pseudobulb. The fleshy flowers are large and showy with spreading sepals and somewhat smaller petals. The 3-lobed lip is attached to the apex of the column foot, has crests and calli inside, and lacks a spur.
CULTIVATION: Plants should be grown in heavy clay pots or in baskets in a coarse bark mixture. While in growth, they need plenty of water, regular fertilizing, high humidity, and moderate shade. In winter, when plants are resting, watering should be reduced and light increased. Propagate by division.

Grammangis ellisii

↔ 20–26 in (50–65 cm) ↑ 20–24 in (50–60 cm) ♀ ☀ ◆ ❄ ▽

From Madagascar. Pseudobulbs 3–8 in (8–20 cm), 4-angled; 3 to 5 leaves at apex. Leaves 6–16 in (15–40 cm) long, fleshy, flat but folded at base, oblong. Arching inflorescences arise from base of pseudobulbs, 20–26 in (50–65 cm) long, with 15 to 20 flowers. Thick-textured flowers, 3 in (8 cm) across; sepals glossy brown with yellow marks, petals smaller and with more yellow; lip striped red and yellow, 3-lobed with large forked callus.

GRAMMATOPHYLLUM

The 11 to 12 species of this genus are among the most impressive of all orchids. They are found throughout Southeast Asia, Indonesia and New Guinea, the Philippines, and several islands in the southwest Pacific. They are medium to large epiphytes, rarely lithophytes, found in tropical forests. There are 2 different groups, which can be separated by their growth. The first group has cane-like stems that grow several meters long and have multiple alternating leaves, giving the impression of a palm frond. The second group has thick compact pseudobulbs, with only a few leaves at the top. Showy long-lasting flowers are borne on long arching inflorescences. Some species reach an enormous size, and *G. speciosum* holds the record as the world's largest and heaviest orchid, with some specimens reaching a weight of several tons and producing several thousand flowers at the same time.
CULTIVATION: Grow in baskets or pots, in direct sunlight with high temperatures and lots of fertilizer. Keep in mind that the plants can double their size in a year! Propagate by division, but small plants won't flower.

Grammatophyllum elegans

↔ 12–60 in (30–150 cm) ↑ 12–48 in (30–120 cm) ♀ ⁜ ☀ ◆/◇ ❄ ▽

Endemic to the Philippines. Large arching inflorescences of up to 50 brown blooms, 3 in (8 cm) across, widely opening, in summer.

Grammatophyllum speciosum

syns *Grammatophyllum fastuosum, G. giganteum, G. papuanum*

↔ 12–20 ft (3.5–6 m) ↑ 3–7 ft (0.9–2 m) ♀ ⁜ ◆ ❄ ▽

From Myanmar, Thailand, Malaysia, to New Guinea and the Solomon Islands; type species of genus. Cane-like stems to 10 ft (3 m) long, palm-like. Inflorescence to 10 ft (3 m), with 30 to 50 blooms in summer–autumn. Flowers 4 in (10 cm) wide, waxy, greenish yellow with fine brownish spots, fragrant.

GRASTIDIUM

GRASS ORCHID
There are around 200 species in this genus, found from India through Southeast Asia to northern Australia and the tropical Pacific Islands (to New Caledonia), with most found in New Guinea. Previously included within *Dendrobium*, they are mostly lowland orchids, requiring warm conditions to thrive. There are some cooler-growing species from higher altitudes. Many of these sympodial species feature grass-like foliage. Produced in pairs (often facing), the flowers are short-lived, rarely lasting past daylight hours. They

bloom prolifically about 9 days after a thunderstorm or a significant weather change. All plants in a region flower on the same day—a cycle repeated numerous times during the warmer months.
CULTIVATION: Grow in pots utilizing a bark-based medium. Larger plants do well on tree-fern slabs. They require warm humid conditions and grow well in shaded to bright situations, as long as the root system is kept relatively moist. They are in active growth year-round. Propagate by division.

Grastidium cathcartii

↔ 36 in (90 cm) ↑ 48 in (120 cm) ♀ ⁜ ◆/◇ ▽

Indian species; one of the few cool-growing members of genus. Yellow-green flowers, 1 in (25 mm), last for 2 or 3 days.

GROBYA

This is a small genus of 4 sympodial epiphytes from Brazil, with 1 species extending to Ecuador. They have ovoid pseudobulbs terminating to a slender neck with 3 or 4 narrow leaves. They produce pendent inflorescences of up to 16 unusually shaped blooms that are in yellow to orange and brown tones. These plants of the humid rainforests are related to *Cyrtopodium*.
CULTIVATION: Readily grown in small pots incorporating a moisture-retentive bark-based medium. Larger plants should also thrive on large tree-fern slabs. Propagate by division of mature specimens.

Grobya amherstiae

↔ 5–10 in (12–25 cm) ↑ 6–12 in (15–30 cm) ♀ ⁜/☀ ◆ ❄ ▽/⊼

From Brazil and Ecuador. Pendulous inflorescences of up to 12 blooms in spring–summer. Light tan flowers, 1¼ in (30 mm) in size, darker brown

spotting over petals and sepals; lip predominantly bright yellow.

GYMNADENIA

syn. *Nigritella*
This terrestrial genus of about 16 species occurs in Europe and in temperate parts of central and eastern Asia, as far east as Japan. The rootstock is tuberous, with lobed tubers. The stem is erect and leafy. The inflorescence is cylindrical or shortly conical, densely many-flowered with small scented flowers. The sepals and petals are free, either all are spreading or the dorsal sepal and petals form a hood; the lip can be 3-lobed and has a spur.
CULTIVATION: Plants usually grow successfully in a well-drained terrestrial compost with added lime. Keep dry after the leaves have died back. Propagate from seed.

Gymnadenia conopsea

FRAGRANT ORCHID
↔ 2–4 in (5–10 cm) ↑ 6–18 in (15–45 cm) ⚤ ⁜ ◇ ❄ ❄ ▽

Widespread in Europe. Leaves 3 to 9, narrow, to 10 in (25 cm) long. Spike cylindrical, densely arranged with many flowers in late spring–summer. Flowers lilac to pink, sweetly scented; lip 3-lobed, slender spur.

Grobya amherstiae

Gymnadenia conopsea, with *Deilephila* hawkmoth pollinator

Habenaria dregeana

Habenaria monorhiza

Habenaria rhodocheila

Haraella retrocalla

syn. *Haraella odorata*

↔ 2½–6 in (6–15 cm) ↕ 2–4 in (5–10 cm)

Dwarf species from Taiwan. Short stem; 4 to 6 leaves, 1¼–3 in (3–8 cm) long, narrowly oblong. Racemes 1–3 in (2.5–8 cm) long, with up to 5 blooms in summer–autumn. Flowers less than 1 in (25 mm) across, scented; sepals and petals pale yellow to green; lip oblong, edges wavy, whitish yellow with deep purple blotch in center.

HABENARIA

This is a cosmopolitan genus, numbering over 600 species of (mostly deciduous) terrestrials with tubers or fleshy roots. They are found throughout the world in the tropics and subtropics, and appear to be a genus well overdue for taxonomic revision. Such studies should reduce the number of species by creating a number of splinter genera. They are generally leafy plants with an upright terminal inflorescence of blooms that are highly variable in shape, size, and color. *Habenaria* species are found in a range of habitats, from heath to grasslands to open forest, with many species found growing in deep shade on the floor of tropical rainforests.

CULTIVATION: Despite the large size of the genus, there are surprisingly few species in cultivation. Most successful growers use a mixture of peat moss, very fine bark, and sand (with large particle size) in various ratios. This ensures good drainage as well as water-holding properties. It is important to dry the pots out after blooming as the plant enters its dormant phase. Excess water during this time could lead to rotting of the tubers. Most species do best in semi-shaded situations. Propagate from seed or by the multiplication of tubers while the plant is dormant.

Habenaria arenaria

↔ 6–12 in (15–30 cm) ↕ 10–16 in (25–40 cm)

Slender plant from South Africa and Mozambique. Tuber ellipsoid, about 1 in (25 mm) long. Leaves several, the 2 largest near the base, spreading, to 7 in (18 cm) long, dark green, often with pale green mottling on uppersurface. Inflorescence laxly arranged with up to 12 flowers in summer. Flowers very small, green; sepals and petals

forming hood, lip deeply 3-lobed; spur about ¾ in (18 mm) long.

Habenaria dregeana

↔ 4–8 in (10–20 cm) ↕ 8–16 in (20–40 cm)

From southeastern Africa. Inflorescences densely arranged with many blooms, just under ¾ in (18 mm) in size, predominantly green, in summer–autumn. Lip star-like with long points radiating in a semi-circle.

Habenaria marginata

syn. *Habenaria aurantiaca*

↔ 2–6 in (5–15 cm) ↕ 3–8 in (8–20 cm)

Occurring from India to Thailand. Tubers 2, about 1 in (25 mm) long. Leaves 3 to 4, spreading, elliptic, to 3 in (8 cm) long. Inflorescence conical, densely arranged with many small flowers in summer. Sepals and petals form hood; sepals green, petals and lip yellow; lip 3-lobed, spur short and club-shaped.

Habenaria monorhiza

↔ 5–10 in (12–25 cm) ↕ 8–20 in (20–50 cm)

From Peru, infrequently seen species; often encountered on the fringes of montane rainforest. Upright inflorescences of numerous small, white, ½ in (12 mm) flowers.

Habenaria rhodocheila

↔ 4–8 in (10–20 cm) ↕ 8–12 in (20–30 cm)

From Indochina and southern China; one of the most impressive members of the genus; quite amenable to cultivation. Upright inflorescences of up to 14 widely opening blooms, 2 in (5 cm) in size, pink to red, dominated by the large lip. Blooms autumn–early winter, dormant through summer.

HARAELLA

The sole member of this genus is a dwarf monopodial epiphyte from Taiwan. It features small blooms that are bee-like in appearance, with up to 5 blooms produced on a short arching to pendent inflorescence. The flowers are green to yellow with a distinctive, glossy, predominantly maroon lip.

CULTIVATION: These moisture- and shade-loving epiphytes grow well on small slabs of cork or tree fern. They must be placed in a humid environment with ample air circulation. They enjoy intermediate temperatures and are best left alone once established. Propagate from seed processed in professional laboratories.

HAWKINSARA

Hawkinsara is a multigeneric artificial genus created by combining members of the sympodial Central and South American genera *Broughtonia*, *Cattleya*, *Laelia*, and *Sophronitis*. The use of the miniature *Broughtonia* and *Sophronitis* has significantly reduced the plant size of these hybrids and contributed to the flowers' round shape and bold color. The flowers are often highly colorful and long lasting, with many intense reds, and they are produced on strong stems well clear of the compact foliage.

CULTIVATION: These orchids grow well in small pots of a coarse bark-based medium or in wooden baskets, as long as they dry out between waterings. They enjoy high light and intermediate to warm temperatures year-round. Propagate by division.

Hawkinsara Keepsake 'Lake View'

↔ 4–12 in (10–30 cm) ↕ 4–20 in (10–50 cm)

Attractive hybrid combining 5 species—*Broughtonia sanguinea*, *Cattleya aclandiae*, *Cattleya aurantiaca*, *Laelia cinnabarina*, and *Sophronitis coccinea*. Compact-growing plant. Brightly colored, orange to red blooms borne in summer. Individual flowers 2 in (5 cm) across.

Hawkinsara Keepsake 'Lake View'

Haraella retrocalla

Hexisea imbricata

HEXISEA

This small genus of sympodial epiphytic species from Central and South America is closely related to *Scaphyglottis*. They have clustered pseudobulbs topped with grass-like foliage. Plants shoot from the base of the pseudobulb as well as from the top of the recently matured bulb, and older plants can have a somewhat straggly appearance. Flowers are small but colorful, from pale orange to deep red. CULTIVATION: These orchids grow readily in pots of a well-drained but moisture-retentive bark-based mixture or on tree-fern slabs. They prefer intermediate growing conditions and regular watering; as they are always growing, they like to be kept moist. Propagate by division.

Hexisea imbricata
↔ 4–16 in (10–40 cm) ↕ 4–20 in (10–50 cm)
♀ ☀ ◆/◆ ⊡/⊠

Colorful species from Venezuela; closely related to *H. bidentata*. Small clusters of bright orange blooms, 1 in (25 mm) in size, from top of pseudobulb. Spring-flowering.

HIMANTOGLOSSUM
syn. *Loroglossum*
LIZARD ORCHID

This genus contains 4 to 5 terrestrial species, which occur in Mediterranean Europe. They resemble *Orchis* in vegetative appearance, but have a very differently shaped lip. They develop subterranean tubers and upright shoots with a few lanceolate leaves. They grow on limy soil in dry grassland and beneath shrubs. The flowers are quite large and attractive. CULTIVATION: Despite being dependant on mycorrhizal fungi in the wild, these plants grow well in a mixture of loam, finely ground limestone, and sand. During the growing season, they like a bit more moisture, but avoid water clogging. Propagate by division of larger colonies of plants.

Himantoglossum adriaticum
syn. *Himantoglossum hircinum* var. *adriaticum*
ADRIATIC LIZARD ORCHID
↔ 6–10 in (15–25 cm) ↕ 12–30 in (30–75 cm) ✱ ☼ ◇ ❄ ❊ ⊡

Found in central Italy, along the southern border of the European Alps into Austria and Slovakia; grows in dry grasslands from sea level to 4,270 ft (1,300 m). Shoot develops 6 to 10 leaves at base, each 3–6 in (8–15 cm) long. Erect terminal inflorescence produces up to 40 flowers, spaced loosely apart, in late spring–early summer. Reddish brown flowers, to 2 in (5 cm) long, lip with shorter mid-lobe than *H. caprinum*.

Himantoglossum caprinum
BALKAN LIZARD ORCHID
↔ 6–12 in (15–30 cm) ↕ 12–40 in (30–100 cm) ✱ ☼/☀ ◇ ❄ ❊ ⊡

Variable species from southeastern Europe. Numerous leaves, to 7 in (18 cm) long, ovate near base, but becoming narrower up stem. Spike cylindrical, rather loosely arranged with 10 to 45 flowers in summer. Flowers purplish, sepals and petals forming a hood; lip 3-lobed, side lobes to 1 in (25 mm) long, mid-lobe 2–3 in (5–8 cm) long, deeply divided into two, twisted in a spiral, spur conical.

Himantoglossum hircinum
syns *Aceras hircinum, Loroglossum hircinum*
LIZARD ORCHID, LIZARD'S TONGUE ORCHID
↔ 6–10 in (15–25 cm) ↕ 12–30 in (30–75 cm) ✱ ☼ ◇ ❄ ❊ ⊡

Robust plant, widespread across the Mediterranean region—in southern Europe, northern Africa, and east to Turkey. Habit similar to *H. caprinum*, but can be distinguished by size and longer mid-lobe of lip in this species; inflorescence also denser and more compact. Flowers are predominantly grayish green with red markings, appear in late spring–early summer. and have a distinct smell of goats.

HOMALOPETALUM
The 5 to 8 species in this genus are miniature epiphytes, distributed from Mexico through Central America and the Caribbean to Colombia and Peru, which are found growing in tropical and subtropical forests. They resemble *Barbosella*, however, they have diminutive pseudobulbs in dense clusters, topped by a single fleshy leaf on a creeping rhizome. The single-flowered inflorescence bears an attractive flower that can be larger than the plant itself in some species, or among the smallest flowers of all orchid species. CULTIVATION: Grow *Homalopetalum* species under intermediate conditions in half-sun, mounted on a piece of cork or similar free-draining bark with a thin layer of living moss. These orchids do not tolerate prolonged periods of drought and should be kept moist and humid throughout the year. Propagation is by division.

Homalopetalum pumilio
syns *Homalopetalum costaricense, H. lehmannianum, Pinelia lehmannianum*
↔ ¾–1¼ in (18–30 mm) ↕ ½–2 in (12–50 mm) ♀ ☼ ◆ ⊡/⊠

Found from Mexico to Peru; grows on trees and larger branches of oak or pine trees at elevations of 1,640–6,560 ft (500–2,000 m). Pseudobulb small, globular, less than ¼ in (6 mm) wide; fleshy leaf, to ½ in (12 mm) long. Single flower, large for size of plant, to 2 in (5 cm) wide, in spring–summer.

HOWEARA
syn. *Zelenkoara*

This trigeneric hybrid genus is composed of the New World epiphytes *Leochilus, Oncidium,* and *Rodriguezia.* There are a number of registered crosses, of which only a few are well known. Plants are generally compact but with an abundant and partly aerial fine root system that often escapes the container. Each pseudobulb has 1 to 2 dark green leathery leaves and some sheathing bracts from which the wiry inflorescence emerges. Plants grow year-round, blooming in autumn, winter, and sometimes in spring. CULTIVATION: Grow in an open mix of bark or coconut husk chips, in small pots or baskets, in a bright, intermediate to warm, bright, well-ventilated area. Maintain high humidity. Water and fertilize throughout the year. Propagate by division.

Howeara Mary Eliza
↔ 4–6 in (10–15 cm) ↕ 4–16 in (10–40 cm) ♀ ☼ ◆/◆ ❊ ⊡

Floriferous hybrid; generic name recently changed to reflect accepted name of *Oncidium* parent, *Zelenkoa onusta.* Leathery leaves to 4 in (10 cm) long, narrow, pointed. Branched raceme 12–16 in (30–40 cm) long. with fragrant flowers, yellow with red speckling, 1 in (25 mm) wide, mainly in autumn–winter.

Himantoglossum hircinum

Homalopetalum pumilio

Howeara Mary Eliza

HUNTLEYA
STAR ORCHID, ESTRELLAS

About 10 species make up this genus, and they are found from Costa Rica to Bolivia, Brazil, Venezuela, and Trinidad. They grow epiphytically in very wet low and medium altitude cloud forests at altitudes of 1,640–3,940 ft (500–1,200 m), and are characterized by small pseudobulbs that are hidden beneath the base of the leaves, and leaves that grow in a fan-shaped manner. They can be separated from the closely related species of *Bollea* by their flexible lip. The star-shaped flowers give rise to the common names.

CULTIVATION: Grow under intermediate and rather wet conditions but with constant air movement and under ample shade. They grow equally well in baskets or mounted on a slab with a layer of living moss or sphagnum. Self-pollination generally leads to infertile seed. Propagation is by division.

Huntleya citrina
syn. *Huntleya waldvogelii*
↔ 8–12 in (20–30 cm) ↕ 8–12 in (20–30 cm)
♀ ☀ ◆ ❄ ⛢/▧

Rare species, found in Colombia and Ecuador, growing at low elevations of 660–825 ft (200–250 m). Leaves to 12 in (30 cm) long, forming fans of a similar diameter. Large citron yellow flowers, to 2 in (5 cm) wide, appear singly in summer–autumn beneath base of leaves.

Huntleya meleagris
syns *Batemannia meleagris*, *Huntleya albidofulva*, *Zygopetalum meleagris*
↔ 8–12 in (20–30 cm) ↕ 8–12 in (20–30 cm)
♀ ☀ ◆/◇ ❄ ⛢/▧

Type species of the genus, found at higher elevations, up to 3,940 ft (1,200 m), in wet cloud forests, from Costa Rica to Brazil; tolerates lower temperatures in culture. Star-shaped fragrant flowers borne in spring, summer, and autumn. Flowers are tricolored; tips of sepals and petals are brown, middle section is yellow, and base is white.

HUTTONAEA

The 5 species of the terrestrial genus *Huttonaea* are all endemic to the southern rainfall region of southern Africa. They grow annually from an underground tuber, producing up to 3 stem-clasping leaves on flowering specimens, while juvenile plants generally produce a single broad, somewhat heart-shaped leaf. The plants have bizarre flowers that have seen this genus isolated without close botanical relatives.

CULTIVATION: These rare orchids are very difficult to maintain, and are best observed in their natural habitat.

Huttonaea grandiflora
↔ 3–8 in (8–20 cm) ↕ 4–36 in (10–90 cm)
⚑ ☼/☀ ◆/◇ ❄ ▧

Species from South Africa. Up to 5 blooms, each 1 in (25 mm) in size, produced in late summer–autumn. Flowers white with heavy fimbriate fringing on sepals, some mauve markings on petals.

HYGROCHILUS

A genus of monopodial orchids, with one, possibly 2 species from Southeast Asia, which was segregated from *Vandopsis* along with numerous other species that are now placed in other genera. The plants are *Vanda*-like with opposite, leathery, strap-like leaves. The strong inflorescence is longer than the leaves and carries few to several fragrant flowers. The very large and thick roots emerge from along the stem. *Hygrochilus parishii* occurs in two distinct forms, which may eventually be separated. *H. subparishii* has been transferred to the genus *Sedirea*, as *S. subparishii*.

CULTIVATION: These plants should be grown in medium to bright light, and they do well in pots or baskets using an open mix with medium- to large-grade bark. They like to be watered frequently, but should be allowed to dry between drenchings. Ensure there is good air movement. Water should be of good quality, and plants should be fed regularly throughout the growing season. Keep drier if weather is cool and dark. Minimum temperature is 59–61°F (15–16°C). Propagation is possible if plant sprouts a secondary growth, or, alternatively, plant stem may be cut if section above cut has its own roots. They can also be propagated from seed.

Hygrochilus parishii

Hygrochilus parishii
syns *Stauropsis parishii*, *Vanda parishii*, *Vandopsis parishii*
↔ 14–18 in (35–45 cm) ↕ 8–12 in (20–30 cm) ♀ ☼/☀ ◆/◇ ❄ ▧

From Myanmar, Thailand, and Vietnam. Leathery opposite leaves to 1 in (25 mm) wide. Flowers around 1½ in (35 mm) tall, fragrant, yellowish green with brown blotches and yellow with rose lip in summer–autumn. *H. p.* var. *mariottianus*, brown to pink and brown flowers with bright rose lip.

Huttonaea grandiflora

Isabelia virginalis

Isochilus linearis

IDA

This genus was first described in 2003. It consists of about 30 species that accommodate the *Lycaste* species that were previously treated within the Section *Fimbriatae*. Most of the plants in this genus grow in very moist areas on the fringes of rainforests throughout the cloudy mountainous regions of South America. This sympodial genus includes epiphytic, lithophytic, and terrestrial members. Produced from the base of the mature pseudobulb, the inflorescences carry a single flower. Most of the species have predominantly green flowers.

CULTIVATION: *Ida* species are best potted in a bark-based mix and grown in a humid environment with ample fresh air circulation. They enjoy bright light, but should not be exposed to direct sunlight as this will burn the thin pleated leaves. Propagation is by division of larger specimens of at least 3 pseudobulbs in spring.

Ida costata
↔ 12–36 in (30–90 cm) ↑ 12–36 in (30–90 cm) ♀/⋀ ☀/☀ ◆/◇ ❋ ▽

From Peru. Tall inflorescences with a single flower in spring. Blooms green,

somewhat nodding, 4 in (10 cm) wide, do not open fully; lip yellow to cream with fine fringed edging.

IONOPSIS

About 7 species are known in this genus, with a distribution range from Florida, USA, through Central America, Mexico, and the Caribbean south to Colombia, Brazil, and Paraguay. They are found growing as epiphytes on small branches in forests and plantations from sea level to 5,250 ft (1,600 m). Some species have small clustered pseudobulbs with a single leaf, others feature a thickened stem with leaves arranged in 2 parallel rows. The flowers are showy with a prominent lip.

CULTIVATION: Grow *Ionopsis* species under intermediate to warm conditions in bright light. Keep plants out of direct sunlight to prevent leaf burning. Humidity should be around 60 percent or higher. These plants thrive best when grown mounted on small sticks or branches with regular misting, at least once daily all year-round, and constant air circulation. No resting period is required. Propagation is by division.

Ionopsis utricularioides
syns *Ionopsis paniculata, I. pulchella*
↔ 6–8 in (15–20 cm) ↑ 12 in (30 cm)
♀ ☀ ◆/◇ ❋ ▧

Very variable species, widespread from Florida, USA, to Brazil and Paraguay, growing at elevations from sea level up to 5,250 ft (1,600 m). Often found in citrus and guava plantations. Small rounded pseudobulbs about ½ in (12 mm) wide, with single, stiff, and lance-shaped leaf, up to 4 in (10 cm) long, which is surrounded by 2 to 3 leaves at base. In bright light, leaves turn reddish. Branched inflorescence to 12 in (30 cm) tall, with up to 50 flowers, mainly in spring or summer. Flowers white to various shades of pink, purple, and lavender, ½ in (12 mm) wide, with large lip.

ISABELIA

This is a small South American genus of sympodial orchids, with Brazil the center of distribution for all 5 species. They are miniature-growing epiphytes, with tight clusters of small pseudobulbs topped with a single leaf, and tend to hug the branches on which they grow. They produce short inflorescences with a solitary flower.

CULTIVATION: These plants are best grown on slabs of cork or tree-fern, or potted in small terracotta pots using sphagnum moss. They prefer humid shaded conditions and do not like to dry out. Good air circulation ensures successful cultivation. Propagation is by division.

Isabelia virginalis
↔ 2–6 in (5–15 cm) ↑ 1½–3 in (3.5–8 cm)
♀ ☀ ◆/◇ ▽/▧

Brazilian species. Pseudobulbs covered in criss-cross pattern of fibrous bracts. Single dark green leaf, to about 2½ in (6 cm) long. Individual white to pale mauve-pink blooms, in winter.

ISOCHILUS

This is a small genus containing about 8 sympodial orchid species that are native to Central America and South America. They grow as epiphytes, lithophytes, and sometimes terrestrials. These graceful botanical species with grass-like foliage look attractive even when they are not in flower. They flower from the top of the thin matured growth, with the top leaves sometimes changing color, taking on purple tones before blooming commences. The flowers are small and colorful, and in some cases do not open fully. Some clones of individual species are self-pollinating.

CULTIVATION: With their thick succulent root system, these plants are very readily grown in pots of a well-drained but moisture-retentive bark-based mixture. All species of *Isochilus* prefer intermediate growing conditions and must be watered regularly, as the plants are invariably in constant growth. Propagate by division.

Isochilus aurantiacus
↔ 4–20 in (10–50 cm) ↕ 4–16 in (10–40 cm)
♀ ☀ ◆/◈ ❋ ☐

Free-flowering species from Brazil. Fine foliage makes it an attractive plant even when not in flower. Small clusters of tiny bright tangerine-orange blooms in winter.

Isochilus linearis
↔ 4–24 in (10–60 cm) ↕ 4–24 in (10–60 cm)
♀ ☀ ◆/◈ ❋ ☐

From Central America and northern South America; most frequently cultivated species. Tubular flowers, ½ in (12 mm) wide, pink to purple, in spring. Some forms self-pollinating and rarely open.

JUMELLEA

This is a monopodial genus of about 70 species of epiphytic and lithophytic orchids from Madagascar, the Mascarene and Comoros Islands and tropical Africa, and into South Africa that are closely related to *Angraecum*. They grow in bright light and have nocturnally fragrant white blooms, with a long, nectar-filled, hollow spur behind the flower. Single flowers are produced from the leaf axils, often in abundance. Most species produce fan-like growths, with leaves in 2 ranks that continue growing for many years, whilst also producing side-growths that take a year or two to reach maturity. Some species are climbing and adhere to the host by producing thick roots randomly along the length of the stem.

CULTIVATION: These are easily grown and popular subjects in cultivation. Most species are amenable to pot or basket culture in a bark-based mix, with some of the climbing and miniature species preferring to be grown on tree-fern or cork slabs. They enjoy bright light levels, constant air circulation, and intermediate to warm conditions, in a humid atmosphere. Propagate by divisions of mature plants, ensuring there is enough root system attached to support the plant as it re-establishes.

Jumellea arachnantha
↔ 20–40 in (50–100 cm) ↕ 18–27 in (45–70 cm) ♀ ☀ ◆ ❋ ☐

Robust plants from the Comoros Islands. Short stems; strap-shaped leaves 18–27 in (45–70 cm) long. Flowers white, fairly large; each segment to 2 in (5 cm) long; lip clawed at base; spur to 1¾ in (45 mm) long. Spring-flowering.

Jumellea comorensis
↔ 4–10 in (10–25 cm) ↕ 5–12 in (12–30 cm) ♀ ☽/☀ ◆/◈ ❋ ☐

From the Comoros Islands. Upright stems with leaves in 2 ranks. Blooms white, just over 1½ in (35 mm) wide, highly fragrant at evening, pollinated by moths. Summer-flowering.

Jumellea confusa
↔ 6–10 in (15–25 cm) ↕ 5–24 in (12–60 cm) ♀/△ ☀ ◆ ❋ ☐

Species from Madagascar. Woody stems; numerous leaves, narrowly strap-shaped, 3–5 in (8–12 cm) long, folded at base. Flowers white; floral segments each to about 1 in (25 mm) long; spur about 5 in (12 cm) long. Spring-flowering.

Jumellea densefoliata
↔ 2½–3 in (6–8 cm) ↕ 2–3 in (5–8 cm) ♀/△ ☀ ◆ ❋ ☐

Short-stemmed plants from Madagascar. Leaves numerous, set close

Jumellea arachnantha

Jumellea confusa

together in 2 rows, each leaf 2–3 in (5–8 cm) long, oblong. Sepals and petals greenish-white, each about ¾ in (18 mm) long; lip white, of similar length; spur slender, 4–5 in (10–12 cm) long. Flowers borne from spring to summer.

Jumellea fragrans
↔ 16–24 in (40–60 cm) ↕ 10–16 in (25–60 cm) ♀ ☀ ◆/◈ ❋ ☐

From the Mascarene Islands. Erect-growing plants, forming dense clumps. Upright woody stem, leafy near apex, produces a single flower in winter. Leaves 4–6 in (10–15 cm) long, narrowly strap-shaped. Medium-sized white flowers; spur about 1¼ in (30 mm) long. Leaves aromatic, can be infused in water to make a sort of tea, known as "fahan."

Jumellea sagittata
↔ 20–30 in (50–75 cm) ↕ 12–15 in (30–45 cm) ♀ ☀ ◆ ❋ ☐

Large plants from Madagascar. Branching at base. Stem short, with about 10 leaves forming a fan. Leaves

Jumellea densefoliata

5–10 in (12–25 cm) long, strap-shaped, folded at base. Pendent inflorescences carry a single flower in winter–spring. Flowers white, floral segments each about 1½ in (35 mm) long; lip diamond-shaped, clawed at base; spur about ¾ in (18 mm) long. Blooms strongly scented at night.

Jumellea comorensis

KEFERSTEINIA

This genus of over 50 species lacks pseudobulbs, having instead a fan of soft leaves. They are epiphytes, rarely terrestrials, found from Nicaragua to Brazil and Bolivia, at elevations of 1,000–8,200 ft (300–2,500 m). The plants are small, compact, and grow in clumps. Each inflorescence produces a single smallish flower, with the plant usually producing few to several flowers at a time in a wide variety of colors and shapes.
CULTIVATION: These plants prefer bright shade, good air movement, high humidity, regular feeding, and good quality water. Winter minimum should be 55–58°F (13–15°C) and maximum not more than 80°F (26°C). Keep plants moist and do not allow to dry out for any period. Do not allow water to stand in the crowns of the fans of leaves overnight or when it is cold, as rot may start and spread. These plants are easy to grow in pots or baskets, and do well in moss, fine bark, and various mixes. As they often produce a massive root system, it is not uncommon to see the plants pushed part-way out of the pot. Propagate by division.

Kefersteinia graminea
syn. *Zygopetalum gramineum*
↔ 8–12 in (20–30 cm) ↕ 8–14 in (20–35 cm)
♀ ☀/☀ ◆/◇ ❀ ▱/☈

From cool montane forests of Venezuela, Colombia, and Ecuador. Short spikes produce a single flower in summer–autumn. Flowers pale green with dense maroon spotting; lip white with maroon blotching. Grows well potted or mounted.

Kefersteinia laminata
↔ 16 in (40 cm) ↕ 12 in (30 cm)
♀ ☀/☀ ◆/◇ ❀ ▱/☈

Uncommon species from Ecuador. Predominantly green, 1¼ in (30 mm) wide, crystalline blooms, overlaid with light mauve suffusions; broad purple lip, white-edged. Spring-flowering.

KUNTHARA

This is a complex generic hybrid, being a combination of *Cochlioda, Miltoniopsis, Odontoglossum*, and *Oncidium*. Many of these hybrids have rich red colors that can be traced back in part to the *Cochlioda* part of their makeup.
CULTIVATION: Kuntharas do not like their roots to dry out, so they need to be potted in sphagnum moss or a fine bark mix. They are suitable for cool growing conditions, but need abundant water year-round and a semi-shaded position. Propagate by division.

Kunthara Hybrids
↔ 12 in (30 cm) ↕ 30 in (75 cm)
♀ ☀ ◆/◇ ❀ ▱

Among the *Kunthara* hybrids available are **Living Fire**, a rich red-flowered

Kefersteinia laminata

hybrid between *Odonchlopsis* Edna and the Central American species *Oncidium maculatum*; **Nelly Isler**, an improvement on its parent *K.* Stefan Isler, has been hybridized with *Miltoniopsis* Kensington; **Stefan Isler**, similar to *K.* Living Fire, is a hybrid between *Odonchlopsis* Edna and *Oncidium leucochilum*. Flowers in spring–summer.

Kunthara Nelly Isler (hybrid)

Kunthara Living Fire (hybrid)

Kunthara Stefan Isler (hybrid)

LAELIA

This genus from Mexico, Central America, and tropical South America is comprised of about 60 easily grown, showy, and colorful sympodial orchids. These *Cattleya* relatives are generally lithophytic, although there are a number of epiphytic species. They also differ from that genus by having 8 pollen bundles or pollinia (*Cattleya* have only 4). They are generally smaller plants than the majority of cattleyas, and mostly have 1 leaf per pseudobulb, although there are a few species with 2 or more leaves. They have been used in numerous artificial hybrids involving a range of related genera, including *Brassavola, Broughtonia, Cattleya, Epidendrum,* and *Sophronitis.*
CULTIVATION: Most species require bright, warm, and moist conditions during summer while the plants are in active growth, and a cooler dry winter, when most species are dormant. Cultivated plants must have unimpeded drainage, and can be mounted or grown in pots using a coarse bark-based medium. Flowering plants may be enjoyed indoors while in bloom. Propagate by division.

Laelia anceps ★

↔ 8–36 in (20–90 cm) ↕ 8–48 in (20–120 cm) ♀ ☀/☀ ◆/◆/◇ ❄ ☐/☒

Native to Mexico. Extremely variable species. Long flattened inflorescences to over 40 in (100 cm) long, with up to 5 large blooms in autumn–winter. Flowers to 5 in (12 cm) across, somewhat starry, colors range from white through shades of pink to deep lavender; lip color just as variable, various combinations of white, yellow, orange,

Laelia anceps

purple, and lilac. Albino (white), bicolored, and splash-petalled forms also in cultivation. *L. a.* var. *veitchiana* 'Fort Caroline', white blooms; pale lilac lip, purple-veined yellow throat.

Laelia blumenscheinii

syn. *Sophronitis blumenscheinii*
↔ 10–16 in (25–40 cm) ↕ 12–14 in (30–35 cm) ∧ ☀/☀ ◆/◇ ❄ ☐

Endemic to eastern Brazil; grows among grasses on rock outcroppings. Elongated pseudobulbs are swollen at base and taper toward apex, with a single, lance-shaped, leathery leaf. Inflorescence to 16 in (40 cm) long, grows from apex of bulb, with up to 12 somewhat sequential flowers in spring. Blooms to 2 in (5 cm) in size, light yellow. Likes cooler drier winters.

Laelia blumenscheinii

Laelia Canariensis

↔ 8–24 in (20–60 cm) ↕ 8–40 in (20–100 cm) ♀/∧ ☀/☀ ◆/◆ ❄ ☐

Popular primary hybrid of *L. anceps* and *L. harpophylla*. Blooms in colors ranging from light purples to orange and yellow tones, in winter–spring.

Laelia Canariensis

Laelia caulescens

↔ 4–10 in (10–25 cm) ↕ 5–14 in (12–35 cm) ∧ ☀/☀ ◆ ❄ ☐

From Brazil; found on rocks near edges of rainforests, in bright light, high humidity, and with plenty of air movement. Upright inflorescences of up to 6 blooms in spring. Flowers almost 2 in (5 cm) wide, flat, musk pink.

Laelia anceps var. *veitchiana* 'Fort Caroline'

Laelia caulescens

L

Laelia crispa

Laelia crispata

Laelia jongheana

Laelia harpophylla

Laelia cinnabarina

syn. *Sophronitis cinnabarina*

↔ 14–16 in (35–40 cm) ↕ 12–20 in (30–50 cm) /\ ☼/☀ ◆/◇ ❈ ▽

Endemic to Brazil; often grows among tall grasses. Elongate pseudobulbs swollen at base, taper to narrower apex. Inflorescence grows from bulb apex, 12–20 in (30–50 cm) tall, with up to 15 large flowers in spring. Blooms 3–4 in (8–10 cm) wide, bright orange, starry; lip also orange, with crisped edge. Needs cool, dry winter.

Laelia crispa

syn. *Sophronitis crispa*

↔ 8–36 in (20–90 cm) ↕ 8–24 in (20–60 cm) ♀/⋀ ☼/☀ ◆/◇ ❈ ▽

From Brazil. Upright spike with up to 7 blooms, in late summer. Flowers 5 in (12 cm) wide, white; lip pre-dominantly purple with yellow markings, floral segments with wavy edges.

Laelia crispata

syns *Laelia rupestris, Sophronitis crispata*

↔ 8–10 in (20–25 cm) ↕ 10–16 in (25–40 cm) /\ ☼ ◆/◇ ❈ ▽

Endemic to eastern Brazil; grows among mosses and grasses. Pseudobulbs nearly cylindrical, narrower at apex; 1 leathery, glaucous, blue-green leaf. Upright spikes arise from apex of bulbs, with up to 10 flowers in spring. Blooms 1½–2 in (35–50 mm) wide, cerise, whitish toward base of petals and sepals; lip cerise and yellow.

Laelia dayana

syn. *Sophronitis dayana*

↔ 5–8 in (12–20 cm) ↕ 6–8 in (15–20 cm) ♀ ☼ ◆ ❈ ▽

Endemic to Brazil; often grows on trees along rivers. Cylindrical pseudobulbs to 2½ in (6 cm) long; 1 ovate leathery leaf at apex. As leaf opens, bud is already present, forming single pink flower, 1½–2 in (35–50mm) wide, in summer–autumn. Lip dark purple with white throat, lined with raised dark purple calli that come to edge of lip. Also blue (coerulea) form.

Laelia harpophylla

syn. *Sophronitis harpophylla*

↔ 14–18 in (35–45 cm) ↕ 14–24 in (35–60 cm) ♀ ☀/☼ ◆ ❈ ▽

Endemic to eastern Brazil. Plants tall; very thin cane-like pseudobulbs; single lance-like leaf. Raceme of 5 to 15 blooms in spring. Flowers to almost

Laelia longipes

3 in (8 cm) wide, bright orange with narrow pointed segments, lip orange.

Laelia jongheana

syn. *Sophronitis jongheana*

↔ 9–14 in (22–35 cm) ↕ 8–12 in (20–30 cm) ♀ ☼/☀ ◆/◇ ❈ ▽

Montane species from Brazil; grows in bright situations. Related to *L. pumila*. Elongate-cylindrical pseudobulbs with a single ovate leathery leaf, with buds already present when leaf separates. Inflorescence with up to 3 large flowers in spring. Blooms 5–6 in (12–15 cm) wide, pink, with golden yellow in throat and calli of lip. Also white form with yellow lip. Species is highly endangered in the wild.

Laelia longipes

syns *Laelia lucasiana, L. ostermeyerii, Sophronitis lucasiana*

↔ 4–6 in (10–15 cm) ↕ 3–4 in (8–10 cm) /\ ☼ ◆ ❈ ▽

Endemic to Brazil; grows in full sun on rocks with mosses. Clustered pseudobulbs with 1 leathery leaf. Short spikes from the apex of bulbs, with 2 to 5 flowers in spring. Blooms bright rose pink with undulate lip. Also white form with yellow lip. Plants have cool, dry, winter rest.

Laelia milleri

syn. *Sophronitis milleri*

↔ 4–16 in (10–40 cm) ↕ 8–27 in (20–70 cm) /\ ☼/☀ ◆/◇ ❈ ▽

Spectacular compact species from Brazil. Tall spikes with up to 8 orange-red to dark red blooms, 2½ in (6 cm) wide, in late spring–summer.

Laelia pumila

syn. *Sophronitis pumila*

↔ 4–16 in (10–40 cm) ↕ 4–8 in (10–20 cm) ♀ ☼ ◆/◇ ❈ ▽/✄

Compact species from Brazil. Single pink to dark purple blooms, almost 4 in (10 cm) wide, produced from developing new growth in summer. Also albino (white) and lilac-colored forms. Prefers more shade than most laelias; may also be grown on slabs of cork or tree fern.

Laelia milleri

Laelia purpurata

Laelia purpurata

syn. *Sophronitis purpurata*

↔ 8–36 in (20–90 cm)　↕ 8–36 in (20–90 cm)

National flower of Brazil; has been called the "Queen of the Laelias."

Up to 5 blooms, 8 in (20 cm) across, produced off mature pseudobulbs in summer. Tall-growing species; wide range and combination of colors, from pure white through all shades of pink, purple, and lilac. Flared and trumpet-like lip in similar color range, with a network of stripes and solid color. Also albino (pure white), semi-alba, splash-petalled, and bicolored forms. Many varieties named, all defining a different color form.

Two of the most popular varieties are *L. p.* var. *carnea* ★, crisp white blooms with a soft pink lip; and *L. p.* var. *werkhauseri*, white blooms with a dark bluish purple lip and a pleasant fragrance.

Laelia purpurata var. *carnea*

Laelia rubescens

Laelia tenebrosa

Laelia sincorana

Laeliocatonia Peggy San 'Galaxy'

Laelia rubescens

syn. *Laelia acuminata*

↔ 10–16 in (25–40 cm) ↑ 10–24 in (25–60 cm) ♀/ʌ ◌/❂ ◆/◇ ❈ ▽/⩘

Found from Mexico to Panama; often in hot dry areas. Pseudobulbs very round, compressed; single leathery leaf. Inflorescences 10–24 in (25–60 cm) long, arise from apex of pseudobulb, with short-lived flowers clustered at end of spike in autumn. Flowers dark pink to nearly white, lip with dark purple spot. *L. r.* var. *roseum*, rich rose pink flowers, darker than normal.

Laelia sincorana

↔ 4–8 in (10–20 cm) ↑ 3–7 in (8–18 cm) ♀ ❂ ◆ ❈ ▽

Compact species from Brazil. Tight clusters of globular pseudobulbs, topped with a single leathery leaf. Blooms produced singly or in pairs in spring–summer. Flowers pink to purple, just over 3 in (8 cm) wide, disproportionally large in relation to size of plant. Tubular lip, cream and deep purple, lightly ruffled at edge. This plant grows well on cork or tree-fern slabs.

Laelia tenebrosa

syn. *Sophronitis tenebrosa*

↔ 8–36 in (20–90 cm) ↑ 8–32 in (20–80 cm) ♀ ◌/❂ ◆/◇ ❈ ▽

Large summer-flowering species from Brazil. Up to 3 blooms, 6 in (15 cm) across. Petals and sepals bronze with coppery hue; lip white with very heavy purple veining.

LAELIOCATONIA

This intergeneric hybrid combines the characteristics of 3 epiphytic New World genera, *Laelia, Cattleya,* and *Broughtonia.* The latter is used to obtain the desirable round flower and to increase both flower count and inflorescence length. The addition of *Cattleya* increases flower size and substance. Yellow- to orange-colored *Laelia* or *Cattleya* parents can produce hybrids with peach to orange blooms. Carried high above dark green fleshy leaves, the fragrant blooms are mostly pink, fuchsia, or plum red, often with darker flares. Compact plants bloom 2 or 3 times a year.

CULTIVATION: Laeliocatonias thrive when grown warm, mounted or with free-draining mix in pots. Allow plants to dry between waterings but always maintain high humidity and good air movement. Fertilize when plants are in active growth. Bright light is needed to achieve flowering potential. Propagate by division of established clumps.

Laeliocatonia Peggy San 'Galaxy'

↔ 6–8 in (15–20 cm) ↑ 8–12 in (20–30 cm) ♀ ❂ ◆/◇ ❈ ▽/⩘

This grex is splash- or flare-petalled, a trait sometimes also repeated in the lip, as with 'Galaxy'. Grown warm and in bright light, branched spike can bear 3 or more flowers, to 2 in (5 cm) wide, whenever new growth matures, mainly in winter, spring, and autumn.

Laeliocattleya Canhamiana 'Coerulea' (hybrid)

LAELIOCATTLEYA

This is an artificial bigeneric group of colorful orchid hybrids between 2 epiphytic New World genera—*Laelia* and *Cattleya*. They are generally robust plants with 1 or 2 leaves per pseudobulb, and come in a wide range of sizes, shapes, and colors—the result of the combination of 2 genera that are themselves highly variable. Almost all colors may be encountered, with the exception of black and sky blue. The flower size varies between 2 in (5 cm) and 10 in (25 cm). Many of the larger-flowering types are grown commercially for the cut-flower trade. CULTIVATION: These attractive hybrids require warmth in winter but will cope with cooler winter temperatures for short periods provided that they are kept dry while dormant. They enjoy bright light conditions and must have unimpeded drainage and a coarse bark-based medium. Healthy plants will develop an extensive system of thick white roots that are long-lived and freely branching. Propagation is by division.

Laeliocattleya Hybrids
↔ 4–30 in (10–75 cm) ↕ 4–36 in (10–90 cm)

Popular and easily grown examples include **C. G. Roebling**, primary hybrid made over a century ago between the "blue-lipped" forms of *Cattleya gaskelliana* and *Laelia purpurata*; **Chit Chat 'Tangerine'**, free-flowering hybrid of *Cattleya aurantiaca* and *Laelia* Coronet, vivid orange blooms; **Edgard van Belle 'Edwin Arthur Hausermann'**, bold pink to purple bloom with a strong fragrance; **Gold Harp**, hybrid between *Laelia harpophylla* and *Laeliocattleya* Golden Blossom, golden yellow blooms, lip with purple ruffled edges; **Jim Burkhalter**, hybrid between *Laeliocattleya* Jalapa and *Cattleya* Chocolate Drop, apricot and pink flowers, deep pinkish red lip; **Mini Purple 'Bette'** ★, popular primary hybrid of compact-growing *Laelia pumila* and *Cattleya walkeriana*, producing pinkish purple flowers; **Myrtle Johnson**, fine "splash-petalled" style, lip colors also appearing on petals; **Pink Favourite 'Jolly'**, primary hybrid of *Laelia milleri* and *Cattleya walkeriana*; **Rojo 'Fiery'**, primary hybrid of *Cattleya aurantiaca* and *Laelia milleri*, bright red flowers with orange tubular lip; **Tropical Pointer 'Cheetah'**, *Cattleya intermedia* hybrid—gets its spots from one of its ancestors, *C. aclandiae*. Depending on parentage, blooms can be produced for most of year.

Laeliocattleya Jim Burkhalter (hybrid)

Laeliocattleya (Cattleya Vaupes Sunrise × *Laeliocattleya* Interglossa) (hybrid)

Laeliocattleya Edgard van Belle 'Edwin Arthur Hausermann' (hybrid)

Laeliocattleya C. G. Roebling (hybrid)

Laeliocattleya Gold Harp (hybrid)

Laeliocattleya Chit Chat 'Tangerine' (hybrid)

Laeliocattleya Rabeiana (hybrid)

Laeliocattleya Kauai Spiders (hybrid)

Laeliocattleya Lauren Oka 'Kristy' (hybrid)

Laeliocattleya (*Laeliocattleya* Blue Ribbon × *Cattleya* Penny Kuroda) (hybrid)

Laeliocattleya 'Maris Song' (hybrid)

Laeliocattleya Mini Purple 'Bette' (hybrid)

Laeliocattleya Mini Purple 'Royale' (hybrid)

Laeliocattleya Orange Embers (hybrid)

Laeliocattleya Myrtle Johnson (hybrid)

Laeliocattleya Pink Favourite 'Jolly' (hybrid)

Laeliocattleya Rojo 'Fiery' (hybrid)

Laeliocattleya Pink Perfume (hybrid)

Laeliocattleya Pre School 'Royale' (hybrid)

Laeliocattleya Royal Emperor 'Wade' (hybrid)

Laeliocattleya Sallieri (hybrid)   *Laeliocattleya* Tropical Pointer 'Cheetah' (hybrid)

Lepanthes species

Lepanthes ligiae, in bud

LANIUM

The 4 or 5 species of this genus are found in the northern parts of South America where they grow as epiphytes. These small plants were formerly included in *Epidendrum*, but separated because of their characteristic creeping rhizome with clustered pseudobulbs, topped by 3 to 4 leaves or small-leafed axils, and the flowers, which have woolly hairs at the back of the sepals, flower stalks, and seed capsules—hence the genus name, meaning "woolly."

CULTIVATION: Best grown mounted, but shallow pots with a free-draining organic substrate are suitable as well. Before flowering, keep the plants under more shade and water frequently; after the flowers have wilted, the plants like more light and less watering. Propagation is by division.

Lanium avicula

syns *Epidendrum avicula, E. lanioides, E. longifolium, Lanium berkeleyi*

↔ 6–12 in (15–30 cm)   ↑ 3–5 in (8–12 cm)

♀ ☀ ◆ 🖅/�ということ

From Brazil and Peru; grows in wet forests at altitudes of about 3,940 ft

(1,200 m). Several subspecies, distinguished by different growth habits. Thickened stems covered in sheaths, upper ones bearing 2 to 3 broad to cylindrical leaves. Unbranched upright inflorescence arises from tip of pseudobulb and carries a number of small flowers in spring and autumn. Flower color ranges from cream to yellowish green or yellowish brown.

LEPANTHES

This is a large genus of over 800 species of dwarf epiphytic or lithophytic orchids from tropical America and the West Indies. They have a short creeping rhizome and slender tufted stems, usually with 1 leaf. The leaves are sometimes attractively patterned and velvety in texture. The inflorescence is a raceme that often lies flat on the leaf surface, bearing one to many small flowers, with the sepals the most prominent parts.

CULTIVATION: Species of *Lepanthes* are not easy to cultivate. They can be grown mounted on bark or in small pots, but require shady, humid, airy conditions and must never be allowed

to dry out. Because of this, they are sometimes most successfully grown in enclosed cases. Propagate by division.

Lepanthes calodictyon

↔ 2–3 in (5–8 cm)   ↑ 2–2½ in (5–6 cm)

♀ ☀ ◇ 🖅/🌿

Dwarf species from Ecuador and southern Colombia. Tufted stems 1½–2 in (3.5–5 cm) long; single leaf. Leaves to 2 in (5 cm) long, elliptic to almost round, bright green, with dense network of red-brown veins. Inflorescence with 1 to several flowers, opening in succession, in winter–spring. Flowers very small, reddish and yellow.

Lepanthes ligiae

↔ 14–18 in (35–45 cm)   ↑ 14–16 in (35–40 cm)   ♀ ☀ ◆/◇ 🖅/🌿

From Colombia; grows in moist mountains. No pseudobulbs, instead there are very thin stems, with 1 soft, oval, pointed leaf. One or more zigzag inflorescences with small flowers bloom consecutively on back of leaves for most of the year. Flowers about ¾ in (18 mm) wide, greenish-yellow with intricate, diminutive, red and yellow petals and lip.

LEPTOTES

This genus contains 5 species, which are found in southern Brazil and Paraguay, where they are found in

Leptotes bicolor

humid montane forests. The small epiphytes or sometimes lithophytes have pencil-shaped pseudobulbs topped by a single cylindrical leaf. The inflorescence with 1 to 5 flowers appears at the base of the leaf. The flowers are quite large and showy for the size of the plants, and colors range from yellowish to white and pink, depending on the species. Overall, the plants resemble a miniature *Brassavola* in their aspects.

CULTIVATION: *Leptotes* species should be grown in bright light under intermediate conditions. Humidity should be high throughout the year and no resting period is required. They do best when mounted on a piece of cork or tree fern with lots of air movement. Propagation is by division.

Leptotes bicolor

syn. *Leptotes serrulata*

↔ 3–6 in (8–12 cm)   ↑ 3–6 in (8–12 cm)

♀ ☀ ◆ 🖅/🌿

Found in the southeastern states of Brazil from Minas Gerais in the north to Santa Catarina in the south and into neighboring Paraguay. Pencil-shaped leaves to 4 in (10 cm) long. Plants from northern part of range are very succulent, with leaves to ½ in (12 mm) wide. Inflorescence with 2 to 3 flowers in spring. Blooms to 1 in (25 mm) wide, white with pink lip. *L. b.* var. *alba*, pure white blooms.

Leptotes unicolor

syn. *Leptotes paranaensis*

↔ 2–3 in (5–8 cm)   ↑ 2–3 in (5–8 cm)

♀ ☀ ◆ 🖅/🌿

From Brazil. Fleshy leaves. Plant somewhat smaller than *L. bicolor*, although the pure pink flowers are same size. Flowers do not open fully and have darker pink veins along sepals and petals. Also a very rare white variety. Spring-flowering.

LIPARIS

This sympodial genus is cosmopolitan, with about 250 species, a large number of which are terrestrial, although in the tropics most members are epiphytes. They are mostly found in shady environments, often near creeks, where there is always high humidity. The epiphytic species often grow on the moss-covered limbs or trunks of trees on the edges of rainforest. Flowers are generally in various shades of yellowish green; some species have contrasting bright orange and red lips.

CULTIVATION: Quick-growing in cultivation if their native environment is simulated. They need to be kept moist and shaded, with circulating fresh air. Most have soft leaves that will burn if exposed to full sun. Some of the creeping species do well on cork or tree-fern slabs, while many grow readily in small pots in a freely draining bark-based medium. Propagate by division.

Liparis latifolia

↔ 4–6 in (10–15 cm)   ↕ 7–12 in (18–30 cm)
🌿 ☀ ◆ ❄ 🗓/📧

Widely distributed throughout Southeast Asia. Pear-shaped pseudobulbs to 1¼ in (30 mm) long, each with 1 leaf, 7–12 in (18–30 cm) long. Flowering stem erect, shorter than leaves, with many closely packed flowers in spring. Blooms small, brick red; fan-shaped lip. Often sold and cultivated as *L. nutans*, a totally different orchid with small green and orange blooms.

Liparis nervosa

↔ 4–8 in (10–20 cm)   ↕ 5–14 in (12–35 cm)
🌿 ☀ ◆/◇ ❄ 🗓

Species has enormous distribution range, found in tropical America, tropical Africa, and in Asia from India to Japan, Indonesia, and the Philippines to western New Guinea. Short-lived pleated leaves. Inflorescence upright with up to 40 greenish yellow to dull red, thin-segmented, odorless blooms, ½ in (12 mm) wide. Spring-flowering. Easy to cultivate.

Liparis nigra

↔ 8–12 in (20–30 cm)   ↕ 10–40 in (25–100 cm) 🌿 ☀ ◆ ❄ 🗓/📧

Taiwanese species. Narrowly cylindrical pseudobulbs, to 8 in (20 cm) tall, with several leaves. Leaves to 6 in (15 cm) long, ovate, pleated. Raceme 10–14 in (25–35 cm) tall, occasionally up to 40 in (100 cm) tall, with many closely packed small flowers in spring. Flowers less than ¾ in (18 mm) across, deep purple-red; lip more or less square, about ½ in (12 mm) long and wide.

Liparis reflexa

↔ 4–36 in (10–90 cm)   ↕ 4–12 in (10–30 cm)
/\ ☀ ◆/◇ 🗓/📧

Australian species. Erect to arching spikes of flowers in autumn and winter. Blooms ½ in (12 mm) long, narrow segments, yellowish green, smelling slightly like wet dog.

Liparis viridiflora

↔ 4–36 in (10–90 cm)   ↕ 4–16 in (10–40 cm)
♀ ☀ ◆/◇ 🗓/📧

From Southeast Asia. Clustered pseudobulbs with 2 to 3 leaves. Long inflorescences densely covered with more than 100 blooms in autumn–spring. Small flowers, ¼ in (6 mm) long, yellow to green, with a most sickly fragrance. Very easy to grow under range of conditions.

LOCKHARTIA

This is a genus of about 30 epiphytic species, which are distributed from Central America to the northern half of South America and the West Indies. Most of the species have a very similar growth habit, and as such are difficult to identify out of bloom. Lacking pseudobulbs, these orchids have upright to pendulous stems with many leaves, which are arranged in 2 ranks and are stem clasping, giving a saw-toothed appearance. Short inflorescences are produced from the leaf axils along the upper part of the stems and bear from 1 to 6 *Oncidium*-like flowers that are typically yellow, with some dark red spotting on the lip. There are also species with white blooms. Most of the species produce their blooms throughout the warmer months of the year.

CULTIVATION: These are easy species to grow in greenhouses or tropical climates. They are best grown and displayed on tree-fern or cork slabs, where they will flourish for years without disturbance. Alternatively, they may be grown in small pots or baskets in a bark-based medium. They enjoy frequent watering, but must be allowed to dry out between applications. They enjoy bright light, circulating air, and intermediate to warm conditions. Propagation is by division of large established clumps in spring.

Lockhartia biserra

Lockhartia biserra

syn. *Epidendrum biserra*

↔ 4–12 in (10–30 cm)   ↕ 4–16 in (10–40 cm)
♀ ☀ ◆/◇ ❄ 🗓/📧

Species found from Venezuela to Ecuador. Tooth-like foliage. Short inflorescences arise from within axils of upper leaves, with up to 4 blooms in summer. Flowers ½ in (12 mm) long, bright yellow, shapely.

Lockhartia pittieri

syn. *Lockhartia integra*

BRAID ORCHID

↔ 5–6 in (12–15 cm)   ↕ 6–8 in (15–20 cm)
♀ ☀/☀ ◆/◇ ❄ 🗓/📧

From humid forests in Ecuador. Cane-like flattened pseudobulbs; braided leaves along their length. Often blooms simultaneously on several short spikes at apex of cane, in autumn–winter. Flowers about ½ in (12 mm) in size, yellow with orange to red on lip.

Liparis nervosa

Liparis viridiflora

Liparis species

L

Ludisia discolor

Ludisia discolor

year, as they are growing almost constantly. Give them plenty of fresh air, to avoid spotting of the leaves, and a shaded position, as direct light will burn the succulent leaves and rhizomes. Propagate by division.

Ludisia discolor
syn. *Haemaria discolor*

↔ 4–24 in (10–60 cm) ↕ 4–16 in (10–40 cm)

🌱 ☀ ◆/◇ ❈ 🪴

Species with variable foliage color and pattern, ranging from dark green to deep purplish brown tints conspicuously veined in gold to coppery red. Leaf surface distinctly velvety. Upright spikes of unusual pure white flowers, yellow at center, arising from new growths, in autumn–winter.

LYCASTE

These deciduous sympodial orchids are native to coastal and mountainous regions from Mexico to Bolivia. There are 45 distinct recognized species. They are cool- to warm-growing epiphytes or terrestrials with fat pseudobulbs and large, thin, pleated leaves. Many of the Central American species (particularly the yellow-flowered group, which also have highly fragrant blooms) often leave sharp spines after the previous season's leaves have fallen. The long-lasting flowers are produced singly, on upright stalks from the base of the pseudobulb, usually in spring and summer, coinciding with new growth. The sepals open fully in most species, with the petals pushed forward, often adjacent to the lip. There are numerous hybrids, mostly based on the magnificent *L. skinneri*, which prefers cooler temperatures.

CULTIVATION: These orchids are best grown in pots, as their roots must not dry out during the growing season. Use a well-drained bark-based mix that incorporates a moisture-retaining medium such as peat moss. They are heavy feeders when in active growth, and require copious watering. The leaves can burn in summer if plants are exposed to direct light. Reduce watering when plants are dormant in winter, allowing the potting medium to dry for a few days before re-wetting. Protect from frost. Propagate by division.

Lycaste aromatica

↔ 8–24 in (20–60 cm) ↕ 8–16 in (20–40 cm)

♀/∧/🌱 ☼/☀ ◆/◇/◇ ❈ 🪴

Found from Mexico to Nicaragua. Spined pseudobulb. Up to 12 flower stems from base of bulb in summer, just after leaves have dropped. Bright yellow blooms 2½ in (6 cm) wide, cinnamon-scented. Easily grown.

LUDISIA
JEWEL ORCHID

This is a sympodial terrestrial genus with only 1 species, which is widely encountered throughout tropical Southeast Asia. It has fleshy creeping stems and small rosettes of succulent leaves. The small flowers are borne in an erect spike arising from the center of the leaf rosette. *Ludisia* is one of the few orchid genera grown primarily for their attractive foliage.

CULTIVATION: Grow in shallow trays or baskets to accommodate its creeping habit. These plants enjoy warm humid conditions throughout the

Lycaste bradeorum

↔ 8–24 in (20–60 cm) ↕ 4–12 in (10–30 cm)

Very floriferous species from Central America. Leafless pseudobulb with numerous flowers, produced singly, from base of bulb in summer. Blooms 2½ in (6 cm) wide, fragrant, greenish yellow sepals and bright yellow-orange petals and lip.

Lycaste macrophylla

↔ 24–32 in (60–80 cm) ↕ 26–32 in (65–80 cm)

Very widespread species with many subspecies, occurring in Nicaragua, Costa Rica, Panama, Colombia, Venezuela, Bolivia and Peru. Pseudobulbs compressed and ovoid; very large pleated leaves, eventually deciduous. Flowers to 4 in (10 cm) wide, variable in color and pattern; sepals reddish, pink, brownish to green; petals white, often flushed or spotted pink or red; lip white, yellow, pinkish, or red. Flowers for most of year. *L. m.* var. *desboisiana,* endemic to northeastern Costa Rica, greenish sepals heavily marked with brown, white, and pink petals.

Lycaste skinneri

syn. *Lycaste guatemalensis*

↔ 8–24 in (20–60 cm) ↕ 4–24 in (10–60 cm)

Highly desirable and variable species from Guatemala, Honduras, and El Salvador. Large light to deep pink blooms, 5 in (12 cm) across, in groups of up to 6, in winter–early spring.

Lycaste tricolor

↔ 8–24 in (20–60 cm) ↕ 4–16 in (10–40 cm)

From Costa Rica and Panama. Somewhat nodding blooms, 2½ in (6 cm) across, sepals greenish bronze, petals white to pale pink, in winter–spring.

Lycaste tricolor

Lycaste aromatica

Lycaste macrophylla var. *desboisiana*

Lycaste skinneri

L

Lycaste bradeorum

Lycaste Albanensis (hybrid)

Lycaste Hybrids

↔ 8–24 in (20–60 cm) ↑ 4–24 in (10–60 cm)

Many of these have hybrid vigor, are easier to grow, and bloom more readily than some of the species. *Lycaste* hybrids mostly flower in winter–spring. **Albanensis**, primary hybrid between *L. lasioglossa* and *L. macrophylla*; **Imschootiana**, primary hybrid made over a century ago between *L. cruenta* and *L. skinneri*; **Koolena** ★, popular hybrid, both as a showbench flower and for breeding, with a high percentage of *L. skinneri* in its genetic make-up; **Leo**, with 3 different species in its background: *L. macrobulbon, L. macrophylla*, and *L. skinneri*; **Macama 'Aline'** and **Macama 'Atlantis'**, are both hybrids between *L.* Sunrise and *L.* Koolena; (**Rowland** × **Shoalhaven**), unregistered hybrid; **Shonan Harmony**, hybrid between *L.* Koolena and *L.* Headington; and **Wyuna 'Pale Beauty'**, hybrid between *L.* Macama and *L. mathiasiae*.

Lycaste Koolena (hybrid)

Lycaste Shonan Harmony (hybrid)

Lycaste Macama 'Aline' (hybrid)

Lycaste Macama 'Atlantis' (hybrid)

Lycaste (Rowland × Shoalhaven) (hybrid)

Lycaste Wyuna 'Pale Beauty' (hybrid)

Lycaste Leo (hybrid)

Lycaste Imschootiana (hybrid)

LYPERANTHUS
BEAK ORCHID, RATTLEBEAKS

This is a small genus of 4 terrestrial orchids unique to Australia, where the deciduous tuberous plants may be found growing, often in groups, in sandy soils of open forest, moist heathland, and coastal areas. There is usually a single leathery leaf and up to 10 fragrant short-lived flowers that "rattle" when shaken, hence one common name. The flower buds resemble bird beaks, hence the other common name. After fruiting, the plants enter dormancy, when they rest for several months before resuming growth in autumn.

CULTIVATION: *Lyperanthus* species can be relatively easy to maintain in cultivation. Plant dormant tubers in a free-draining mix of coarse sand, loam, and leaf mold or bark chips. Provide bright, cool, airy conditions. They should be watered carefully once the shoots emerge in autumn, and the mix should not be allowed to dry out excessively while plants are in active growth. Propagation is from seed and from any extra tubers that may form.

Lyperanthus serratus
RATTLE BEAK

↔ 4–8 in (10–20 cm) ↑ 10–20 in (25–50 cm)
🌱 ☀/🌤 ◈/◇ ❀ ⊡

From Western Australia. Single leaf to 12 in (30 cm) long, narrow elongate. Raceme 10–20 in (25–50 cm) long with fragrant flowers, dull maroon brown, prominent bright yellow brush-like callus on recurved lip, in spring.

Lyperanthus serratus

MACODES

This evergreen terrestrial genus includes about 9 species occurring from Malaysia to New Guinea, the Solomon Islands, and Vanuatu. It is one of several genera known collectively as "jewel orchids," grown for the beauty of their leaves, which are marked with colored veins, rather than for their flowers. Short, erect, fleshy stems with several leaves arise from a short creeping rhizome. Erect inflorescences carry rather small dull-colored flowers, with the 3-lobed lip held uppermost.

CULTIVATION: Plants should be grown in a shallow pan in a free-draining terrestrial compost in intermediate to warm, humid, shady conditions. It is better to water from below, to avoid getting water on the leaves. Propagation is by division.

Macodes petola

↔ 6–8 in (15–20 cm) ↑ 7–8 in (18–20 cm)
🌾 ☀ ◆/◈ 🗓

Found from Sumatra in Indonesia to the Philippines. Several broadly ovate leaves 2–4 in (5–10 cm) long, in loose rosette on each stem, dark green with 5 longitudinal pale silvery green veins and numerous cross-veins. Raceme to 8 in (20 cm) tall, with many small brownish flowers in summer.

Macodes sanderiana

↔ 6–8 in (15–20 cm) ↑ 7–8 in (18–20 cm)
🌾 ☀ ◆/◈ 🗓

Creeping plants from New Guinea. Leaves to 3 in (8 cm) long, broadly ovate to almost round, bright green or bronze-green with a network of golden veins. Flowers brownish with a white lip. Summer-flowering.

MACROCLINIUM

There are about 30 species in this genus, which was formerly included in *Notylia*. Occurring in Costa Rica, Colombia, and Peru, they grow as epiphytes at altitudes of 1,330–6,230 ft (400–1,900 m) in hot to cool humid forests. They can be separated from *Notylia* by their fan-shaped growth of compressed succulent leaves and sheaths. Sometimes the base of the leaves is thickened to form a small pseudobulb. The pendent or upright inflorescence carries a cluster of delicate, almost translucent, flowers at the tip. They grow on small twigs in nature and are generally not very long-lived in cultivation.

CULTIVATION: Grow mounted on a piece of cork or tree fern with a layer of living moss to retain the moisture. They need intermediate to warm conditions and high humidity year-round.

They do not require a resting period. Propagation is possible by division of larger clumps or colonies, but this is not recommended as the plants do not like to be disturbed.

Macroclinium bicolor

syn. *Notylia bicolor*

↔ 16–60 in (40–150 cm) ↑ 16–40 in (40–100 cm) ♀ ☀ ◆/◈ 🐟

Found from Mexico to Costa Rica, growing at altitudes of 5,250–5,900 ft (1,600–1,800 m). Small compressed pseudobulbs reach only ¼ in (6 mm) wide. Leaves to 2 in (5 cm) long, clustered in dense colonies. Arching inflorescence bears up to 15 flowers, which faintly smell of freshly ironed washing. Sepals white to translucent green; lip and petals purple. Summer-flowering.

MALAXIS

This sympodial terrestrial genus is of cosmopolitan distribution, with most of its more than 300 species occurring in tropical Asia. The mid-green leaves are thin, pleated, and usually deciduous. The small flowers range from green to orange or even purple. It is a poorly studied genus with many dissimilar groups likely to be transferred into other new genera. The flowers are generally of botanical interest only.

Masdevallia coccinea

CULTIVATION: Rarely seen in cultivation. These plants need warm humid conditions year-round, especially during the growing season. Pot in a moisture-retentive medium that is also well drained. Propagate by division.

Malaxis taurina

↔ 8 in (20 cm) ↑ 4–16 in (10–40 cm)
🌾 ☀ ◆ 🗓

From New Caledonia. Pseudobulb green with a purplish tinge; up to 4 pleated leaves. Upright inflorescences produce up to 16 small green flowers in summer.

MASDEVALLIA

FLAG ORCHID

There are almost 500 species in this genus, distributed in Central and

Masdevallia amabilis

South America. They are generally found in cloud forests in mountainous regions with fairly uniform conditions throughout the year. They have no pseudobulbs, produce clumps of single fleshy leaves, and store moisture in the roots and foliage. Species bloom at different times; peak seasons are winter and spring. They come in an amazing range of shapes, sizes, and bright colors, and most are single-flowered; larger-flowered species produce fewer blooms. The sepals often terminate with short or long tails, while the petals and lip are generally tiny. The many hybrids are more vigorous in cultivation.

CULTIVATION: Flag orchids prefer small pots, and sphagnum moss is the preferred medium. They will grow in pots with a bark and perlite mix if it does not dry out. Keep plants slightly potbound, moist, shaded, and in a cool humid environment throughout the year, out of direct sunlight. Propagation is by division.

Masdevallia amabilis
↔ 4–12 in (10–30 cm) ↑ 6–12 in (15–30 cm)
♀/⋀ ☼/☀ ◇ ✿ ⊔

From Peru. Wiry inflorescences bear a single flower in winter–early spring. Individual blooms 2½ in (6 cm) tall, range in color from bright purple to white. Strictly a cool-growing species—plants grown in warm climates will not flower, and suffer leaf drop during the summer months.

Masdevallia coccinea ★
↔ 8 in (20 cm) ↑ 4–20 in (10–50 cm)
♥ ☀ ◇/◇ ✿ ⊔

Spectacular summer-blooming orchid from Colombia. Large, round, 5 in (12 cm) wide flowers, on tall leafless stalks above foliage, in spring. Most variable in color—red, purple, pink, yellow, and white.

Masdevallia veitchiana

Masdevallia floribunda

Masdevallia floribunda
syn. *Masdevallia tuerckheimii*
↔ 4–8 (10–20 cm) ↑ 3–6 in (8–15 cm)
♀ ☼/☀ ◆/◇ ✿ ⊔

From Central America and the Caribbean. Widespread species, found over a wide altitudinal range and growing within numerous forest types. Single blooms, 1 in (25 mm) tall, in winter–spring. Flower color varies from greenish yellow to reddish tones.

Masdevallia ignea
↔ 4–5 in (10–12 cm) ↑ 4–12 in (10–30 cm)
♥ ☀ ◇ ✿ ⊔

Species from Colombia; relatively large. Stems 1–3 in (2.5–8 cm) long, single erect leaf, 3–8 in (8–20 cm) long. Single-flowered inflorescence 7–12 in (18–30 cm) long. Flowers showy, 2 in (5 cm) long, sepals joined for half their length to form a narrow tube. Flowers variable in color, yellow, orange, or red. Summer-flowering.

Masdevallia infracta
↔ 8 in (20 cm) ↑ 4–12 in (10–30 cm)
♥ ☀ ◆/◇ ✿ ⊔

Intermediate-sized orchid from Brazil. Up to 4 flowers, 2 in (5 cm) wide, yellow, orange, and red-purple, in spring. Can re-bloom next season from same inflorescence.

Masdevallia nidifica
↔ 2–3 in (5–8 cm) ↑ 1–3 in (2.5–8 cm)
♀ ☀ ◇ ✿ ⊔

Small tufted orchid from Costa Rica, Panama, Colombia, and Ecuador. Stems very short; leaf erect, 1–2½ in (2.5–6 cm) long, including stalk,

Masdevallia tridens

Masdevallia princeps 'Long Stem'

Masdevallia nidifica

Masdevallia ophioglossa

elliptic. Inflorescence produces a single flower in winter–summer. Translucent white to pink flowers, reddish-purple flushed; sepals partly joined to form a tube, sepal tails to 1 in (25 mm) long.

Masdevallia ophioglossa
↔ 2½–4 in (6–10 cm) ↑ 4–7 in (10–18 cm)
♀ ☀ ◇ ✿ ⊔

Small species from Ecuador. Stems short; leaves to 3 in (8 cm) long, including stalk. Inflorescence carries single small flower in autumn–winter. Sepals white, partly joined to form a tube, sepal tails short, thick, yellowish.

Masdevallia princeps
↔ 8–16 in (20–40 cm) ↑ 8–20 in (20–50 cm)
♀ ☼/☀ ◆ ✿ ⊔

From Peru. Large blooms, can be up to 12 in (30 cm) tall, produced singly on a wiry inflorescence in spring. Individual flowers brownish red and very slender. More warmth tolerant than many other masdevallias. '**Long Stem**', orange-flowered cultivar.

Masdevallia tovarensis
↔ 12 in (30 cm) ↑ 12 in (30 cm)
♀ ☀ ◆/◇ ✿ ⊔

From Venezuela. Groups of up to 4 long-lived white flowers, 3 in (8 cm) wide, in spring. Inflorescence can re-bloom next season.

Masdevallia tridens
syn. *Masdevallia ova-avis*
↔ 4–8 in (10–20 cm) ↑ 4–12 in (10–30 cm)
♥ ☀ ◇/◇ ✿ ⊔

Multi-flowered orchid from Ecuador. Up to 8 nodding flowers, 1½ in (35 mm) wide, open simultaneously in spring. Blooms pinkish cream, dark maroon spots; sepal tails bright yellow.

Masdevallia veitchiana ★
↔ 12 in (30 cm) ↑ 24 in (60 cm)
♥ ☀ ◇/◇ ✿ ⊔

From Peru, known from the Aztec city of Machu Picchu. Spikes of orange flowers, 5 in (12 cm) wide, with tiny bright purple tubercles, incandescent sheen in sunlight, in spring–summer.

M

Masdevallia Angelita 'Royale' (hybrid)

Masdevallia Angelita (hybrid)

Masdevallia Adelina (hybrid)

Masdevallia Hybrids

↔ 4–12 in (10–30 cm) ↕ 4–24 in (10–60 cm)

Many hybrids have been developed. They exhibit hybrid vigor and many bloom several times a year. Popular hybrids include: **Adelina**, between *M. velifera* and *M. deformis*, gold and red flowers; **Angelita**, between *M. sanctae-inesae*, *M. strobelii*, and *M. veitchiana*, golden yellow centers; **Carousel 'Parade'**, pink blooms, darker veining; **Charisma**, between *M. coccinea* and the striped *M. yungasensis*, pale pink blooms, magenta striped; **Cinnamon Twist**, orange flowers, heavily spotted red-brown; **Copper Angel 'Highland'**, orange flowers; **Copperwing**, between *M. veitchiana* and *M. decumana*, deep yellow blooms, copper spotting; **Dean Haas**, orange blooms; **Delma Hart 'Paddy'**, creamy white flowers, gold throat; **Elegance**, yellow flowers, flushed pink; **Falcata 'North Degree'**, orange blooms, highlighted with red; **Machu Picchu**, between *M. ayabacana* and *M. coccinea*, superb magenta flowers; **(Magdalene × Marguerite)**, between 2 hybrids, deep red flowers, center fading slightly; **Marguerite**, between *M. infracta* and *M. veitchiana*, flowers with copper-red spotting; **Pixie Shadow**, between *M. infracta* and *M. schroederiana*, rich red flowers; **Prince Charming**, between *M. angulata* and *M. veitchiana*, flowers with ruby red banding deepening at center; **Redwing**, magenta blooms; **Rose-Mary**, between *M. coccinea* and pink-spotted *M. glandulosa*, rose pink flowers, orange at center; **Urubamba**, between *M. ayabacana* and *M. veitchiana*, orange blooms; and **Winter Blush**, between *M.* Angel Frost *(M. veitchiana × M. strobelii)* and *M. chaparensis*, golden orange blooms.

Masdevallia (Bright Spice × Galaxy) (hybrid)

Masdevallia Elegance (hybrid)

Masdevallia Charisma 'Gina' (hybrid)

Masdevallia Dean Haas (hybrid)

Masdevallia Charisma (hybrid)

Masdevallia Carousel Parade (hybrid)

Masdevallia Copper Angel 'Highland' (hybrid)

Masdevallia Copperwing (hybrid)

Masdevallia Cinnamon Twist (hybrid)

Masdevallia Delma Hart 'Paddy' (hybrid)　　　*Masdevallia* Falcata 'North Degree' (hybrid)

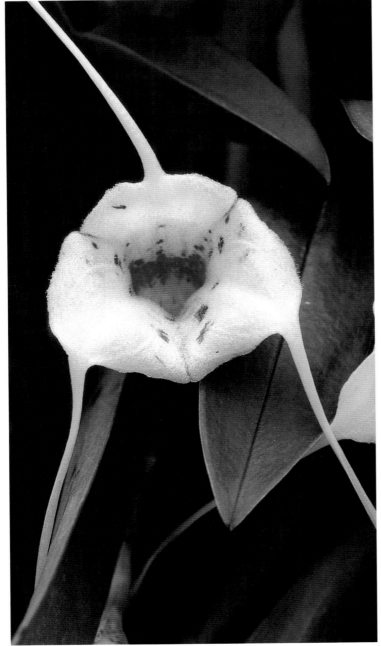

Masdevallia Marguerite (hybrid)

Masdevallia Geneva Spots 'Royale' (hybrid)　　　*Masdevallia* Machu Picchu (hybrid)　　　*Masd.* (Magdalene × Marguerite) (hybrid)

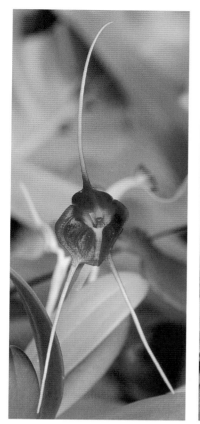

Masdevallia Pixie Shadow (hybrid)   *Masdevallia* Prince Charming (hybrid)

Masdevallia Redwing (hybrid)

Masdevallia Watercolor Dreamer 'Monet's
Garden' (hybrid)

Masdevallia Winter Blush (hybrid)   *Masdevallia* Rose-Mary (hybrid)   *Masdevallia* Urubamba (hybrid)

Maxillaria biolleyi, in the wild, Cerro de la Muerte, Costa Rica

Maxillaria acuminata

Maxillaria chrysantha

MAXILLARIA

This is a complex genus of some 600 epiphytic and lithophytic sympodial orchids from Mexico, and Central and South America. They exhibit an enormous range in plant habit and floral shape, size, and color. In most species, solitary blooms emerge from the base of the pseudobulbs, and petals are smaller than sepals. They produce 1 to 3 leaves at the top of the pseudobulb. For such a large genus, there have been surprisingly few artificial hybrids, despite their obvious potential. They are related to *Lycaste*.

CULTIVATION: These orchids have varying growing requirements, but most species established in cultivation are cool- to intermediate-growing plants, enjoy bright light in a humid environment, and are easily grown in pots of a coarse bark-based mix. Many species, particularly the miniatures, also grow well on slabs of tree fern or cork. Propagate by division.

Maxillaria acuminata

↔ 4–12 in (10–30 cm) ↕ 4–8 in (10–20 cm)
♀ ☼/☀ ◆/◈/◇ ❉ ⊡

Found from Mexico to Peru. Creeping growth habit; 2 leaves produced at apex of pseudobulbs. Greenish yellow blooms, 1¼ in (30 mm) tall, produced singly, with color constant throughout flower. Spring-flowering.

Maxillaria biolleyi

↔ 20 in (50 cm) ↕ 36 in (90 cm)
♀ ☼ ◆/◈ ⊡

Uncommon, tall, leafy orchid from Costa Rica and Panama. Upright habit; leaves dark green, narrow lance-shaped. Masses of white to pale pink, ¾ in (18 mm) wide flowers, from leaf axils along upper part, most of year.

Maxillaria chrysantha

↔ 10–14 in (25–35 cm) ↕ 10–14 in (25–35 cm) ♀ ☼ ◆ ❉ ⊡

From Brazil, related to *M. porphyrostele*. Oval compressed pseudobulbs; 2 to 3 long narrow leaves, less than ¾ in (18 mm) long. Single-flowered inflorescences originate from base of bulbs in spring. Golden yellow cupped flowers. Grows well potted in bark.

Maxillaria cucullata

Maxillaria fractiflexa

Maxillaria marginata

Maxillaria picta

Maxillaria cogniauxiana
↔ 8 in (20 cm) ↕ 24 in (60 cm)

Miniature-growing, clumping, and branching orchid from Brazil. Strappy leaves, deep olive green. Long-lived claret flowers, 1¼ in (30 mm) wide, glossy, cup-shaped. Flowers in spring–summer.

Maxillaria cucullata
↔ 8–32 in (20–80 cm) ↕ 8–16 in (20–40 cm)

Variable species found from Mexico to Ecuador. Vigorous plant, readily grown over a wide range of climatic conditions. Golden blooms overlaid with deep maroon spotting, glossy dark chocolate brown lip. Main blooming season is summer, with odd flowers produced throughout the year.

Maxillaria fractiflexa
↔ 8 in (20 cm) ↕ 4–24 in (10–60 cm)

From Colombia; large-flowered orchid. Tall mid-green leaves, strappy. Flowers to 6 in (15 cm) wide, narrow sepals, mustard yellow to brown; twisted petals, cream; relatively small white lip. Summer-flowering.

Maxillaria marginata
↔ 4–16 in (10–40 cm) ↕ 4–8 in (10–20 cm)

Found from Brazil to Ecuador. Flowers produced in groups of up to 8 from base of recently matured pseudobulb in summer. Blooms not widely opening, deep cream to yellow; all segments with a banded edge of deep maroon.

Maxillaria nigrescens
↔ 4–8 in (10–20 cm) ↕ 4–24 in (10–60 cm)

Native to Colombia and Venezuela. Leaves mid-green, develop spots if grown in conditions that are too warm. Thick spidery blooms, 3 in (8 cm) wide, rich reddish brown, in spring–summer.

Maxillaria picta
↔ 10–16 in (25–40 cm) ↕ 10–14 in (25–35 cm)

From the cool mountains of eastern Brazil; similar growth habit to *M. chrysantha*. Clustered pseudobulbs, ovoid, single-leafed. Strap-shaped to oblong leaves, 8–12 in (20–30 cm) long. Inflorescences to 6 in (30 cm) long, bear numerous fragrant blooms in summer, autumn, and spring. Flowers variable in pattern and color intensity, but usually creamy white with brown blotches on outside of segments and a solid yellow interior. Lobed lip, often paler in color than tepals. Grows well potted, and can be grown outside in frost-free areas.

Maxillaria cogniauxiana

Maxillaria porphyrostele

Maxillaria porphyrostele

↔ 4–8 in (10–20 cm) ↕ 4–24 in (10–60 cm)
♀/◺ ☼/◖ ◆/◆/◇ ✽ ☐

From Brazil; hardy orchid. Round pseudobulbs; 2 strap-like leaves. Bright yellow flowers, 2 in (5 cm) wide, long-lasting. Yellow lip, red-brown markings near base. Blooms in early spring.

Maxillaria sanderiana

↔ 20–27 in (50–70 cm) ↕ 18–20 in (45–50 cm) ♀/◢ ☼ ◆/◇ ✽ ☐

From Colombia, Ecuador, and Peru; grows on steep slopes in very wet montane forests. Medium to large species; leathery pseudobulb; 3 large leaves. Erect, horizontal, or pendent inflorescence with single, quite large bloom in summer. Flowers 4–6 in (10–15 cm) wide, white with light to dense purpled-red spotting or blotches at base of petals and sepals; lip white, yellow, or blackish-purple. Grows best in baskets.

Maxillaria variabilis ★

↔ 4–8 in (10–20 cm) ↕ 4–24 in (10–60 cm)
♀ ☼/◖ ◆/◆/◇ ✽ ☐

Variable species found from Mexico to Panama. Upright habit, somewhat branching in older specimens. Leaves green, long, strap-like. Flowers vary from yellow, orange, brown, and red to a dark claret-black, in spring–summer.

MEDIOCALCAR

CHERRY ORCHID

This small group of creeping and scrambling, cool- to intermediate-growing sympodial orchids come from the highland areas of New Guinea and parts of the Pacific Islands. There are about 20 recognized species. They have varying growth habits, but the spherical glossy blooms that appear from the immature new growth, either singly or in pairs, are very similar. They have been called "cherry orchids" because

Maxillaria variabilis

of these unique blooms. Most species flower from autumn to early spring.
CULTIVATION: The small species perform well in shallow pots of sphagnum moss, while larger plants can be grown on tree-fern rafts, as long as the substrate is kept moist. They detest hot dry conditions and must be kept moist and heavily shaded in a buoyant atmosphere. Propagate by division.

Mediocalcar bifolium

↔ 4–12 in (10–30 cm) ↕ 3–10 in (8–25 cm)
♀ ☼ ◆/◇ ❋ ✽ ☐/◿

From New Guinea; upright-growing, 2-leafed, branching and clumping orchid. Small bright red flowers, ½ in (12 mm) wide, pure white tips to segments. Winter-blooming.

Mediocalcar decoratum ★

↔ 4–24 in (10–60 cm) ↕ 2–6 in (5–15 cm)
♀ ☼ ◆/◇ ❋ ✽ ☐/◿

Creeping orchid, native to New Guinea. Petite pseudobulbs; 3 or 4 small, succulent, green- to purple-stained leaves. Tiny bright orange

flowers, with yellow tips to segments, appear in autumn–winter.

MEXICOA

A monotypic genus, which was formerly included into *Oncidium*. The plants grow epiphytically in mixed oak forests in Mexico, in the States of Guerrero, Oaxaca, Michoacan, and Mexico, at altitudes of 5,900–7,550 ft (1,800–2,300 m). They form dense clumps because the pseudobulbs grow very close to each other. It was separated from *Oncidium* because of its unique flower aspect.
CULTIVATION: Grow under cool to temperate conditions between 54–68°F (12–20°C) in bright light, but not in full sun. Needs cool temperatures at night. When grown in pots, use a coarse organic substrate and leave to dry out between watering. Propagation is by division.

Mexicoa ghiesbreghtiana

syns *Odontoglossum warneri*, *Oncidium ghiesbreghtiana*

↔ 6–8 in (15–20 cm) ↕ 5–6 in (12–15 cm)
♀ ☼ ◇ ❋ ✽ ☐

Mexican species. Pseudobulbs 1¼ in (30 mm) high and somewhat flattened; 2 narrow leaves, to 5 in (12 cm) long. New shoots have supporting leaves at base of pseudobulb. Inflorescence carries 2 to 3 flowers, to 1½ in (35 mm) in size, from spring to autumn. Sepals and petals yellowish with pink to brown marking, lip bright yellow with orange callus.

MICROCOELIA

This is a leafless monopodial genus of about 30 epiphytes from tropical Africa and Madagascar. As they have no leaves, they use their vast flattened root system to perform this function. The roots are gray when dry but quickly turn to green when moist. All species have white or cream blooms, and though they are quite small, they are produced in significant numbers.
CULTIVATION: These twig epiphytes respond well to cultivation as long as they are kept in warm conditions with

Mediocalcar decoratum

Mediocalcar bifolium

bright light. They will quickly rot if over-watered (especially if coupled with cool temperatures), or placed in an area with poor air circulation, so they are best grown on pieces of cork that will allow for quick drainage and drying after watering. Established plants should not be disturbed. Propagation is from seed sown in professional laboratories specializing in orchids.

Microcoelia exilis
↔ 8–10 in (20–25 cm) ↑ 6–10 in (15–25 cm)
♀ ☀ ◆/◈ ☔

From eastern and central Africa, South Africa, and Madagascar. Long gray-green roots, forming a tangled mass. Several racemes, to 10 in (25 cm) long, densely arranged with many very small, white, spurred flowers. Blooms off and on through year.

Microcoelia globulosa
↔ 4–8 in (10–20 cm) ↑ 4–8 in (10–20 cm)
♀ ☀ ◆ ☔

Leafless species found from Ethiopia to Zimbabwe, east to the Democratic Republic of the Congo; grows in open tropical forest. Arching inflorescences carry up to 20 flowers in autumn–winter. Flowers less than ¼ in (6 mm) in size, dull white.

Microcoelia stolzii
↔ 4–12 in (10–30 cm) ↑ 4–10 in (10–25 cm)
♀ ☀ ◆/◈ ☔

Attractive species from eastern Africa. Arching inflorescences of up to 40 round crystalline white flowers, less than ¼ in (6 mm) in size, that give the impression that they are covered in sugar. Mature plants may produce multiple flower spikes.

Mexicoa ghiesbreghtiana

MICROTERANGIS

This is a genus of 7 short-stemmed fine-rooted species from Madagascar, the Comoros Islands, and the Mascarene Islands that was formerly classified as *Chamaeangis* and differs from that genus only in botanical detail. The racemes are densely arranged with many flowers, which are tiny, with spreading sepals and petals that can be straw yellow, orange, or reddish-brown in color.

CULTIVATION: These orchids usually do better mounted on a bark slab than in a pot. They require shady humid conditions with good air movement, in intermediate temperatures. Propagate from seed.

Microterangis hariotiana
↔ 3–4 in (8–10 cm) ↑ 4–8 in (10–20 cm)
♀ ☀ ◆ ▭/☔

From Madagascar and the Comoros Islands; short-stemmed species. Several leaves, bright green, 2–3 in (5–8 cm) long. Racemes pendent, 4–8 in (10–20 cm) long, densely arranged with many flowers in summer. Flowers minute, orange or reddish-brown, showy in spite of their small size.

MICROTIS
ONION ORCHID

Microtis includes about 9 species of deciduous terrestrial orchids from eastern Asia, Australia, and New Zealand. They are slender plants, with a single, long, narrow leaf and a dense raceme of small flowers, usually green or

Microterangis hariotiana

greenish-white. The dorsal sepal forms a hood with the petals, the lateral sepals are spreading. The name comes from the Greek, *mikros* meaning small, and *ous* meaning ear, thought to refer to the wings on the column on either side of the anther. The leaves resemble those of onion seedlings—hence the common name.

CULTIVATION: Plants should be grown in a standard terrestrial mixture and watered freely while in growth, with weak doses of fertilizer. After flowering, while the plants are dormant, they should be kept dry; they can be repotted at this time. Propagate by division or from seed.

Microtis orbicularis
↔ 1–2 in (2.5–5 cm) ↑ 8–12 in (20–30 cm)
❦ ☀ ◇ ▭

Slender plants from Australia; leaf to 8 in (20 cm) long, narrowly cylindrical, almost thread-like. Inflorescence to 12 in (30 cm) tall, with up to 30 flowers in spring–summer. Flowers very small, greenish or reddish.

M

Microcoelia exilis

Microtis orbicularis

MILTASSIA

This hardy bigeneric orchid hybrid is a combination of *Miltonia* and *Brassia*. These spidery sympodial hybrids, an influence from the *Brassia* parent, are more tolerant of both cool and high temperatures and flower reliably every year. They grow in a range of conditions and have long-lasting blooms, often fragrant, making them popular flowering pot plants. Most *Miltassia* hybrids bloom in spring and summer. CULTIVATION: These orchids grow well in pots of a bark-based medium, with larger plants looking good in hanging baskets. In frost-free climates they can also be attached to garden trees that do not shed their bark. They are vigorous and worth cultivating, and bloom best when grown as large specimens. They appreciate bright humid conditions throughout the year. Propagate by division.

Miltassia 'Charles M. Fitch'
↔ 24 in (60 cm) ↕ 32 in (80 cm)
♀ ☼/☀ ◆/◇ ❄ ☐

Popular easily grown hybrid between *Brassia verrucosa* and *Miltonia spectabilis*. Mid-green strappy leaves. Pale to dark pink starry blooms, darker spots over segments, in summer.

Miltassia 'Mourier Bay' × Miltonia 'Sao Paulo'
↔ 24 in (60 cm) ↕ 32 in (80 cm)
♀ ☼/☀ ◆/◇ ❄ ☐

Unregistered hybrid that combines 3 *Miltonia* species and 2 *Brassia* species. Paler green strap-like leaves. Green to creamy white blooms blotched with orange marks, in summer.

MILTONIA

This is a genus of sympodial orchids, containing about 10 epiphytic species, mostly found in Brazil. They have showy blooms in a large variety of colors, and are vigorous plants that quickly grow into specimen size. *Miltonia* species have been hybridized with many of the related genera, including *Brassia*, to produce *Miltassia*, and with *Oncidium* to create the genus *Miltonidium*. However, many of the hybrids labeled as *Miltonia* species in collections often refer to the closely related genus of pansy orchids, *Miltoniopsis*. CULTIVATION: *Miltonia* species can be grown on large slabs or plaques of cork or tree fern, or potted in squat-style pots, as they do not have a deep root system. They will take bright light and high temperatures in summer, as long as the humidity remains high. They require a cooler dry rest period in winter. They are reliable bloomers and, for best results, they should be fed regularly throughout the growing season. However, the plants will still perform well even with a level of neglect. Propagation is by division.

Miltonia clowesii
↔ 8–24 in (20–60 cm) ↕ 8–27 in (20–70 cm)
♀ ☀ ◆/◇ ❄ ☐/⋙

Striking Brazilian orchid. Tall spikes of up to 8 yellow-brown, starry, 3 in (8 cm) wide flowers, overlaid with chestnut-brown bars and blotches, in summer–autumn. Lip white, purple markings at base.

Miltonia cuneata
↔ 8–24 in (20–60 cm) ↕ 8–20 in (20–50 cm)
♀ ☀ ◆ ❄ ☐/⋙

From Brazil; closely related to *M. clowesii*. Compressed pseudobulbs to 4 in (10 cm) long; leaves 12–18 in (30–45 cm) long, dark green. Raceme to 18 in (45 cm) tall, with 7 to 10 flowers, each 2–3 in (5–8 cm) across, in winter–spring. Sepals and petals yellowish, heavily barred with chocolate brown, with a slight undulation over these segments; lip white, fan-shaped, with a basal callus of 2 ridges.

Miltonia flavescens
↔ 8–36 in (20–90 cm) ↕ 8–20 in (20–50 cm)
♀ ☼/☀ ◆/◇ ❄ ☐/⋙

Vigorous orchid from Brazil. Spikes of up to 12 somewhat spidery blooms in summer. Flowers 3 in (8 cm) wide, narrow segments, pale creamy yellow.

Miltonia moreliana
syn. *Miltonia spectabilis* var. *moreliana*
↔ 5–6 in (12–15 cm) ↕ 10–16 in (25–40 cm)
♀ ☀ ◆ ❄ ☐/⋙

Species from Brazil. Pseudobulbs yellowish, laterally compressed, to 4 in (10 cm) long, ovoid, 2-leafed at apex. Leaves 4–6 in (10–15 cm) long, narrowly strap-shaped, yellow-green.

Miltassia 'Charles M. Fitch'

Miltonia spectabilis

Single-flowered inflorescence to 10 in (25 cm) long, in summer. Flowers flat, to 4 in (10 cm) across; sepals and petals plum-purple; lip pink, heavily veined with purple.

Miltonia regnellii

↔ 8–24 in (20–60 cm) ↕ 8–24 in (20–60 cm)
♀ ☀ ◆/◈ ❄ ▽/🌧

Striking orchid from Brazil. White flowers, with contrasting pink to mauve lip, up to 5 blooms, 2½ in (6 cm) wide, on arching spike, in summer. Also a pure white form.

Miltonia Sandy's Cove

↔ 8–24 in (20–60 cm) ↕ 8–24 in (20–60 cm)
♀ ☀ ◆/◈ ❄ ▽/🌧

Hybrid orchid, of unusual color combination, with 5 species in its ancestry. Golden brown tepals, contrasting plum-colored lip. Spring-flowering.

Miltonia spectabilis

↔ 8–24 in (20–60 cm) ↕ 8–16 in (20–40 cm)
♀ ☀ ◆/◈ ❄ ▽/🌧

Variable species from Brazil. Flowers 3 in (8 cm) wide, singly or in pairs, in spring. Common form features white petals and sepals, broad lip, 2-tone purple; also pink and purple forms and rare albino cultivars.

MILTONIDIUM

This bigeneric hybrid is a combination of *Miltonia* and *Oncidium*. These compact sympodial hybrids tolerate both cool and high temperatures and are reliable flowerers. Able to be grown in a wide range of conditions and with long-lasting, often fragrant, blooms, *Miltonidium* hybrids are very popular flowering pot plants. Due to the diversity within the genus

Miltonia Sandy's Cove

Oncidium, there are countless hybridizing possibilities for these hybrids. Most *Miltonidium* plants produce colorful blooms in spring and summer.

CULTIVATION: These hybrids like bright humid conditions throughout the year and grow well in pots of a bark-based medium, preferring to be somewhat pot-bound. In frost-free climates they may also be attached to garden trees that do not shed their bark. They are particularly vigorous and worth cultivating, and bloom best when grown as large specimens. Propagate by division.

Miltonidium Bartley Schwarz 'Highland'

↔ 8–24 in (20–60 cm) ↕ 8–36 in (20–90 cm)
♀ ◐/◑ ◆/◈ ❄ ▽

Orchid hybrid with strong influence from *Oncidium leucochilum*. Superb blooms with striking strong reddish color and white lip, in summer.

Miltonidium Pupukea Sunset 'H & R'

↔ 8–24 in (20–60 cm) ↕ 8–36 in (20–90 cm)
♀ ◐/◑ ◆/◈ ❄ ▽

Popular hybrid between tricolored *Miltonia warscewiczii* and the small buttercup yellow-flowered species *Oncidium cheirophorum*. Brownish blooms, often rust-like, with red and yellow lip.

Miltonia clowesii   *Miltonia regnellii*

Miltonidium Bartley Schwarz 'Highland'   *Miltonidium* Pupukea Sunset 'H & R'

MILTONIOPSIS

PANSY ORCHID

This genus is made up of 6 different sympodial orchids, mainly from Colombia and Ecuador. They were once included within *Miltonia*, but botanically, *Miltoniopsis* is closer to *Odontoglossum* than *Miltonia*. Many artificial hybrids have been created within this showy genus, known as "pansy orchids" because of their floral shape and color markings. These plants are fragile with thin foliage. The leaves are usually bluish green and narrow. The large flat blooms come in a range of colors. Care should be taken with handling, as all parts scorch and bruise easily.

CULTIVATION: These orchids prefer a narrow temperature range; they do not want to go below 50°F (10°C) in winter or go over 79°F (26°C) in summer. The foliage prefers a shaded humid position. Blooms will readily mark if not provided with ample air movement. They are best in small pots, with sphagnum moss used exclusively as the growing medium. The hybrids are generally easier to grow than the species, due to hybrid vigor. Propagate by division.

Miltoniopsis phalaenopsis

↔ 15 in (38 cm)   ↕ 12 in (30 cm)

Colombian species, occurring at altitudes of 3,940–4,920 ft (1,200–1,500 m). Clumping species; grass-like foliage. Up to 5 shapely white flowers, 2½ in (6 cm) wide, in spring. Outstanding broad white lip, yellow at base, distinguished by a waterfall pattern of bright purple markings often passed on to hybrids.

Miltoniopsis Cute 'Rodeo' (hybrid)

Miltoniopsis vexillaria

↔ 8–24 in (20–60 cm)   ↕ 8–16 in (20–40 cm)

From Colombia and Peru; a major parent among *Miltoniopsis* hybrids. Upright to arching spikes of up to 8 flowers, to 4 in (10 cm) wide, palest pink to deep rose, in spring.

Miltoniopsis Hybrids

↔ 32 in (80 cm)   ↕ 20 in (50 cm)

These hybrids offer a range of colors and patterns in white, pinks, purples, reds, and yellows. Many are fragrant. **Beall's Strawberry Joy**, rose pink blooms, deep strawberry red markings; **Cute 'Rodeo'**, white-edged blooms, deep ruby red centers; **First Love 'Pink Lady'**, yellow-throated pink blooms; **Herralexandre**, white blooms, rich ruby centers; **Hudson Bay**, white blooms brushed with rose pink; **Jean Carlson**, striking hot pink blooms; **Red Knight**, pink and purple blooms; **Robert Strauss**, creamy white blooms, red to orange marking at centers; **Rouge 'California Plum'** ★, 2-tone plum blooms, white-edged; and **Zorro 'Yellow Delight'**, pale yellow blooms with orange-red marking.

Miltoniopsis phalaenopsis

Miltoniopsis Beall's Strawberry Joy (hybrid)

Miltoniopsis Herralexandre (hybrid)

Miltoniopsis Robert Strauss (hybrid)

Miltoniopsis Zorro 'Yellow Delight' (hybrid)

Miltoniopsis Jean Carlson (hybrid)

Miltoniopsis First Love 'Pink Lady' (hybrid)

Miltoniopsis Hudson Bay (hybrid)

Miltoniopsis Red Knight (hybrid)

Miltoniopsis Rouge 'California Plum' (hybrid)

M

Myrmecophila tibicinis

MYRMECOPHILA

This genus of large-growing, sympodial, tropical epiphytes and lithophytes was previously treated within *Schomburgkia*. The genus contains close to 10 species, which are found from Mexico to Venezuela, and the West Indies. These orchids produce robust and hollow pseudobulbs, which become home for specific ant species in the wild that in turn protect the plant from predators. The long inflorescences produce loose clusters of flowers near the tip. The blooms are long-lived and showy, and come in a range of bright and pastel colors. CULTIVATION: *Myrmecophila* species are ideally suited to garden culture in tropical climates, with large specimens becoming feature plants. They take up

a lot of room in the greenhouse—a factor that should be taken into consideration if the available growing area is only small. They do best when grown in warm conditions on large slabs of cork or tree fern or potted in baskets or large shallow pots in a bark-based medium. They must be given strong light, and mature plants can be acclimatized to full sun. They enjoy frequent watering during their growing period, with a reduction of watering in winter when the plants go into a short dormant phase. Large plants may be divided in the early spring before the new season's flush of roots and new growths commences. Even though in the wild these plants support ant colonies, ants are not required in cultivation.

Myrmecophila tibicinis
syn. *Schomburgkia tibicinis*
↔ 1–3 ft (0.3–0.9 m)   ↕ 1–8 ft (0.3–2.4 m)
♀ ◐/☀ ◆/◈ ❋ ▽/☈

Central American species. Hollow pseudobulbs. Inflorescence to over 7 ft (2 m) tall. Bright pink, red, and yellow flowers, 3 in (8 cm) in size, in early summer.

MYSTACIDIUM

This genus contains about a dozen species, found in southern Africa with 1 species ranging north into Tanzania. The plants are monopodial epiphytes, found in a variety of habitats, from open forests, along rivers, and in solitary trees in savannah up to 5,900 ft (1,800 m) in montane forests in higher elevations. The star-shaped showy flowers are produced on a pendent inflorescence in winter. Well over 100 species have been described under this name, but are now grouped in different genera such as *Aeranthes*, *Angraecum*, *Jumellea*, or *Microcoelia*. CULTIVATION: Grow under intermediate to warm conditions in moderate light and humidity. They like to be mounted with lots of air around the roots. Pot culture is not recommended. Water only in the morning as the roots should be dry by nightfall. The plants prefer a drier resting period in winter. Propagate from seed, or by division when lateral offshoots are produced.

Mystacidium brayboniae
↔ 2½–6 in (6–15 cm)   ↕ 2–4 in (5–10 cm)
♀ ◐/☀ ◆ ☈

Miniature species from South Africa; grows in humid forests. Pendulous inflorescences of up to 12 pure crystalline white blooms, to 1 in (25 mm) across, in spring. Known to shed its leaves in times of drought, regrowing these when conditions improve.

Mystacidium capense
syn. *Mystacidium filicorne*
↔ 6–10 in (15–25 cm)   ↕ 4–6 in (10–15 cm)
♀ ◐/☀ ◆/◈ ❋ ☈

Found in South Africa in dry *Acacia* woodland and montane forests, from sea level up to 2,300 ft (700 m). Fleshy roots with fine white streaks. Short stem; 4 to 8 leaves, each 4–5 in (10–12 cm) long. Pendent racemes carry up to 15 white flowers in winter.

Mystacidium capense

Mystacidium brayboniae

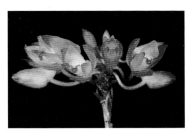

Nageliella purpurea

NAGELIELLA

syn. *Hartwegia*

This genus contains 2 species from Mexico and Central America that are closely related to *Epidendrum*. They grow as epiphytes, rarely terrestrial, at altitudes from sea level up to 6,890 ft (2,100 m). The acute, succulent, and spotted leaves, to 6 in (15 cm) long, sit on a slender stem up to 3 in (8 cm) long. The inflorescence can reach a length of 20 in (50 cm).

CULTIVATION: These orchids do best when mounted on a piece of cork or tree fern under moderate light and intermediate temperature conditions. Humidity and water supply should be high year-round. Do not cut away old inflorescences after blooming, as they produce new flowers, even in the next season. Propagate by division.

Nageliella purpurea

syns *Hartwegia comosa, H. purpurea*
↔ 4–6 in (10–15 cm) ↕ 5–6 in (12–15 cm)
♀ ☼ ◆ ▽/≋

Small species from Mexico, Guatemala, El Salvador, and Honduras; found growing on mossy branches from sea level up to 4,920 ft (1,500 m) in altitude. Rather rounded leaves, green with purple spots, on short stems. Pink to lavender flowers in summer.

NAKAMOTOARA

This is a genus of artificial monopodial hybrids between *Ascocentrum*, *Neofinetia*, and *Vanda*. Crossing *Ascocenda* (*Ascocentrum* × *Vanda*) with *Neofinetia* has created most of these hybrids. These erect-growing epiphytes have strap-like channeled leaves in 2 ranks; the inflorescences appear from the stem at the base of the leaf. Larger plants may branch at the base and have numerous, very thick, cord-like roots. The colorful, showy, long-lived blooms are mostly produced in spring and summer; large plants can bloom throughout the year in the tropics.

CULTIVATION: Ideal for bark-filled wooden baskets, these plants enjoy humid intermediate to warm conditions and high light levels. Their thick roots will often venture outside the confines of the pot or basket, and this culture should be encouraged, as

the roots require unimpeded air circulation and must dry out quickly after watering. Propagate by division.

Nakamotoara Rainbow Gem

↔ 4–12 in (10–30 cm) ↕ 4–16 in (10–40 cm)
♀ ☼/☀ ◆/◇ ❈ ▽/≋

Hybrid between *Neofinetia falcata* and *Ascocenda* Flambeau; progeny have shown some variation in color. Flowers from spring to autumn. 'Pink Star', deep green strappy leaves, bright pink, almost glowing flowers; 'White Lady', dark green leaves, white flowers.

NANODES

This small genus of 3 distinct sympodial species was formerly included within *Epidendrum*. These orchids are native to parts of Central America and South America. Their fleshy leaves are 2-ranked and long lived. Up to 3 waxy flowers are produced from a sheath at the end of the current growth.

CULTIVATION: These orchids are very popular in cultivation; however, the various species have quite different growing requirements. All must have humidity and ample air circulation. Propagate by division.

Nanodes discolor

syn. *Epidendrum discolor*
↔ 3–4 in (8–10 cm) ↕ 3–5 in (8–12 cm)
♀ ☼ ◆ ❈ ▽/≋

From Central and South America. Pseudobulbs cane-like, clustered. Leaves to 1¼ in (30 mm) long. Flowers usually 2, to ½ in (12 mm) wide, greenish yellow, greenish brown, or pink-purple; lip shape variable. Blooms in spring–summer.

NEOBATHIEA

This small genus of 5 species comes from Madagascar, with 1 species also found on the Comoros Islands. They are small or medium-sized epiphytes with white, green, or rarely yellow flowers. The sepals and petals are spreading, the lip can be 3-lobed, and the spur is long and slender with a wide mouth.

CULTIVATION: Species of *Neobathiea* can be grown mounted on bark or in a pot with a free-draining compost. Plants need high humidity, moderate shade, intermediate temperatures, and good ventilation, but should be kept drier in winter. Propagate from seed.

Neobathiea grandidierana

syn. *Neobathiea filicornu*
↔ 3–4 in (8–10 cm) ↕ 2–2½ in (5–6 cm)
♀ ☀ ◆ ❈ ▽/≋

Short-stemmed species from Madagascar and the Comoros Islands.

Nakamotoara Rainbow Gem 'Pink Star'

Leaves 4 to 5, to 2 in (5 cm) long. Single-flowered inflorescence slightly shorter than leaves. Flowers about 1 in (25 mm) across, greenish-white or white, turning yellow with age; lip unlobed, ¾ in (18 mm) long; spur slender from a wide mouth, 5–6 in (12–15 cm) long. Summer-flowering.

NEOFINETIA

This small-growing monopodial genus from Japan and Korea, with just one variable species, is a distant relative of *Angraecum*. The sole member is an erect-growing epiphyte, with small, thin, strap-like, channeled leaves in 2 ranks. Older plants may branch at the base and usually have numerous, very thick, cord-like roots. The inflorescences are produced from the stem at the base of the leaf.

CULTIVATION: *Neofinetia* enjoys humid cool to intermediate growing conditions in bright light. Larger specimens grow well on cork plaques, while they are also suitable for culture in terracotta pots, in a well-drained gravel and bark-based mix. Propagate by division of clumps.

Neofinetia falcata

↔ 3–10 in (8–25 cm) ↕ 3–8 in (8–20 cm)
♀ ☼/☀ ◆ ❈ ▽/≋

Variable species from Japan and Korea; considered a sacred plant in Japan. Leaves arranged in 2 ranks. Small clusters of up to 8 flowers are produced on compact clumping plants in summer. Flowers fragrant, white, with long 2 in (5 cm) spurs. The variegated-leafed forms are highly prized.

Neobathiea grandidierana

Nakamotoara Rainbow Gem 'White Lady'

NEOLAUCHEA

This is a monotypic genus from southern Brazil. The plant produces chains of round pseudobulbs that are topped with a single needle-like leaf. Short single-flowered inflorescences appear from the base of the leaf after it has matured.

CULTIVATION: These orchids are best grown on long rafts of tree fern or cork, and they will quickly ramble over and cover the host, forming a specimen plant in a few years. They will take a range of temperatures, and enjoy abundant water in the warmer months. Propagate by division.

Neolauchea pulchella

syn. *Isabelia pulchella*
↔ 4–20 in (10–50 cm) ↕ 2½–5 in (6–12 cm)
♀ ☼/☀ ◆/◆/◇ ❈ ≋

From southern Brazil. Bright magenta blooms, less than ¾ in (18 mm) wide, do not open fully, in winter–spring.

N

Neolauchea pulchella, seed capsules

Neolauchea pulchella

NEOPABSTOPETALUM

This is a recently registered trigeneric hybrid combining *Neogardneria, Pabstia,* and *Zygopetalum*. These hybrids come in a range of colors, however, most feature green petals and sepals, with a white lip that is often stained with purple.

CULTIVATION: Grow these hybrids in pots, in a coarse bark mix. Keep moist year-round, with increased watering and fertilizing while actively growing. They need high humidity and good air circulation. Propagate by division of mature multigrowth specimens.

Neopabstopetalum Adelaide Alive
syn. *Woodwardara Adelaide Alive*

↔ 4–16 in (10–40 cm) ↑ 6–24 in (15–60 cm)
🌼 🔆 ◆/◇ ❄ 🗑

Hybrid with dark chocolate brown flowers, lip bright purple. Flowers produced in autumn–spring.

Neostylis Lou Sneary

Neopabstopetalum Beverley Lou
syn. *Woodwardara Beverley Lou*

↔ 4–16 in (10–40 cm) ↑ 6–24 in (15–60 cm)
🌼 🔆 ◆/◇ ❄ 🗑

Hybrid with green flowers, petals and sepals striped with deep maroon markings, white lip suffused with lilac. Flowers in autumn–spring.

Neopabstopetalum Warooka

↔ 8–20 in (20–50 cm) ↑ 10–24 in (25–60 cm) 🌼 🔆/🔆 ◆/◆/◇ ❄ 🗑

Fifth generation hybrid between *Zygoneria* Adelaide Meadows and *Zygopabstia* Kiwi; with a number of infusions of *Zygopetalum*, and single injections of *Neogardneria* and *Pabstia*. Blooms from summer to winter.

NEOSTYLIS

Neostylis is a genus of horticultural monopodial hybrids between *Neofinetia* and *Rhynchostylis*. These epiphytes are erect-growing, with strap-like channeled leaves in 2 ranks. Larger plants may branch at the base, and have numerous, very thick, cord-like roots. Flowers appear from the stem at the base of the leaf. These hybrids are mostly spring- and summer-blooming, but can bloom throughout the year in the tropics, with their colorful showy blooms being long lived.

CULTIVATION: Ideal plants for bark-filled wooden baskets, in humid warm

Neopabstopetalum Adelaide Alive

Neopabstopetalum Beverley Lou

to intermediate conditions and high light levels. The roots can venture outside the pot or basket, and this should be encouraged, as the roots need unimpeded air circulation and must dry out quickly after watering. Propagate by division of mature basal shoots.

Neostylis Lou Sneary

↔ 4–12 in (10–30 cm) ↑ 4–16 in (10–40 cm)
🌼 🔆/🔆 ◆/◆ ❄ 🗑/🌿

Primary hybrid between *Neofinetia falcata* and *Rhynchostylis coelestis*. Leaves mid-green, strap-like. Flowers range from whites through pinks to pale blues, very long lasting. Pleasant scent. Blooms from spring to autumn.

NIDEMA

Nidema is a genus of 2 species of sympodial epiphytes from tropical South and Central America and the West Indies. Plants have long creeping

rhizomes and pseudobulbs, often laterally compressed, which bear one fleshy leaf, folded at the base. The erect inflorescence is terminal on the pseudobulb, and is few-flowered. The flowers are small with conspicuous bracts; the sepals and petals are free, the petals shorter than the sepals. The lip is hinged to the column-foot.

CULTIVATION: Plants can be grown either mounted or in a shallow pan in a bark mixture. They need plenty of moisture while in active growth but should be kept drier, although not completely dry, when resting. Propagate by division.

Nidema ottonis
syn. *Epidendrum ottonis*

↔ 4–6 in (10–15 cm) ↑ 4–6 in (10–15 cm)
🌼 🔆 ◆ ❄ 🗑/🌿

Small species from the West Indies. Pseudobulbs clustered, elliptic, about

Nidema ottonis, in Jardín Botánico Lankester, Costa Rica

1½ in (35 mm) long. Leathery leaves to 6 in (15 cm) long, narrowly oblong. Upright inflorescence, to about 4 in (10 cm) long, laxly arranged with 3 to 6 flowers in spring. Flowers creamy white, sometimes tinged with green or yellow, rather fleshy, about ¾ in (18 mm) in diameter.

NOTYLIA

About 50 species are known in this neotropical genus, distributed from Mexico in the north to Paraguay in the south. They grow as epiphytes in lowland forests up to elevations of about 1,640 ft (500 m), with only one species found at higher altitudes in montane forests up to 4,920 ft (1,500 m). They are easily recognized by their clustered single-leafed pseudobulbs with 2 foliaceous sheaths and mostly long pendent inflorescences with numerous small flowers, around ½ in (12 mm) in diameter.

CULTIVATION: Grow these orchids under intermediate to warm conditions and moderate light. They do best when mounted on a piece of tree fern or similar moisture-retaining slab. They do not like prolonged periods of dryness, so water frequently. They do not require a resting period. Propagation is by division of larger clumps.

Notylia barkeri

↔ 8–10 in (20–25 cm)   ↕ 8–10 in (20–25 cm)
♀ ☀ ◆ 🏐

Found from Mexico to Panama; grows in humid forests, swamps, and even in coffee plantations at altitudes of up to 4,920 ft (1,500 m). Single leaf, light green, leathery, to about 8 in (20 cm) long. Pendent inflorescence, to 12 in (30 cm) long, appears at base of sheaths of pseudobulb, with many small, slightly fragrant, greenish flowers in spring.

OBERONIA

This is a sympodial epiphytic genus with over 300 species, found from Africa through Southeast Asia to the Pacific Islands. It is a poorly studied genus due to the very tiny blooms and similarity when not in flower. The succulent leaves, produced in 2 ranks, are generally broad, flattened, and pointed at the apex. They bloom only once off the main growth, from between the last 2 leaves, and the inflorescence is often longer than the plant. They are clump-forming and many are attractive plants even when not in bloom. The genus is named for Oberon, king of the fairies.

CULTIVATION: These botanical orchids are seen only in specialist orchid collections. They require warm, humid, shaded conditions throughout the year and are best grown on slabs of moisture-retentive tree fern or cork, with some sphagnum moss covering the rootball. These plants rarely succeed in pots, as the roots require a lot of aeration. Propagate from seed.

Oberonia gracilis

↔ 4–8 in (10–20 cm)   ↕ 4–16 in (10–40 cm)
♀ ☀ ◆ 🏐

Species from New Guinea. Pendent habit; strappy bright green leaves. Inflorescences produce up to 100 tiny, round, tan to brown flowers in autumn–winter.

Oberonia species

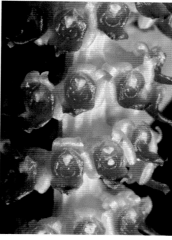

Oberonia gracilis

Oberonia gracilis

Octomeria alpina

Octomeria juncifolia

OCTOMERIA

This genus from South America contains about 150 species. They grow as miniature epiphytes or lithophytes and are characterized by sympodial growths without pseudobulbs. There are 2 leaf types—cylindrical pencil-shaped leaves, or broader flat leaves. Most species produce a dense cluster of flowers at the junction of the shoot and the leaf. CULTIVATION: Grow mounted on a piece of tree fern or cork with a layer of living moss, or in small shallow pots in a fine organic substrate. Keep humidity high year-round and water regularly. Propagate by division of larger clumps of shoots.

Octomeria alpina

↔ 4–8 in (10–20 cm)   ↕ 3–6 in (8–15 cm)
♀ ☀/☀ ◇/◇ ☐/☒

Small tufted South American species. Pale yellow translucent blooms, less than ½ in (12 mm) in size, in spring. Do not expose to direct sunlight.

Octomeria grandiflora

syns *Octomeria arcuata, O. surinamensis*
↔ 4–6 in (10–15 cm)   ↕ 6–8 in (15–20 cm)
♀ ☀/☀ ◆/◇ ☐/☒

From the lower Caribbean, Suriname, Colombia, Peru, and Bolivia; found

growing at altitudes of 330–8,200 ft (100–2,500 m) in wet forests. Broad acute leaves on a cylindrical shoot. Single flower, yellowish, about 1 in (25 mm) in size. Blooms from autumn to spring.

Octomeria juncifolia

↔ 4–10 in (10–25 cm)   ↕ 12–16 in (30–40 cm)   ♀ ☀/☀ ◆/◇ ☐/☒

From cool humid mountain forests of Brazil. Lacks pseudobulbs; descending cylindrical leaves, under ¼ in (6 mm) across. Clusters of up to 15 small, cupped, yellow blooms with a little red on lip, from base of leaves. Blooms sporadically throughout the year. Grow mounted, or in baskets using moss.

Odontioda Avranches (hybrid)

ODONTIODA

This is a cool-growing bigeneric hybrid between the sympodial genera *Odontoglossum* and *Cochlioda*, with *C. noezliana* giving bright red color to many of its hybrids. Sometimes the *Cochlioda* influence is barely noticeable as the hybrids have been repeatedly backcrossed onto other odontoglossums. CULTIVATION: These plants like cool, moist, humid conditions in a part-

shaded position, and thrive in pots. Use sphagnum moss or a fine-grade bark mixture with perlite. Keep well-watered. Propagate by division.

Odontioda Hybrids

↔ 8–24 in (20–60 cm)   ↕ 8–36 in (20–90 cm)
♀ ☀ ◇ ❀ ☐

Most of these hybrids are winter and spring flowerers, with the bloom size from 2–5 in (5–12 cm). **Avranches ★**, albino hybrid developed from white-flowered forms of species; **Bugle Boy**, red-orange blooms; **Durham River**, full shape from *Odontoglossum* parent, with intense color coming from *Cochlioda*; (**Erik Jaeger** × **Helen Stead** '**Geyserland**'), pink and white blooms with darker markings; **Heatonensis** × *Odontoglossum* **Starlight**, unregistered hybrid, spidery shape inherited from *Odontoglossum cirrhosum*; **La Fosse**, most unusual color combination of maroon, white, and yellow. (**Nichirei Sunrise** × **Ingmar**), vermilion and hot pink blooms; **Ruby Eyes**, pink flowers with maroon patterning; **Sheila Hands**, white blooms overlaid with brown and edged with pink; and **Wearside Gate**, bright red blooms.

Odontioda Durham River (hybrid)

Odontioda Bugle Boy (hybrid)

Odontioda (Erik Jaeger × Helen Stead 'Geyserland') (hybrid)

Odontioda Heatonensis × *Odontoglossum* Starlight (hybrid)

Odontioda (Nichirei Sunrise × Ingmar) (hybrid)

Odontioda Ruby Eyes (hybrid)

Odontioda La Fosse (hybrid)

Odontioda Phoenix Way × (Mount Diablo × Tiffany) (hybrid)

Odontioda Wearside Gate (hybrid)

Odontioda Sheila Hands (hybrid)

Odontobrassia Kenneth Biven 'Santa Barbara'

ODONTOBRASSIA

A cool- to warm-growing bigeneric hybrid between the sympodial genera *Odontoglossum* and *Brassia*. These spidery-bloomed hybrids, an influence from the *Brassia* parent, are more tolerant of both cool and high temperatures and are reliable flowerers every year. They may bloom at any time, but the long-lasting flowers are more frequently produced in the warmer months. They grow in a wide range of conditions and are popular pot plants. CULTIVATION: These hybrids grow well in pots of a bark-based medium and they require frequent watering and fertilizing when in active growth. They are suitable for bright humid conditions, out of direct sunlight, and require moisture throughout the year, with the frequency tapered off in winter months. Propagate by division.

Odontobrassia Kenneth Biven 'Santa Barbara'

↔ 8–27 in (20–70 cm) ↕ 8–40 in (20–100 cm) ♧ ☀ ◆/◈/◇ ❉ ▽

Primary hybrid between *Odontoglossum cariniferum* and *Brassia arcuigera*. Blooms 5 in (12 cm) wide, dark chocolate with yellowish tips, white lip. Flowers in spring–summer.

ODONTOCIDIUM

This is a hardy bigeneric hybrid, a combination of *Odontoglossum* and *Oncidium*. These sympodial hybrids have long-lasting blooms and are increasing in popularity as pot plants. CULTIVATION: These plants grow well in pots and must be kept well watered. Use sphagnum moss or a fine-grade bark mixture with perlite. Grow in part-shade. More warmth tolerant than odontoglossums, these hybrids will thrive in a range of temperatures if kept in a humid environment out of direct sunlight. Propagate by division.

Odontocidium Hybrids

↔ 8–24 in (20–60 cm) ↕ 8–36 in (20–90 cm) ♧ ☀ ◆/◈/◇ ❉ ▽

These hybrids often have tall spikes of abundant medium-sized flowers. Most flower in winter–spring. **Artur Elle**, yellow blooms with reddish peppering; **Bittersweet 'Sophie'** and **Bittersweet 'Toffee'**, popular and variable hybrids; **Dark Charmer 'Antigua'**, yellow and maroon blooms, lip white, maroon, and yellow; **Dorothy Wisnom 'Golden Gate'** ★, one of the finest odontocidiums, large infusions of *Odontoglossum crispum*, *Oncidium leucochilum*, and *Oncidium tigrinum* in its ancestry; **Golden Trident**, large yellow flowers, lip with dark marking; **Hansueli Isler**, mahogany and yellow blooms; **Mayfair 'RFW'**, golden yellow blooms; **Tigersun 'Nugget'**, yellow blooms, tan markings; and **Tropic Tiger**, 7 different species in its pedigree, green blooms with dark maroon-brown blotches, deep red lip.

Odontocidium Artur Elle (hybrid)

Odontocidium Bittersweet 'Sophie' (hybrid)

Odontocidium Dark Charmer 'Antigua' (hybrid)

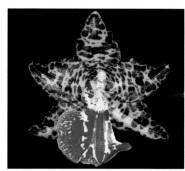

Odontocidium Tropic Tiger (hybrid)

Odontocidium Dorothy Wisnom 'Golden Gate' (hybrid)

Odontocidium Mayfair 'RFW' (hybrid)

Odontocidium Golden Trident (hybrid)

Odontocidium Bittersweet 'Toffee' (hybrid)

Odontocidium Hansueli Isler (hybrid)

Odontocidium Tigersun 'Nugget' (hybrid)

Odontoglossum trilobum

Odontoglossum gloriosum

ODONTOGLOSSUM

This genus of about 60 cool-growing orchids from mountainous regions of South America is related to *Oncidium* and *Miltoniopsis*. Most have short to long spikes of large, showy, yellow and brown blooms, often spidery. The popular ornamentals have been the species with white and pink flowers and wider segments, giving the effect of a round bloom. There are many hybrids in *Odontoglossum* and its combinations with related genera. Some of the more popular combinations include *Colmanara* (× *Miltonia* × *Oncidium*), *Odontioda* (× *Cochlioda*), and *Odontocidium* (× *Oncidium*).

CULTIVATION: Odontoglossums thrive in cool growing conditions in a part-shaded position. Grow in pots in a fine-grade bark mixture with perlite in a 5:1 ratio or in sphagnum moss. Keep well-watered. Propagate by division.

Odontoglossum crispum
↔ 4–16 in (10–40 cm) ↕ 5–32 in (12–80 cm) ♀ ☀ ◇ ✿ ⛢

From Colombia. Compressed pseudobulbs, each with 2 strap-like leaves. Up to 12 or more large, widely opening blooms, 3 in (8 cm) wide, with broad segments. Flowers white to pale rose, spotted or blotched with red or purple. Blooms in autumn–winter.

Odontoglossum gloriosum
↔ 14–16 in (35–40 cm) ↕ 24–36 in (60–90 cm) ♀ ☀ ◇ ✿ ⛢

From cool humid forests at 6,560– 9,840 ft (2,000–3,000 m) elevation

Odontoglossum wyattianum

in Colombia and western Venezuela. Oval compressed pseudobulbs; 2 to 3 apical linear leaves. Inflorescences 24–36 in (60–90 cm) in height, arise from base of bulbs, with up to 35 flowers in spring. Flowers creamy-white with red spots and blotches, base of lip yellow.

Odontoglossum harryanum
↔ 14–16 in (35–40 cm) ↕ 14–18 in (35–45 cm) ♀ ☀ ◆/◇ ✿ ⛢

From Colombia; grows in lower cloud forest at altitudes of 5,900–7,550 ft (1,800–2,300 m). Oval compressed pseudobulbs; 2 to 3 leaves at apex. Inflorescences 16–18 in (40–45 cm) long, with several flowers in summer. Brown flowers about 3 in (8 cm) wide, yellow markings, petals point forward, white lip with basal half-streaked.

Odontoglossum trilobum
syn. *Oncidium trilobum*
↔ 44–50 in (110–130 cm) ↕ 48–55 in (120–140 cm) ♀ ☀/☀ ◆/◆/◇ ✿ ⛢

Species from Bolivia and Peru; grows in wet montane forests. Pseudobulbs ovate, laterally compressed, 2-leafed. Inflorescence pendulous, much-branched, 3 to 5 flowers per branch; often 50 to 80 flowers open at a time, usually in spring. Flowers to 2 in (5 cm) in diameter. Sepals and petals yellow to green, marked with large brown blotches; lip white, prominently 3-lobed at about the middle, with red-purple markings.

Odontoglossum wyattianum
↔ 4–12 in (10–30 cm) ↕ 5–24 in (12–60 cm) ♀ ☀ ◇ ✿ ⛢

From Peru and Ecuador; found in mossy cloud forests at altitudes of around 6,560 ft (2,000 m). Up to 25 tan-brown, 3 in (8 cm) wide blooms, contrasting, broad, 2-toned purple lip, in late winter–spring. Closely related to *O. harryanum*.

Odontoglossum Hybrids
↔ 8–24 in (20–60 cm) ↕ 8–36 in (20–90 cm) ♀ ☀ ◇ ✿ ⛢

Mostly winter- and spring-flowering hybrids. Blooms 1½–5 in (3.5–12 cm) in size. (**Augres** × *nobile*), unregistered hybrid, white blooms, contrasting yellow lip, deep pink border; (**Holiday Gold** × **Geyser Gold**), golden yellow hybrid; **Illustre**, red-brown blooms with white markings; **La Hougue Bie**, blooms with well-defined yellow, white, and tan blotches; **Margarete Holm**, blooms with white, yellow, and maroon markings; and **Mimosa 'Oda Marcet'**, vivid plum-purple blooms with a velvety texture.

Odontoglossum harryanum

Odontoglossum (Augres × *nobile*) (hybrid)

Odontoglossum (Holiday Gold × Geyser Gold) (hybrid)

Odontoglossum Illustre (hybrid*)*

Odontoglossum La Hougue Bie (hybrid)

Odontoglossum Mimosa 'Oda Marcet' (hybrid)

Odontoglossum Margarete Holm (hybrid)

Odontonia Papageno

Odontonia Papageno 'Fiesta'

Odontonia Susan Bogdanow

ODONTONIA

This bigeneric hybrid genus is a combination of *Odontoglossum* and *Miltonia*. These sympodial hybrids often have spikes of up to 12 medium-sized flowers. They are more warmth tolerant than odontoglossums and will thrive in a range of temperatures if kept in a humid environment out of direct sunlight. These orchids have long-lasting blooms and sometimes flower more than once a year. Most are spring flowerers.

CULTIVATION: Grow these orchids in pots, in sphagnum moss or a fine-grade bark mixture with 10 percent perlite added. They require abundant water throughout the year and prefer a part-shaded position. Propagation is by division.

Odontonia Bartley Schwarz ★
syn. *Oncidopsis Bartley Schwarz*
↔ 8–24 in (20–60 cm) ↕ 8–36 in (20–90 cm)
♀ ☀ ◈/◇ ❁ ⊟

Hybrid with upright inflorescences of up to 10 plum-colored blooms, 2 in (5 cm) wide; lip predominantly pure white. Flowers in spring–summer.

Odontonia Papageno
↔ 8–16 in (20–40 cm) ↕ 8–20 in (20–50 cm)
♀ ☀ ◈/◇ ❁ ⊟

Heavily dominated by influences from *Miltoniopsis vexillaria* and *Odontoglossum crispum*. White blooms overlaid with purple; lip white, orange at base. 'Fiesta', selected cultivar. Flowers from spring to autumn.

Odontonia Susan Bogdanow
↔ 8–24 in (20–60 cm) ↕ 8–36 in (20–90 cm)
♀ ☀ ◈/◇ ❁ ⊟

Hybrid with large blooms, up to 3½ in (9 cm) wide, pinkish cream overlaid with darker purple to red spotting. Flowers from spring to autumn.

OECEOCLADES

About 30 species make up this genus, found mainly in Africa and Madagascar, but with 1 also found in the Americas from Florida in the north to Argentina in the south. They are terrestrial, rarely epiphytes, with ovoid pseudobulbs topped by 1 to 3 leaves that are often variegated. The main habitat is dry woodlands at lower altitudes—only one species, from Madagascar, is found in higher elevations up to 4,270 ft (1,300 m). The erect inflorescence appears at the base of the pseudobulb and produces numerous small flowers.

CULTIVATION: Because of the extreme conditions in the natural habitat, these orchids are rather difficult to cultivate. Try to grow them in a sandy free-draining substrate in the same way as hot-growing succulents. Only water when the plants are in growth and never wet the leaves. A distinct resting period is necessary in winter. Propagate by division.

Oeceoclades maculata
syns *Eulophidium ledienii*, *E. maculatum*
↔ 6–8 in (15–20 cm) ↕ 8–12 in (20–30 cm)
✿ ◈ ◆ ⊟

Found in the Americas from Florida, USA to Paraguay, and in Africa from Senegal to Sudan and from Tanzania to Zimbabwe; grows in leaf litter between trees and rocks at altitudes

Odontonia Bartley Schwarz

up to 5,900 ft (1,800 m). Pseudobulbs to 1 in (25 mm) high; single
tough leaf, up to 10 in (25 cm) long.
Inflorescence to 12 in (30 cm) high,
with up to 12 reddish flowers from
autumn to spring.

Oeceoclades pulchra

syn. *Eulophia pulchra*

↔ 8–20 in (20–50 cm) ↕ 8–40 in
(20–100 cm) ✹ ☀/☀ ◆/◆ ⬜

Widespread species, found from
Madagascar to Asia and Southeast
Asia to New Guinea, Australia, and
the tropical Pacific Islands. Variable
flowering period and flower color.
Up to a dozen blooms, 2 in (5 cm)
in size, ranging in color from white
to yellow-green, predominantly white
lip. Usually spring-flowering.

OEONIELLA

This genus contains 2 monopodial
epiphytic species occurring in Madagascar, the Mascarene Islands, and the
Seychelles. Plants have long, often
branched, leafy stems with numerous
roots and racemes of white flowers.
The sepals and petals are free, the lip
is 3-lobed with a short conical spur.
The name is a diminutive of *Oeonia*,
a related genus.

CULTIVATION: Because of their long
stems, plants are usually either grown
mounted on a bark slab or potted in
a coarse bark mix with a moss pole
to climb. They need high humidity,
good ventilation, and moderate shade.
Propagate by division of mature basal
shoots or from seed.

Oeoniella polystachys

↔ 4–12 in (10–30 cm) ↕ 4–12 in (10–30 cm)
♀ ☀ ◆/◆ ❉ ⬜/🔺

From Madagascar, the Comoros and
Mascarene Islands, and the Seychelles.
Stem branched, usually about 6 in
(15 cm) long, sometimes up to 12 in

Oeceoclades species

Oerstedella schweinfurthiana

(30 cm). Narrowly oblong leaves,
1–4 in (2.5–10 cm) long. Upright
or arching inflorescences, 6–10 in
(15–25 cm) long, arise on stem
opposite leaves, with 12 to 15 flowers
in spring. Flowers scented, white,
1–1½ in (25–35 mm) across; lip
funnel-shaped, 3-lobed near apex.

OERSTEDELLA

About 30 species are known in this
genus, which occurs in Central
America and northern South America.
They grow as epiphytes, lithophytes,
or terrestrials, and are characterized
by a creeping sympodial rhizome with
short stems and distichous lanceolate
leaves. The thick and very succulent
white roots are very prominent. The
terminal inflorescence carries few to
many attractive fleshy flowers with a
prominent lip. The genus was formerly
included in *Epidendrum*, but can be
distinguished by the structure of the
column and its attachment to the lip.

CULTIVATION: Grow these orchids in
moderate to bright light. Water regularly and keep humidity high all year.
When the stems are mature, a short
period of reduced watering, but still
high humidity, is appreciated. Best
grown in small baskets or mounted
because of the thick and succulent
roots. Propagation is by division.

Oerstedella centropetala

syns *Epidendrum centradenia, E. tenuiflorum, Oerstedella centradenia*

↔ 4–10 in (10–25 cm) ↕ 6–20 in (15–50 cm)
♀/◭ ☀ ◆ ❉ ⬜/🔺

Found from Nicaragua through Costa
Rica south into Panama; grows in wet
montane forests at altitudes of 3,940–
4,920 ft (1,200–1,500 m); often found
in fruit plantations. Short stems to
about 6 in (15 cm) long, with several
lanceolate leaves, each to 2 in (5 cm)
long. Inflorescence produces up to

Oerstedella centropetala

10 bright pink to lavender flowers
from late winter to early summer.

Oerstedella schweinfurthiana

syn. *Epidendrum schweinfurthianum*

↔ 16–36 in (40–90 cm) ↕ 36–88 in
(90–210 cm) ✹ ☀/☀ ◆/◇ ❉ ⬜/🔺

Tall species, endemic to Guatemala;
found growing on the upper slopes
of mountains. Cane-like pseudobulbs;
several opposite leaves. Several to
many blooms on a branched inflorescence in autumn. Flowers 1¼–1½ in
(30–35 mm) long, orange sepals and
petals, bright pink lip.

Oerstedella wallisii

syn. *Epidendrum wallisii*

↔ 8–12 in (20–30 cm) ↕ 10–30 in
(25–75 cm) ♀/✹ ☀ ◆/◆/◇ ❉ ⬜/🔺

From Costa Rica, Panama, and Colombia; grows in wet montane forests
at 1,640–6,560 ft (500–2,000 m) altitude. Cane-like stems, covered in leaf
sheaths; lanceolate leaves. Terminal
arching to pendulous inflorescence,
4–6 in (10–15 cm) long, with 2 to 4
flowers in autumn–early winter. Yellow
flowers, can be marked with reddish
spots on tepals; lip white with yellow
base to white with pink striations.

Oeoniella polystachys

ONCIDIUM

DANCING LADY ORCHID

This large genus of sympodial orchids from tropical America contains over 650 different species. In general, they bear yellow and brown flowers on long branching inflorescences. Most have a distinct pseudobulb with up to 4 leaves at the apex. Inflorescences generally appear from the leaf axil of recently matured growth. In many species, the lip is the most prominent feature. They bloom only once from the pseudobulb.

CULTIVATION: Most species are frequently grown mounted, which permits unimpeded development of the root system and allows for quick drying after watering. Some smaller species may be grown in pots. Cultural requirements are varied, and depend largely on the habitat and altitude of particular species. Most prefer intermediate growing conditions. Propagate by division.

Oncidium baueri

syns *Oncidium altissimum*, *O. wydleri*
↔ 1–4 ft (0.3–1.2 m)   ↑ 1–10 ft (0.3–3 m)
♀ ☼/☀ ◆/◇ ❉ ▼

From Central America and Brazil; closely related to *O. sphacelatum*. Huge branched inflorescences, up to 10 ft

Oncidium baueri

(3 m) in height, produce numerous yellow and brown blooms, each 1¼ in (30 mm) across, in spring–summer.

Oncidium Cameo Sunset

↔ 5–16 in (12–40 cm)   ↑ 4–20 in (10–50 cm)
♀ ☼ ◆/◇ ❉ ▼

Richly colored hybrid that has only 2 species in its background—*O. crispum* and *O. concolor*. Produces up to 16 blooms, around 2½–3 in (6–8 cm) in size, brownish petals and sepals, bright yellow lip. Autumn-flowering.

Oncidium crispum

↔ 4–16 in (10–40 cm)   ↑ 8–27 in (20–70 cm)
♀ ☼/☀ ◆/◇ ❉ ▼

From Brazil. Ovoid pseudobulbs; 2-leafed. Leathery leaves to 8 in (20 cm) long. Branching inflorescence carries

Oncidium Cameo Sunset

Oncidium croesus

3 in (8 cm) wide blooms, predominantly brown, with some yellow patches, in summer.

Oncidium croesus ★

↔ 4–12 in (10–30 cm)   ↑ 4–8 in (10–20 cm)
♀ ☼ ◆/◇ ❉ ▼

From Brazil; miniature clump-forming species. Short spikes produce up to 5 flowers, glossy, yellow and brown, 1¼ in (30 mm) wide, in spring.

Oncidium flexuosum

↔ 8–36 in (20–90 cm)   ↑ 8–60 in (20–150 cm)   ♀ ☼/☀ ◆/◇ ❉ ⬟

Common and widespread species from South America. Climbing habit; long rhizomes between pseudobulbs. Tall branching spikes bear masses of long-lasting, bright yellow, ¾ in (18 mm) wide flowers, in mid-summer.

Oncidium fuscatum

syn. *Miltonia warscewiczii*
↔ 8–18 in (20–45 cm)   ↑ 12–24 in (30–60 cm)   ♀ ☼/☀ ◆ ❉ ▼

From Panama, Colombia, and Peru. Ovoid, compressed, ribbed pseudobulbs; 2 to 3 leaves, broadly-linear, somewhat tessellated. Inflorescences 12–24 in (30–60 cm) long, usually branched; should not be cut until brown as they often rebloom. Flowers around 1½ in (35 mm) in size; sepals and petals usually pink with white, undulate edges; lip white, pink, and reddish, with oval, smooth, shiny, often orange spot. Plants flower any time of year. Used in hybridization.

Oncidium hintonii

↔ 14–18 in (35–45 cm)   ↑ 18–26 in (45–65 cm)   ♀ ☼ ◆ ❉ ▼

From Mexico; found growing in seasonal dry forests. Oval, compressed, ribbed pseudobulbs; 2 to 3 leaves. Inflorescences 18–26 in (45–65 cm) long, branched, with flowers around 2 in (5 cm) long, in spring–summer. Yellow and brown petals and sepals; white, brown, and yellow lip.

Oncidium leucochilum

↔ 12–18 in (30–45 cm)   ↑ 2–8 ft (0.6–2.4 m)
♀ ☼ ◆/◇ ❉ ▼

From Mexico, Guatemala, and Honduras; grows in mountainous forests.

Compressed, oval, ribbed pseudobulbs; 2 apical leaves. Tall inflorescences, 2–8 ft (0.6–2.4 m) high, branched, with many flowers in spring. Flowers around 2 in (5 cm) wide, yellow to greenish, spotted brown, large lip, white with a little pink.

Oncidium maculatum

↔ 14–18 in (35–45 cm) ↕ 14–24 in (35–60 cm) ☿ ☀ ◆ ❄ ⛉

From Mexico, Guatemala, Honduras, and El Salvador; found in semi-arid woodlands and shady canyons at 3,600–7,220 ft (1,100–2,200 m) altitude. Pseudobulbs oval, compressed, ribbed; 2 to 3 apical leaves. Inflorescences 14–24 in (35–60 cm) long, arise from base of bulbs, with several flowers in winter. Flowers around 2 in (5 cm) long, light yellow with large brown blotches, lip light yellow and white with a few red markings.

Oncidium marshallianum

↔ 6–16 in (15-40 cm) ↕ 8–40 in (20–100 cm) ☿ ☀ ◆/◇ ❄ ⛉

From Brazil. Inflorescence, which can branch on robust specimens, carries up to 30 blooms in spring. Bright golden yellow blooms, over 2½ in (6 cm) wide, with a degree of brown markings and blotches throughout center of segments.

Oncidium ornithorynchum

↔ 4–24 in (10–60 cm) ↕ 6–36 in (15–90 cm) ☿ ☀ ◆/◇ ❄ ⛉

From Central America. Pendent spikes, heavily branched, with long-lasting pink and purple, chocolate-scented flowers, 1 in (25 mm) tall, in winter.

Oncidium phymatochilum

↔ 8–16 in (20–40 cm) ↕ 8–27 in (20–70 cm) ☿ ☀/☀ ◆/◆ ❄ ⛉

From Central America and Brazil. Branching inflorescences of numerous well-spaced blooms in spring–summer. Flowers to 2 in (5 cm) wide, thin segments, dull cream to yellow overlaid with dark brown and purple barring; lip predominantly white with gold crest.

Oncidium leucochilum

Oncidium maculatum

Oncidium phymatochilum

Oncidium marshallianum

Oncidium ornithorynchum

Oncidium sphacelatum

Oncidium Tai

Oncidium sarcodes

↔ 8–20 in (20–50 cm) ↕ 8–32 in (20–80 cm)

From Brazil. Clustered pseudobulbs; 2 to 3 leathery leaves. Branching inflorescences, upright to arching, with up to 40 blooms in spring. Flowers around 1¼ in (30 mm) in size, green to yellow-green in color; lip yellow with tan-brown spots.

Oncidium Sharry Baby 'Sweet Fragrance'

↔ 8–36 in (20–90 cm) ↕ 8–48 in (20–120 cm)

One of the most popular orchids used for the flowering pot-plant industry. Hybrid with upright branched spikes of reddish pink, brown, and white flowers, 1½ in (35 mm) wide, highly fragrant, smelling like chocolate. Can bloom a number of times during year.

Oncidium sphacelatum

↔ 8–36 in (20–90 cm) ↕ 8–60 in (20–150 cm)

Vigorous species native to Central America; adaptable throughout a range of climates in cultivation. Long, branched, and upright to arching inflorescences of typical brown and yellow blooms, each 1¼ in (30 mm) wide. Spring-flowering. Very hardy and reliable species.

Oncidium Sweet Sugar

↔ 8–36 in (20–90 cm) ↕ 8–48 in (20–120 cm)

Attractive hybrid with long branching inflorescences of bright yellow blooms, 2 in (5 cm) wide, some tan

Oncidium sarcodes

markings on top of floral segments. Flowers in summer–autumn. Plant enjoys high temperatures, as long as humidity is also high.

Oncidium Tai

↔ 12–48 in (30–120 cm) ↕ 12–60 in (30–150 cm)

Vigorous primary hybrid between *O. maculatum* and *O. sphacelatum*, both yellow and brown flowered species, taking a wide range of climatic conditions. Flowers in spring–summer.

Oncidium Sweet Sugar

Oncidium varicosum

DANCING LADY ORCHID

↔ 4–16 in (10–40 cm) ↕ 5–32 in (12–80 cm)

From Brazil; species has been dominant in the production of "varicosum-type" *Oncidium* hybrids. Clustered pseudobulbs, each with up to 3 leaves. Upright branching inflorescences carry up to 70 long-lasting blooms in summer. Flowers 2 in (5 cm) across; petals and sepals small, yellow with brown markings; lip large, flat, round, bright yellow, dominating the flower.

Oncidium viperinum

↔ 5–6 in (12–15 cm) ↕ 5–7 in (12–18 cm)

From southern Brazil, Paraguay, Uruguay, and northern Argentina. Oval purple-speckled pseudobulbs; 1 to 2 elongate leaves. Inflorescence 5–7 in (12–18 cm) tall, arises from base of bulbs, producing several flowers in summer. Flowers 1–1¼ in (25–30 mm) in size; brown and/or green petals and sepals, lip large, bright yellow with a bright red area.

Ophrys insectifera

OPHRYS

BEE ORCHID

This genus is distributed in Europe
and the Mediterranean from the
Canary Islands east to the Caucasus
and into southern Scandinavia in the
north. They grow terrestrially in various habitats from dry grass lands to
open forests and bush and prefer free-
draining calceolous soil with a higher
pH-value. The plants reach a height
of 2–30 in (5–75 cm) and the flowers
imitate certain bee species and are
pollinated by male bees, which are
further attracted to the flowers by
their fragrance, which imitates female
pheromones. The common name is
derived from the appearance of the
flower. There are currently 56 accepted
species in this genus, and many natural
hybrids. They are extremely variable
and form hybrid swarms in nature.
CULTIVATION: These plants need a dry
resting period in summer as the dormant subterranean tuberoids are prone
to rot if kept too moist. Flowers appear
in spring or late summer to autumn
in Mediterranean species when nights
become cooler and more humid. Grow
them in a free-draining mineral substrate in bright light. Direct sun is
necessary. Frost hardiness depends
on the species; those from northern
regions will tolerate temperatures of
0°F (–18°C). Propagate from extra
tubers that may form, or from seed.

Ophrys apifera
syns *Ophrys bicolor, O. boteroni,
O. trollii*
BEE ORCHID
↔ 2–4 in (5–10 cm) ↕ 8–24 in (20–60 cm)

Occurs in coastal regions of Europe,
North Africa, and Turkey to the
Caucasus, up to elevations of 5,900 ft
(1,800 m). Ovate to lanceolate basal
leaves. Upright inflorescence bears 2 to
17 flowers in summer. White to reddish pink or lilac sepals, green petals,
yellow and brown marked lip.

Ophrys holoserica
syn. *Ophrys fuciflora*
LATE SPIDER ORCHID
↔ 2–4 in (5–10 cm) ↕ 4–20 in (10–50 cm)

Species from continental Europe
and the Mediterranean region. Ovate
basal leaves. Flower stalk produces
2 to 10 blooms in late spring. Light
pink sepals, greenish petals, reddish
brown hairy lip.

Ophrys insectifera
syns *Ophrys muscifera, O. myodes*
FLY ORCHID
↔ 2–4 in (5–10 cm) ↕ 6–16 in (15–40 cm)

Found in central and northern Europe
in dry grasslands. Erect flower stalk
bears 2 to 20 flowers in spring–early
summer. Green sepals; thin purple-
black petals; dark reddish brown lip,
metallic blue spot in center.

Ophrys lutea
YELLOW BEE ORCHID
↔ 2–7 in (5–18 cm) ↕ 4–12 in (10–30 cm)

From the Mediterranean region. Basal
rosette of 3 to 6 leaves, to 4 in (10 cm)
long; 1 or 2 stem leaves above. Raceme
loosely arranged with up to 7 flowers;
bracts longer than ovary. Flowers about
¾ in (18 mm) across; sepals and petals
yellow-green, petals much shorter
than sepals; lip about ¾ in (18 mm)
long, 3-lobed, oblong, deep brown to
purple-black with yellow edge; speculum iridescent bluish gray. Flowers
from late winter to late spring.

Ophrys sphegodes
syn. *Ophrys aranifera*
EARLY SPIDER ORCHID
↔ 2–4 in (5–10 cm) ↕ 4–18 in (10–45 cm)

Found in central and southern
Europe. Erect flower stalk carries 3 to
12 flowers in spring. Yellowish to olive
green sepals, greenish petals, hairy
brown lip, H-shaped mark in middle.

Ophrys tenthredinifera
SAWFLY ORCHID
↔ 3–10 in (8–25 cm) ↕ 4–18 in (10–45 cm)

From the Mediterranean region. Basal
rosette of 3 to 5 leaves, each to 5 in
(12 cm) long; up to 4 sheathing leaves
on stem. Raceme carries up to 10
blooms in late spring–early summer.
Flowers about 1 in (25 mm) across;
sepals and petals red or pink; sepals
broadly ovate, petals smaller, triangular. Lip brownish-purple with yellow
to light brown hairy edge; speculum
small, blue-gray edged with yellow.

ORCHIS

This genus contains about 33 species
of terrestrial orchids from Europe, particularly from around the Mediterranean, North Africa, and temperate
Asia. Recent DNA work has led to
several species previously included here
being moved to other genera. Plants
have 2 or 3 round or ovoid tubers and
a rosette of basal leaves, sometimes
spotted. The inflorescence is cylindrical with thin floral bracts. The smallish flowers come in a range of colors.
The sepals and petals usually form a
hood, the lip is 3-lobed, with the mid-
lobe often divided; usually spurred.
CULTIVATION: Some species can be
planted in temperate gardens and will
become naturalized. Others are better
in an alpine house, usually grown in
pans, in a free-draining terrestrial compost, with added lime if the species
grows in calcareous soils in the wild.
After the leaves die back, plants should
be kept dry until signs of new growth
appear. Propagate from seed.

Ophrys apifera

Osmoglossum pulchellum 'Royale'

Orchis militaris
MILITARY ORCHID
↔ 3–6 in (8–15 cm) ↑ 8–26 in (20–65 cm)
❧ ❂/◐ ◇ ❄ ❀ ▽

Widespread in Europe, including England, where it is very rare; found growing on lime-rich soil. Basal leaves 3 to 5, elliptic, 3–7 in (8–18 cm) long. Inflorescence fairly densely arranged with many flowers in spring–summer. Sepals and petals forming a hood, pale pink outside, purple-veined inside; lip 3-lobed, mid-lobe divided again, pink or purplish, paler in center with tufts of reddish hairs forming spots.

Orchis purpurea
LADY ORCHID
↔ 3–5 in (8–12 cm) ↑ 12–36 in (30–90 cm)
❧ ❂/◐ ◇ ❄ ❀ ▽

Robust species from Europe, including England, where it is rare; found on calcareous soil. From 3 to 6 basal leaves, 2–8 in (5–20 cm) long, glossy green, semi-erect. Inflorescence densely arranged with many flowers in spring–summer. Sepals and petals brownish red, forming a hood; lip white or pale pink with tufts of hair forming purple spots, 3-lobed, side lobes narrow, mid-lobe broadly triangular, emarginate, almost 1 in (25 mm) long and wide; spur short, pointing down.

ORNITHOCEPHALUS
This widely distributed genus contains approximately 30 species, which occur from Mexico in the north to Bolivia and Brazil in the south. They grow as epiphytes in humid lowland and montane forests from sea level up to 4,920 ft (1,500 m), preferring rather shady spots on moss-covered twigs and branches. The genus is easily recognized by its fan-shaped equitant leaves. They are easy to cultivate and flower profusely.
CULTIVATION: Depending on the origin of the species, grow under warm to intermediate conditions, in shade to half-sun, with high humidity year-round. They do not like to be kept dry for long periods. These orchids are well suited to for slab culture—a piece of moss-covered cork is ideal. Propagate from seed or by division.

Ornithocephalus bicornis
↔ 3–6 in (8–15 cm) ↑ 3–6 in (8–15 cm)
❧ ❂/◑/◐/◉ ◆/◇ ❄ ▩

Miniature species from Central America. Fan-shaped leaves. Short inflorescences bear up to 30 flowers in spring. Tiny flowers, under ½ in (12 mm) across, greenish yellow. Attractive even when not in bloom.

Ornithocephalus gladiatus
syns *Ornithocephalus falcatus,*
O. inflexus, O. tripterus
↔ 2–5 in (5–12 cm) ↑ 2–4 in (5–10 cm)
❧ ❂/◉ ◇ ❄ ▩

Found from Mexico to French Guiana and on Trinidad, Tobago, and Grenada, also extending into Bolivia and Brazil; found growing at altitudes of 3,000–4,920 ft (900–1,500 m). Type species of genus and most common species encountered in culture. Leaves large for genus. Inflorescences longer than leaves, with many tiny, greenish yellow flowers from early spring to late summer.

Ornithocephalus myrticola
↔ 1–2 in (25–50 mm) ↑ 1–3 in (2.5–8 cm)
❧ ❂/◉ ◆ ❄ ▩

Distributed from Bolivia to Brazil, south to the States of Minas Gerais and Rio Grande do Sul in forests up to elevations of 1,985 ft (650 m). Very small plants; leaves do not exceed 2 in (5 cm) long. Hairy spikes, longer than leaves, carry white flowers with greenish striations; petals larger than sepals. Flowering occurs mainly in autumn.

OSMOGLOSSUM
A genus of about 6 species, 4 of which are found in cultivation. They range from Mexico to Ecuador and grow as epiphytes, sometimes as lithophytes, in humid montane forests and cloud forests at altitudes of 3,280–8,200 ft (1,000–2,500 m). They grow in dense clumps, with each of the flattened pseudobulbs bearing 2 grass-like leaves, with adjacent leaves covering the pseudobulb. The genus was formerly included into *Odontoglossum* but separated because of the very different flower morphology. The flowers have a very pleasant smell and some species were used to create the modern perfumed *Odontoglossum* hybrids.
CULTIVATION: Grow under cool to temperate conditions in bright light. During the growing season, keep temperatures at night above 59°F (15°C), in winter they may drop to 43–46°F (6–8°C). The day temperature should be between 59–68°F (15–20°C). Keep humidity high (50–80 percent). Grow in pots in coarse organic substrate; leave to dry between waterings. They need a resting period in late summer. Propagate by division.

Osmoglossum convallarioides
syn. *Odontoglossum convallarioides*
LILY-OF-THE-VALLEY ORCHID
↔ 8–12 in (20–30 cm) ↑ 8–12 in (20–30 cm)
❧ ❂ ◆/◇ ❄ ▽

Found from Mexico to Costa Rica, possibly also in Panama. Upright inflorescences emerge from base of pseudobulb. Up to 6 or 7 small white flowers, less than ¾ in (18 mm) wide; sometimes washed with red on outside. Sepals and petals fused at base; lip faces upward. Spring flowers, smell faintly like hyacinths (*Hyacinthus*) or lily-of-the-valley (*Convallaria*).

Osmoglossum pulchellum
syn. *Odontoglossum pulchellum*
↔ 8–12 in (20–30 cm) ↑ 8–12 in (20–30 cm)
❧ ❂ ◆/◇ ❄ ▽

Found from Mexico through Guatemala to El Salvador, Nicaragua, and possibly in Honduras. Similar to *O. convallarioides,* but flowers larger, to 1½ in (35 mm) in diameter, in autumn–winter. 'Royale', large, white, scented flowers.

Ornithocephalus bicornis

PABSTIA

syn. *Colax*

The 5 species in this genus are endemic to Brazil. The medium-sized epiphytes, lithophytes, or sometimes terrestrials grow in humid rainforests or cloud forests at altitudes of 660–4,920 ft (200–1,500 m). They prefer rather shady locations and have densely clustered ovoid pseudobulbs with 2 rather soft leaves. The erect or arching inflorescence carries up to 4 showy flowers. CULTIVATION: Grow under warm conditions in shade and with high humidity levels in pots with a coarse substrate. Regular watering is essential when the plants are growing, and the plants do not like to dry out for prolonged periods. Once the pseudobulbs have matured, reduce watering. Propagation is by division.

Pabstia jugosa

syn. *Colax jugosus*

↔ 6–10 in (15–25 cm)   ↕ 8–12 in (20–30 cm)
♀/⋀   ☀   ◆   ❄   ▭

Occurs in southeastern Brazil in cloud forests, at altitudes of 2,300 ft (700 m) and above. Erect or arching inflorescence to about 6–9 in (15–22 cm) long, with up to 4 showy, fragrant, waxy flowers, in spring–early summer. Sepals white, petals and lip white with dark purple spots.

PAPHIOPEDILUM

SLIPPER ORCHID

The slipper orchids, with their distinctive modified lip or "pouch," have long been highly prized in horticulture. They are cultivated throughout the world, and countless hybrids have been produced from the 80 or so species. The range extends from India eastward across southern China to the Philippines and throughout Southeast Asia and Malaysia to New Guinea and the Solomon Islands. New species continue to be discovered, particularly in remote rainforest areas of Borneo and China. There is a huge amount of diversity within the genus: some are terrestrial, growing through the leaf litter on the forest floor; others are lithophytes that show a preference for limestone cliffs; others are epiphytes, happy to live in the major forks of rainforest trees. Most species produce a single flower, but some may have up to a dozen or more open at one time, and then there are others that flower sequentially. They are generally found in quite bright situations, but not receiving direct sunlight. These flowers, which come in a wide range of colors and forms, often last for well over a month in pristine condition. Most

have plain green strap leaves; others have distinctive mottled foliage, which makes them attractive plants even when they are not in flower. Slipper orchids generally grow in quite moist and humid environments. They do not have pseudobulbs but store water in their fleshy leaves and thick hairy root system. This genus name comes from the temple to Aphrodite (Venus) at Paphos, and the Greek *pedilon,* meaning a slipper.

CULTIVATION: Slipper orchids are best grown in pots, in a well-drained bark-based medium. Select a pot size that fits the roots snugly, as they will not tolerate stagnant conditions around the root system. Pot the plant so that it is slightly buried, as often the roots will push it out of the mix, and any exposed new roots can become dry and not develop further. Keep plants shaded and moist during the warmer months, and mist foliage frequently. Many of the multi-flowered species need a drier rest in winter, along with a significant drop in day and night-time temperature. There are cool-, intermediate-, and warm-growing species. Propagation is by division.

Paphiopedilum appletonianum

syn. *Paphiopedilum wolterianum*

↔ 8–12 in (20–30 cm)   ↕ 6–24 in (15–60 cm)
⋀/♀   ☀/☀   ◆   ❄   ▭

From Thailand, Laos, Cambodia, Vietnam, Peninsular Malaysia, and Hainan Island, China; grows in leaf litter, occasionally in mossy rock crevices. Leaves with light and dark green tessellation. Tall inflorescence, 8–24 in (20–60 cm) high. Flowers variable, narrow outstretched petals with purple-pink tips, small greenish dorsal sepal, reddish to green pouch. Blooms in winter–spring. '**Jan**', one of a number of attractive cultivars.

Paphiopedilum barbatum

↔ 6–16 in (15–40 cm)   ↕ 6–12 in (15–30 cm)
⋀   ☀   ◆/◇   ❄   ▭

From Peninsular Malaysia. Tessellated foliage; single 3 in (8 cm) bloom,

white and green overlaid with distinct purple stripes and suffusions. Flowers in spring–summer.

Paphiopedilum bellatulum

↔ 8–12 in (20–30 cm)   ↕ 2½–6 in (6–15 cm)
♥   ☀   ◆/◇   ❄   ▭

Native to Thailand and Myanmar. Waxy tessellated leaves; very short flower stem with single 3 in (8 cm) wide bloom that rests on leaves, in summer. Flowers large, white, with sizeable dark maroon spots.

Paphiopedilum boxallii

↔ 8–16 in (20–40 cm)   ↕ 4–20 in (10–50 cm)
♀/♥   ☀   ◆/◇   ❄   ▭

From Myanmar; grows in humid areas, mainly on mossy trees. Plain green leaves, lance-shaped, to 10 in (25 cm) long. Velvety upright flower stem carries a single bloom in winter–spring. Flowers 5 in (12 cm) in size, predominantly brown and mustard-colored with heavy maroon-brown blotches on dorsal sepal. Some taxonomists consider this a variety of *P. villosum.*

Paphiopedilum barbatum

Paphiopedilum bellatulum

Paphiopedilum boxallii

Paphiopedilum appletonianum 'Jan'

Paphiopedilum bullenianum

Paphiopedilum concolor

Paphiopedilum fowliei

Paphiopedilum bullenianum

↔ 4–12 in (10–30 cm) ↕ 4–16 in (10–40 cm)
🌿 ☀ ◆ ❄ ▭

From Malaysia and Indonesia. Tessellated foliage; flower stem to 12 in (30 cm) long, with 1 bloom in winter–spring. Flowers 4 in (10 cm) wide, predominantly olive green to pink.

Paphiopedilum callosum

↔ 8–12 in (20–30 cm) ↕ 5–6 in (12–15 cm)
🌿 ☀/☀ ◆/◈ ❄ ▭

From Thailand, Laos, Cambodia, and Vietnam; usually grows in leaf litter, in evergreen forests. Alternate leaves, tessellated, light and dark green; upright

inflorescence with 1, occasionally 2, blooms in spring–autumn. Flowers 3–4 in (8–10 cm) across; outstretched purple, green, and white petals; red-purple pouch-like lip; white with green and purple dorsal sepal and synsepal.

Paphiopedilum charlesworthii

↔ 10–12 in (25–30 cm) ↕ 6–10 in (15–25 cm) ⋀ ☀ ◈ ❄ ▭

From Myanmar, Thailand, and Yunnan, China; grows on mossy limestone cliffs. Leaves green, often with purplish markings on both surfaces, to 8 in (20 cm) long. Flower single, glossy, to 3 in (8 cm) wide, with

striking rose-lavender dorsal sepal, in autumn–winter. *P. c.* var. *album*, pure white flower, 4 in (10 cm) across; very rare specimen. Flowers in early winter.

Paphiopedilum concolor

syn. *Cypripedium concolor*

↔ 8–12 in (20–30 cm) ↕ 6–10 in (15–25 cm)
⋀/🌿 ☀/☀ ◆ ❄ ▭

Widespread species from Thailand, Myanmar, Cambodia, Vietnam, and southwestern China; often grows on steep slopes with limestone soils. Green leaves, mottled with white, densely spotted purple-red underneath. Up to 3 flowers, 1½–2½ in (3.5–6 cm) wide,

cream to soft yellow, lightly to densely spotted reddish to purple. Flowers in spring–autumn in cultivation.

Paphiopedilum delenatii

syn. *Cypripedium delenatii*

↔ 7–9 in (18–22 cm) ↕ 6–10 in (15–25 cm)
🌿 ☀/☀ ◆/◈ ❄ ▭

Endemic to Vietnam; found in humus soils. Beautiful mottled leaves, dark green with greenish white mottling and spotted reddish purple underneath. Spike 6–10 in (15–25 cm) tall, with 1 to 2 fragrant flowers in winter–spring. Flowers to 3 in (8 cm) wide; soft, fuzzy, whitish petals and dorsal sepal, globular pink pouch.

Paphiopedilum exul

↔ 8–16 in (20–40 cm) ↕ 4–12 in (10–30 cm)
🌿 ☀/☀ ◆ ❄ ▭

Small tropical species from Thailand; closely related to *P. insigne*. Stiff plain green leaves; single, 2½ in (6 cm) wide, green and white bloom with bold maroon spotting on base of dorsal sepal. Summer-flowering,

Paphiopedilum fowliei

↔ 6–7 in (15–18 cm) ↕ 8–10 in (20–25 cm)
🌿 ☀/☀ ◆/◈ ❄ ▭

Endemic to Palawan in the Philippines; grows in humus soils. Leaves light and dark green. Inflorescence to 10 in (25 cm) tall, with 1 flower in spring. Flowers 2–2½ in (5–6 cm) in size; petals and sepals white, green, and maroon, with maroon pouch.

Paphiopedilum glanduliferum

syn. *Paphiopedilum gardineri*

↔ 12–14 in (30–35 cm) ↕ 14–18 in (35–45 cm) ⋀/🌿 ☀ ◆/◈ ❄ ▭

Native to highlands of New Guinea; often grows in humus-filled crevices. Leaves green and leathery. Upright inflorescence carries 2 to 4 flowers in winter. Flowers to 8 in (20 cm) wide; dark, twisted, outstretched petals, dorsal sepal and synsepal white with dark striping, yellowish to reddish pouch.

Paphiopedilum delenatii

Paphiopedilum exul

Paphiopedilum glaucophyllum

↔ 8–20 in (20–50 cm) ↕ 4–24 in (10–60 cm) ✿ ☀ ◆/◇ ❋ ⊔

From Java, Indonesia. Plain bluish green foliage; long spikes of sequentially flowering yellowish green, pink, and white, 3 in (8 cm) wide flowers. Can bloom throughout year. 'Lee', maroon veining and spotting on floral segments.

Paphiopedilum gratrixianum

↔ 8–16 in (20–40 cm) ↕ 4–16 in (10–40 cm) ✿ ☀ ◆/◆/◇ ❋ ⊔

From Vietnam and Laos. Single bloom, 3 in (8 cm) wide, predominantly glossy orange-brown with some maroon spotting, dorsal sepal with white edges. Winter-flowering.

Paphiopedilum glanduliferum

Paphiopedilum glaucophyllum

Paphiopedilum glaucophyllum 'Lee'

Paphiopedilum gratrixianum

P

Paphiopedilum hainanense

↔ 8–12 in (20–30 cm) ↑6–20 in (15–50 cm)
⋀/⅄ ☼/☀ ◆ ✿ ⊔

From Hainan Island, China. Tessellated foliage. Single 3 in (8 cm) wide bloom, mainly green and pale purple, in late winter–spring. Some botanists consider this species to be within the range for the related *P. appletonianum.*

Paphiopedilum haynaldianum

↔ 12–24 in (30–60 cm) ↑4–32 in
(10–80 cm) ♀//⋀/⅄ ☼ ◆/◇ ✿ ⊔

From the Philippines. Plain green leathery leaves. Up to 5 flowers produced at the same time, 5 in (12 cm) wide, yellow to green, white, and mauve, marked with dark red blotches. Spring- and summer-blooming.

Paphiopedilum henryanum

↔ 8–12 in (20–30 cm) ↑4–16 in (10–40 cm)
⋀ ☼ ◆/◇ ✿ ⊔

Stunning and distinctive species from China and Vietnam. Plain green leaves; single, 2½ in (6 cm) wide, colorful bloom. Dorsal sepal green with bold maroon spots, petals brownish purple, lip bright dark pink. Spring-flowering species.

Paphiopedilum hirsutissimum

↔ 8–16 in (20–40 cm) ↑4–16 in (10–40 cm)
⅄ ☼ ◆/◇ ✿ ⊔

Found from India to Indochina. Hairy flower stems; flowers yellow to green, with brown, and purple markings, 6 in (15 cm) wide, also covered in hairs. Winter- to spring-flowering.

Paphiopedilum hookerae

↔ 4–12 in (10–30 cm) ↑4–20 in (10–50 cm)
⅄ ☼ ◆ ✿ ⊔

Uncommon species from northern Borneo; found growing among decaying leaf litter on fringes of tropical rainforests. Boldly tessellated leaves. Single bloom, 3 in (8 cm) wide, predominantly green with solid purple coloration at ends of petals, which are also peppered with deep maroon. Flowers produced in summer. *P. h.* var. *volonteanum*, leaves with purple spotting on undersides.

Paphiopedilum insigne ★

↔ 8–12 in (20–30 cm) ↑4–16 in (10–40 cm)
⅄ ☼ ◆/◇ ✿ ⊔

From Nepal and northern India; commonly grown variable species, readily grows into a specimen. Leaves to 12 in (30 cm) long. Glossy, brownish yellow, 5 in (12 cm) wide flowers, heavily spotted in red-brown, in winter.

Paphiopedilum kolopakingii

↔ 12–20 in (30–50 cm) ↑30–50 in
(75–130 cm) ⅄ ☼ ◆/◇ ✿ ⊔

From Kalimantan, Borneo; grows on mossy rocks above rivers. Similar to *P. stonei*, but blooms smaller and more numerous. Green strap-like leaves to 10 in (25 cm) long. Erect inflorescence bears about 10 flowers in spring. Flowers to 2½ in (6 cm) wide, dorsal sepal green to white, striped dark brown; petals yellow with stripes; lip yellow. *P. k.* var. *topperii*, tawny yellow, striped maroon.

Paphiopedilum henryanum

Paphiopedilum liemianum

↔ 14–18 in (35–45 cm) ↑18 in (45 cm)
⅄ ☼/☀ ◆/◇ ✿ ⊔

From northern Sumatra, Indonesia; grows in limestone soils, often among tree roots. Undulated green leaves, some populations with strong greenish yellow and dark green tessellation. Inflorescence to 18 in (45 cm) long, with large bracts behind each of 15 to 25 sequential flowers, 1 to 2 open at once, virtually ever-blooming. Green dorsal sepal with circular white border, white with reddish marking on petals, pink pouch-like lip.

Paphiopedilum lowii

↔ 12–24 in (30–60 cm) ↑8–40 in
(20–100 cm) ⋀/⅄ ☼ ◆/◇ ✿ ⊔

Variable multi-flowered species from Peninsular Malaysia, Borneo, and Indonesia. Similar to *P. haynaldianum*, but lacking spotting on dorsal sepal. Tall inflorescences, to 20 in (50 cm), produce up to 6 blooms in spring–summer. Flowers green, white, and deep purple, 6 in (15 cm) wide. 'Select', attractive cultivar.

Paphiopedilum malipoense

↔ 10–12 in (25–30 cm) ↑18–24 in
(45–60 cm) ⅄ ☼/☀ ◇ ✿ ⊔

Stoloniferous species from northern Vietnam and southern China; grows in deciduous forests in limestone soils. Leaves dark green mottled light, wavy edges, red-purple spotting underneath. Tall inflorescences, 18–24 in (45–60 cm), with 1 to 2 fragrant flowers almost 4 in (10 cm) wide, green with purple markings. White and blackish purple staminode; inflated pouch, dark spotted inside. Blooms late autumn–spring. *P. m.* var. *jackii* (syn. *P. jackii*) grows in same area as *P. malipoense,* but differs in less purple on flower, nearly white staminode, and lighter-colored plant.

Paphiopedilum hainanense

Paphiopedilum haynaldianum

Paphiopedilum kolopakingii

Paphiopedilum insigne

Paphiopedilum lowii 'Select'

Paphiopedilum hirsutissimum

Paphiopedilum liemianum

Paphiopedilum malipoense

Paphiopedilum hookerae var. *volonteanum*

Paphiopedilum malipoense var. *jackii*

Paphiopedilum moquetteanum

Paphiopedilum niveum

Blooms throughout year. *P. p.* **var.** *purpurescens*, purple-tinged flowers.

Paphiopedilum rothschildianum

↔ 8–32 in (20–80 cm)　↕ 8–36 in (20–90 cm)
/\/⤋　☀　◆/◈　✤　▽

From Sabah in north Borneo; endemic to Mt Kinabalu, where it often occurs in large clumps; a most impressive and majestic species. Up to 5 dark-striped flowers on an upright spike; each flower to 12 in (30 cm) across the extended petals. Spring- to summer-blooming.

Paphiopedilum spicerianum

↔ 8–12 in (20–30 cm)　↕ 4–16 in (10–40 cm)
⤋　☀　◆/◇　✤　▽

Native to India. Blooms to 3 in (8 cm) across. Olive green undulating petals; broad dorsal sepal, white with green base and with a narrow, central, purple stripe; bronze pouch. Blooms in autumn.

Paphiopedilum mastersianum

↔ 8–12 in (20–30 cm)　↕ 4–20 in (10–50 cm)
⤋　☀　◆/◈　✤　▽

From Ambon, Indonesia. Tessellated-leafed species, single bloom in summer. Flower 4 in (10 cm) wide, very glossy, mainly tan; olive green dorsal sepal with pale to pure white border.

Paphiopedilum moquetteanum

↔ 6–24 in (15–60 cm)　↕ 4–20 in (10–50 cm)
⤋　☀　◆　✤　▽

From Java, Indonesia. Sequentially flowered species, can bloom all through year. Individual flowers to 4 in (10 cm) across, in a combination of pale yellows and greens with a pink lip. Some taxonomists consider this to be a variety of *P. glaucophyllum*.

Paphiopedilum niveum

↔ 4–8 in (10–20 cm)　↕ 4–12 in (10–30 cm)
⤋　☀　◆　✤　▽

From Thailand; grows on limestone cliffs near sea level in the wild. Tessellated leaves. Wide-segmented, 3 in (8 cm) wide flowers, white with maroon peppering. Summer-blooming.

Paphiopedilum philippinense

↔ 8–16 in (20–40 cm)　↕ 8–24 in (20–60 cm)
/\/⤋　☀　◆/◈　✤　▽

From the Philippines and north Borneo. Multi-flowered, green-leafed. Up to 5 blooms, 4 in (10 cm) wide, white dorsal sepal with maroon stripes; reddish brown, elongated, often twisted petals; mustard lip. Summer-flowering. *P. p.* **var.** *roebelenii* has larger flowers.

Paphiopedilum primulinum

↔ 8–16 in (20–40 cm)　↕ 4–24 in (10–60 cm)
⤋　☀　◆/◈　✤　▽

From Sumatra, Indonesia. Long spikes of many sequentially opening flowers, each 3 in (8 cm) wide, bright canary yellow, dorsal sepal tinged green.

Paphiopedilum sukhakulii

↔ 4–10 in (10–25 cm)　↕ 4–12 in (10–30 cm)
⤋　☀　◆/◈　✤　▽

From northern Thailand; discovered in 1964, one of the most popular species in cultivation. Mottled foliage; single distinctive bloom in autumn–spring. Flowers 5 in (12 cm) across, pale green-striped dorsal sepal; flat and broad green petals, boldly spotted with deep maroon; chiefly reddish-purple lip.

Paphiopedilum mastersianum

Paphiopedilum spicerianum

Paphiopedilum primulinum

Paphiopedilum primulinum var.
purpurescens

Paphiopedilum rothschildianum

Paphiopedilum philippinense var. *roebelenii*

Paphiopedilum philippinense

Paphiopedilum sukhakulii

Paphiopedilum tonsum

Paphiopedilum villosum

Paphiopedilum tonsum

↔ 8–12 in (20–30 cm) ↑14–16 in (35–40 cm) /\/✹ ☀ ◆ ❋ ⊡

Endemic to Sumatra, Indonesia; grows in humus-filled limestone cracks. Beautiful tessellated leaves, reddish underneath. Flower spike, 14–16 in (35–40 cm) tall, with 1 flower, 3–4 in (8–10 cm) wide, in late winter–spring. Greenish-brown petals and pouch, white on dorsal sepal.

Paphiopedilum venustum

↔ 12–16 in (30–40 cm) ↑10–14 in (25–35 cm) ✹ ☀/☀ ◇ ❋ ⊡

Species with many forms, from Himalayan foothills of India, Bangladesh, Bhutan, and Nepal in very wet habitats; often found in humus soils near cliff bases. Unusual coloring on foliage; leaves tessellated, often gray-green and dark green, with reddish purple underneath. Inflorescence

usually bears 1, occasionally 2, flowers in autumn–winter. Flowers very variable, generally white dorsal sepal with green stripes, black-spotted petals usually tipped with orange or red, and yellowish to orangeish pouch marbled green. *P. v.* var. *measuresianum* lacks the reddish pigment, producing a green, yellow, and white flower; also lacks purple pigment under leaves. *P. v.* 'Red Lip', reddish pouch.

Paphiopedilum victoria-regina

syn. *Paphiopedilum chamberlainianum*

↔ 8–24 in (20–60 cm) ↑4–27 in (10–70 cm) /\/✹ ☀ ◆/◇ ❋ ⊡

From central Sumatra in Indonesia; grows on forest floor or on mossy rocks. Leaves green with wavy edges. Arching to erect spikes, with up to 20 sequentially produced blooms. Large persistent bracts behind each flower. Blooms to 3 in (8 cm) wide;

Paphiopedilum victoria-regina

white-edged green dorsal sepal with dark lines or reddish spotting overlay, white to yellow-green and reddish undulated petals, pink lip. Can bloom throughout the year.

Paphiopedilum villosum

↔ 8–12 in (20–30 cm) ↕ 4–16 in (10–40 cm)
❦ ☀ ◆/◇ ❉ ⊟

Found from India to Indochina. Commonly grown. Flowers, 5 in (12 cm) wide, glossy, bronze overlay. Dorsal sepal yellow to green with dark brown markings at base. Petals 2-tone; top half reddish brown, bottom half yellowish green. Blooms in winter–spring.

Paphiopedilum wardii

BLACK ORCHID, RAINBOW ORCHID

↔ 10–12 in (25–30 cm) ↕ 8–18 in (20–45 cm) ∧/❦ ☀ ◆ ❉ ⊟

From northern Myanmar and southern China; grows in humus. Blooms in winter–spring, to 6 in (15 cm) wide; petals greenish sometimes with red suffusion, densely spotted dark brown to maroon; lip green with brown veining. *P. w.* var. *album*, greenish blooms. *P. w.* 'Coco', Chinese form, petals heavily dotted dark red.

Paphiopedilum wardii var. *album*

Paphiopedilum wardii 'Coco'

Paphiopedilum venustum var. *measuresianum*

Paphiopedilum venustum 'Red Lip'

Paphiopedilum Delophyllum (hybrid)

Paphiopedilum Flame Dragon (hybrid)

Paphiopedilum Dragon Callos (hybrid)

Paphiopedilum Hybrids

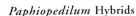

↔ 4–8 in (10–20 cm) ↕ 4–24 in (10–60 cm)

While there are hundreds of possible combinations, there have been 3 basic styles of hybrids popular for over a century. "Maudiae"-type hybrids *(P.* Maudiae, an antique hybrid between *P. callosum* and *P. lawrenceanum)* have tessellated 2-tone foliage and single blooms with prominent stripes on the broad, white, dorsal sepal. Of these, the "albino" hybrids have green stripes on the dorsal sepal, with green petals and pouch; the "coloratum" hybrids are the same, but with purple stripes, while the "vinicolors" have deep beet-root-colored flowers and almost black stripes. Multifloral hybrids have grown in popularity, and often feature larger-flowered spectacular species, such as *P. rothschildianum, P. philippinense, P. stonei,* and, since its rediscovery, *P. sanderianum.* The third group are the "complex hybrids;" these are the large, round, single-flowered plants often seen at orchid shows. Ironically, despite being developed for over a century, there is only a handful of species in their pedigree. They are mostly multiple generation hybrids, with high ratios of *P. insigne, P. spicerianum,* and *P. villosum,* with minor influences of *P. bellatulum, P. charlesworthii, P.*

druryi, P. exul, and *P. niveum.* Obviously, many of today's desirable species were unknown when most of this breeding was undertaken. Here is a selection of slipper orchid hybrids. **Booth's Sand Lady,** multi-flowered hybrid; **Darling,** hybrid of *P.* Madame Martinet and *P. lawrenceanum;* **Delophyllum,** hybrid between *P. delenatii* and *P. glaucophyllum;* **Gael,** albino "Maudiae-type"; **Gold Dollar,** hybrid of the yellow-flowered species *P. armeniacum* and *P. primulinum;* **Honey,** hybrid of *P. philippinense* and *P. primulinum;* **Lawrebel,** hybrid of *P. lawrenceanum* and *P. bellatulum;* **Lebaudyanum,** hybrid of the multi-flowered species *P. haynaldianum* and *P. philippinense;* **Limidolli,** hybrid of *P. henryanum* and *P. liemianum;* **Madame Martinet,** hybrid between *P. delenatii* and *P. callosum;* **Mitylene** and **Onyx,** albino "Maudiae-type" hybrids; **Oriental Enchantment,** albino "Maudiae-type" with white blooms striped with bright green; **Pathfinder Norm,** "complex" or "exhibition" style; **Pinocchio,** hybrid of *P. primulinum* and *P. glaucophyllum;* **Red Fusion,** vinicolor "Maudiae-type" with deep claret-colored blooms; **Rolfei,** hybrid between *P. bellatulum* and *P. rothschildianum;* **Saint Swithin,** hybrid between *P. philippinense* and *P. rothschildianum* with large flowers; **Sioux,** "complex" or "exhibition" style; and **Yospur,** hybrid of *P. delenatii* and *P. conco-bellatulum,* with round white blooms overlaid with some fine pepper spotting of purple.

Paphiopedilum Booth's Sand Lady (hybrid)

Paphiopedilum Darling (hybrid)

Paphiopedilum Faire-Maud (hybrid)

Paphiopedilum Gael (hybrid)

Paphiopedilum Lebaudyanum (hybrid)

Paphiopedilum Juno (hybrid)

Paphiopedilum Gold Dollar (hybrid)

Paphiopedilum Honey (hybrid)

Paphiopedilum Lawrebel (hybrid)

Paphiopedilum Limidolli (hybrid)

Paphiopedilum Madame Martinet (hybrid)

Paphiopedilum Morganiae (hybrid)

Paphiopedilum Nirvana (hybrid)

Paphiopedilum Mitylene (hybrid)

Paphiopedilum Oriental Enchantment (hybrid)

Paphiopedilum Pathfinder Norm (hybrid)

Paphiopedilum Onyx (hybrid)

P

Paphiopedilum Petula (hybrid)

Paphiopedilum Pinocchio (hybrid)

Paphiopedilum (Raisin Eyes × Maudiae) (hybrid)

Paphiopedilum Pinocchio 'Yellow' (hybrid)

Paphiopedilum Rolfei (hybrid)

Paphiopedilum Red Fusion (hybrid)

Paphiopedilum Red Prince (hybrid)

Paphiopedilum Smaug 'Peats Ridge' (hybrid)

Paphiopedilum (sukhakulii × Virgo*)* (hybrid)

Paphiopedilum Sioux (hybrid)

Paphiopedilum Song of Love (hybrid)

Paphiopedilum Wossner Perle (hybrid)

Paphiopedilum Yospur (hybrid)

Paphiopedilum (sukhakulii × Tuxedo Junction*)* (hybrid)

Paracaleana nigrita

PAPILIONANTHE

About 10 species are known from southeastern Asia, from India through the Himalayas, to Sumatra and Borneo, Indonesia. They grow as monopodial epiphytes or terrestrials in hot and humid swamps and forests from sea level to altitudes of about 5,580 ft (1,700 m). The species were separated from *Vanda* and *Aerides* because of their elongated stems, pencil-shaped leaves, and different flower structure with upward-facing lateral lobes of the lip. They grow very tall and are often used in tropical countries as garden plants.
CULTIVATION: Those species that were formerly included in *Aerides* are best grown mounted or in small baskets and need warm to intermediate conditions, bright light, and a distinct resting period in winter. The species formerly included in *Vanda* need hot and humid conditions and direct sun all year. The long and thick aerial roots need a lot of space. It is not easy to get flowers on plants cultivated in greenhouses in temperate zones of North America or Europe. Propagate by division of longer portions of stems.

Papilionanthe hookeriana
syn. *Vanda hookeriana*
↔ 6–8 in (15–20 cm) ↑ 5–7 ft (1.5–2 m)
♀/🌂 ☼ ◆ ❄ ☷/🗮

Largest member of the genus; found in Vietnam, Malaysia, Borneo, and Sumatra in Indonesia; grows in coastal swamps. Leaves to about 4 in (10 cm) long. Inflorescence carries 2 to 3 or more showy flowers, each about 3 in (8 cm) in diameter, in spring–summer. Sepals and petals white with carmine-colored spots; lip tinted carmine. A completely white variety is known.

Papilionanthe Miss Joaquim
syn. *Vanda* Miss Joaquim
↔ 8–16 in (20–40 cm) ↑ 1–7 ft (0.3–2 m)
♀ ☼ ◆/◇ ❄ ☷/🗮

Primary hybrid between *P. hookeriana* and *P. teres*; registered in 1893. The national flower of Singapore, features prominently, under the name of *Vanda* Miss Joaquim, on the country's currency, stamps, and official documents. Pale pink to purple blooms (also a white-flowered form) borne throughout year.

Papilionanthe teres
syn. *Vanda teres*
↔ 8–10 in (20–25 cm) ↑ 5–7 ft (1.5–2 m)
♀/🌂 ☼ ◆ ❄ ☷/🗮

Occurs in southeastern Asia, especially in hot valleys; type species of genus. Leaves longer and thicker than those of *P. hookeriana*. Light pink flowers with a darker pink lip.

Papilionanthe vandarum
↔ 12–16 in (30–40 cm) ↑ 27–36 in (70–90 cm) ♀ ☼/◗ ◆/◇ ❄ ☷/🗮

Monopodial orchid from northern India and Myanmar; found in open, seasonally dry forests. Rambling plant; very narrow, pencil-shaped, opposite leaves. Flowers to 3 in (8 cm) across, white with open clawed petals, some pink on lip. Blooms in autumn–spring.

PARACALEANA
SMALL DUCK ORCHID
This is a small genus of 10 diminutive species of deciduous terrestrial orchids from southern Australia, with one species, *P. minor*, extending to New Zealand. Most of the species are endemic to the southwestern corner of Western Australia. They grow in sandy soils in heathlands and on the fringes of swamps. At one time they were included within the now monotypic genus, *Caleana*. All species have their bizarre blooms with the modified and pheromone-laced lip uppermost, to attract their wasp pollinators. These wasps in turn accidentally pollinate the bloom while they are trying to "mate" with the lip, which flips the insect onto the reproductive parts of the bloom. This is known as pseudocopulation.
CULTIVATION: Unfortunately these specialized orchids have proved to be very difficult to maintain in cultivation and are best observed in the wild.

Paracaleana nigrita
↔ ¾–2½ in (18–60 mm) ↑ 2–6 in (5–15 cm)
🌂 ☼/◗ ◆/◇ ☷

From southwestern Australia. Erect wiry inflorescence, produced from a single small leaf less than 1 in (25 mm) long, carries 1 or 2 blooms, each 1 in (25 mm) in size, in spring. Petals and sepals predominantly green to dull red; highly modified lip, pimpled in texture, dark maroon.

Papilionanthe vandarum

Papilionanthe Miss Joaquim

PARAPHALAENOPSIS

Four species are known in this genus and are found as epiphytes in Borneo between sea level and 2,300 ft (700 m) on upper branches in the canopy. The short monopodial stems have very long cylindrical and hanging leaves that reach 7 ft (2 m) in some species, and long spreading roots. These features make them instantly recognizable. The flowers resemble those of *Phalaenopsis*, the genus in which they were formerly included. They differ in leaf shape and the structure of the lip.

CULTIVATION: Grow mature plants under warm humid conditions and bright light. Juvenile plants do well in shade or semi-shade. Keep out of direct sunlight. During spring and summer, the plants need lots of water. Be careful when fertilizing—the roots easily turn brown when the concentration is too high. Keep a bit drier in winter. Grow mounted on cork or

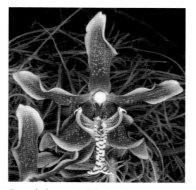

Paraphalaenopsis labukensis

Pescatorea cerina

tree-fern slabs, to cater for the hanging leaves. Propagation is from seed.

Paraphalaenopsis denevei

syn. *Phalaenopsis denevei*

↔ 4–8 in (10–20 cm) ↑ 16–27 in (40–70 cm)

From western Borneo; usually has 3 to 6 cylindrical leaves, to 27 in (70 cm) long. Short inflorescence; flowers to 2 in (5 cm) in diameter. Sepals and petals yellow to greenish yellow or brown, lip white with dark purple lobes. Flowering can occur at several times of year.

Paraphalaenopsis labukensis

↔ 4–8 in (10–20 cm) ↑ 40–84 in (100–200 cm)

From Borneo; grows to an impressive size, leaves can reach 7 ft (2 m) in cultivation. Short raceme bears up to 15 flowers in spring. Sepals and petals brownish violet, spotted yellow, with yellow rim, yellow lip finely barred with purplish brown.

Pescatorea lehmannii

Paraphalaenopsis laycockii

syn. *Phalaenopsis laycocki*

↔ 4–8 in (10–20 cm) ↑ 24–40 in (60–100 cm)

Species from western Borneo. Inflorescence with up to 15 flowers, each to ½ in (12 mm) in size. Sepals and petals light pink; pink lip with darker purple stripes and yellow callus. Summer-flowering.

PESCATOREA

This is a genus of about 15 sympodial epiphytes, occurring in Central and South America, from Costa Rica to Ecuador. They have a fan-shaped growth habit with quite thin narrow leaves. The large, colorful, fragrant, long-lived blooms are extremely attractive, and appear singly from

the leaf axils, in spring and summer. These orchids are increasing in popularity as seedlings of a number of the species have become available.

CULTIVATION: *Pescatorea* species require humid, shaded, intermediate conditions throughout the year, with no rest period. Direct sunlight will invariably burn the soft leaves. They need to be kept moist, as they have no pseudobulbs for water storage. Constant, fresh, moving air around the thin foliage is essential. Propagate by division.

Pescatorea cerina

↔ 8–16 in (20–40 cm) ↑ 4–16 in (10–40 cm)

From Panama and Costa Rica. Highly fragrant creamy white to pale lemon yellow blooms, 3 in (8 cm) long, with broad segments; lip yellow with fine, dark red, longitudinal stripes. Flowers in spring–summer.

Pescatorea lehmannii

↔ 8–16 in (20–40 cm) ↑ 4–20 in (10–50 cm)

From Colombia and Ecuador. White flowers, 4 in (10 cm) long, longitudinally striped with maroon on petals and sepals; some clones appear to be almost solid purple; dark purple lip, covered with cream-colored bristle-like hairs. Flowers in spring–summer.

PHAIOCALANTHE

This group of about 30 hybrids is composed of two terrestrial genera, *Calanthe* and *Phaius*. The first hybrids were made about 100 years ago. The leaves are pointed, accordion-pleated, to 30 in (75 cm) long, and arise from ovoid pseudobulbs. *Phaius* tends to dominate plant form, while the influence of *Calanthe* is seen in the flowers, especially in the more open and often lobed lips, with white to red blooms on erect spikes in the cooler months.

Paraphalaenopsis laycockii

CULTIVATION: Members of this genus are robust and warm-growing to warmth tolerant. Use an open terrestrial mix with added composted manure. Raise in bright light. Water copiously and fertilize weekly with a dilute liquid applied directly to the compost during periods of active growth. Do not let water accumulate in emerging shoots. Provide good air movement, as foliage can be prone to spotting. Propagate by division.

Phaiocalanthe Schroederiana
↔ 16–24 in (40–60 cm) ↑12–32 in (30–80 cm) ❁ ☀ ◆/◇ ❈ ⛁

Hybrid registered in 1901. Arching leaves to 24 in (60 cm) long. Richly colored bloom with an open lip, shows the result of crossing a large yellowish *Phaius* with a pink- to red-flowered *Calanthe*. Bears about 10 to 15 flowers, to 4 in (10 cm) wide, in winter–spring.

PHAIOCYMBIDIUM
This intergeneric hybrid is composed of two Old World genera, *Phaius* and *Cymbidium*. There are only a small number of known hybrids. The warmth-tolerant plants resemble the *Phaius* parent, which in all these hybrids has been one of the highly variable forms of *Phaius tankervilleae*. The influence of *Cymbidium*, which is difficult to see in the hybrids, has given rise to some controversy. Flowers are usually yellow with contrasting lips, and are borne in winter and spring.

CULTIVATION: Use an open terrestrial mix. Raise in bright humid conditions with good air circulation. Water copiously and fertilize with a dilute liquid applied directly to the compost during periods of active growth. Do not allow water to accumulate in the emerging shoots or leaf axils. Reduce watering somewhat for a few weeks after pseudobulbs have matured. Propagate by division.

Phaiocymbidium Chardwarense
↔ 12–16 in (30–40 cm) ↑20–27 in (50–70 cm) ❁ ☀ ◆/◇ ❈ ⛁

This hybrid resembles its *Phaius* parent, with broad pleated leaves to 20 in (50 cm) long. Inflorescence, to 27 in (70 cm) tall, with about 15 flowers, arises from base of ovoid pseudobulb in winter–spring. Bright yellow flowers, to 3 in (8 cm) wide, ruffled red lip.

PHAIUS
SWAMP ORCHID
This is a group of some 50 distinct, evergreen, terrestrial species, found in Africa, Madagascar, and India, and throughout Southeast Asia, south to Australia and the Pacific Islands. They have clustered pseudobulbs, with large, pleated, broad but thin leaves. They produce tall spikes of showy colorful flowers in spring and summer.

CULTIVATION: Generally, these plants enjoy intermediate to warm conditions and bright light, and need to be kept moist. If grown in pots, these should be deep with a well-drained medium incorporating pine bark, sand, and peat moss. The pots can be sat in a saucer of water, about 2 in (5 cm) deep, during summer. They need less water in winter, when the plants are semi-dormant. Propagate by division.

Phaius flavus
syn. *Limodorum flavum*
↔ 24–30 in (60–75 cm) ↑18–26 in (45–65 cm) ❁ ☀/☀ ◆/◇ ❈ ⛁

Found throughout much of tropical Asia; grows on forest floors. Roundish pseudobulbs; large, broad, pleated leaves, spotted distinctively with

Phaiocalanthe Schroederiana

yellow. Inflorescence to 16 in (40 cm) tall, from base of bulb. Light to bright yellow flowers, 2–3 in (5–8 cm) across, wavy edged lip with orange, brown, or reddish lines. Blooms in spring.

Phaius tankervilleae
↔ 8–36 in (20–90 cm) ↑12–48 in (30–120 cm) ❁ ☀/☀ ◆/◇ ❈ ⛁

From Southeast Asia, Australia, and the Pacific Islands. Most commonly cultivated species, has become naturalized in some tropical countries. Up to 20 blooms, 5 in (12 cm) long, tan-brown on inside, white trumpet-like lip with some purple markings. Summer-flowering.

Phaiocymbidium Chardwarense

Phaius flavus

Phaius tankervilleae, in the wild

Phalaenopsis aphrodite subsp. *formosana*

PHALAENOPSIS

MOTH ORCHID

These orchids are popular with florists and are often used for weddings. The 60 or so species in the genus are found throughout the tropical rainforests of Asia, and south to New Guinea and northern Australia. Most species exist in the wild as epiphytes, and the monopodial plants consist of only a few leathery, often deep green, leaves. There are also some species with attractive tessellated foliage.

CULTIVATION: *Phalaenopsis* species and hybrids need warm, humid, damp conditions, and will grow and bloom in quite deep shade. These orchids are mostly grown in pots in a bark-based medium, but a number of species perform well on long slabs of tree fern or cork when grown in the greenhouse. They are marketed as flowering pot plants, and are one of the most majestic flowers in horticulture; even better, they are the best orchids to grow indoors as they are compact in habit,

will grow in a range of light conditions, and prefer a temperature range that is also pleasant for humans. Cut off the flower spike only after it has died and turned brown. As long as the stem remains green, there is the potential for more flowers to be produced along dormant eyes of the peduncle—the part of the flowering stem between the plant and the first flower. Most species and their hybrids can bloom throughout the year, but peak flowering occurs in spring and summer.

Phalaenopsis amabilis ★

↔ 8–20 in (20–50 cm) ↕ 12–36 in (30–90 cm) ♀ ☼ ◆ ❄ ⛊/⛆

Species from Indonesia, Borneo, and the Philippines. Leaves broadly oval, to 20 in (50 cm) long. Long arching sprays of large, flat, pure white flowers, 3 in (8 cm) wide. *P. rosenstromii* is a closely related species from northeastern Australia and New Guinea.

Phalaenopsis aphrodite

↔ 8–24 in (20–60 cm) ↕ 4–24 (10–60 cm) ♀ ☼ ◆ ❄ ⛊/⛆

From the Philippines. Closely related to *P. amabilis* and at times has been considered as a variety of that species; differs primarily in its smaller milky white blooms, 2½ in (6 cm) wide,

different lip structure, and shorter broader leaves. Flowers in spring–summer. *P. a.* subsp. *formosana*, smaller, shapelier blooms.

Phalaenopsis equestris

↔ 5–12 in (12–30 cm) ↕ 4–12 in (10–30 cm) ♀ ☼ ◆ ❄ ⛊/⛆

Popular miniature-flowered species from the Philippines and Taiwan. Branched sprays of numerous pink to rose-purple blooms, 1¼ in (30 mm) wide. Flowers in autumn–spring.

Phalaenopsis gibbosa

↔ 3–8 in (8–20 cm) ↕ 2–3 in (5–8 cm) ♀ ◑/☼ ◆/◈ ❄ ⛊/⛆

Monopodial orchid from Vietnam and Laos; grows in forests with cool dry winters. Alternate oval leaves, can be deciduous (less so in cultivation). Flowers small, less than 1 in (25 mm) in size, white, bright yellow spots on white lip. Blooms in spring.

Phalaenopsis lueddemanniana

↔ 6–16 in (15–40 cm) ↕ 4–16 in (10–40 cm) ♀ ☼ ◆ ❄ ⛊

Highly variable species from the Philippines. Greenish white flowers, 1½ in (35 mm) wide, with concentric purple barring that may give blooms an overall pink appearance. Old

Phalaenopsis amabilis

Phalaenopsis equestris

Phalaenopsis gibbosa

Phalaenopsis lueddemanniana

inflorescences often produce plantlets, which can be removed when roots have formed.

Phalaenopsis mannii
syn. *Polychilos mannii*
↔ 10–16 in (25–40 cm) ↕ 8–12 in (20–30 cm) ♀ ☼/☀ ♦/◆ ❄ �/☂

Monopodial orchid from northeastern India, Nepal, China, and Vietnam; found growing in lightly shaded to dense forests at altitudes of 1,640–4,600 ft (500–1,400 m). Leathery shiny leaves. Flowers yellow with heavy red to brown barring and spotting, white lip. Blooms in spring–summer.

Phalaenopsis parishii
↔ 5–8 in (12–20 cm) ↕ 4–8 in (10–20 cm) ♀ ☀ ♦ ❄ ☂/☁

Compact-growing miniature-flowered species found from India to Thailand; can become deciduous during dry

winters. Short sprays of white blooms, ¾ in (18 mm) wide; contrasting bright wine-colored lip.

Phalaenopsis pulcherrima
syn. *Doritis pulcherrima*
↔ 5–12 in (12–30 cm) ↕ 4–36 in (10–90 cm) ∧/✄ ☼/☀ ♦/◆ ❄ ☂/☁

From Southeast Asia; often found in sandy soils near the coast. Stiff leathery leaves, often have purple pigment. Upright inflorescences carry up to 20 blooms, each 1 in (25 mm) wide, varying from light pink to dark purple, in summer. Also rare white, lilac, and unusual splash-petalled cultivars.

Phalaenopsis schilleriana
↔ 8–20 in (20–50 cm) ↕ 12–36 in (30–90 cm) ♀ ☼ ♦ ❄ ☂

From the Philippines. Showy foliage mottled in green and silver. Branched inflorescence with numerous large

flowers, pale pink to lilac to deep rose, 4 in (10 cm) wide, in winter–spring.

Phalaenopsis wilsonii
↔ 4–5 in (10–12 cm) ↕ 6–8 in (15–20 cm) ♀/∧ ☼/☀ ♦/◆ ❄ ☁

Species from southwestern China and eastern Tibet, found growing in

seasonally dry forests. Alternate flat leaves can be deciduous at times, but plants rarely lose them completely in cultivation. Pink flowers, ¾–1 in (18–25 mm) in size, darker lip, usually all open simultaneously in spring. Likes to grow mounted, preferring cooler drier winter.

Phalaenopsis pulcherrima

Phalaenopsis schilleriana

P

Phalaenopsis mannii, dark form

Phalaenopsis parishii

Phalaenopsis Artemis (hybrid)

Phalaenopsis Antique Gold (hybrid)

Phalaenopsis Brother Cefiro (hybrid)

Phalaenopsis Brother Golden Potential (hybrid)

Phalaenopsis Hybrids

↔ 5–24 in (12–60 cm) ↕ 8–36 in (20–90 cm)

Many *Phalaenopsis* hybrids have been produced, and this is almost certainly the most important commercial genus of orchids grown. Tens of thousands of plants are sold in flower annually throughout the world to cater for the growing flowering pot-plant trade. White *Phalaenopsis* hybrids, mostly derived from *P. amabilis*, are still one of the most popular flowers, and they are often used in wedding bouquets; these include **Cottonwood, Oregon Delight, Snow City,** and **Taisuco Adian.** Previously there were similar hybrids known under the generic name of *Doritaenopsis*, but these are all now classified as *Phalaenopsis*. There is some variation in color, apart from the classic white and pink standard hybrids. Bicolored hybrids include: **Brother Pico Sweetheart,** City Girl, Livingston's Gem, Luchia Lip,** and **Quevedo.** Hybrids in pink and purple include: **Brother Juno, Brother Pico Vallezac, Cosmic Star, Ho's Amaglad, Hwafeng Redqueen, Little Kiss, Night Shine, Queen Beer, Sogo Firework, Sogo Yukidian, Sonoma Spots, Taisuco Pixie,** and (Timothy Christopher × *pulcherrima*). Candy stripe hybrids include: **Brother Pico Pink, Brother Showpiece, Formosa Mini, Hsinying Facia, Minho Stripes, Quilted Beauty,** and **Striped Eagle.** Hybrids in yellow-bronze shades include: **Antique Gold, Brother Cefiro, Brother Golden Potential, Brother Golden Wish, Coral Harbor, Hakugin, Pumpkin Patch, Sand Stone,** and **Taida Sunset.** More recently, new hybrids have been bred from some of the smaller, often rather unusual or brightly colored species, which have provided new shapes, sizes, and color combinations.

Phalaenopsis Brother Golden Wish (hybrid)

Phalaenopsis Brother Kaiser (hybrid)

Phalaenopsis Brother Little Spotty (hybrid)

Phalaenopsis Brother Juno (hybrid)

Phalaenopsis Brother Pico Sweetheart
(hybrid)

Phalaenopsis Brother Pico Vallezac (hybrid)

Phalaenopsis Brother Pico Pink (hybrid)

Phalaenopsis Brother Showpiece (hybrid)

Phalaenopsis (Ching Her John × Dou-dii Rose) (hybrid)

Phalaenopsis City Girl (hybrid)

Phalaenopsis Coral Harbor (hybrid)

Phalaenopsis Cosmic Star (hybrid)

Phalaenopsis Chancellor (hybrid)

Phalaenopsis Cottonwood (hybrid)

Phalaenopsis Hsinying Facia (hybrid)

Phalaenopsis (Dou-dii Rose × Ching Her John) (hybrid)

Phalaenopsis Hwafeng Redqueen (hybrid)

Phalaenopsis (Golden Peoker 'B' ×
stuartiana 'Larkin Valley') (hybrid)

Phalaenopsis Little Kiss (hybrid)

Phalaenopsis Hakugin (hybrid)

Phalaenopsis Formosa Mini (hybrid)

Phalaenopsis Luchia Lip (hybrid)

Phalaenopsis Livingston's Gem (hybrid)

Phalaenopsis Minho Stripes (hybrid)

Phalaenopsis Queen Beer (hybrid)

Phalaenopsis Oregon Delight (hybrid)

Phalaenopsis (Morgenrot × Opaline) (hybrid)

Phalaenopsis Night Shine (hybrid)

Phalaenopsis (Malibu Tiger × Vladimir Horowitz) (hybrid)

Phalaenopsis Pumpkin Patch (hybrid)

Phalaenopsis Quevedo (hybrid)

Phalaenopsis Snow City (hybrid)

Phalaenopsis Sogo Firework (hybrid)

Phalaenopsis Quilted Beauty (hybrid)

Phalaenopsis Sand Stone (hybrid)

Phalaenopsis Sogo Yukidian (hybrid)

Phalaenopsis Sonoma Spots (hybrid)

Phalaenopsis Sonnentau × (Doritaenopsis Mosel × self) (hybrid)

Phalaenopsis Striped Eagle (hybrid)

Phalaenopsis Sylvania Fair 'Sacha' × (Wilma Hughes × Diana Hampton) 'Petula' (hybrid)

Phalaenopsis Taisuco Adian (hybrid)

Phalaenopsis Taisuco Firebird (hybrid)

Phalaenopsis Taida Sunset (hybrid)

Phalaenopsis (Timothy Christopher × *pulcherrima*) (hybrid)

PHOLIDOTA

syns *Acanthoglossum, Camelostalix, Chelonanthera, Crinonia, Ptilocnema*

RATTLESNAKE ORCHID

This genus contains about 70 species and is spread from India to southern China, through the Malay Archipelago, Indonesia, and New Guinea to New Caledonia and northern Australia. They grow as epiphytes or lithophytes in montane forests at altitudes up to 6,560 ft (2,000 m). They have a creeping or pendent rhizome with densely packed or widely separated pseudobulbs topped by 1 or 2 leaves. The flower stalks have very large, overlapping bracts that resemble the tail of a rattlesnake.
CULTIVATION: Grow under warm conditions in semi-shade. The species with clustered pseudobulbs do well in pots with a free-draining substrate; those with the pseudobulbs spaced apart do better when mounted on a slab with a layer of moisture-retaining moss. The plants need a short resting period after the growth is completed. Propagation is by division.

Pholidota articulata
↔ 8–12 in (20–30 cm) ↕ 8–12 in (20–30 cm)
♀/∧ ☀ ◆/◈ ▯/☂

Widespread robust species from India, Myanmar, Thailand, Laos, Vietnam, and the Philippines; grows on rocks and tree bases. Slender pseudobulb, to 6 in (15 cm) long, arises from the apex of an older growth. Leaves leathery, to 6 in (15 cm) long. Arching inflorescence to 10 in (25 cm) long, with about 15 fragrant creamy white to pink flowers, less than ½ in (12 mm) wide, in spring–summer.

Pholidota bracteata
↔ 4–12 in (10–30 cm) ↕ 6–14 in (15–35 cm)
♀ ☀/☀ ◆ ▯/☂

From Thailand; closely related to *P. imbricata*, with some authorities including it with that variable and widespread species. Pendulous flaccid inflorescence, densely packed with pinkish to white blooms in spring.

Pholidota chinensis
↔ 8–10 in (20–25 cm) ↕ 12–16 in (30–40 cm) ♀/∧ ☀ ◆ ▯/☂

From southern China, Myanmar, and Vietnam; grows on rainforest trees and rocks. Round pseudobulbs; somewhat narrow pointed leaves. Arching inflorescence holds 8 to 20 nearly translucent orange-white flowers with white lip. Flowers in spring.

Phalaenopsis Taisuco Pixie (hybrid)

Pholidota imbricata
syns *Pholidota conchoidea, P. loricata, P. triotos, Ptilocnema bracteatum*

NECKLACE ORCHID, RATTLESNAKE ORCHID
↔ 8–12 in (20–30 cm) ↕ 10–14 in (25–35 cm) ♀ ☀ ◆ ▯/☂

Occurs in tropical Asia, from India to Australia and even on some Pacific islands at altitudes up to about 5,250 ft (1,600 m). Type species of genus, may even be split into several species. Clustered conical pseudobulbs to 3 in (8 cm) high; single thick leaf to 12 in (30 cm) long. Erect or arching inflorescence with up to 50 small, fragrant, white flowers. Flowering time variable, from spring to mid-winter.

PHRAGMIPEDIUM

SOUTH AMERICAN SLIPPER ORCHID
This genus from Central and South America has about 20 species. The sympodial plants have multiple flowers, generally blooming sequentially; some robust species have branching spikes of blooms. They are well known to orchid growers; their popularity rose dramatically in the early 1980s with the discovery of the bright red species *P. besseae*, which has been used to create a number of attractive orange and red hybrids. Most flower during warmer months, but very productive plants can bloom throughout the year.
CULTIVATION: These orchids have similar requirements to those of *Paphiopedilum*, but require stronger light levels and frequent watering. They grow well in a bark-based medium with the addition of washed pea-sized river gravel and perlite. Some growers use pure sphagnum moss. The plants prefer deep plastic pots, and much success has been achieved by placing them in shallow saucers of water, 2 in (5 cm) deep. Propagate by division.

Phragmipedium besseae
↔ 8–16 in (20–40 cm) ↕ 8–20 in (20–50 cm)
∧/⊻ ☀ ◆/◈ ❉ ▯

From Ecuador and Peru. Broadly segmented orange to bright red flowers, 2½ in (6 cm) across. Also a rare yellow-flowered form. Flowers in spring–summer.

Phragmipedium caudatum
↔ 12–24 in (30–60 cm) ↕ 8–36 in (20–90 cm) ♀/∧ ☀ ◆ ❉ ▯

From Central America and western South America; largest-flowered member of the genus. Up to 4 yellow-green to brown blooms; long pendulous sepals to 24 in (60 cm) long. Flowers in spring–autumn.

Phragmipedium longifolium
↔ 12–24 in (30–60 cm) ↕ 8–36 in (20–90 cm) ⊻ ☀ ◆ ❉ ▯

Variable species found from Costa Rica to Ecuador. Predominantly green blooms, 6 in (15 cm) across, red-brown markings on the narrow outstretched petals. Autumn-flowering.

Phragmipedium longifolium

Pholidota chinensis

Pholidota bracteata

Phragmipedium Hybrids

↔ 8–24 in (20–60 cm)   ↑ 8–36 in (20–90 cm)

🌱 ☀ ◆/◇ ❄ 🪴

There has been an upsurge of interest in hybrids in this genus. Two styles come to the fore: the long-sepalled types from *P. caudatum* and *P. longifolium*, and the pink and red types from *P. schlimii* and *P. besseae* respectively. Most of the following hybrids can have up to 6 blooms 2–4 in (5–10 cm) across: **Don Wimber ★**, between *P.* Eric Young and *P. besseae*; **Eric Young**, between *P. besseae* and *P. longifolium*; **Jason Fischer**, between *P. besseae* and *P.* Memoria Dick Clements; **Lutz Rollke**, between *P. besseae* and *P. boissierianum*; **Memoria Dick Clements**, between *P. sargentianum* and *P. besseae*; **Nitidissimum 'Raybar'**, between *P. caudatum* and *P.* Conchiferum; **Noirmont 'Red Albatross'** between *P.* Memoria Dick Clements and *P. longifolium*; **Saint Ouen**, between *P. besseae* and *P.* Hanne Popow; and **Sergeant Eric**, between *P.* Eric Young and *P. sargentianum*.

Phragmipedium Eric Young (hybrid)

Phragmipedium Don Wimber (hybrid)

Phragmipedium Lutz Rollke (hybrid)

Phragmipedium Memoria Dick Clements (hybrid)

Phragmipedium Noirmont 'Red Albatross' (hybrid)

Phragmipedium Nitidissimum 'Raybar' (hybrid)

Phragmipedium Jason Fischer (hybrid)

Phragmipedium Saint Ouen (hybrid)

Phragmipedium Sergeant Eric (hybrid)

P

PLATANTHERA

BUTTERFLY ORCHID

This genus contains about 85 species that spread across temperate, subtropical, and tropical regions of the world. They are found from Greenland to Mexico and New Guinea and grow terrestrially in meadows, bushland, forests, and swamps from sea level to about 8,200 ft (2,500 m). Very variable genus; some species have a single basal leaf topped by an upright inflorescence, others have stems covered in multiple sheaths and leaves. Leaf shape is rounded to lanceolate. The flowers range from white to greenish and soft pink. The lip is usually unlobed and always carries a spur.
CULTIVATION: A lime-free mixture of peat moss, mixed with sieved peat is suitable for almost all species. Prevent the substrate from clogging, as this will invariably lead to root rot. The plants grow under cool conditions in shade or semi-shade, some will even tolerate full sun. Propagate by division.

Platanthera bifolia

syns *Gymnadenia bifolia*, *Habenaria bifolia*, *Platanthera solstitialis*

LESSER BUTTERFLY ORCHID

↔ 4–10 in (10–25 cm) ↑ 6–20 in (15–50 cm)
🌱 ◐/◑/☀ ◇ ❄ ✿ ⊔

From Europe and the Mediterranean region, in light deciduous or coniferous forests, dry meadows, and bushland. Usually 2, rarely 3 to 4, basal leaves. Erect inflorescence with about 10 white fragrant flowers with distinct spur in late spring–summer.

Platanthera chlorantha

syns *Habenaria chlorantha*, *Platanthera montana*, *P. virescens*

GREATER BUTTERFLY ORCHID

↔ 6–14 in (15–35 cm) ↑ 8–20 in (20–50 cm)
🌱 ◐/◑/☀ ◇ ❄ ✿ ⊔

From Europe and the Mediterranean region; found growing in meadows,

Platanthera ciliaris

bushland, and forests. Basal leaves are almost opposite. Erect inflorescence carries many small greenish white flowers in late spring–summer.

Platanthera ciliaris

↔ 4–6 in (10–15 cm) ↑ 27–40 in (70–100 cm) 🌱 ◐/◑ ◇ ❄ ✿ ⊔

From eastern and southeastern USA. Stem erect, leafy; leaves 2–12 in (5–30 cm) long, glossy green. Inflorescence densely or loosely arranged with many flowers in summer–autumn. Orange flowers; dorsal sepal forming a hood with petals, lateral sepals reflexed; lip deeply fringed; spur slender, 1–1½ in (25–35 mm) long.

Platanthera integra

↔ 2–3 in (5–8 cm) ↑ 16–24 in (40–60 cm)
🌱 ◐/◑ ◇ ❄ ✿ ⊔

From eastern and southeastern USA. Erect stem with 1 or 2 large leaves near base, each 2–8 in (5–20 cm) long, grading into bracts up stem. Inflorescence cylindrical, densely arranged with many flowers in summer–autumn. Flowers small, yellow; lip unlobed, not fringed; spur short and slender.

Platanthera integra

Platanthera leucophaea

EASTERN PRAIRIE FRINGED ORCHID

↔ 8–10 in (20–25 cm) ↑ 16–26 in (40–65 cm) 🌱 ◐ ◇ ❄ ✿ ⊔

Species from wet fens and prairie in Canada and the USA east of the Mississippi River, where it is threatened due to habitat loss and drought. Leaves lance-like to 8 in (20 cm) long. Leafy stem carries about 20 blooms in summer. Flowers to 1 in (25 mm) wide, white, fragrant, with fringed lips. Pollinators are sphinx moths.

PLECTORRHIZA

TANGLE ORCHID

This is a genus of 3 species of small monopodial epiphytic orchids, 2 of which are native to the east coast of Australia, the third endemic to Lord Howe Island. Narrow strap-like leaves are in 2 rows, and the stem is supported by a tangle of crooked wiry roots that attach to the outer twigs of trees and shrubs, in rainforests and other moist forests. Flowers are small but scented, with narrow greenish

sepals and petals and a whitish lip. Plants may be abundant but inconspicuous among foliage. They have had limited appeal to collectors. The genus name comes from two Greek words; *plektos* meaning twisted, *rhiza* meaning root.
CULTIVATION: Tangle orchids are easily grown in a humid shady environment with good ventilation. Attach to a suspended slab of cork or old weathered hardwood. Spray sparingly in summer with very weak liquid manure. Propagation is by stem division.

Plectorrhiza tridentata

TANGLE ORCHID, TANGLEROOT ORCHID

↔ 4–6 in (10–15 cm) ↑ 2½–6 in (6–15 cm)
🌸 ◑/☀ ◈/◇ 🍃

From rainforests and sclerophyll forests of eastern Australia. Leaves lance-shaped to narrowly oval or oblong, to 4 in (10 cm) long. Flowers fragrant, green to brown, lip white marked red, yellow, or green, on 5 in (12 cm) racemes. Summer-flowering.

Plectorrhiza tridentata

P

PLEIONE

This small genus of about 20 mostly semi-alpine bulbous orchids is related to *Coelogyne*. Pleiones are found in a wide variety of mountain habitats, at high altitudes, from Nepal to China. They grow as terrestrials or epiphytes on mossy limbs or fallen rotting logs and produce *Cattleya*-like blooms, singly or in pairs, in early spring.

CULTIVATION: Pleiones are easy to cultivate in cool climates and do best if repotted annually in a rich, well-drained, terrestrial mix. Healthy plants will produce 2 new growths, which develop into new plants, as older pseudobulbs will shrivel and die. Keep the potting mix moist from spring to early autumn while plants are actively growing. They need to be kept cool and dry during the winter months. Propagate by division of the dormant pseudobulbs in late winter.

Pleione bulbocodioides

↔ 3–4 in (8–10 cm) ↑ 4–7 in (10–18 cm)
/\/�ిన ☀ ◇ ❄ ❂

Variable species widespread in China. Pseudobulbs conical, single-leafed.

Pleione formosana

Leaf to 6 in (15 cm) long, developing after flowering. Flowers to 4 in (10 cm) across, pink to deep red-purple; lip with darker marks and fringed edges. Spring-flowering.

Pleione formosana

↔ 16 in (40 cm) ↑ 16 in (40 cm)
/\/✿ ☀ ◇ ❄ ❂ ❒

From China and Taiwan; hardiest species. Flowers to 4 in (10 cm), in size, in shades of pink; many named cultivars, also pure white forms, such as '**Clare**'. Fringed lip with white and yellow base and small red-brown blotches. Some botanists consider *P. bulbocodioides* to be the same species.

Pleione formosana 'Clare'

Pleione praecox

AUTUMN-FLOWERING PLEIONE
↔ 8–12 in (20–30 cm) ↑ 6–10 in (15–25 cm)
✿ ☀ ◇ ❂ ❒

Found from China to India; grows on mossy slopes. Top-shaped pseudobulb; 2 leaves, pleated, oval, pointed, to 10 in (25 cm) long. Stem to 3 in (8 cm) tall, with 1 or 2 flowers appearing in autumn when leaves wither.

Flowers to 4 in (10 cm) in diameter, white to deep pink, slightly fragrant, with fringed lip.

Pleione Hybrids

↔ 8–16 in (20–40 cm) ↑ 8–16 in (20–40 cm)
✿ ☀ ◇ ❄ ❂ ❒

There have been numerous hybrids created, using *P. formosana* as a foundation with other pink- and

Pleione Soufrière (hybrid)

purple-flowered species, as well as incorporating some of the more difficult-to-grow, yellow-flowered species from China. **Alishan**, creamy-colored hybrid between *P. Versailles* and *P. formosana*; **Britannia**, cerise-flowered hybrid between *P. formosana* and *P. Tongariro*; **El Pico**, cerise-flowered hybrid between *P. Versailles* and *P. bulbocodioides*; **Shantung**, hybrid between *P. formosana* and *P. Confusa* (*P. albiflora* × *P. forrestii*), flowers vary from peach and cream tones through to pale pink to lilac, due to the influence of the yellow-flowered *P. forrestii*; **Soufrière**, pale pink flowers, white-fringed lip with brownish red and yellow markings, hybrid between *P. Versailles* and *P. confusa*; **Tolima**, purple-flowered hybrid between *P. formosana* and *P. speciosa*; **Tongariro**, purple-flowered hybrid between *P. Versailles* and *P. speciosa*; **Versailles**, vigorous pink- to purple-flowered hybrid between *P. formosana* and *P. limprichtii*, and **Zeus Weinstein**, hybrid between *P. formosana* and *P. forrestii*, flowers lilac-pink, lip yellowish with red markings.

Pleione Britannia (hybrid)

Pleione Tongariro (hybrid)

Pleione Versailles (hybrid)

Pleione Alishan (hybrid)

Pleione El Pico (hybrid)

Pleione Tolima (hybrid)

Pleione Shantung (hybrid)

Pleione Zeus Weinstein (hybrid)

P

Pleurothallis immersa

PLEUROTHALLIS

This is a large genus of over 1,000 species of sympodial orchids from the American tropics. They are generally epiphytes of the mountainous rain-forests, but there are many species that grow in open situations, on rocks, or as terrestrials, generally in thick mosses. A single leaf is produced, often on a thin flattened "stem," called a ramicaul, as they lack pseudobulbs. The flowers are produced from a spathe or sheath at the base of the leaf, either singly or on an inflorescence. There is an amazing range of color, shape, and size within the blooms of the various species. Plants range from miniatures to species that can grow over 3 ft (0.9 m) tall. Most are cool-growing, but there are also examples from lowland regions that require warm conditions in cultivation. They are mainly of interest to species orchid enthusiasts, who enjoy the challenge of growing these more unusual botanical subjects in their collections.

CULTIVATION: Members of this genus have similar cultural requirements to *Masdevallia*, but will generally tolerate a wider range of temperatures and stronger light intensities. They like to be somewhat potbound and prefer small pots. Keep them moist, shaded, and generally in a humid environment throughout the year, but avoid direct sunlight. Most species may be grown in sphagnum moss or in a fine bark mix, with some of the creeping species suitable for mounting on tree fern. Propagation is by root division.

Pleurothallis cordata

↔ 4–12 in (10–30 cm)   ↕ 4–16 in (10–40 cm)
♀ ☀/☼ ◆/◈/◇ ☐

Widespread and variable species from Venezuela, Colombia, Ecuador, Peru, and Bolivia. Small blooms, less than ½ in (12 mm) in size, produced almost continuously from where base of leaf meets its "stem." Flowers usually from greenish yellow to orange-brown.

Pleurothallis cordata

Pleurothallis praecipua

Pleurothallis viduata 'Fox Den'

Pleurothallis grobyi
↔ 2½–12 in (6–30 cm) ↕ 1½–6 in (3.5–15 cm) ⚲ ☀ ◆/◆/◇ ⊔

Common and variable species from Central America, the West Indies, Brazil, and Peru. Attractive compact foliage, with leaves colored purplish green on undersurface. Small lax spikes of tiny green to yellow-orange flowers, striped maroon; often do not open fully. Summer-flowering.

Pleurothallis immersa
↔ 8–10 in (20–25 cm) ↕ 18–24 in (45–60 cm) ⚲ ☀ ◆/◇ ⊔

Variable species found from Mexico to Colombia and Venezuela. Lacks pseudobulbs; leathery elongate-oval leaves emerge directly from rhizome. Unusual inflorescence arises out of leaf mid-vein, toward the apex, eventually reaching 18–24 in (45–60 cm). Several orange-yellow to reddish-brown fleshy flowers open

simultaneously, but spike continues to grow and flower for months. Blooms in autumn–spring.

Pleurothallis macroblepharis
↔ 2–8 in (5–20 cm) ↕ 2–6 in (5–15 cm) ⚲ ☀/☀ ◆/◇ ⊔

From Ecuador. Ever-expanding, wiry, zig-zagged inflorescence produces a number of dainty starry blooms, just under ¾ in (18 mm) in size, creamy-green, heavily striped with deep maroon. May bloom throughout the year.

Pleurothallis marthae
↔ 6–14 in (15–35 cm) ↕ 8–20 in (20–50 cm) ⚲ ☀/☀ ◆ ⊔

From Colombia; one of the larger-growing species in genus. Large, heart-shaped, broad leaves. Yellow through pink to purple blooms, may be bi-colored with combinations of these tones. Blooms in spring–summer.

Pleurothallis phalangifera
↔ 14–16 in (35–40 cm) ↕ 12–14 in (30–35 cm) ⚲ ☀ ◆/◇ ⊔

Occurs in Colombia and Ecuador; grows in coolish moist forests. Leaves leathery, elongate-oval, pointed, on thin stem. Arching inflorescence, arising from leaf base, carries 12 or so blooms, to 2 in (5 cm) in size, in light green or wine-red forms. Plants seem to prefer intermediate conditions in cultivation. Blooms in any season.

Pleurothallis praecipua
↔ 14–16 in (35–40 cm) ↕ 12–14 in (30–35 cm) ⚲ ☀ ◆/◇ ⊔

Species from Colombia and Ecuador; grows in coolish moist forests. Lacks pseudobulbs; leaves leathery, elongate-oval, pointed, on thin stem. Plants can bloom anytime, with many flowers, but only 1 or 2 open at a time. Flowers just under ½ in (12 mm) in size, purplish pink, white petal tips, dark purple lip. Grows well potted or mounted, using moss.

Pleurothallis tuerckheimii
↔ 4–20 in (10–50 cm) ↕ 8–20 in (20–50 cm) ⚲ ☀ ◆ ⊔

Robust Central American species. Long inflorescences of up to 20 reddish brown blooms, about 1 in (25 mm) tall, in summer.

Pleurothallis viduata
↔ 4–12 in (10–30 cm) ↕ 4–12 in (10–30 cm) ⚲ ☀/☀ ◆/◆/◇ ⊔

From Ecuador; a most interesting species that appears to have been collected only once, with this single plant entering cultivation. *Viduatus*

Pleurothallis marthae

is Latin for "lost," and this refers to the missing collection data from when it was collected and described in 1981. It is believed that all plants of this species in cultivation throughout the world have been divisions, or aerial growths produced in the leaf axil, of the original collected plant. White blooms, just under ½ in (12 mm) in size, with deep maroon "eyes." Blooms appear throughout the year. Very easy to cultivate, enjoys a range of temperatures. 'Fox Den', attractive cultivar.

Pleurothallis villosa
syn. *Pleurothallis schiedei*
↔ 1½–6 in (3.5–15 cm) ↕ 1½–6 in (3.5–15 cm) ⚲ ☀ ◆/◇ ⊔

Somewhat bizarre miniature species found in Mexico and Guatemala. Short fine spikes of up to 5 tiny flowers, ranging from greenish yellow through orange-brown to deep maroon, darker spotting over sepals. White filaments dangle from edges of sepals, and move in the slightest breeze. Flowers in spring–autumn.

Pleurothallis macroblepharis

Pleurothallis phalangifera

PODANGIS

This genus contains one species of monopodial epiphytic orchid from western and central Africa. The stem is short, sometimes branching at the base, with fleshy, bilaterally flattened leaves forming a fan. Inflorescences are racemose, arising from below the leaves and from the axils of the lower leaves. The name is derived from the Greek *pous*, meaning foot, and *angos*, meaning vessel.

CULTIVATION: The sole species grows in evergreen forest and so requires shade and high humidity. However, it rots easily if over-watered, so if it is grown in a pot, it must be allowed to dry out before watering again. It does well mounted if the humidity is sufficiently high. Propagate by seed.

Podangis dactyloceras

↔ 4–6 in (10–15 cm) ↕ 4–5 in (10–12 cm)
♀ ☀ ◆ ▭/⬚

From western and central Africa. Leaves several, 4–6 in (10–15 cm) long, sword-shaped. Racemes to 2 in (5 cm) long, with up to 20 flowers set close together, almost in a head, in summer. Flowers small, cup-shaped, translucent white with a green anthercap. Spur about ½ in (12 mm) long, wide-mouthed then narrower at middle and swollen again and sometimes lobed at apex.

POGONIA

About 10 species are known in this genus. They are found in all temperate regions of the Northern Hemisphere except Europe. These terrestrial orchids grow in wet meadows, bogs, and swamps. The subterranean rhizome produces small rounded tuberoids and downy roots. The erect shoot has 1 or 2 leaves and a mostly single-flowered inflorescence. The plants quickly form large colonies with their branching rhizome.

CULTIVATION: Grow potted in an acid- and lime-free substrate like fresh peat and sphagnum, mixed with 10 percent sand, perlite, or vermiculite. They prefer wet sunny spots in the garden and may even be planted out. They are easily propagated by division.

Pogonia ophioglossoides

syn. *Arethusa ophioglossoides*

ADDER'S MOUTH, ROSE POGONIA, SNAKE MOUTH

↔ 4–8 in (10–20 cm) ↕ 6–10 in (15–25 cm)
✄ ☼ ◇ ❋ ❊ ⬚

Found in North America from eastern Canada south to Florida in the USA, and in East Asia in China, Japan, and Korea; grows in bogs and swamps in full sun. Single flower, to 1 in (25 mm) in size, pink to red; even white forms have been found. Lip decorated with frills and hairs. Flowering occurs in spring in the south and summer in the northern parts of the range.

POLYSTACHYA

This is a large genus of sympodial, mostly epiphytic, orchids from Africa, with a few outlying species in other tropical countries. They are mostly miniature clumping species with small pseudobulbs. Interesting, upside-down, botanical flowers are produced on upright inflorescences, from between the leaves of the immature new growth. The lip is uppermost in the bloom. The flowers are found in a range of colors, with yellows and oranges dominating.

CULTIVATION: Most of their active growth takes place during the warmer months, with the plants entering a dormant phase during winter. Reduce watering during this time. They prefer humid intermediate growing conditions, with ample light. Propagate by division.

Polystachya bella

↔ 4–12 in (10–30 cm) ↕ 4–12 in (10–30 cm)
♀ ☀ ◆ ❊ ⬚

Species from Kenya. Oval pseudobulbs with 1 to 2 leaves. Flowering inflorescences, sometimes branching, carry 1 in (25 mm) bright orange-yellow blooms that darken with age. Summer-flowering.

Polystachya gerrardii

↔ 4–10 in (10–25 cm) ↕ 3–12 in (8–30 cm)
♀ ☼/☀ ◆ ❊ ⬚

Species from eastern central Africa and Madagascar; related to *P. cultriformis*. Branched inflorescences of numerous white-cream to pale pink blooms, just under ½ in (12 mm) in size, that do not open widely. Flowers in spring–summer.

Polystachya johnstonii

↔ 2–6 in (5–15 cm) ↕ 2–4 in (5–10 cm)
♀ ☀ ◆ ❊ ⬚

Small-growing variable species from Malawi. Greenish blooms, ¾ in (18 mm) long, with purple suffusions, contrasting pink lip. Spring-flowering.

Polystachya longiscapa

↔ 6–8 in (15–20 cm) ↕ 12–36 in (30–90 cm)
⋀ ☀ ◆/◇ ❊ ⬚

From eastern Tanzania. Leaves to 15 in (38 cm) long, grass-like, arching. Inflorescence to 36 in (90 cm) tall, with 1 to 3 branches, several-flowered. Flowers 2 in (5 cm) across, pale pink to lilac-pink. Blooms off and on through year.

Polystachya ottoniana

↔ 2½–8 in (6–20 cm) ↕ 2½–8 in (6–20 cm)
♀ ☼/☀ ◆/◇ ❊ ⬚

Small-growing species from South Africa. Short inflorescences bear up

Podangis dactyloceras

Pogonia ophioglossoides

Polystachya gerrardii

Polystachya ottoniana

to 5 blooms, to ½ in (12 mm) across, in spring–summer. White-cream to yellowish flowers, do not open fully, having a clawed appearance.

Polystachya pubescens
↔ 6–8 in (15–20 cm) ↕ 6–10 in (15–25 cm)

From South Africa and Swaziland. Pseudobulbs conical, forming clumps. Leaves 2 to 3, dark green, elliptic, to 4 in (5–10 cm) long. Inflorescences with short hairs, to 5 in (12 cm) tall, with 7 to 12 flowers in autumn–early winter. Flowers opening wide, to ¾ in (18 mm) across, bright yellow, lateral sepals with red-brown lines on upper half. '**Gleneyrie**', attractive cultivar.

Polystachya johnstonii

Polystachya species

Polystachya pubescens 'Gleneyrie'

Porroglossum olivaceum

Porroglossum teaguei

Porroglossum meridionale

PORROGLOSSUM

syn. *Lothiana*

About 30 species are known in this genus. They occur from Venezuela to Bolivia and Peru and are found as epiphytes or occasionally as lithophytes in montane cloud forests. The genus is closely related to *Masdevallia* and the plants have a similar habit with clustered shoots and short-stemmed leaves. They differ from that genus in the sensitive lip that traps insects between the lip and the column to aid pollination.

CULTIVATION: They prefer small pots, and sphagnum moss is the recommended medium. Keep cool and moist year-round in shade or semishade. Propagation is by division.

Porroglossum amethystinum
syns *Masdevallia amethystinum, Scaphosepalum amethystinum*

↔ 4–6 in (10–15 cm) ↕ 6–10 in (15–25 cm)
♀/∧ ☀/◑ ◆/◊ ❈ ▽

From Ecuador, growing at altitudes of 4,920–7,880 ft (1,500–2,400 m); mostly in wet cloud forests. Short bract-covered stems with 1 leaf. Erect inflorescence to 10 in (25 cm) high, with several small pink flowers produced in succession throughout year.

Porroglossum echidnum
syns *Masdevallia echidna, M. mucosa, Scaphosepalum echidnum*

↔ 4–6 in (10–15 cm) ↕ 2–8 in (5–20 cm)
♀/∧ ☀/◑ ◇ ❈ ▨

From Venezuela, Colombia, Peru, and Ecuador; grows in Andean cloud forests at altitudes of 8,550–10,500 ft (2,600–3,200 m). Short stems, covered in bracts; single obovate to elliptical leaf. Inflorescence to 8 in (20 cm) high, with a single greenish flower. Flowers throughout the year.

Porroglossum meridionale

↔ 1½–4 in (3.5–10 cm) ↕ 1¼–5 in (3–12 cm) ♀ ☀ ◆/◊ ❈ ▽

Small-growing tufted species from Peru. Dull purple blooms, just under ¾ in (18 mm) in size, on a few-flowered inflorescence. Peak blooming in late winter–spring, but occasional flowers produced throughout the year.

Porroglossum olivaceum

↔ 2½–4 in (6–10 cm) ↕ 2½–8 in (6–20 cm) ♀ ☀ ◆/◊ ❈ ▽

From Ecuador and Colombia; cloud forest species, variable in both flower size and color. Olive green to orange-tan blooms, just under 1 in (25 mm) in diameter, produced in spring.

Porroglossum teaguei

↔ 2–3 in (5–8 cm) ↕ 4–10 in (10–25 cm) ♀ ☀ ◆ ❈ ▽

Small species from Ecuador. Leaves dark green, to 5 in (12 cm) long. Inflorescence erect, 6–10 in (15–25 cm) tall. Flowers small; sepals translucent purple with long, slender, pink to red tails, lip pink. Summer-flowering.

POTINARA

Potinara has 4 genera in its genetic make-up, being a combination of the sympodial genera *Brassavola, Cattleya, Laelia,* and *Sophronitis*. They are like sophrolaeliocattleyas, but differ in having an extra infusion of *Brassavola*. Generally, the flowers are also slightly larger than those of the parents.

CULTIVATION: These hybrids require part-shade to strong light, but will burn in direct sunlight. They grow best in pots incorporating a coarse bark-based medium to ensure unimpeded drainage. Healthy plants will develop an extensive system of thick white roots, which are long lived and branch freely. Plants will withstand cooler winter temperatures for short periods if kept dry while dormant. Flowers are long lasting and the plant can be enjoyed indoors when in bloom. Propagate by division after flowering.

Potinara Hybrids

↔ 8–24 in (20–60 cm) ↕ 8–24 in (20–60 cm)
♀ ☀ ◆/◊ ❈ ▽

There is a huge color range in these attractive hybrids with bright yellow and reds predominating. Many can bloom more than once a year; however most flower in spring. **Afternoon Delight 'Magnificent'**, rich orange blooms; **Atomic Fireball**, solid red blooms, 4 in (10 cm) across; *(Brassolaeliocattleya* Orange Nugget × *Potinara* Wattana Gold)*, yellow blooms; *(Brassolaeliocattleya* Regal Pokai × *Potinara* Pastushin's Gold)*, reddish pink blooms, ruffled deep red lip with yellow markings; **Burana Beauty ★**, distinctive 2-tone yellow and red splash-petalled hybrid; **Dal's Moon**, creamy flowers with ruffled edges and dark markings; **Little Toshie 'Gold Country'**, pure yellow, 3 in (8 cm) blooms, contrasting deep red lip; **Little Toshie 'Lake Land'**, yellow to orange blooms, lip edged with dark red; **Netrasiri Starbright**, varies from pale orange to red; **Super Nova**, very round well-shaped golden yellow flower, red markings on lip.

Potinara Dal's Moon (hybrid)

Potinara Afternoon Delight 'Magnificent' (hybrid)

Potinara Atomic Fireball (hybrid)

Potinara Netrasiri Starbright (hybrid)

Potinara (Brassolaeliocattleya Regal Pokai × *Potinara* Pastushin's Gold*)* (hybrid)

Potinara Little Toshie 'Gold Country' (hybrid)

Potinara Little Toshie 'Lake Land' (hybrid)

Potinara Super Nova (hybrid)

Potinara (Brassolaeliocattleya Orange Nugget × *Potinara* Wattana Gold*)* (hybrid)

Potinara Burana Beauty (hybrid)

Prosthechea chacaoensis

PROMENAEA

This genus is found only in Brazil and contains about 15 species. They are distributed from the States of Minas Gerais in the north to Rio Grande do Sul in the south and grow epiphytically or lithophytically in medium altitude montane forests. The densely clustered pseudobulbs generally have 2 soft leaves and 2 leaf-carrying lateral sheaths. The basal inflorescences appear with the new shoot and carry 1 to 2 showy flowers with a movable lip. In some species, the flowers change their color from yellow to white with ageing.
CULTIVATION: These species are generally easy to grow, needing medium light levels, year-round high humidity, and lots of air movement. Reduce

watering in winter. The thin leaves are prone to leaf spotting. Grow in small pots, baskets, or mounted, in shade to semi-shade. The fine roots do not like to be waterlogged, so use a fast-draining substrate. Propagation is by division.

Promenaea stapelioides
↔ 6–8 in (15–20 cm)   ↕ 2–4 in (5–10 cm)
♀ ☀/☀ ◆ ❄ ▽/≈

Found in southern Brazil, in the States of Rio de Janeiro, Sao Paulo, Parana, and Santa Catarina. Flowers resemble those of *Stapelia*. Waxy fragrant flowers, to about 2 in (5 cm) in diameter; greenish sepals and petals, densely spotted and banded with dark purple, mid-lobe of lip almost black. Summer-flowering.

Promenaea xanthina
syn. *Promenaea citrina*
↔ 6–8 in (15–20 cm)   ↕ 2–4 in (5–10 cm)
♀ ☀/☀ ◆ ❄ ▽/≈

Brazilian species, found from Minas Gerais and Espirito Santo in the north, south to Parana; grows in montane forests at elevations up to 5,580 ft (1,700 m). Waxy flowers, to 2 in (5 cm) in diameter, light to dark yellow sepals, red spots and band on petals and lip. Some plants have pure yellow flowers. Blooms in summer.

PROSTHECHEA
COCKLESHELL ORCHID
This is a genus of around 100 species found from Florida, USA, to Brazil. They were previously included within the vast genus *Encyclia*. Many species of these sympodial epiphytes and lithophytes are known as cockleshell orchids on account of the lip shape, which is often striped and always the uppermost part of the flower. In general, the individual blooms are long lived, with many having a strong pleasant fragrance. The pseudobulbs are spindle-shaped, generally flattened with two distinctive edges along their length. Flowering inflorescences are produced from the apex of the 1 to 5 leaves, after the pseudobulbs have fully developed.
CULTIVATION: *Prosthechea* species are readily grown, either on cork or tree-fern slabs, wooden slatted baskets, or

potted in a well-drained bark-based medium. Most species have a dormant period from late autumn to early spring, when growth recommences. The majority of the species are summer flowering and enjoy bright light conditions. They are reliable bloomers in cultivation, with most species also tolerating a wide variation in temperature. Propagate by division of large specimens in spring.

Prosthechea brassavolae
syns *Encyclia brassavolae*, *Epidendrum brassavolae*, *Panarica brassavolae*
↔ 14–18 in (35–45 cm)   ↕ 14–18 in (35–45 cm)   ♀/⟋ ☀/☀ ◆/◇ ❄ ▽/≈

Species found from Mexico to Panama; grows in open forests. Pseudobulbs swollen at base, tapering toward apex; 2 to 3 leathery leaves. Spikes, 6–16 in (15–40 cm) long, bloom from bulb apex, with 3 to 12 or more flowers. Individual blooms around 2½–3 in (6–8 cm) in size, yellowish narrow segments, white and violet lip. Blooms at various times during year.

Prosthechea chacaoensis
syn. *Encyclia chacaoensis*
↔ 6–12 in (15–30 cm)   ↕ 8–14 in (20–35 cm)
♀ ☀ ◆/◆/◇ ❄ ▽/≈

Found from Mexico to Colombia and Venezuela. Highly fragrant species; small clusters of cream blooms, 2 in (5 cm) wide, lip with purple stripes. Spring- to summer-flowering.

Prosthechea cochleata
syns *Anacheilium cochleatum*, *Encyclia cochleata*, *Epidendrum cochleatum*
COCKLESHELL ORCHID
↔ 9–18 in (22–45 cm)   ↕ 8–24 in (20–60 cm)
♀ ☀ ◆/◆ ❄ ▽/≈

Widespread in tropical America; found in deciduous, evergreen, and oak forests. Compressed ovoid pseudobulbs; 1 to 3 thin elongate leaves. Flower spikes, 8–24 in (20–60 cm) tall, arise from apex of pseudobulbs, with many sequential flowers. Spikes bloom continually for up to a year, nearly ever-blooming. Upside-down flowers, greenish narrow segments, blackish-purple striped lip. Easy to grow, potted or mounted.

Prosthechea crassilabia
syn. *Encyclia vespa*
↔ 8–14 in (20–35 cm)   ↕ 8–27 in (20–70 cm)
♀ ☀ ◆/◆ ❄ ▽/≈

Widespread throughout Costa Rica to Brazil. Upright inflorescence with numerous blooms, less than ¾ in (18 mm) wide, in spring. Fleshy flowers, yellowish green, spotted with dark maroon. Spring-flowering.

Prosthechea brassavolae

Prosthechea cochleata

Prosthechea michuacana

syn. *Encyclia michuacana*

↔ 8–16 in (20–40 cm) ↑8–48 in (20–120 cm) ⚲ ☀ ◆ ✿ ☐/≋

From Central America. Tall, upright, branched inflorescences bear numerous reddish brown to olive green flowers, 1 in (25 mm) wide, with predominantly white lip. Summer-flowering.

Prosthechea prismatocarpa

syn. *Epidendrum prismatocarpum*

↔ 8–16 in (20–40 cm) ↑8–27 in (20–70 cm) ⚲ ☀ ◆/◆ ✿ ☐/≋

From Costa Rica and Panama. Up to 20 blooms, 2 in (5 cm) wide, fragrant, long lasting. Waxy flowers, pale cream to dull greenish yellow, blotched with deep maroon, cream lip tipped with pink. Flowers in summer–autumn.

Prosthechea radiata

syns *Anacheilium radiatum, Encyclia radiata, Epidendrum radiatum*

↔ 12–16 in (30–40 cm) ↑8–16 in (20–40 cm) ⚲/⋀ ☀ ◆ ✿ ☐/≋

Found from Mexico to Venezuela. Ovoid pseudobulbs with 2 to 3 leaves. Upside-down flowers, to 1¼ in (3 cm)

in size, very fragrant, greenish-white; white lip with several dark purple vertical lines. Spring-blooming. Easy to grow potted or mounted.

Prosthechea Sunburst

syn. *Encyclia* Sunburst

↔ 8–20 in (20–50 cm) ↑8–20 in (20–50 cm) ⚲ ☀ ◆/◆ ✿ ☐/≋

Primary hybrid of *P. radiata* and *P. vitellina*; characteristics intermediate between these 2 species. Flowers, about 1¼ in (30 mm) tall, yellow to creamy orange. Flowers from summer to autumn.

Prosthechea prismatocarpa

Prosthechea Sunburst

Prosthechea crassilabia

Prosthechea michuacana

Prosthechea radiata

Psychopsis Mendenhall

PSEUDOLAELIA

This is a small poorly known genus of about 10 species of seldom seen epiphytic and lithophytic orchids that are endemic to Brazil. They are related to *Schomburgkia* but are smaller plants. They generally grow as epiphytes, almost exclusively on stunted *Vellozia* bushes and small trees, in exposed positions at high altitude. Each pseudobulb bears up to 7 leaves, and there is a long rhizome between these, giving the plant an untidy rambling appearance. Not every growth blooms, and they appear to be shy blooming. Most species produce an upright to arching branched (or unbranched) inflorescence holding up to 16 successively opening blooms. Most species have light pink to dark purple flowers.

CULTIVATION: Due to their rambling habit, these rarely seen orchids are best grown on horizontal plaques of cork bark and must be allowed to dry out fully between waterings. They require high light levels and ample air circulation, coupled with cool to intermediate temperatures. Keep them dry during their winter dormant period. Only overgrown specimens should be divided, in early spring, as these plants resent excessive root disturbance.

Pseudolaelia vellozicola
syn. *Schomburgkia vellozicola*
↔ 4–32 in (10–80 cm) ↕ 4–20 in (10–50 cm)
♀ ☼/◐ ◆/◇ ❄ 🍃

From Brazil; first species in this genus to be described. Spikes of up to 14 sequentially produced, light to deep pink, 1½ (35 mm) blooms, which have a remarkable similarity to the distantly related *Encyclia adenocaula*. Blooms in summer.

PSYCHILIS

The 15 species in this genus are found in the Caribbean. They grow as epiphytes, lithophytes, and terrestrials in exposed positions on or between rocks, and on trees. The rigid slender pseudobulbs resemble those of *Schomburgkia* and are thickened at the base and carry about 1 to 3 stiff leaves. The inflorescence is capable of producing flowers in successive seasons. These species were formerly included in the huge genera of *Epidendrum* or *Encyclia*.

CULTIVATION: The thick white roots do not like to be enclosed in pots, so growing these species mounted on cork in a rather xerophytic way is best. They need plenty of light and warm conditions year-round. High

humidity is more important than irrigation and a resting period with reduced watering is required in winter. In tropical regions, they can be naturalized in trees and will flower almost at any time of the year. Propagation is by division.

Psychilis kraenzlinii
syns *Encyclia kraenzlinii*, *Epidendrum kraenzlinii*
↔ 8–20 in (20–50 cm) ↕ 16–40 in (40–100 cm) ♀ ☼ ◆ ❄ 🍃

Endemic to the island of Puerto Rico; generally found growing in shrubby dry bushes. Long inflorescence with a cluster of 10 to 15 dark purple flowers, with a trilobed lip. Flowering is mostly in spring or summer.

Psychilis krugii
syns *Encyclia krugii*, *Epidendrum krugii*
↔ 8–20 in (20–50 cm) ↕ 16–40 in (40–100 cm) ♀ ☼ ◆ ❄ 🍃

Endemic to the island of Puerto Rico; grows in hot and exposed positions, in dry shrub or on cacti. Very long inflorescence carries many successively opening flowers with yellowish brown sepals and petals and a whitish lip. Flowering occurs mainly in spring.

Psychilis truncata
syns *Encyclia truncata*, *Epidendrum eggersii*, *E. truncata*
↔ 6–8 in (15–20 cm) ↕ 8–12 in (20–30 cm)
♀/\ ☼ ◆ ❄ 🍃

Found on the island of Hispaniola; grows in dry shrubs or on cliff walls. Smaller than its relatives; pseudobulbs carry only a single leaf. Branching inflorescence carries many small flowers in spring–summer. Greenish brown sepals and petals, pink lip.

PSYCHOPSIS
BUTTERFLY ORCHIDS
This genus of about 5 species from Central and South America is closely related to *Oncidium*. Plants have clustered, laterally compressed pseudobulbs, and a single, leathery, tessellated, broad, and upright leaf. The erect unbranched inflorescences arise from the base of the pseudobulbs. The flowers are showy, usually striped, and produced in succession over a long period. The dorsal sepal and petals are erect, narrow at the base and broader at the tips; the lateral sepals are broad and spreading, often with undulate margins. The lip is large with a callus at the base. The name comes from Greek, *psyche* meaning butterfly, and *opsis*, meaning resembling, referring to the butterfly-like appearance of the flowers.

CULTIVATION: Plants of *Psychopsis* can be grown either potted in a coarse epiphyte mix or mounted on a bark slab. They need a bright airy situation and should be watered freely while in growth but kept cooler while resting, when they only need to be misted every few days. Old flower spikes should not be cut off as they will sometimes flower again. Propagation is by division.

Psychopsis kramerianum
syn. *Oncidium kramerianum*
↔ 5–24 in (12–60 cm) ↕ 8–36 in (20–90 cm)
♀ ☼/◐ ◆ ❄ 🍂/🍃

Species found from Costa Rica to Peru. Large brown and yellow flowers, to 5 in (12 cm) tall, produced singly on a tall cylindrical inflorescence throughout the year.

Psychopsis Mendenhall
syn. *Oncidium* Mendenhall
↔ 5–24 in (12–60 cm) ↕ 8–36 in (20–90 cm)
♀ ☼/◐ ◆/◇ ❄ 🍂/🍃

Vigorous hybrid; backcross of *P.* Butterfly (*P. papilio* × *P. sanderae*) onto *P. papilio*. Yellow and brown blooms, up to 8 in (20 cm) tall. Flowers at any time of year.

Psychopsis papilio
syns *Oncidium papilio*, *Psychopsis picta*
BUTTERFLY ORCHID
↔ 5–24 in (12–60 cm) ↕ 8–36 in (20–90 cm)
♀ ☼/◐ ◆ ❄ 🍂/🍃

Striking species from West Indies, Guyana, Venezuela, Ecuador, Peru, Colombia, and Brazil. Oval compressed pseudobulbs; single lance-shaped leaf, often attractively patterned with red overlay on green. Inflorescences arise from base of bulbs, can reach 20–24 in (50–60 cm) tall, and may bloom for several years. Nearly ever-blooming, with single flower at a time. Large flowers to 6 in (15 cm) tall; elongate narrow petals and dorsal sepal dark red mottled yellow, flared ventral sepals orange and yellow barred, lip yellow edged with red-orange. Spikes should not be cut until dry.

Pseudolaelia vellozicola

Psychopsis kramerianum

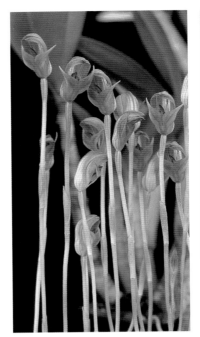

Pterostylis curta

Pterostylis pedunculata

PTEROSTYLIS
GREENHOOD ORCHID

This is a genus of around 120 species of temperate, deciduous, terrestrial orchids, known as "greenhoods," with the majority of the species occurring in Australia. There are also representatives from New Zealand, New Caledonia, and New Guinea. Most species have a rosette of leaves, with the single bloom produced on a slender stem, originating from the crown of the foliage. Blooms are usually green with reddish brown suffusions and transparent "light windows" to deceive pollinators that would normally avoid a darker area. The dorsal sepals and petals overlap to form a hood. The lip is sensitive, mobile, and capable of rapid movement, and an important attractant for pollinators. CULTIVATION: The colony-forming species are relatively easy to cultivate, flower, and multiply. They require moist, humid, and cool conditions when in growth from autumn to spring. They are best grown in a well-drained terrestrial mix, containing a high proportion of peat moss and coarse sand. They go dormant in summer, at which time they should be kept dry, and revert to round white tubers about ½ in (12 mm) across. Repot annually, repositioning the dormant tubers 2 in (5 cm) below the soil surface. Propagate from extra tubers that may form, or from seed.

Pterostylis curta
↔ 1½–3 in (3.5–8 cm)   ↕ 4–12 in (10–30 cm)
✿ ☀ ◆/◇ ✳ ❁ ⊟

From Australia. Dark green and yellowish green flowers, 1½ in (35 mm)

wide, light brown lip has a distinctive slight twist. Blooms in early spring.

Pterostylis nutans
NODDING GREENHOOD
↔ 1½–3 in (3.5–8 cm)   ↕ 1½–12 in (3.5–30 cm) ✿ ☀ ◆/◇ ✳ ❁ ⊟

From Australia; one of the most common species. Distinctive green and white, nodding, 1¼ in (30 mm) blooms in winter. Vigorous grower, multiplies well in cultivation.

Pterostylis pedunculata
MAROONHOOD
↔ 3–5 in (8–12 cm)   ↕ 6–8 in (15–20 cm)
✿ ☀ ◆/◇ ✳ ❁ ⊟

From wet open forest of southern and eastern Australia, including Tasmania. Leaves 3 to 6, oval, to 2½ in (6 cm) long, in a ground-hugging rosette. Flower solitary, to ¾ in (18 mm) wide, on a stalk to 8 in (20 cm) tall; "hood" and fused pointed sepals green and white with darker tips. Blooms in winter–spring.

Pterostylis planulata
↔ 1½–4 in (3.5–10 cm)   ↕ 1½–14 in (3.5–35 cm) ✿ ☀ ◆/◇ ✳ ❁ ⊟

From southeastern Australia; closely related to *P. biseta*. Up to 6 translucent greenish blooms, 1½ in (35 mm) in size. Flowers in spring–early summer. Species was recently reclassified as *Oligochaetochilus planulatus*, but it is still too early to tell if the botanical community will adopt this name.

PTERYGODIUM

This is a genus of about 20 deciduous terrestrial species that are endemic to

Pterostylis planulata, in the wild, Grampians National Park, Victoria, Australia

Pterostylis nutans

Pterygodium hastatum

South Africa, with the exception of
P. ukingense, which is from Tanzania.
They produce upright inflorescences
of often bunched flowers in a range
of colors, generally with a somewhat
hooded dorsal sepal. While a number
of species are difficult to locate in the
wild, others have outstanding brightly
colored blooms that have enormous
potential for cultivation.
CULTIVATION: These terrestrial
species are relatively easy to cultivate,
flower, and multiply. They require
moist, humid, and cool conditions
when in growth, which is from late
winter to summer. The plants are best
grown in a well-drained terrestrial
mix, containing a high proportion
of peat moss and coarse sand. They
become dormant in autumn, at which
time they should be kept dry. They
are best repotted annually, repositioning the dormant tubers 2 in (5 cm)
below the soil surface. Propagation
is from seed.

Pterygodium hastatum

↔ 5–10 in (12–25 cm)   ↕ 6–14 in (15–35 cm)
� ☀ ◆/◇ ❄ ▽

From eastern South Africa. Up to 4
leaves; inflorescence with up to 10
blooms, just under 1 in (25 mm) in
size, pale green to white with some
fine purple dots on petals and sepals.
Flowers in late summer.

PYRORCHIS

FIRE ORCHID

This is a genus of 2 species of deciduous terrestrial orchids from southern
Australia. *P. nigricans* is widespread,
however *P. forrestii* is confined to
the southwestern corner of western
Australia. These 2 species were

Pyrorchis nigricans

previously included with *Lyperanthus*,
but differ in their leaf morphology,
floral structure, and their biology.
The name *Pyrorchis* literally translates
to fire orchid, as these spring-flowering species generally only bloom after
a summer forest fire the previous year.
They reproduce vegetatively, forming
new tubers at the end of long slender
roots and from seed, as native bees
pollinate them.
CULTIVATION: Unfortunately these
orchids are very difficult to maintain

in cultivation. Specialist growers of
deciduous terrestrial orchids have had
limited success growing the plants in
pots in a very sandy well-drained
medium, but report that the plants
rarely ever bloom. Laboratory tests
using "smoke water" have been
encouraging to trigger the plants into
blooming but these techniques are not
readily available. Alternatively, terracotta or clay pots would need to be
used if a small fire was lit over the
dormant tubers in summer.

Pyrorchis nigricans

syn. *Lyperanthus nigricans*
POTATO ORCHID, RED BEAK,
UNDERTAKER ORCHID

↔ 2–3 in (5–8 cm)   ↕ 4–12 in (10–30 cm)
✚ ☼/☀ ◆ ❄ ▽

From western and southern Australia,
including Tasmania. Leaf single, basal,
oval, pointed, to 3 in (8 cm) long.
Flowers fragrant, white, heavily striped
red, lip white, purple-red centrally,
on long racemes in spring. Flowers
blacken with age.

RANGAERIS

This genus contains about 5 species and is found in Africa from Sierra Leone and Senegal, east to Kenya and Eritrea and south to northern South Africa. They grow as epiphytes, sometimes as lithophytes or terrestrials, and are characterized by an elongated monopodial stem with rigid, almost succulent, strap-shaped leaves arranged in 2 rows, and star-shaped, white, fragrant flowers with a long spur. The inflorescence, which can be arching or pendent, appears in the upper sections of the stem.

CULTIVATION: These orchids thrive on slabs or in shallow pots or baskets in a free-draining substrate to accommodate the thick roots. They do not need bright light; shade or semi-shade is sufficient, and a short resting period after flowering is recommended. Propagation is by division.

Rangaeris muscicola

↔ 8–12 in (20–30 cm)   ↕ 6–8 in (15–20 cm)
♀/⋀ ☀ ◆ ❄ ⊟/☋

Type species of genus; widely spread in Africa from Kenya to South Africa; found growing in coastal forest to dense upper montane forests at altitudes of up to 6,200 ft (2,500 m). Short stems carry fan of dark green leaves. Up to 15 white flowers are produced per inflorescence, each with a spur to almost 4 in (10 cm) long. Winter-blooming.

Rangaeris rhipsalisocia

↔ 8–12 in (20–30 cm)   ↕ 6–8 in (15–20 cm)
♀ ☀ ◆ ❄ ⊟/☋

Somewhat aberrant species; resembles *Podangis* when not in flower due to the sickle-shaped leaves. Occurs in tropical regions of Africa from Senegal to Uganda and Angola. Short-stemmed, small, white flowers do not open completely. Blooms any time of year.

RENANTANDA

This is an artificial monopodial genus between *Renanthera* and *Vanda*. These epiphytic orchids are erect-growing, with strap-like channeled leaves in 2 ranks. Larger plants may branch at the base and have numerous, very thick, cord-like roots. The inflorescences appear from the stem at the base of the leaf. The hybrids are not as tall as many of the *Renanthera* species, as the *Vanda* influence has reduced the plant size while increasing the floral size and imparting wider petals to the bloom.

Renantanda Tuanku Bainun

Rangaeris muscicola

In the tropics they bloom throughout the year, with a peak during the summer months.

CULTIVATION: These vandaceous epiphytes require warm to hot conditions with bright light, and are suited to tropical gardens and greenhouses in climates away from the tropics. They are best grown in pots using a coarse grade of pine bark as the potting medium. The thick roots will often venture outside the confines of the pot or basket, and this culture should be encouraged, as the roots require unimpeded air circulation and must dry out quickly after watering. Propagate from cuttings with at least 3 roots attached.

Renantanda Tuanku Bainun
↔ 8–32 in (20–80 cm) ↑ 8–48 in (20–120 cm) ♀ ☼ ◆ ❁ ☐

Hybrid between *Vanda* Keeree's Delight and *Renanthera storiei*. Shapely blooms, 3 in (8 cm) tall, red, with darker tessellation throughout flower.

RENANTHERA
FIRE ORCHID

This robust monopodial genus, with some 15 species, is found throughout Malaysia, Indonesia, the Philippines, and New Guinea, where they grow in hot, humid, lowland conditions. Most species bear very bright long-lasting flowers on branched inflorescences. There have been a number of hybrids made both within the genus and with related genera, particularly to exploit the bright red colors and to improve the overall shape of the bloom.

CULTIVATION: These tall-growing vandaceous epiphytes require warm to hot conditions with strong light, and are best suited to tropical gardens and large greenhouses in climates away from the tropics. Because of their rambling habit they can prove difficult to confine to pots, and are best grown in wooden baskets or on large slabs of cork. In the tropics they bloom throughout the year, with a peak during summer. In this habitat they can be tied to the trunks of trees and grown in full sun. They will not withstand temperatures below 54°F (12°C). Propagation is from cuttings with at least 3 roots attached.

Renanthera coccinea
↔ 8–32 in (20–80 cm) ↑ 8–48 in (20–120 cm) ♀ ☼ ◆ ❁ ☐/〽

Widespread and variable species from Southeast Asia. Numerous blooms, 2 in (5 cm) wide, dark orange to deep red, with darker spotting peppered over flower, in spring–autumn.

Renanthera monachica

Renanthera imschootiana
↔ 36–48 in (90–120 cm) ↑ 48–60 in (120–150 cm) ♀ ☼/☀ ◆ ❁ ☐/〽

Occurs from Myanmar, northern India, Yunnan Province in China, and Laos to South Vietnam; grows on trees on limestone cliffs at altitudes of 1,640–4,920 ft (500–1,500 m). Large, long-stemmed, scrambling species; stems woody, bare at base; numerous leaves, 2–4 in (5–10 cm) long, fleshy and leathery. Inflorescences usually branched, to 18 in (45 cm) long, with 10 to 30 flowers in spring–summer. Flowers showy, about 2 in (5 cm) across; sepals red or orange, yellow at base; petals orange-red or yellow, spotted with red; very small lip, whitish with red spots.

Renanthera monachica
↔ 20–24 in (50–60 cm) ↑ 12–24 in (30–60 cm) ♀ ☀ ◆/◆ ❁ ☐/〽

From the Philippines. Fairly erect plant; leaves 2–5 in (5–12 cm) long, narrowly strap-shaped. Inflorescences unbranched, 7–18 in (18–45 cm) long, loosely arranged with 6 to 30 flowers in spring. Flowers 1–1½ in (25–35 mm) across, yellow, spotted with red.

Renanthera Hybrids
↔ 8–36 in (20–90 cm) ↑ 1–8 ft (0.3–2.4 m) ♀ ☼ ◆ ❁ ☐/〽

Vandaceous hybrids; blooming occurs in warmer months of year, or throughout year in the tropics; generally hardier than the species. Some of the attractive hybrids are: **Monaseng**, bright orange blooms, heavily overlaid with red, has *R. imschootiana, R. monachica,* and *R. storiei* in its pedigree; **Tan Keong Choon**, striking red hybrid bred from *R. matutina, R. philippinensis,* and *R. storiei*; **Tom Thumb**, red-flowered primary hybrid between *R. monachica* and *R. imschootiana*.

Renanthera imschootiana

Renanthera Tan Keong Choon (hybrid)

Renanthera Tom Thumb (hybrid)

Renanthera Monaseng (hybrid)

R

Restrepia antennifera

Restrepia antennifera 'Cow Hollow'

Restrepia contorta

Restrepia guttulata

RESTREPIA

COCKROACH ORCHID

This is an increasingly popular genus of around 40 species of miniature sympodial orchids. They are single-leafed and single-flowered epiphytes from Central and South America that are easily recognized, even when not in flower. Related to *Pleurothallis* and *Masdevallia*, they have comparatively large flowers, to 3 in (8 cm) tall, which are fairly uniform in shape, in a range of bright and subtle colors. The lateral sepals are invariably fused together to form a synsepal, which is the most prominent feature of a *Restrepia* flower. The length and color pattern of the synsepal are important features for species identification. The common name refers to the flowers' resemblance to some types of cockroach.

CULTIVATION: These orchids are tolerant of a wide temperature range, as long as they are kept moist, in a humid environment, with ample air circulation. They enjoy being copiously watered throughout the year. Sphagnum moss is the preferred medium for potted plants, while larger specimens can be grown on slabs or plaques of cork or tree fern. They benefit from bright light, but will not take direct sun. When the lighting levels are correct, the leaves will often take on a slight purplish tone. *Restrepia* is one of the few genera of orchids that can be propagated from leaf-cuttings as well as by division.

Restrepia antennifera
syn. *Restrepia hemsleyana*
↔ 10–14 in (25–35 cm) ↑ 8–10 in (20–25 cm) ♀ ☀ ◆/◇ ❄ ☐

From Colombia, Venezuela, and Ecuador; found growing in moist montane forests. Lacks pseudobulbs; oval pointed leaves on a thin stem. Flowers bloom from back of leaves at base, at any time of year, and will continue to do so for years. Blooms about 3 in (8 cm) long, probably largest in genus, with synsepal very variable in both color and patterning. Blooms range from yellow, orangish, pink, and red and can be striped or spotted. '**Cow Hollow**' (syn. *R. hemsleyana* 'Cow Hollow'), very large striped form of species.

Restrepia contorta
syn. *Restrepia caucana*
↔ 5–6 in (12–15 cm) ↑ 7–8 in (18–20 cm) ♀ ☀ ◆/◇ ❄ ☐/☈

Usually grows high in trees in montane forests of Venezuela, Colombia, Ecuador, and Peru. Oval leaves, to about 2 in (5 cm) long, on thin stems. Flowers 1–1½ in (25–35 mm) long, extremely variable in color and pattern, with synsepal usually yellow, orange, rose, or red, spotted or striped. Blooms anytime. Grows well in pots, baskets, or mounted, using moss or fine bark.

Restrepia guttulata
↔ 3–8 in (8–20 cm) ↑ 3–6 in (8–15 cm) ♀ ☀ ◆/◇ ❄ ☐

Found from Venezuela to Peru. Blooms 2 in (5 cm) wide, range in color from orange to red and pink to deep purple, synsepal strikingly peppered with bold dark reddish purple blotches. Spring-blooming.

RESTREPIELLA

This genus contains a single species from Central America. It is found growing epiphytically in riverine and swamp forests and even in coffee plantations at altitudes of 130–5,250 ft (40–1,600 m). They are medium-sized plants, with clustered erect stems, each with a single leathery leaf. The species was first described as a *Pleurothallis*, and then moved with 7 other species to *Restrepiella*; these other species were later placed in *Restrepiopsis*, a genus more closely related to *Octomeria* and *Pleurothallopsis*. Up to 4 strongly scented flowers with mobile lips are produced in succession and last a couple of days each. The flower resembles a snake's head, which is reflected in the botanical name.

CULTIVATION: Grow these orchids under warm to intermediate conditions in moderately bright light, high humidity, and good ventilation. Plants can be mounted or grown in pots in a fine substrate. Water regularly. Propagation is by division.

Restrepiella ophiocephala
syns *Pleurothallis ophiocephala*, *Restrepia ophiocephala*
↔ 6–8 in (15–20 cm) ↑ 6–16 in (15–40 cm) ♀ ☀ ◆/◇ ☐/☈

Found in Mexico, Belize, Guatemala, El Salvador, and Costa Rica. Stems 3–9 in (8–22 cm) long, covered with papery bracts; oblong-lanceolate leaf

Restrepiella ophiocephala

Rhinerrhiza divitiflora

3–9 in (8–22 cm) long. Yellowish brown blooms with purple spots, produced at base of leaf in winter–spring.

RHINERRHIZA

This genus, related to *Sarcochilus*, contains a single epiphytic species from eastern Australia and lowland parts of New Guinea. They are relatively large monopodial plants, with durable leathery leaves and a strong root system. The long pendent inflorescences produce up to 60 flowers that only last for 2 days.
CULTIVATION: These orchids resent having their roots covered, so are best mounted on narrow but long sections of cork or tree fern, to accommodate the extensive root system. They must be kept in a part-shaded position in a humid environment, with plenty of free circulating air. This is not an easy genus to maintain in cultivation. Propagate from seed.

Rhinerrhiza divitiflora
RASPY ROOT ORCHID
↔ 3–12 in (8–30 cm) ↕ 3–16 in (8–40 cm)
♀ ☀ ◆ ❁ ➘

Distinctive Australian species; flat roots with rough surface. Spidery, yellowish orange, 2½ in (6 cm) wide blooms, covered with fine red spots. Comparatively tiny lip, white, marked with yellow and red. Spring-flowering.

RHIPIDOGLOSSUM

This African genus, which contains around 40 species, was established in 1918 by German botanist Rudolf Schlechter but until recently, most authorities placed it in synonymy with *Diaphananthe*, described 4 years earlier by Schlechter. However, recent DNA work indicates that the genera should be kept separate. Plants of both genera look very much alike, the difference is mainly based on the character of the pollinarium. In *Rhipidoglossum* each pollinium has its own stipes (stalk) and viscidium (sticky gland), while in *Diaphananthe*, the pollinia each have their own stipes but share a common viscidium. The peg-like callus on the lip of most species of *Diaphananthe* is absent in *Rhipidoglossum*. Rhipidoglossums are long- or short-stemmed with numerous roots, often with white streaks when wet; the flowers are usually small, white, greenish, or yellowish, with a long or short spur.
CULTIVATION: Grow short-stemmed types in pots in a medium bark-based compost; those with long stems and many roots do better mounted on bark. Most species require intermediate to warm conditions with fairly heavy shade and high humidity. When not actively growing, they should be kept drier but not allowed to dry out completely. Propagate by division of mature basal shoots or from seed.

Rhipidoglossum xanthopollinium
syn. *Diaphananthe xanthopollinia*
↔ 6–12 in (15–30 cm) ↕ 4–12 in (10–30 cm)
♀ ☀ ◆ ❁ ➘

From central and eastern Africa and South Africa; variable short- or long-stemmed species. Strap-shaped leaves, sometimes fleshy, to 6 in (15 cm) long. Racemes arising along stem, to around 4 in (10 cm) long, densely arranged with many blooms in spring–summer. Flowers small, creamy yellow or straw-colored to orange, lilac-scented.

RHIZANTHELLA
UNDERGROUND ORCHID
This is a bizarre saprophytic genus that grows and blooms entirely underground, with the ripe seed capsules barely reaching the soil surface. There are 2 known species, one occurring in eastern Australia *(Rhizanthella slateri)*, the other *(R. gardneri)* endemic to Western Australia. They are generally only found by accident. The heads of small succulent blooms resemble fungi, and it is thought that ants or fungus gnats that co-exist in the leaf litter may pollinate the flowers. They are known to flower in spring and summer.
CULTIVATION: This orchid is rarely seen and its cultivation has never been attempted except in a laboratory.

Rhizanthella slateri
↔ 3–12 in (8–30 cm) ↕ 3–8 in (8–20 cm)
✿ ☀ ◆ ▭

From eastern Australia. Branched rhizome; mature plants produce a rounded inflorescence crowded with many tiny, fleshy, cream to purplish blooms that are protected by triangular bracts, in spring–summer.

RHYNCHOLAELIA
The 2 species in this genus are found from Mexico to Costa Rica at altitudes of up to 4,920 ft (1,500 m). They grow as epiphytes in hot, rather dry, mountainous forests or thorn bush, and on cacti. The long white roots run up and down the bark for several

Rhyncholaelia digbyana 'Mrs Chase'

meters. The 2 species were formerly placed in *Brassavola*, but separated because of the *Cattleya*-like growth habit and differences in flower structure. The hybrids still carry the name, e.g. *Brassocattleya* or *Brassolaelia*. They were used to introduce substance, fragrance, and frilled petals and lips into many famous hybrids.
CULTIVATION: These plants can be grown in small containers or mounted on a piece of cork or similar material under warm to hot and humid conditions in very bright light. Careful watering is essential, with the amount reduced once the pseudobulbs have matured. Rhyncholaelias are very brittle and new shoots can easily break off when the plants are handled. Propagate by division.

Rhyncholaelia digbyana
syn. *Brassavola digbyana*
↔ 8–14 in (20–35 cm) ↕ 8–14 in (20–35 cm)
♀ ☀ ◆ ❁ ▭/➘

From Costa Rica, Belize, Guatemala, Honduras, and Mexico; similar to a tough and succulent *Cattleya;* distinct glaucous sheen. Clustered pseudobulbs, each with single leathery leaf to 8 in (20 cm) long. Single lemon-scented flower, to 7 in (18 cm) wide; apple green sepals and petals, cream-colored lip with frilled hairy edge. Some clones have maroon flushes along tepals. Summer-flowering. *R. d.* var. *fimbripetala*, from Honduras, finely frilled petals. *R. d.* 'Mrs Chase', attractive cultivar.

Rhyncholaelia glauca
syn. *Brassavola glauca*
↔ 8–14 in (20–35 cm) ↕ 8–14 in (20–35 cm)
♀ ☀ ◆/◇ ❁ ▭/➘

Species from Guatemala and Mexico; similar to *R. digbyana*. Spindle-shaped pseudobulbs; 1-leafed. Single flower emerges from 4 in (10 cm) long sheath in spring. Fragrant blooms; green sepals and petals, sometimes flushed with soft purple; cream lip with small purple spot at base; edges of flower segments are complete.

R

Rhizanthella slateri

Rhizanthella slateri

RHYNCHOSTELE

This is a genus consisting of some 16 species of sympodial orchids found from Mexico to the northern part of South America. They are related to *Odontoglossum*, and were previously included within that genus. They have egg-shaped, somewhat flattened pseudobulbs topped with up to 3 thin textured leaves. Most of the species in this genus have showy colorful flowers on short or long stems.

CULTIVATION: These plants grow well potted in a fine-grade bark mixture with the addition of 20 percent perlite. Sphagnum moss is also a popular potting medium. *Rhynchostele* orchids are most suitable for humid intermediate growing conditions, and require abundant water throughout the year. They prefer a position in part-shade, and are more tolerant of warm conditions than *Odontoglossum* species. Propagation is by division.

Rhynchostele bictoniensis

syn. *Odontoglossum bictoniense*

↔ 8–16 in (20–40 cm)   ↕ 8–24 in (20–60 cm)
♀ ☀ ◆ ❈ ▽

Found from Mexico to Panama. Upright inflorescences of up to 14 blooms in winter–spring. Flowers 2 in (5 cm) across; petals and sepals vary from yellowish green to brown, darker spotting and barring over segments; broad white lip.

Rhynchostele cordata

syn. *Odontoglossum cordatum*

↔ 8–16 in (20–40 cm)   ↕ 8–16 in (20–40 cm)
♀ ☀ ◆ ❈ ▽

Species found from Mexico to Venezuela. Starry blooms, 3 in (8 cm) wide, mustard-colored with dark brown blotches, in summer–autumn.

Rhynchostele bictoniensis

Rhynchostele cordata

Rhynchostele Stanfordiense

Rhynchostele maculata

syns *Lemboglossum maculatum*, *Odontoglossum maculatum*

↔ 8–12 in (20–30 cm)   ↕ 8–14 in (20–35 cm)
♀ ☀ ◆/◇ ❈ ▽

From Mexico, Guatemala, and Costa Rica; found in oak and pine forests. Compressed oval pseudobulbs; few thinnish leaves. Inflorescences grow from base of bulbs, erect to arching, with several blooms in winter–spring. Flowers 2½–3 in (6–8 cm) in size; rusty brown sepals, yellow petals, lip spotted red to brown.

Rhynchostele rossii

syns *Lemboglossum rossii*, *Odontoglossum rossii*

↔ 6–8 in (15–20 cm)   ↕ 5–7 in (12–18 cm)
♀ ☀ ◆/◇ ❈ ▽

From cool humid forests of Mexico, Guatemala, Honduras, and Nicaragua. Somewhat compressed, thickish, round pseudobulbs; single leaf. Inflorescences from base of matured bulbs, with up to 4 blooms in autumn–winter, sometimes in other seasons. Flowers white to light pink with reddish-brown spotting on sepals and base of petals; lip white with yellow callus. Often confused with *R. ehrenbergii*, but that species blooms alongside new growth.

Rhynchostele Stanfordiense

↔ 8–16 in (20–40 cm)   ↕ 8–27 in (20–70 cm)
♀ ☀ ◆ ❈ ▽

Primary hybrid between *R. bictoniensis* and *R. uro-skinneri*. Upright inflorescences of 2 in (5 cm) wide flowers, green, blotched and barred brown; pink lip. Flowers in spring–summer.

Rhynchostele uro-skinneri

syns *Lemboglossum uro-skinneri*, *Odontoglossum uro-skinneri*

↔ 14–18 in (35–45 cm)   ↕ 12–16 in (30–40 cm)   ♀ ☀ ◆/◇ ❈ ▽

From Guatemala and Honduras. Large, oval, compressed pseudobulbs; few, broad, strap-like leaves. Spike to 40 in (100 cm) high, originates from base of mature bulbs. Flowers 1¼–3 in (3–5 cm) in size; mottled brown petals and sepals; large, rose pink and white, mottled lip. Blooms in various seasons.

RHYNCHOSTYLIS

FOXTAIL ORCHIDS

This genus of monopodial plants contains only 4 or 5 species. These tropical, lowland, vandaceous species are erect-growing epiphytes, with thick, strap-like, channeled leaves in 2 ranks. Larger plants may branch at the base, and have numerous, cord-like, very

thick roots. The inflorescences appear from the stem at the base of the leaf.

CULTIVATION: These plants grow in brightly lit situations, and require year-round warm conditions. They are best grown in wooden baskets, with the thick fleshy roots attaching to the timber and being allowed to ramble, as the roots require unimpeded air circulation and must dry out quickly after watering. Propagate from seed.

Rhynchostylis gigantea

↔ 8–20 in (20–50 cm)   ↕ 8–24 in (20–60 cm)
♀ ☼/☀ ◆ ❈ ▽/⋑

From Thailand and Indochina; most popular cultivated species. Blooms 1¼ in (30 mm) wide, range in color from white with pink spotting and blotching to various shades of purple to red. Also bicolored and pure white strains. Flowers in late winter–spring.

Rhynchostylis retusa

↔ 8–20 in (20–50 cm)   ↕ 8–30 in (20–75 cm)
♀ ☼/☀ ◆/◆ ❈ ▽/⋑

Widespread species from Southeast Asia. Long pendulous inflorescences of up to 60 flowers, ¾ in (18 mm) wide, white with pink markings. Also a rare pure white form. Flowers in summer.

RIMACOLA

This is a monotypic genus found only in sandstone areas near Sydney, New South Wales, Australia. It grows in sandstone rock crevices that always have water flowing through them so the plants never dry out. Plant bears several arching to pendulous leaves, and, while it lacks a pseudobulb, water and nutrients are stored in its fleshy, brittle, and extensive root system.

CULTIVATION: Unfortunately this species has proved to be impossible to maintain in cultivation due to its highly specialized habitat.

Rimacola elliptica

↔ 4–12 in (10–30 cm)   ↕ 2½–12 in (6–30 cm)   ✱ ☀ ◆/◇ ❈ ▽

Distinctive Australian species. Inflorescences with up to 12 blooms in late spring–summer. Green flowers,

Rhynchostylis gigantea

Rimacola elliptica

each 1 in (25 mm) wide; lip with purple-brown markings.

ROBIQUETIA

This genus consists of about 40 species, distributed from India and Sri Lanka through Southeast Asia to northern Australia and some Pacific Islands. Generally tropical species of the lowlands, they are monopodial epiphytes, with leathery leaves produced in 2 ranks. They produce large numbers of relatively small but colorful fleshy flowers. Flowering occurs during the warmer months of the year, with some species blooming throughout the year in tropical regions.

CULTIVATION: These orchids are best grown on cork or tree-fern slabs (either vertical or horizontal), as few of them like their roots covered. Keep them moist year-round. Larger specimens can be grown in small baskets. Most species enjoy part-shade and are best suited to greenhouse culture in all but tropical climates. They require warm conditions year-round, disliking temperatures below 50°F (10°C). Propagate from seed.

Robiquetia cerina

↔ 5–14 in (12–35 cm)　↕ 4–20 in (10–50 cm)
🌵 ☀ ◆ ❄ 🏞

From the Philippines. Thick bluish green leaves. Short densely packed inflorescences in spring–summer. Hot pink to purple blooms, just over ¼ in (6 mm) wide, do not open fully.

Robiquetia succisa

syn. *Robiquetia paniculata*

↔ 8–20 in (20–50 cm)　↕ 8–27 in (20–70 cm)
🌵 ☼/☀/☀ ◆/◈ ❄ 🏞

Fast-growing monopodial species from mainland Southeast Asia. Branched inflorescences of up to 80 blooms in summer. Flowers ½ in (12 mm) wide, golden yellow to green.

Robiquetia succisa

Robiquetia cerina

R

Rodriguezia lanceolata

Rodriguezia decora

RODRIGUEZIA

This genus contains some 40 species of sympodial orchids from tropical Mexico, Central America, and South America, often found growing in cloud forests as twig epiphytes, rarely found growing on the trunks or main branches of trees. The small pseudobulbs are flattened with 1 or 2 leaves at the apex. Flowering is in autumn and winter, with inflorescences produced from the leaf axil at the base of the recently matured pseudobulb. Related to *Oncidium*, many of the species have showy colorful blooms.
CULTIVATION: These epiphytic orchids are best mounted on sections of cork or tree fern, to accommodate the extensive and wiry root system. They must be kept in a humid environment, with plenty of free circulating air. Propagation is by division of large clumps.

Rodriguezia decora
↔ 4–24 in (10–60 cm) ↕ 4–16 in (10–40 cm)

From Brazil. Long rhizome between pseudobulbs; requires a long mount in cultivation. Egg-shaped pseudobulbs; stiff leathery leaves to 6 in (15 cm) long. Spikes of up to 12 blooms in autumn–winter. Lightly scented flowers, 1 in (25 mm) wide, pale pink to purple-brown; flared lip, white to pink, with dark spotting.

Rodriguezia lanceolata
syn. *Rodriguezia secunda*
↔ 6–8 in (15–20 cm) ↕ 10–16 in (25–40 cm)

From South America, Central America, and the West Indies. Narrowly ovoid, laterally compressed pseudobulbs, to around 1½ in (35 mm) long; single leaf to 10 in (25 cm) long, narrowly oblong. Unbranched inflorescences 3–16 in (8–40 cm) long, densely covered with many blooms in winter–spring. Flowers rich rose-purple, rather small.

Rodriguezia venusta
↔ 6–8 in (15–20 cm) ↕ 6–7 in (15–18 cm)

From Brazil and Peru. Pseudobulbs 1–1¼ in (25–30 mm) long, narrowly ovoid; single leaf to 6 in (15 cm) long. Arching inflorescences, 3–7 in (8–18 cm) long, with a few blooms in spring. Flowers strongly scented, about 1½ in (35 mm) across, white, with yellow callus on lip.

ROSSIOGLOSSUM
CLOWN ORCHIDS, TIGER ORCHIDS
This is a small group of 6 different but similar Central American species, which at one time were included under *Odontoglossum*. They have a distinct somewhat flattened pseudobulb with up to 3 broad leathery leaves at the apex. Flower spikes, which generally appear from the leaf axil of the semi-matured new growth, develop from late summer to autumn and bloom in late autumn and winter. They bloom only once from the pseudobulb.
CULTIVATION: These orchids like warm moist conditions and bright light during the main growing period, from late spring to autumn. Keep on the dry side during winter and only water enough to keep the pseudobulbs from shriveling. They are best grown potted, in a bark-based mix, under cool to intermediate conditions. Propagate by division of large clumps.

Rossioglossum grande ★
syn. *Odontoglossum grande*
↔ 8–20 in (20–50 cm) ↕ 8–20 in (20–50 cm)

From Mexico and Guatemala. Stiff spikes of up to 8 blooms in winter. Flowers 6 in (15 cm) across; chestnut brown bars across sepals, yellow and brown petals, lip creamy with red-brown markings.

Rossioglossum Rawdon Jester
↔ 8–20 in (20–50 cm) ↕ 8–20 in (20–50 cm)

Cross between *R. grande* and *R. Williamsianum* (*R. grande* × *R. schlieperianum*); resembles robust forms of *R. grande*. Flowers in winter–spring.

Rossioglossum Rawdon Jester

Rossioglossum grande

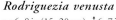

R

Sarcochilus aequalis

Sarcochilus aequalis, albino form

SACCOLABIOPSIS

This genus is related to *Sarcochilus* and contains about 8 monopodial epiphytic species from northern Australia, New Guinea, and Indonesia. They often grow on the edges of rainforests as twig epiphytes, rarely on the trunks or main branches of trees. The small plants have leaves in 2 ranks and a network of coarse wiry roots. They produce short spikes of mainly green flowers that face the apex of the inflorescence.

CULTIVATION: These plants resent having their roots covered, so they are best mounted on long narrow sections of cork. Keep in a part-shaded position in a warm humid environment, with plenty of free circulating air. They are not easy to maintain in cultivation. Propagate by division of mature basal shoots or from seed.

Saccolabiopsis armitii

↔ 2½–6 in (6–15 cm)   ↕ 2½–8 in (6–20 cm)
♀ ☀ ◆ ☈

From North Queensland, Australia. Pendent spikes, crowded with up to 50 tiny yellowish green blooms, in summer.

SARCOCHILUS

FAIRY ORCHID

This genus contains about 20 diminutive monopodial species. They are native to eastern Australia and New Caledonia, and may be epiphytic or lithophytic. The short inflorescences bear showy blooms in many shapes and colors, and are mostly spring- and summer-flowering. Mainly cultivated are the lithophytic species; the tree-dwelling species often grow as twig epiphytes. The lithophytes are clump-forming, whereas the epiphytes generally only have one growth.

CULTIVATION: Lithophytic species are easily cultivated in pots, in a coarse mixture such as 2 parts medium-grade pine bark, 1 part pea-sized gravel, and a handful of perlite. Epiphytic species should be grown on long narrow slabs of weathered timber or cork. They can easily succumb to crown rot. Most species will take cool to cold conditions, but need at least 70 percent

shade in a humid environment. Protect from frost and avoid excessive heat. Keep moist, with high humidity and good air circulation. The clumping species may be propagated by division; epiphytes from seed.

Sarcochilus aequalis

syn. *Sarcochilus hartmannii* Southern form
WAXY SARCOCHILUS
↔ 6–10 in (15–25 cm)   ↕ 4–6 in (10–15 cm)
⋀ ☼/☀ ◈/◇ ❄ ☒

From eastern New South Wales, Australia; grows in breezy shaded places up to 1,970 ft (600 m) in altitude. Thin leaves, to 6 in (15 cm) long, spreading. Flowers to ¾ in (18 mm) wide, cream, small pale brown markings, on arching racemes, in winter–spring.

Sarcochilus ceciliae

FAIRY BELLS, PINK BELLS
↔ 6–12 in (15–30 cm)   ↕ 4–8 in (10–20 cm)
⋀ ☼/☀ ◈/◇ ❄ ☒

From sunny dry areas of Queensland and northern New South Wales, Australia. Leaves to 4 in (10 cm) long. Erect racemes to 8 in (20 cm) tall, with tiny pink flowers, lip marked yellow, in spring–summer.

Sarcochilus falcatus

ORANGE BLOSSOM ORCHID
↔ 4–8 in (10–20 cm)   ↕ 2½–8 in (6–20 cm)
♀ ☼/☀ ◈/◇ ❄ ☈

From eastern Australia. Up to 12 white to cream flowers, to 1½ in (35 mm) wide, gold and purple markings on lip, in late spring.

Saccolabiopsis armitii

Sarcochilus fitzgeraldii

Sarcochilus hartmannii 'Giant Frost'

Sarcochilus hirticalcar

Sarcochilus fitzgeraldii

↔ 4–16 in (10–40 cm) ↕ 4–16 in (10–40 cm)
⋀ ☀/☀ ◈/◇ ❁ ⛶

From Australia; grows in cool heavily shaded situations. Up to 12 white blooms, 1¼ in (30 mm) wide, light pink to dark crimson spots or bands in center, in spring.

Sarcochilus hartmannii ★

↔ 4–16 in (10–40 cm) ↕ 4–16 in (10–40 cm)
⋀ ☀ ◈/◇ ❁ ⛶

Variable species from Australia; often grows in strong light. Thick leaves. Upright to arching sprays produce up to 25 flowers in spring. Flowers pure white, round, 1 in (25 mm) wide, tiny lip, may have reddish brown markings in center. 'Giant Frost', attractive cultivar.

Sarcochilus hillii

LITTLE GEM SARCOCHILUS
↔ 2½–5 in (6–12 cm) ↕ 2½–5 in (6–12 cm)
♀ ☀/☀ ◈/◇ ↯

Small-growing orchid found from subtropical coastal Queensland to southeastern New South Wales in Australia. Very narrow fleshy leaves, to 4 in (10 cm) long. Round, crystalline white to pale pink blooms, ½ in (12 mm) wide, in spring–summer.

Sarcochilus hirticalcar

syns *Parasarcochilus hirticalcar*, *Pteroceras hirticalcar*
↔ 2½–6 in (6–15 cm) ↕ 2½–6 in (6–15 cm)
♀ ☀ ◈ ❁ ↯

From Queensland's Cape York Peninsula in Australia. Blooms greenish yellow, ½ in (12 mm) wide, petals and sepals edged in reddish brown. Flowers in summer–autumn.

Sarcochilus olivaceus

↔ 4–12 in (10–30 cm) ↕ 4–8 in (10–20 cm)
♀/⋀ ☀ ◈/◇ ❁ ↯

From eastern Australia. Up to 12 yellowish green to bright green blooms, angular, fragrant, 1 in (25 mm) wide, from mid-summer to early autumn.

Sarcochilus serrulatus

↔ 4–8 in (10–20 cm) ↕ 2½–6 in (6–15 cm)
♀ ☀/☀ ◈ ❁ ↯

Rare shade-loving orchid from northern Queensland, Australia. Short spikes with brick red to brown flowers, ¾ in (18 mm) long, in spring.

Sarcochilus Hybrids

↔ 4–16 in (10–40 cm) ↕ 4–16 in (10–40 cm)
♀/⋀ ☀/☀ ◈/◇ ❁ ⛶/↯

Sarcochilus has been extensively linebred and hybridized. Popular combinations link hardy lithophytic types such as *S. ceciliae, S. fitzgeraldii,* and *S. hartmannii* with smaller-flowered but colorful epiphytic species. Use of *S. hirticalcar* expanded both color range and flowering times, so some hybrids bloom year-round. Individual blooms range from ¾ in (18 mm) to 1½ in (35 mm) wide. **Armstrong**, orange-toned blooms; **Bobby-Dazzler**, pink and purple flowers, year-round; **Burgundy on Ice 'Arctic Circle'**, white flowers, red marking at center and on lip; **First Light ★**, blooms with brown and tan tones and spotting; **Fitzhart**, white blooms, purple bands and suffusions; **Heidi**, backcross of *S.* Fitzhart and *S. hartmannii*; **Kate**, pink blooms, cross between *S. roseus* and *S.* Heidi; **Melba**, between *S. falcatus* and *S. hartmannii*; **Velvet**, pale to deep purple and pink flowers, year-round.

Sarcochilus serrulatus

Sarcochilus Armstrong (hybrid)

Sarcochilus Bobby-Dazzler (hybrid)

Sarcochilus First Light (hybrid)

Sarcochilus Kate (hybrid)

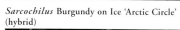

Sarcochilus Burgundy on Ice 'Arctic Circle' (hybrid)

Sarcochilus Burgundy on Ice 'Arctic Circle', foliage (hybrid)

Sarcochilus Fitzhart (hybrid)

Sarcochilus Velvet (hybrid)

Sartylis Blue Knob

SARTYLIS

This bigeneric monopodial hybrid between *Sarcochilus* and *Rhynchostylis* was created to make many of the tropical vandaceous orchids more amenable to lower winter temperatures. There have only been a small number of these monopodial hybrids registered. They can bloom throughout the year, and will grow and flower in a wide range of temperatures.
CULTIVATION: They are ideal plants for bark-filled wooden baskets, enjoying humid cool to warm conditions and high light levels, and their colorful showy blooms are long lived. The thick roots will often venture outside the confines of the pot or basket, and this culture should be encouraged, as the roots require unimpeded air circulation and must dry out quickly after watering. They generally stay as single growth plants and are generally multiplied by seed or tissue culture in specialist laboratories.

Sartylis Blue Knob
↔ 4–20 in (10–50 cm) ↕ 4–24 in (10–60 cm)
♀ ☀ ◆/◆/◇ ❊ ▭

Primary hybrid between *Sarcochilus hartmannii* and *Rhynchostylis retusa*. Long foxtails of blooms, each 1¼ in (30 mm) wide, white to pale pink with purple spotting. Flowers throughout year, peaking in spring–autumn.

Sartylis Jannine Banks
↔ 4–20 in (10–50 cm) ↕ 4–24 in (10–60 cm)
♀ ☀ ◆/◆ ❊ ▭

Primary hybrid between *Sarcochilus hartmannii* and *Rhynchostylis gigantea*. Inflorescences with dark claret and pink blooms, 2 in (5 cm) wide, produced repeatedly throughout warmer months of year.

SATYRIUM

This is a genus of over 100 different species of deciduous terrestrial orchids primarily from southern Africa. There are outlying taxa found in Madagascar, and *Satyrium nepalense* extends from Pakistan to southwestern China. They are related to *Disa*, and have their blooms produced on generally upright inflorescences, and in most cases the few to many flowers are densely crowded. The lip is uppermost in all species and is helmet-shaped. The flowers, which are protected by a leaf-like bract, come in a wide range of colors and color combinations.
CULTIVATION: These orchids should be potted in a well-drained terrestrial mix and appreciate a high proportion of coarse sand with some organic matter. Some species are easily grown, while others have proved difficult to maintain over more than 2 seasons. They require bright light to induce flowering and like to be kept moist when in active growth. The potting medium should be allowed to dry out during the dormant period. Propagation is from seed.

Satyrium carneum
↔ 12–18 in (30–45 cm) ↕ 12–32 in (30–80 cm) ❧ ☼/☀ ◇ ❊ ▭

Robust species from western South Africa. Basal leaves 2, ovate, to 9 in (22 cm) long, tightly pressed to the ground. Flowering stem with several sheathing leaves; spike with many densely packed flowers in spring–summer. Blooms pink, relatively large; spurs about ¾ in (18 mm) long, parallel to ovary.

Satyrium coriifolium
↔ 6–10 in (15–25 cm) ↕ 8–30 in (20–75 cm) ❧ ☼ ◆/◇ ❊ ▭

Robust species from western South Africa. Leaves to 6 in (15 cm) long, erect or spreading, elliptic. Inflorescence with many densely packed flowers in early spring. Flowers bright orange or bright yellow, relatively large; spurs about ½ in (12 mm) long, lying along ovary.

Satyrium erectum
↔ 4–12 in (10–30 cm) ↕ 4–20 in (10–50 cm) ❧ ☼/☀ ◆/◇ ❊ ▭

Robust species from western South Africa. Two basal leaves, almost round, to 6 in (15 cm) long, pressed to the ground. Flowering stem with several sheathing leaves; spike with several to many densely packed flowers, mostly in spring. Flowers relatively large, strongly and sweetly scented, pale to deep pink with darker marks on petals and lip; spurs short.

Satyrium hallackii
↔ 8–16 in (20–40 cm) ↕ 8–24 in (20–60 cm) ❧ ☼/☀ ◆/◇ ❊ ▭

From southeastern Africa. Loose rosette of leaves is followed by thick upright inflorescence of up to 60 flowers in summer. Blooms about 1 in (25 mm) across, pink.

Satyrium longicauda
↔ 8–16 in (20–40 cm) ↕ 8–27 in (20–70 cm) ❧ ☼/☀ ◆/◇ ❊ ▭

From southeastern Africa. Plant has 1 or 2 leaves and lax inflorescence of up to 40 white to pink flowers, each about 1½ in (35 mm) in size. Summer-flowering.

Satyrium nepalense
↔ 8–20 in (20–50 cm) ↕ 6–30 in (15–75 cm) ❧ ☀ ◆/◇ ❊ ▭

Erect species from India, Sri Lanka, and Myanmar. Leaves semi-erect or spreading, 4–10 in (10–25 cm) long, oblong, rather fleshy. Flowering stem stout, with some sheathing leaves; densely packed with many flowers in summer; bracts longer than flowers.

Satyrium hallackii

Satyrium longicauda

Satyrium pumilum

Flowers scented, bright pink, rarely white, about ½ in (12 mm) wide.

Satyrium pumilum
↔ 2–4 in (5–10 cm) ↑ 1–2 in (2.5–5 cm)
🌱 ☼/☀ ◆/◇ ❄ ☐

Endemic to South Africa. Distinctive species with very short stems, so the proportionally large flowers, 1¼ in (30 mm) in size, actually rest on the ground. Flowers greenish yellow to deep maroon; resemble members of unrelated succulent genus *Stapelia*; smell of carrion and are pollinated by flies. Flowers in spring–summer.

SCAPHOSEPALUM
This is a genus of about 60 different small-growing epiphytes and some-times lithophytes, which are related to *Pleurothallis* and *Porroglossum*. They are found throughout Central America and the northern half of South America, growing in rain and mist forests. The multiflowered inflorescence emerges from leaf base; successive flowering allows the plant to remain blooming throughout the year. The lateral sepals, with their extended "tails,"

are the dominant feature of these brightly colored flowers that are held with the lip uppermost.
CULTIVATION: These orchids should be kept moist, shaded, and generally in a humid environment throughout the year, and they must avoid direct sunlight. Most *Scaphosepalum* species may be grown in small pots of sphagnum moss or in a fine bark mix, with some of the clumping species suitable for mounting on tree fern. Propagate by division.

Scaphosepalum breve
↔ 4–6 in (10–15 cm) ↑ 5–6 in (12–15 cm)
♀ ☀ ◇ ☐/☒

Dwarf plant occurring in Guyana, Venezuela, Colombia, Ecuador, and Bolivia. Stems to 1¼ in (30 mm) long, with a single leaf. Leaves narrowly elliptic, to 6 in (15 cm) long. Racemes to 10 in (25 cm) long, loosely arranged with several to many flowers throughout year. Sepals 1 in (25 mm) long including tails ½ in (12 mm) long; orange or yellow marked with red. Petals and lip very small.

Scaphosepalum swertiifolium
↔ 5–6 in (12–15 cm) ↑ 6–9 in (15–22 cm)
♀ ☀ ◇ ☐/☒

Tufted plants from Colombia and Ecuador. Stems to 1 in (25 mm) long; leaves about 8 in (20 cm) long. Inflorescences to 6 in (15 cm) long; flowers to 3 in (8 cm) across, white or pale yellow, with pink or brown marks. Lateral sepals to 2 in (5 cm) long, including spreading tails to almost 2 in (5 cm) long. Petals and lip very small. Flowers throughout year.

Scaphosepalum verrucosum
↔ 6–8 in (15–20 cm) ↑ 8–20 in (20–50 cm)
♀/\ ☀ ◇ ☐/☒

Tufted plants from Colombia. Stems to 1¼ in (30 mm) long; fleshy or leathery leaves 2–6 in (5–15 cm) long. Upright inflorescences 8–20 in (20–50 cm) long, carry numerous blooms on warty flower stalks. Flowers small, fleshy, yellow or yellow-green marked with reddish-brown or purple. Blooms produced throughout year.

S

Scaphosepalum swertiifolium

Scaphyglottis violacea

SCAPHYGLOTTIS

This genus, related to *Hexisea*, has its 50 plus members distributed throughout Central America, the West Indies, and South America to Brazil and Bolivia. This is a poorly understood genus botanically, and there are few species in cultivation. They are sympodial epiphytes and lithophytes that have an unusual growth habit. The pseudobulbs, as well as being produced at their base, are also superposed: they proliferate on top of each other, from the apex of the previous vegetative growth. The flowers are produced between the leaf axils, and in most species are tiny, green, and fairly insignificant. There are some species that produce larger and more colorful flowers. These are plants for the serious species orchid enthusiasts, particularly those who enjoy the unusual miniatures.

CULTIVATION: These small-growing miniatures are readily grown in pots of well-drained, but moisture-retentive bark-based mixture or on tree-fern slabs. They prefer intermediate growing conditions and regular watering, as the plants are invariably in constant growth and like to be kept moist. Propagate by division of established specimens, and removal of small plantlets formed as aerial growths.

Scaphyglottis prolifera
syn. *Scaphyglottis cuneata*
↔ 3–4 in (8–10 cm)　↑ 4–5 in (10–12 cm)
♀ ☀/☼ ◆ ❋ ☖/📐

Species from Central and South America. Pseudobulbs superposed, clustered, branching, cylindrical or spindle-shaped, with 2 leaves. Narrow leaves, to just under 2 in (5 cm) long. Inflorescences in clusters, with a single, very small, white flower, slightly tinged with pink or yellow. Spring-flowering.

Scaphyglottis stellata
syn. *Scaphyglottis amethystina*
↔ 3–6 in (8–15 cm)　↑ 3–6 in (8–15 cm)
♀/⋀ ☀/☼ ◆ ❋ ☖/📐

From Central and South America. Pseudobulbs superposed, to 5 in (12 cm) long, often purple-tinged, with 2 oblong leaves to 5 in (12 cm) long. Inflorescences in clusters, with a single bloom in spring. Flowers small, pink, purple or rarely white.

Scaphyglottis violacea
↔ 2–8 in (5–20 cm)　↑ 2½–6 in (6–15 cm)
♀ ☀/☼ ◆/◇ ❋ ☖/📐

Small clumping species from Venezuela, Brazil, and Peru. Small clusters of very tiny (3 mm wide) bright rose pink and white blooms that do not open fully. Spring-flowering.

SCHISTOSTYLUS

This monotypic genus is related to *Sarcochilus*, and comes from eastern Australia. The small plants are often found growing as twig epiphytes on small branches overhanging water, rarely growing on the trunks or main branches of trees. They have leaves in 2 ranks and a network of coarse wiry roots. They produce short spikes of mainly green flowers that face the apex of the inflorescence.

CULTIVATION: These orchids do not like having their roots covered, so are best mounted on narrow but long sections of cork. They are best kept in a semi-shaded position in a humid environment, with plenty of free circulating air. This is not an easy genus to maintain in cultivation. Propagation is from seed.

Schistostylus purpuratus
↔ 2½–5 in (6–12 cm)　↑ 2½–5 in (6–12 cm)
♀ ☀ ◆ 📐

Species with a restricted range in eastern Australia. Short pendent spikes of up to 6 reddish to green blooms, ¼ in (6 mm) wide, predominantly white lip, in spring.

SCHOENORCHIS

About 22 species are known in this genus from tropical regions of Asia, from India and Sri Lanka to Indonesia, the Philippines, New Guinea, and northern Australia. They grow as epiphytes and have erect or hanging, monopodial, sometimes branching stems with broad or slender, in some species even cylindrical leaves. The minute flowers appear in large numbers on a simple or branched inflorescence.

CULTIVATION: *Schoenorchis* species are best grown mounted on a slab of cork or tree fern under warm conditions, high humidity, and in semishade. The terete-leafed species need regular watering year-round, while the broad-leafed species need less water and should get their roots dry quickly after watering. These plants need to be kept somewhat cooler and drier during winter. Propagation is from seed.

Schoenorchis fragrans
syn. *Saccolabium fragrans*
↔ 1¼–2 in (3–5 cm)　↑ 2–4 in (5–10 cm)
♀ ☀ ◆ 📐

Found in Myanmar and Thailand at elevations up to 3,280 ft (1,000 m). Leaves broad, fleshy, elliptic. Axillary short pendent inflorescence with many bright pink minute flowers in summer.

Schoenorchis micrantha
syn. *Schoenorchis densiflora*
↔ 2–4 in (5–10 cm)　↑ 2–4 in (5–10 cm)
♀ ☀ ◆ 📐

Species from New Guinea; found at lower altitudes; differs from *S. fragrans* in its cylindrical, sickle-shaped leaves and whitish fragrant flowers on a hanging inflorescence. Blooms in spring–summer.

Schoenorchis pachyacris
↔ 1½–3 in (3.5–8 cm)　↑ ¾–2½ in (1.8–6 cm)　♀ ☀/☼ ◆/◆ 📐

From Thailand, Malaysia, and Indonesia. Very small-growing, vandaceous, monopodial orchid with thick succulent leaves arranged in 2 ranks. Short inflorescences produce small blooms in summer. Flowers ¼ in (6 mm) in size, sparkling bright pink.

SCHOMBURGKIA

This is a small sympodial genus, with about 20 species that resemble some of the closely related larger *Laelia* species. They are found in the West Indies and from Mexico to Brazil. They have elongated pseudobulbs, sometimes hollow, with 2 or 3 rigid leathery leaves at the apex. Long inflorescences emerge from the most recently matured growth, and clusters of large, colorful, often waxy blooms usually make their appearance in late spring, summer, and autumn.

CULTIVATION: Most species need high light levels and warm temperatures to grow and flower well. They dislike

Schistostylus purpuratus

Schoenorchis pachyacris

temperatures below 50°F (10°C).
Rambling growth makes them difficult
to contain in pots; often they will only
bloom once they are pot bound or
have grown out of their pots. Mature
plants should be grown in pots over
18 in (45 cm) in diameter. They can
be mounted on large slabs of cork or
tree fern. Most species need protection
from mid-summer heat, and light
shading; some can be grown in full sun
in the tropics. Propagate by division.

Schomburgkia lueddemanniana
↔ 20–40 in (50–100 cm) ↕ 24–55 in
(60–140 cm) ♀/Λ ☀ ◆ ❄ ☐/☂

Large plants found from Costa Rica
to Colombia. Pseudobulbs stalked, to
16 in (40 cm) long, ellipsoid or club-
shaped; 2 to 3 oblong or strap-shaped
leaves, to 12 in (30 cm) long. Inflorescence terminal on pseudobulb, more
or less erect, with several flowers in
spring. Flowers 2–2½ in (5–6 cm)
across; sepals and petals light brown,
lip pinkish, with 3 lobes.

Schomburgkia superbiens
syns *Cattleya superbiens*, *Laelia
superbiens*
↔ 4–6 ft (1.2–1.8 m) ↕ 2–12 ft
(0.6–3.5 m) ♀/❧ ☀ ◆/◆/◇ ❄ ☐/☂

Large plants from Mexico, Guatemala,
and Honduras. Pseudobulbs to 12 in
(30 cm) long, narrowly oblong, furrowed, slightly compressed; 1 to 2
leaves at apex. Leaves to 12 in (30 cm)
long, narrowly oblong. Inflorescence
terminal, unbranched, erect or arching,
to 48 in (120 cm) long, with many
flowers in autumn. Flowers large and
showy, to 5 in (12 cm) across, scented,
long-lasting, lilac-mauve, lip darker
with yellow callus.

Schomburgkia undulata
↔ 4–6 ft (1.2–1.8 m) ↕ 3–7 ft (0.9–2 m)
♀ ☀ ◆/◆ ❄ ☐/☂

Large plant from Colombia, Trinidad,
and Venezuela. Pseudobulbs to 10 in
(25 cm) long, spindle-shaped; 2 to 3
leaves at apex. Leaves to 12 in (30 cm)
long, oblong to strap-shaped, rigid.
Inflorescence 2–6 ft (0.6–1.8 m) long,

Schoenorchis fragrans

unbranched, with about 20 loosely
arranged flowers toward apex in late
autumn–spring. Flowers sometimes
scented, waxy, short-lived, showy,
about 2 in (5 cm) across; sepals and
petals shiny maroon-purple, edges
undulate; lip bright magenta.

Schomburgkia weberbaueriana
↔ 3–4 ft (0.9–1.2 m) ↕ 3–4 in (0.9–1.2 m)
♀ ☀ ◆ ❄ ☐

Large plants found growing in montane forests in Peru. Pseudobulbs to
16 in (40 cm) long, spindle-shaped to
cylindrical, with 2 leaves. Inflorescence
to 32 in (80 cm) long, unbranched,
with several to many loosely arranged
flowers, with prominent, narrow,
pointed floral bracts. Flowers about
1 in (25 mm) across, greenish yellow
marked with brown, lip white, tinged
with mauve. Flowers in late spring.

Schomburgkia lueddemanniana

SCUTICARIA

This genus of 5 medium-sized sympodial epiphytes comes from tropical Central and South America. Plants have small pseudobulbs, with a single leaf at the apex. The long, pendent, fleshy leaves are more or less cylindrical but grooved on the uppersurface. The inflorescences are lateral, with 1 to a few flowers. The flowers are showy, with spreading sepals and petals and a concave 3-lobed lip with a slightly notched mid-lobe. The name comes from the Latin *scutica*, meaning whip, referring to the long thin leaves.
CULTIVATION: Because of their long pendent leaves, these orchids should be grown mounted on a vertical bark slab. They need plenty of water while in active growth; keep drier after flowering. Propagate by division.

Scuticaria hadwenii

↔ 6–8 in (15–20 cm)   ↕ 8–18 in (20–45 cm)
♀ ☀ ◆ ❀ ⧖

Pendent plants from Brazil and Guyana. Leaves to 18 in (45 cm) long. Inflorescences arching or pendent, to 2 in (5 cm) long, with 1 to 2 flowers in spring–autumn. Flowers about 3 in (8 cm) across, scented, long-lasting, yellow, heavily blotched with brown; lip white or pale yellow, spotted and marked with red or brown.

Scuticaria steelei

↔ 6–8 in (15–20 cm)   ↕ 40–60 in
(100–150 cm) ♀ ☀ ◆ ❀ ⧖

From tropical South America and Central America; large plant. Pseudobulbs to 1¼ in (30 mm) long; leaves pendent, to 60 in (150 cm) long. Short raceme with 1 to 3 flowers in spring–summer. Flowers showy, to 3 in (8 cm) across, waxy and long-lasting, yellow or greenish yellow with maroon-brown spots; lip paler, with reddish streaks.

SEDIREA

This genus includes only one short-stemmed, monopodial, epiphytic species, which is found in Korea and

Sedirea japonica

Japan, including the Ryukyu Islands. Plants have stout fleshy roots, several leaves, and racemes of scented flowers.
CULTIVATION: Grow these plants in pots in a medium epiphyte compost in a humid, partially shaded situation in a cool or intermediate greenhouse. They can be kept drier in winter but should not dry out completely. Propagate from seed.

Sedirea japonica

↔ 6–12 in (15–30 cm)   ↕ 4–6 in (10–15 cm)
♀ ☀ ◆/◇ ❀ ⧖

Strap-shaped leaves, to 6 in (15 cm) long. Raceme to 6 in (15 cm) long, with 2 to 12 scented white flowers, about 1 in (25 mm) across, in summer. Lateral sepals with purplish bars on basal half; pink-purple spots and bars on lip; spur conical.

SEIDENFADENIA

This monotypic genus is found in Thailand and Myanmar growing as an epiphyte in forests between sea level and 5,900 ft (1,800 m). The long cylindrical leaves are pendent on a very short monopodial stem and may reach 20 in (50 cm) long. The erect inflorescence bears many showy flowers. The thick white roots are very prominent.
CULTIVATION: Grow these plants under warm and humid conditions, similar to *Phalaenopsis*. Because of the hanging habit, the plants are best mounted with a thin layer of sphagnum or moss. Propagate from seed.

Seidenfadenia mitrata

syn. *Aerides mitrata*
↔ 4–6 in (10–15 cm)   ↕ 12–20 in (30–50 cm)
♀ ☀ ◆ ❀ ⧖

Found in humid forests of Thailand and Myanmar. Unbranched erect inflorescence to 6–8 in (15–20 cm) long, with 15 to 30 flowers in spring. Flowers fragrant, light pink, with showy dark pink lip.

Serapias lingua

Serapias neglecta

SERAPIAS

HEART-FLOWERED ORCHID, TONGUE ORCHID
There are 7 to 12 species known in this genus. They are terrestrial orchids found in the Mediterranean region of Europe, eastward to the Caucasus; several species spread north to France, Switzerland, and even Britain, and south to parts of northern Africa and the Canary Islands. They are similar in habit to *Orchis*, but are easily recognized by the spurless flowers with a prominent tongue-shaped lip. The plants survive in winter with subterranean tuberoids.
CULTIVATION: These orchids are among the easier to cultivate terrestrial species. Grow them in an alpine house, with a dry resting period in summer. They need a free-draining mineral substrate in bright light and will quickly form large colonies. They need direct sun. Frost hardiness is dependent on the species, but it is safer to place them in a sheltered place with temperatures above freezing. Propagate by division.

Serapias cordigera

HEART-FLOWERED ORCHID
syns *Serapias azorica*, *S. ovalis*
↔ 6–10 in (15–25 cm)   ↕ 8–14 in (20–35 cm)
⚘ ☼/☀ ◇ ❀ ⧖

Found in Mediterranean Europe and northern Africa; grows in dry and wet grasslands, dunes, and forests up to altitudes of 3,280 ft (1,000 m). Subterranean tubers give rise to 5 to 9 lanceolate leaves and an erect inflorescence covered in bracts with 2 to 10 maroon flowers in spring.

Serapias lingua

syns *Serapias excavata*, *S. hirsuta*, *S. stenopetala*

TONGUE ORCHID
↔ 6–10 in (15–25 cm)   ↕ 4–14 in (10–35 cm)
⚘ ☼/☀ ◇ ❀ ⧖

Found in Mediterranean Europe and northern Africa; grows in dry and wet

Serapias vomeracea subsp. *laxiflora*

grasslands, dunes, shrubs, and forests, up to altitudes of 6,560 ft (2,000 m). Subterranean tubers give rise to 4 to 8 lanceolate leaves and an erect inflorescence with large bracts with 2 to 6 brownish pink flowers in spring.

Serapias neglecta

↔ 3–7 in (8–18 cm)   ↕ 4–12 in (10–30 cm)
⚘ ☼/☀ ◇ ❀ ⧖

From the Mediterranean region. Leaves 4 to 10, semi-erect, to 5 in (12 cm) long, broad or narrow, can be folded. Raceme with 2 to 8, occasionally more, rather densely packed flowers. Sepals and petals form hood, yellow-green to lilac; lip 3-lobed, to 2 in (5 cm) long, mid-lobe red-brown to yellow. Flowers in late spring–early summer.

Serapias parviflora

syns *Serapias elongata*, *S. laxiflora*, *S. occultata*

TONGUE ORCHID
↔ 6–10 in (15–25 cm)   ↕ 6–12 in (15–30 cm)
⚘ ☼/☀ ◇ ❀ ⧖

Found on all Mediterranean Islands and in neighboring North African and southern European countries; grows in meadows, among shrubs, and in coniferous forests, up to 3,940 ft (1,200 m) altitude. Lanceolate leaves. Erect inflorescence covered in bracts with 3 to 10 reddish flowers in spring.

Serapias vomeracea

↔ 5–6 in (12–15 cm)   ↕ 8–24 in (20–60 cm)
⚘ ☼/☀ ◇ ❀ ⧖

From the Mediterranean region. Leaves 4 to 7, to 8 in (20 cm) long, semi-erect. Raceme with 3 to 10 flowers in spring-summer, bracts longer than flowers. Sepals and petals form hood, light red with darker veins; lip about 1½ in (35 mm) long, densely hairy, rust-red to violet-brown. *S. v.* subsp. *laxiflora* (sometimes treated as a separate species, *S. laxiflora*), is smaller, usually less than 12 in (30 cm) tall.

S

Serapias vomeracea

Smitinandia micrantha

Sobralia macrantha var. *alba*

SMITINANDIA

This is a small genus of 3 monopodial vandaceous species that are found from the Himalayas through Southeast Asia to Indonesia. They produce sprays of chunky, small, colorful blooms that are long lived. They were previously included within the genus *Saccolabium*.
CULTIVATION: Ideal plants for bark-filled wooden baskets, they enjoy warm conditions and high light levels. The thick roots will often venture outside the confines of the pot or basket, and this culture should be encouraged, as the roots require unimpeded air circulation and must dry out quickly after watering. Propagate by division of mature basal shoots or from seed.

Smitinandia micrantha

syns *Saccolabium fissum*, *S. micranthum*
↔ 5–10 in (12–25 cm) ↕ 4–10 in (10–25 cm)
♀ ☼ ◆/◈ ❋ ☐

Found from northern India through Southeast Asia; the most commonly seen species in cultivation. Thick inflorescence with up to 30 flowers in spring–summer. Blooms just over ¼ in (6 mm) wide, white to pale pink with bright lilac-colored lip.

SOBRALIA

A genus of about 100 species, mostly terrestrials, found from Mexico to tropical South America. Few are cultivated but availability is increasing. Popular species have huge *Cattleya*-like blooms, which are often short-lived, and are produced from the top of the leafy cane-like growths in summer.
CULTIVATION: To accommodate the extensive roots, pot these plants into large deep containers in a well-drained terrestrial mix with bark added. Intermediate to warm conditions suit most species. These plants enjoy strong light, coupled with frequent watering and feeding during warmer months. Sit

plants in saucers of water in summer. Keep dry in winter. Hardy species can be planted in gardens in frost-free climates in soil with a high percentage of organic matter. Propagation is by division in spring.

Sobralia decora

↔ 24–36 in (60–90 cm) ↕ 30–32 in (75–80 cm) ♀//▲/❆ ☼ ◆/◈ ❋ ☐

Tall and bamboo-like plants found from Mexico to Costa Rica in shaded ravines and oak and pine forests. Lacks pseudobulbs; opposite, pleated, hairy leaves to 9 in (22 cm) long. Large flowers, to 4 in (10 cm) wide, white to lilac with lavender to purple lip. Flowers bloom sequentially from apex of growths, each bloom lasting one day. Flowers in spring–summer.

Sobralia macrantha

↔ 1–4 ft (0.3–1.2 m) ↕ 1–7 ft (0.3–2 m)
❆ ☼/☼ ◆/◈ ❋ ☐

Found from Mexico to Costa Rica. Stems to 7 ft (2 m) tall, often less in cultivation. Large flowers, to 10 in (25 cm) wide, rose-purple, in summer. *S. m.* var. *alba*, white flowers.

Sobralia Mirabilis

↔ 36 in (90 cm) ↕ 36 in (90 cm)
❆ ☼/☼ ◆/◈ ❋ ☐

Registered in 1903; cross between *S. macrantha* and *S.* Veitchii. Original cross had white petals with faintest pink blush around mid-pink wavy-edged lip much elongated at base. Later forms vary, mainly in lip color. Summer-flowering.

Sobralia xantholeuca ★

↔ 1–4 ft (0.3–1.2 m) ↕ 1–5 ft (0.3–1.5 m)
❆ ☼/☼ ◆/◈ ❋ ☐

From Mexico and Guatemala. Similar habit to *S. macrantha*. Slightly nodding lemon yellow flowers, to 8 in (20 cm) wide, in summer.

Sobralia macrantha

Sobralia Mirabilis

Sobralia Yellow Kiss

↔ 12–84 in (30–200 cm) ↑ 20–84 in (50–200 cm) ✤ ☼/◑ ◆/◈/◇ ❈ ☐

Third-generation hybrid involving *S. xantholeuca* and *S. macrantha*. Large robust plants make ideal garden subjects in frost-free climates, taking wide range of temperatures. Summer-flowering.

SOPHROCATTLEYA

Sophrocattleya is a bigeneric hybrid between the sympodial genera *Sophronitis* and *Cattleya*. Most of these hybrids have the cool-growing *Sophronitis coccinea* in their background, which leads to smaller-growing plants, flowers that have a more filled-in shape, and many of the red tones. The yellow-flowered hybrids often have *Cattleya luteola* in their lineage. They mostly bloom in spring and summer, with some flowering in autumn.

CULTIVATION: These hybrids enjoy bright light and cool to warm temperatures. They require a cooler and drier rest in winter when the plants are in a dormant phase. They must all have unimpeded drainage and a coarse bark-based medium. They grow best in plastic or terracotta pots and must dry out between waterings. Healthy plants will develop an extensive system of thick white roots, which are long lived and freely branch. Propagate by division.

Sophrocattleya Beaufort

↔ 4–16 in (10–40 cm) ↑ 4–16 in (10–40 cm) ♀ ☼/◑ ◆/◈ ❈ ☐

Very popular miniature primary hybrid between *Sophronitis coccinea* and *Laelia luteola*. Generally has bright yellow blooms; some clones in orange tones. Flowers throughout year.

Sophrocattleya Lana Coryell ★

↔ 4–16 in (10–40 cm) ↑ 4–16 in (10–40 cm) ♀ ☼/◑ ◆/◈ ❈ ☐

Popular compact-growing hybrid between *Sophrocattleya* Beaufort and *Cattleya walkeriana*. Disproportionally large flowers, salmon pink to purple, throughout year. Has received many awards.

Sobralia xantholeuca

SOPHROLAELIA

A bigeneric hybrid combining the sympodial genera *Sophronitis* and *Laelia*. In general, they are brightly colored hybrids with long thin pseudobulbs, each with a single leathery leaf. They produce small clusters of flowers from spring to autumn, and are called "cocktail orchids," referring to their diminutive size, and the wide range of bright to pastel colors that are produced.

CULTIVATION: These hybrids enjoy bright light and cool to warm temperatures. They need a cooler and drier rest in winter when they enter a dormant phase. They must have unimpeded drainage and like to dry out between waterings. They are best grown in a coarse bark-based medium, and do well in pots, enjoying being potbound. They look best grown into specimen plants, producing a mass of showy flowers. Propagation is by division.

Sophrolaelia Gratrixiae

↔ 4–16 in (10–40 cm) ↑ 4–16 in (10–40 cm) ♀ ☼/◑ ◆/◈ ❈ ☐

Primary hybrid between *Sophronitis coccinea* and *Laelia tenebrosa*, registered over 100 years ago. Clusters of attractive, small, bright red flowers with a tubular lip, are produced in spring–summer.

Sophrolaelia Orpetii

↔ 4–16 in (10–40 cm) ↑ 4–16 in (10–40 cm) ♀ ☼/◑ ◆/◈ ❈ ☐

Popular primary hybrid between *Sophronitis coccinea* and *Laelia pumila*. Compact-growing hybrid; clusters of striking purple flowers, sometimes yellow-throated. Blooms produced throughout the year.

Sophrocattleya Lana Coryell

Sophrolaelia Gratrixiae

Sophrolaeliocattleya Ann Komine (hybrid)

Sophrolaeliocattleya Ann Topper (hybrid)

SOPHROLAELIOCATTLEYA

This is a 3-way orchid hybrid from 3 sympodial genera: *Sophronitis, Laelia,* and *Cattleya*. Most of the hybrids have the cool-growing *Sophronitis coccinea* somewhere in their background, using its influence for shapely red blooms as well as its compact to miniature growth habit. The yellow-flowered hybrids often have *Cattleya luteola* in their lineage.

CULTIVATION: These hybrids do well in bright light and cool to warm temperatures. Give them a cooler and drier rest in winter when the plants are in a dormant state. Best grown in plastic or terracotta pots, they require excellent drainage and a coarse bark-based medium. Allow to dry out between waterings. Healthy plants will develop an extensive system of thick white roots, which are long lived and freely branch. Propagate by division.

Sophrolaeliocattleya Hybrids

↔ 4–16 in (10–40 cm) ↕ 4–16 in (10–40 cm)

Depending on hybrid, flower size varies from 1½ in (35 mm) to 6 in (15 cm) across petals. Mostly spring- and summer-blooming, some flower in autumn. **Ann Komine**, glossy claret colored blooms; **Fire Lighter**, blooms readily off young plants, purplish red blooms; **Hazel Boyd 'Apricot Glow'** ★ very popular clone of this successful American-bred hybrid between *S.* California Apricot and *S.* Jewel Box; **Jannine Louise**, popular orange- to red-flowered hybrid between *S.* Kauai Starbright and *S.* Hazel Boyd; **Jeweler's Art**, 5 in (12 cm) wide blooms, unusual orange-pink shades; **Mahalo Jack**, deep pink blooms, hybrid between *Sophrolaelia* Orpetii and *Cattleya walkeriana*; **Memoria Ken Martin**, deep salmon pink to red flowers; **Mine Gold 'Orchid Centre'**, yellow blooms, deep red lip; **Sunset Nugget**, burnt orange blooms, overlaid with fine red veining, deep red lip; **Trizac**, older hybrid, cerise blooms, darker lip.

Sophrolaeliocattleya Memoria Ken Martin (hybrid)

Sophrolaeliocattleya Jeweler's Art (hybrid)

Sophrolaeliocattleya Mine Gold 'Orchid Centre' (hybrid)

Sophrolaeliocattleya Fire Lighter (hybrid)

Sophrolaeliocattleya Red Elf (hybrid)   *Sophrolaeliocattleya* Kevin (hybrid)

Sophrolaeliocattleya Mahalo Jack (hybrid)

Sophrolaeliocattleya Seagull's Mini-Cat Heaven 'Dainty Lady' (hybrid)

Sophrolaeliocattleya Hazel Boyd 'Apricot Glow' (hybrid)

Sophrolaeliocattleya Sunset Nugget (hybrid)

Sophrolaeliocattleya Hazel Boyd (hybrid)   *Sophrolaeliocattleya* Trizac (hybrid)

Sophronitella violacea

SOPHRONITELLA

This genus from southeastern Brazil contains a single species, which was formerly included in the genus *Sophronitis*. The creeping plants are epiphytes or lithophytes, and form small clusters in bright spots in humid montane forests at intermediate altitudes.
CULTIVATION: Grow under intermediate conditions, bright light, and good humidity. Grow mounted on a piece of cork; they do not thrive in pots. Propagate by division.

Sophronitella violacea
syns *Cattleya violacea*, *Sophronitis violacea*

↔ 4–6 in (10–15 cm) ↕ 3–6 in (8–15 cm)

Species from Brazil. Slender, ovoid, strongly ridged pseudobulb on a branching rhizome; single grass-like leaf. Inflorescence with 1 to 2, rarely 3, star-shaped pink flowers, to 1 in (25 mm) wide, in late autumn–winter. White variety was described but no specimens are known to exist today.

SOPHRONITIS

A small genus of about 8 brightly colored, sympodial, epiphytic and lithophytic orchids from Brazil and Bolivia. They are closely related to the genus *Laelia*, in particular the Section Hadrolaelia, which includes species such as *L. dayana* and *L. pumila*. These laelias and *Sophronitis* share similarities in having single colorful blooms, and an inflorescence without a sheath but the young leaf folds around the buds.
CULTIVATION: Most species are best grown in cool to intermediate conditions, in pots, using a bark-based mix for larger plants, and sphagnum moss for smaller ones. Repot every other year as they lose their roots in stale mix. They need medium light levels, a humid and part-shaded environment, and fresh air, and will not tolerate stagnant conditions. Reduce watering in winter. *Sophronitis* have been extensively used within the *Cattleya* alliance, creating compact plants and brightly colored full blooms. Propagate by division.

Sophronitis cernua
↔ 2½–7 in (6–18 cm) ↕ 1½–3 in (3.5–8 cm)

Creeping orchid, native to Brazil and Bolivia. Groups of up to 6 flowers on short nodding sprays in autumn. Blooms ½ in (12 mm) wide, bright tangerine-orange, some yellow on lip. Will not tolerate cold; best grown on cork mounts.

Sophronitis coccinea
syn. *Sophronitis grandiflora*

↔ 2½–8 in (6–20 cm) ↕ 1½–5 in (3.5–12 cm)

Magnificent Brazilian orchid. Large, round, flat blooms, to 3 in (8 cm) wide, bright orange to scarlet-red; very narrow lip, often yellow and orange markings. Flowers in autumn–winter. Clones such as 'Jannine' display improved vigor.

Sophronitis wittigiana
syn. *Sophronitis rosea*

↔ 2–4 in (5–10 cm) ↕ 2–4 in (5–10 cm)

From Brazil. Pseudobulbs rounded to oval, leaf reddish on underside. Flowers 1, rarely 2, from the tip of the pseudobulb, bright rose to pink, sometimes with slightly darker veining; lip yellow in the center. Blooms in autumn.

SPATHOGLOTTIS

This group of 40 evergreen to semi-deciduous, tropical, terrestrial orchids is found from Southeast Asia, New Guinea, and northern Australia to nearby islands of the Pacific. They grow in grasslands and open forests in moist places. They have small, conical, and somewhat flattened pseudobulbs on or just below the soil surface. A few large pleated leaves and tall inflorescences of mainly pink and purple, occasionally yellow or white, showy flowers are produced. They bloom throughout the year in the tropics, and during warmer months in greenhouses in temperate climates.

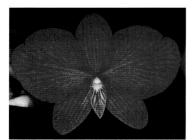

Sophronitis coccinea 'Jannine'

CULTIVATION: These plants are best in bright light. Warm conditions throughout the year are required as they dislike temperatures below 50°F (10°C). Grow in deep pots in a well-drained medium incorporating pine bark, sand, and peat moss. Keep moist—pots can be placed in a saucer of water, about 2 in (5 cm) deep, during the period of active growth in the summer. Reduce watering during the winter when the plants are semi-dormant. Propagate by division.

Spathoglottis plicata
syn. *Spathoglottis vieillardii*

↔ 8–48 in (20–120 cm) ↕ 12–40 in (30–100 cm)

From Southeast Asia, Australia, and nearby Pacific Islands, naturalized in Hawaii, USA, where it is marketed as a native. Erect spikes of up to 20 pink to purple, 1½ in (35 mm) wide blooms all through the year.

SPIRANTHES
LADIES' TRESSES

This genus contains about 300 species and is found in temperate, subtropical, or tropical regions all over the world. They primarily grow as terrestrials, but may be found on branches or on rocks occasionally. The thick, almost tuberous roots are fibrous and support a slender plant with lanceolate leaves and an erect inflorescence with little flowers spiraling around it.
CULTIVATION: While some species turn out to be almost impossible to cultivate, others do very well when grown in small pots in a mixture of loam and leaf compost or peat. Water well when growing, and keep a bit drier in winter after the leaves have died off. They are easily propagated by division, as the plants quickly form large colonies.

Spiranthes odorata
syn. *Spiranthes cernua*
FRAGRANT LADIES' TRESSES, NODDING LADIES' TRESSES

↔ 4–6 in (10–15 cm) ↕ 12–36 in (30–90 cm)

One of the larger species in genus. Essentially from North America,

Spathoglottis plicata

Spathoglottis plicata

S

Stanhopea anfracta

where it is found in the southeast in grassy alkaline marshes and wet meadows, with some naturalized populations in the Netherlands in Europe. Flowers white, smell of jasmine. Blooms in autumn–winter.

Spiranthes sinensis

CHINESE LADIES' TRESSES

↔ 4–6 in (10–15 cm) ↕ 4–10 in (10–25 cm)

Found in eastern Russia, Malaysia, Australia, and some Pacific Islands south to New Zealand; grows in grassy areas, open forests, and bogs. Basal leaf rosette supports erect inflorescence; flowers tiny, bright pink sepals and petals, white lip. Flowers in summer.

Spiranthes spiralis

syn. *Spiranthes autumnalis*

AUTUMN LADIES' TRESSES

↔ 4–6 in (10–15 cm) ↕ 4–12 in (10–30 cm)

Found in central and southern Europe eastward to the western Himalayas; grows in grasslands and open forest, between sea level and 4,920 ft (1,500 m). White flowers in late summer–autumn.

STANHOPEA

UPSIDE-DOWN ORCHID

This large popular genus, containing about 70 epiphytic orchids, is found from Mexico to Brazil. They feature egg-shaped pseudobulbs, each with a single leaf. They are grown for their large, bizarre, and colorful blooms and amazing lip structure. The waxy blooms are fragrant and last for only a few days.

CULTIVATION: Grow these orchids in baskets to allow their pendent spikes to spear through the medium and burst into bloom. Use *Cymbidium* compost, sphagnum moss, fine-grade pine bark, or a combination of these materials. Mounted plants rarely stay moist enough, resulting in a bunch of yellowish shriveled back-bulbs. They appreciate constant moisture throughout the year and grow best in a part-shaded position. Leaves will burn in very strong light and low humidity. There are species suitable for cool

Stanhopea nigroviolacea

to tropical climates, which flower over several months. Propagate by division.

Stanhopea anfracta

↔ 12–20 in (30–50 cm) ↕ 20–30 in (50–75 cm)
Large species found in the eastern Andes from Ecuador to Bolivia. Leaves to 16 in (40 cm) long. Inflorescence with 7 to 13 flowers in summer–autumn. Flowers about 2 in (5 cm) across. Sepals and petals fleshy, spreading, pale to deep orange; lip orange with dark brownish eyespot on either side near base.

Stanhopea embreei

↔ 8–20 in (20–50 cm) ↕ 8–20 in (20–50 cm)
Species from Ecuador. Up to 5, white, 5 in (12 cm) wide flowers, with random dark red spots and deep purple spotting on white and yellow lip. Summer-blooming.

Stanhopea nigroviolacea ★

syn. *Stanhopea tigrina* var. *nigroviolacea*

↔ 8–24 in (20–60 cm) ↕ 8–20 in (20–50 cm)
From Mexico; the most commonly seen species in cultivation. Pairs of yellowish green, 7 in (18 cm) wide blooms, heavily blotched with dark reddish brown. Pleasant powerful vanilla fragrance, which is often detected before sighting the blooms. Summer-flowering.

Stanhopea oculata

Stanhopea wardii

Stanhopea oculata

↔ 8–20 in (20–50 cm)   ↑ 8–20 in (20–50 cm)

Elegant variable orchid found from Mexico to Brazil. Up to 8 flowers in late summer–autumn. Blooms ½ in (12 mm) wide, pale yellow overlaid with red-purple circular spots; cream lip marked with fine reddish pepper spotting, bright orange base.

Stanhopea wardii

↔ 8–20 in (20–50 cm)   ↑ 8–20 in (20–50 cm)

Variable orchid found in Nicaragua, Costa Rica, Panama, Colombia, and Venezuela. Up to 10, bright yellow to orange, 5 in (12 cm) wide blooms, with fine maroon spotting, in summer or autumn. Distinguished by very dark purple patch at lip base.

STAUROCHILUS

This genus of vandaceous monopodial orchids consists of about 14 species, many of which were previously classified within the related genus *Trichoglottis*. They are found throughout Southeast Asia, with their center of distribution in the Philippines. These erect-growing epiphytes produce their leathery strap-like leaves in 2 ranks. Their long-lasting attractive flowers have ensured their popularity in cultivation among orchid fanciers.
CULTIVATION: These tropical orchids are readily grown in wooden baskets, thriving in bright, humid, intermediate to warm conditions, and are suited to tropical gardens and greenhouses in climates away from the tropics. They are best grown in pots using a coarse grade of pine bark as the potting medium. The thick roots will often venture outside the confines of the pot or basket, and this culture should be encouraged, as the roots require unimpeded air circulation and must dry out quickly after watering. They may also be grown on slabs of tree fern or cork, or attached to suitable trees in tropical climates. Propagate from cuttings with at least 3 roots attached.

Staurochilus fasciatus

↔ 6–12 in (15–30 cm)   ↑ 10–32 in (25–80 cm)

Widespread throughout Southeast Asia; type species of genus. Upright inflorescences of up to 8 blooms in spring–summer. Flowers long lived and highly fragrant, less than 2 in (5 cm) wide, mustard yellow with dark brown barring.

Staurochilus luchuensis

syn. *Trichoglottis ionosma*

↔ 8–16 in (20–40 cm)   ↑ 8–24 in (20–60 cm)

From the Philippines and Taiwan. Branched inflorescences of numerous, flat, 1¼ in (30 mm) wide, yellow and honey, long-lasting blooms in spring.

STELIS

This is a huge genus of over 1,000 species, closely related to *Pleurothallis*, which is found throughout the rainforests and open forests of Central America and South America. These tufted plants lack pseudobulbs and often have succulent water-holding leaves. They grow as epiphytes and lithophytes, and some species also grow as terrestrials, among grasses with their roots in moss. The flowers are produced on slender spikes, and are presented alternately, often in a somewhat zig-zagged fashion, with 20 being an average number. The individual blooms have a similar structure, with 3 prominent similar-looking sepals, tiny petals, and a comparable lip. Flower color ranges from white to yellows and greens through browns to dark red-purples. Interestingly, some species have noctural blooms that close during the day. Because of their apparent similarity, and small size, these botanicals have only been popular in specialist collections.
CULTIVATION: These orchids will generally tolerate a wide range of temperatures and stronger light intensities. They like to be somewhat potbound and prefer small pots. For best results they should be kept moist, shaded, and generally in a humid environment throughout the year, avoiding direct sunlight. Most species may be grown in sphagnum moss or in a fine bark mix, with some of the creeping species suitable for mounting on tree fern. Propagate by division.

Stelis argentata

↔ 2–4 in (5–10 cm)   ↑ 7–12 in (18–30 cm)

Widespread in Central America and South America. Stems 1¼–2½ in (3–6 cm) long, with 1 leaf. Leaves 2–4 in (5–10 cm) long, elliptic. Inflorescence 6–10 in (15–25 cm) long, erect or suberect, with many loosely arranged flowers. Flowers very small, pale green tinged with maroon or pale maroon. Blooms more than once a year, in spring–autumn.

Stelis imraei

syn. *Pleurothallis imraei*

↔ 2½–6 in (6–15 cm)   ↑ 4–8 in (10–20 cm)

Found from Costa Rica to Bolivia. Short spikes, often appear from underside of leaf, with up to 12 blooms in spring. Flowers deep purple to yellowish green, ¼ in (6 mm) in size, covered in fine short hairs.

STENOGLOTTIS

This is a genus of 5 species, possibly more, from southern Africa and eastern tropical Africa, with one species reaching as far north as Tanzania. They are terrestrial or lithophytic, occasionally epiphytic, with tuberous roots and basal rosettes of spotted or unspotted leaves. The inflorescence arises from the middle of a rosette, with racemes of many small pink or white flowers, often spotted with purple. The sepals and petals form a hood, the lip is 3- or 5-lobed, with or without a spur, the lobes often fringed.
CULTIVATION: These plants should be grown in shallow pots in a free-

Staurochilus fasciatus

Staurochilus luchuensis

Stelis species, in bud

Stelis imraei

draining terrestrial mix. After flowering, the leaves die off, and the dead remnants should be removed. Plants should be kept dry until signs of new growth appear, when careful watering can be resumed. Propagate by division when plants are dormant.

Stenoglottis fimbriata

↔ 10–12 in (25–30 cm) ↑ 1½–6 in (3.5–15 cm) /\/❈ ☀ ◆/◇ ❈ ⊡

From South Africa and Swaziland. Leaves 6–10 in a basal rosette, 1–6 in (2.5–15 cm) long, dark green spotted with purple (rarely unspotted), wavy-edged. Inflorescence fairly densely many-flowered; flowers small, lilac pink with darker spots; lip 3-lobed with no spur. Flowers in summer.

Stenoglottis longifolia

↔ 8–12 in (20–30 cm) ↑ 12–40 in (30–100 cm) /\/❈ ☀ ◆/◇ ❈ ⊡

From South Africa. Numerous, light green, wavy-edged leaves, 4–10 in (10–25 cm) long, form basal rosette. Raceme densely packed with many flowers in late summer–autumn. Pale to deep pink flowers; lip with some purple spots, almost ¾ in (18 mm) long, 5-lobed, lobes often fringed.

STENORRHYNCHOS

There are about 30 species in this genus, which is distributed in tropical and subtropical regions of the Americas. They grow as terrestrials and have thick roots and an erect inflorescence with often very bright and showy flowers in pink, orange, or red. The leaves often appear after, in some species before, flowering. CULTIVATION: Grow in small pots or shallow pans in a mixture of loam, sand, and leaf compost. The plants need regular watering when growing; reduce watering after the leaves have died back. Grow under intermediate light conditions. Propagate by division.

Stenorrhynchos lanceolatum

syns *Spiranthes lanceolata, S. orchioides, Stenorrhynchos orchioides*

LEAFLESS BEAKED ORCHID, SCARLET LADIES' TRESSES

↔ 8–14 in (20–35 cm) ↑ 16–36 in (40–90 cm) ❈ ☼ ◆ ❈ ⊡

Found in Florida in the USA, Central America, South America, and the Caribbean; grows at altitudes of 330–3,940 ft (100–1,200 m) in open wet meadows and disturbed areas such as along roadsides. Basal leaves form small rosette. Long erect stem with numerous showy flowers about 1 in (25 mm)

Stenorrhynchos speciosum

Symphoglossum sanguineum

wide. Blooms usually bright coral red, but greenish and yellow forms also known. Flowers in spring–summer.

Stenorrhynchos speciosum

↔ 4–6 in (10–15 cm) ↑ 12–24 in (30–60 cm) ❈ ☀ ◆ ❈ ⊡

Erect plant from Central America and northern South America and the West Indies. Fleshy roots. Leaves in basal rosette, sometimes marked with white. Inflorescence to 24 in (60 cm) long, with many densely packed flowers, with colored bracts as long as, or longer than the flowers, in winter–spring. Flowers showy; sepals and petals orange or red, lip white.

SYMPHOGLOSSUM

About 6 species or probably only 1 variable species are known in this genus that is distributed in Ecuador and Peru. It is found as an epiphyte in montane cloud forests at elevations of 3,940–8,530 ft (1,200–2,600 m), forming dense clumps of laterally compressed pseudobulbs, each with 2 apical leaves and several smaller leaf sheaths. The arching to pendent inflorescence bears numerous showy flowers in spring. The genus was separated from *Cochlioda* because of its different flower structure. CULTIVATION: Keep these orchids under shade during hot summer days and water regularly throughout the growth season. They grow equally well in pots in a free-draining organic substrate, or mounted on a slab with a moisture-retaining layer of sphagnum or moss. Propagate by division, but the plants do not like to be disturbed too often.

Symphoglossum sanguineum

syns *Cochlioda sanguinea, Mesospinidium sanguineum*

↔ 10–14 in (25–35 cm) ↑ 8–12 in (20–30 cm) ♀ ☼ ◆/◇ ❈ ⊡

Found in cloud forests, especially on western side of the Andes in Peru and Ecuador. Arching inflorescence, 32 in (80 cm) or more, produces up to 30 flowers in spring. Flower color is variable, ranging from light to dark pink, lip lighter colored.

Stenoglottis longifolia

S

Telipogon octavoi

TELIPOGON

This genus contains about 100 species, found from Nicaragua in the north to Venezuela in the west and east to Peru, with the highest concentration in Colombia. They grow as epiphytes, some species also as terrestrials, in high altitude, cool and wet, Andean cloud forests at altitudes of 4,600–11,480 ft (1,400–3,500 m). The plants have no pseudobulbs, and have short or elongated stems with distichous leaves. The flowers are quite showy in some species and have small sepals; the petals and lip are larger, often with prominent veining.
CULTIVATION: Species of *Telipogon* are reputedly difficult to cultivate successfully for longer periods. They need cool conditions, shade to semi-shade, and high humidity. The plants need to be watered regularly, and almost constant misting is essential. No resting period is required. Good air movement is necessary to prevent fungal diseases. The plants thrive in small pots or mounted. A key to successful cultivation is to keep the temperature below 68°F (20°C), which can be difficult during the summer months. Propagation is by division.

Telipogon octavoi
↔ 2–2½ in (5–6 cm)　↑ 10–14 in (25–35 cm)

From Ecuador; grows in very moist montane forests. Lacks pseudobulbs; opposite leaves on short cane-like growths, eventually forming small tufts. Upright inflorescence with roundish flowers, to 1¼ in (30 mm) in size, that bloom sequentially, at any time of year. Requires cool, moist, humid conditions in cultivation.

THELYMITRA

SUN ORCHID
This large genus contains about 100 terrestrial orchid species, and is primarily from Australia, with smaller outlying populations in New Zealand, New Guinea, New Caledonia, the Philippines, and Borneo. Plants produce a single thick and fleshy leaf and an upright inflorescence with a few to many flowers in late spring and summer, depending on the species. The un-orchid-like blooms have similar floral segments and lack the highly modified and specialized lip seen on most orchid species. Blues, pinks, and purples are the most common colors encountered, yet there are species with yellow, brown, and white flowers, some with additional spotting. However, it is the bright sky-blue-flowered species that has given these orchids international recognition. They are called sun orchids because the flowers will rarely open on cloudy days and evenings, relying on bright sunlight and warm temperatures for the blooms to open. The plants are dormant throughout the hot and dry Australian summers, where they retreat to underground tubers.
CULTIVATION: These colorful sun orchids rely on a mycorrhizal fungus for their survival and have proved very difficult to maintain in cultivation, with the plants annually declining in vigor before fading away. Specialist growers have had some success by growing some species in a free-draining sandy mixture incorporating a small percentage of organic matter. Propagate by division of clumps.

Thelymitra aristata
syn. *Thelymitra grandiflora*
GREAT SUN-ORCHID, SPIKED THELYMITRA
↔ 6–8 in (15–20 cm)　↑ 16–24 in (40–60 cm)

From southern and eastern Australia; grows in wooded grasslands. Lance-like leaf, to 16 in (40 cm) long, precedes an erect multi-flowered inflorescence, to 24 in (60 cm) tall. Fragrant blue

Thelymitra aristata

Thunia Veitchiana

flowers, to 1 in (25 mm) wide, open on warm sunny days in spring.

Thelymitra ixioides
↔ 4–8 in (10–20 cm)　↑ 4–40 in (10–100 cm)

Robust species from Australia. Narrow grooved leaf. Numerous flowers, to 1¼ in (30 mm) wide, pinkish blue to deep blue, often with some darker pepper spotting in center of flower. Spring-blooming.

Thelymitra matthewsii
SPIRAL SUN-ORCHID
↔ 2½–4 in (6–10 cm)　↑ 4–6 in (10–15 cm)

From open woodlands of northern New Zealand and eastern Australia. Narrow, fleshy, spiral leaf twists around flower stem at its base. Single flower, rose purple, often veined darker purple, less than ¾ in (18 mm) wide, with 2 yellow column arms above the large yellow anther cap. Spring blooms.

THUNIA

Thunia is a genus of 5 medium to large terrestrial orchids from India, Nepal, China, and Southeast Asia. The cane-like biennial stems are erect and clustered, the lower part covered with sheaths, the upper part leafy, with the leaves arranged in 2 ranks. The inflorescence is terminal, with prominent bracts. The flowers are large, showy, and scented—each one is short-lived but they are produced in succession. The sepals and petals are free, spreading, and somewhat similar; the lip is trumpet-shaped, and frilled at the apex. The name was given in honor of Graf von Thun of Tetschin (1786–1873).
CULTIVATION: The canes should be potted in a terrestrial mix and watered and fertilized freely while in growth. After flowering, plants should be dried off and kept in a cool bright place. Propagate by division or from stem cuttings.

Thelymitra ixioides

Thunia alba

syn. *Thunia marshalliana*

↔ 12–20 in (30–50 cm) ↑ 30–50 in (75–125 cm) ❦ ☀/◐ ◇/◊ ❈ ⊔

Robust plant from India, Myanmar, and China. Leaves 4–6 in (10–15 cm) long, lanceolate, gray-green. Drooping inflorescences, to 12 in (30 cm) long, of 4 to 9 flowers in summer. Fragrant flowers, about 5 in (12 cm) across; sepals and petals pure white, lip orange or yellow with purple stripes.

Thunia Veitchiana

↔ 6–20 in (15–50 cm) ↑ 8–40 in (20–100 cm) ❦ ☀/◐ ◆/◐/◊ ❈ ⊔

Primary hybrid between the seldom seen pink-flowered *T. bensoniae* and *T. marshalliana*. Vigorous-growing. Up to 5 blooms, 6 in (15 cm) in size, white, with a pale pink flush; lip heavily flushed purple coupled with orange markings. Summer-blooming.

TOLUMNIA

About 20 species are grouped in this genus, which is exclusively distributed in the Caribbean. They grow as epiphytes and lithophytes in arid forests, shrubs, grasslands, and mangroves from sea level up to 6,560 ft (2,000 m). Once known as the "variegated oncidiums," they can be easily distinguished by their growth, with the fan-shaped leaves either growing in dense clusters or on a climbing rhizome. The inflorescences are longer than the leaves and reach 32 in (80 cm) in one species.

CULTIVATION: Cultural requirements vary, depending on the species. Most species are difficult to keep alive for long periods; the hybrids are easier to grow. In general, they like bright, sunny, and rather dry conditions and intermediate to warm conditions. The minimum temperature for all species is 59°F (15°C). They should be mounted on slender twigs and misted daily, but do not wet too thoroughly. Old inflorescences should not be clipped, as often new flowers or even new shoots (keikis) appear. Propagation is by division, but separate only mature leaf fans.

Tolumnia pulchella

syn. *Oncidium pulchellum*

↔ 4–6 in (10–15 cm) ↑ 4–6 in (10–15 cm) ♀ ☼ ◆/◐ ❈ ⊔/➘

Type species of genus; found in Jamaica. Compact leaf fans. Paniculate inflorescence with up to 20 showy flowers in spring–summer. Flowers wine red to pink with a prominent lip. *T. p.* var. *concava*, rare white or whitish variety.

Tolumnia variegata

Tolumnia triquetra

syns *Olgasias triquetra, Oncidium triquetrum*

↔ 4–6 in (10–15 cm) ↑ 4–8 in (10–20 cm) ♀ ☼ ◆/◐ ❈ ➘

Compact-growing species from Jamaica. Inflorescence to 8 in (20 cm) long with showy flowers in summer–winter. Cream flowers, reddish markings on floral segments; petals distinctly triangular.

Tolumnia variegata

syn. *Oncidium variegatum*

↔ 4–6 in (10–15 cm) ↑ 4–6 in (10–15 cm) ♀ ☼ ◆/◐ ❈ ⊔/➘

Very widespread species, occurring in southern Florida in the USA, on the Bahamas, Cuba, Hispaniola, Puerto Rico, and the Virgin Islands. White flowers, sometimes washed with faint pink, with light brown markings. Flowers mainly in spring–autumn.

TRIAS

This small genus of about 10 epiphytic species comes from Southeast Asia. It is closely related to *Bulbophyllum*, but has almost triangular flowers with fleshy spreading sepals that are much larger than the petals and lip. The anther cap is elongated and often cleft. The plants are small, with a creeping rhizome, almost round single-leafed pseudobulbs, and solitary flowers, usually relatively large for the size of plant. The inflorescences arise from the base of the pseudobulb. The name

Tolumnia (hybrid)

comes from the Greek *trias*, meaning three, referring to the triangular shape of the flowers.

CULTIVATION: Species of *Trias* should be grown either mounted on a slab or grown in a shallow pan. They need high humidity and plenty of water while in growth and kept drier when resting. Propagate by division.

Trias oblonga

↔ 3–4 in (8–10 cm) ↑ 1–1½ in (25–35 mm) ♀ ☀ ◆ ❈ ⊔/➘

Dwarf species from Myanmar and Thailand. Pseudobulbs just under 1 in (25 mm) high, angled, set close together. Leaves to 1½ in (35 mm) tall; inflorescences about 1 in (25 mm) tall. Flowers yellow to yellow-green, about 1 in (25 mm) across. Spring-flowering species.

Trias picta

↔ 2½–6 in (6–15 cm) ↑ 1–1½ in (25–35 mm) ♀ ☼ ◆ ❈ ⊔/➘

Mat-forming species from Thailand and Myanmar. Single bloom, fleshy, less than ¾ in (18 mm) across, heavily peppered with fine purple dots that can give the impression of solid color. Petals and lip quite minute, sepals form bulk of flower. Flowers in spring–early summer.

Trias oblonga

Trias picta

Trichocentrum cebolleta

Trichocentrum ascendens

TRICHOCENTRUM
syn. *Acoidium*

About 20 species of this neotropical genus are known. They are found in Florida in the USA, and from Mexico to southeastern Brazil, and grow in small clusters as epiphytes in wet or seasonally dry forest at altitudes of 1,000–4,600 ft (300–1,400 m). The small pseudobulbs carry a single apical leaf. The inflorescences bear few to many very showy flowers with a prominent flat lip. Recently, some species from the related genus *Oncidium* have been moved to *Trichocentrum*.

CULTIVATION: Grow in bright light without direct sun in intermediate to warm conditions, mounted on small pieces of cork or similar material, and water regularly without a distinct resting period. The plants can be propagated by division, but do not like to be transplanted too often, as they grow very slowly.

Trichocentrum ascendens
syn. *Oncidium ascendens*
↔ 6–20 in (15–50 cm)　↕ 8–27 in (20–70 cm)
♀ ☼/☀ ◆/◈ ❄ ☌

Climbing species from the West Indies, Central America, and Colombia. Cylindrical leaves. Branching inflorescences of numerous blooms in summer. Flowers just under 1 in (25 mm) in size, red-brown and yellow.

Trichocentrum cebolleta
syns *Oncidium cebolleta, O. longifolium*
↔ 4–16 in (10–40 cm)　↕ 8–48 in (20–120 cm)　♀ ☼ ◆ ❄ ☌

Tropical species from West Indies and Central America. Reduced

pseudobulbs; long cylindrical leaves resemble a rat's tail. Sprays of up to 30 blooms, to 1½ in (35 mm) across, in summer. Greenish sepals and petals with brown spotting; large golden yellow lip.

Trichocentrum luridum
syns *Oncidium guttatum, O. luridum*
↔ 18–36 in (45–90 cm)　↕ 30–36 in (75–90 cm)　♀/⋀ ☼/☀ ◆/◈ ❄ ☌

Widespread in tropical America, from southern Florida in the USA, the West Indies, and Mexico, south to Guyana and Peru, in a variety of habitats. Very reduced pseudobulbs; large "mule ear" leaves, very stiff, thick, leathery, and erect. Tall branched inflorescences, 30–36 in (75–90 cm) high. Flowers 1–1½ in (25–35 mm) wide, yellowish or reddish with brown mottling, lip white to pink. Can bloom in any season.

Trichocentrum pulchrum
syns *Trichocentrum maculatum, T. speciosum, T. verruciferum*
↔ 4–6 in (10–15 cm)　↕ 6–8 in (15–20 cm)　♀ ☼ ◆ ❄ ☌

From Venezuela, Colombia, and southern Peru, usually found in wet montane forests at altitudes of 3,280–5,250 ft (1,000–1,600 m). Inflorescence carries 1 to 2 blooms in summer. Flowers to 2 in (5 cm) across, white or cream with red spots.

Trichocentrum splendidum
syn. *Oncidium splendidum*
↔ 20–24 in (50–60 cm)　↕ 24–48 in (60–120 cm)　♀/⋀ ☼/☀ ◆/◈ ❄ ☌

From Guatemala and Honduras; grows in lowland forests. Quite small pseudobulbs for size of plant; large, leathery, thick, "mule-ear" leaves. Tall branched inflorescences, 24–48 in (60–120 cm) high, bear long-lasting

blooms in winter. Flowers around 2½–3 in (6–8 cm) long, sepals and petals reddish brown and yellow banded, very large lip, bright yellow.

Trichocentrum tigrinum
↔ 4–6 in (10–15 cm)　↕ 6–8 in (15–20 cm)　♀ ☼ ◆ ❄ ☌

From Ecuador and northern Peru. Leaves prominently spotted with red. Flowers to 2 in (5 cm) across; sepals and petals greenish with dark purple markings, lip white with purple base and yellow center. Flowers from summer to autumn.

TRICHOGLOTTIS
syn. *Stauropsis*

About 60 species are known in this genus from eastern Asia, Malaysia, the Philippines, Indonesia, and several Polynesian islands. The monopodial epiphytes grow in lowland forests and have pendent or climbing stems with succulent distichous leaves. The small fleshy or waxy flowers appear on short stems in the leaf axils or on many-flowered racemes. The lip has the mid-lobe covered with very fine hairs.

CULTIVATION: These plants need warm temperatures, not below 59°F (15°C); light levels vary from shade to bright sun, depending on the species. They grow best in pots in a free-draining substrate or mounted. No resting period is required. Propagation is by division.

Trichoglottis atropurpurea
syn. *Trichoglottis brachiata*
↔ 3–5 in (8–12 cm)　↕ 16–32 in (40–80 cm)　♀ ☼ ◆ ❄ ☖/☌

Found in the Philippines; grows to 1,000 ft (300 m) in low rainforest. Long stems; short, ovate, distichous leaves; thick white roots. Flowers in spring–summer. Blooms light to dark purple, some looking almost velvety.

Trichocentrum splendidum

Trichocentrum splendidum, leaf

Trichoglottis geminata

syn. *Trichoglottis wenzelii*

↔ 5–10 in (12–25 cm) ↑ 8–32 in (20–80 cm)
♀ ☼/☀ ◆/◇ ❄ ☐/☀

Climbing species from Borneo, the Philippines, and Sulawesi, Indonesia. Upright habit, producing aerial roots along length of stem for support on forest trees in bright light. Highly and pleasantly fragrant blooms produced either individually or in pairs opposite leaves, in spring–summer. Flowers less than ¾ in (18 mm) in size, greenish yellow, boldly banded with 3 or 4 deep maroon stripes; long lip is predominantly white.

Trichoglottis philippinensis

syns *Arachnis philippinensis, Staurochilus philippinensis, Stauropsis philippinensis*

↔ 3–5 in (8–12 cm) ↑ 16–32 in (40–80 cm)
♀ ☼ ◆ ❄ ☐/☀

From the Philippines, range also extends to Borneo. Very similar to *T. geminata;* almost indistinguishable when not in flower. Yellowish flowers with variable brown markings; white to pink lip, can age to yellowish. Flowering mainly in spring–summer.

TRICHOPILIA

syn. *Pilumna*

Around 22 species are known in this genus, and they are distributed from Mexico to Brazil. They grow as epiphytes in medium altitude montane forests up to elevations of 9,200 ft (2,800 m). The ovate pseudobulbs are covered in bracts and carry a single leathery leaf. The hanging inflorescence appears at the base of the pseudobulbs and carries up to 5, rarely up to 8, attractive fragrant flowers with a very showy tubular lip.

CULTIVATION: *Trichopilia* species grow best under intermediate conditions in moderate shade. Because of their hanging inflorescences, they are accommodated in small baskets or mounted. When the pseudobulbs are growing, the plants need plenty of water, which should be reduced for several weeks after the pseudobulbs have matured. Otherwise, a new shoot will be produced, rather than flowers. Propagation is by division.

Trichopilia fragrans

syns *Pilumna fragrans, Trichopilia albida, T. candida, T. lehmannii*

↔ 8–12 in (20–30 cm) ↑ 8–18 in (20–45 cm)
♀ ☀ ◇ ❄ ☐/☀

Found in Peru and Ecuador at altitudes of 3,940–9,200 ft (1,200–2,800 m). Clustered pseudobulbs to 5 in (12 cm) high; leaf adds another 12 in (30 cm) to size of plant. From 2 to 5 flowers,

Trichoglottis geminata

to 4 in (10 cm) in diameter, are produced in late autumn–winter. Sepals and petals cream with light reddish spots, large white lip with bright red markings along outer lobe.

Trichopilia marginata

↔ 5–10 in (12–25 cm) ↑ 5–12 in (12–30 cm)
♀ ☼/☀ ◆/◇ ❄ ☐/☀

Found from Guatemala to Colombia. Small pendent inflorescences with up to 5 impressive blooms in spring. Flowers about 4 in (10 cm) wide; dark reddish petals and sepals; large, trumpet-like, dark red-purple lip. '**Faye**', rich pink and white flowers.

Trichopilia suavis

syn. *Trichopilia kienastiana*

↔ 8–12 in (20–30 cm) ↑ 6–12 in (15–30 cm)
♀ ☀ ◇ ❄ ☐/☀

From Costa Rica and Colombia; grows at elevations of 3,280–4,920 ft (1,000–1,500 m) in the lower forest

Trichoglottis philippinensis

story, on large moss-covered branches and trunks. Short inflorescence bears 2 to 5 blooms in early summer. Flowers to 4 in (10 cm) wide; sepals and petals cream with light reddish spots, large white lip with bright red markings along outer lobe. Also a pure white variety.

Trichopilia tortilis

↔ 5–10 in (12–25 cm) ↑ 5–10 in (12–25 cm)
♀ ☀ ◇ ❄ ☐/☀

Type species of the genus; found from Mexico to Costa Rica, at altitudes of 3,280–4,600 ft (1,000–1,400 m) in humid forests. Usually bears a single flower per inflorescence in early summer. Spirally twisted sepals and petals, yellowish with reddish brown central stripe, showy white lip.

TRIGONIDIUM

This genus contains about 20 sympodial, epiphytic and semi-terrestrial species from Central and South America. They have small clustered pseudobulbs topped with 2 or 3 long strap-like leaves. The flowers are produced singly on long peduncles, and have a most unusual shape with the 3 reflexing sepals dominating the bloom. The petals and lip are disproportionally smaller. These spring-flowering orchids are rarely seen in cultivation, being found in specialist collections and botanical gardens.

CULTIVATION: These orchids will grow well in pots using a bark-based medium. They appreciate regular watering and fertilizing and enjoy humid conditions combined with high light and intermediate to warm temperatures throughout the year. Propagate by division.

Trigonidium egertonianum

↔ 8–24 in (20–60 cm) ↑ 8–20 in (20–50 cm)
♀ ☼/☀ ◆/◇ ❄ ☐

Found from Mexico to Colombia. Mid-green strap-like leaves. Cup-shaped, pale yellow to pinkish tan, 1½ in (35 mm) wide blooms that also have finer and darker striping over the flower. Spring-blooming.

Trigonidium egertonianum

Trichopilia marginata 'Faye'

VANDA
syn. *Trudelia*

This is a group of about 50 species of sturdy monopodial orchids found from Sri Lanka and India, across Southeast Asia to New Guinea and northeastern Australia. They are erect-growing, with strap-like channeled leaves, in 2 ranks. Larger plants may branch at the base, and have numerous, very thick, cord-like roots. The inflorescences appear from the stem at the base of the leaf. They have showy long-lasting blooms, which come in a range of colors and combinations. What were previously known as the "terete-leafed vandas" have been transferred to the genus *Papilionanthe*, but in horticulture they continue to be known by their well-known, earlier name. This is one of the most important genera of plants for cut flower production in Thailand and Singapore. An extensive hybridizing program has developed using a handful of species, both within *Vanda* and in combinations with related genera.

CULTIVATION: Vandas are readily grown in wooden baskets, with the majority thriving in bright, humid, and intermediate to warm conditions, and are suited to tropical gardens and greenhouses in climates away from the tropics. They are best grown in pots using a coarse grade of pine bark as the potting medium. The thick roots will often venture outside the confines of the pot or basket, and this should be encouraged as the roots require unimpeded air circulation and must dry out quickly after watering. In the tropics many species and their hybrids bloom throughout the year, peaking in spring and summer. Propagate from cuttings with at least 3 roots attached.

Vanda alpina
syn. *Trudelia alpina*
↔ 12–20 in (30–50 cm) ↕ 3–7 in (8–18 cm)
🌺 ☀ ◆ ❋ 🍶

From northeastern India; often forms clumps. Leaves in 2 rows, 2–6 in (5–15 cm) long, narrowly oblong. Short inflorescence with 1 to 3 flowers in summer. Flowers pendent, about ¾–1 in (18–25 mm) across; sepals and petals green to yellow-green, lip green with purple markings.

Vanda coerulea ★
↔ 4–10 in (10–25 cm) ↕ 6–36 in (15–90 cm)
🌺 ❂/☀ ◆/◇ ❋ 🍶

Mountainous species found from India to China; one of the best known vandas. Erect spikes, frequently with over 12 blooms in late summer–autumn. Large, flat, spectacular, pale to deep lilac-blue, tessellated flowers, 4 in (10 cm) across. Many improved clones in cultivation.

Vanda coerulescens
↔ 10–14 in (25–35 cm) ↕ 14–20 in (35–50 cm) 🌺 ❂/☀ ◆ ❋ 🍶

Monopodial species from northeastern India, southern China, Thailand, and Myanmar; found growing in deciduous forests at altitudes of 1,640–4,920 ft (500–1,500 m). Lacks pseudobulbs; alternate leaves, to 5 in (12 cm) long, narrow, strap-like, leathery. Erect inflorescences, to 20 in (50 cm) high, appear from between leaves, with clusters of 10 to 30 blooms in autumn–spring. Fragrant flowers, 1–1½ in (25–35 mm) across, bluish-lavender to nearly white, with purple lip. '**Magnificent**', deeper blue flowers.

Vanda coerulescens

Vanda coerulescens 'Magnificent'

Vanda cristata
syn. *Trudelia cristata*
↔ 8–24 in (20–60 cm) ↕ 8–20 in (20–50 cm)
🌺 ❂/☀ ◆/◆ ❋ 🍶

Found from Nepal to China. Leathery green leaves. Greenish yellow blooms, 2 in (5 cm) wide, blood-red-marked lip divided into 2 lobes at tip. Flowers appear in summer.

Vanda denisoniana
↔ 8–16 in (20–40 cm) ↕ 8–36 in (20–90 cm)
🌺 ☀/☀ ◆/◆ ❋ 🍶

From Thailand and southern China. Arching to upright inflorescences of up to 8 long-lasting blooms in winter–spring. Flowers around 2½ in (6 cm) wide, pale yellow-green to honey-colored blooms.

Vanda hindsii
↔ 8–16 in (20–40 cm) ↕ 8–48 in (20–120 cm) 🌺 ❂/☀ ◆/◆ ❋ 🍶

From Australia and New Guinea. Up to 10 blooms, 1½ in (35 mm) in size, shiny brown with yellow edges on floral segments. Spring-flowering.

Vanda javierae
↔ 7–12 in (18–30 cm) ↕ 8–36 in (20–90 cm)
🌺 ☀ ◆/◆ ❋ 🍶

Endemic to Luzon Island in the Philippines; rare and spectacular, recently discovered species; usually found growing near water. Leathery strap-like leaves. Inflorescence with up to 8 blooms in spring. Flowers white, 2½ in (6 cm) tall, with wide segments. Related to *V. roeblingiana*, lip similar anchor shape, but coloring is white with faint pink and brown markings at base. Likes cooler temperatures and heavier shade than most vandas.

Vanda lamellata
↔ 16–18 in (40–45 cm) ↕ 16–20 in (40–50 cm) 🌺 ❂/☀ ◆/◆ ❋ 🍶

Variable species with several forms; found in seasonally dry forests in the Philippines, Taiwan, and Borneo. Typical *Vanda* habit; many strappy leaves. Inflorescence carries several to many blooms in winter–spring. Flowers around 1½–2 in (35–50 mm) wide, usually pale to greenish yellow to white with brown overlay. *V. l.* var. *boxallii*, creamy-white flowers, reddish-brown overlay on bottom half, pink lip.

Vanda luzonica
↔ 8–20 in (20–50 cm) ↕ 8–40 in (20–100 cm) 🌺 ❂/☀ ◆/◆ ❋ 🍶

Species from the Philippines. Upright inflorescence. Attractive, white, 2½ in (6 cm) flowers, pink to purple splashing and blotching on the petals and sepals. Spring-flowering.

Vanda pumila
syn. *Trudelia pumila*
↔ 10–12 in (25–30 cm) ↕ 10–20 in (25–50 cm) 🌺 ❂/☀ ◆/◆ ❋ 🍶

Erect species found from India to Indochina. Leaves narrowly lance-shaped, 4–6 in (10–15 cm) long. Short inflorescence carries 2 to 4 blooms in summer. Flowers cream, 2 in (5 cm) wide, with red and white markings on lip.

Vanda sanderiana
syn. *Euanthe sanderiana*
↔ 8–20 in (20–50 cm) ↕ 8–48 in (20–120 cm) 🌺 ❂ ◆ ❋ 🍶

Large monopodial orchid; grows in forests on Mindanao in the Philippines; from sea level up to 1,640 ft (500 m); used extensively in hybrids. Upright inflorescence with up to 10 flowers, each 4 in (10 cm) in diameter, in autumn. Dorsal sepal and petals are faint violet-pink with chocolate brown spots near base. Lateral sepals are ochre-yellow with reddish-brown veining. There is much variation in the coloring and several varieties have been described.

Vanda testacea
syn. *Vanda parviflora*
↔ 5–10 in (12–25 cm) ↕ 6–24 in (15–60 cm) 🌺 ❂/☀ ◆/◆ ❋ 🍶

Compact-growing species; found from Sri Lanka and India through to Thailand. Numerous small flowers, light yellow in color, 1 in (25 mm) in diameter, lip dark mauve-blue. Blooms in spring–summer.

Vanda tricolor
↔ 8–20 in (20–50 cm) ↕ 8–48 in (20–120 cm) 🌺 ❂/☀ ◆/◆ ❋ 🍶

From Java, Indonesia; found on rocks or trees on the fringes of lowland forest; distinctive and common species. Perfumed flowers, 2½ in (6 cm) wide, white with dark reddish brown spots; lip purple, with yellow and white patches at base. Blooms in autumn–winter.

Vanda cristata

Vanda coerulea

Vanda javierae

Vanda denisoniana

Vanda lamellata

Vanda pumila

Vanda sanderiana

Vanda tricolor

Vanda Rothschildiana (hybrid)

Vanda (hybrid)

Vanda Gordon Dillon (hybrid)

Vanda Happy Smile (hybrid)

Vanda Lumpini Red 'AM' (hybrid)

Vanda Bangkok Pink (hybrid)

Vanda Marlie Dolera (hybrid)

Vanda Pat Delight (hybrid)

Vanda Robert's Delight (hybrid)

Vanda Pranerm Prai (hybrid)

Vanda (Gordon Dillon × Robert Fuchs) (hybrid)

Vanda Manisaki (hybrid)

Vanda Sansai Blue (hybrid)

Vanda Tailor Blue (hybrid)

Vanda Hybrids

↔ 8–20 in (20–50 cm)　↑ 8–48 in
(20–120 cm)

Thousands of *Vanda* hybrids have been produced over the past century. Most of the breeding has been centered on 2 important and spectacular species, *V. coerulea* and *V. sanderiana* (syn. *Euanthe sanderiana*). *V. coerulea* is behind all of the "blue" hybrids, many of which have darker tessellations throughout the bloom, and it has also made these hybrids more adaptable to cooler growing conditions. *V. sanderiana* has passed its large round flowers on to its progeny, and is responsible for many of the pink- and brown-flowered combinations. The albino form has also been used to produce many of the green and yellow hybrids. The individual blooms of the hybrid flowers vary in size from 1½–4 in (3.5–10 cm), and are produced all year round. **Bangkok Pink**, pinkish to purple blooms with fine spotting over flower; **Gordon Dillon**, round and very dark purple-black tessellated flowers; **Happy Smile**, mustard-colored blooms, prominently spotted with brown; **Manisaki**, 4 species in its background, *V. dearei*, *V. tricolor*, *V. luzonica*, and *V. sanderiana*; **Marlie Dolera**, needs strong light to bloom well; **Pat Delight**, deep pink blooms overlaid with prominent red markings; **Reverend Masao Yamada**, well-shaped, colorful hybrid, characteristics from *V. sanderiana*; **Robert's Delight**, pink-flowered hybrid with heavy influence from *V. sanderiana*; **Rothschildiana** ★, popular blue- to purple-flowered vanda, primary hybrid between *V. sanderiana* and *V. coerulea*; **Sansai Blue**, deep blue hybrid, with heavy influence from *V. coerulea*.

Vanda Reverend Masao Yamada (hybrid)

Vandopsis warocqueana

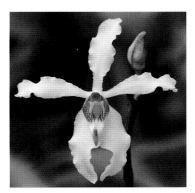

Vandopsis undulata

VANDOPSIS

This is a tropical genus of about 10 large-growing monopodial vandaceous species that are found in exposed situations, near lowland forests, throughout coastal regions of Southeast Asia. They have impressive branched flower spikes producing numerous long-lived, fleshy, and often fragrant blooms.

CULTIVATION: These orchids demand strong light to full sun and hot humid conditions to grow and bloom successfully. Because of the rambling habit of some of the species, they may be difficult to confine to pots, and are best grown on trees, being incorporated into tropical gardens. Propagate by taking off sections of the main plant with at least 3 active roots attached.

Vandopsis undulata

syns *Stauropsis undulata*, *Vanda undulata*
↔ 5–10 in (12–25 cm) ↕ 8–20 in (20–50 cm)
♀ ☼ ◆/◇ ❄ ▢/☈

From Nepal; quite different to other species in genus, does not require constant high temperatures. Erect inflorescences of up to 8 well-spaced blooms in spring. Flowers 2 in (5 cm) tall, white flushed with pink, petals and sepals with wavy edges.

Vandopsis warocqueana

syns *Sarcanthopsis nagarensis*, *Stauropsis warocqueana*
↔ 20–84 in (50–200 cm) ↕ 20–96 in (50–240 cm) ♀ ☼ ◆ ❄ ☈

Large robust species from New Guinea; grows on the fringes of lowland rainforests. Upright branched inflorescence with numerous blooms in summer–autumn. Fleshy flowers, just under 2 in (5 cm) in size, yellowish green overlaid with maroon to dark brown spotting.

VANILLA

The genus *Vanilla* consists of about 100 orchid species, which are found throughout the wetter tropical regions of the world. They are unusual in having a vine-like growth habit, with adventitious roots being produced along nodes of the stem, adjacent to the succulent leaves. Many species start life as terrestrials before becoming epiphytic. The flowers bear a similarity to the unrelated *Cattleya*, and can be quite showy, but generally only last a day. In heavy flowerings, fresh blooms are produced daily from the short racemes.

CULTIVATION: They need plenty of room to grow to their full potential. Commercially, they are often grown in pots with very long totems supporting the orchids' climbing habit, the roots adhering to the substrate. In private collections, they are often in hanging baskets, with many of the flexible stems manually turned back into the center of the plant. They need bright light and warm conditions, in a very humid environment, throughout the year. Propagate from cuttings.

Vanilla planifolia

VANILLA
↔ 1–10 ft (0.3–3 m) ↕ 1–10 ft (0.3–3 m)
♀ ☼ ◆/◇ ❄ ▢/☈

Native to Central and South America; vanilla essence is extracted from the seed capsules of this species. Often grown as a conversation piece in botanical gardens and enthusiasts' collections. Pale yellow-green flowers, 2½ in (6 cm) in size, trumpet-like lip. Also a variegated leafed form in cultivation. Spring-flowering.

Vanilla polylepis

↔ 20–80 in (50–200 cm) ↕ 40–200 in (100–500 cm) ♀ ☼/☼ ◆/◇ ▢/☈

Climbing species from tropical Africa. Leaves fleshy, to almost 10 in (25 cm) long. Sequentially flowering, short, fleshy inflorescence with up to 20 blooms in summer. Fragrant flowers, 5 in (12 cm) in size, cream to green, outstanding purple-red flared lip. Blooms only last for one day; replaced the next day by developing buds. Vine needs to be over 10–14 ft (3–4 m) tall before it will bloom.

VASCOSTYLIS

This is a trigeneric hybrid composed of the epiphytic tropical Asian genera, *Ascocentrum*, *Rhynchostylis*, and *Vanda*. There are numerous registered hybrids. The influence of *Ascocentrum* is seen in the compact plant habit and the many colorful, small to medium-sized flowers on erect spikes. *Vanda* increases flower size, and improves flower shape and substance. *Rhynchostylis* increases flower count and adds fragrance. Flower color ranges from white through yellow, pink, and red, to shades of blue and mauve. Plants grow year round, blooming mostly in autumn, winter or spring.

CULTIVATION: Vegetative offsets (keikis) forming at the base of a plant can be left in place as they will flower and increase the showiness of a specimen. Plants are best grown in bark-filled wooden baskets, under warm conditions and high light levels. Propagate by division of mature basal shoots or from seed.

Vascostylis Pine Rivers 'Pink'

↔ 8–12 in (20–30 cm) ↕ 10–20 in (25–50 cm) ♀ ☼ ◆/◇ ❄ ▢

Strap-like leaves to 8 in (20 cm) long. Erect inflorescence bears up to 50 blooms in spring. Fragrant flowers, flat, round, 1½ in (35 mm) wide, deep cherry pink. Valued in the cut flower trade.

Vanilla polylepis

Vascostylis Pine Rivers 'Pink'

V

VUYLSTEKEARA

This is a trigeneric sympodial hybrid involving *Cochlioda*, *Miltonia*, and *Odontoglossum*. Generally, the crossing of *Odontodia* with *Miltonia* has formed these colorful hybrids. They produce long, erect to arching inflorescences of shapely blooms that come in a range of colors and patterns.

CULTIVATION: *Vuylstekeara* orchids do not like their roots to dry out, so plant in sphagnum moss or a fine bark mix. They are suitable for intermediate to cool growing conditions, and need abundant water throughout the year and a part-shaded position. Give them a humid environment and plenty of air circulation. Propagate by division.

Vuylstekeara Hybrids

↔ 4–20 in (10–50 cm)   ↕ 4–24 in (10–60 cm)

Members of the *Odontoglossum* alliance. Flowers range from 1½–5 in (3.5–12 cm) across the petals, and bloom in spring–autumn. **Cambria ★**, popular hybrid, mass-produced using modern tissue culture techniques, white and maroon blooms with yellow blotch on lip; **Edna 'Stamperland'**, medium-sized vibrant red and orange flowers on tall inflorescences; **Ephyra**, raspberry-colored blooms with white edging to segments; **Everglades Promise**, showy pink and red blooms, large flared lip; **Linda Isler**, numerous claret blooms, white lip; **Memoria Hanna Lassfolk** highlights the variation once 3 different genera become involved; **Memoria Mary Kavanaugh**, large purple flowers, a legacy of its parent *Miltonia spectabilis*.

Vuylstekeara Cambria (hybrid)

Vuylstekeara Everglades Promise (hybrid)

Vuylstekeara Edna 'Stamperland' (hybrid)

Vuylstekeara Ephyra (hybrid)

Vuylstekeara Memoria Hanna Lassfolk (hybrid)

Vuylstekeara Linda Isler (hybrid)

Vuyl. Memoria Mary Kavanaugh (hybrid)

WILSONARA

This is a trigeneric hybrid that combines the sympodial genera *Cochlioda*, *Odontoglossum*, and *Oncidium*. Generally, the crossing of *Odontodia* with *Oncidium* has formed these colorful hybrids, which are more tolerant of higher temperatures than most of the pure odontoglossums. They produce long, erect to arching inflorescences of shapely blooms that come in a range of colors and patterns.

CULTIVATION: These orchids do not like their roots to dry out, so the plants need to be potted in sphagnum moss or a fine bark mix. They are suitable for cool to intermediate growing conditions, and require abundant water throughout the year and a part-shaded position in a humid environment with plenty of air circulation. Propagate by division.

Wilsonara Hybrids

↔ 4–20 in (10–50 cm)   ↑ 4–24 in (10–60 cm)

Blooms may be produced at any time of year. Flowers from 1½–3½ in (3.5–9 cm) across the petals. **Athol Bell**, pale cream blooms, caramel spotting; **Blazing Lustre**, peach flowers with darker maroon spotting, contrasting white lip; **Dorset Gold**, cream blooms heavily suffused in gold tones; **Firecracker**, orange to red blooms last for up to 2 months in good conditions; **Kendrick Williams 'Rosslow'**, deep pink flowers; and **Russiker Tiger**, brown and yellow hybrid heavily influenced by *Oncidium tigrinum*.

Wilsonara Athol Bell (hybrid)

Wilsonara Blazing Lustre (hybrid)

Wilsonara Dorset Gold (hybrid)

Wilsonara Firecracker (hybrid)

Wilsonara Russiker Tiger (hybrid)

Wilsonara Kendrick Williams 'Rosslow' (hybrid)

W

Xylobium variegatum

Zygopabstia Gumeracha

XYLOBIUM

About 30 species are known in this genus. They are found throughout Central and South America, growing as epiphytes, rarely terrestrials, in forests at altitudes up to 9,840 ft (3,000 m). The greatest diversity of species is found in Andean regions from Venezuela to Peru. They are characterized by slender, almost pencil-shaped pseudobulbs with erect pleated leaves, on a sympodial rhizome. The basal inflorescence carries numerous small, rather inconspicuous, flowers.

CULTIVATION: These plants grow best in a free-draining substrate, in pots or baskets, and require intermediate to cool and bright conditions. After growth is finished, reduce watering, but keep humidity high. Propagation is by division.

Xylobium variegatum

syns *Xylobium carnosum, X. scabrilingua, X. squalens, X. supinum*

↔ 8–12 in (20–30 cm) ↕ 16–24 in (40–60 cm) ♀ ☼ ◆ ❀ ▣ ▽

Found from Costa Rica south to Peru, Bolivia, Venezuela, and Brazil at altitudes of 660–3,280 ft (200–1,000 m). Dark green ovate pseudobulbs to 3 in (8 cm) high; 2 pleated leaves. Short basal inflorescence carries a dense cluster of flowers, mostly in summer–autumn. Flowers yellowish cream with faint reddish markings, lip has darker spots, especially at tip.

ZYGOPABSTIA

syn. *Zygocolax*

Zygopabstia is a hybrid combination between the sympodial orchid genera *Zygopetalum* and *Pabstia* (syn. *Colax*). These are more compact plants than many of the zygopetalums, and have the advantage of blooming more than once a year. The individual flowers are 1½–3½ in (35–90 mm) across.

CULTIVATION: These plants enjoy intermediate to cool temperatures, under moist and shaded conditions. Avoid direct sunlight, as the leaves are prone to scorching if exposed for even short periods. The plants must be in a humid environment with plenty of air circulation, otherwise the leaf tips will dry off and the foliage may spot. Sphagnum moss or fine-grade bark is a suitable medium, and they must not be over potted. Their main bloom period is winter and spring, but many will also bloom at other times of the year once a new growth is semi-mature. Propagation is by division.

Zygopabstia Gumeracha

↔ 4–20 in (10–50 cm) ↕ 8–24 in (20–60 cm) ♀ ☼ ◆/◇ ❀ ▽

Fourth generation hybrid with *Zygopetalum maxillare, Z. intermedium,*

Z. crinitum, and *Pabstia jugosa* in its background. Blooms are green, overlaid with dark brown and maroon markings; magenta lip sometimes marked with white or cream. Flowers in winter–spring.

ZYGOPETALUM

This small genus of about 16 hardy terrestrial and epiphytic sympodial orchids is native to South America. They have tall spikes of large, showy, long-lasting, and highly fragrant flowers. There have been many hybrids made, within both *Zygopetalum* and related genera, to produce compact plants and expand and intensify the color range of the blooms.

CULTIVATION: Most zygopetalums may be grown in commercially available "orchid composts," which are generally free draining but retain some

moisture. Some growers use fine-grade pine bark, others make up their own combinations to suit their conditions and watering frequency. The epiphytic species prefer a mix incorporating a high percentage of coarse bark. They like deep pots to accommodate the vigorous root system. The plants respond to frequent watering and feeding, and like to be kept moist all year, with increased watering and fertilizing from spring to autumn while actively growing. They need high humidity and good air circulation, or leaf tips will dry off and foliage may spot. Propagate by division.

Zygopetalum crinitum

↔ 4–16 in (10–40 cm) ↕ 8–24 in (20–60 cm) ♀ ☼/☼ ◆/◇ ❀ ▽

From Brazil. Upright inflorescences of up to 8 blooms are produced in

Zygopetalum crinitum

Zygopetalum intermedium

Zygopetalum mackayi

winter–spring. Flowers to 3 in (8 cm) wide, petals and sepals yellow-green streaked with dark brown, lip white with purplish red veins and dense, fine, short hairs.

Zygopetalum intermedium

↔ 4–16 in (10–40 cm) ↕ 4–16 in (10–40 cm)
🌱 ☀ ◆/◇ ❄ ⊟

From Brazil; similar to *Z. mackayi*. Up to 6 blooms, 3 in (8 cm) wide, are carried on thick erect spikes, in autumn–winter. Fleshy green petals and sepals blotched with deep maroon-purple; fan-shaped lip, white with dark lilac veining.

Zygopetalum mackayi

↔ 4–16 in (10–40 cm) ↕ 4–16 in (10–40 cm)
🌱 ☀ ◆/◇ ❄ ⊟

From Brazil. Up to 10 blooms, 3 in (8 cm) wide, on thick erect spikes, in autumn–winter. Fleshy green petals and sepals blotched with maroon-purple; fan-shaped lip, white with dark lilac veining.

Zygopetalum maxillare

↔ 4–16 in (10–40 cm) ↕ 4–16 in (10–40 cm)
🌱 ☀ ◆/◇ ❄ ⊟/🔺

From Brazil and Paraguay. Climbing species; long distinct rhizome between pseudobulbs. Flat leaves with marked veining. Up to 6 flowers per inflorescence in winter–spring. Flowers 2½ in (6 cm) wide, bright green with varying degrees of red-brown blotches; lip bright bluish purple. Suitable for slab culture using tree fern as the medium.

Zygopetalum Hybrids

↔ 4–16 in (10–40 cm) ↕ 4–16 in (10–40 cm)
🌱/🔽 ☀ ◆/◇ ❄ ⊟

Most of the *Zygopetalum* hybrids have a heavy influence from *Z. mackayi* in their background, and this has led to similarities between many of the crossings. Plants that are more compact have been obtained by the use of *Z. maxillare* as a parent, and these may also bloom more than once a year. Flower size is 2½–3 in (6–8 cm) across the petals. (**106 'Royale Romp'** × **Redvale 'Heir Apparent'**), yellow-green flowers with dark chocolate markings, lip white with deep purple markings; **Alan Greatwood**, very shapely and round dark brownish maroon blooms with distinctive greenish edge to petals and sepals, white lip, with dark lilac veining; **Blanchetown**, light tan blooms, purple lip with darker striping;

Zygopetalum (106 'Royale Romp' × Redvale 'Heir Apparent') (hybrid)

Zygopetalum Alan Greatwood (hybrid)

Zygopetalum Blanchetown (hybrid)

Zygopetalum (hybrid)

Zygopetalum **Imagination** (hybrid)

Zygopetalum **Kiwi Dusk** (hybrid)

Imagination, dark brown blooms, deep purple lip; **Kiwi Dusk**, green blooms barred with maroon markings, contrasting white and deep lilac lip; and **Titanic**, robust fragrant hybrid.

ZYGOSEPALUM
syn. *Menadenium*

This genus contains about 6 species from northern parts of South America, where they are found in the basins of the Amazon and Orinoco rivers and their tributaries. They grow as epiphytes or terrestrials in wet lowland or montane forests at altitudes of 330–7,880 ft (100–2,400 m). The ovoid pseudobulbs, with up to 4 apical pleated leaves, are clustered or spaced apart on a creeping or climbing rhizome. The lateral inflorescence carries only one or few showy flowers with a 3-lobed lip.
CULTIVATION: Grow the epiphytic climbing species under warm conditions in shade and with ample watering throughout the year. Their habit makes them suitable for long slabs rather than pots. The terrestrial species must be grown in cool to intermediate conditions, in pots, without a resting period. Propagate by division.

Zygosepalum lindeniae
syns *Menadenium lindeniae*, *Zygopetalum lindeniae*

↔ 8–12 in (20–30 cm) ↕ 10–16 in (25–40 cm) ♀ ☀ ◆ ❀ ▢/🅵

Found in Venezuela, Brazil, and Peru; grows in rainforests and montane forests. Climbing rhizome; laterally compressed pseudobulbs. Flowers to about 3 in (8 cm) across, sepals and petals yellowish brown, lip light pink to white with prominent reddish striations. Flowers in spring–summer.

ZYGOSTATES

This genus contains approximately 9 species, occurring in southeastern Brazil, with 2 species extending into adjacent Argentina and Paraguay. They grow as epiphytes in low to medium altitude forests up to 1,640 ft (500 m). They are closely related to *Dipteranthus*, but can easily be distinguished by the lack of pseudobulbs. Leaves are glossy green, leathery, and up to 4 in (10 cm) in length. Their relatively easy culture and masses of tiny flowers make them attractive specimens.

CULTIVATION: These orchids prefer to grow in warmer areas of the intermediate section of a greenhouse. The humidity should be high year-round. Keep in shade to half-sun. The delicate plants don't like to be kept dry for longer periods. Their habit makes them most suitable to slab culture—a cork slab with moss cover is ideal. Be somewhat careful with watering in winter and provide lots of ventilation to dry the leaves after spraying. Do not replant or divide too often, plants flower more profusely when left undisturbed. Propagate by division.

Zygostates alleniana
↔ 1¼–2 in (30–50 mm) ↕ ¾–1¼ in (18–30 mm) ♀ ☀/☀ ◆ ❀ 🅵

From southern Brazil, occurring in Parana, Santa Catarina, and Rio Grande do Sul, and to the west into Argentina and Paraguay. Forms dense cushions of slender leaves, each to 1 in (25 mm) long. Masses of sprays with tiny white flowers, lip with greenish yellow side lobes, in spring.

Zygostates lunata
↔ 2–4 in (5–10 cm) ↕ 2–4 in (5–10 cm) ♀ ☀/☀ ◆ ❀ 🅵

From Brazil; occurring in Minas Gerais in the north, south to Santa Catarina; type species of the genus. Flowers in dense spikes; green sepals, greenish to orange-yellow petals, white lip. Blooms in autumn–winter.

Zygopetalum **Titanic** (hybrid)

Glossary

Acid (of soils) Having a pH below about 6. Strongly acid soils are high in organic materials such as peat; lime (calcium carbonate) is completely absent from them. Acid soils dominate in regions of higher rainfall.

Adventitious (of roots or buds) Arising at various points along a stem rather than at the base or apex or another such specific zone.

Aerial (of plant parts) Arising anywhere above the ground.

Alkaline (of soils) Having a pH above about 8. Alkaline soils usually contain lime in the form of calcium carbonate or calcium hydroxide. They occur naturally in regions of lower rainfall.

Alternate (of the arrangement of leaves on a stem) Arising one from each node in a staggered formation. Many alternate leaf arrangements are also spiral, their points of attachment forming a spiral around the stem; others are alternate and distichous, forming two rows more or less in the one plane.

Anther The pollen-containing part of a stamen, the other part being the filament (stalk).

Aphid Small sap-sucking insect of the family Aphididae, mostly wingless and translucent. Aphids feed on young foliage in large numbers and may weaken a plant. They excrete sugary droplets that attract ants.

Aquatic A plant species that grows in water for at least the greater part of its life cycle. Aquatics are divided into submerged, emergent, and floating.

Arctic (of climates) Those of lands above the Arctic Circle (latitude 66 deg 30 min North).

Aromatic As normally used, of plant smells; those of a spicy, resinous, or musky character, and often associated with foliage or fruit, in contrast to the sweet smells of flowers normally described as "fragrant."

Ascending (of stems, branches, inflorescences) Rising at a steep angle but not vertical.

Aspect The way a slope faces, which determines how much sunshine it gets, and whether in morning, evening, or at midday; or more generally the outlook of a part of a house or garden especially in relation to sunlight.

Axil The inner angle between an organ such as a leaf and the organ that supports it, usually a stem.

Axillary (of buds, flowers, inflorescences) Arising from a leaf axil.

Axis General term for any stem, rachis of inflorescence, or compound leaf, or center-line of a flower.

Backcross A hybrid resulting from crossing an existing hybrid with one of its parents, thereby increasing the proportion of genes from that parent.

Bark Outer layer of stem containing protective corky and fibrous tissues as well as the phloem, which conducts sugary sap downward. Best developed in trees, often becoming very thick with age.

Basal At or near the base of a plant's trunk, stem, leaf, etc.

Bifoliate Having only 2 leaves per shoot; used in particular for species and hybrids of the orchid genus *Cattleya* with 2 leaves per pseudobulb, as opposed to the unifoliates with only one.

Bigeneric hybrid Generic hybrid (especially of orchids) with genes from 2 different genera, as opposed to multigeneric hybrids with genes from 3 or more genera.

Binomial A scientific name consisting of two parts, the genus name and the specific epithet. *Homo sapiens* and *Cymbidium insigne* are both binomials.

Bloom General term for a flower or flower-like inflorescence; or, on leaf or fruit surfaces, a thin, delicate, white, or bluish film of wax, as on grapes or plums.

Botanical name The internationally recognized name of a plant species, genus, family, etc., usually derived from Latin or Latinized Greek elements, and published in conformity with the *International Code of Botanical Nomenclature*.

Botany The scientific study of plants.

Botrytis Botanically, a genus of microscopic fungi that cause rots in various flowers and fruits.

Bud The early stage of a flower or group of flowers, or of a leafy shoot (vegetative bud), before expanding or elongating.

Calcareous (of soils) Containing particles or nodules of calcium salts, especially calcium carbonate. Calcareous soils are formed on chalk, coral, limestone, or dolomite, but are also common in arid regions.

Calyx (plural calyces) The lowest or outermost of the layers attached to the receptacle of a flower. The calyx consists of sepals, that may be separate or partly or fully fused to one another and which are commonly green in contrast to the more colorful petals.

Cane (in gardening) A long straight branch produced by one season's growth.

Canopy (of a tree) The whole of the foliage and outer branches, the part of the tree that shades the ground; (of a forest) the uppermost layer of tree crowns.

Carpel The fundamental unit of a flower's gynoecium (female organ), usually differentiated into an ovary containing ovules (embryonic seeds), and a narrower style tipped by a stigma which receives pollen. Carpels may be single or multiple in one flower, and multiple carpels are often fused together.

Chlorophyll The green pigment in plants, mainly in the leaves, that with the aid of light energy combines carbon dioxide from the air and water from the soil to create the sap sugars that are the building blocks of plant cell-wall materials such as cellulose and lignin. The process is called photosynthesis.

Cleistogamous Having small inconspicuous flowers that are pollinated from their own anthers but do not open.

Cloud forest Also called "mist forest," "elfin forest." Forest type occurring mainly on tropical mountains frequently enveloped in cloud throughout the year, with moisture-saturated air. Trees are evergreen, often low and crooked, with trunks and limbs draped in epiphytes such as mosses, lichens, ferns, orchids, and bromeliads. Plants from these environments require high humidity and a narrow temperature range, and are usually frost-tender.

Column (in orchids) The fleshy structure in the flower's center consisting of fused style, stigma, and stamens. Similar structures are found in some other plant families.

Common name Name of a plant species that is not its botanical or scientific name and has no scientific status. Common names are generally in the language of the country where the plant is growing. A species may have many common names, or if obscure may never have acquired any.

Compound (of a plant organ) Consisting of smaller units grouped together, so a compound leaf consists of two to many discrete leaflets, a compound inflorescence is a branched structure consisting of two or more basic units such as spikes, umbels, or heads.

Container Any item in which a plant may be grown out of the ground. In the nursery industry container-grown plants are the major alternative to bare-rooted plants at point of sale. Common containers are tubes, pots, tubs, and hanging baskets.

Cool-temperate (of climatic regions) Those in the cooler half of the temperate zone, where winter frosts and snow are of regular occurrence; lands at sea level that lie approximately 40–60 degrees latitude.

Corolla Collective term for the petals of a flower, which may be separate or wholly or partly fused into a tube, bell, or disc; the tubular part is then termed the corolla tube and the flared part the corolla limb, which may consist of corolla lobes (the free ends of the petals).

Cross A less formal term for hybrid, also applicable to plants resulting from cross-pollination of different races or cultivars within a species.

Cross-pollination The transmission of pollen from one plant to another plant that is not part of the same clone or cultivar, with resulting fertilization of its flowers.

Cultivar A cultivated variety that has been given a distinguishing name. A cultivar is assumed to be constant in its horticultural qualities and able to be propagated with those qualities unaltered. Modern cultivars must be given names of non-Latin form, enclosed in single quotes and capitalized, e.g., 'Our Tropics'.

Cultivated (of a plant species) Established in cultivation with its requirements known to gardeners.

Cutting A piece of plant stem (more rarely of leaf, root, or rhizome) cut off the parent plant for propagation; its lower end is inserted in soil or a sterile medium such as sand until roots form and a new plant is obtained.

Deciduous (of a plant species) Losing all leaves at a certain season of the year, usually winter in the case of cool-climate species, usually the dry season in the case of tropical species.

Decussate Arrangement of opposite leaves in which each leaf pair is oriented at right angles to the next pair below it, resulting in four vertical ranks of leaves.

Dicotyledon (or dicot) The larger of the two great classes into which the flowering plants (angiosperms) are divided, the other being the monocotyledons. As the name implies, dicotyledons have two seed leaves and additionally they mostly have net-veined leaves, flower parts in multiples of four or five, and a cambium layer in the stems.

Dioecious (of a plant species) With male and female flowers borne on different plants, so that plants of both sexes need to be present for pollination and fruit set. Flowers can be termed dioecious if of different sexes though borne on the same plant.

Diploid Plant having 2 matching sets of chromosomes, as in most wild plants. Diploids reproduce sexually with greater freedom than polyploids.

Disease Any kind of ill health or disfigurement of a plant caused by micro-organisms such as viruses, bacteria, fungi, or nematodes, or by deficiency or excess of a particular nutrient element. Distinct from pests, a term applied to more visible insects or other fauna which attack the plant.

Dispersal The natural spread of a plant to new sites, usually by seed but sometimes by bulbs, pieces of stem, or even detached leaves. A species' dispersal mechanism is the way it ensures this spread, e.g., by wind-carried seed, fruits eaten by birds which pass the seed, fruits that hook onto animal fur or human clothing.

Distichous (of leaf arrangement) Forming two rows or ranks, regardless of whether leaves are opposite or alternate; contrasted with spiral, decussate.

Diurnal (of a species' flowering habit) Opening its flowers during the daytime, generally in the morning; contrasted with nocturnal, flowers opening late afternoon or at dusk.

Division The most simple means of propagation of most clump-forming perennials, usually achieved by lifting the whole plant out of the soil or its container and cutting through the root-crown or rhizomes with a sharp blade or, for some kinds of plants, simply pulling apart, into two or more pieces, which are then replanted. Also one of the higher levels of plant classification; the flowering plants are now treated as the division Magnoliophyta.

Dormant In a state of suspended growth of a plant, usually during winter or other adverse season, and usually in a leafless state.

Dorsal The side of a plant organ that, when it is expanding from the bud, faces away from the axis to which it is attached; thus in a normal leaf the dorsal side is the underside; in an orchid flower the apparent upper sepal is referred to as the dorsal sepal, but that is because the stalks of most orchid flowers are twisted through 180 degrees.

Drainage (of soils or growing media) The means by which excess water is enabled to flow away by gravity, so opening up air spaces needed by the roots of most plants for absorption of gases, principally oxygen. In gardens, good drainage is ensured by raising of beds, improving soil texture, or inserting special drainage pipes and/or gravel beds beneath the soil. In container-grown plants drainage is achieved by adequate number and size of holes in the base, and sometimes by a layer of coarse, rot-resistant material (traditionally "crocks" from broken clay pots) below the growing medium, which itself should be open and free-draining.

Elliptic (of leaves, petals, etc.) In the shape of an ellipse but commonly with both ends more or less pointed.

Emarginate (of leaf apex) Slightly indented, though not with a very large, broad indentation.

Endemic (of a species, genus, etc.) Occurring in the wild only in one readily defined geographical region, e.g., *Aerides lawrenciae* is endemic to the island of Mindanao in the Philippines.
Epiphyte (of a plant species) One that habitually grows in the wild on the branches or trunk of a tree, well above the ground. Epiphytes do not feed on living tissues of their host but on dead bark, leaf litter, and dust, often using a symbiotic fungus to extract nutrients from these. Most cultivated orchids are epiphytes.
Equitant (of leaves) Overlapping at the bases.
Erect Directed vertically upward or almost so.
Evergreen (of a plant species) Maintaining its foliage through all seasons, although old leaves may be shed in larger numbers in certain seasons.
Exotic (of a plant species) One that is not native to the country or region in question.
Fertilize (in gardening and agriculture) To add nutrients to soil; (in botany) to bring pollen to a stigma and effectively pollinate it so that the pollen nucleus combines with the egg nucleus in the ovule.
Fertilizer Any material added to the soil to provide nutrients for plants, including compost, manure, manufactured chemicals such as urea, potassium sulfate, or superphosphate, and liquid extracts such as fish emulsion.
Filament The stalk of a stamen, bearing the anther at its tip.
Flower The reproductive organ of all members of the flowering plants (angiosperms) consisting typically of a perianth which is often differentiated into calyx and corolla, a group of stamens that release pollen, and one or more carpels containing ovules that on fertilization develop into seeds. Many flowers are reduced in structure with some of these parts missing.
Foliage Leaves and twigs in mass, a term used only in the singular.
Frost The condition of air temperature falling below the freezing point of water (32°F or 0°C), resulting in formation of ice crystals if the air contains moisture. Because cold air sinks, frost may occur at soil level when temperature at standard meteorological measuring height (5 ft or 1.5 m) is several degrees above freezing. In dry air there may be no ice crystals (hoar frost) formed but plant foliage may be killed; such an event is known as a "black frost."
Fungicide A chemical applied for the control of fungal parasites of plants.
Fusiform (of roots) Spindle-shaped, so that they taper from the middle to each end.
Genus (plural genera) The next level of botanical classification above species. The genus name can stand by itself, e.g., *Dendrobium*, but it also forms the first part of a species name, e.g., *Dendrobium kingianum*.
Germination The emergence of a new plant from a seed, mostly requiring absorption of water by the seed and certain temperature and light levels.
Greenhouse An enclosed structure with roof of transparent or translucent material, traditionally glass but nowadays usually plastic, in which plants are grown, its purpose being to raise the temperature of their environment and so protect them from winter frost and/or promote faster growth even in summer in cool climates. Greenhouses may be heated artificially or unheated, relying on their capacity to absorb and trap solar radiation. In normal use a greenhouse is a high-roofed structure distinguished from a frame, cloche, tunnel, or "igloo." The term greenhouse is now preferred over both "glasshouse" and "hothouse."
Grex All the progeny of a cross between two species, two gregi (plural of grex), or a species and a grex, regardless of when and where the crossing occurred; a concept applied in practice in only in a few groups of plants, notably orchid and rhododendron hybrids. A grex name is similar in form to a cultivar name but without quotation marks, and may precede a cultivar name, e.g., *Masdevallia* Carousel 'Parade'. A single grex may include many named cultivars.
Growing season The season in which growth of a particular plant takes place, in cool-temperate climates nearly always between spring and the end of summer, in drier tropical climates nearly always the wet season.
Growth habit The overall form or shape of a plant.
Habitat (of a species) The sum of geographical location, soil, topography, and vegetation type in which a species is normally found wild.
Horticulture The practice of growing plants, and other aspects of gardening. Commercial horticulture (as opposed to agriculture) embraces the growing of fruit, nuts, and cut-flowers, as well as the nursery and landscape industries.
House plant Any plant grown full-time for ornament inside a house, generally being a species or cultivar able to tolerate low light levels and other adverse environmental factors associated with house interiors.
Humus The organic matter in soil, derived in nature from leaf and twig litter, dead roots, and decayed tree trunks; in gardens it can be added in the form of compost, manure, or peat. Humus greatly improves soil by retaining moisture and mineral nutrients and keeping the soil open and well aerated.
Hybrid The progeny resulting from fertilization of a species, variety, or cultivar by a different species, variety, or cultivar, combining the genetic makeup of both. The progeny of hybrids continue to be hybrids. Botanical names of hybrids between 2 species are indicated by the multiplication sign "×" inserted in one of 2 positions, namely: (a) where no hybrid name has been published—between the names of the two parent species, e.g., *Paphiopedilum* (Raisin Eyes × Maudiae); (b) where a hybrid name has been published for a hybrid between 2 species—before the epithet, e.g., *Cattleya* × *guatemalensis* [*C. skinneri* × *C. aurantiaca*]. Where 3 or more species are involved in a hybrid, the "×" sign is not used; the resulting hybrid may be given a grex name, or a cultivar name is used directly following the genus name.
Indigenous (of plant species or subspecies) Forming part of the original natural flora of a country or region (though not necessarily endemic); thus, *Dendrobium speciosum* is indigenous to Australia.
Inflorescence Specialized flower-bearing branch of a plant, together with the flowers on it.
Insecticide A substance, nowadays usually of synthetic chemical origin, used to kill insect pests (see also pesticide). Modern insecticides are mostly designed to target biochemical processes specific to insects or even particular types of insects, and to have low toxicity to humans and other vertebrate animals.
Intergeneric hybrid Hybrid with species of 2 or more different genera in its parentage, most commonly created in orchids. Generally distinguished by a hybrid botanical name, formed in accordance with the following rules: (a) where published for a hybrid between species of 2 different genera (a bigeneric hybrid), the name combines elements of the names of the parent genera and may be (but is not necessarily) preceded by a multiplication sign "×," e.g., *Laeliocattleya* [*Laelia* × *Cattleya*]; (b) where published for a hybrid between 3 or more genera, the name is taken from a person's name followed by the suffix *–ara*, e.g., *Wilsonara*, which has species of *Odontoglossum, Oncidium,* and *Cochlioda* in its parentage. Alternatively, so as to cover existing names such as *Sophrolaeliocattleya*, the rule allows for names of trigeneric hybrids to be formed in the same way as bigeneric.
Internode The interval between two successive nodes on a plant stem or twig.
Keiki An orchid's aerial growth, which is produced randomly along a section of pseudobulb.
Labellum In an orchid flower, the usually large and distinctively shaped petal that commonly juts forward from the flower's center; it is technically the upper of the 3 petals (or inner perianth segments), but because most orchid flowers have stalks twisted through 180 degrees, it may appear to be the lower. The various protuberances and color patterns on an orchid labellum are nearly always adaptations to attract and guide pollinating agents, principally insects.
Leaf The plant organ that is primarily responsible for photosynthesis.
Lip An upper or lower lobe, or group of several lobes, of the usually tubular corolla of a flower with a single vertical plane of symmetry (zygomorphic). Most such flowers are 2-lipped.
Lithophyte A plant species that habitually grows on rocks, virtually in the absence of soil. Many epiphytes are also capable of growing as lithophytes.
Mealybug Small sap-sucking insects of the family Coccidae (to which scale insects also belong), wingless, slow-moving, and covered in a whitish water-repellent powder. They infest and weaken plants, often hiding among leaf bases or underground parts, and may be difficult to control.
Mericlone A plant resulting from the division of a selected cultivar's meristem tissue into minute pieces and culturing them in a sterile medium in a laboratory, using auxins to initiate root and shoot development. Mericloning allows rapid production of large numbers of identical and disease-free plants.
Microclimate The climate of any small area as modified by local topography, vegetation, structures, or activities, in contrast to the regional climate. For example, the shelter of trees or masonry walls may create a frost-free microclimate in an otherwise frosty climate. Microclimates are an important part of plant habitats, both in gardens and in the wild.
Monocotyledon (or monocot) A plant belonging to the smaller of the two great classes into which the flowering plants (angiosperms) are divided, the larger being the dicotyledons. As the name implies, monocotyledons have only one seed leaf and additionally they mostly have parallel-veined leaves, flower parts in multiples of three, and no cambium layer in the stems. Only a minority of monocotyledons are trees or shrubs, for example the palms, aloes, yuccas, dracaenas, and cordylines.
Monopodial (of a species' growth habit) Characterized by each shoot having a continuing apical growing point which, at least for a period of years, maintains dominance over the lateral shoots that branch from its leaf axils. Contrasted with sympodial, in which growth is always continued by lateral shoots. This distinction is important in orchid genera, which are always either monopodial (as in *Vanda* and its allies) or sympodial (as in *Cattleya*).
Monotypic Describes a taxon, in particular a genus, family, order, class, or division, that has only one member at the next lower level in the hierarchy. Thus *Schistostylus* is a monotypic genus, with only a single species, *S. purpuratus*.
Mycorrhiza A fungus that invades the root tissues of a plant and forms a symbiotic relationship with it. The plant benefits because the fungus can digest organic matter that occurs in the surrounding soil, converting it to simpler molecules such as sugars that the plant can absorb more easily, while the fungus is assured of access to moisture.
Native (of a species) Forming part of the original wild flora of the country or region under consideration. See also indigenous.
New World Traditional term for all of the Americas, going back to Columbus's time. Contrasted with the Old World.
Node The region of a stem to which a leaf or leaves are attached. If leaves are alternately arranged then there is only one leaf per node, but if opposite then there are two, and if whorled, three or more. Nodes alternate with internodes on a stem.
Non-resupinate (of flowers) Not upside down.
Old World Traditional collective term for Europe, Asia, Africa, Australia, and all nearby islands, as contrasted to the New World. The concept only arose following Columbus's discovery of the Americas.
Opposite (of leaves) Attached to the stem in pairs, on opposite sides of a node.
Orchid Any member of the very large monocot family Orchidaceae, exceeded in number of species only by the dicot family Asteraceae (composites or daisies), occurring in most of the world's lands but most diverse in the tropics, where the great majority grow as epiphytes. Orchids have zygomorphic flowers of elaborate structure, capsular fruits containing vast numbers of minute seeds featuring no food reserves, and roots that contain symbiotic fungal mycorrhiza, essential for the orchid's nutrition. They are little used by humans except as ornaments, but are grown and collected by a

vast number of enthusiasts around the world, and their flowers are sold in every florist's shop.

Ovary (in flowers) The swollen part of the female organ containing the ovules.

Ovule The future seed but before fertilization; in flowering plants enclosed in the ovary but in conifers and cycads borne on the scale of a cone.

Peat The remains of dead plants that have been preserved in a wet acid environment for long periods (thousands, even millions of years), becoming compressed and darkened. Large deposits are mined, the peat used for fuel, for soil improvement, and for horticultural potting media. The best peat is moss peat, derived largely from sphagnum moss, but sedge peat is also available.

Perianth The parts of a flower that enclose the sexual organs in bud, normally the combined petals (corolla) and sepals (calyx). Used mainly for flowers where petals are not clearly distinguishable from sepals, in which case they are all termed perianth-segments.

Pest (in gardening) Mostly insects or other small fauna that feed on plants, either weakening them or disfiguring them. Contrast with disease.

Pesticide General term for chemicals used to kill undesirable organisms, whether weeds, fungi, insects, snails, etc.—though the more precise terms are herbicide, fungicide, insecticide, molluscicide, etc.

Petal One of the inner layer of the 2 layers of organs that surround the sexual organs of a flower, the outer being the sepals. Petals are often thin and colorful or white, and are seldom green like sepals. The petals of one flower are collectively termed the corolla. They may be fused into a tube, bell, or funnel, or may be absent.

Photosynthesis The process that takes place in green leaves of plants. With the aid of the pigment chlorophyll and the sun's energy, water from the soil and carbon dioxide from the air are combined to produce the carbohydrates (initially sugars) essential to the formation of new tissues.

Pollen The dust-like material produced by the male organs of both flowering plants and gymnosperms, each tiny grain containing a male nucleus that combines with a female nucleus in an ovule to produce a seed. In flowering plants a pollen grain is received on the stigma and "germinates," producing an extremely fine tube that grows down through the style and into an ovule, the nucleus descending through this tube.

Pollination The mechanism by which pollen is transferred from stamens to stigma, whether in the same flower or different flowers, or on different plants. Agents of pollination include wind, insects, and birds; pollen can be deliberately transferred by humans.

Polyploid A species, subspecies, or cultivar having more than 2 matching sets of chromosomes; includes triploids (3 sets), tetraploids (4 sets), and hexaploids (6 sets). Polyploids may show increases in size and vigor compared with the more usual wild diploids, but often have impediments to normal sexual reproduction.

Pot A container for growing a plant in, in common usage being one of small to medium size (under about 12 in or 30 cm diameter) and usually tapering slightly from top to bottom, with a drainage hole or holes in the base. Smaller, more elongated containers are generally called "tubes"; broad shallow containers for bulbs or orchids are "pans"; larger pots, heavy to lift, are "tubs."

Propagation The practice of multiplying plants artificially, whether by seed, cuttings, layers, grafts, divisions, or tissue culture.

Pseudobulb A bulb-like storage organ that is not a bulb, i.e., does not consist of concentrically arranged leaves modified for food storage. Used almost exclusively for the stems of sympodial orchid genera, based on the bulb-like form of some, e.g., *Cymbidium*, *Lycaste*, but among orchid growers its use has extended to some much more elongated or slender stems, as in many *Dendrobium* species.

Raceme An unbranched inflorescence consisting of an elongated stem or rachis bearing a succession of stalked flowers, the youngest at the tip.

Rachis (rhachis) Any elongated stem other than a leafy shoot bearing organs distributed along its length, as in the central stalk of a pinnate leaf or the stem of a raceme.

Rainforest Luxuriant forest with a completely closed canopy developed in areas of high rainfall. Tropical rainforest is characterized by a great diversity of tree species and abundance of lianes and epiphytes, while temperate rainforest may have only three to six tree species.

Rhizomatous (of a plant species) Having rhizomes as its form of food storage or mode of spread.

Rhizome A stem that runs horizontally along or below the soil surface, putting out roots along its length and sending up erect shoots at intervals; it may be swollen and behave as a storage or overwintering organ.

Root The organ of absorption of water and mineral nutrients, as well as of anchorage to the soil, in the higher plants. Roots are distinguished from underground stems (such as rhizomes) by their anatomical structure.

Sand The coarsest component of most soils, defined as having particles more than 0.5 mm but less than 2 mm in diameter (larger particles are classed as gravel). Sands are composed of hard minerals, in most cases predominantly quartz which is almost pure silica, extremely hard, and virtually insoluble in water; but beach sands may also contain shell grit, which is chemically similar to limestone.

Saprophyte A plant or fungus that is able to make use of dead organic matter (such as leaf litter, fallen logs, or straw) as its source of nutrition. A large proportion of the fungi are saprophytes, but saprophytic flowering plants require a symbiotic relationship with a lower organism, usually a fungus, in or around their roots.

Savanna (savannah) A common vegetation type in the tropics consisting of grassland with sparsely scattered trees, occurring on plains in regions of highly seasonal rainfall.

Scale insect Any of a group of sap-sucking insect of the family Coccidae (to which mealybugs also belong) that in its adult state covers itself with a layer of wax and becomes virtually immobile. Some scale insect species are garden pests and may cause major damage to commercial plantings.

Sclerophyll Term describing a species whose leaves are somewhat harsh and rigid due to containing a high proportion of cellulose and woody tissues. Especially common among Australian shrubs, it is believed to be an adaptation to very infertile soils.

Seed Organ of reproduction and dispersal of flowering plants and gymnosperms (collectively called the seed plants), developing enclosed in the fruit of the former or on scales of female cones of the latter. A seed consists of a plant embryo, food storage tissue, and a protective seed coat. A seed may remain dormant for a long period before its germination is initiated by moisture and warmth.

Sepal One segment of the calyx of a flower. Sepals are usually green in contrast to the colored petals; they may be fused to one another, at least toward their bases.

Species (abbreviation sp., plural spp.) The basic unit of plant classification, usually consisting of a population of individuals that are fairly uniform in character and breed freely with one another over many generations without obvious change in their progeny. A species is normally unable to breed with another species or if it does, the resulting progeny do not remain constant or do not produce viable seed. The scientific name of a species consists of the name of the genus to which it belongs, followed by a name referred to as the specific epithet, e.g., *Fernandezia subbiflora*.

Speculum Shiny square to U-shaped area found on the lip of some orchids.

Sphagnum Mosses belonging to the genus *Sphagnum*, found in largest quantities in cooler regions of world where they grow in extensive bogs. Sphagnum can absorb and retain many times its own weight of water while remaining well aerated and is therefore valued in horticultural growing media. Peat, or at least moss peat, is mainly fossilized sphagnum.

Stamen The male reproductive organ in a flower, consisting typically of a slender stalk (filament) and a pollen-sac (anther), which opens by a slit or pore to release pollen. The stamens form the third row of organs from the outside of a flower, inside the sepals and petals.

Stem The organ of a plant that supports leaves and flowers, and to which the roots attach; in the broadest sense, any shoot, trunk, branch, or twig is a stem. Distinguished from a stalk.

Stigma The apical part of a carpel, or of two or more fused carpels, that is receptive to pollen, often separated from the ovary by a slender style.

Style The slender portion of a carpel, or of several fused carpels, between the ovary and the stigma.

Subarctic (of climates) Those characteristic of lands just outside the Arctic Circle.

Substrate Any material on or in which a plant is rooted, e.g., soil, sand, rock, bark.

Subtropical (of climates) Those characteristic of lands just outside the tropical zones, generally warm and frost free, at least in coastal regions.

Sympodial (of a species' growth habit) Characterized by each shoot having limited growth, stopping after one to several nodes are formed and often terminating in an inflorescence, with growth continuing from a lateral shoot, the process being repeated indefinitely and often following a seasonal rhythm. Contrasted with monopodial, the distinction being especially important between orchid genera.

Synonym Any name referring to the same species or genus as another name, though usually taken to mean the name that is currently not accepted; thus *Neolehmannia porpax* is a synonym of *Epidendrum porpax*, now the accepted name for the beetle orchid. When a genus has been merged with or split from another genus, the synonym is never the larger or older genus.

Synsepal Section of a flower where two or more sepals are fully or partly fused together.

Taxonomy The science and practice of classifying and naming living organisms.

Temperate (of climates) Those of lands lying between the Tropic of Cancer and the Arctic Circle, or between the Tropic of Capricorn and the Antarctic Circle—but climates close to the tropics (within about 10 degrees of latitude) are generally termed subtropical, and those close to the Arctic Circle are termed subarctic. Temperate climates may also be found at high altitudes in the tropics. See also cool-temperate and warm-temperate.

Tepal Alternative term for perianth-segment in flowers where the petals and sepals are not strongly differentiated. Used mainly for plants in the lily group of monocot families.

Terrestrial (of a species) Normally found in the ground and on dry land, as opposed to epiphytic or aquatic.

Tessellated (of tree bark) Broken up into small squares or other angular shapes, like floor tiles.

Tetraploid (of a hybrid or cultivar) One with double the normal set of chromosomes of its diploid wild relatives, i.e., with four matching sets of chromosomes instead of two sets. Tetraploids are sometimes created artificially by plant breeders and tend to be larger in all their parts. See also polyploid.

Tropical (of climates, species) Occurring in the tropics, that is, in lands between the Tropic of Cancer and Tropic of Capricorn.

Truncate (of leaf apex or base) Cut off more or less squarely.

Vandaceous Those monopodial genera of orchids comprising *Vanda* and its close allies, frequently combined in generic hybrids.

Variegated (of leaves) Mottled, streaked, edged, or striped with colors (mostly white to yellow) other than the normal green of wild plants. They are mostly found in ornamental cultivars; the term is less commonly applied to flowers.

Vein A visible strand of conducting tissue in a leaf or a petal.

Viscidium Sticky substance in flowers that allows pollen to attach to or be removed from the pollinating insect.

Warm-temperate (of climates) Those of lands in the warmer halves of the temperate zones, at latitudes between about 25 and 40 degrees.

Xerophyte A plant adapted to dry climates and capable of surviving through droughts other than by seeds or bulbs.

Zygomorphic (of flowers) Having only one vertical plane of symmetry, e.g., as in nearly all orchids. Contrasted with "actinomorphic," in which a plane of symmetry passes through each petal and sepal.

Cultivation Table

The following cultivation table features at-a-glance information for every species or hybrid with an individual entry in *Flora's Orchids*. Simply find the plant you wish to know more about, and run your eye along the row to discover its height and spread, whether it has showy and/or scented flowers, whether it is drought and/or frost tolerant, the aspect it prefers, and more. The last column is marked for the plant if that plant is protected by Appendix I of CITES.

The type of plant is abbreviated to **E**, **L**, or **T**:

E = the plant is an epiphyte.

L = the plant is a lithophyte.

T = the plant is a terrestrial.

The temperature requirements that each plant needs to thrive are given (some plants will grow in more than one temperature range), abbreviated to **W**, **I**, or **C**:

W = warm-growing plants that prefer a winter nighttime minimum of 60°F (16°C); these plants are very unforgiving if temperatures drop below 50°F (10°C), but can take high temperatures as long as the humidity is high.

I = intermediate-growing plants that prefer a winter nighttime minimum of 50°F (10°C); these plants can take cooler temperatures for short lengths of time.

C = cool-growing plants that prefer a winter nighttime minimum of 39°F (4°C); keep these plants cooler in summer.

Plant name	Height	Spread	Type	Temp.	Showy flowers	Scented flowers	Grow in pot	Grow on mount	Keep moist	Dry winter	Drought tolerant	Frost tolerant	Full sun	Half sun	Shade	CITES listed
Acacallis cyanea	6–12 in (15–30 cm)	8–12 in (20–30 cm)	E	W			♦	♦						♦	♦	
Acampe ochracea	16–24 in (40–60 cm)	16–24 in (40–60 cm)	E	W/I	♦	♦							♦			
Acampe papillosa	24–36 in (60–90 cm)	12–24 in (30–60 cm)	E	W/I	♦	♦								♦		
Acampe rigida	8–60 in (20–150 cm)	12–24 in (30–60 cm)	E	W/I	♦	♦								♦		
Acanthephippium mantinianum	24–30 in (60–75 cm)	12–24 in (30–60 cm)	T	I	♦		♦								♦	
Aceras anthropophorum	4–24 in (10–60 cm)	4–12 in (10–30 cm)	T	C			♦				♦		♦			
Acianthus confusus	2½–4 in (6–10 cm)	1 in (25 mm)	T	I			♦		♦						♦	
Acianthus exsertus	2–4 in (5–10 cm)	½–1½ in (12–35 mm)	T	I/C			♦		♦					♦	♦	
Ada aurantiaca	10–16 in (25–40 cm)	8–16 in (20–40 cm)	E/L	C			♦				♦			♦	♦	
Ada glumacea	8–12 in (20–30 cm)	8–16 in (20–40 cm)	E/L	C			♦				♦			♦		
Ada keiliana	6–12 in (15–30 cm)	8–16 in (20–40 cm)	E	C	♦	♦	♦				♦			♦	♦	
Aerangis biloba	5–8 in (12–20 cm)	4–16 in (10–40 cm)	E	W/I	♦	♦		♦	♦						♦	
Aerangis citrata	2½–5 in (6–12 cm)	5–12 in (12–30 cm)	E	W/I	♦	♦	♦	♦	♦					♦		
Aerangis cryptodon	6–15 in (15–38 cm)	6–15 in (15–38 cm)	E	W/I	♦	♦	♦	♦	♦					♦		
Aerangis distincta	6–8 in (15–20 cm)	5–10 in (12–25 cm)	E	I	♦	♦		♦							♦	
Aerangis ellisii	16–32 in (40–80 cm)	8–16 in (20–40 cm)	E/L	I	♦	♦	♦	♦	♦						♦	♦
Aerangis kotschyana	4–8 in (10–20 cm)	6–18 in (15–45 cm)	E	W/I	♦	♦		♦							♦	
Aerangis rhodosticha	2½–7 in (6–18 cm)	4–10 in (10–25 cm)	E	W/I	♦	♦		♦							♦	
Aeranthes caudata	32–48 in (80–120 cm)	12–16 in (30–40 cm)	E	I			♦		♦						♦	
Aeranthes grandiflora	6–12 in (15–30 cm)	12–16 in (30–40 cm)	E	W			♦	♦	♦						♦	

Plant name	Height	Spread	Type	Temp.	Showy flowers	Scented flowers	Grow in pot	Grow on mount	Keep moist	Dry winter	Drought tolerant	Frost tolerant	Full sun	Half sun	Shade	CITES listed
Aerides crassifolia	8–20 in (20–50 cm)	8–16 in (20–40 cm)	E	W/I	◆	◆	◆	◆	◆				◆	◆		
Aerides falcata	8–40 in (20–100 cm)	8–20 in (20–50 cm)	E	W/I	◆	◆	◆	◆	◆				◆	◆		
Aerides houlletiana	8–24 in (20–60 cm)	8–20 in (20–50 cm)	E	W/I	◆	◆	◆	◆	◆				◆	◆		
Aerides krabiensis	8–24 in (20–60 cm)	6–10 in (15–25 cm)	E	W	◆	◆	◆	◆	◆				◆	◆		
Aerides lawrenciae	12–48 in (30–120 cm)	12–27 in (30–70 cm)	E	W	◆	◆	◆	◆	◆				◆	◆		
Aerides leeana	8–16 in (20–40 cm)	12–20 in (30–50 cm)	E	W/I	◆	◆	◆	◆	◆						◆	
Aerides multiflora	8–36 in (20–90 cm)	8–24 in (20–60 cm)	E	I	◆	◆	◆	◆	◆				◆	◆		
Aerides odorata	8–72 in (20–180 cm)	8–40 in (20–100 cm)	E	W/I	◆	◆	◆	◆	◆				◆	◆		
Aerides quinquevulnera	8–40 in (20–100 cm)	8–16 in (20–40 cm)	E	W/I	◆	◆	◆	◆	◆				◆	◆		
Aerides rosea	8–36 in (20–90 cm)	8–24 in (20–60 cm)	E	I	◆	◆	◆	◆	◆				◆	◆		
Amesiella monticola	2–4 in (5–10 cm)	4–6 in (10–15 cm)	E	I	◆		◆	◆	◆					◆	◆	
Amesiella philippinensis	1¼–2 in (3–5 cm)	2–4 in (5–10 cm)	E	W	◆		◆	◆	◆					◆	◆	
Anacamptis pyramidalis	8–32 in (20–80 cm)	4–10 in (10–25 cm)	T	C		◆					◆	◆	◆			
Ancistrochilus rothschildianus	4–14 in (10–35 cm)	6–10 in (15–25 cm)	E/T	I	◆		◆	◆	◆	◆			◆			
Angraecum calceolus	10–12 in (25–30 cm)	12–15 in (30–38 cm)	E	I/C	◆	◆	◆	◆	◆						◆	
Angraecum didieri	4–6 in (10–15 cm)	4–6 in (10–15 cm)	E	I	◆	◆		◆	◆				◆			
Angraecum distichum	6–10 in (15–25 cm)	6–8 in (15–20 cm)	E	W/I	◆	◆	◆		◆						◆	
Angraecum eburneum	12–30 in (30–75 cm)	20–40 in (50–100 cm)	E/L	W/I	◆	◆	◆		◆				◆			
Angraecum firthii	3–4 ft (0.9–1.2 m)	4–6 in (10–15 cm)	E	I	◆	◆	◆	◆	◆					◆	◆	
Angraecum infundibulare	3–10 ft (0.9–3 m)	6–8 in (15–20 cm)	E	W	◆	◆	◆		◆						◆	
Angraecum Lemforde White Beauty	8–12 in (20–30 cm)	8–12 in (20–30 cm)	E	I	◆	◆	◆		◆					◆	◆	
Angraecum scottianum	3–12 in (8–30 cm)	3–6 in (8–15 cm)	E	I/C	◆	◆	◆	◆	◆				◆			
Angraecum sesquipedale	8–36 in (20–90 cm)	12–24 in (30–60 cm)	E	W/I	◆	◆	◆		◆				◆			
Angraecum Veitchii	8–40 in (20–100 cm)	12–24 in (30–60 cm)	E/L	W/I	◆	◆	◆		◆				◆			
Anguloa clowesii	16–24 in (40–60 cm)	12–24 in (30–60 cm)	T	I/C	◆		◆		◆					◆		
Anguloa hohenlohii	16–24 in (40–60 cm)	12–24 in (30–60 cm)	T	I/C	◆		◆		◆					◆		
Anguloa uniflora	16–24 in (40–60 cm)	12–24 in (30–60 cm)	T	I/C	◆		◆		◆					◆		
Angulocaste Jupiter × *Anguloa hohenlohii*	16–24 in (40–60 cm)	24–36 in (60–90 cm)	E/T	I/C	◆		◆		◆						◆	
Angulocaste Rosemary	16–24 in (40–60 cm)	24–36 in (60–90 cm)	E/T	I/C	◆		◆		◆				◆			
Anoectochilus koshunensis	2–6 in (5–15 cm)	8–12 in (20–30 cm)	T	I	◆		◆		◆						◆	
Ansellia africana	16–40 in (40–100 cm)	16–60 in (40–150 cm)	E	I	◆	◆	◆	◆		◆		◆	◆			

Plant name	Height	Spread	Type	Temp.	Showy flowers	Scented flowers	Grow in pot	Grow on mount	Keep moist	Dry winter	Drought tolerant	Frost tolerant	Full sun	Half sun	Shade	CITES listed
Arachnis flos-aeris	3–15 ft (0.9–4.5 m)	20–32 in (50–80 cm)	E/L	W	♦	♦		♦	♦				♦			
Arachnis hookeriana	3–15 ft (0.9–4.5 m)	12–20 in (30–50 cm)	E/L	W	♦			♦	♦				♦			
Aranda Noorah Alsagoff	16–24 in (40–60 cm)	12–20 in (30–50 cm)	E	W	♦		♦	♦	♦				♦			
Aranthera Beatrice Ng	16–84 in (40–200 cm)	12–24 in (30–60 cm)	E	W	♦			♦	♦				♦			
Arpophyllum giganteum	16–32 in (40–80 cm)	12–36 in (30–90 cm)	E	W/I	♦		♦							♦		
Arpophyllum spicatum	32–48 in (80–120 cm)	12–20 in (30–50 cm)	E/L/T	W/I	♦		♦							♦		
Arundina graminifolia	16–84 in (40–200 cm)	12–36 in (30–90 cm)	T	W	♦		♦						♦			
Ascocenda Hybrids	16–48 in (40–120 cm)	12–24 in (30–60 cm)	E	W	♦		♦						♦			
Ascocentrum ampullaceum	6–10 in (15–25 cm)	8–12 in (20–30 cm)	E	W/I	♦		♦							♦	♦	
Ascocentrum aurantiacum subsp. *philippinense*	4–16 in (10–40 cm)	8–12 in (20–30 cm)	E	W/I	♦		♦	♦	♦				♦			
Ascocentrum christensonianum	4–8 in (10–20 cm)	8–12 in (20–30 cm)	E	W	♦		♦							♦	♦	
Ascocentrum garayi	5–12 in (12–30 cm)	5–10 in (12–25 cm)	E	W			♦						♦			
Ascoglossum calopterum	12–20 in (30–50 cm)	8–16 in (20–40 cm)	E	W				♦	♦				♦			
Ascoglossum purpureum	12–20 in (30–50 cm)	8–16 in (20–40 cm)	E	W				♦	♦				♦			
Ascorachnis Shah Alam City	8–40 in (20–100 cm)	8–20 in (20–50 cm)	E	W	♦		♦	♦	♦				♦	♦		
Aspasia lunata	10–16 in (25–40 cm)	8–12 in (20–30 cm)	E	W			♦					♦		♦		
Aspasia psittacina	10–16 in (25–40 cm)	8–12 in (20–30 cm)	E	W	♦	♦	♦					♦		♦	♦	
Barbosella cucullata	3–6 in (8–15 cm)	2–4 in (5–10 cm)	E	I/C			♦	♦	♦				♦			
Barkeria lindleyana	16–24 in (40–60 cm)	16–32 in (40–80 cm)	E	W/I	♦		♦	♦		♦				♦	♦	
Barkeria melanocaulon	12–16 in (30–40 cm)	6–8 in (15–20 cm)	L	W/I	♦		♦	♦		♦				♦	♦	
Barkeria scandens	5–16 in (12–40 cm)	4–8 in (10–20 cm)	E/L	W/I	♦		♦	♦		♦			♦	♦		
Barlia robertiana	12–32 in (30–80 cm)	10–12 in (25–30 cm)	T	C		♦	♦					♦		♦		
Bartholina etheliae	8–12 in (20–30 cm)	2½–4 in (6–10 cm)	T	I/C	♦		♦						♦			
Beallara Marfitch 'Howard's Dream'	30 in (75 cm)	12 in (30 cm)	E	I	♦		♦					♦		♦		
Beallara Tahoma Glacier	8–30 in (20–75 cm)	8–12 in (20–30 cm)	E	I/C			♦					♦			♦	
Bifrenaria harrisoniae	8–12 in (20–30 cm)	8–24 in (20–60 cm)	E/L	I/C	♦	♦	♦							♦	♦	
Bletia purpurea	20–60 in (50–150 cm)	16–24 in (40–60 cm)	T	C	♦		♦					♦		♦		
Bletilla striata	12–24 in (30–60 cm)	12–48 in (30–120 cm)	T	C	♦		♦			♦		♦	♦	♦		
Bollea coelestis	10–20 in (25–50 cm)	10–20 in (25–50 cm)	E	I	♦		♦		♦					♦		
Bonatea polypodantha	10–14 in (25–35 cm)	6–10 in (15–25 cm)	T	I/C			♦				♦			♦	♦	

Plant name	Height	Spread	Type	Temp.	Showy flowers	Scented flowers	Grow in pot	Grow on mount	Keep moist	Dry winter	Drought tolerant	Frost tolerant	Full sun	Half sun	Shade	CITES listed
Bonatea speciosa	16–24 in (40–60 cm)	8–12 in (20–30 cm)	T	C			♦			♦				♦	♦	
Brassavola cucullata	12 in (30 cm)	24 in (60 cm)	E	W/I	♦	♦		♦		♦			♦	♦		
Brassavola flagellaris	8–24 in (20–60 cm)	8–12 in (20–30 cm)	E/L	W/I	♦	♦	♦	♦		♦			♦	♦		
Brassavola nodosa	12–18 in (30–45 cm)	8–12 in (20–30 cm)	E/L	I	♦	♦	♦	♦		♦			♦			
Brassavola subulifolia	6–8 in (15–20 cm)	8–12 in (20–30 cm)	E	I	♦	♦	♦	♦		♦			♦			
Brassia arcuigera	12–24 in (30–60 cm)	8–16 in (20–40 cm)	E	W/I	♦	♦	♦	♦	♦					♦		
Brassia gireoudiana	12–16 in (30–40 cm)	16–20 in (40–50 cm)	E	W/I	♦	♦	♦	♦						♦	♦	
Brassia lawrenceana	12–16 in (30–40 cm)	12–20 in (30–50 cm)	E	W/I	♦	♦	♦	♦						♦	♦	
Brassia maculata	10–14 in (25–35 cm)	12–16 in (30–40 cm)	E	W/I	♦	♦	♦	♦						♦		
Brassia verrucosa	8–12 in (20–30 cm)	8–24 in (20–60 cm)	E	I	♦	♦	♦	♦						♦		
Brassia Hybrids	12 in (30 cm)	24 in (60 cm)	E	W/I	♦	♦	♦							♦		
Brassidium Fly Away 'Taida'	8–12 in (20–30 cm)	8–24 in (20–60 cm)	E	W/I	♦		♦							♦		
Brassidium Shooting Star × *Brassia* Rex	8–20 in (20–50 cm)	8–20 in (20–50 cm)	E	I	♦		♦						♦	♦		
Brassidium Wild Warrior 'Santa Barbara'	8–12 in (20–30 cm)	8–24 in (20–60 cm)	E	W/I	♦		♦							♦		
Brassocattleya Hybrids	10 in (25 cm)	12 in (30 cm)	E	W/I/C	♦	♦	♦	♦		♦				♦		
Brassolaeliocattleya Hybrids	8–24 in (20–60 cm)	8–24 in (20–60 cm)	E	W/I/C	♦	♦	♦			♦				♦		
Broughtonia negrilensis	8–27 in (20–70 cm)	8–16 in (20–40 cm)	E	W/I			♦	♦	♦				♦	♦		
Broughtonia sanguinea	8–24 in (20–60 cm)	6–8 in (15–20 cm)	E	W			♦	♦	♦				♦			
Brownleea parviflora	8–24 in (20–60 cm)	8–16 in (20–40 cm)	T	I/C		♦						♦	♦	♦		
Bulbophyllum absconditum	1–2 in (2.5–5 cm)	4–6 in (10–15 cm)	E	W			♦	♦							♦	
Bulbophyllum ambrosia	6–8 in (15–20 cm)	4–6 in (10–15 cm)	E	W/I	♦	♦	♦	♦						♦	♦	
Bulbophyllum appendiculatum	2–4 in (5–10 cm)	8–14 in (20–35 cm)	E	W/I	♦		♦	♦						♦	♦	
Bulbophyllum carunculatum	24 in (60 cm)	10 in (25 cm)	E	W		♦		♦	♦				♦			
Bulbophyllum contortisepalum	6–8 in (15–20 cm)	6–8 in (15–20 cm)	E	W				♦	♦					♦	♦	
Bulbophyllum corolliferum	4–6 in (10–15 cm)	6–8 in (15–20 cm)	E	W/I	♦	♦	♦	♦						♦	♦	
Bulbophyllum Daisy Chain	5 in (12 cm)	12 in (30 cm)	E	W	♦		♦	♦						♦		
Bulbophyllum dearei	6–8 in (15–20 cm)	5–6 in (12–15 cm)	E	I	♦	♦	♦	♦	♦						♦	
Bulbophyllum exiguum	¾–2 in (1.8–5 cm)	8–16 in (20–40 cm)	E/L	I/C				♦	♦					♦	♦	
Bulbophyllum falcatum	5–12 in (12–30 cm)	8–24 in (20–60 cm)	E	W/I			♦	♦		♦						
Bulbophyllum fletcherianum	12–40 in (30–100 cm)	10–24 in (25–60 cm)	L	W	♦	♦		♦	♦				♦	♦		
Bulbophyllum globuliforme	½–¾ in (12–18 mm)	1¼–4 in (3–10 cm)	E/L	I/C				♦	♦					♦	♦	

Plant name	Height	Spread	Type	Temp.	Showy flowers	Scented flowers	Grow in pot	Grow on mount	Keep moist	Dry winter	Drought tolerant	Frost tolerant	Full sun	Half sun	Shade	CITES listed
Bulbophyllum graveolens	20 in (50 cm)	24 in (60 cm)	E	W	♦	♦	♦	♦	♦					♦		
Bulbophyllum guttulatum	10 in (25 cm)	10 in (25 cm)	E	W/I	♦			♦	♦					♦		
Bulbophyllum levatii	6–8 in (15–20 cm)	6–8 in (15–20 cm)	E	W/I				♦	♦					♦		
Bulbophyllum lingulatum	1½–2 in (3.5–5 cm)	3–4 in (8–10 cm)	E	W/I				♦	♦						♦	
Bulbophyllum longissimum	6–12 in (15–30 cm)	6–12 in (15–30 cm)	E	W/I	♦	♦	♦	♦	♦					♦	♦	
Bulbophyllum Louis Sander	6–8 in (15–20 cm)	8–12 in (20–30 cm)	E	W	♦		♦	♦	♦					♦	♦	
Bulbophyllum macrobulbum	12–40 in (30–100 cm)	10–24 in (25–60 cm)	L	W	♦	♦	♦	♦	♦					♦		
Bulbophyllum morphologorum	6–8 in (15–20 cm)	6–8 in (15–20 cm)	E	W				♦	♦					♦	♦	
Bulbophyllum ngoyense	1–2 in (2.5–5 cm)	4–12 in (10–30 cm)	E	W/I				♦	♦						♦	
Bulbophyllum nymphopolitanum	8–10 in (20–25 cm)	4–8 in (10–20 cm)	E	W				♦	♦						♦	
Bulbophyllum ornatissimum	4–6 in (10–15 cm)	6–10 in (15–25 cm)	E	W	♦		♦	♦						♦	♦	
Bulbophyllum patella	2–2½ in (5–6 cm)	2½–4 in (6–10 cm)	E	I/C			♦	♦	♦					♦		
Bulbophyllum pectenveneris	3–6 in (8–15 cm)	16 in (40 cm)	E	W				♦	♦				♦			
Bulbophyllum picturatum	10–12 in (20–30 cm)	4–6 in (15–30 cm)	E	W	♦		♦	♦	♦						♦	
Bulbophyllum pulchellum	6–10 in (15–25 cm)	4–8 in (10–20 cm)	E	W	♦			♦	♦					♦	♦	
Bulbophyllum rothschildianum	10 in (25 cm)	24 in (60 cm)	E	W/I/C	♦	♦	♦		♦					♦		
Bulbophyllum rufinum	4–8 in (10–20 cm)	12–20 in (30–50 cm)	E	W/I	♦	♦	♦	♦	♦					♦	♦	
Bulbophyllum schillerianum	2½–8 in (6–20 cm)	3–6 in (8–15 cm)	E/L	I/C				♦	♦					♦		
Bulbophyllum speciosum	3–8 in (8–20 cm)	4–10 in (10–25 cm)	E	I/C	♦		♦	♦	♦						♦	
Bulbophyllum sulawesii	10–16 in (25–40 cm)	16–20 in (40–50 cm)	E	W	♦	♦		♦	♦					♦	♦	
Bulbophyllum tridentatum	10 in (25 cm)	12 in (30 cm)	E	W		♦		♦	♦					♦		
Bulbophyllum unitubum	5–8 in (12–20 cm)	8 in (20 cm)	E	W	♦			♦	♦					♦		
Bulbophyllum wendlandianum	8–12 in (20–30 cm)	4–12 in (10–30 cm)	E	W/I/C	♦		♦	♦	♦					♦	♦	
Cadetia taylori	4–6 in (10–15 cm)	4–8 in (10–20 cm)	E/L	I		♦	♦	♦						♦		
Caladenia arenicola	12–24 in (30–60 cm)	6–10 in (15–25 cm)	T	I/C	♦		♦					♦				
Caladenia chapmanii	6–18 in (15–45 cm)	4–8 in (10–20 cm)	T	C	♦		♦						♦			
Caladenia flava	8–12 in (20–30 cm)	4–10 in (10–25 cm)	T	I/C	♦		♦						♦	♦		
Caladenia harringtoniae	8–16 in (20–40 cm)	6–10 in (15–25 cm)	T	I/C	♦		♦					♦				
Caladenia latifolia	8–18 in (20–45 cm)	4–10 in (10–25 cm)	T	I/C	♦		♦						♦	♦		
Caladenia longicauda	14–24 in (35–60 cm)	7–10 in (18–25 cm)	T	I/C	♦	♦	♦					♦				

Plant name	Height	Spread	Type	Temp.	Showy flowers	Scented flowers	Grow in pot	Grow on mount	Keep moist	Dry winter	Drought tolerant	Frost tolerant	Full sun	Half sun	Shade	CITES listed
Caladenia nana	2–6 in (5–15 cm)	2–4 in (5–10 cm)	T	I/C	♦		♦						♦			
Calanthe discolor	16–20 in (40–50 cm)	8–12 in (20–30 cm)	T	C	♦		♦			♦					♦	
Calanthe Rose Georgene	12–24 in (30–60 cm)	8–20 in (20–50 cm)	T	W/I	♦		♦							♦	♦	
Calanthe rosea	12–20 in (30–50 cm)	10–20 in (25–50 cm)	T	W/I	♦		♦			♦					♦	
Calanthe striata	12–20 in (30–50 cm)	16–18 in (40–45 cm)	T	C	♦		♦								♦	
Calanthe sylvatica	20–30 in (50–75 cm)	12–20 in (30–50 cm)	T	I	♦		♦								♦	
Calanthe triplicata	32–40 in (80–100 cm)	20–40 in (50–100 cm)	T	I	♦		♦								♦	
Calanthe vestita	24–36 in (60–90 cm)	16–30 in (40–75 cm)	T	W/I	♦		♦								♦	
Calochilus campestris	16–24 in (40–60 cm)	2–4 in (5–10 cm)	T	I/C	♦									♦		
Calochilus paludosus	10–14 in (25–35 cm)	2–3 in (5–8 cm)	T	I/C	♦	♦	♦						♦	♦		
Calopogon tuberosus	12–16 in (30–40 cm)	2–4 in (5–10 cm)	T	C	♦		♦		♦				♦			
Calypso bulbosa	6–8 in (15–20 cm)	1–2 in (2.5–5 cm)	T	C	♦	♦	♦			♦		♦		♦		
Cannaeorchis verruciferum	16–48 in (40–120 cm)	8–20 in (20–50 cm)	E/T	W/I	♦		♦						♦	♦		
Catasetum saccatum	12–24 in (30–60 cm)	12–16 in (30–40 cm)	E	I	♦		♦			♦				♦		
Catasetum tenebrosum	12–18 in (30–45 cm)	12–16 in (30–40 cm)	E	W/I	♦		♦			♦			♦	♦		
Cattleya aclandiae	3–6 in (8–15 cm)	4–12 in (10–30 cm)	E	W/I	♦		♦	♦						♦		
Cattleya amethystoglossa	30–50 in (75–130 cm)	12–20 in (30–50 cm)	E/L	I	♦		♦	♦					♦			
Cattleya aurantiaca	5–24 in (12–60 cm)	6–24 in (15–60 cm)	E	W/I			♦						♦	♦		
Cattleya bicolor	8–48 in (20–120 cm)	8–24 in (20–60 cm)	E/L	W/I	♦		♦						♦	♦		
Cattleya bowringiana	6–36 in (15–90 cm)	4–24 in (10–60 cm)	L	W/I	♦		♦						♦	♦		
Cattleya gaskelliana	8–16 in (20–40 cm)	8–20 in (20–50 cm)	E	W/I	♦	♦	♦							♦		
Cattleya × *guatemalensis*	12–14 in (30–35 cm)	12–16 in (30–40 cm)	E	I	♦		♦						♦	♦		
Cattleya intermedia	6–16 in (15–40 cm)	4–12 in (10–30 cm)	E	W/I	♦		♦							♦		
Cattleya loddigesii	6–24 in (15–60 cm)	4–12 in (10–30 cm)	E	W/I	♦		♦							♦		
Cattleya lueddemanniana	6–20 in (15–50 cm)	4–12 in (10–30 cm)	L	W/I	♦		♦							♦		
Cattleya mendelii	16–18 in (40–45 cm)	16–18 in (40–45 cm)	E/L	I	♦	♦	♦							♦		
Cattleya nobilior	5–8 in (12–20 cm)	7–12 in (18–30 cm)	E/L	W	♦	♦	♦						♦	♦		
Cattleya schilleriana	4–6 in (10–15 cm)	4–12 in (10–30 cm)	E	W/I	♦			♦	♦					♦		
Cattleya schofieldiana	12–40 in (30–100 cm)	8–20 in (20–50 cm)	E	W/I	♦		♦							♦		
Cattleya schroderae	16–18 in (40–45 cm)	16–18 in (40–45 cm)	E	I	♦	♦	♦							♦		
Cattleya skinneri	12–14 in (30–35 cm)	12–16 in (30–40 cm)	E	I	♦		♦							♦		

Plant name	Height	Spread	Type	Temp.	Showy flowers	Scented flowers	Grow in pot	Grow on mount	Keep moist	Dry winter	Drought tolerant	Frost tolerant	Full sun	Half sun	Shade	CITES listed
Cattleya walkeriana	3–6 in (8–15 cm)	4–10 in (10–25 cm)	E	I	♦		♦							♦		
Cattleya Hybrids	8–32 in (20–80 cm)	8–24 in (20–60 cm)	E	I	♦		♦							♦		
Cattleyopsis lindenii	4–6 in (10–15 cm)	4–6 in (10–15 cm)	E	W	♦		♦				♦	♦	♦			
Cattleytonia Maui Maid	4–20 in (10–50 cm)	4–12 in (10–30 cm)	E	W/I	♦		♦	♦					♦	♦		
Cattleytonia Starrlyn	4–20 in (10–50 cm)	4–12 in (10–30 cm)	E	W/I	♦		♦	♦					♦	♦		
Caularthron bicornutum	8–24 in (45–60 cm)	14–18 in (35–45 cm)	E/L	W		♦	♦	♦			♦		♦			
Cephalanthera austiniae	20–26 in (50–65 cm)	3–4 in (8–10 cm)	T	C	♦		♦					♦		♦		
Cephalanthera damasonium	8–24 in (20–60 cm)	4–8 in (10–20 cm)	T	C	♦		♦					♦		♦		
Cephalanthera longifolia	6–24 in (15–60 cm)	3–4 in (8–10 cm)	T	C	♦		♦							♦		
Cephalanthera rubra	4–24 in (10–60 cm)	4–8 in (10–20 cm)	T	C	♦		♦					♦		♦		
Ceratostylis incognita	3–7 in (8–18 cm)	4–8 in (10–20 cm)	E	I/C			♦	♦	♦						♦	
Ceratostylis retisquama	8–16 in (20–40 cm)	4–6 in (10–15 cm)	E	W			♦	♦					♦	♦		
Chiloglottis formicifera	4–12 in (10–30 cm)	3–6 in (8–15 cm)	T	I/C			♦							♦		
Chiloglottis gunnii	3–12 in (8–30 cm)	3–8 in (8–20 cm)	T	I/C			♦	♦						♦		
Chiloschista lunifera	1–5 in (2.5–12 cm)	2½–8 in (6–20 cm)	E	W/I	♦			♦	♦					♦	♦	
Chiloschista parishii	2–4 in (5–10 cm)	2–3 in (5–8 cm)	E	W				♦	♦				♦			
Chysis aurea	8–24 in (20–60 cm)	8–10 in (20–25 cm)	E	I	♦		♦	♦		♦				♦		
Chysis bractescens	6–10 in (15–25 cm)	6–8 in (15–20 cm)	E	I	♦		♦	♦		♦				♦		
Cirrhaea dependens	10–14 in (25–35 cm)	8–12 in (20–30 cm)	E	I			♦	♦		♦				♦		
Cleisostoma racemiferum	10–20 in (25–50 cm)	20–27 in (50–70 cm)	E	I.			♦	♦	♦						♦	
Cleisostoma recurvum	8–18 in (20–45 cm)	8–18 in (20–45 cm)	E	I			♦	♦							♦	
Cleisostoma weberi	6–18 in (15–45 cm)	4–8 in (10–20 cm)	E	W			♦	♦					♦	♦		
Clowesia rosea	12–20 in (30–50 cm)	8–12 in (20–30 cm)	E	I		♦	♦			♦				♦		
Clowesia warscewiczii	8–20 in (20–50 cm)	6–10 in (15–25 cm)	E	W/I	♦	♦	♦			♦			♦	♦		
Cochleanthes amazonica	4–20 in (10–50 cm)	4–10 in (10–25 cm)	E	W/I			♦		♦					♦		
Cochleanthes discolor	4–8 in (10–20 cm)	6–8 in (15–20 cm)	E	I			♦		♦						♦	
Cochlioda noezliana	8–14 in (20–35 cm)	6–8 in (15–20 cm)	E	I			♦	♦						♦		
Cochlioda rosea	12–18 in (30–45 cm)	5–6 in (12–15 cm)	E	I/C			♦	♦							♦	
Cochlioda vulcanica	8–14 in (20–35 cm)	5–6 in (12–15 cm)	E	I/C			♦	♦							♦	
Coelia bella	16–32 in (40–80 cm)	6–20 in (15–50 cm)	E	I	♦	♦	♦	♦	♦				♦	♦	♦	
Coelogyne Burfordiense	10–36 in (25–90 cm)	8–32 in (20–80 cm)	E	W	♦	♦	♦							♦		

Plant name	Height	Spread	Type	Temp.	Showy flowers	Scented flowers	Grow in pot	Grow on mount	Keep moist	Dry winter	Drought tolerant	Frost tolerant	Full sun	Half sun	Shade	CITES listed
Coelogyne chloroptera	6½–12 in (16–30 cm)	6–12 in (15–30 cm)	E	I	◆	◆	◆								◆	
Coelogyne corymbosa	5–10 in (12–25 cm)	4–8 in (10–20 cm)	E	I/C		◆	◆							◆		
Coelogyne cristata	8–12 in (20–30 cm)	12–16 in (30–40 cm)	E	I/C	◆	◆	◆							◆		
Coelogyne flaccida	5–15 in (12–38 cm)	4–27 in (10–70 cm)	E	I/C	◆	◆	◆							◆		
Coelogyne huettneriana	4–8 in (10–20 cm)	6–12 in (15–30 cm)	E	I/C	◆	◆	◆							◆	◆	
Coelogyne lawrenceana	10–12 in (25–30 cm)	12–18 in (30–45 cm)	E	I/C	◆	◆	◆							◆		
Coelogyne Memoria W. Micholitz	8–27 in (20–70 cm)	8–20 in (20–50 cm)	E	I/C	◆		◆							◆		
Coelogyne nitida	6–10 in (15–25 cm)	6–12 in (15–30 cm)	E	I/C	◆	◆	◆							◆	◆	
Coelogyne ovalis	3–4 in (8–10 cm)	6–12 in (15–30 cm)	E	I/C		◆								◆		
Coelogyne pandurata	8–24 in (20–60 cm)	8–48 in (20–120 cm)	E	W	◆	◆	◆							◆		
Coelogyne speciosa	10–27 in (25–70 cm)	15–20 in (38–50 cm)	E	W/I	◆		◆							◆		
Coelogyne tomentosa	40–50 in (100–130 cm)	10–12 in (25–30 cm)	E	I/C	◆	◆	◆							◆		
Colmanara Hybrids	8–30 in (20–75 cm)	8–12 in (20–30 cm)	E	I/C	◆		◆		◆					◆		
Comparettia falcata	4–6 in (10–15 cm)	3–5 in (8–12 cm)	E	I	◆		◆	◆	◆				◆			
Comparettia speciosa	4–6 in (10–15 cm)	3–5 in (8–12 cm)	E	I	◆		◆	◆	◆				◆			
Comperia comperiana	10–24 in (25–60 cm)	6–8 in (15–20 cm)	T	C			◆				◆				◆	
Condylago rodrigoi	10 in (25 cm)	3 in (8 cm)	E	I/C			◆	◆	◆						◆	
Corallorhiza striata	12–20 in (30–50 cm)	3–4 in (8–10 cm)	T	C			◆					◆			◆	
Corallorhiza trifida	5–8 in (12–20 cm)	¾–1¼ in (18–30 mm)	T	C			◆					◆		◆	◆	
Coryanthes macrantha	30–40 in (75–100 cm)	24–30 in (60–75 cm)	E	W/I	◆	◆	◆	◆	◆					◆		
Coryanthes speciosa	30–40 in (75–100 cm)	24–30 in (60–75 cm)	E	W/I	◆	◆	◆	◆						◆		
Corybas barbarae	½–2 in (12–50 mm)	¾–1½ in (18–35 mm)	T	I/C			◆		◆						◆	
Corybas diemenicus	1–4 in (25–100 mm)	1–1½ in (25–35 mm)	T	I/C			◆		◆						◆	
Corybas montanus	½–2 in (12–50 mm)	¾–1½ in (18–35 mm)	T	I/C			◆								◆	
Corybas pruinosus	½–1½ in (12–35 mm)	1–1¼ in (25–30 mm)	T	I/C			◆		◆					◆		
Cryptopus elatus	20–40 in (50–100 cm)	6–12 in (15–30 cm)	E/L	I		◆	◆	◆						◆		
Cuitlauzina pendula	6–12 in (15–30 cm)	8–14 in (20–35 cm)	E	C		◆		◆		◆			◆	◆		
Cycnoches barthiorum	14–20 in (35–50 cm)	14–20 in (35–50 cm)	E	I	◆	◆									◆	
Cycnoches ventricosum	12–26 in (30–65 cm)	12–27 in (30–70 cm)	E	I	◆	◆								◆		
Cymbidiella flabellata	12–28 in (30–70 cm)	12–32 in (30–80 cm)	T	W/I	◆		◆	◆					◆	◆		
Cymbidiella pardalina	16–40 in (40–100 cm)	16–60 in (40–150 cm)	E	W	◆		◆		◆				◆			

Plant name	Height	Spread	Type	Temp.	Showy flowers	Scented flowers	Grow in pot	Grow on mount	Keep moist	Dry winter	Drought tolerant	Frost tolerant	Full sun	Half sun	Shade	CITES listed
Cymbidium bicolor	16–26 in (40–65 cm)	18–24 in (45–60 cm)	E	W	✦	✦	✦		✦				✦	✦		
Cymbidium canaliculatum	16–26 in (40–65 cm)	18–24 in (45–60 cm)	E	W/I/C	✦	✦	✦		✦		✦		✦			
Cymbidium erythrostylum	12–27 in (30–70 cm)	8–24 in (20–60 cm)	E	C	✦		✦		✦				✦	✦		
Cymbidium insigne	27–32 in (70–80 cm)	24–36 in (60–90 cm)	T	C	✦		✦		✦				✦			
Cymbidium lancifolium	4–20 in (10–50 cm)	4–18 in (10–45 cm)	T	I	✦		✦		✦						✦	
Cymbidium lowianum	12–48 in (30–120 cm)	8–36 in (20–90 cm)	T	I/C	✦		✦		✦				✦	✦		
Cymbidium madidum	20–32 in (50–80 cm)	24–36 in (60–90 cm)	E	I	✦		✦		✦				✦			
Cymbidium parishii	12–16 in (30–40 cm)	12–16 in (30–40 cm)	E/T	I/C	✦	✦	✦		✦				✦			
Cymbidium sanderae	20–30 in (50–75 cm)	20–27 in (50–70 cm)	E	C	✦		✦		✦				✦			
Cymbidium sinense	20–30 in (50–75 cm)	20–24 in (50–60 cm)	E/T	I/C	✦	✦	✦		✦				✦	✦	✦	
Cymbidium suave	12–48 in (30–120 cm)	8–32 in (20–80 cm)	E	I/C	✦	✦	✦		✦				✦	✦		
Cymbidium tracyanum	12–48 in (30–120 cm)	8–36 in (20–90 cm)	E	C	✦	✦	✦		✦			✦	✦	✦		
Cymbidium Hybrids	12–48 in (30–120 cm)	8–36 in (20–90 cm)	T	I/C	✦		✦		✦				✦	✦		
Cypripedium acaule	8–18 in (20–45 cm)	6–8 in (15–20 cm)	T	C	✦		✦		✦			✦			✦	
Cypripedium calceolus	8–24 in (20–60 cm)	10–12 in (25–30 cm)	T	C	✦	✦	✦		✦			✦			✦	
Cypripedium californicum	20–48 in (50–120 cm)	4–6 in (10–15 cm)	T	C	✦	✦	✦		✦			✦			✦	
Cypripedium formosanum	4–10 in (10–25 cm)	4–12 in (10–30 cm)	T	C	✦		✦		✦					✦		
Cypripedium montanum	8–16 in (20–40 cm)	6–8 in (15–20 cm)	T	I/C	✦	✦	✦		✦			✦		✦	✦	
Cypripedium parviflorum	6–20 in (15–50 cm)	4–10 in (10–25 cm)	T	C	✦	✦	✦		✦			✦	✦	✦	✦	
Cypripedium reginae	16–32 in (40–80 cm)	8–12 in (20–30 cm)	T	C	✦		✦		✦			✦	✦	✦		
Cyrtochilum falcipetalum	10–20 ft (3–6 m)	32–48 in (80–120 cm)	E/L	C	✦		✦			✦					✦	
Cyrtochilum microxiphium	12–60 in (30–150 cm)	8–24 in (20–60 cm)	T	I/C	✦		✦		✦					✦	✦	
Cyrtopodium holstii	32–40 in (80–100 cm)	20–40 in (50–100 cm)	T	W		✦							✦			
Cyrtopodium punctatum	3–5 ft (0.9–1.5 m)	3–4 ft (0.9–1.2 m)	E/T	W		✦							✦			
Cyrtorchis arcuata	12–20 in (30–50 cm)	16–20 in (40–50 cm)	E/L	W/I		✦		✦					✦			
Cyrtostylis reniformis	1¼–5 in (3–12 cm)	¾–2 in (18–50 mm)	T	I/C			✦				✦			✦	✦	
Dactylorhiza elata	24 in (60 cm)	6 in (15 cm)	T	C	✦		✦			✦		✦	✦	✦		
Dactylorhiza foliosa	12–27 in (30–70 cm)	4–10 in (10–25 cm)	T	C	✦		✦			✦		✦	✦	✦		
Dactylorhiza fuchsii	8–24 in (20–60 cm)	4–10 in (10–25 cm)	T	C	✦		✦			✦		✦	✦	✦		
Dactylorhiza incarnata	8–24 in (20–60 cm)	4–10 in (10–25 cm)	T	C	✦		✦			✦		✦	✦	✦		

Plant name	Height	Spread	Type	Temp.	Showy flowers	Scented flowers	Grow in pot	Grow on mount	Keep moist	Dry winter	Drought tolerant	Frost tolerant	Full sun	Half sun	Shade	CITES listed
Dactylorhiza majalis	8–30 in (20–75 cm)	5–12 in (12–30 cm)	T	C	♦		♦			♦		♦	♦			
Dactylorhiza praetermissa	8–27 in (20–70 cm)	8–12 in (20–60 cm)	T	C	♦		♦			♦		♦	♦			
Dactylorhiza romana	6–14 in (15–35 cm)	8–12 in (20–30 cm)	T	C	♦		♦			♦		♦	♦			
Dactylorhiza sambucina	4–12 in (10–30 cm)	6–8 in (15–20 cm)	T	C	♦		♦			♦		♦	♦	♦		
Dactylorhiza urvilleana	10–32 in (25–80 cm)	4–10 in (10–25 cm)	T	C	♦		♦		♦			♦	♦	♦		
Darwinara Pretty Girl	8–24 in (20–60 cm)	8–15 in (20–38 cm)	E	W/I	♦		♦						♦			
Degarmoara Skywalker 'Red Star'	8–32 in (20–80 cm)	8–16 in (20–40 cm)	E	I/C	♦		♦			♦			♦			
Degarmoara Starshot 'Fashion'	8–32 in (20–80 cm)	8–16 in (20–40 cm)	E	I/C	♦		♦			♦			♦			
Degarmoara Winter Wonderland 'White Fairy'	8–32 in (20–80 cm)	8–16 in (20–40 cm)	E	I/C	♦		♦			♦			♦			
Dendrobium aduncum	12–24 in (30–60 cm)	18–24 in (45–60 cm)	E	W/I	♦		♦			♦			♦			
Dendrobium aemulum	4–6 in (10–15 cm)	8 in (20 cm)	E	C	♦	♦		♦					♦			
Dendrobium albosanguineum	14–16 in (35–40 cm)	14–16 in (35–40 cm)	E	I	♦		♦						♦			
Dendrobium alexandrae	8–27 in (20–70 cm)	8–20 in (20–50 cm)	E	W/I	♦		♦						♦			
Dendrobium amethystoglossum	34–38 in (85–95 cm)	18–27 in (45–70 cm)	E	I/C		♦	♦	♦		♦			♦	♦		
Dendrobium anosmum	8–48 in (20–120 cm)	8–16 in (20–40 cm)	E	W/I	♦	♦	♦							♦	♦	
Dendrobium antennatum	8–24 in (20–60 cm)	4–12 in (10–30 cm)	E	W	♦		♦	♦					♦	♦		
Dendrobium atroviolaceum	8–20 in (20–50 cm)	8–24 in (20–60 cm)	E	I	♦		♦						♦			
Dendrobium bigibbum	4–24 in (10–60 cm)	8–24 in (20–60 cm)	E	W	♦		♦				♦		♦			
Dendrobium bracteosum	6–14 in (15–35 cm)	5–15 in (12–38 cm)	E	W	♦		♦						♦			
Dendrobium bulbophylloides	½–1¼ in (12–30 mm)	2–8 in (5–20 cm)	E	I		♦	♦	♦					♦			
Dendrobium bullenianum	8–40 in (20–100 cm)	8–16 in (20–40 cm)	E	W/I	♦		♦	♦					♦	♦		
Dendrobium cacatua	4–12 in (10–30 cm)	4–12 in (10–30 cm)	E	I/C	♦			♦	♦						♦	
Dendrobium canaliculatum	4–16 in (10–40 cm)	4–16 in (10–40 cm)	E	W	♦			♦		♦			♦			
Dendrobium capitisyork	6–24 in (15–60 cm)	4–20 in (10–50 cm)	E	I	♦			♦	♦						♦	
Dendrobium capituliflorum	6–12 in (15–30 cm)	8–12 in (20–30 cm)	E/L	I		♦	♦						♦			
Dendrobium ceraula	6–16 in (15–40 cm)	4–10 in (10–25 cm)	E	I/C	♦		♦		♦				♦			
Dendrobium chameleon	5–24 in (12–60 cm)	4–8 in (10–20 cm)	E	I	♦		♦		♦				♦			
Dendrobium chittimae	4–12 in (10–30 cm)	4–10 in (10–25 cm)	E	I	♦	♦							♦	♦		
Dendrobium chrysocrepis	8–12 in (20–30 cm)	4–6 in (10–15 cm)	E/L	C	♦	♦	♦			♦			♦	♦		
Dendrobium chrysotoxum	8–16 in (20–40 cm)	8–24 in (20–60 cm)	E	W/I	♦		♦			♦		♦	♦			
Dendrobium crumenatum	8–24 in (20–60 cm)	8–24 in (20–60 cm)	E	W	♦	♦	♦	♦					♦	♦		

Plant name	Height	Spread	Type	Temp.	Showy flowers	Scented flowers	Grow in pot	Grow on mount	Keep moist	Dry winter	Drought tolerant	Frost tolerant	Full sun	Half sun	Shade	CITES listed
Dendrobium cucullatum	27–36 in (70–90 cm)	10–16 in (25–40 cm)	E/L	I	◆	◆	◆	◆						◆		
Dendrobium curvicaule	8–36 in (20–90 cm)	12–48 in (30–120 cm)	E/L	W/I/C	◆	◆	◆					◆	◆	◆		
Dendrobium cuthbertsonii	1–3 in (2.5–8 cm)	2–8 in (5–20 cm)	E	I/C	◆		◆	◆	◆					◆		
Dendrobium × delicatum	12–20 in (30–50 cm)	16–20 in (40–50 cm)	E/L	I/C	◆	◆	◆						◆	◆		
Dendrobium densiflorum	12–18 in (30–45 cm)	16–20 in (40–50 cm)	E	I	◆		◆			◆				◆		
Dendrobium dichaeoides	2–3 in (5–8 cm)	2½–8 in (6–20 cm)	E/L	I/C	◆		◆	◆	◆					◆	◆	
Dendrobium discolor	1–6 ft (0.3–1.8 m)	1–4 ft (0.3–1.2 m)	E/L	W	◆		◆		◆				◆			
Dendrobium dixanthum	8–30 in (20–75 cm)	6–12 in (15–30 cm)	E	W/I	◆		◆							◆	◆	
Dendrobium engae	8–27 in (20–70 cm)	8–20 in (20–50 cm)	E	I	◆	◆	◆							◆		
Dendrobium farmeri	12–18 in (30–45 cm)	12–18 in (30–45 cm)	E	I	◆	◆	◆	◆		◆				◆		
Dendrobium fimbriatum	1–7 ft (0.3–2 m)	1–4 ft (0.3–1.2 m)	E	I/C	◆		◆			◆			◆	◆		
Dendrobium findleyanum	14–24 in (35–60 cm)	16–24 in (40–60 cm)	E	I	◆	◆							◆	◆		
Dendrobium flaviflorum	8–20 in (20–50 cm)	8–16 in (20–40 cm)	E	I/C	◆		◆							◆	◆	◆
Dendrobium formosum	16–18 in (40–45 cm)	14–18 in (35–45 cm)	E/L	I	◆		◆						◆	◆		
Dendrobium gibsonii	12–48 in (30–120 cm)	12–24 in (30–60 cm)	E	I	◆		◆						◆	◆		
Dendrobium goldschmidtianum	8–36 in (20–90 cm)	8–24 in (20–60 cm)	E	W/I	◆		◆	◆					◆	◆		
Dendrobium gracilicaule	8–24 in (20–60 cm)	8–36 in (20–90 cm)	E/L	I/C		◆	◆	◆					◆	◆		
Dendrobium × gracillimum	18–24 in (45–60 cm)	24–30 in (60–75 cm)	E	I/C		◆	◆						◆	◆		
Dendrobium harveyanum	8–16 in (20–40 cm)	8–16 in (20–40 cm)	E	W	◆		◆							◆		
Dendrobium hercoglossum	6–16 in (15–40 cm)	8–24 in (20–60 cm)	E	W/I/C	◆		◆	◆						◆	◆	
Dendrobium jenkinsii	2½–4 in (6–10 cm)	4–5 in (10–12 cm)	E	I		◆		◆		◆				◆		
Dendrobium johnsoniae	8–20 in (20–50 cm)	8–20 in (20–50 cm)	E	W	◆	◆	◆							◆		
Dendrobium keithii	4–16 in (10–40 cm)	6–16 in (15–40 cm)	E	W/I/C			◆	◆					◆	◆	◆	
Dendrobium kingianum	2–36 in (5–90 cm)	4–48 in (10–120 cm)	E/L	I/C	◆	◆	◆							◆		
Dendrobium laevifolium	2½–6 in (6–15 cm)	2½–8 in (6–20 cm)	E	I/C	◆		◆		◆					◆		
Dendrobium lawesii	6–20 in (15–50 cm)	4–12 in (10–30 cm)	E	W/I	◆		◆		◆					◆		
Dendrobium lichenastrum	½–¾ in (12–18 mm)	4–6 in (10–15 cm)	E/L	I				◆						◆		
Dendrobium lindleyi	8–16 in (20–40 cm)	8–16 in (20–40 cm)	E	W/I	◆								◆	◆		
Dendrobium lituiflorum	24–27 in (60–70 cm)	18–27 in (45–70 cm)	E	I	◆	◆	◆			◆			◆	◆		
Dendrobium macrophyllum	8–27 in (20–70 cm)	8–24 in (20–60 cm)	E	W	◆		◆						◆	◆		
Dendrobium masarangense	1–2 in (2.5–5 cm)	2–5 in (5–12 cm)	E	I/C			◆	◆						◆		

Plant name	Height	Spread	Type	Temp.	Showy flowers	Scented flowers	Grow in pot	Grow on mount	Keep moist	Dry winter	Drought tolerant	Frost tolerant	Full sun	Half sun	Shade	CITES listed
Dendrobium melaleucaphilum	8–24 in (20–60 cm)	8–20 in (20–50 cm)	E	I/C	♦	♦		♦						♦	♦	
Dendrobium moniliforme	4–10 in (10–25 cm)	8–24 in (20–60 cm)	E	I/C		♦	♦						♦	♦		
Dendrobium monophyllum	2½–8 in (6–20 cm)	8–12 in (20–30 cm)	E/L	I/C		♦		♦					♦	♦		
Dendrobium mutabile	8–36 in (20–90 cm)	16–60 in (40–150 cm)	E/L	W/I	♦		♦						♦	♦		
Dendrobium nobile	8–24 in (20–60 cm)	8–24 in (20–60 cm)	E	W/I/C	♦		♦			♦			♦	♦		
Dendrobium pandanicola	4–24 in (10–60 cm)	4–16 in (10–40 cm)	E	I/C	♦		♦	♦							♦	
Dendrobium peguanum	1½–3 in (3.5–8 cm)	2½–3 in (6–7 cm)	E	I		♦	♦			♦				♦		
Dendrobium phalaenopsis	8–32 in (20–80 cm)	4–12 in (10–30 cm)	E	W	♦		♦							♦		
Dendrobium primulinum	16–32 in (40–80 cm)	12–20 in (30–50 cm)	E	I	♦	♦	♦		♦	♦			♦	♦		
Dendrobium pseudoglomeratum	8–27 in (20–70 cm)	8–20 in (20–50 cm)	E	W/I			♦							♦		
Dendrobium pulchellum	1–7 ft (0.3–2 m)	1–3 ft (0.3–0.9 m)	E	W	♦	♦							♦	♦		
Dendrobium rex	12–48 in (30–120 cm)	12–60 in (30–150 cm)	E/L	W/I/C	♦	♦	♦					♦	♦	♦		
Dendrobium roseipes	14–24 in (35–60 cm)	18–24 in (45–60 cm)	E	I		♦			♦					♦		
Dendrobium rupestre	1–2 in (2.5–5 cm)	2–4 in (5–10 cm)	E	I/C		♦				♦				♦		
Dendrobium sanderae	27–36 in (70–90 cm)	20–24 in (50–60 cm)	E	W/I	♦		♦							♦		
Dendrobium scabrilingue	10–14 in (25–35 cm)	12–18 in (30–45 cm)	E	W/I	♦	♦	♦		♦					♦		
Dendrobium schildhaueri	12–16 in (30–40 cm)	14–18 in (35–45 cm)	E	W/I	♦		♦			♦			♦	♦		
Dendrobium secundum	40 in (100 cm)	12–24 in (30–60 cm)	E	W/I			♦							♦		
Dendrobium smillieae	8–48 in (20–120 cm)	8–27 in (20–70 cm)	E	W	♦		♦						♦	♦		
Dendrobium speciosum	4–48 in (10–120 cm)	1–10 ft (0.3–3 m)	E/L	I/C	♦	♦	♦	♦			♦		♦	♦		
Dendrobium spectabile	8–32 in (20–80 cm)	8–24 in (20–60 cm)	E	W	♦		♦						♦	♦		
Dendrobium subclausum	6–20 in (15–50 cm)	4–12 in (10–30 cm)	E	W/I	♦		♦							♦		
Dendrobium sulphureum	1–2 in (2.5–5 cm)	2–5 in (5–12 cm)	E	I/C	♦		♦		♦					♦		
Dendrobium tapiniense	8–32 in (20–80 cm)	8–24 in (20–60 cm)	E	W/I	♦		♦						♦	♦		
Dendrobium tarberi	8–44 in (20–110 cm)	12–60 in (30–150 cm)	E/L	W/I/C	♦	♦	♦				♦		♦	♦		
Dendrobium tetragonum	4–27 in (10–70 cm)	4–20 in (10–50 cm)	E	I/C	♦	♦	♦	♦						♦		
Dendrobium thrysiflorum	8–24 in (20–60 cm)	8–36 in (20–90 cm)	E	W/I	♦		♦							♦		
Dendrobium tortile	16–20 in (40–50 cm)	20–24 in (50–60 cm)	E/L/T	W/I	♦	♦	♦						♦	♦		
Dendrobium trilamellatum	18–24 in (45–60 cm)	16–24 in (40–60 cm)	E	W/I	♦		♦	♦						♦		
Dendrobium vexillarius	1–5 in (2.5–12 cm)	2–5 in (5–12 cm)	E	I/C	♦		♦		♦					♦		
Dendrobium victoriae-reginae	8–24 in (20–60 cm)	8–20 in (20–50 cm)	E	I/C	♦		♦		♦					♦		

Plant name	Height	Spread	Type	Temp.	Showy flowers	Scented flowers	Grow in pot	Grow on mount	Keep moist	Dry winter	Drought tolerant	Frost tolerant	Full sun	Half sun	Shade	CITES listed
Dendrobium wardianum	8–27 in (20–70 cm)	8–16 in (20–40 cm)	E	W/I	◆	◆	◆						◆	◆		
Dendrobium wentianum	8–32 in (20–80 cm)	4–12 in (10–30 cm)	E	I	◆		◆		◆					◆		
Dendrobium williamsonii	8–16 in (20–40 cm)	8–12 in (20–30 cm)	E	W/I			◆							◆		
Dendrobium, Australian Hybrids	4–24 in (10–60 cm)	8–30 in (20–75 cm)	E	I/C	◆	◆	◆							◆		
Dendrobium, "Hardcane" Hybrids	8–40 in (20–100 cm)	8–32 in (20–80 cm)	E	W	◆		◆						◆	◆		
Dendrobium, "Nigrohirsute" Hybrids	8–16 in (20–40 cm)	8–16 in (20–40 cm)	E	W/I	◆		◆						◆	◆		
Dendrobium, "Softcane" Hybrids	8–24 in (20–60 cm)	6–16 in (15–40 cm)	E	I/C	◆		◆						◆	◆		
Dendrochilum arachnites	6–8 in (15–20 cm)	8–12 in (20–30 cm)	E	I	◆		◆		◆					◆	◆	
Dendrochilum cobbianum	6–20 in (15–50 cm)	8–20 in (20–50 cm)	E	W/I	◆	◆	◆		◆					◆		
Dendrochilum filiforme	14–18 in (35–45 cm)	14–18 in (35–45 cm)	E	I/C	◆	◆	◆		◆						◆	
Dendrochilum glumaceum	8–16 in (20–40 cm)	8–24 in (20–60 cm)	E	W/I	◆		◆		◆					◆		
Dendrochilum latifolium	6–20 in (15–50 cm)	8–20 in (20–50 cm)	E	W/I	◆		◆		◆					◆		
Dendrochilum niveum	6–8 in (15–20 cm)	6–8 in (15–20 cm)	E	I	◆	◆	◆								◆	
Dendrochilum saccolabium	8–16 in (20–40 cm)	8–24 in (20–60 cm)	E	I	◆		◆		◆					◆		
Dendrochilum simile	20–30 in (50–75 cm)	20–30 in (50–75 cm)	E	I	◆		◆		◆						◆	
Dendrochilum tenellum	8–16 in (20–40 cm)	8–32 in (20–80 cm)	E	I	◆	◆	◆		◆					◆		
Diaphananthe fragrantissima	20–30 in (50–75 cm)	10–12 in (25–30 cm)	E	W/I	◆	◆	◆								◆	
Dichaea glauca	16–24 in (40–60 cm)	6–8 in (15–20 cm)	E	I	◆	◆	◆	◆	◆						◆	
Dichaea muricata	12–18 in (30–45 cm)	4–5 in (10–12 cm)	E	I		◆	◆		◆						◆	
Dichaea pendula	16–24 in (40–60 cm)	12–20 in (30–50 cm)	E	I				◆	◆						◆	
Dichaea sodiroi	3–20 in (8–50 cm)	4–8 in (10–20 cm)	E	I/C	◆			◆	◆						◆	
Dimorphorchis lowii	60–80 in (150–200 cm)	40–60 in (100–150 cm)	E	W	◆		◆		◆				◆			
Diplocaulobium aratriferum	5–6 in (12–15 cm)	5–6 in (12–15 cm)	E	I/C		◆	◆	◆						◆		
Dipteranthus estradae	¾–3 in (1.8–8 cm)	1½–4 in (3.5–10 cm)	E	I	◆			◆	◆						◆	
Disa aurata	4–24 in (10–60 cm)	8–12 in (20–30 cm)	T	C	◆		◆		◆					◆		
Disa cardinalis	12–27 in (30–70 cm)	4–8 in (10–20 cm)	T	C	◆		◆		◆				◆			
Disa lugens	18–40 in (45–100 cm)	1½–4 in (3.5–10 cm)	T	C	◆		◆		◆				◆	◆		
Disa racemosa	3–40 in (8–100 cm)	3–5 in (8–12 cm)	T	C	◆		◆		◆				◆			
Disa tripetaloides	4–20 in (10–50 cm)	8–12 in (20–30 cm)	T	C	◆		◆		◆				◆			
Disa uniflora	6–32 in (15–80 cm)	4–10 in (10–25 cm)	T	C	◆		◆		◆				◆	◆		
Disa Hybrids	8–32 in (20–80 cm)	4–10 in (10–25 cm)	T	C	◆				◆				◆	◆		

Plant name	Height	Spread	Type	Temp.	Showy flowers	Scented flowers	Grow in pot	Grow on mount	Keep moist	Dry winter	Drought tolerant	Frost tolerant	Full sun	Half sun	Shade	CITES listed
Diuris maculata	4–16 in (10–40 cm)	4–8 in (10–20 cm)	T	C	◆		◆					◆	◆			
Dockrillia cucumerina	1½–2 in (3.5–5 cm)	6–10 in (15–25 cm)	E	I/C				◆						◆		
Dockrillia linguiformis	1–5 in (2.5–12 cm)	4–24 in (10–60 cm)	E/L	I/C	◆	◆	◆				◆		◆	◆		
Dockrillia schoenina	4–32 in (10–80 cm)	4–20 in (10–50 cm)	E	I/C		◆	◆							◆	◆	
Dockrillia striolata	4–30 in (10–75 cm)	4–20 in (10–50 cm)	L	C	◆		◆	◆				◆	◆	◆		
Dockrillia teretifolia	1–10 ft (0.3–3 m)	1–3 ft (0.3–0.9 m)	E	I/C	◆	◆			◆				◆	◆		
Dockrillia wassellii	2½–6 in (6–15 cm)	2½–8 in (6–20 cm)	E	W/I	◆			◆					◆	◆		
Dracula bella	7–12 in (18–30 cm)	10–12 in (25–30 cm)	E	I/C	◆		◆		◆						◆	
Dracula Cafe Mocha	8–14 in (20–35 cm)	8–16 in (20–40 cm)	E	I/C	◆		◆		◆						◆	
Dracula chimaera	7–18 in (18–45 cm)	12–16 in (30–40 cm)	E	C	◆		◆		◆						◆	
Dracula gigas	14–18 in (35–45 cm)	10–14 in (25–35 cm)	E	I/C	◆		◆		◆						◆	
Dracula polyphemus	20–24 in (50–60 cm)	12–16 in (30–40 cm)	E	I/C	◆		◆		◆						◆	
Dracula Quasimodo	8–14 in (20–35 cm)	8–16 in (20–40 cm)	E	I/C	◆		◆		◆						◆	
Dracula tubeana	4–16 in (10–40 cm)	4–16 in (10–40 cm)	E	I	◆		◆		◆					◆		
Dracula vampira	20–24 in (50–60 cm)	12–16 in (30–40 cm)	E	I/C	◆		◆		◆						◆	
Dracula velutina	4–16 in (10–40 cm)	4–16 in (10–40 cm)	E	I/C	◆		◆		◆					◆		
Drakaea glyptodon	4–14 in (10–35 cm)	½–1½ in (12–35 mm)	T	I/C	◆		◆					◆	◆			
Dryadella edwallii	1–2 in (2.5–5 cm)	1–2 in (2.5–5 cm)	E	I/C			◆	◆	◆						◆	
Dryadella pusiola	2½–3 in (6–8 cm)	2–3 in (5–8 cm)	E	I			◆	◆	◆						◆	
Dryadella zebrina	2–2½ in (5–6 cm)	1½–2 in (3.5–5 cm)	E	I			◆	◆							◆	
Dyakia hendersoniana	3–8 in (8–20 cm)	2½–6 in (6–15 cm)	E	W	◆	◆	◆		◆				◆	◆		
Elythranthera brunonis	6–12 in (15–30 cm)	1–3 in (2.5–8 cm)	T	I/C	◆		◆						◆	◆		
Encyclia alata	8–36 in (20–90 cm)	8–20 in (20–50 cm)	E	W/I	◆		◆				◆		◆	◆		
Encyclia hanburyi	8–27 in (20–70 cm)	8–20 in (20–50 cm)	E	W/I	◆		◆			◆			◆	◆		
Encyclia randii	12–24 in (30–60 cm)	12–24 in (30–60 cm)	E	W/I	◆	◆	◆	◆								
Epiblastus basalis	4–12 in (10–30 cm)	4–12 in (10–30 cm)	E/T	I	◆		◆		◆					◆		
Epicattleya Purple Glory 'Moir's Pride'	8–20 in (20–50 cm)	6–16 in (15–40 cm)	E	W/I	◆	◆	◆						◆			
Epicattleya Siam Jade	8–16 in (20–40 cm)	4–16 in (10–40 cm)	E	W/I/C		◆	◆						◆	◆		
Epidendrum anceps	24–36 in (60–90 cm)	16–20 in (40–50 cm)	E/L	W/I	◆		◆	◆						◆		
Epidendrum barbeyanum	4–10 in (10–25 cm)	4–10 in (10–25 cm)	E	W/I	◆		◆	◆						◆		

Plant name	Height	Spread	Type	Temp.	Showy flowers	Scented flowers	Grow in pot	Grow on mount	Keep moist	Dry winter	Drought tolerant	Frost tolerant	Full sun	Half sun	Shade	CITES listed
Epidendrum ciliare	8–24 in (20–60 cm)	8–36 in (20–90 cm)	E	W/I	♦		♦	♦		♦			♦	♦		
Epidendrum ibaguense	8–48 in (20–120 cm)	8–48 in (20–120 cm)	E/T	W/I/C	♦		♦						♦	♦		
Epidendrum ilense	8–48 in (20–120 cm)	8–24 in (20–60 cm)	E	W	♦		♦	♦	♦					♦		
Epidendrum lacustre	12–44 in (30–110 cm)	12–24 in (30–60 cm)	T	W/I	♦		♦						♦	♦		
Epidendrum medusae	4–12 in (10–30 cm)	4–16 in (10–40 cm)	E	I/C	♦		♦			♦				♦		
Epidendrum × obrienianum	6–30 ft (1.8–9 m)	30–50 in (75–130 cm)	T	I	♦		♦						♦			
Epidendrum parkinsonianum	1–7 ft (0.3–2 m)	8–24 in (20–60 cm)	E	W/I	♦		♦	♦					♦	♦		
Epidendrum porpax	1–2½ in (2.5–6 cm)	2–12 in (5–30 cm)	E	W/I/C	♦		♦	♦	♦					♦	♦	
Epidendrum pseudepidendrum	8–40 in (20–100 cm)	4–16 in (10–40 cm)	E	W	♦		♦							♦		
Epidendrum secundum	8–36 in (20–90 cm)	8–48 in (20–120 cm)	T	W/I	♦		♦						♦	♦		
Epidendrum stanfordianum	10–20 in (25–50 cm)	8–30 in (20–75 cm)	E	W/I	♦		♦							♦		
Epidendrum Hybrids	8–48 in (20–120 cm)	8–48 in (20–120 cm)	E	W/I/C	♦		♦							♦		
Epigeneium triflorum	5–12 in (12–30 cm)	8–16 in (20–40 cm)	E	W/I	♦		♦	♦					♦	♦		
Epipactis gigantea	24–40 in (60–100 cm)	8–16 in (20–40 cm)	T	C	♦		♦					♦	♦			
Epipactis helleborine	8–40 in (20–100 cm)	4–12 in (10–30 cm)	T	C	♦		♦						♦		♦	
Epipactis palustris	12–16 in (30–40 cm)	4–6 in (10–15 cm)	T	C	♦		♦						♦	♦		
Epipactis viridiflora	8–36 in (20–90 cm)	4–8 in (10–20 cm)	T	C	♦		♦						♦		♦	
Epiphronitis Veitchii	4–20 in (10–50 cm)	2–6 in (5–15 cm)	E/T	W/I	♦		♦	♦						♦		
Eria aporoides	4–10 in (10–25 cm)	4–10 in (10–25 cm)	E	W/I			♦						♦	♦		
Eria gigantea	8–36 in (20–90 cm)	8–24 in (20–60 cm)	E	I			♦							♦		
Eria mysorensis	4–16 in (10–40 cm)	4–24 in (10–60 cm)	E	I			♦							♦		
Eria spicata	4–14 in (10–35 cm)	6–20 in (15–50 cm)	E	I			♦								♦	
Eria stricta	4–10 in (10–25 cm)	4–10 in (10–25 cm)	E	W/I			♦							♦		
Eria xanthocheila	6–16 in (15–40 cm)	4–16 in (10–40 cm)	E	I			♦						♦	♦	♦	
Eriopsis biloba	18–40 in (45–100 cm)	16–20 in (40–50 cm)	E/T	I	♦		♦		♦					♦		
Erycina echinata	4–8 in (10–20 cm)	5–8 in (12–20 cm)	E	W	♦			♦		♦			♦	♦		
Esmeralda cathcartii	40–80 in (100–200 cm)	16–24 in (40–60 cm)	E	I	♦		♦		♦						♦	
Esmeralda clarkei	8–40 in (20–100 cm)	8–20 in (20–50 cm)	E	W/I	♦		♦		♦					♦		
Euchile mariae	6–10 in (15–25 cm)	4–6 in (10–15 cm)	E	I	♦		♦	♦		♦			♦			
Eulophia clavicornis	4–36 in (10–90 cm)	4–16 in (10–40 cm)	T	I/C	♦		♦						♦	♦		
Eulophia ovalis	6–27 in (15–70 cm)	4–16 in (10–40 cm)	T	I/C	♦		♦						♦	♦		

Plant name	Height	Spread	Type	Temp.	Showy flowers	Scented flowers	Grow in pot	Grow on mount	Keep moist	Dry winter	Drought tolerant	Frost tolerant	Full sun	Half sun	Shade	CITES listed
Eulophia spectabilis	18–40 in (45–100 cm)	8–12 in (20–30 cm)	T	I	◆		◆							◆	◆	
Eulophia welwitschii	10–36 in (25–90 cm)	4–16 in (10–40 cm)	T	I/C	◆		◆						◆	◆		
Eulophiella elisabethae	24–36 in (60–90 cm)	16–20 in (40–50 cm)	E	W	◆			◆	◆					◆		
Eurychone rothschildiana	4–6 in (10–15 cm)	8–12 in (20–30 cm)	E	W	◆	◆	◆		◆						◆	
Fernandezia subbiflora	1¼–5 in (3–12 cm)	1¼–4 in (3–10 cm)	E	C	◆		◆		◆						◆	
Galeandra baueri	12–16 in (30–40 cm)	8–12 in (20–30 cm)	E	I		◆	◆			◆				◆		
Gastrochilus calceolaris	4–6 in (10–15 cm)	6–8 in (15–20 cm)	E	W			◆	◆						◆		
Gastrochilus formosanus	3–4 in (8–10 cm)	1–2 in (2.5–5 cm)	E	W	◆		◆	◆						◆		
Gastrochilus japonicus	2–6 in (5–15 cm)	4–12 in (10–30 cm)	E	W/I	◆		◆	◆						◆	◆	
Gastrochilus obliquus	2–6 in (5–15 cm)	4–14 in (10–35 cm)	E	W/I	◆		◆	◆						◆	◆	
Gastrochilus suavis	2–6 in (5–15 cm)	4–12 in (10–30 cm)	E	W/I	◆		◆	◆						◆	◆	
Gastrorchis pulcher	24–30 in (60–75 cm)	20–24 in (50–60 cm)	T	I	◆		◆			◆				◆	◆	
Gastrorchis steinhardtiana	8–20 in (20–50 cm)	8–16 in (20–40 cm)	T	I	◆		◆			◆				◆	◆	
Georgeblackara Tribute	3–10 in (8–25 cm)	3–6 in (8–15 cm)	E	W/I	◆		◆	◆						◆		
Glossodia major	4–14 in (10–35 cm)	2–4 in (5–10 cm)	T	I/C	◆	◆	◆					◆	◆	◆		
Gomesa crispa	6–8 in (15–20 cm)	6–8 in (15–20 cm)	E	C	◆	◆	◆		◆						◆	
Gongora histrionica	36 in (90 cm)	27 in (70 cm)	E	W/I	◆	◆	◆		◆					◆		
Gongora nigropunctata	20–27 in (50–70 cm)	20–24 in (50–60 cm)	E	W/I	◆	◆	◆		◆					◆	◆	
Gongora pleiochroma	8–20 in (20–50 cm)	8–24 in (20–60 cm)	E	W/I	◆	◆	◆		◆						◆	
Goodyera biflora	2–6 in (5–15 cm)	2½–3 in (6–8 cm)	T	I/C			◆		◆					◆	◆	
Goodyera tesselata	4–10 in (10–25 cm)	2½–4 in (6–10 cm)	T	I/C		◆	◆							◆	◆	
Grammangis ellisii	20–24 in (50–60 cm)	20–26 in (50–65 cm)	E	I	◆		◆		◆						◆	
Grammatophyllum elegans	12–48 in (30–120 cm)	12–60 in (30–150 cm)	E	W/I	◆		◆						◆	◆		
Grammatophyllum speciosum	3–7 ft (0.9–2 m)	12–20 ft (3.5–6 m)	E	W	◆	◆	◆						◆			
Grastidium cathcartii	48 in (120 cm)	36 in (90 cm)	E	I/C			◆		◆					◆		
Grobya amherstiae	6–12 in (15–30 cm)	5–10 in (12–25 cm)	E	I	◆		◆	◆						◆	◆	
Gymnadenia conopsea	6–18 in (15–45 cm)	2–4 in (5–10 cm)	T	C	◆	◆	◆					◆	◆			
Habenaria arenaria	10–16 in (25–40 cm)	6–12 in (15–30 cm)	T	I			◆		◆						◆	

Plant name	Height	Spread	Type	Temp.	Showy flowers	Scented flowers	Grow in pot	Grow on mount	Keep moist	Dry winter	Drought tolerant	Frost tolerant	Full sun	Half sun	Shade	CITES listed
Habenaria dregeana	8–16 in (20–40 cm)	4–8 in (10–20 cm)	T	I/C	♦		♦		♦				♦	♦		
Habenaria marginata	3–8 in (8–20 cm)	2–6 in (5–15 cm)	T	I/C			♦		♦				♦			
Habenaria monorhiza	8–20 in (20–50 cm)	5–10 in (12–25 cm)	T	I	♦		♦		♦					♦		
Habenaria rhodocheila	8–12 in (20–30 cm)	4–8 in (10–20 cm)	T	W/I	♦		♦		♦					♦	♦	
Haraella retrocalla	2–4 in (5–10 cm)	2½–6 in (6–15 cm)	E	I		♦	♦	♦	♦						♦	
Hawkinsara Keepsake 'Lake View'	4–20 in (10–50 cm)	4–12 in (10–30 cm)	E	W/I	♦		♦						♦	♦		
Hexisea imbricata	4–20 in (10–50 cm)	4–16 in (10–40 cm)	E	W/I			♦	♦						♦		
Himantoglossum adriaticum	12–30 in (30–75 cm)	6–10 in (15–25 cm)	T	C	♦		♦					♦	♦			
Himantoglossum caprinum	12–40 in (30–100 cm)	6–12 in (15–30 cm)	T	C	♦		♦					♦	♦	♦		
Himantoglossum hircinum	12–30 in (30–75 cm)	6–10 in (15–25 cm)	T	C	♦	♦	♦					♦	♦			
Homalopetalum pumilio	½–2 in (12–50 mm)	¾–1¼ in (18–30 mm)	E	I			♦	♦	♦					♦		
Howeara Mary Eliza	4–16 in (10–40 cm)	4–6 in (10–15 cm)	E	W/I	♦	♦	♦							♦		
Huntleya citrina	8–12 in (20–30 cm)	8–12 in (20–30 cm)	E	W	♦		♦	♦							♦	
Huntleya meleagris	8–12 in (20–30 cm)	8–12 in (20–30 cm)	E	W/I	♦	♦	♦	♦	♦						♦	
Huttonaea grandiflora	4–36 in (10–90 cm)	3–8 in (8–20 cm)	T	I/C	♦		♦							♦	♦	
Hygrochilus parishii	8–12 in (20–30 cm)	14–18 in (35–45 cm)	E	W/I	♦	♦	♦			♦			♦	♦		
Ida costata	12–36 in (30–90 cm)	12–36 in (30–90 cm)	E/L	I/C	♦	♦	♦							♦	♦	
Ionopsis utricularioides	12 in (30 cm)	6–8 in (15–20 cm)	E	W/I	♦			♦	♦				♦			
Isabelia virginalis	1½–3 in (3.5–8 cm)	2–6 in (5–15 cm)	E	W/I			♦	♦	♦					♦		
Isochilus aurantiacus	4–16 in (10–40 cm)	4–20 in (10–50 cm)	E	W/I	♦		♦		♦					♦		
Isochilus linearis	4–24 in (10–60 cm)	4–24 in (10–60 cm)	E	W/I	♦		♦		♦					♦		
Jumellea arachnantha	18–27 in (45–70 cm)	20–40 in (50–100 cm)	E	I	♦	♦	♦								♦	
Jumellea comorensis	5–12 in (12–30 cm)	4–10 in (10–25 cm)	E	W/I	♦	♦	♦							♦	♦	
Jumellea confusa	5–24 in (12–60 cm)	6–10 in (15–25 cm)	E/L	I	♦	♦	♦								♦	
Jumellea densefoliata	2–3 in (5–8 cm)	2½–3 in (6–8 cm)	E/L	I	♦	♦	♦								♦	
Jumellea fragrans	10–16 in (25–60 cm)	16–24 in (40–60 cm)	E	W/I	♦	♦	♦								♦	
Jumellea sagittata	12–15 in (30–45 cm)	20–30 in (50–75 cm)	E	I	♦	♦	♦								♦	
Kefersteinia graminea	8–14 in (20–35 cm)	8–12 in (20–30 cm)	E	I/C	♦		♦	♦	♦					♦	♦	

Plant name	Height	Spread	Type	Temp.	Showy flowers	Scented flowers	Grow in pot	Grow on mount	Keep moist	Dry winter	Drought tolerant	Frost tolerant	Full sun	Half sun	Shade	CITES listed
Kefersteinia laminata	12 in (30 cm)	16 in (40 cm)	E	I/C	♦		♦	♦	♦					♦	♦	
Kunthara Hybrids	30 in (75 cm)	12 in (30 cm)	E	I/C	♦		♦		♦					♦		
Laelia anceps	8–48 in (20–120 cm)	8–36 in (20–90 cm)	E	W/I/C	♦	♦	♦	♦		♦			♦	♦		
Laelia blumenscheinii	12–14 in (30–35 cm)	10–16 in (25–40 cm)	L	I/C	♦		♦			♦			♦	♦		
Laelia Canariensis	8–40 in (20–100 cm)	8–24 in (20–60 cm)	E/L	W/I	♦		♦						♦	♦		
Laelia caulescens	5–14 in (12–35 cm)	4–10 in (10–25 cm)	L	I	♦		♦						♦	♦		
Laelia cinnabarina	12–20 in (30–50 cm)	14–16 in (35–40 cm)	L	I/C	♦		♦			♦			♦	♦		
Laelia crispa	8–24 in (20–60 cm)	8–36 in (20–90 cm)	E/L	W/I	♦		♦						♦	♦		
Laelia crispata	10–16 in (25–40 cm)	8–10 in (20–25 cm)	L	I/C	♦		♦				♦		♦			
Laelia dayana	6–8 in (15–20 cm)	5–8 in (12–20 cm)	E	I	♦		♦							♦		
Laelia harpophylla	14–24 in (35–60 cm)	14–18 in (35–45 cm)	E	I	♦		♦							♦	♦	
Laelia jongheana	8–12 in (20–30 cm)	9–14 in (22–35 cm)	E	I/C	♦		♦						♦	♦		♦
Laelia longipes	3–4 in (8–10 cm)	4–6 in (10–15 cm)	L	I	♦		♦			♦			♦			
Laelia milleri	8–27 in (20–70 cm)	4–16 in (10–40 cm)	L	W/I	♦		♦			♦			♦	♦		
Laelia pumila	4–8 in (10–20 cm)	4–16 in (10–40 cm)	E	W/I	♦		♦	♦						♦		
Laelia purpurata	8–36 in (20–90 cm)	8–36 in (20–90 cm)	E	W/I	♦	♦	♦						♦	♦		
Laelia rubescens	10–24 in (25–60 cm)	10–16 in (25–40 cm)	E/L	W/I	♦		♦	♦		♦			♦	♦		
Laelia sincorana	3–7 in (8–18 cm)	4–8 in (10–20 cm)	E	I	♦		♦							♦		
Laelia tenebrosa	8–32 in (20–80 cm)	8–36 in (20–90 cm)	E	W/I	♦	♦	♦						♦	♦		
Laeliocatonia Peggy San 'Galaxy'	8–12 in (20–30 cm)	6–8 in (15–20 cm)	E	W/I	♦	♦	♦	♦						♦		
Laeliocattleya Hybrids	4–36 in (10–90 cm)	4–30 in (10–75 cm)	E	W/I	♦		♦					♦	♦	♦		
Lanium avicula	3–5 in (8–12 cm)	6–12 in (15–30 cm)	E	I		♦	♦							♦		
Lepanthes calodictyon	2–2½ in (5–6 cm)	2–3 in (5–8 cm)	E	C			♦	♦	♦						♦	
Lepanthes ligiae	14–16 in (35–40 cm)	14–18 in (35–45 cm)	E	I/C			♦	♦	♦						♦	
Leptotes bicolor	3–6 in (8–12 cm)	3–6 in (8–12 cm)	E	I			♦	♦	♦					♦		
Leptotes unicolor	2–3 in (5–8 cm)	2–3 in (5–8 cm)	E	I			♦	♦	♦					♦		
Liparis latifolia	7–12 in (18–30 cm)	4–6 in (10–15 cm)	T	I	♦		♦	♦	♦						♦	
Liparis nervosa	5–14 in (12–35 cm)	4–8 in (10–20 cm)	T	I/C	♦		♦		♦						♦	
Liparis nigra	10–40 in (25–100 cm)	8–12 in (20–30 cm)	T	I	♦	♦	♦	♦	♦						♦	
Liparis reflexa	4–12 in (10–30 cm)	4–36 in (10–90 cm)	L	I/C		♦	♦	♦	♦					♦		

Plant name	Height	Spread	Type	Temp.	Showy flowers	Scented flowers	Grow in pot	Grow on mount	Keep moist	Dry winter	Drought tolerant	Frost tolerant	Full sun	Half sun	Shade	CITES listed
Liparis viridiflora	4–16 in (10–40 cm)	4–36 in (10–90 cm)	E	W/I		♦	♦	♦	♦					♦		
Lockhartia biserra	4–16 in (10–40 cm)	4–12 in (10–30 cm)	E	W/I	♦		♦	♦	♦					♦		
Lockhartia pittieri	6–8 in (15–20 cm)	5–6 in (12–15 cm)	E	W/I	♦		♦	♦	♦					♦	♦	
Ludisia discolor	4–16 in (10–40 cm)	4–24 in (10–60 cm)	T	W/I	♦		♦		♦						♦	
Lycaste aromatica	8–16 in (20–40 cm)	8–24 in (20–60 cm)	E/L/T	W/I/C	♦	♦	♦							♦	♦	
Lycaste bradeorum	4–12 in (10–30 cm)	8–24 in (20–60 cm)	E	W/I	♦	♦	♦						♦	♦		
Lycaste macrophylla	26–32 in (65–80 cm)	24–32 in (60–80 cm)	E/T	I	♦	♦	♦							♦		
Lycaste skinneri	4–24 in (10–60 cm)	8–24 in (20–60 cm)	E	I/C	♦	♦	♦							♦		
Lycaste tricolor	4–16 in (10–40 cm)	8–24 in (20–60 cm)	E	W/I	♦	♦	♦							♦		
Lycaste Hybrids	4–24 in (10–60 cm)	8–24 in (20–60 cm)	E/T	W/I	♦		♦							♦		
Lyperanthus serratus	10–20 in (25–50 cm)	4–8 in (10–20 cm)	T	I/C	♦	♦	♦						♦	♦		
Macodes petola	7–8 in (18–20 cm)	6–8 in (15–20 cm)	T	W/I			♦		♦						♦	
Macodes sanderiana	7–8 in (18–20 cm)	6–8 in (15–20 cm)	T	W/I			♦		♦						♦	
Macroclinium bicolor	16–40 in (40–100 cm)	16–60 in (40–150 cm)	E	W/I		♦		♦	♦					♦		
Malaxis taurina	4–16 in (10–40 cm)	8 in (20 cm)	T	W			♦		♦					♦		
Masdevallia amabilis	6–12 in (15–30 cm)	4–12 in (10–30 cm)	E/L	C	♦		♦		♦					♦	♦	
Masdevallia coccinea	4–20 in (10–50 cm)	8 in (20 cm)	T	I/C	♦		♦		♦					♦		
Masdevallia floribunda	3–6 in (8–15 cm)	4–8 in (10–20 cm)	E	W/I	♦		♦		♦					♦	♦	
Masdevallia ignea	4–12 in (10–30 cm)	4–5 in (10–12 cm)	T	C	♦		♦		♦						♦	
Masdevallia infracta	4–12 in (10–30 cm)	8 in (20 cm)	T	W/I	♦		♦		♦						♦	
Masdevallia nidifica	1–3 in (2.5–8 cm)	2–3 in (5–8 cm)	E	C	♦		♦		♦						♦	
Masdevallia ophioglossa	4–7 in (10–18 cm)	2½–4 in (6–10 cm)	E	C	♦		♦		♦						♦	
Masdevallia princeps	8–20 in (20–50 cm)	8–16 in (20–40 cm)	E	I	♦		♦		♦					♦	♦	
Masdevallia tovarensis	12 in (30 cm)	12 in (30 cm)	E	W/I	♦		♦		♦					♦		
Masdevallia tridens	4–12 in (10–30 cm)	4–8 in (10–20 cm)	T	I/C	♦		♦		♦					♦		
Masdevallia veitchiana	24 in (60 cm)	12 in (30 cm)	T	I/C	♦		♦		♦					♦		
Masdevallia Hybrids	4–24 in (10–60 cm)	4–12 in (10–30 cm)	T	I/C	♦		♦		♦					♦		
Maxillaria acuminata	4–8 in (10–20 cm)	4–12 in (10–30 cm)	E	W/I/C	♦		♦							♦	♦	
Maxillaria biolleyi	36 in (90 cm)	20 in (50 cm)	E	W/I			♦							♦		
Maxillaria chrysantha	10–14 in (25–35 cm)	10–14 in (25–35 cm)	E	I	♦		♦							♦		

Plant name	Height	Spread	Type	Temp.	Showy flowers	Scented flowers	Grow in pot	Grow on mount	Keep moist	Dry winter	Drought tolerant	Frost tolerant	Full sun	Half sun	Shade	CITES listed
Maxillaria cogniauxiana	24 in (60 cm)	8 in (20 cm)	E	W/I	◆		◆							◆		
Maxillaria cucullata	8–16 in (20–40 cm)	8–32 in (20–80 cm)	E/L/T	W/I/C	◆		◆							◆		
Maxillaria fractiflexa	4–24 in (10–60 cm)	8 in (20 cm)	E	I/C	◆		◆							◆		
Maxillaria marginata	4–8 in (10–20 cm)	4–16 in (10–40 cm)	E	W/I/C	◆		◆							◆		
Maxillaria nigrescens	4–24 in (10–60 cm)	4–8 in (10–20 cm)	E	I/C	◆		◆							◆		
Maxillaria picta	10–14 in (25–35 cm)	10–16 in (25–40 cm)	E/L	I/C	◆	◆	◆							◆		
Maxillaria porphyrostele	4–24 in (10–60 cm)	4–8 in (10–20 cm)	E/L	W/I/C	◆		◆						◆	◆		
Maxillaria sanderiana	18–20 in (45–50 cm)	20–27 in (50–70 cm)	E/T	I/C	◆		◆		◆					◆		
Maxillaria variabilis	4–24 in (10–60 cm)	4–8 in (10–20 cm)	E	W/I/C	◆		◆						◆	◆		
Mediocalcar bifolium	3–10 in (8–25 cm)	4–12 in (10–30 cm)	E	I/C	◆		◆	◆	◆			◆		◆		
Mediocalcar decoratum	2–6 in (5–15 cm)	4–24 in (10–60 cm)	E	I/C	◆		◆	◆	◆			◆		◆		
Mexicoa ghiesbreghtiana	5–6 in (12–15 cm)	6–8 in (15–20 cm)	E	C	◆		◆					◆		◆		
Microcoelia exilis	6–10 in (15–25 cm)	8–10 in (20–25 cm)	E	W/I					◆					◆		
Microcoelia globulosa	4–8 in (10–20 cm)	4–8 in (10–20 cm)	E	W					◆					◆		
Microcoelia stolzii	4–10 in (10–25 cm)	4–12 in (10–30 cm)	E	W/I					◆					◆		
Microterangis hariotiana	4–8 in (10–20 cm)	3–4 in (8–10 cm)	E	I				◆	◆							◆
Microtis orbicularis	8–12 in (20–30 cm)	1–2 in (2–5 cm)	T	C			◆			◆						◆
Miltassia 'Charles M. Fitch'	32 in (80 cm)	24 in (60 cm)	E	I/C	◆		◆						◆	◆		
Miltassia 'Mourier Bay' × *Miltonia* 'Sao Paulo'	32 in (80 cm)	24 in (60 cm)	E	I/C	◆		◆						◆	◆		
Miltonia clowesii	8–27 in (20–70 cm)	8–24 in (20–60 cm)	E	W/I	◆		◆	◆		◆				◆		
Miltonia cuneata	8–20 in (20–50 cm)	8–24 in (20–60 cm)	E	I	◆		◆	◆		◆				◆		
Miltonia flavescens	8–20 in (20–50 cm)	8–36 in (20–90 cm)	E	W/I	◆		◆	◆		◆			◆	◆		
Miltonia moreliana	10–16 in (25–40 cm)	5–6 in (12–15 cm)	E	I	◆		◆	◆		◆					◆	
Miltonia regnellii	8–24 in (20–60 cm)	8–24 in (20–60 cm)	E	W/I	◆		◆	◆						◆		
Miltonia Sandy's Cove	8–24 in (20–60 cm)	8–24 in (20–60 cm)	E	W/I	◆		◆	◆		◆				◆		
Miltonia spectabilis	8–16 in (20–40 cm)	8–24 in (20–60 cm)	E	W/I	◆		◆	◆		◆				◆		
Miltonidium Bartley Schwarz 'Highland'	8–36 in (20–90 cm)	8–24 in (20–60 cm)	E	W/I	◆		◆						◆	◆		
Miltonidium Pupukea Sunset 'H & R'	8–36 in (20–90 cm)	8–24 in (20–60 cm)	E	W/I	◆		◆						◆	◆		
Miltoniopsis phalaenopsis	12 in (30 cm)	15 in (38 cm)	E	W/I	◆		◆		◆					◆		
Miltoniopsis vexillaria	8–16 in (20–40 cm)	8–24 in (20–60 cm)	E	W/I	◆		◆		◆					◆		
Miltoniopsis Hybrids	20 in (50 cm)	32 in (80 cm)	E	W/I	◆	◆	◆		◆					◆		

Plant name	Height	Spread	Type	Temp.	Showy flowers	Scented flowers	Grow in pot	Grow on mount	Keep moist	Dry winter	Drought tolerant	Frost tolerant	Full sun	Half sun	Shade	CITES listed
Myrmecophila tibicinis	1–8 ft (0.3–2.4 m)	1–3 ft (0.3–0.9 m)	E	W/I	◆		◆	◆					◆	◆		
Mystacidium brayboniae	2–4 in (5–10 cm)	2½–6 in (6–15 cm)	E	I				◆		◆				◆	◆	
Mystacidium capense	4–6 in (10–15 cm)	6–10 in (15–25 cm)	E	W/I	◆			◆		◆				◆	◆	
Nageliella purpurea	5–6 in (12–15 cm)	4–6 in (10–15 cm)	E	I		◆	◆	◆						◆		
Nakamotoara Rainbow Gem	4–16 in (10–40 cm)	4–12 in (10–30 cm)	E	W/I	◆		◆	◆					◆	◆		
Nanodes discolor	3–5 in (8–12 cm)	3–4 in (8–10 cm)	E	I	◆		◆	◆	◆						◆	
Neobathiea grandidierana	2–2½ in (5–6 cm)	3–4 in (8–10 cm)	E	I	◆		◆	◆		◆					◆	
Neofinetia falcata	3–8 in (8–20 cm)	3–10 in (8–25 cm)	E	I	◆	◆	◆	◆	◆				◆	◆		
Neolauchea pulchella	2½–5 in (6–12 cm)	4–20 in (10–50 cm)	E	W/I/C	◆		◆	◆						◆	◆	
Neopabstopetalum Adelaide Alive	6–24 in (15–60 cm)	4–16 in (10–40 cm)	E	I/C	◆	◆	◆							◆		
Neopabstopetalum Beverley Lou	6–24 in (15–60 cm)	4–16 in (10–40 cm)	E	I/C	◆		◆							◆		
Neopabstopetalum Warooka	10–24 in (25–60 cm)	8–20 in (20–50 cm)	E	W/I/C	◆	◆	◆							◆	◆	
Neostylis Lou Sneary	4–16 in (10–40 cm)	4–12 in (10–30 cm)	E	W/I	◆	◆	◆	◆					◆	◆		
Nidema ottonis	4–6 in (10–15 cm)	4–6 in (10–15 cm)	E	I	◆		◆	◆							◆	
Notylia barkeri	8–10 in (20–25 cm)	8–10 in (20–25 cm)	E	W		◆		◆						◆		
Oberonia gracilis	4–16 in (10–40 cm)	4–8 in (10–20 cm)	E	W			◆	◆						◆		
Octomeria alpina	3–6 in (8–15 cm)	4–8 in (10–20 cm)	E	I/C		◆	◆	◆						◆	◆	
Octomeria grandiflora	6–8 in (15–20 cm)	4–6 in (10–15 cm)	E	W/I		◆		◆						◆	◆	
Octomeria juncifolia	12–16 in (30–40 cm)	4–10 in (10–25 cm)	E	I/C		◆	◆	◆						◆	◆	
Odontioda Hybrids	8–36 in (20–90 cm)	8–24 in (20–60 cm)	E	C	◆		◆		◆					◆		
Odontobrassia Kenneth Biven 'Santa Barbara'	8–40 in (20–100 cm)	8–27 in (20–70 cm)	E	W/I/C	◆		◆		◆					◆		
Odontocidium Hybrids	8–36 in (20–90 cm)	8–24 in (20–60 cm)	E	W/I/C	◆		◆							◆		
Odontoglossum crispum	5–32 in (12–80 cm)	4–16 in (10–40 cm)	E	C	◆		◆		◆					◆		
Odontoglossum gloriosum	24–36 in (60–90 cm)	14–16 in (35–40 cm)	E	C	◆		◆		◆					◆		
Odontoglossum harryanum	14–18 in (35–45 cm)	14–16 in (35–40 cm)	E	I/C	◆		◆		◆					◆		
Odontoglossum trilobum	48–55 in (120–140 cm)	44–50 in (110–130 cm)	E	W/I/C	◆		◆		◆					◆	◆	
Odontoglossum wyattianum	5–24 in (12–60 cm)	4–12 in (10–30 cm)	E	C	◆		◆		◆					◆		
Odontoglossum Hybrids	8–36 in (20–90 cm)	8–24 in (20–60 cm)	E	C	◆		◆		◆					◆		
Odontonia Bartley Schwarz	8–36 in (20–90 cm)	8–24 in (20–60 cm)	E	I/C	◆	◆	◆		◆					◆		

Plant name	Height	Spread	Type	Temp.	Showy flowers	Scented flowers	Grow in pot	Grow on mount	Keep moist	Dry winter	Drought tolerant	Frost tolerant	Full sun	Half sun	Shade	CITES listed
Odontonia Papageno	8–20 in (20–50 cm)	8–16 in (20–40 cm)	E	I/C	◆		◆		◆						◆	
Odontonia Susan Bogdanow	8–36 in (20–90 cm)	8–24 in (20–60 cm)	E	I/C	◆		◆		◆					◆		
Oeceoclades maculata	8–12 in (20–30 cm)	6–8 in (15–20 cm)	T	W			◆			◆			◆			
Oeceoclades pulchra	8–40 in (20–100 cm)	8–20 in (20–50 cm)	T	W/I			◆			◆				◆	◆	
Oeoniella polystachys	4–12 in (10–30 cm)	4–12 in (10–30 cm)	E	W/I	◆	◆	◆	◆							◆	
Oerstedella centropetala	6–20 in (15–50 cm)	4–10 in (10–25 cm)	E/L	W	◆		◆	◆	◆					◆		
Oerstedella schweinfurthiana	36–88 in (90–210 cm)	16–36 in (40–90 cm)	T	I/C	◆		◆	◆					◆	◆		
Oerstedella wallisii	10–30 in (25–75 cm)	8–12 in (20–30 cm)	E/T	W/I/C	◆		◆	◆	◆					◆		
Oncidium baueri	1–10 ft (0.3–3 m)	1–4 ft (0.3–1.2 m)	E	W/I	◆		◆						◆	◆		
Oncidium Cameo Sunset	4–20 in (10–50 cm)	5–16 in (12–40 cm)	E	I/C	◆		◆							◆		
Oncidium crispum	8–27 in (20–70 cm)	4–16 in (10–40 cm)	E	W/I	◆		◆						◆	◆		
Oncidium croesus	4–8 in (10–20 cm)	4–12 in (10–30 cm)	E	W/I	◆		◆							◆		
Oncidium flexuosum	8–60 in (20–150 cm)	8–36 in (20–90 cm)	E	W/I	◆				◆				◆	◆		
Oncidium fuscatum	12–24 in (30–60 cm)	8–18 in (20–45 cm)	E	I	◆		◆						◆	◆		
Oncidium hintonii	18–26 in (45–65 cm)	14–18 in (35–45 cm)	E	I	◆		◆							◆		
Oncidium leucochilum	2–8 ft (0.6–2.4 m)	12–18 in (30–45 cm)	E	I/C	◆	◆	◆									
Oncidium maculatum	14–24 in (35–60 cm)	14–18 in (35–45 cm)	E	I	◆		◆							◆		
Oncidium marshallianum	8–40 in (20–100 cm)	6–16 in (15–40 cm)	E	I/C	◆		◆							◆		
Oncidium ornithorynchum	6–36 in (15–90 cm)	4–24 in (10–60 cm)	E	I/C	◆	◆	◆							◆		
Oncidium phymatochilum	8–27 in (20–70 cm)	8–16 in (20–40 cm)	E	W/I	◆		◆							◆	◆	
Oncidium sarcodes	8–32 in (20–80 cm)	8–20 in (20–50 cm)	E	W/I/C	◆		◆							◆	◆	
Oncidium Sharry Baby 'Sweet Fragrance'	8–48 in (20–120 cm)	8–36 in (20–90 cm)	E	W/I	◆	◆	◆						◆	◆		
Oncidium sphacelatum	8–60 in (20–150 cm)	8–36 in (20–90 cm)	E	W/I	◆	◆	◆	◆					◆	◆		
Oncidium Sweet Sugar	8–48 in (20–120 cm)	8–36 in (20–90 cm)	E	W/I	◆		◆						◆	◆		
Oncidium Tai	12–60 in (30–150 cm)	12–48 in (30–120 cm)	E	W/I/C	◆		◆						◆	◆		
Oncidium varicosum	5–32 in (12–80 cm)	4–16 in (10–40 cm)	E	W/I	◆		◆	◆					◆	◆		
Oncidium viperinum	5–7 in (12–18 cm)	5–6 in (12–15 cm)	E	I	◆		◆							◆		
Ophrys apifera	8–24 in (20–60 cm)	2–4 in (5–10 cm)	T	C	◆		◆						◆	◆		
Ophrys holoserica	4–20 in (10–50 cm)	2–4 in (5–10 cm)	T	C	◆		◆					◆	◆			
Ophrys insectifera	6–16 in (15–40 cm)	2–4 in (5–10 cm)	T	C	◆		◆					◆	◆			
Ophrys lutea	4–12 in (10–30 cm)	2–7 in (5–18 cm)	T	C	◆		◆						◆	◆		

Plant name	Height	Spread	Type	Temp.	Showy flowers	Scented flowers	Grow in pot	Grow on mount	Keep moist	Dry winter	Drought tolerant	Frost tolerant	Full sun	Half sun	Shade	CITES listed
Ophrys sphegodes	4–18 in (10–45 cm)	2–4 in (5–10 cm)	T	C	◆		◆					◆	◆			
Ophrys tenthredinifera	4–18 in (10–45 cm)	3–10 in (8–25 cm)	T	C	◆		◆						◆	◆		
Orchis militaris	8–26 in (20–65 cm)	3–6 in (8–15 cm)	T	C	◆		◆					◆	◆	◆		
Orchis purpurea	12–36 in (30–90 cm)	3–5 in (8–12 cm)	T	C	◆		◆					◆		◆	◆	
Ornithocephalus bicornis	3–6 in (8–15 cm)	3–6 in (8–15 cm)	E	W/I	◆			◆	◆				◆	◆	◆	
Ornithocephalus gladiatus	2–4 in (5–10 cm)	2–5 in (5–12 cm)	E	I	◆			◆	◆					◆	◆	
Ornithocephalus myrticola	1–2 in (25–50 mm)	1–2 in (25–50 mm)	E	W	◆			◆	◆					◆	◆	
Osmoglossum convallarioides	8–12 in (20–30 cm)	8–12 in (20–30 cm)	E	I/C	◆	◆	◆						◆			
Osmoglossum pulchellum	8–12 in (20–30 cm)	8–12 in (20–30 cm)	E	W	◆	◆	◆						◆			
Pabstia jugosa	8–12 in (20–30 cm)	6–10 in (15–25 cm)	E/L	W	◆	◆	◆		◆					◆		
Paphiopedilum appletonianum	6–24 in (15–60 cm)	8–12 in (20–30 cm)	L/T	W	◆		◆							◆	◆	◆
Paphiopedilum barbatum	6–12 in (15–30 cm)	6–16 in (15–40 cm)	L	W/I	◆		◆							◆		◆
Paphiopedilum bellatulum	2½–6 in (6–15 cm)	8–12 in (20–30 cm)	T	W/I	◆		◆							◆		◆
Paphiopedilum boxallii	4–20 in (10–50 cm)	8–16 in (20–40 cm)	E/T	I/C	◆		◆							◆	◆	◆
Paphiopedilum bullenianum	4–16 in (10–40 cm)	4–12 in (10–30 cm)	T	W	◆		◆							◆		◆
Paphiopedilum callosum	5–6 in (12–15 cm)	8–12 in (20–30 cm)	T	W/I	◆		◆							◆	◆	◆
Paphiopedilum charlesworthii	6–10 in (15–25 cm)	10–12 in (25–30 cm)	L	I	◆		◆							◆		◆
Paphiopedilum concolor	6–10 in (15–25 cm)	8–12 in (20–30 cm)	L/T	W	◆		◆							◆	◆	◆
Paphiopedilum delenatii	6–10 in (15–25 cm)	7–9 in (18–22 cm)	T	W/I	◆	◆	◆							◆	◆	◆
Paphiopedilum exul	4–12 in (10–30 cm)	8–16 in (20–40 cm)	T	W	◆		◆					◆	◆			◆
Paphiopedilum fowliei	8–10 in (20–25 cm)	6–7 in (15–18 cm)	T	W/I	◆		◆						◆	◆		◆
Paphiopedilum glanduliferum	14–18 in (35–45 cm)	12–14 in (30–35 cm)	L/T	W/I	◆		◆							◆		◆
Paphiopedilum glaucophyllum	4–24 in (10–60 cm)	8–20 in (20–50 cm)	T	W/I	◆		◆							◆		◆
Paphiopedilum gratrixianum	4–16 in (10–40 cm)	8–16 in (20–40 cm)	T	W/I/C	◆		◆							◆		◆
Paphiopedilum hainanense	6–20 in (15–50 cm)	8–12 in (20–30 cm)	L/T	W	◆		◆							◆	◆	◆
Paphiopedilum haynaldianum	4–32 in (10–80 cm)	12–24 in (30–60 cm)	E/L/T	W/I	◆		◆							◆		◆
Paphiopedilum henryanum	4–16 in (10–40 cm)	8–12 in (20–30 cm)	L	W/I	◆		◆							◆		◆
Paphiopedilum hirsutissimum	4–16 in (10–40 cm)	8–16 in (20–40 cm)	T	I/C	◆		◆							◆		◆
Paphiopedilum hookerae	4–20 in (10–50 cm)	4–12 in (10–30 cm)	T	W	◆		◆								◆	◆
Paphiopedilum insigne	4–16 in (10–40 cm)	8–12 in (20–30 cm)	T	I/C			◆							◆		◆

Plant name	Height	Spread	Type	Temp.	Showy flowers	Scented flowers	Grow in pot	Grow on mount	Keep moist	Dry winter	Drought tolerant	Frost tolerant	Full sun	Half sun	Shade	CITES listed
Paphiopedilum kolopakingii	30–50 in (75–130 cm)	12–20 in (30–50 cm)	T	W/I	◆		◆							◆		◆
Paphiopedilum liemianum	18 in (45 cm)	14–18 in (35–45 cm)	T	W/I	◆		◆							◆	◆	◆
Paphiopedilum lowii	8–40 in (20–100 cm)	12–24 in (30–60 cm)	L/T	W/I	◆		◆							◆		◆
Paphiopedilum malipoense	18–24 in (45–60 cm)	10–12 in (25–30 cm)	T	I	◆	◆	◆							◆	◆	◆
Paphiopedilum mastersianum	4–20 in (10–50 cm)	8–12 in (20–30 cm)	T	W/I	◆		◆							◆		◆
Paphiopedilum moquetteanum	4–20 in (10–50 cm)	6–24 in (15–60 cm)	T	W	◆		◆								◆	◆
Paphiopedilum niveum	4–12 in (10–30 cm)	4–8 in (10–20 cm)	T	W	◆		◆							◆		◆
Paphiopedilum philippinense	8–24 in (20–60 cm)	8–16 in (20–40 cm)	L/T	W/I	◆		◆							◆		◆
Paphiopedilum primulinum	4–24 in (10–60 cm)	8–16 in (20–40 cm)	T	W/I	◆		◆							◆		◆
Paphiopedilum rothschildianum	8–36 in (20–90 cm)	8–32 in (20–80 cm)	L/T	W/I	◆		◆							◆		◆
Paphiopedilum spicerianum	4–16 in (10–40 cm)	8–12 in (20–30 cm)	T	I/C	◆		◆							◆		◆
Paphiopedilum sukhakulii	4–12 in (10–30 cm)	4–10 in (10–25 cm)	T	W/I	◆		◆								◆	◆
Paphiopedilum tonsum	14–16 in (35–40 cm)	8–12 in (20–30 cm)	L/T	W	◆		◆								◆	◆
Paphiopedilum venustum	10–14 in (25–35 cm)	12–16 in (30–40 cm)	T	I	◆		◆		◆					◆	◆	◆
Paphiopedilum victoria-regina	4–27 in (10–70 cm)	8–24 in (20–60 cm)	L/T	W/I	◆		◆							◆		◆
Paphiopedilum villosum	4–16 in (10–40 cm)	8–12 in (20–30 cm)	T	I/C	◆		◆							◆		◆
Paphiopedilum wardii	8–18 in (20–45 cm)	10–12 in (25–30 cm)	L/T	I	◆		◆								◆	◆
Paphiopedilum Hybrids	4–24 in (10–60 cm)	4–8 in (10–20 cm)	T	I/C	◆		◆							◆	◆	
Papilionanthe hookeriana	5–7 ft (1.5–2 m)	6–8 in (15–20 cm)	E/T	W	◆		◆	◆					◆			
Papilionanthe Miss Joaquim	1–7 ft (0.3–2 m)	8–16 in (20–40 cm)	E	W/I	◆		◆	◆					◆	◆		
Papilionanthe teres	5–7 ft (1.5–2 m)	8–10 in (20–25 cm)	E/T	W	◆		◆	◆					◆			
Papilionanthe vandarum	27–36 in (70–90 cm)	12–16 in (30–40 cm)	E	W/I	◆		◆	◆					◆	◆		
Paracaleana nigrita	2–6 in (5–15 cm)	¾–2½ in (18–60 mm)	T	I/C			◆						◆	◆		
Paraphalaenopsis denevei	16–27 in (40–70 cm)	4–8 in (10–20 cm)	E	W	◆			◆	◆				◆	◆		
Paraphalaenopsis labukensis	40–84 in (100–200 cm)	4–8 in (10–20 cm)	E	W	◆			◆		◆			◆	◆		
Paraphalaenopsis laycockii	24–40 in (60–100 cm)	4–8 in (10–20 cm)	E	W	◆			◆		◆			◆	◆		
Pescatorea cerina	4–16 in (10–40 cm)	8–16 in (20–40 cm)	E	W/I	◆	◆	◆		◆					◆		
Pescatorea lehmannii	4–20 in (10–50 cm)	8–16 in (20–40 cm)	E	W/I	◆	◆	◆		◆					◆		
Phaiocalanthe Schroederiana	12–32 in (30–80 cm)	16–24 in (40–60 cm)	T	W/I	◆		◆		◆					◆		
Phaiocymbidium Chardwarense	20–27 in (50–70 cm)	12–16 in (30–40 cm)	T	W/I	◆		◆							◆		
Phaius flavus	18–26 in (45–65 cm)	24–30 in (60–75 cm)	T	W/I	◆		◆		◆					◆	◆	

Plant name	Height	Spread	Type	Temp.	Showy flowers	Scented flowers	Grow in pot	Grow on mount	Keep moist	Dry winter	Drought tolerant	Frost tolerant	Full sun	Half sun	Shade	CITES listed
Phaius tankervilleae	12–48 in (30–120 cm)	8–36 in (20–90 cm)	T	W/I	◆		◆		◆				◆	◆		
Phalaenopsis amabilis	12–36 in (30–90 cm)	8–20 in (20–50 cm)	E	W	◆		◆	◆	◆					◆		
Phalaenopsis aphrodite	4–24 in (10–60 cm)	8–24 in (20–60 cm)	E	W	◆		◆	◆	◆						◆	
Phalaenopsis equestris	4–12 in (10–30 cm)	5–12 in (12–30 cm)	E	W	◆		◆	◆	◆					◆		
Phalaenopsis gibbosa	2–3 in (5–8 cm)	3–8 in (8–20 cm)	E	W/I	◆		◆	◆		◆				◆	◆	
Phalaenopsis lueddemanniana	4–16 in (10–40 cm)	6–16 in (15–40 cm)	E	W	◆		◆		◆					◆		
Phalaenopsis mannii	8–12 in (20–30 cm)	10–16 in (25–40 cm)	E	W/I	◆		◆	◆	◆					◆	◆	
Phalaenopsis parishii	4–8 in (10–20 cm)	5–8 in (12–20 cm)	E	W	◆		◆	◆	◆					◆		
Phalaenopsis pulcherrima	4–36 in (10–90 cm)	5–12 in (12–30 cm)	L/T	W	◆		◆		◆				◆	◆		
Phalaenopsis schilleriana	12–36 in (30–90 cm)	8–20 in (20–50 cm)	E	W	◆		◆		◆					◆		
Phalaenopsis wilsonii	6–8 in (15–20 cm)	4–5 in (10–12 cm)	E/L	W/I	◆			◆		◆				◆	◆	
Phalaenopsis Hybrids	8–36 in (20–90 cm)	5–24 in (12–60 cm)	E	W	◆		◆		◆					◆		
Pholidota articulata	8–12 in (20–30 cm)	8–12 in (20–30 cm)	E/L	W/I		◆	◆	◆						◆		
Pholidota bracteata	6–14 in (15–35 cm)	4–12 in (10–30 cm)	E	I		◆	◆	◆						◆	◆	
Pholidota chinensis	12–16 in (30–40 cm)	8–10 in (20–25 cm)	E/L	I		◆	◆	◆						◆		
Pholidota imbricata	10–14 in (25–35 cm)	8–12 in (20–30 cm)	E	W		◆	◆	◆				◆				
Phragmipedium besseae	8–20 in (20–50 cm)	8–16 in (20–40 cm)	L/T	W/I	◆		◆		◆					◆		◆
Phragmipedium caudatum	8–36 in (20–90 cm)	12–24 in (30–60 cm)	E/L	W	◆		◆		◆					◆		◆
Phragmipedium longifolium	8–36 in (20–90 cm)	12–24 in (30–60 cm)	T	W	◆		◆		◆				◆			◆
Phragmipedium Hybrids	8–36 in (20–90 cm)	8–24 in (20–60 cm)	T	W/I	◆		◆		◆				◆			
Platanthera bifolia	6–20 in (15–50 cm)	4–10 in (10–25 cm)	T	C	◆	◆	◆					◆	◆	◆	◆	
Platanthera chlorantha	8–20 in (20–50 cm)	6–14 in (15–35 cm)	T	C	◆	◆	◆					◆	◆	◆	◆	
Platanthera ciliaris	27–40 in (70–100 cm)	4–6 in (10–15 cm)	T	C	◆	◆	◆					◆	◆	◆		
Platanthera integra	16–24 in (40–60 cm)	2–3 in (5–8 cm)	T	C	◆	◆	◆					◆	◆	◆		
Platanthera leucophaea	16–26 in (40–65 cm)	8–10 in (20–25 cm)	T	C	◆	◆	◆					◆	◆			
Plectorrhiza tridentata	2½–6 in (6–15 cm)	4–6 in (10–15 cm)	E	I/C		◆		◆	◆					◆	◆	
Pleione bulbocodioides	4–7 in (10–18 cm)	3–4 in (8–10 cm)	L/T	C	◆		◆			◆					◆	
Pleione formosana	16 in (40 cm)	16 in (40 cm)	L/T	C	◆		◆			◆		◆		◆		
Pleione praecox	6–10 in (15–25 cm)	8–12 in (20–30 cm)	T	C	◆	◆	◆			◆				◆		
Pleione Hybrids	8–16 in (20–40 cm)	8–16 in (20–40 cm)	T	C	◆		◆			◆		◆				
Pleurothallis cordata	4–16 in (10–40 cm)	4–12 in (10–30 cm)	E	W/I/C			◆		◆					◆	◆	

Plant name	Height	Spread	Type	Temp.	Showy flowers	Scented flowers	Grow in pot	Grow on mount	Keep moist	Dry winter	Drought tolerant	Frost tolerant	Full sun	Half sun	Shade	CITES listed
Pleurothallis grobyi	1½–6 in (3.5–15 cm)	2½–12 in (6–30 cm)	E	W/I/C			◆		◆					◆		
Pleurothallis immersa	18–24 in (45–60 cm)	8–10 in (20–25 cm)	E	I/C			◆		◆						◆	
Pleurothallis macroblepharis	2–6 in (5–15 cm)	2–8 in (5–20 cm)	E	I/C			◆		◆					◆	◆	
Pleurothallis marthae	8–20 in (20–50 cm)	6–14 in (15–35 cm)	E	I			◆		◆					◆	◆	
Pleurothallis phalangifera	12–14 in (30–35 cm)	14–16 in (35–40 cm)	E	I/C			◆		◆						◆	
Pleurothallis praecipua	12–14 in (30–35 cm)	14–16 in (35–40 cm)	E	I/C			◆		◆						◆	
Pleurothallis tuerckheimii	8–20 in (20–50 cm)	4–20 in (10–50 cm)	E	I			◆		◆					◆		
Pleurothallis viduata	4–12 in (10–30 cm)	4–12 in (10–30 cm)	E	W/I/C			◆		◆					◆	◆	
Pleurothallis villosa	1½–6 in (3.5–15 cm)	1½–6 in (3.5–15 cm)	E	I/C			◆		◆						◆	
Podangis dactyloceras	4–5 in (10–12 cm)	4–6 in (10–15 cm)	E	I			◆	◆							◆	
Pogonia ophioglossoides	6–10 in (15–25 cm)	4–8 in (10–20 cm)	T	C	◆		◆		◆			◆	◆			
Polystachya bella	4–12 in (10–30 cm)	4–12 in (10–30 cm)	E	W	◆		◆			◆				◆		
Polystachya gerrardii	3–12 in (8–30 cm)	4–10 in (10–25 cm)	E	I	◆		◆							◆	◆	
Polystachya johnstonii	2–4 in (5–10 cm)	2–6 in (5–15 cm)	E	W	◆		◆			◆				◆		
Polystachya longiscapa	12–36 in (30–90 cm)	6–8 in (15–20 cm)	L	I/C	◆		◆			◆			◆			
Polystachya ottoniana	2½–8 in (6–20 cm)	2½–8 in (6–20 cm)	E	W/I/C	◆		◆			◆				◆	◆	
Polystachya pubescens	6–10 in (15–25 cm)	6–8 in (15–20 cm)	E/L	I/C	◆	◆	◆	◆		◆	◆			◆	◆	
Porroglossum amethystinum	6–10 in (15–25 cm)	4–6 in (10–15 cm)	E/L	I/C	◆		◆		◆					◆	◆	
Porroglossum echidnum	2–8 in (5–20 cm)	4–6 in (10–15 cm)	E/L	C	◆		◆		◆					◆	◆	
Porroglossum meridionale	1¼–5 in (3–12 cm)	1½–4 in (3.5–10 cm)	E	I/C	◆		◆		◆						◆	
Porroglossum olivaceum	2½–8 in (6–20 cm)	2½–4 in (6–10 cm)	E	I/C	◆		◆		◆						◆	
Porroglossum teaguei	4–10 in (10–25 cm)	2–3 in (5–8 cm)	E	I	◆		◆		◆						◆	
Potinara Hybrids	8–24 in (20–60 cm)	8–24 in (20–60 cm)	E	W/I	◆		◆			◆				◆		
Promenaea stapelioides	2–4 in (5–10 cm)	6–8 in (15–20 cm)	E	I	◆	◆	◆	◆						◆	◆	
Promenaea xanthina	2–4 in (5–10 cm)	6–8 in (15–20 cm)	E	I	◆		◆	◆						◆	◆	
Prosthechea brassavolae	14–18 in (35–45 cm)	14–18 in (35–45 cm)	E/L	W/I	◆		◆	◆					◆	◆		
Prosthechea chacaoensis	8–14 in (20–35 cm)	6–12 in (15–30 cm)	E	W/I/C	◆	◆	◆	◆						◆		
Prosthechea cochleata	8–24 in (20–60 cm)	9–18 in (22–45 cm)	E	W/I	◆		◆	◆						◆		
Prosthechea crassilabia	8–27 in (20–70 cm)	8–14 in (20–35 cm)	E	W/I	◆		◆	◆						◆		
Prosthechea michuacana	8–48 in (20–120 cm)	8–16 in (20–40 cm)	E	I	◆		◆	◆						◆		
Prosthechea prismatocarpa	8–27 in (20–70 cm)	8–16 in (20–40 cm)	E	W/I	◆	◆	◆	◆						◆		

Plant name	Height	Spread	Type	Temp.	Showy flowers	Scented flowers	Grow in pot	Grow on mount	Keep moist	Dry winter	Drought tolerant	Frost tolerant	Full sun	Half sun	Shade	CITES listed
Prosthechea radiata	8–16 in (20–40 cm)	12–16 in (30–40 cm)	E/L	I	◆	◆	◆	◆						◆		
Prosthechea Sunburst	8–20 in (20–50 cm)	8–20 in (20–50 cm)	E	W/I	◆	◆	◆	◆						◆		
Pseudolaelia vellozicola	4–20 in (10–50 cm)	4–32 in (10–80 cm)	E	I/C	◆			◆		◆			◆	◆		
Psychilis kraenzlinii	16–40 in (40–100 cm)	8–20 in (20–50 cm)	E	W	◆			◆		◆			◆			
Psychilis krugii	16–40 in (40–100 cm)	8–20 in (20–50 cm)	E	W	◆			◆					◆			
Psychilis truncata	8–12 in (20–30 cm)	6–8 in (15–20 cm)	E/L	W	◆					◆			◆			
Psychopsis kramerianum	8–36 in (20–90 cm)	5–24 in (12–60 cm)	E	W	◆		◆	◆					◆	◆		
Psychopsis Mendenhall	8–36 in (20–90 cm)	5–24 in (12–60 cm)	E	W/I	◆		◆	◆					◆	◆		
Psychopsis papilio	8–36 in (20–90 cm)	5–24 in (12–60 cm)	E	W	◆		◆	◆					◆	◆		
Pterostylis curta	4–12 in (10–30 cm)	1½–3 in (3.5–8 cm)	T	I/C	◆		◆					◆		◆		
Pterostylis nutans	1½–12 in (3.5–30 cm)	1½–3 in (3.5–8 cm)	T	I/C	◆		◆					◆			◆	
Pterostylis pedunculata	6–8 in (15–20 cm)	3–5 in (8–12 cm)	T	I/C	◆		◆					◆		◆		
Pterostylis planulata	1½–14 in (3.5–35 cm)	1½–4 in (3.5–10 cm)	T	I/C	◆		◆					◆		◆		
Pterygodium hastatum	6–14 in (15–35 cm)	5–10 in (12–25 cm)	T	I/C	◆		◆				◆			◆		
Pyrorchis nigricans	4–12 in (10–30 cm)	2–3 in (5–8 cm)	T	I/C	◆	◆	◆						◆	◆		
Rangaeris muscicola	6–8 in (15–20 cm)	8–12 in (20–30 cm)	E/L	W	◆	◆	◆	◆							◆	
Rangaeris rhipsalisocia	6–8 in (15–20 cm)	8–12 in (20–30 cm)	E	W	◆	◆	◆	◆							◆	
Renantanda Tuanku Bainun	8–48 in (20–120 cm)	8–32 in (20–80 cm)	E	W	◆		◆		◆				◆			
Renanthera coccinea	8–48 in (20–120 cm)	8–32 in (20–80 cm)	E	W	◆		◆	◆					◆			
Renanthera imschootiana	48–60 in (120–150 cm)	36–48 in (90–120 cm)	E	I	◆		◆	◆					◆	◆		◆
Renanthera monachica	12–24 in (30–60 cm)	20–24 in (50–60 cm)	E	W/I	◆		◆	◆						◆		
Renanthera Hybrids	1–8 ft (0.3–2.4 m)	8–36 in (20–90 cm)	E	W	◆		◆	◆					◆			
Restrepia antennifera	8–10 in (20–25 cm)	10–14 in (25–35 cm)	E	I/C	◆		◆		◆						◆	
Restrepia contorta	7–8 in (18–20 cm)	5–6 in (12–15 cm)	E	I/C	◆		◆	◆							◆	
Restrepia guttulata	3–6 in (8–15 cm)	3–8 in (8–20 cm)	E	I/C	◆		◆		◆					◆		
Restrepiella ophiocephala	6–16 in (15–40 cm)	6–8 in (15–20 cm)	E	W/I		◆	◆		◆					◆		
Rhinerrhiza divitiflora	3–16 in (8–40 cm)	3–12 in (8–30 cm)	E	I	◆			◆						◆		
Rhipidoglossum xanthopollinium	4–12 in (10–30 cm)	6–12 in (15–30 cm)	E	I	◆	◆	◆	◆							◆	
Rhizanthella slateri	3–8 in (8–20 cm)	3–12 in (8–30 cm)	T	I			◆								◆	
Rhyncholaelia digbyana	8–14 in (20–35 cm)	8–14 in (20–35 cm)	E	W	◆	◆	◆	◆					◆			

Plant name	Height	Spread	Type	Temp.	Showy flowers	Scented flowers	Grow in pot	Grow on mount	Keep moist	Dry winter	Drought tolerant	Frost tolerant	Full sun	Half sun	Shade	CITES listed
Rhyncholaelia glauca	8–14 in (20–35 cm)	8–14 in (20–35 cm)	E	W/I	◆	◆	◆	◆					◆			
Rhynchostele bictoniensis	8–24 in (20–60 cm)	8–16 in (20–40 cm)	E	I	◆		◆		◆					◆		
Rhynchostele cordata	8–16 in (20–40 cm)	8–16 in (20–40 cm)	E	I	◆		◆		◆					◆		
Rhynchostele maculata	8–14 in (20–35 cm)	8–12 in (20–30 cm)	E	I/C	◆		◆		◆					◆		
Rhynchostele rossii	5–7 in (12–18 cm)	6–8 in (15–20 cm)	E	I/C	◆		◆		◆					◆		
Rhynchostele Stanfordiense	8–27 in (20–70 cm)	8–16 in (20–40 cm)	E	I	◆		◆		◆					◆		
Rhynchostele uro-skinneri	12–16 in (30–40 cm)	14–18 in (35–45 cm)	E	I/C	◆		◆		◆					◆		
Rhynchostylis gigantea	8–24 in (20–60 cm)	8–20 in (20–50 cm)	E	W	◆		◆	◆					◆	◆		
Rhynchostylis retusa	8–30 in (20–75 cm)	8–20 in (20–50 cm)	E	W/I	◆		◆	◆					◆	◆		
Rimacola elliptica	2½–12 in (6–30 cm)	4–12 in (10–30 cm)	T	I/C	◆				◆					◆		
Robiquetia cerina	4–20 in (10–50 cm)	5–14 in (12–35 cm)	E	W	◆			◆	◆					◆		
Robiquetia succisa	8–27 in (20–70 cm)	8–20 in (20–50 cm)	E	W/I	◆			◆	◆				◆	◆	◆	
Rodriguezia decora	4–16 in (10–40 cm)	4–24 in (10–60 cm)	E	W/I	◆	◆		◆	◆					◆		
Rodriguezia lanceolata	10–16 in (25–40 cm)	6–8 in (15–20 cm)	E	I	◆			◆	◆					◆	◆	
Rodriguezia venusta	6–7 in (15–18 cm)	6–8 in (15–20 cm)	E	I	◆	◆		◆	◆						◆	
Rossioglossum grande	8–20 in (20–50 cm)	8–20 in (20–50 cm)	E	I/C	◆		◆			◆			◆	◆		
Rossioglossum Rawdon Jester	8–20 in (20–50 cm)	8–20 in (20–50 cm)	E	I/C	◆		◆			◆			◆	◆		
Saccolabiopsis armitii	2½–8 in (6–20 cm)	2½–6 in (6–15 cm)	E	W				◆	◆					◆		
Sarcochilus aequalis	4–6 in (10–15 cm)	6–10 in (15–25 cm)	L	I/C	◆		◆		◆					◆	◆	
Sarcochilus ceciliae	4–8 in (10–20 cm)	6–12 in (15–30 cm)	L	I/C	◆		◆		◆			◆	◆	◆		
Sarcochilus falcatus	2½–8 in (6–20 cm)	4–8 in (10–20 cm)	E	I/C	◆	◆		◆	◆					◆	◆	
Sarcochilus fitzgeraldii	4–16 in (10–40 cm)	4–16 in (10–40 cm)	L	I/C	◆		◆		◆					◆	◆	
Sarcochilus hartmannii	4–16 in (10–40 cm)	4–16 in (10–40 cm)	L	I/C	◆		◆		◆					◆		
Sarcochilus hillii	2½–5 in (6–12 cm)	2½–5 in (6–12 cm)	E	I/C		◆		◆	◆					◆	◆	
Sarcochilus hirticalcar	2½–6 in (6–15 cm)	2½–6 in (6–15 cm)	E	I	◆			◆	◆					◆		
Sarcochilus olivaceus	4–8 in (10–20 cm)	4–12 in (10–30 cm)	E/L	I/C	◆	◆		◆	◆						◆	
Sarcochilus serrulatus	2½–6 in (6–15 cm)	4–8 in (10–20 cm)	E	I	◆		◆		◆					◆	◆	
Sarcochilus Hybrids	4–16 in (10–40 cm)	4–16 in (10–40 cm)	E/L	I/C	◆	◆	◆		◆					◆	◆	
Sartylis Blue Knob	4–24 in (10–60 cm)	4–20 in (10–50 cm)	E	W/I/C	◆		◆							◆		
Sartylis Jannine Banks	4–24 in (10–60 cm)	4–20 in (10–50 cm)	E	W/I	◆		◆		◆					◆		

Plant name	Height	Spread	Type	Temp.	Showy flowers	Scented flowers	Grow in pot	Grow on mount	Keep moist	Dry winter	Drought tolerant	Frost tolerant	Full sun	Half sun	Shade	CITES listed
Satyrium carneum	12–32 in (30–80 cm)	12–18 in (30–45 cm)	T	C	◆		◆			◆			◆			
Satyrium coriifolium	8–30 in (20–75 cm)	6–10 in (15–25 cm)	T	I/C	◆		◆			◆			◆			
Satyrium erectum	4–20 in (10–50 cm)	4–12 in (10–30 cm)	T	I/C	◆	◆	◆			◆			◆	◆		
Satyrium hallackii	8–24 in (20–60 cm)	8–16 in (20–40 cm)	T	I/C	◆		◆			◆			◆	◆		
Satyrium longicauda	8–27 in (20–70 cm)	8–16 in (20–40 cm)	T	I/C	◆		◆			◆			◆	◆		
Satyrium nepalense	6–30 in (15–75 cm)	8–20 in (20–50 cm)	T	I/C	◆	◆	◆			◆				◆		
Satyrium pumilum	1–2 in (2.5–5 cm)	2–4 in (5–10 cm)	T	I/C	◆	◆	◆			◆			◆	◆		
Scaphosepalum breve	5–6 in (12–15 cm)	4–6 in (10–15 cm)	E	C			◆	◆	◆						◆	
Scaphosepalum swertiifolium	6–9 in (15–22 cm)	5–6 in (12–15 cm)	E	C			◆	◆	◆						◆	
Scaphosepalum verrucosum	8–20 in (20–50 cm)	6–8 in (15–20 cm)	E/L	C			◆	◆	◆						◆	
Scaphyglottis prolifera	4–5 in (10–12 cm)	3–4 in (8–10 cm)	E	I	◆		◆	◆	◆				◆	◆		
Scaphyglottis stellata	3–6 in (8–15 cm)	3–6 in (8–15 cm)	E/L	I			◆	◆					◆	◆		
Scaphyglottis violacea	2½–6 in (6–15 cm)	2–8 in (5–20 cm)	E	I/C	◆		◆	◆						◆	◆	
Schistostylus purpuratus	2½–5 in (6–12 cm)	2½–5 in (6–12 cm)	E	I			◆	◆						◆		
Schoenorchis fragrans	2–4 in (5–10 cm)	1¼–2 in (3–5 cm)	E	W		◆	◆	◆						◆	◆	
Schoenorchis micrantha	2–4 in (5–10 cm)	2–4 in (5–10 cm)	E	W		◆	◆	◆						◆		
Schoenorchis pachyacris	¾–2½ in (1.8–6 cm)	1½–3 in (3.5–8 cm)	E	W/I				◆	◆					◆	◆	
Schomburgkia lueddemanniana	24–55 in (60–140 cm)	20–40 in (50–100 cm)	E/L	I	◆		◆								◆	
Schomburgkia superbiens	2–12 ft (0.6–3.5 m)	4–6 ft (1.2–1.8 m)	E/T	W/I/C	◆	◆	◆							◆		
Schomburgkia undulata	3–7 ft (0.9–2 m)	4–6 ft (1.2–1.8 m)	E	W/I	◆	◆	◆	◆						◆		
Schomburgkia weberbaueriana	3–4 ft (0.9–1.2 m)	3–4 ft (0.9–1.2 m)	E	I	◆		◆							◆		
Scuticaria hadwenii	8–18 in (20–45 cm)	6–8 in (15–20 cm)	E	I	◆	◆			◆	◆					◆	
Scuticaria steelei	40–60 in (100–150 cm)	6–8 in (15–20 cm)	E	I	◆				◆	◆					◆	
Sedirea japonica	4–6 in (10–15 cm)	6–12 in (15–30 cm)	E	I/C	◆	◆	◆			◆					◆	
Seidenfadenia mitrata	12–20 in (30–50 cm)	4–6 in (10–15 cm)	E	W	◆	◆			◆	◆				◆		
Serapias cordigera	8–14 in (20–35 cm)	6–10 in (15–25 cm)	T	C	◆		◆						◆	◆		
Serapias lingua	4–14 in (10–35 cm)	6–10 in (15–25 cm)	T	C	◆		◆						◆	◆		
Serapias neglecta	4–12 in (10–30 cm)	3–7 in (8–18 cm)	T	C	◆		◆						◆	◆		
Serapias parviflora	6–12 in (15–30 cm)	6–10 in (15–25 cm)	T	C	◆		◆						◆	◆		
Serapias vomeracea	8–24 in (20–60 cm)	5–6 in (12–15 cm)	T	C	◆		◆						◆	◆		
Smitinandia micrantha	4–10 in (10–25 cm)	5–10 in (12–25 cm)	E	W/I	◆	◆	◆							◆		

Plant name	Height	Spread	Type	Temp.	Showy flowers	Scented flowers	Grow in pot	Grow on mount	Keep moist	Dry winter	Drought tolerant	Frost tolerant	Full sun	Half sun	Shade	CITES listed
Sobralia decora	30–32 in (75–80 cm)	24–36 in (60–90 cm)	E/L/T	W/I	◆		◆			◆				◆		
Sobralia macrantha	1–7 ft (0.3–2 m)	1–4 ft (0.3–1.2 m)	T	W/I	◆		◆			◆			◆	◆		
Sobralia Mirabilis	36 in (90 cm)	36 in (90 cm)	T	W/I	◆		◆			◆				◆	◆	
Sobralia xantholeuca	1–5 ft (0.3–1.5 m)	1–4 ft (0.3–1.2 m)	T	W/I	◆		◆			◆			◆	◆		
Sobralia Yellow Kiss	20–80 in (50–200 cm)	12–84 in (30–200 cm)	T	W/I/C	◆		◆			◆			◆	◆		
Sophrocattleya Beaufort	4–16 in (10–40 cm)	4–16 in (10–40 cm)	E	W/I	◆		◆			◆			◆	◆		
Sophrocattleya Lana Coryell	4–16 in (10–40 cm)	4–16 in (10–40 cm)	E	W/I	◆		◆			◆			◆	◆		
Sophrolaelia Gratrixiae	4–16 in (10–40 cm)	4–16 in (10–40 cm)	E	W/I	◆		◆			◆			◆	◆		
Sophrolaelia Orpetii	4–16 in (10–40 cm)	4–16 in (10–40 cm)	E	W/I	◆		◆			◆			◆	◆		
Sophrolaeliocattleya Hybrids	4–16 in (10–40 cm)	4–16 in (10–40 cm)	E	W/I	◆		◆			◆			◆	◆		
Sophronitella violacea	3–6 in (8–15 cm)	4–6 in (10–15 cm)	E/L	I	◆			◆					◆	◆		
Sophronitis cernua	1½–3 in (3.5–8 cm)	2½–7 in (6–18 cm)	E	W/I	◆		◆	◆					◆	◆		
Sophronitis coccinea	1½–5 in (3.5–12 cm)	2½–8 in (6–20 cm)	E	I/C	◆		◆	◆						◆		
Sophronitis wittigiana	2–4 in (5–10 cm)	2–4 in (5–10 cm)	E	I	◆		◆	◆	◆					◆		
Spathoglottis plicata	12–40 in (30–100 cm)	8–48 in (20–120 cm)	T	W/I	◆		◆		◆				◆			
Spiranthes odorata	12–36 in (30–90 cm)	4–6 in (10–15 cm)	T	C	◆	◆	◆			◆			◆			
Spiranthes sinensis	4–10 in (10–25 cm)	4–6 in (10–15 cm)	T	I			◆			◆			◆			
Spiranthes spiralis	4–12 in (10–30 cm)	4–6 in (10–15 cm)	T	I/C			◆			◆			◆			
Stanhopea anfracta	20–30 in (50–75 cm)	12–20 in (30–50 cm)	E	I	◆	◆	◆		◆					◆		
Stanhopea embreei	8–20 in (20–50 cm)	8–20 in (20–50 cm)	E	W/I	◆	◆	◆		◆					◆		
Stanhopea nigroviolacea	8–20 in (20–50 cm)	8–24 in (20–60 cm)	E	W/I/C	◆	◆	◆		◆					◆		
Stanhopea oculata	8–20 in (20–50 cm)	8–20 in (20–50 cm)	E	W/I	◆	◆	◆		◆					◆		
Stanhopea wardii	8–20 in (20–50 cm)	8–20 in (20–50 cm)	E	W/I	◆	◆	◆		◆					◆		
Staurochilus fasciatus	10–32 in (25–80 cm)	6–12 in (15–30 cm)	E	W/I	◆	◆	◆	◆					◆	◆		
Staurochilus luchuensis	8–24 in (20–60 cm)	8–16 in (20–40 cm)	E	W/I	◆	◆	◆	◆					◆	◆		
Stelis argentata	7–12 in (18–30 cm)	2–4 in (5–10 cm)	E	I			◆	◆							◆	
Stelis imraei	4–8 in (10–20 cm)	2½–6 in (6–15 cm)	E	I/C			◆								◆	
Stenoglottis fimbriata	1½–6 in (3.5–15 cm)	10–12 in (25–30 cm)	L/T	I/C	◆		◆			◆					◆	
Stenoglottis longifolia	12–40 in (30–100 cm)	8–12 in (20–30 cm)	L/T	I/C	◆		◆			◆					◆	
Stenorrhynchos lanceolatum	16–36 in (40–90 cm)	8–14 in (20–35 cm)	T	I	◆		◆		◆			◆				
Stenorrhynchos speciosum	12–24 in (30–60 cm)	4–6 in (10–15 cm)	T	I	◆		◆		◆					◆		

Plant name	Height	Spread	Type	Temp.	Showy flowers	Scented flowers	Grow in pot	Grow on mount	Keep moist	Dry winter	Drought tolerant	Frost tolerant	Full sun	Half sun	Shade	CITES listed
Symphoglossum sanguineum	8–12 in (20–30 cm)	10–14 in (25–35 cm)	E	I/C	◆		◆		◆					◆		
Telipogon octavoi	10–14 in (25–35 cm)	2–2½ in (5–6 cm)	E	C	◆		◆	◆	◆					◆	◆	
Thelymitra aristata	16–24 in (40–60 cm)	6–8 in (15–20 cm)	T	I	◆	◆	◆							◆		
Thelymitra ixioides	4–40 in (10–100 cm)	4–8 in (10–20 cm)	T	I/C	◆		◆						◆			
Thelymitra matthewsii	4–6 in (10–15 cm)	2½–4 in (6–10 cm)	T	I	◆		◆							◆		
Thunia alba	30–50 in (75–125 cm)	12–20 in (30–50 cm)	T	I/C	◆	◆	◆		◆				◆	◆		
Thunia Veitchiana	8–40 in (20–100 cm)	6–20 in (15–50 cm)	T	W/I/C	◆	◆	◆		◆				◆	◆	◆	
Tolumnia pulchella	4–6 in (10–15 cm)	4–6 in (10–15 cm)	E	W/I	◆		◆	◆					◆			
Tolumnia triquetra	4–8 in (10–20 cm)	4–6 in (10–15 cm)	E	W/I	◆		◆	◆					◆			
Tolumnia variegata	4–6 in (10–15 cm)	4–6 in (10–15 cm)	E	W/I	◆		◆	◆					◆			
Trias oblonga	1–1½ in (25–35 mm)	3–4 in (8–10 cm)	E	I	◆		◆	◆	◆						◆	
Trias picta	1–1½ in (25–35 mm)	2½–6 in (6–15 cm)	E	I	◆		◆	◆	◆					◆		
Trichocentrum ascendens	8–27 in (20–70 cm)	6–20 in (15–50 cm)	E	W/I	◆			◆	◆				◆	◆		
Trichocentrum cebolleta	8–48 in (20–120 cm)	4–16 in (10–40 cm)	E	W	◆			◆					◆			
Trichocentrum luridum	30–36 in (75–90 cm)	18–36 in (45–90 cm)	E/L	W/I	◆			◆					◆	◆		
Trichocentrum pulchrum	6–8 in (15–20 cm)	4–6 in (10–15 cm)	E	W	◆			◆					◆			
Trichocentrum splendidum	24–48 in (60–120 cm)	20–24 in (50–60 cm)	E/L	W/I	◆			◆					◆	◆		
Trichocentrum tigrinum	6–8 in (15–20 cm)	4–6 in (10–15 cm)	E	W	◆			◆					◆			
Trichoglottis atropurpurea	16–32 in (40–80 cm)	3–5 in (8–12 cm)	E	W	◆		◆	◆	◆				◆			
Trichoglottis geminata	8–32 in (20–80 cm)	5–10 in (12–25 cm)	E	W/I	◆	◆	◆	◆					◆	◆		
Trichoglottis philippinensis	16–32 in (40–80 cm)	3–5 in (8–12 cm)	E	W	◆		◆	◆	◆				◆			
Trichopilia fragrans	8–12 in (20–30 cm)	8–18 in (20–45 cm)	E	I	◆	◆	◆	◆							◆	
Trichopilia marginata	5–12 in (12–30 cm)	5–10 in (12–25 cm)	E	W/I	◆	◆	◆							◆	◆	
Trichopilia suavis	6–12 in (15–30 cm)	8–12 in (20–30 cm)	E	I	◆	◆	◆	◆	◆						◆	
Trichopilia tortilis	5–10 in (12–25 cm)	5–10 in (12–25 cm)	E	I	◆	◆	◆	◆							◆	
Trigonidium egertonianum	8–20 in (20–50 cm)	8–24 in (20–60 cm)	E	W/I	◆								◆	◆		
Vanda alpina	3–7 in (7–18 cm)	12–20 in (30–50 cm)	E	I	◆		◆								◆	
Vanda coerulea	6–36 in (15–90 cm)	4–10 in (10–25 cm)	E	I/C	◆		◆						◆	◆		
Vanda coerulescens	14–20 in (35–50 cm)	10–14 in (25–35 cm)	E	I	◆	◆	◆						◆	◆		

Plant name	Height	Spread	Type	Temp.	Showy flowers	Scented flowers	Grow in pot	Grow on mount	Keep moist	Dry winter	Drought tolerant	Frost tolerant	Full sun	Half sun	Shade	CITES listed
Vanda cristata	8–20 in (20–50 cm)	8–24 in (20–60 cm)	E	W/I	◆		◆						◆	◆		
Vanda denisoniana	8–36 in (20–90 cm)	8–16 in (20–40 cm)	E	W/I	◆		◆						◆	◆		
Vanda hindsii	8–48 in (20–120 cm)	8–16 in (20–40 cm)	E	W/I	◆		◆						◆	◆		
Vanda javierae	8–36 in (20–90 cm)	7–12 in (18–30 cm)	E	W/I	◆		◆							◆		
Vanda lamellata	16–20 in (40–50 cm)	16–18 in (40–45 cm)	E	W/I	◆		◆						◆	◆		
Vanda luzonica	8–40 in (20–100 cm)	8–20 in (20–50 cm)	E	W/I	◆		◆						◆	◆		
Vanda pumila	10–20 in (25–50 cm)	10–12 in (25–30 cm)	E	W/I	◆		◆						◆	◆		
Vanda sanderiana	8–48 in (20–120 cm)	8–20 in (20–50 cm)	E	W	◆		◆						◆			
Vanda testacea	6–24 in (15–60 cm)	5–10 in (12–25 cm)	E	W/I	◆		◆						◆	◆		
Vanda tricolor	8–48 in (20–120 cm)	8–20 in (20–50 cm)	E	W/I	◆		◆						◆	◆		
Vanda Hybrids	8–48 in (20–120 cm)	8–20 in (20–50 cm)	E	W/I	◆		◆						◆	◆		
Vandopsis undulata	8–20 in (20–50 cm)	5–10 in (12–25 cm)	E	W/I	◆		◆	◆						◆		
Vandopsis warocqueana	20–96 in (50–240 cm)	20–84 in (50–200 cm)	E	W	◆			◆					◆			
Vanilla planifolia	1–10 ft (0.3–3 m)	1–10 ft (0.3–3 m)	E	W/I		◆	◆	◆					◆			
Vanilla polylepis	40–200 in (100–500 cm)	20–80 in (50–200 cm)	E	W/I		◆	◆	◆						◆	◆	
Vascostylis Pine Rivers 'Pink'	10–20 in (25–50 cm)	8–12 in (20–30 cm)	E	W/I	◆	◆	◆							◆		
Vuylstekeara Hybrids	4–24 in (10–60 cm)	4–20 in (10–50 cm)	E	I/C	◆		◆		◆					◆		
Wilsonara Hybrids	4–24 in (10–60 cm)	4–20 in (10–50 cm)	E	I/C	◆		◆		◆					◆		
Xylobium variegatum	16–24 in (40–60 cm)	8–12 in (20–30 cm)	E	I	◆		◆						◆			
Zygopabstia Gumeracha	8–24 in (20–60 cm)	4–20 in (10–50 cm)	E	I/C	◆	◆	◆		◆					◆		
Zygopetalum crinitum	8–24 in (20–60 cm)	4–16 in (10–40 cm)	E	I/C	◆	◆	◆		◆				◆	◆		
Zygopetalum intermedium	4–16 in (10–40 cm)	4–16 in (10–40 cm)	E	I/C	◆	◆	◆							◆		
Zygopetalum mackayi	4–16 in (10–40 cm)	4–16 in (10–40 cm)	E	I/C	◆	◆	◆							◆		
Zygopetalum maxillare	4–16 in (10–40 cm)	4–16 in (10–40 cm)	E	I/C	◆	◆	◆	◆	◆					◆		
Zygopetalum Hybrids	4–16 in (10–40 cm)	4–16 in (10–40 cm)	E/T	I/C	◆	◆	◆		◆					◆		
Zygosepalum lindeniae	10–16 in (25–40 cm)	8–12 in (20–30 cm)	E	W	◆		◆	◆	◆						◆	
Zygostates alleniana	¾–1¼ in (18–30 mm)	1¼–2 in (30–50 mm)	E	W	◆			◆	◆					◆	◆	
Zygostates lunata	2–4 in (5–10 cm)	2–4 in (5–10 cm)	E	W	◆			◆	◆					◆	◆	

Index

Italicized page numbers indicate reference in caption. Plain page numbers indicate reference in text. Genus page ranges cover pages on which text or photographs for that genus appear.

A

Acacallis 58
Acacallis coerulea see *Acacallis cyanea* 58, *58*
Acacallis cyanea 58, *58*
Acacallis fimbriata see *Acacallis cyanea* 58, *58*
Acacallis hoehnei see *Acacallis cyanea* 58, *58*
Acacallis oliveriana see *Acacallis cyanea* 58, *58*
Acampe 58–59
Acampe dentata see *Acampe ochracea* 58
Acampe multiflora see *Acampe rigida* 58–59, *58*
Acampe ochracea 58
Acampe papillosa 58
Acampe rigida 58–59, *58*
Acanthephippium 58–59
Acanthephippium mantinianum 58, 59
Acanthoglossum see *Pholidota* 265
Aceras 59
Aceras anthropophorum 59, *59*
Aceras hircinum see *Himantoglossum hircinum* 190, *190*
Acianthella confusa see *Acianthus confusus* 59, *59*
Acianthus 59
Acianthus confusus 59, *59*
Acianthus exsertus 59, *59*
Acianthus reniformis see *Cyrtostylis reniformis* 132, *132*
Acoidium see *Trichocentrum* 308
Acoridium simile see *Dendrochilum simile* 163, *163*
Ada 60
Ada aurantiaca 60, *60*
Ada glumacea 60, *60*
Ada keiliana 60, *60*
  'Our Tropics' 60
Ada lehmanni see *Ada aurantiaca* 60, *60*
adder's mouth (*Pogonia ophioglossoides*) 272, *272*
Adriatic lizard orchid (*Himantoglossum adriaticum*) 190
Aerangis 60–61
Aerangis alata see *Aerangis ellisii* 61
Aerangis biloba 61
Aerangis caulescens see *Aerangis ellisii* 61
Aerangis citrata 60, 61
Aerangis cryptodon 61, *61*
Aerangis distincta 61
Aerangis ellisii 61
Aerangis kotschyana 61
Aerangis luteoalba var. *rhodosticta* see *Aerangis rhodosticta* 61, *61*

Aerangis platyphylla see *Aerangis ellisii* 61
Aerangis rhodosticta 61, *61*
Aeranthes 61
Aeranthes brachycentron see *Aeranthes grandiflora* 61, *61*
Aeranthes caudata 61
Aeranthes grandiflora 61, *61*
Aeranthes imerinensis see *Aeranthes caudata* 61
Aeranthus see *Aeranthes* 61
Aerides 62–63
Aerides calceolare see *Gastrochilus calceolaris* 185
Aerides crassifolia 62, *62*
Aerides falcata 62
Aerides fieldingii see *Aerides rosea* 63
Aerides houlletiana 62, *62*
Aerides krabiensis 62, *62*
Aerides lawrenciae 62, *62*
Aerides leeana 62, *63*
Aerides mitrata see *Seidenfadenia mitrata* 296
Aerides multiflora 62
Aerides odorata 62, *63*
Aerides quinquevulnera 63
Aerides rosea 63
African tiger orchid (*Ansellia*) 66–67
Amesiella 63
Amesiella monticola 63, *63*
Amesiella philippinensis 63
Anacamptis 64
Anacamptis pyramidalis 64, *64*
Anacamptis urvilleana see *Anacamptis pyramidalis* 64, *64*
Anacheilium cochleatum see *Prosthechea cochleata* 276, *276*
Anacheilium radiatum see *Prosthechea radiata* 277, *277*
Ancistrochilus 64
Ancistrochilus hirsutissimus see *Ancistrochilus rothschildianus* 64, *64*
Ancistrochilus rothschildianus 64, *64*
Angraecum 64–65
Angraecum calceolus 64
Angraecum didieri 64, 65
Angraecum distichum 64
Angraecum eburneum 64–65
Angraecum eburneum subsp. *eburneum* 65
Angraecum eburneum subsp. *giryamae* 65
Angraecum eburneum subsp. *superbum* 65
Angraecum eburneum subsp. *superbum* var. *longicalcar* 65
Angraecum eburneum subsp. *xerophilum* 65
Angraecum firthii 65, *65*
Angraecum grandiflorum see *Aeranthes grandiflora* 61, *61*
Angraecum infundibulare 65
Angraecum Lemforde White Beauty 65
Angraecum Lemforde White Beauty 'Max' 65
Angraecum Lemforde White Beauty 'Mr. Wonderful' 65
Angraecum philippinense see *Amesiella philippinensis* 63
Angraecum rothschildianum see *Eurychone rothschildiana* 184, *184*

Angraecum scottianum 65, *65*
Angraecum sedeni see *Cyrtorchis arcuata* 132, *132*
Angraecum sesquipedale 65
Angraecum Veitchii 65, *65*
Anguloa 65
Anguloa clowesii 65
Anguloa hohenlohii 65
Anguloa uniflora 65, *65*
Angulocaste 66
Angulocaste Jupiter × *Anguloa hohenlohii* 66, *66*
Angulocaste Rosemary 66, *66*
Anoectochilus 66
Anoectochilus koshunensis 66
Ansellia 66–67
Ansellia africana 66, *67*
  'Alba' 66, *67*
  'Kruger Rand' 66, *67*
  'Tinonee' 66, *67*
Ansellia confusa see *Ansellia africana* 66, *67*
Ansellia congoensis see *Ansellia africana* 66, *67*
Ansellia gigantea see *Ansellia africana* 66, *67*
Ansellia humilis see *Ansellia africana* 66, *67*
Ansellia nilotica see *Ansellia africana* 66, *67*
ant orchid (*Chiloglottis formicifera*) 104, *104*
Arachnanthe see *Arachnis* 67
Arachnanthe alba see *Arachnis hookeriana* 67
Arachnanthe lowii see *Dimorphorchis lowii* 164, 165
Arachnis 67
Arachnis alba see *Arachnis hookeriana* 67
Arachnis flos-aeris 67
Arachnis hookeriana 67
Arachnis moschifera see *Arachnis flos-aeris* 67
Arachnis philippinensis see *Trichoglottis philippinensis* 309, *309*
Aranda 67
Aranda Noorah Alsagoff 67, *67*
Aranthera 67
Aranthera Beatrice Ng 67, *67*
Arethusa ophioglossoides see *Pogonia ophioglossoides* 272, *272*
Arpophyllum 68
Arpophyllum giganteum 68, *68*
Arpophyllum spicatum 68
Arundina 68
Arundina graminifolia 68, *68*
Ascocenda 68–69
Ascocenda Carolaine 'Kathleen' 68, 69
Ascocenda Fuchs Gold 68
Ascocenda Fuchs Serval 68, *69*
Ascocenda Guo Chia Long 68
Ascocenda Hybrids 68–69
Ascocenda Kwa Geok Choo 68, *69*
Ascocenda Pramote 68, *69*
Ascocenda 'Pranam' 68
Ascocenda Princess Mikasa 68, *69*
Ascocenda Udomchai Beauty 68, *69*
Ascocenda (*Vanda* Pimsai) × (*Vanda* Keeree × Prackypetch) 69
Ascocenda Wichot 68, *69*

Ascocenda Yip Sum Wah × *Vanda* Bitty Hearthrob 'Pink' 69
Ascocentrum 70–71
Ascocentrum ampullaceum 70, *70*
Ascocentrum aurantiacum subsp. *philippinense* 70, *70*
Ascocentrum christensonianum 70, *70*
Ascocentrum garayi 70, *71*
Ascocentrum hendersoniana see *Dyakia hendersoniana* 172, *172*
Ascoglossum 71
Ascoglossum calopterum 71
Ascoglossum purpureum 71
Ascorachnis 71
Ascorachnis Shah Alam City 71, *71*
Aspasia 71
Aspasia lunata 71
Aspasia psittacina 71, *71*
autumn bulbophyllum (*Bulbophyllum exiguum*) 85
autumn ladies' tresses (*Spiranthes spiralis*) 303
autumn-flowering pleione (*Pleione praecox*) 268

B

Balkan lizard orchid (*Himantoglossum caprinum*) 190
bamboo orchid (*Arundina*) 68
Barbosella 72
Barbosella cucullata 72
  'Hillside' 72, *72*
Barkeria 72
Barkeria lindleyana 72, *72*
Barkeria melanocaulon 72, *72*
Barkeria scandens 72, *72*
Barlia 73
Barlia robertiana 73
Bartholina 73
Bartholina etheliae 73, *73*
Batemannia meleagris see *Huntleya meleagris* 191
beak orchid (*Lyperanthus*) 207
Beallara 73
Beallara Marfitch 'Howard's Dream' 73, *73*
Beallara Tahoma Glacier 73, *73*
beard orchid (*Calochilus*) 94
bee orchid (*Ophrys*) 237
bee orchid (*Ophrys apifera*) 237, *237*
bee swarm orchid (*Cyrtopodium punctatum*) 132, *132*
Bifrenaria 74–75
Bifrenaria harrisoniae 74, 75
bird orchid (*Chiloglottis*) 104
black orchid (*Paphiopedilum wardii*) 247
Bletia 75
Bletia purpurea 75
Bletilla 75
Bletilla striata 75, *75*
Bollea 75
Bollea coelestis 75, *75*
Bonatea 76
Bonatea polypodantha 76, *76*
Bonatea speciosa 76
  'Green Egret' 76, *76*
Bothriochilus bellus see *Coelia bella* 106, 107

bottlebrush orchid (*Dendrobium smillieae*) 148, *149*

braid orchid (*Lockhartia pittieri*) 203

Brassavola 76–77

Brassavola cordata see *Brassavola subulifolia* 77

Brassavola cucullata 76, *76*

Brassavola digbyana see *Rhyncholaelia digbyana* 285

Brassavola flagellaris 76, *76*

Brassavola glauca see *Rhyncholaelia glauca* 285

Brassavola nodosa 76

Brassavola subulifolia 77

Brassia 77–79

Brassia arcuigera 77, *77*

Brassia brachiata see *Brassia verrucosa* 77, *77*

Brassia Chieftain *78, 79*

Brassia Chieftain × *B.* Rex *78, 79*

Brassia Edvah Loo *78, 79*

Brassia gireoudiana 77, *77*

Brassia glumacea see *Ada glumacea* 60, *60*

Brassia Hybrids 78–79

Brassia keiliana see *Ada keiliana* 60, *60*

Brassia lawrenceana 77, *77*

Brassia longissima see *Brassia arcuigera* 77, *77*

Brassia maculata 77

Brassia Memoria Fritz Boedeker *78, 79*

Brassia Rex 'Christine' *78, 79*

Brassia Rising Star *78, 79*

Brassia Spider's Feast *78, 79*

Brassia Spider's Gold *78, 79*

Brassia verrucosa 77, *77*

Brassidium 79

Brassidium Fly Away 'Taida' *79, 79*

Brassidium Shooting Star × *Brassia* Rex 79, *79*

Brassidium Wild Warrior 'Santa Barbara' 79, *79*

Brassocattleya 79–80

Brassocattleya Binosa 79, *79*

Brassocattleya Hybrids 79–80

Brassocattleya Island Charm 'Carmela' 79, *79*

Brassocattleya Maikai 80, *80*

Brassocattleya November Bride 'Santa Clara' 80, *80*

Brassocattleya Sunny Delight 80, *80*

Brassolaeliocattleya 80–83

Brassolaeliocattleya Alma Kee 'Tipmalee' 80, *80*

Brassolaeliocattleya Ann Cleo 'Hallona' 80, *81*

Brassolaeliocattleya Bingham Vick 80, *81*

Brassolaeliocattleya Dundas 'Olga' 80, *82*

Brassolaeliocattleya Erin Kobayashi × *Cattleya walkeriana* 80, *80*

Brassolaeliocattleya George King × *Laeliocattleya* Janet *82*

Brassolaeliocattleya Gold Bug 80, *81*

Brassolaeliocattleya Golden Tang 80, *82*

Brassolaeliocattleya Hawaiian Satisfaction 'Romantic' 80, *81*

Brassolaeliocattleya Hybrids 80–83

Brassolaeliocattleya Lucky 'Golden Ring' 80, *82*

Brassolaeliocattleya Mem. Helen Brown × *Laeliocattleya* Tokyo Magic *82*

Brassolaeliocattleya (Memoria Benigno Aquino × Golden Embers) 80, *82*

Brassolaeliocattleya Memoria Julia Piferrer 80, *81*

Brassolaeliocattleya Rosemary Hayden 'Paradise' 80, *82*

Brassolaeliocattleya Samba Splendor 80

Brassolaeliocattleya (Shades of Jade × Waikiki Gold) 80, *83*

Brassolaeliocattleya Sunstate's Easter Parade 80, *81*

Brassolaeliocattleya Toshi Aoki 'Blumen Insel' 80, *82*

Brassolaeliocattleya Toshi Aoki 'Pokai' 80, *81*

Brassolaeliocattleya Waianae Leopard 80, *83*

Brassolaeliocattleya Williette Wong 80, *83*

bridal veil orchid (*Dockrillia teretifolia*) 168

broad-leafed helleborine (*Epipactis helleborine*) 180, 181

broad-leafed marsh orchid (*Dactylorhiza majalis*) 134

Broughtonia 83–84

Broughtonia negrilensis 83, *83*

Broughtonia sanguinea 84, *84*

Brownleea 84

Brownleea parviflora 84, *84*

Bulbophyllum 84–90

Bulbophyllum absconditum 84, *84*

Bulbophyllum ambrosia 84, *85*

Bulbophyllum appendiculatum 85, *85*

Bulbophyllum carunculatum 85, *85*

Bulbophyllum collettii see *Bulbophyllum wendlandianum* 90, *90*

Bulbophyllum contortisepalum 85

Bulbophyllum corolliferum 85, *85*

Bulbophyllum Daisy Chain 85, *85*

Bulbophyllum dearei 85

Bulbophyllum exiguum 85

Bulbophyllum falcatum 86, *86*

Bulbophyllum flaviflorum see *Bulbophyllum pectenveneris* 88, *88*

Bulbophyllum fletcherianum 86, *86*

Bulbophyllum globuliforme 86

Bulbophyllum graveolens 86, *87*

Bulbophyllum guttulatum 87, *87*

Bulbophyllum levanae see *Bulbophyllum nymphopolitanum* 88, *88*

Bulbophyllum levatii 87, *87*

Bulbophyllum lingulatum 87, *87*

Bulbophyllum longissimum 87, *87*

Bulbophyllum Louis Sander 87

Bulbophyllum macrobulbum 87, *87*

Bulbophyllum morphologorum 88

Bulbophyllum neocaledonicum see *Bulbophyllum absconditum* 84, *84*

Bulbophyllum ngoyense 88, *88*

Bulbophyllum nymphopolitanum 88, *88*

Bulbophyllum ornatissimum see *Bulbophyllum rothschildianum* 88, *88*

Bulbophyllum patella 88, *88*

Bulbophyllum pectenveneris 88, *88*

Bulbophyllum picturatum 88, *88*

Bulbophyllum pulchellum 88

Bulbophyllum putidum see *Bulbophyllum appendiculatum* 85, *85*

Bulbophyllum rothschildianum 88, *88*

Bulbophyllum rufinum 88, *89*

Bulbophyllum schillerianum 90, *90*

Bulbophyllum speciosum 90, *90*

Bulbophyllum sulawesii 90, *90*

Bulbophyllum tridentatum 90, *90*

Bulbophyllum unitubum 90, *90*

Bulbophyllum wendlandianum 90, *90*

butterfly orchid (*Platanthera*) 267

butterfly orchid (*Psychopsis papilio*) 278

butterfly orchids (*Psychopsis*) 278–79

C

Cadetia 91

Cadetia taylori 91, *91*

Caladenia 91–92

Caladenia arenicola 91, *91*

Caladenia chapmanii 91, *91*

Caladenia flava 91, *91*

Caladenia harringtoniae 92, *92*

Caladenia latifolia 92, *92*

Caladenia longicauda 92, *92*

Caladenia nana 92, *92*

Calanthe 92–93

Calanthe discolor 93

Calanthe discolor var. *flava* see *Calanthe striata* 93, *93*

Calanthe masuca see *Calanthe sylvatica* 93, *93*

Calanthe natalensis see *Calanthe sylvatica* 93, *93*

Calanthe Rose Georgene 93, *93*

Calanthe rosea 93

Calanthe sieboldii see *Calanthe striata* 93, *93*

Calanthe striata 93, *93*

Calanthe sylvatica 93, *93*

Calanthe triplicata 93

Calanthe veratrifolia see *Calanthe triplicata* 93

Calanthe vestita 93

Calanthe volkensii see *Calanthe sylvatica* 93, *93*

Calochilus 94

Calochilus campestris 94

Calochilus paludosus 94, *94*

Caloglossum see *Cymbidiella* 113

Calopogon 94

Calopogon pulchellus see *Calopogon tuberosus* 94, *94*

Calopogon tuberosus 94, *94*

Calypso 94

calypso (*Calypso bulbosa*) 94, *94*

Calypso borealis see *Calypso bulbosa* 94, *94*

Calypso bulbosa 94, *94*

Calypso bulbosa var. *americana* 94

Calypso bulbosa var. *bulbosa* 94

Calypso bulbosa var. *occidentalis* 94

Calypso japonica see *Calypso bulbosa* 94, *94*

Calypso occidentalis see *Calypso bulbosa* 94, *94*

Camelostalix see *Pholidota* 265

candle orchid (*Arpophyllum*) 68

Cannaeorchis 94–95

Cannaeorchis verruciferum 94, *95*

Cape York spider orchid (*Dendrobium capitisyork*) 138

Catasetum 95

Catasetum roseum see *Clowesia rosea* 106

Catasetum saccatum 95

Catasetum tenebrosum 95

Cattleya 95–102

Cattleya aclandiae 95, *95*

Cattleya amethystoglossa 95

Cattleya amethystoglossa var. *coerulea* 95, *95*

Cattleya aurantiaca 96
  'Golden Dew' 96, *96*
  'Marigold' 96, *96*
  'Red' 96, *96*

Cattleya bicolor 96
  'Golden Gate' 96, *96*

Cattleya bicolor var. *braziliensis* 96

Cattleya Bow Bells 'July' 101, *101*

Cattleya Bowgata 101, *101*

Cattleya bowringiana 96

Cattleya (Browniae × *loddigesii*) 101, *101*

Cattleya Earl 'Imperialis' 101, *102*

Cattleya Eclipse 101, *102*

Cattleya Frasquita 101, *102*

Cattleya gaskelliana 96, *96*

Cattleya gaskelliana var. *alba* 96

Cattleya × *guatemalensis* 96, *96*

Cattleya Hawaiian Comfort 101, *102*

Cattleya Humming Bird Hybrids 101, *102*

Cattleya Hybrids 101–02

Cattleya intermedia 96–97, *97*
  'Breckenridge Snow' 97
  'Do Hector' 97, *97*
  'Do Hector' × var. *alba gigantea* 97
  'Irrorata' 97, *97*

Cattleya intermedia var. *alba* 97, *97*

Cattleya intermedia var. *amethystina* 97, *97*

Cattleya intermedia var. *aquinii* 97, *97*

Cattleya labiata var. *mendelii* see *Cattleya mendelii* 99, *99*

Cattleya loddigesii 98, *98*
  'Bella Vista' 98, *98*
  'Blue Sky' 98, *98*
  'Impassionata' 98
  ('Pink Spots' × 'Dark Pink') 98, *98*
  ('Pink Spots' × 'Monty') 98, *98*
  ('Shorty' × 'Sweetheart') 98, *98*

Cattleya lueddemanniana 99, *99*

Cattleya Luteous Forb 101, *102*

Cattleya mendelii 99, *99*

Cattleya Miyuki 'Abe' 101, *102*

Cattleya nobilior 99

Cattleya Penny Kuroda 'Spots' 101, *102*

Cattleya schilleriana 99, *99*

Cattleya schofieldiana 99, *99*

Cattleya schroderae 99

Cattleya skinneri 100, *100*
  'Casa Luna' 100, *100*
Cattleya skinneri var. *alba* 'Rebemic' 100, *100*
Cattleya skinneri var. *coerulescens* 100, *100*
Cattleya speciosissima see *Cattleya lueddemanniana* 99, *99*
Cattleya superbiens see *Schomburgkia superbiens* 295
Cattleya violacea see *Sophronitella violacea* 302, *302*
Cattleya walkeriana 100, *101*
Cattleya walkeriana var. *alba* 100, *101*
Cattleya walkeriana var. *alba* 'Pendentive' 100, *101*
Cattleyopsis 103
Cattleyopsis lindenii 103
Cattleytonia 103
Cattleytonia Maui Maid 103, *103*
Cattleytonia Starrlyn 103, *103*
Caularthron 103
Caularthron bicornutum 103
Cephalanthera 103
Cephalanthera alba see *Cephalanthera damasonium* 103
Cephalanthera austiniae 103, *103*
Cephalanthera damasonium 103
Cephalanthera grandiflora see *Cephalanthera damasonium* 103
Cephalanthera longifolia 103
Cephalanthera rubra 103
Ceratostylis 104
Ceratostylis incognita 104, *104*
Ceratostylis retisquama 104, *104*
chain orchid (*Dendrochilum*) 162–63
Chelonanthera see *Pholidota* 265
cherry orchid (*Mediocalcar*) 216
Chiloglottis 104
Chiloglottis formicifera 104, *104*
Chiloglottis gunnii 104, *104*
Chiloschista 104–05
Chiloschista lunifera 104, *105*
Chiloschista parishii 105, *105*
Chinese ground orchid (*Bletilla*) 75
Chinese ladies' tresses (*Spiranthes sinensis*) 303
Chysis 105
Chysis aurea 105
Chysis bractescens 105, *105*
Chysis limminghei see *Chysis aurea* 105
Chysis maculata see *Chysis aurea* 105
cigar orchid (*Cyrtopodium*) 132
cigar orchid (*Cyrtopodium punctatum*) 132, *132*
Cirrhaea 105
Cirrhaea dependens 105, *105*
Cirrhaea hoffmanseggii see *Cirrhaea dependens* 105, *105*
Cirrhaea nasuta see *Cirrhaea dependens* 105, *105*
Cirrhaea tristis see *Cirrhaea dependens* 105, *105*
Cirrhaea viridipurpurea see *Cirrhaea dependens* 105, *105*
Cirrhaea warreana see *Cirrhaea dependens* 105, *105*

Cirrhopetalum Daisy Chain see *Bulbophyllum* Daisy Chain 85, *85*
Cleisostoma 105
Cleisostoma racemiferum 105, *105*
Cleisostoma recurvum 105, *105*
Cleisostoma rostratum see *Cleisostoma recurvum* 105, *105*
Cleisostoma weberi 105, *105*
Clowesia 106
Clowesia rosea 106
Clowesia warscewiczii 106, *106*
clown orchids (*Rossioglossum*) 288
Cochleanthes 106
Cochleanthes amazonica 106, *106*
Cochleanthes discolor 106
Cochlioda 106–07
Cochlioda noezliana 106
Cochlioda rosea 106–07, *107*
Cochlioda sanguinea see *Symphoglossum sanguineum* 305, *305*
Cochlioda vulcanica 106, 107
cockleshell orchid (*Prosthechea*) 276–77
cockleshell orchid (*Prosthechea cochleata*) 276, *276*
cockroach orchid (*Restrepia*) 284
Coelia 106–07
Coelia bella 106, 107
Coelogyne 107–08
Coelogyne Burfordiense 107, *107*
Coelogyne chloroptera 107, *107*
Coelogyne corymbosa 107, *107*
Coelogyne cristata 107
Coelogyne flaccida 107, *107*
  'Caramel' 107, *107*
  'Dark' 107, *107*
Coelogyne huettneriana 108, *108*
Coelogyne lawrenceana 108, *108*
Coelogyne massangeana see *Coelogyne tomentosa* 108, *108*
Coelogyne Memoria W. Micholitz 108, *108*
Coelogyne nitida 108, *108*
Coelogyne ochracea see *Coelogyne nitida* 108, *108*
Coelogyne ovalis 108
Coelogyne pandurata 108
Coelogyne speciosa 108, *108*
Coelogyne tomentosa 108, *108*
Colax see *Pabstia* 239
Colax jugosus see *Pabstia jugosa* 239
Colmanara 109
Colmanara Hybrids 109
Colmanara Wildcat 'Carmela' 109, *109*
Colmanara Wildcat 'Exile' 109, *109*
Colmanara Wildcat 'Gemma Webb' 109, *109*
Colmanara Wildcat 'Hildos' 109, *109*
comet orchid (*Angraecum*) 64–65
common bird orchid (*Chiloglottis gunnii*) 104, *104*
common spotted orchid (*Dactylorhiza fuchsii*) 133, *133*
Comparettia 110
Comparettia falcata 110
Comparettia rosea see *Comparettia falcata* 110
Comparettia speciosa 110, *110*
Comperia 110

Comperia comperiana 110
Condylago 110
Condylago rodrigoi 110, *110*
Cooktown orchid (*Dendrobium bigibbum*) 137
Cooktown orchid (*Dendrobium phalaenopsis*) 146
copper beard orchid (*Calochilus campestris*) 94
coral root (*Corallorrhiza*) 110
Corallorrhiza 110
Corallorrhiza innata see *Corallorrhiza trifida* 110
Corallorrhiza striata 110, *110*
Corallorrhiza trifida 110
Coryanthes 110–11
Coryanthes macrantha 111
Coryanthes speciosa 111
Corybas 111
Corybas barbarae 111, *111*
Corybas diemenicus 111, *111*
Corybas montanus 111, *111*
Corybas pruinosus 111, *111*
cowslip orchid (*Caladenia flava*) 91, *91*
Crinonia see *Pholidota* 265
Cryptopus 113
Cryptopus elatus 113, *113*
cucumber orchid (*Dockrillia cucumerina*) 168, *169*
Cuitlauzina 113
Cuitlauzina pendula 113
  'Shin Soon' 113, *113*
Cycnoches 112–13
Cycnoches barthiorum *112*, 113
Cycnoches ventricosum 113
Cymbidiella 113
Cymbidiella flabellata 113, *113*
Cymbidiella pardalina 113, *113*
Cymbidiella rhodocheila see *Cymbidiella pardalina* 113, *113*
Cymbidium 114–29
Cymbidium African Adventure 'Sahara Gold' 116, *117*
Cymbidium Alegria 'Saint Lita' *117*
Cymbidium Alexfrida 'The Queen' *117*
Cymbidium Anita 'Pymble' 116, *117*
Cymbidium aspidistrifolium see *Cymbidium lancifolium* 114, 115
Cymbidium Astronaut 'Raja' 116, *117*
Cymbidium (Atalanta × Gottianum) *117*
Cymbidium Aunty MacKovich *117*
Cymbidium Australian Midnight *117*
Cymbidium Baldoyle 'Melbury' *117*
Cymbidium bambusifolium see *Cymbidium lancifolium* 114, 115
Cymbidium Belle Park 'Orange Gleam' *118*
Cymbidium bicolor 114
Cymbidium Bisou Bisou 'Geyserland' *118*
Cymbidium Black Forest 'Just Desserts' *118*
Cymbidium Blazing Fury 'Fatboy' *118*
Cymbidium Bolton Grange *118*

Cymbidium Bulbarrow 'Friar Tuck' 116, *118*
Cymbidium canaliculatum 114, *114*
Cymbidium canaliculatum var. *sparkesii* 114, *114*
Cymbidium Cape Crystal *118*
Cymbidium Castle of Mey 'Pinkie' 116, *118*
Cymbidium Champagne Robin *118*
Cymbidium Clauboda 'Sydney Rothwell' *119*
Cymbidium Colina 'Ember' *119*
Cymbidium Cranbourne 'Chase' *119*
Cymbidium Desirée 'Elizabeth A. Logan' *119*
Cymbidium Dilly 'Del Mar' 116, *119*
Cymbidium (Disney Girl × Robin) *119*
Cymbidium Dolly 'Featherhill' *119*
Cymbidium (Dolly × Kimberley Szabo) *119*
Cymbidium (Dream Temple × Pure Ice) *120*
Cymbidium (Eastern Star × Sleeping Nymph) *120*
Cymbidium Electric Ladyland 'Peats Ridge' *120*
Cymbidium Emerald Glory 'Valerie' *120*
Cymbidium erythrostylum 114, *114*
Cymbidium Esmeralda *120*
Cymbidium Fair Delight 'Highfields' *120*
Cymbidium Fanfare 'Spring' 116, *120*
Cymbidium Fare Wand 'Numan' *120*
Cymbidium Finetta 'Glendessary' *120*
Cymbidium Gibson Girl 'Mephisto Waltz' *121*
Cymbidium (Globetrotter × Minniken) *121*
Cymbidium Gripper 'Royale' *121*
Cymbidium Highland Advent *121*
Cymbidium Highland Glen 'Cooksbridge' *121*
Cymbidium Highland Lassie 'Jersey' *121*
Cymbidium hoosai see *Cymbidium sinense* 116
Cymbidium Hybrids 116–29
Cymbidium Ice Ranch 116, *121*
Cymbidium insigne 114–15
  'Mrs. Carl Holmes' 115
Cymbidium Iris Cooper 'Drama Queen' *125*
Cymbidium 'James Tee Kirk 81' *121*
Cymbidium James Toya 'Royale' *122*
Cymbidium Jeanette 'Enid Harper' *122*
Cymbidium John Woden 116, *122*
Cymbidium Joker 'Foul Play' *122*
Cymbidium Joker 'Irish Mist' *122*
Cymbidium Kabuki Moon 'Alice' *122*
Cymbidium (Katy Shaw × Southborough) *122*
Cymbidium (Khyber Pass × Dolly) *123*

Cymbidium Kiku Ono *123*

Cymbidium Kiri te Kanawa *123*

Cymbidium Lady McAlpine 'Jersey' 116, *123*

Cymbidium Lancashire Rose 'Maureen' *123*

Cymbidium lancifolium *114,* 115

Cymbidium leroyi see *Cymbidium madidum* 116, *116*

Cymbidium Levis Duke 'Bella Vista' *123*

Cymbidium Little Bighorn 'Calga' *123*

Cymbidium Little Bighorn 'Prairie' 116, *123*

Cymbidium lowianum 115, *115*

Cymbidium lowianum var. *concolor* 115, *115*

Cymbidium (Lustrous Damsell × Alvin Bryant) *124*

Cymbidium Lynette Artemis *124*

Cymbidium madidum 116, *116*

Cymbidium Marie Bashir *124*

Cymbidium Marilyn Sharp 'Curvaceous' *124*

Cymbidium Mary Smith 'Lucy' *124*

Cymbidium Mavourneen 'Jester' 116, *124*

Cymbidium (Melinga × Pharaoh's Gold) × Dural *124*

Cymbidium Mighty Margaret *124*

Cymbidium (Mighty Mouse × Beach Girl) 'Carly' *124*

Cymbidium Mighty Tracey 'Royale' *125*

Cymbidium Mini Goddess 'Apricot' *125*

Cymbidium Mini Verd 'Captain Cook' 116, *125*

Cymbidium Orange Crush *125*

Cymbidium Orchid Conference 'Green Light' 116, *125*

Cymbidium parishii 116

Cymbidium parishii var. *sanderae* see *Cymbidium sanderae* 116

Cymbidium Paul Robeson *122*

Cymbidium (Paul Robeson × Mighty Mouse) 'It's Nice' *125*

Cymbidium Pontac 'Trinity' 116, *126*

Cymbidium Pywacket 'Royale' *126*

Cymbidium (Red Beauty × Cronulla) *126*

Cymbidium Red Idol 'Royale' *126*

Cymbidium Rievaulx *126*

Cymbidium 'Royale Jester' *126*

Cymbidium Rumours 'Desiree' *126*

Cymbidium Saint Aubins Bay *127*

Cymbidium San Francisco *127*

Cymbidium sanderae 116

Cymbidium sinense 116
   'Red Star' 116

Cymbidium Sleeping Nymph 'Glacier' *127*

Cymbidium Sleeping Nymph 'Perfection' *127*

Cymbidium (So Bold × Rajah's Ruby) *127*

Cymbidium Spanish Lullaby 'Douce Josephine' *127*

Cymbidium Spotted Leopard 'Showtime' *127*

Cymbidium suave 116, *116*

Cymbidium Sumatra 'Astrid' 116, *129*

Cymbidium Sunshine Falls 'Green Fantasy' 116, *128*

Cymbidium Surman's Rose 'Gosford Gold' *129*

Cymbidium Sylvia Miller 'Gold Cup' 116, *129*

Cymbidium Tea Time 'Afternoon Delight' *129*

Cymbidium Tinsel 'Harriet' 116, *129*

Cymbidium tracyanum 116, *116*

Cymbidium Valley Legend 'Gee Wizz' 116, *129*

Cymbidium Wallacia 'Burnt Gold' *129*

Cymbidium (Wallara × Huckleberry Mountain) 'Royal Jewels' *129*

Cymbidium Wesley Davidson 'Geyserland' *129*

Cymbidium Wesley Davidson 'Netty' *129*

Cymbidium Yowie Rose 'Cabernet' *129*

Cypripedium 130–31

Cypripedium acaule 130, *130*

Cypripedium calceolus 130

Cypripedium calceolus var. *parviflorum* see *Cypripedium parviflorum* 130, *131*

Cypripedium californicum 130, *130*

Cypripedium concolor see *Paphiopedilum concolor* 240, *240*

Cypripedium delenatii see *Paphiopedilum delenatii* 240, *240*

Cypripedium formosanum 130, *130*

Cypripedium montanum 130

Cypripedium parviflorum 130, *131*

Cypripedium parviflorum var. *pubescens* 130

Cypripedium pubescens see *Cypripedium parviflorum* var. *pubescens* 130

Cypripedium reginae 130

Cyrtochilum 130–31

Cyrtochilum falcipetalum 131

Cyrtochilum microxiphium 131, *131*

Cyrtopodium 132

Cyrtopodium gigas see *Cyrtopodium punctatum* 132, *132*

Cyrtopodium holstii 132

Cyrtopodium punctatum 132, *132*

Cyrtopodium tigrinum see *Cyrtopodium punctatum* 132, *132*

Cyrtorchis 132

Cyrtorchis arcuata 132, *132*

Cyrtorchis sedeni see *Cyrtorchis arcuata* 132, *132*

Cyrtorchis whitei see *Cyrtorchis arcuata* 132, *132*

Cyrtostylis 132

Cyrtostylis reniformis 132, *132*

D

Dactylorhiza 133–34

Dactylorhiza elata 133

Dactylorhiza foliosa 133, *133*

Dactylorhiza fuchsii 133, *133*
   'Cruickshank' 133, *133*
   'Rachel' 133, *133*

Dactylorhiza incarnata 134, *134*

Dactylorhiza latifolia see *Dactylorhiza majalis* 134

Dactylorhiza majalis 134

Dactylorhiza majalis subsp. *praetermissa* see *Dactylorhiza praetermissa* 134

Dactylorhiza praetermissa 134

Dactylorhiza romana 134

Dactylorhiza sambucina 134

Dactylorhiza sulphurea see *Dactylorhiza romana* 134

Dactylorhiza sulphurea subsp. *pseudosambucina* see *Dactylorhiza romana* 134

Dactylorhiza urvilleana 134, *134*

dancing lady orchid (*Oncidium*) 234–36

dancing lady orchid (*Oncidium varicosum*) 236

Darwinara 134

Darwinara Pretty Girl 134, *134*

Degarmoara 135

Degarmoara Skywalker 'Red Star' 135, *135*

Degarmoara Starshot 'Fashion' 135, *135*

Degarmoara Winter Wonderland 'White Fairy' 135, *135*

Dendrobium 136–61

Dendrobium aduncum 136, *136*

Dendrobium aemulum 136

Dendrobium aggregatum see *Dendrobium lindleyi* 144

Dendrobium aggregatum var. *jenkinsii* see *Dendrobium jenkinsii* 142, *143*

Dendrobium Akatuki Queen 158, *159*

Dendrobium albosanguineum 136, *136*

Dendrobium alexandrae 136, *136*

Dendrobium amethystoglossum 136, 137

Dendrobium Andree Miller 157

Dendrobium (Angelline × Ellen Glow) 152, *152*

Dendrobium anosmum 136, 137

Dendrobium antennatum 137

Dendrobium aphyllum see *Dendrobium cucullatum* 139, *139*

Dendrobium atroviolaceum 136, 137

Dendrobium, Australian Hybrids 152–55

Dendrobium Bardo Rose 152, *152*

Dendrobium Barry Simpson 152, *152*

Dendrobium beckleri see *Dockrillia schoenina* 168, *169*

Dendrobium Bellingen 152, *153*

Dendrobium Biddy 152, *152*

Dendrobium bigibbum 137

Dendrobium bigibbum subsp. *phalaenopsis* 137

Dendrobium bigibbum var. *compactum* 137, *137*

Dendrobium bigibbum var. *superbum* see *Dendrobium phalaenopsis* 146

Dendrobium Bohemian Rhapsody 158, *159*

Dendrobium bracteosum 137, *137*

Dendrobium Brinawa Sunset 152, *153*

Dendrobium bulbophylloides 137, *137*

Dendrobium bullenianum 137

Dendrobium Burgundy Cream 152, *152*

Dendrobium cacatua 138, *138*

Dendrobium canaliculatum 138, *138*

Dendrobium capitisyork 138

Dendrobium capituliflorum 138, *138*

Dendrobium ceraula 138, *138*

Dendrobium chameleon 138, *139*

Dendrobium Chao Praya Rose 156, *156*

Dendrobium chittimae 139, *139*

Dendrobium Christmas Chime 'Azuka' 158, *159*

Dendrobium chrysocrepis 139

Dendrobium chrysotoxum 139, *139*

Dendrobium chrysotoxum var. *suavissimum* 139

Dendrobium Colorado Springs 158, *158*

Dendrobium crumenatum 139

Dendrobium cucullatum 139, *139*

Dendrobium cucumerinum see *Dockrillia cucumerina* 168, *169*

Dendrobium curvicaule 139, *139*
   'Bee Creek' 139, *139*

Dendrobium curvicaule subsp. *curvicale* see *Dendrobium curvicaule* 139, *139*

Dendrobium cuthbertsonii 140, *140*

Dendrobium dartoisianum see *Dendrobium tortile* 150, 151

Dendrobium × *delicatum* 140
   'Pretty Good' 140, *140*

Dendrobium densiflorum 140, *140*

Dendrobium dichaeoides 140, *141*

Dendrobium discolor 140, *141*

Dendrobium dixanthum 140, *141*

Dendrobium Elegant Heart 152, *152*

Dendrobium engae 140–41, *141*

Dendrobium exiguum see *Bulbophyllum exiguum* 85

Dendrobium farmeri 141

Dendrobium farmeri var. *albiflorum* 141, *141*

Dendrobium fimbriatum 141

Dendrobium fimbriatum var. *oculatum* 141, *141*

Dendrobium findleyanum 141, *141*

Dendrobium flaviflorum 142, *142*

Dendrobium (*fleckeri* × *discolor*) 153

Dendrobium Floralia 156, *157*

Dendrobium formosum 142, *142*

Dendrobium Frosty Dawn 158

Dendrobium galactanthum see *Dendrobium scabrilingue* 148, *149*

Dendrobium Gatton Monarch 158, *159*

Dendrobium gibsonii 142, *142*

Dendrobium Golden Blossom 'Kogane' 158, *159*

Dendrobium Golden Blossom 'Venus' 158, *161*

Dendrobium Golden Dorn *153*

Dendrobium goldschmidtianum 142, *142*

Dendrobium gonzalesii see *Dendrobium ceraula* 138, *138*

Dendrobium gracilicaule 142

Dendrobium × gracillimum 142

Dendrobium guibertii see *Dendrobium densiflorum* 140, *140*

Dendrobium Hanafubuki 158, *158*

Dendrobium hanburyanum see *Dendrobium lituiflorum* 144, *144*

Dendrobium, "Hardcane" Hybrids 156–57

Dendrobium harveyanum 142, *142*

Dendrobium hedyosmum see *Dendrobium scabrilingue* 148, *149*

Dendrobium hercoglossum 142

Dendrobium Hilda Poxon 152, *152*

Dendrobium Honey Leen 158, *161*

Dendrobium Hybrids 151–61

Dendrobium jenkinsii 142, *143*

Dendrobium johnsoniae 143, *143*

Dendrobium Jonathan's Glory 152, *154*

Dendrobium Kay Lynette 158, *159*

Dendrobium Kayla 152, *154*

Dendrobium keithii 143, *143*

Dendrobium kesteveni see *Dendrobium × delicatum* 140

Dendrobium Kim 152, *155*

Dendrobium kingianum 143, *143* 'Steve' 143, *143*

Dendrobium kingianum var. *album* 143, *143*

Dendrobium laevifolium 144, *144*

Dendrobium lawesii 144, *144*

Dendrobium lichenastrum 144, *144*

Dendrobium Lilac Frost 158, *160*

Dendrobium lindleyi 144

Dendrobium linguiforme see *Dockrillia linguiformis* 168, *168*

Dendrobium lituiflorum 144, *144*

Dendrobium Lorikeet 152, *154*

Dendrobium Lovely Virgin 'Angel' 158, *161*

Dendrobium macrophyllum 144, 145

Dendrobium Maihime 'Beauty' 158, *161*

Dendrobium Maroon Star 152, *155*

Dendrobium masarangense 145, *145*

Dendrobium melaleucaphilum 145, *145*

Dendrobium Memoria Kevin Conroy 152, *154*

Dendrobium miyakei see *Dendrobium goldschmidtianum* 142, *142*

Dendrobium moniliforme 145, *145*

Dendrobium monophyllum 145, *145*

Dendrobium mutabile 146, *146*

Dendrobium Nagasaki 156, *157*

Dendrobium, "Nigrohirsute" or Black-haired Style Hybrids 158

Dendrobium nobile 146, *146*

Dendrobium nobile var. *cooksonianum* 146

Dendrobium nobile var. *nobilius* 146

Dendrobium nobile var. *virginale* 146, *146*

Dendrobium Nora Tokunaga 156

Dendrobium obtusisepalum see *Dendrobium wentianum* 150, 151

Dendrobium Oriental Paradise 'Aurora' 158, *161*

Dendrobium Our Reg 152, *154*

Dendrobium pandanicola 146, *146*

Dendrobium peguanum 146, *147*

Dendrobium phalaenopsis 146

Dendrobium pierardii see *Dendrobium cucullatum* 139, *139*

Dendrobium prenticei see *Dendrobium lichenastrum* 144, *144*

Dendrobium primulinum 146, *147*

Dendrobium pseudoglomeratum 146, *147*

Dendrobium Pua'ala 156, *156*

Dendrobium pulchellum 146

Dendrobium rex 146, *147*

Dendrobium Ronnie Gee 152, *155*

Dendrobium roseipes 146, *147*

Dendrobium rupestre 146, *147*

Dendrobium Sagamusmi 158, *160*

Dendrobium Sailor Boy 158, *161*

Dendrobium Sailor Boy 'Pinkie' 158, *161*

Dendrobium sanderae 148

Dendrobium sanderae var. *luzonicum* 148

Dendrobium sanderae var. *major* 148

Dendrobium sanderae var. *milleri* 148

Dendrobium sanderae var. *parviflorum* 148

Dendrobium sanderae var. *surigaense* 148, *149*

Dendrobium scabrilingue 148, *149*

Dendrobium schildhaueri 148, *148*

Dendrobium schroderi Hort. see *Dendrobium densiflorum* 140, *140*

Dendrobium secundum 148 'White' 148, *148*

Dendrobium Sedona 156, *157*

Dendrobium semifuscum see *Dendrobium trilamellatum* 150, 151

Dendrobium smillieae 148, *149*

Dendrobium, "Softcane" Hybrids 158–61

Dendrobium speciosum 148

Dendrobium speciosum subsp. *hillii* see *Dendrobium tarberi* 150, 151

Dendrobium speciosum var. *grandiflorum* see *Dendrobium rex* 146, *147*

Dendrobium spectabile 148, *148*

Dendrobium Stardust 158, *160*

Dendrobium striolatum see *Dockrillia striolata* 168, *169*

Dendrobium subclausum 148, *149*

Dendrobium sulphureum 148, *149*

Dendrobium Super Star 'Dandy' 158, *161*

Dendrobium superbum see *Dendrobium anosmum* 136, 137

Dendrobium Suzanne Neil 156, *156*

Dendrobium tapiniense 150, 151

Dendrobium tarberi 150, 151

Dendrobium teretifolium see *Dockrillia teretifolia* 168

Dendrobium tetragonum 150, 151 'Black Boy' *150*, 151

Dendrobium tetragonum var. *giganteum* see *Dendrobium capitisyork* 138

Dendrobium tetragonum var. *melaleucaphilum* see *Dendrobium melaleucaphilum* 145, *145*

Dendrobium Thai Pinky 156, *157*

Dendrobium Thanaid Stripes 156, 156

Dendrobium thyrsiflorum 150, 151

Dendrobium topaziacum see *Dendrobium bullenianum* 137

Dendrobium tortile 150, 151

Dendrobium triflorum see *Epigeneium triflorum* 180

Dendrobium trilamellatum 150, 151

Dendrobium verruciferum see *Cannaeorchis verruciferum* 94, 95

Dendrobium vexillarius 151, *151*

Dendrobium victoriae-reginae 151, *151*

Dendrobium virgineum see *Dendrobium schildhaueri* 148, *148*

Dendrobium wardianum 150, 151

Dendrobium Warrior 152, *154*

Dendrobium wassellii see *Dockrillia wassellii* 168, *169*

Dendrobium wentianum 150, 151

Dendrobium White Fairy 156, *157*

Dendrobium williamsonii 150, 151

Dendrobium Wonga 152, *155*

Dendrobium Yondi Brolga 152, *155*

Dendrobium Yukidaruma 'King' 158, *160*

Dendrobium Zeus 152, *154*

Dendrochilum 162–63

Dendrochilum arachnites 162, *162*

Dendrochilum cobbianum 162, *162*

Dendrochilum filiforme 162

Dendrochilum glumaceum 162, *162*

Dendrochilum latifolium 162, 163

Dendrochilum niveum 163, *163*

Dendrochilum saccolabium 163

Dendrochilum simile 163, *163*

Dendrochilum tenellum 163, *163*

Diacrium see *Caularthron* 103

Diaphananthe 164

Diaphananthe fragrantissima 164

Diaphananthe xanthopollinia see *Rhipidoglossum xanthopollinium* 285

Dichaea 164–65

Dichaea glauca 164–65, *164*

Dichaea muricata 165

Dichaea pendula 165

Dichaea sodiroi 164, 165

Dimorphorchis 164–65

Dimorphorchis lowii 164, *165*

Diplocaulobium 165

Diplocaulobium aratriferum 165, *165*

Dipteranthus 165

Dipteranthus estradae 165, *165*

Disa 166–67

Disa aurata 166

Disa cardinalis 166

Disa Diores 166, *167*

Disa Hybrids 166–67

Disa Kewbett 166, *167*

Disa Kewensis 166, *167*

Disa lugens 166, *166*

Disa racemosa 166

Disa tripetaloides 166

Disa tripetaloides var. *aurata* see *Disa aurata* 166

Disa uniflora 166, *166*

Disa Watsonii 166, *167*

Diuris 166–67

Diuris maculata 166, 167

Dockrillia 168–69

Dockrillia cucumerina 168, *169*

Dockrillia linguiformis 168, *168*

Dockrillia schoenina 168, *169*

Dockrillia striolata 168, *169*

Dockrillia teretifolia 168

Dockrillia wassellii 168, *169*

Dr. Keil's ada (*Ada keiliana*) 60, *60*

donkey orchids (*Diuris*) 166–67

Doritis pulcherrima see *Phalaenopsis pulcherrima* 257, *257*

doubletails (*Diuris*) 166–67

dove orchid (*Dendrobium crumenatum*) 139

Dracula 170–71

Dracula bella 170

Dracula Cafe Mocha 170, *170*

Dracula chimaera 170, *170*

Dracula gigas 170, *170* 'Mamie' 170, *170*

Dracula polyphemus 170, *170*

Dracula Quasimodo *170*, 171

Dracula tubeana 171, *171*

Dracula vampira 171 'Bela Lugosi' 171

Dracula velutina 171, *171*

Drakaea 171

Drakaea glyptodon 171, *171*

Dryadella 172

Dryadella albicans see *Dryadella pusiola* 172, *172*

Dryadella edwallii 172

Dryadella pusiola 172, *172*

Dryadella zebrina 172, *172*

Dyakia 172

Dyakia hendersoniana 172, *172*

E

early coral root (*Corallorrhiza trifida*) 110

early marsh orchid (*Dactylorhiza incarnata*) 134, *134*

early spider orchid (*Ophrys sphegodes*) 237

eastern prairie fringed orchid (*Platanthera leucophaea*) 267

elderflower orchid (*Dactylorhiza sambucina*) 134

Elythranthera 173

Elythranthera brunonis 173, *173*

enamel orchids *(Elythranthera)* 173
Encyclia 173
Encyclia alata 173
Encyclia alata subsp. *virella* 173, *173*
Encyclia belizensis see *Encyclia alata* subsp. *virella* 173, *173*
Encyclia brassavolae see *Prosthechea brassavolae* 276, *276*
Encyclia chacaoensis see *Prosthechea chacaoensis* 276, *276*
Encyclia cochleata see *Prosthechea cochleata* 276, *276*
Encyclia hanburyi 173, *173*
Encyclia kraenzlinii see *Psychilis kraenzlinii* 278
Encyclia krugii see *Psychilis krugii* 278
Encyclia mariae see *Euchile mariae* 184
Encyclia michuacana see *Prosthechea michuacana* 277, *277*
Encyclia radiata see *Prosthechea radiata* 277, *277*
Encyclia randii 173, *173*
Encyclia Sunburst see *Prosthechea* Sunburst 277, *277*
Encyclia truncata see *Psychilis truncata* 278
Encyclia vespa see *Prosthechea crassilabia* 276, *277*
Epiblastus 174
Epiblastus basalis 174, *174*
Epicattleya 174
Epicattleya Purple Glory 'Moir's Pride' 174, *174*
Epicattleya Siam Jade 174, *174*
Epidendrum 175–79
Epidendrum anceps 175, *175*
Epidendrum avicula see *Lanium avicula* 202
Epidendrum barbeyanum 175, *175*
Epidendrum biserra see *Lockhartia biserra* 203, *203*
Epidendrum brassavolae see *Prosthechea brassavolae* 276, *276*
Epidendrum centradenia see *Oerstedella centropetala* 233, *233*
Epidendrum ciliare 175, *175*
Epidendrum cochleatum see *Prosthechea cochleata* 276, *276*
Epidendrum Cosmo Dream Color 'Momo 1' 177, *177*
Epidendrum discolor see *Nanodes discolor* 223
Epidendrum eggersii see *Psychilis truncata* 278
Epidendrum elongatum see *Epidendrum secundum* 176
Epidendrum Hokulea 177, *177*
Epidendrum Hokulea 'Santa Barbara' 177, *177*
Epidendrum Hybrids 177–79
Epidendrum ibaguense 175, *175*
Epidendrum ilense 175, *175*
Epidendrum Joseph Glow 'Seto Raspberry' 177, *178*
Epidendrum Joseph Lii 'Reiddy' 177, *178*
Epidendrum kraenzlinii see *Psychilis kraenzlinii* 278

Epidendrum krugii see *Psychilis krugii* 278
Epidendrum lacustre 176, *176*
Epidendrum lanioides see *Lanium avicula* 202
Epidendrum longifolium see *Lanium avicula* 202
Epidendrum mariae see *Euchile mariae* 184
Epidendrum medusae 176, *176*
Epidendrum × *obrienianum* 176
Epidendrum Orange Glow 177, *178*
Epidendrum ottonis see *Nidema ottonis* 224–25, *224*
Epidendrum Pacific Ember 177, *178*
Epidendrum Pacific Girl 177, *178*
Epidendrum Pacific Vista *178*
Epidendrum parkinsonianum 176, *176*
Epidendrum Pom Pom 177, *178*
Epidendrum porpax 176, *176*
Epidendrum Pretty Princess *179*
Epidendrum prismatocarpum see *Prosthechea prismatocarpa* 277, *277*
Epidendrum pseudepidendrum 176, *177*
Epidendrum punctatum see *Cyrtopodium punctatum* 132, *132*
Epidendrum radiatum see *Prosthechea radiata* 277, *277*
Epidendrum Salmon Sunset *179*
Epidendrum schweinfurthianum see *Oerstedella schweinfurthiana* 233, *233*
Epidendrum secundum 176 'Clark' 176, *177*
Epidendrum stanfordianum 176 'Tabitha Davis' 176, *177*
Epidendrum tenuiflorum see *Oerstedella centropetala* 233, *233*
Epidendrum Tiny Red *179*
Epidendrum Tokyo Snow *179*
Epidendrum truncata see *Psychilis truncata* 278
Epidendrum Venus Valley 'Lemon' 177, *179*
Epidendrum wallisii see *Oerstedella wallisii* 233
Epigeneium 180–81
Epigeneium triflorum 180
Epigeneium triflorum var. *orientale* 180, *181*
Epipactis 180–81
Epipactis americana see *Epipactis gigantea* 180, 181
Epipactis atropurpurea see *Cephalanthera rubra* 103
Epipactis gigantea 180, 181
Epipactis helleborine 180, 181
Epipactis palustris 181
Epipactis purpurata see *Epipactis viridiflora* 181
Epipactis viridiflora 181
Epiphronitis 181
Epiphronitis Veitchii 181, *181*
Eria 181–83
Eria aporoides 181, *181*
Eria flava see *Eria mysorensis* 183
Eria gigantea *182*, 183

Eria mysorensis 183
Eria pubescens see *Eria mysorensis* 183
Eria spicata 183
Eria stricta 183
Eria xanthocheila 183, *183*
Eriopsis 183
Eriopsis biloba 183, *183*
Eriopsis rutidobulbon see *Eriopsis biloba* 183, *183*
Erycina 183
Erycina echinata 183
Esmeralda 183
Esmeralda cathcartii 183
Esmeralda clarkei 183, *183*
estrellas *(Huntleya)* 191
Euanthe sanderiana see *Vanda sanderiana* 310, *311*
Euchile 184
Euchile mariae 184
Eulophia 184
Eulophia clavicornis 184, *184*
Eulophia nuda see *Eulophia spectabilis* 184
Eulophia ovalis 184, *184*
Eulophia pulchra see *Oeceoclades pulchra* 233
Eulophia spectabilis 184
Eulophia squalida see *Eulophia spectabilis* 184
Eulophia welwitschii 184, *184*
Eulophidium ledienii see *Oeceoclades maculata* 232–33
Eulophidium maculatum see *Oeceoclades maculata* 232–33
Eulophiella 184
Eulophiella elisabethae 184
Eulophiella perrieri see *Eulophiella elisabethae* 184
Eurychone 184
Eurychone rothschildiana 184, *184*

F
fairy bells *(Sarcochilus ceciliae)* 289
fairy orchid *(Sarcochilus)* 289–91
fairy slipper *(Calypso bulbosa)* 94, *94*
Fernandezia 185
Fernandezia subbiflora 185, *185*
fire orchid *(Pyrorchis)* 281
fire orchid *(Renanthera)* 283
flag orchid *(Masdevallia)* 208–13
fly orchid *(Ophrys insectifera)* 237, *237*
foxtail orchids *(Rhynchostylis)* 286
fragrant ladies' tresses *(Spiranthes odorata)* 302–03
fragrant orchid *(Gymnadenia conopsea)* 188, *188*

G
Galeandra 185
Galeandra baueri 185, *185*
Galeandra cristata see *Galeandra baueri* 185, *185*
Gastrochilus 185–86
Gastrochilus calceolaris 185
Gastrochilus formosanus 185
Gastrochilus japonicus 186, *186*
Gastrochilus nebulosus see *Gastrochilus formosanus* 185
Gastrochilus obliquus 186, *186*
Gastrochilus quercetorum see *Gastrochilus formosanus* 185

Gastrochilus somai see *Gastrochilus japonicus* 186, *186*
Gastrochilus suavis 186, *186*
Gastrorchis 186
Gastrorchis pulcher 186
Gastrorchis pulcher var. *alba* 186, *186*
Gastrorchis steinhardtiana 186, *186*
Georgeblackara 186–87
Georgeblackara Tribute 186, *187*
gherkin orchid *(Dockrillia cucumerina)* 168, *169*
giant helleborine *(Epipactis gigantea)* 180, 181
giant orchid *(Barlia robertiana)* 73
Glossodia 186–87
Glossodia major 186–87, *187*
gnat orchid *(Acianthus)* 59
gnat orchid *(Cyrtostylis)* 132
Gomesa 187
Gomesa crispa 187, *187*
Gomesa polymorpha see *Gomesa crispa* 187, *187*
Gomesa undulata see *Gomesa crispa* 187, *187*
Gongora 187
Gongora histrionica 187, *187*
Gongora nigropunctata 187, *187*
Gongora pleiochroma 187, *187*
Goodyera 187
Goodyera biflora 187
Goodyera tesselata 187
Grammangis 188
Grammangis ellisii 188, *188*
Grammangis pardalina see *Cymbidiella pardalina* 113, *113*
Grammatophyllum 188
Grammatophyllum elegans 188, *188*
Grammatophyllum fastuosum see *Grammatophyllum speciosum* 188
Grammatophyllum giganteum see *Grammatophyllum speciosum* 188
Grammatophyllum papuanum see *Grammatophyllum speciosum* 188
Grammatophyllum speciosum 188
grass orchid *(Grastidium)* 188
grass pink *(Calopogon tuberosus)* 94, *94*
Grastidium 188
Grastidium cathcartii 188
great sun-orchid *(Thelymitra aristata)* 306, *306*
greater butterfly orchid *(Platanthera chlorantha)* 267
greenhood orchid *(Pterostylis)* 280
Grobya 188
Grobya amherstiae 188, *188*
Gymnadenia 188
Gymnadenia bifolia see *Platanthera bifolia* 267
Gymnadenia conopsea 188, *188*

H
Habenaria 189
Habenaria arenaria 189
Habenaria aurantiaca see *Habenaria marginata* 189
Habenaria bifolia see *Platanthera bifolia* 267

Habenaria bonatea see *Bonatea speciosa* 76
Habenaria chlorantha see *Platanthera chlorantha* 267
Habenaria dregeana 189, *189*
Habenaria marginata 189
Habenaria monorhiza 189, *189*
Habenaria rhodocheila 189, *189*
Haemaria discolor see *Ludisia discolor* 204, *204*
hammer orchid (*Drakaea*) 171
Hapalochilus speciosus see *Bulbophyllum speciosum* 90, *90*
Haraella 189
Haraella odorata see *Haraella retrocalla* 189, *189*
Haraella retrocalla 189, *189*
Hartwegia see *Nageliella* 223
Hartwegia comosa see *Nageliella purpurea* 223, *223*
Hartwegia purpurea see *Nageliella purpurea* 223, *223*
Hawkinsara 189
Hawkinsara Keepsake 'Lake View' 189, *189*
hay-scented orchid (*Dendrochilum glumaceum*) 162, *162*
heart-flowered orchid (*Serapias*) 296–97
heart-flowered orchid (*Serapias cordigera*) 296
helleborine (*Cephalanthera*) 103
helmet orchid (*Corybas*) 111
Hexisea 190
Hexisea imbricata 190, *190*
Himantoglossum 190
Himantoglossum adriaticum 190
Himantoglossum caprinum 190
Himantoglossum hircinum 190, *190*
Himantoglossum hircinum var. *adriaticum* see *Himantoglossum adriaticum* 190
Homalopetalum 190
Homalopetalum costaricense see *Homalopetalum pumilio* 190, *190*
Homalopetalum lehmannianum see *Homalopetalum pumilio* 190, *190*
Homalopetalum pumilio 190, *190*
Hormidium mariae see *Euchile mariae* 184
Howeara 190
Howeara Mary Eliza 190, *190*
Huntleya 191
Huntleya albidofulva see *Huntleya meleagris* 191
Huntleya citrina 191
Huntleya meleagris 191
Huntleya waldvogelii see *Huntleya citrina* 191
Huttonaea 191
Huttonaea grandiflora 191, *191*
Hygrochilus 191
Hygrochilus parishii 191, *191*
Hygrochilus parishii var. *mariottianus* 191

I

Ida 192
Ida costata 192
Ionopsis 192
Ionopsis paniculata see *Ionopsis utricularioides* 192

Ionopsis pulchella see *Ionopsis utricularioides* 192
Ionopsis utricularioides 192
ironbark orchid (*Dendrobium aemulum*) 136
Isabelia 192
Isabelia pulchella see *Neolauchea pulchella* 223, *223*
Isabelia virginalis 192, *192*
Isochilus 192–93
Isochilus aurantiacus 193
Isochilus linearis *192*, 193

J

jewel orchid (*Goodyera*) 187
jewel orchid (*Ludisia*) 204
Jumellea 193
Jumellea arachnantha 193, *193*
Jumellea comorensis 193, *193*
Jumellea confusa 193, *193*
Jumellea densefoliata 193, *193*
Jumellea fragrans 193
Jumellea sagittata 193

K

Kefersteinia 194
Kefersteinia graminea 194
Kefersteinia laminata 194, *194*
king orchid (*Dendrobium speciosum*) 148
Komper's orchid (*Comperia comperiana*) 110
Kunthara 194
Kunthara Hybrids 194
Kunthara Living Fire 194, *194*
Kunthara Nelly Isler 194, *194*
Kunthara Stefan Isler 194, *194*

L

ladies' tresses (*Spiranthes*) 302–03
lady of the night orchid (*Brassavola*) 76–77
lady orchid (*Orchis purpurea*) 238
lady's slipper (*Cypripedium*) 130–31
lady's slipper orchid (*Cypripedium calceolus*) 130
Laelia 195–98
Laelia acuminata see *Laelia rubescens* 198, *198*
Laelia anceps 195, *195*
Laelia anceps var. *veitchiana* 'Fort Caroline' 195, *195*
Laelia blumenscheinii 195, *195*
Laelia Canariensis 195, *195*
Laelia caulescens 195, *195*
Laelia cinnabarina 196
Laelia crispa 196, *196*
Laelia crispata 196, *196*
Laelia dayana 196
Laelia harpophylla 196, *196*
Laelia jongheana 196, *196*
Laelia longipes 196, *196*
Laelia lucasiana see *Laelia longipes* 196, *196*
Laelia milleri 196, *197*
Laelia ostermeyerii see *Laelia longipes* 196, *196*
Laelia pumila 196
Laelia purpurata 197, *197*
Laelia purpurata var. *carnea* 197, *197*
Laelia purpurata var. *werkhauseri* 197
Laelia rubescens 198, *198*

Laelia rubescens var. *roseum* 198
Laelia rupestris see *Laelia crispata* 196, *196*
Laelia sincorana 198, *198*
Laelia superbiens see *Schomburgkia superbiens* 295
Laelia tenebrosa 198, *198*
Laeliocatonia 198
Laeliocatonia Peggy San 'Galaxy' 198, *198*
Laeliocattleya 199–201
Laeliocattleya C. G. Roebling 199, *199*
Laeliocattleya Canhamiana 'Coerulea' *199*
Laeliocattleya (*Cattleya* Vaupes Sunrise × *Laeliocattleya* Interglossa) *199*
Laeliocattleya Chit Chat 'Tangerine' 199, *199*
Laeliocattleya Edgard van Belle 'Edwin Arthur Hausermann' 199, *199*
Laeliocattleya Gold Harp 199, *199*
Laeliocattleya Hybrids 199–201
Laeliocattleya Jim Burkhalter 199, *199*
Laeliocattleya Kauai Spiders 200
Laeliocattleya (*Laeliocattleya* Blue Ribbon × *Cattleya* Penny Kuroda) *200*
Laeliocattleya Lauren Oka 'Kristy' *200*
Laeliocattleya 'Maris Song' *200*
Laeliocattleya Mini Purple 'Bette' 199, *200*
Laeliocattleya Mini Purple 'Royale' *200*
Laeliocattleya Myrtle Johnson 199, *200*
Laeliocattleya Orange Embers *200*
Laeliocattleya Pink Favourite 'Jolly' 199, *200*
Laeliocattleya Pink Perfume *201*
Laeliocattleya Pre School 'Royale' *201*
Laeliocattleya Rabeiana *200*
Laeliocattleya Rojo 'Fiery' 199, *201*
Laeliocattleya Royal Emperor 'Wade' *201*
Laeliocattleya Sallieri *201*
Laeliocattleya Tropical Pointer 'Cheetah' 199, *201*
Laeliopsis lindenii see *Cattleyopsis lindenii* 103
Lanium 202
Lanium avicula 202
Lanium berkeleyi see *Lanium avicula* 202
large bird orchid (*Chiloglottis gunnii*) 104, *104*
large mosquito orchid (*Acianthus exsertus*) 59, *59*
large wax-lip orchid (*Glossodia major*) 186–87, *187*
large-flowered goodyera (*Goodyera biflora*) 187
late spider orchid (*Ophrys holoserica*) 237
leafless beaked orchid (*Stenorrhynchos lanceolatum*) 305

Lemboglossum maculatum see *Rhynchostele maculata* 286
Lemboglossum rossii see *Rhynchostele rossii* 286
Lemboglossum uro-skinneri see *Rhynchostele uro-skinneri* 286
leopard orchid (*Ansellia*) 66–67
Lepanthes 202
Lepanthes calodictyon 202
Lepanthes ligiae 202, *202*
Leptotes 202
Leptotes bicolor 202, *202*
Leptotes bicolor var. *alba* 202
Leptotes paranaensis see *Leptotes unicolor* 202
Leptotes serrulata see *Leptotes bicolor* 202, *202*
Leptotes unicolor 202
lesser butterfly orchid (*Platanthera bifolia*) 267
Lichterfeldia see *Cuitlauzina* 113
lily-of-the-valley orchid (*Osmoglossum convallarioides*) 238
Limodorum flavum see *Phaius flavus* 255, *255*
Liparis 203
Liparis latifolia 203
Liparis nervosa 203, *203*
Liparis nigra 203
Liparis reflexa 203
Liparis viridiflora 203, *203*
little gem sarcochilus (*Sarcochilus hillii*) 290
lizard orchid (*Himantoglossum*) 190
lizard orchid (*Himantoglossum hircinum*) 190, *190*
lizard's tongue orchid (*Himantoglossum hircinum*) 190, *190*
Lockhartia 203
Lockhartia biserra 203, *203*
Lockhartia integra see *Lockhartia pittieri* 203
Lockhartia pittieri 203
Loroglossum see *Himantoglossum* 190
Loroglossum hircinum see *Himantoglossum hircinum* 190, *190*
Lothiana see *Porroglossum* 274
Ludisia 204
Ludisia discolor 204, *204*
Lycaste 204–06
Lycaste Albanensis 206, *206*
Lycaste aromatica 204, *205*
Lycaste bradeorum 205, *205*
Lycaste guatemalensis see *Lycaste skinneri* 205, *205*
Lycaste Hybrids 206
Lycaste Imschootiana 206, *206*
Lycaste Koolena 206, *206*
Lycaste Leo 206, *206*
Lycaste Macama 'Aline' 206, *206*
Lycaste Macama 'Atlantis' 206, *206*
Lycaste macrophylla 205
Lycaste macrophylla var. *desboisiana* 205, *205*
Lycaste (Rowland × Shoalhaven) 206, *206*
Lycaste Shonan Harmony 206, *206*
Lycaste skinneri 205, *205*
Lycaste tricolor 205, *205*

Lycaste Wyuna 'Pale Beauty' 206, *206*
Lyperanthus 207
Lyperanthus nigricans see *Pyrorchis nigricans* 281, *281*
Lyperanthus serratus 207, *207*

M

Macodes 208
Macodes petola 208
Macodes sanderiana 208
Macroclinium 208
Macroclinium bicolor 208
madeiran orchid (*Dactylorhiza foliosa*) 133, *133*
Malaxis 208
Malaxis taurina 208
man orchid (*Aceras*) 59
maroonhood (*Pterostylis pedunculata*) 280, *280*
marsh helleborine (*Epipactis palustris*) 181
marsh orchid (*Dactylorhiza*) 133–34
Masdevallia 208–13
Masdevallia Adelina 210, *210*
Masdevallia albicans see *Dryadella pusiola* 172, *172*
Masdevallia amabilis 208, *208*
Masdevallia amethystinum see *Porroglossum amethystinum* 274
Masdevallia Angelita 210, *210*
Masdevallia Angelita 'Royale' 210, *210*
Masdevallia bella see *Dracula bella* 170
Masdevallia (Bright Spice × Galaxy) *210*
Masdevallia Carousel 'Parade' 210, *211*
Masdevallia Charisma 210, *211*
Masdevallia Charisma 'Gina' *211*
Masdevallia chimaera see *Dracula chimaera* 170, *170*
Masdevallia Cinnamon Twist 210, *211*
Masdevallia coccinea 208, *208*
Masdevallia Copper Angel 'Highland' 210, *211*
Masdevallia Copperwing 210, *211*
Masdevallia Dean Haas 210, *211*
Masdevallia Delma Hart 'Paddy' 210, *212*
Masdevallia echidna see *Porroglossum echidnum* 274
Masdevallia edwallii see *Dryadella edwallii* 172
Masdevallia Elegance 210, *210*
Masdevallia Falcata 'North Degree' 210, *212*
Masdevallia floribunda 209, *209*
Masdevallia Geneva Spots 'Royale' *212*
Masdevallia gigas see *Dracula gigas* 170
Masdevallia Hybrids 210–13
Masdevallia ignea 209
Masdevallia infracta 209
Masdevallia Machu Picchu 210, *212*
Masdevallia (Magdalene × Marguerite) 210, *212*
Masdevallia Marguerite 210, *212*

Masdevallia mucosa see *Porroglossum echidnum* 274
Masdevallia nidifica 209, *209*
Masdevallia ophioglossa 209, *209*
Masdevallia ova-avis see *Masdevallia tridens* 209, *209*
Masdevallia Pixie Shadow 210, *213*
Masdevallia polyphemus see *Dracula polyphemus* 170, *170*
Masdevallia Prince Charming 210, *213*
Masdevallia princeps 209 'Long Stem' 209, *209*
Masdevallia Redwing 210, *213*
Masdevallia Rose-Mary 210, *213*
Masdevallia tovarensis 209
Masdevallia tridens 209, *209*
Masdevallia tuerckheimii see *Masdevallia floribunda* 209, *209*
Masdevallia Urubamba 210, *213*
Masdevallia vampira see *Dracula vampira* 171
Masdevallia veitchiana 209, *209*
Masdevallia Watercolor Dreamer 'Monet's Garden' *213*
Masdevallia Winter Blush 210, *213*
Masdevallia zebrina see *Dryadella zebrina* 172, *172*
Maxillaria 214–16
Maxillaria acuminata 214, *214*
Maxillaria biolleyi 214, *214*
Maxillaria chrysantha 214, *214*
Maxillaria cogniauxiana 215, *215*
Maxillaria cucullata 215, *215*
Maxillaria fractiflexa 215, *215*
Maxillaria marginata 215, *215*
Maxillaria nigrescens 215
Maxillaria picta 215, *215*
Maxillaria porphyrostele 216, *216*
Maxillaria sanderiana 216
Maxillaria variabilis 216, *216*
Mediocalcar 216
Mediocalcar bifolium 216, *216*
Mediocalcar decoratum 216, *216*
Megaclinium falcatum see *Bulbophyllum falcatum* 86, *86*
Menadenium see *Zygosepalum* 320
Menadenium lindeniae see *Zygosepalum lindeniae* 320
Mendel's cattleya (*Cattleya mendelii*) 99, *99*
Mesospinidium sanguineum see *Symphoglossum sanguineum* 305, *305*
Mexicoa 216–17
Mexicoa ghiesbreghtiana 216, *217*
Microcoelia 216–17
Microcoelia exilis 217, *217*
Microcoelia globulosa 217
Microcoelia stolzii 217
Microterangis 217
Microterangis hariotiana 217, *217*
Microtis 217
Microtis orbicularis 217, *217*
military orchid (*Orchis militaris*) 238
Miltassia 218
Miltassia 'Charles M. Fitch' 218, *218*
Miltassia 'Mourier Bay' × *Miltonia* 'Sao Paulo' 218
Miltonia 218–19
Miltonia clowesii 218, *219*

Miltonia cuneata 218
Miltonia flavescens 218
Miltonia moreliana 218
Miltonia regnellii 219, *219*
Miltonia Sandy's Cove 219, *219*
Miltonia spectabilis 219, *219*
Miltonia spectabilis var. *moreliana* see *Miltonia moreliana* 218
Miltonia warscewiczii see *Oncidium fuscatum* 234
Miltonidium 219
Miltonidium Bartley Schwarz 'Highland' 219, *219*
Miltonidium Pupukea Sunset 'H & R' 219, *219*
Miltoniopsis 220–21
Miltoniopsis Beall's Strawberry Joy 220, *220*
Miltoniopsis Cute 'Rodeo' 220, *220*
Miltoniopsis First Love 'Pink Lady' 220, *221*
Miltoniopsis Herralexandre 220, *220*
Miltoniopsis Hudson Bay 220, *221*
Miltoniopsis Hybrids 220–21
Miltoniopsis Jean Carlson 220, *221*
Miltoniopsis phalaenopsis 220, *220*
Miltoniopsis Red Knight 220, *221*
Miltoniopsis Robert Strauss 220, *221*
Miltoniopsis Rouge 'California Plum' 220, *221*
Miltoniopsis vexillaria 220
Miltoniopsis Zorro 'Yellow Delight' 220, *221*
moccasin flower (*Cypripedium acaule*) 130, *130*
mosquito orchid (*Acianthus*) 59
mosquito orchid (*Acianthus confusus*) 59, *59*
moth orchid (*Phalaenopsis*) 256–65
mountain lady's-slipper (*Cypripedium montanum*) 130
Myrmecophila 222
Myrmecophila tibicinis 222, *222*
Mystacidium 222
Mystacidium brayboniae 222, *222*
Mystacidium capense 222, *222*
Mystacidium filicorne see *Mystacidium capense* 222, *222*

N

Nageliella 223
Nageliella purpurea 223, *223*
Nakamotoara 223
Nakamotoara Rainbow Gem 223
Nakamotoara Rainbow Gem 'Pink Star' 223, *223*
Nakamotoara Rainbow Gem 'White Lady' 223, *223*
Nanodes 223
Nanodes discolor 223
Nanodes mathewsii see *Epidendrum porpax* 176, *176*
Nanodes medusae see *Epidendrum medusae* 176, *176*
necklace orchid (*Pholidota imbricata*) 265
Neobathiea 223
Neobathiea filicornu see *Neobathiea grandidierana* 223, *223*
Neobathiea grandidierana 223, *223*
Neofinetia 223
Neofinetia falcata 223

Neolauchea 223
Neolauchea pulchella 223, *223*
Neolehmannia porpax see *Epidendrum porpax* 176, *176*
Neopabstopetalum 224
Neopabstopetalum Adelaide Alive 224, *224*
Neopabstopetalum Beverley Lou 224, *224*
Neopabstopetalum Warooka 224
Neostylis 224
Neostylis Lou Sneary 224, *224*
Nidema 224–25
Nidema ottonis 224–25, *224*
Nigritella see *Gymnadenia* 188
noble cattleya (*Cattleya nobilior*) 99, *99*
nodding greenhood (*Pterostylis nutans*) 280, *280*
nodding ladies' tresses (*Spiranthes odorata*) 302–03
northern coral root (*Corallorrhiza trifida*) 110
Notylia 225
Notylia barkeri 225
Notylia bicolor see *Macroclinium bicolor* 208

O

Oberonia 225
Oberonia gracilis 225, *225*
Octomeria 226
Octomeria alpina 226, *226*
Octomeria arcuata see *Octomeria grandiflora* 226
Octomeria grandiflora 226
Octomeria juncifolia 226, *226*
Octomeria surinamensis see *Octomeria grandiflora* 226
Odontioda 226–27
Odontioda Avranches 226, *226*
Odontioda Bugle Boy 226, *226*
Odontioda Durham River 226, *226*
Odontioda (Erik Jaeger × Helen Stead 'Geyserland') 226, *227*
Odontioda Heatonensis × *Odontoglossum* Starlight 226, *227*
Odontioda Hybrids 226–27
Odontioda La Fosse 226, *227*
Odontioda (Nichirei Sunrise × Ingmar) 226, *227*
Odontioda Phoenix Way × (Mount Diablo × Tiffany) *227*
Odontioda Ruby Eyes 226, *227*
Odontioda Sheila Hands 226, *227*
Odontioda Wearside Gate 226, *227*
Odontobrassia 228
Odontobrassia Kenneth Biven 'Santa Barbara' 228, *228*
Odontocidium 228–29
Odontocidium Artur Elle 228, *228*
Odontocidium Bittersweet 'Sophie' 228, *228*
Odontocidium Bittersweet 'Toffee' 228, *229*
Odontocidium Dark Charmer 'Antigua' 228, *228*
Odontocidium Dorothy Wisnom 'Golden Gate' 228, *229*
Odontocidium Golden Trident 228, *229*
Odontocidium Hansueli Isler 228, *229*

Odontocidium Hybrids 228–29
Odontocidium Mayfair 'RFW' 228, *229*
Odontocidium Tigersun 'Nugget' 228, *229*
Odontocidium Tropic Tiger 228, *229*
Odontoglossum 230–31
Odontoglossum (Augres × *nobile*) 230, *231*
Odontoglossum bictoniense see *Rhynchostele bictoniensis* 286, *286*
Odontoglossum citrosmum see *Cuitlauzina pendula* 113
Odontoglossum convallarioides see *Osmoglossum convallarioides* 238
Odontoglossum cordatum see *Rhynchostele cordata* 286, *286*
Odontoglossum crispum 230
Odontoglossum gloriosum 230, *230*
Odontoglossum grande see *Rossioglossum grande* 288, *288*
Odontoglossum harryanum 230, *230*
Odontoglossum (Holiday Gold × Geyser Gold) 230, *231*
Odontoglossum Hybrids 230–31
Odontoglossum Illustre 230, *231*
Odontoglossum La Hougue Bie 230, *231*
Odontoglossum maculatum see *Rhynchostele maculata* 286
Odontoglossum Margarete Holm 230, *231*
Odontoglossum Mimosa 'Oda Marcet' 230, *231*
Odontoglossum pendulum see *Cuitlauzina pendula* 113
Odontoglossum pulchellum see *Osmoglossum pulchellum* 238
Odontoglossum rossii see *Rhynchostele rossii* 286
Odontoglossum trilobum 230, *230*
Odontoglossum uro-skinneri see *Rhynchostele uro-skinneri* 286
Odontoglossum warneri see *Mexicoa ghiesbreghtiana* 216, *217*
Odontoglossum wyattianum 230, *230*
Odontonia 232
Odontonia Bartley Schwarz 232, *232*
Odontonia Papageno 232, *232*
Odontonia Papageno 'Fiesta' 232, *232*
Odontonia Susan Bogdanow 232, *232*
Oeceoclades 232–33
Oeceoclades maculata 232–33
Oeceoclades pulchra 233
Oeoniella 233
Oeoniella polystachys 233, *233*
Oerstedella 233
Oerstedella centradenia see *Oerstedella centropetala* 233, *233*
Oerstedella centropetala 233, *233*
Oerstedella schweinfurthiana 233, *233*
Oerstedella wallisii 233
Olgasias triquetra see *Tolumnia triquetra* 307
Oncidium 234–36

Oncidium altissimum see *Oncidium baueri* 234, *234*
Oncidium ascendens see *Trichocentrum ascendens* 308, *308*
Oncidium baueri 234, *234*
Oncidium Cameo Sunset 234, *234*
Oncidium cebolleta see *Trichocentrum cebolleta* 308, *308*
Oncidium crispum 234
Oncidium croesus 234, *234*
Oncidium echinatum see *Erycina echinata* 183
Oncidium falcipetalum see *Cyrtochilum falcipetalum* 131
Oncidium flexuosum 234
Oncidium fuscatum 234
Oncidium ghiesbreghtiana see *Mexicoa ghiesbreghtiana* 216, *217*
Oncidium guttatum see *Trichocentrum luridum* 308
Oncidium hintonii 234
Oncidium kramerianum see *Psychopsis kramerianum* 278, *279*
Oncidium leucochilum 234–35, *235*
Oncidium longifolium see *Trichocentrum cebolleta* 308, *308*
Oncidium luridum see *Trichocentrum luridum* 308
Oncidium maculatum 235, *235*
Oncidium marshallianum 235, *235*
Oncidium Mendenhall see *Psychopsis* Mendenhall 278, *278*
Oncidium microxiphium see *Cyrtochilum microxiphium* 131, *131*
Oncidium ornithorynchum 235, *235*
Oncidium papilio see *Psychopsis papilio* 278
Oncidium phymatochilum 235, *235*
Oncidium pulchellum see *Tolumnia pulchella* 307
Oncidium sarcodes 236, *236*
Oncidium Sharry Baby 'Sweet Fragrance' 236
Oncidium sphacelatum 236, *236*
Oncidium splendidum see *Trichocentrum splendidum* 308, *308*
Oncidium Sweet Sugar 236, *236*
Oncidium Tai 236, *236*
Oncidium trilobum see *Odontoglossum trilobum* 230, *230*
Oncidium triquetrum see *Tolumnia triquetra* 307
Oncidium varicosum 236
Oncidium variegatum see *Tolumnia variegata* 307, *307*
Oncidium viperinum 236
Oncidium wydleri see *Oncidium baueri* 234, *234*
Oncidopsis Bartley Schwarz see *Odontonia* Bartley Schwarz 232, *232*
onion orchid (*Dendrobium canaliculatum*) 138, *138*
onion orchid (*Microtis*) 217
Ophrys 237
Ophrys apifera 237, *237*

Ophrys aranifera see *Ophrys sphegodes* 237
Ophrys bicolor see *Ophrys apifera* 237, *237*
Ophrys boteroni see *Ophrys apifera* 237, *237*
Ophrys fuciflora see *Ophrys holoserica* 237
Ophrys holoserica 237
Ophrys insectifera 237, *237*
Ophrys lutea 237
Ophrys muscifera see *Ophrys insectifera* 237, *237*
Ophrys myodes see *Ophrys insectifera* 237, *237*
Ophrys sphegodes 237
Ophrys tenthredinifera 237
Ophrys trollii see *Ophrys apifera* 237, *237*
orange blossom orchid (*Sarcochilus falcatus*) 289
Orchis 237–38
Orchis elata see *Dactylorhiza elata* 133
Orchis fuchsii see *Dactylorhiza fuchsii* 133, *133*
Orchis incarnata see *Dactylorhiza incarnata* 134, *134*
Orchis militaris 238
Orchis purpurea 238
Ornithocephalus 238
Ornithocephalus bicornis 238, *238*
Ornithocephalus falcatus see *Ornithocephalus gladiatus* 238
Ornithocephalus gladiatus 238
Ornithocephalus inflexus see *Ornithocephalus gladiatus* 238
Ornithocephalus myrticola 238
Ornithocephalus tripterus see *Ornithocephalus gladiatus* 238
Osmoglossum 238
Osmoglossum convallarioides 238
Osmoglossum pulchellum 238
'Royale' 238, *238*

P

Pabstia 239
Pabstia jugosa 239
Panarica brassavolae see *Prosthechea brassavolae* 276, *276*
pansy orchid (*Miltoniopsis*) 220–21
Paphiopedilum 239–52
Paphiopedilum appletonianum 239 'Jan' 239, *239*
Paphiopedilum barbatum 239, *239*
Paphiopedilum bellatulum 239, *239*
Paphiopedilum Booth's Sand Lady 248, *248*
Paphiopedilum boxallii 239, *239*
Paphiopedilum bullenianum 240, *240*
Paphiopedilum callosum 240
Paphiopedilum chamberlainianum see *Paphiopedilum victoria-regina* 246, *246*
Paphiopedilum charlesworthii 240
Paphiopedilum charlesworthii var. *album* 240
Paphiopedilum concolor 240, *240*
Paphiopedilum Darling 248, *248*
Paphiopedilum delenatii 240, *240*
Paphiopedilum Delophyllum 248, *248*
Paphiopedilum Dragon Callos 248

Paphiopedilum exul 240, *240*
Paphiopedilum Faire-Maud 249
Paphiopedilum Flame Dragon 248
Paphiopedilum fowliei 240, *240*
Paphiopedilum Gael 248, *249*
Paphiopedilum gardineri see *Paphiopedilum glanduliferum* 240, *241*
Paphiopedilum glanduliferum 240, *241*
Paphiopedilum glaucophyllum 241, *241*
'Lee' 241, *241*
Paphiopedilum Gold Dollar 248, *249*
Paphiopedilum gratrixianum 241, *241*
Paphiopedilum hainanense 242, *242*
Paphiopedilum haynaldianum 242, *242*
Paphiopedilum henryanum 242, *242*
Paphiopedilum hirsutissimum 242, *243*
Paphiopedilum Honey 248, *249*
Paphiopedilum hookerae 242
Paphiopedilum hookerae var. *volonteanum* 242, *243*
Paphiopedilum Hybrids 248–52
Paphiopedilum insigne 242, *243*
Paphiopedilum jackii see *Paphiopedilum malipoense* var. *jackii* 242, *243*
Paphiopedilum Juno 249
Paphiopedilum kolopakingii 242, *243*
Paphiopedilum Lawrebel 248, *249*
Paphiopedilum Lebaudyanum 248, *249*
Paphiopedilum liemianum 242, *243*
Paphiopedilum Limidolli 248, *249*
Paphiopedilum lowii 242
'Select' 242, *243*
Paphiopedilum Madame Martinet 248, *250*
Paphiopedilum malipoense 242, *243*
Paphiopedilum malipoense var. *jackii* 242, *243*
Paphiopedilum mastersianum 244, *244*
Paphiopedilum Mitylene 248, *250*
Paphiopedilum moquetteanum 244, *244*
Paphiopedilum Morganiae 250
Paphiopedilum Nirvana 250
Paphiopedilum niveum 244, *244*
Paphiopedilum Onyx 248, *250*
Paphiopedilum Oriental Enchantment 248, *250*
Paphiopedilum Pathfinder Norm 248, *250*
Paphiopedilum Petula 251
Paphiopedilum philippinense 244, *245*
Paphiopedilum philippinense var. *roebelenii* 244, *245*
Paphiopedilum Pinocchio 248, *251*
Paphiopedilum Pinocchio 'Yellow' 251
Paphiopedilum primulinum 244, *245*
Paphiopedilum primulinum var. *purpurescens* 244, *245*

Paphiopedilum (Raisin Eyes × Maudiae) *251*

Paphiopedilum Red Fusion 248, *251*

Paphiopedilum Red Prince *251*

Paphiopedilum Rolfei 248, *251*

Paphiopedilum rothschildianum 244, *245*

Paphiopedilum Saint Swithin 248

Paphiopedilum Sioux 248, *252*

Paphiopedilum Smaug 'Peats Ridge' *252*

Paphiopedilum Song of Love *252*

Paphiopedilum spicerianum 244, *244*

Paphiopedilum sukhakulii 244, *245*

Paphiopedilum (sukhakulii × Tuxedo Junction) *252*

Paphiopedilum (sukhakulii × Virgo) *252*

Paphiopedilum tonsum 246, *246*

Paphiopedilum venustum 246 'Red Lip' 246, *247*

Paphiopedilum venustum var. *measuresianum* 246, *247*

Paphiopedilum victoria-regina 246, *246*

Paphiopedilum villosum 246, 247

Paphiopedilum wardii 247 'Coco' 247, *247*

Paphiopedilum wardii var. *album* 247, *247*

Paphiopedilum wolterianum see *Paphiopedilum appletonianum* 239

Paphiopedilum Wosner Perle *252*

Paphiopedilum Yospur 248, *252*

Papilionanthe 253

Papilionanthe hookeriana 253

Papilionanthe Miss Joaquim 253, *253*

Papilionanthe teres 253

Papilionanthe vandarum 253, *253*

Paracaleana 253

Paracaleana nigrita 253, *253*

Paraphalaenopsis 254

Paraphalaenopsis denevei 254

Paraphalaenopsis labukensis 254, *254*

Paraphalaenopsis laycockii 254, *254*

Parasarcochilus hirticalcar see *Sarcochilus hirticalcar* 290, *290*

pencil orchid (*Dockrillia*) 168–69

Pescatorea 254

Pescatorea cerina 254, *254*

Pescatorea lehmannii 254, *254*

Phaiocalanthe 254–55

Phaiocalanthe Schroederiana 255, *255*

Phaiocymbidium 255

Phaiocymbidium Chardwarense 255, *255*

Phaius 255

Phaius flavus 255, *255*

Phaius tankervilleae 255, *255*

Phalaenopsis 256–65

Phalaenopsis amabilis 256, *256*

Phalaenopsis Antique Gold 258, *258*

Phalaenopsis aphrodite 256

Phalaenopsis aphrodite subsp. *formosana* 256, *256*

Phalaenopsis Artemis *258*

Phalaenopsis Brother Cefiro 258, *258*

Phalaenopsis Brother Golden Potential 258, *258*

Phalaenopsis Brother Golden Wish 258, *258*

Phalaenopsis Brother Juno 258, *259*

Phalaenopsis Brother Kaiser *259*

Phalaenopsis Brother Little Spotty *259*

Phalaenopsis Brother Pico Pink 258, *259*

Phalaenopsis Brother Pico Sweetheart 258, *259*

Phalaenopsis Brother Pico Vallezac 258, *259*

Phalaenopsis Brother Showpiece 258, *260*

Phalaenopsis Chancellor *260*

Phalaenopsis (Ching Her John × Dou-dii Rose) *260*

Phalaenopsis City Girl 258, *260*

Phalaenopsis Coral Harbor 258, *260*

Phalaenopsis Cosmic Star 258, *260*

Phalaenopsis Cottonwood 258, *260*

Phalaenopsis denevei see *Paraphalaenopsis denevei* 254

Phalaenopsis (Dou-dii Rose × Ching Her John) *261*

Phalaenopsis equestris 256, *257*

Phalaenopsis Formosa Mini 258, *261*

Phalaenopsis gibbosa 256, *257*

Phalaenopsis (Golden Poeker 'B' × stuartiana 'Larkin Valley') *261*

Phalaenopsis Hakugin 258, *261*

Phalaenopsis Ho's Amaglad 258

Phalaenopsis Hsinying Facia 258, *261*

Phalaenopsis Hwafeng Redqueen 258, *261*

Phalaenopsis Hybrids 258–65

Phalaenopsis laycocki see *Paraphalaenopsis laycockii* 254, *254*

Phalaenopsis Little Kiss 258, *261*

Phalaenopsis Livingston's Gem 258, *262*

Phalaenopsis Luchia Lip 258, *262*

Phalaenopsis lueddemanniana 256–57, *257*

Phalaenopsis (Malibu Tiger × Vladimir Horowitz) *263*

Phalaenopsis mannii 257, *257*

Phalaenopsis Minho Stripes 258, *262*

Phalaenopsis (Morgenrot × Opaline) *263*

Phalaenopsis Night Shine 258, *262*

Phalaenopsis Oregon Delight 258, *262*

Phalaenopsis parishii 257, *257*

Phalaenopsis pulcherrima 257, *257*

Phalaenopsis Pumpkin Patch 258

Phalaenopsis Queen Beer 258, *262*

Phalaenopsis Quevedo 258, *263*

Phalaenopsis Quilted Beauty 258, *263*

Phalaenopsis Sand Stone 258, *263*

Phalaenopsis schilleriana 257, *257*

Phalaenopsis Snow City 258, *263*

Phalaenopsis Sogo Firework 258, *263*

Phalaenopsis Sogo Yukidian 258, *264*

Phalaenopsis Sonnentau × (*Doritaenopsis* Mosel × self) *264*

Phalaenopsis Sonoma Spots 258, *264*

Phalaenopsis Striped Eagle 258, *264*

Phalaenopsis Sylvania Fair 'Sacha' × (Wilma Hughes × Diana Hampton) 'Petula' *264*

Phalaenopsis Taida Sunset 258, *264*

Phalaenopsis Taisuco Adian 258, *264*

Phalaenopsis Taisuco Firebird *264*

Phalaenopsis Taisuco Pixie 258, *265*

Phalaenopsis (Timothy Christopher × *pulcherrima*) 258, *265*

Phalaenopsis wilsonii 257

phantom orchid (*Cephalanthera austiniae*) 103, *103*

Pholidota 265

Pholidota articulata 265

Pholidota bracteata 265, *265*

Pholidota chinensis 265, *265*

Pholidota conchoidea see *Pholidota imbricata* 265

Pholidota imbricata 265

Pholidota loricata see *Pholidota imbricata* 265

Pholidota triotos see *Pholidota imbricata* 265

Phragmipedium 265–66

Phragmipedium besseae 265

Phragmipedium caudatum 265

Phragmipedium Don Wimber 266, *266*

Phragmipedium Eric Young 266, *266*

Phragmipedium Hybrids 266

Phragmipedium Jason Fischer 266, *266*

Phragmipedium longifolium 265, *265*

Phragmipedium Lutz Rollke 266, *266*

Phragmipedium Memoria Dick Clements 266, *266*

Phragmipedium Nitidissimum 'Raybar' 266, *266*

Phragmipedium Noirmont 'Red Albatross' 266, *266*

Phragmipedium Saint Ouen 266, *266*

Phragmipedium Sergeant Eric 266, *266*

pigeon orchid (*Dendrobium crumenatum*) 139

Pilumna see *Trichopilia* 309

Pilumna fragrans see *Trichopilia fragrans* 309

Pinelia lehmannianum see *Homalopetalum pumilio* 190, *190*

pinepink (*Bletia purpurea*) 75

pink bells (*Sarcochilus ceciliae*) 289

pink fairies (*Caladenia latifolia*) 92, *92*

pink lady's slipper (*Cypripedium acaule*) 130, *130*

Platanthera 267

Platanthera bifolia 267

Platanthera chlorantha 267

Platanthera ciliaris 267, *267*

Platanthera integra 267, *267*

Platanthera leucophaea 267

Platanthera montana see *Platanthera chlorantha* 267

Platanthera solstitialis see *Platanthera bifolia* 267

Platanthera virescens see *Platanthera chlorantha* 267

Plectorrhiza 267

Plectorrhiza tridentata 267, *267*

Pleione 268–69

Pleione Alishan 269, *269*

Pleione Britannia 269, *269*

Pleione bulbocodioides 268

Pleione El Pico 269, *269*

Pleione formosana 268, *268* 'Clare' 268, *268*

Pleione Hybrids 268–69

Pleione praecox 268

Pleione Shantung 269, *269*

Pleione Soufrière 268, *269*

Pleione Tolima 269, *269*

Pleione Tongariro 269, *269*

Pleione Versailles 269, *269*

Pleione Zeus Weinstein 269, *269*

Pleurothallis 270–71

Pleurothallis cordata 270, *270*

Pleurothallis grobyi 271

Pleurothallis immersa 270, 271

Pleurothallis imraei see *Stelis imraei* 304, *305*

Pleurothallis macroblepharis 271, *271*

Pleurothallis marthae 271, *271*

Pleurothallis ophiocephala see *Restrepiella ophiocephala* 284–85, *284*

Pleurothallis phalangifera 271, *271*

Pleurothallis praecipua 271, *271*

Pleurothallis schiedei see *Pleurothallis villosa* 271

Pleurothallis tuerckheimii 271

Pleurothallis viduata 271 'Fox Den' 271, *271*

Pleurothallis villosa 271

Podangis 272

Podangis dactyloceras 272, *272*

Pogonia 272

Pogonia ophioglossoides 272, *272*

Polychilos mannii see *Phalaenopsis mannii* 257, *257*

Polystachya 272–73

Polystachya bella 272

Polystachya gerrardii 272, *273*

Polystachya johnstonii 272, *273*

Polystachya longiscapa 272

Polystachya ottoniana 272–73, *273*

Polystachya pubescens 273 'Gleneyrie' *273*, *273*

Porroglossum 274

Porroglossum amethystinum 274

Porroglossum echidnum 274

Porroglossum meridionale 274, *274*

Porroglossum olivaceum 274, *274*

Porroglossum teaguei 274

potato orchid (*Pyrorchis nigricans*) 281, *281*

Potinara 274–75

Potinara Afternoon Delight 'Magnificent' 274, *274*

Potinara Atomic Fireball 274, *274*

Potinara (*Brassolaeliocattleya* Orange Nugget × *Potinara* Wattana Gold) 274, *275*

Potinara (*Brassolaeliocattleya* Regal Pokai × *Potinara* Pastushin's Gold) 274, *275*

Potinara Burana Beauty 274, *275*

Potinara Dal's Moon 274, *274*

Potinara Hybrids 274–75

Potinara Little Toshie 'Gold Country' 274, *275*

Potinara Little Toshie 'Lake Land' 274, *275*

Potinara Netrasiri Starbright 274, *275*

Potinara Super Nova 274, *275*

Promenaea 276

Promenaea citrina see *Promenaea xanthina* 276

Promenaea stapelioides 276

Promenaea xanthina 276

Prosthechea 276–77

Prosthechea brassavolae 276, *276*

Prosthechea chacaoensis 276, *276*

Prosthechea cochleata 276, *276*

Prosthechea crassilabia 276, *277*

Prosthechea michuacana 277, *277*

Prosthechea prismatocarpa 277, *277*

Prosthechea radiata 277, *277*

Prosthechea Sunburst 277, *277*

Pseudolaelia 278

Pseudolaelia vellozicola 278, *278*

Psychilis 278

Psychilis kraenzlinii 278

Psychilis krugii 278

Psychilis truncata 278

Psychopsis 278–79

Psychopsis kramerianum 278, *279*

Psychopsis Mendenhall 278, *278*

Psychopsis papilio 278

Psychopsis picta see *Psychopsis papilio* 278

Pteroceras hirticalcar see *Sarcochilus hirticalcar* 290, *290*

Pterostylis 280

Pterostylis curta 280, *280*

Pterostylis nutans 280, *280*

Pterostylis pedunculata 280, *280*

Pterostylis planulata 280, *280*

Pterygodium 280–81

Pterygodium hastatum 281, *281*

Ptilocnema see *Pholidota* 265

Ptilocnema bracteatum see *Pholidota imbricata* 265

purple enamel orchid (*Elythranthera brunonis*) 173, *173*

purple helmet (*Corybas diemenicus*) 111, *111*

pyramidal orchid (*Anacamptis*) 64

pyramidal orchid (*Anacamptis pyramidalis*) 64, *64*

Pyrorchis 281

Pyrorchis nigricans 281, *281*

Q

queen's lady's-slipper (*Cypripedium reginae*) 130

R

rainbow orchid (*Paphiopedilum wardii*) 247

Rangaeris 282

Rangaeris muscicola 282, *282*

Rangaeris rhipsalisocia 282

raspy root orchid (*Rhinerrhiza divitiflora*) 285, *285*

rattle beak (*Lyperanthus serratus*) 207, *207*

rattlebeaks (*Lyperanthus*) 207

rattlesnake orchid (*Goodyera*) 187

rattlesnake orchid (*Pholidota*) 265

rattlesnake orchid (*Pholidota imbricata*) 265

rattlesnake plantain (*Goodyera*) 187

red beak (*Pyrorchis nigricans*) 281, *281*

red beard orchid (*Calochilus paludosus*) 94, *94*

red fox bulbophyllum (*Bulbophyllum rufinum*) 88, *89*

red helleborine (*Cephalanthera rubra*) 103

Renantanda 282–83

Renantanda Tuanku Bainun *282*, 283

Renanthera 283

Renanthera coccinea 283

Renanthera Hybrids 283

Renanthera imschootiana 283, *283*

Renanthera monachica 283, *283*

Renanthera Monaseng 283, *283*

Renanthera Tan Keong Choon 283, *283*

Renanthera Tom Thumb 283, *283*

Restrepia 284

Restrepia antennifera 284, *284* 'Cow Hollow' 284, *284*

Restrepia caucana see *Restrepia contorta* 284, *284*

Restrepia contorta 284, *284*

Restrepia guttulata 284, *284*

Restrepia hemsleyana see *Restrepia antennifera* 284, *284*

Restrepia hemsleyana 'Cow Hollow' see *Restrepia antennifera* 'Cow Hollow' 284, *284*

Restrepia ophiocephala see *Restrepiella ophiocephala* 284–85, *284*

Restrepiella 284–85

Restrepiella ophiocephala 284–85, *284*

Rhinerrhiza 285

Rhinerrhiza divitiflora 285, *285*

Rhipidoglossum 285

Rhipidoglossum xanthopollinium 285

Rhizanthella 285

Rhizanthella slateri 285, *285*

Rhyncholaelia 285

Rhyncholaelia digbyana 285 'Mrs Chase' 285, *285*

Rhyncholaelia digbyana var. *fimbripetala* 285

Rhyncholaelia glauca 285

Rhynchostele 286

Rhynchostele bictoniensis 286, *286*

Rhynchostele cordata 286, *286*

Rhynchostele maculata 286

Rhynchostele rossii 286

Rhynchostele Stanfordiense 286, *286*

Rhynchostele uro-skinneri 286

Rhynchostylis 286

Rhynchostylis gigantea 286, *286*

Rhynchostylis retusa 286

Rimacola 286–87

Rimacola elliptica 286–87, *286*

Robiquetia 287

Robiquetia cerina 287, *287*

Robiquetia paniculata see *Robiquetia succisa* 287, *287*

Robiquetia succisa 287, *287*

robust marsh orchid (*Dactylorhiza elata*) 133

rock lily (*Dendrobium speciosum*) 148

Rodriguezia 288

Rodriguezia decora 288, *288*

Rodriguezia lanceolata 288, *288*

Rodriguezia secunda see *Rodriguezia lanceolata* 288, *288*

Rodriguezia venusta 288

rose pogonia (*Pogonia ophioglossoides*) 272, *272*

Rossioglossum 288

Rossioglossum grande 288, *288*

Rossioglossum Rawdon Jester 288, *288*

S

Saccolabiopsis 289

Saccolabiopsis armitii 289, *289*

Saccolabium calceolaris see *Gastrochilus calceolaris* 185

Saccolabium fissum see *Smitinandia micrantha* 298, *298*

Saccolabium fragrans see *Schoenorchis fragrans* 294, *295*

Saccolabium micranthum see *Smitinandia micrantha* 298, *298*

Saccolabium nebulosum see *Gastrochilus formosanus* 185

Saccolabium purpureum see *Ascoglossum purpureum* 71

Sarcanthopsis nagarensis see *Vandopsis warocqueana* 314, 315

Sarcochilus 289–91

Sarcochilus aequalis 289, *289*

Sarcochilus Armstrong 290, *291*

Sarcochilus Bobby-Dazzler 290, *291*

Sarcochilus Burgundy on Ice 'Arctic Circle' 290, *291*

Sarcochilus ceciliae 289

Sarcochilus falcatus 289

Sarcochilus First Light 290, *291*

Sarcochilus fitzgeraldii 290, *290*

Sarcochilus Fitzhart 290, *291*

Sarcochilus hartmannii 290 'Giant Frost' 290, *290* Southern form see *Sarcochilus aequalis* 289, *289*

Sarcochilus Heidi 290

Sarcochilus hillii 290

Sarcochilus hirticalcar 290, *290*

Sarcochilus Hybrids 290–91

Sarcochilus Kate 290, *291*

Sarcochilus Melba 290

Sarcochilus olivaceus 290

Sarcochilus serrulatus 290, *290*

Sarcochilus Velvet 290, *291*

Sarcoglossum see *Cirrhaea* 105

Sarcorhynchus see *Diaphananthe* 164

Sartylis 292

Sartylis Blue Knob 292, *292*

Sartylis Jannine Banks 292

Satyrium 292–93

Satyrium carneum 292

Satyrium coriifolium 292

Satyrium erectum 292

Satyrium hallackii 292, *292*

Satyrium longicauda 292, *292*

Satyrium nepalense 292–93

Satyrium pumilum 293, *293*

sawfly orchid (*Ophrys tenthredinifera*) 237

Scaphosepalum 293

Scaphosepalum amethystinum see *Porroglossum amethystinum* 274

Scaphosepalum breve 293

Scaphosepalum echidnum see *Porroglossum echidnum* 274

Scaphosepalum swertiifolium 293, *293*

Scaphosepalum verrucosum 293

Scaphyglottis 294

Scaphyglottis amethystina see *Scaphyglottis stellata* 294

Scaphyglottis cuneata see *Scaphyglottis prolifera* 294

Scaphyglottis prolifera 294

Scaphyglottis stellata 294

Scaphyglottis violacea 294, *294*

scarlet ladies' tresses (*Stenorrhynchos lanceolatum*) 305

Schistostylus 294

Schistostylus purpuratus 294, *294*

Schoenorchis 294–95

Schoenorchis densiflora see *Schoenorchis micrantha* 294

Schoenorchis fragrans 294, *295*

Schoenorchis micrantha 294

Schoenorchis pachyacris 294, *295*

Schomburgkia 294–95

Schomburgkia lueddemanniana 295, *295*

Schomburgkia superbiens 295

Schomburgkia tibicinis see *Myrmecophila tibicinis* 222, *222*

Schomburgkia undulata 295

Schomburgkia vellozicola see *Pseudolaelia vellozicola* 278, *278*

Schomburgkia weberbaueriana 295

Schroder's cattleya (*Cattleya schroderae*) 99

Scleropteris see *Cirrhaea* 105

scorpion orchid (*Arachnis*) 67

Scuticaria 296

Scuticaria hadwenii 296

Scuticaria steelei 296

Sedirea 296

Sedirea japonica 296, *296*

Seidenfadenia 296

Seidenfadenia mitrata 296

Serapias 296–97

Serapias azorica see *Serapias cordigera* 296

Serapias cordigera 296

Serapias elongata see *Serapias parviflora* 296

Serapias excavata see *Serapias lingua* 296, *296*

Serapias hirsuta see *Serapias lingua* 296, *296*

Serapias laxiflora see *Serapias parviflora* 296

Serapias lingua 296, *296*

Serapias neglecta 296, *296*

Serapias occultata see *Serapias parviflora* 296

Serapias ovalis see *Serapias cordigera* 296

Serapias parviflora 296

Serapias stenopetala see *Serapias lingua* 296, *296*

Serapias vomeracea 296, *297*

Serapias vomeracea subsp. *laxiflora* 296, *296*

showy lady's-slipper (*Cypripedium reginae*) 130

sickle-leafed arpophyllum (*Arpophyllum spicatum*) 68

Skinner's cattleya (*Cattleya skinneri*) 100, *100*

slipper orchid (*Paphiopedilum*) 239–52

small duck orchid (*Paracaleana*) 253

Smitinandia 298

Smitinandia micrantha 298, *298*

snake mouth (*Pogonia ophioglossoides*) 272, *272*

snow orchid (*Cephalanthera austiniae*) 103, *103*

Sobralia 298–99

Sobralia decora 298

Sobralia macrantha 298, *298*

Sobralia macrantha var. *alba* 298, *298*

Sobralia Mirabilis 298, *299*

Sobralia xantholeuca 298, *299*

Sobralia Yellow Kiss 299

Sophrocattleya 299

Sophrocattleya Beaufort 299

Sophrocattleya Lana Coryell 299, *299*

Sophrolaelia 299

Sophrolaelia Gratrixiae 299, *299*

Sophrolaelia Orpetii 299

Sophrolaeliocattleya 300–01

Sophrolaeliocattleya Ann Komine 300, *300*

Sophrolaeliocattleya Ann Topper *300*

Sophrolaeliocattleya Fire Lighter 300, *301*

Sophrolaeliocattleya Hazel Boyd *301*

Sophrolaeliocattleya Hazel Boyd 'Apricot Glow' 300, *301*

Sophrolaeliocattleya Hybrids 300–01

Sophrolaeliocattleya Jannine Louise 300

Sophrolaeliocattleya Jeweler's Art 300, *300*

Sophrolaeliocattleya Kevin *301*

Sophrolaeliocattleya Mahalo Jack 300, *301*

Sophrolaeliocattleya Memoria Ken Martin 300, *300*

Sophrolaeliocattleya Mine Gold 'Orchid Centre' 300, *300*

Sophrolaeliocattleya Red Elf *301*

Sophrolaeliocattleya Seagull's Mini-Cat Heaven 'Dainty Lady' *301*

Sophrolaeliocattleya Sunset Nugget 300, *301*

Sophrolaeliocattleya Trizac 300, *301*

Sophronitella 302

Sophronitella violacea 302, *302*

Sophronitis 302

Sophronitis blumenscheinii see *Laelia blumenscheinii* 195, *195*

Sophronitis cernua 302

Sophronitis cinnabarina see *Laelia cinnabarina* 196

Sophronitis coccinea 302 'Jannine' 302, *302*

Sophronitis crispa see *Laelia crispa* 196, *196*

Sophronitis crispata see *Laelia crispata* 196, *196*

Sophronitis dayana see *Laelia dayana* 196

Sophronitis grandiflora see *Sophronitis coccinea* 302

Sophronitis harpophylla see *Laelia harpophylla* 196, *196*

Sophronitis jongheana see *Laelia jongheana* 196, *196*

Sophronitis lucasiana see *Laelia longipes* 196, *196*

Sophronitis milleri see *Laelia milleri* 196, *197*

Sophronitis pumila see *Laelia pumila* 196

Sophronitis purpurata see *Laelia purpurata* 197, *197*

Sophronitis rosea see *Sophronitis wittigiana* 302

Sophronitis tenebrosa see *Laelia tenebrosa* 198, *198*

Sophronitis violacea see *Sophronitella violacea* 302, *302*

Sophronitis wittigiana 302

South American slipper orchid (*Phragmipedium*) 265–66

southern marsh orchid (*Dactylorhiza praetermissa*) 134

Spathoglottis 302

Spathoglottis plicata 302, *302*

Spathoglottis vieillardii see *Spathoglottis plicata* 302, *302*

spider orchid (*Arachnis*) 67

spider orchid (*Bonatea speciosa*) 76

spider orchid (*Brassia*) 77–79

spider orchid (*Caladenia*) 91–92

spiked thelymitra (*Thelymitra aristata*) 306, *306*

spiral sun-orchid (*Thelymitra matthewsii*) 306

Spiranthes 302–03

Spiranthes autumnalis see *Spiranthes spiralis* 303

Spiranthes cernua see *Spiranthes odorata* 302–03

Spiranthes lanceolata see *Stenorrhynchos lanceolatum* 305

Spiranthes odorata 302–03

Spiranthes orchioides see *Stenorrhynchos lanceolatum* 305

Spiranthes sinensis 303

Spiranthes spiralis 303

Stanhopea 303–04

Stanhopea anfracta 303, *303*

Stanhopea embreei 303

Stanhopea nigroviolacea 303, *303*

Stanhopea oculata 304, *304*

Stanhopea tigrina var. *nigroviolacea* see *Stanhopea nigroviolacea* 303, *303*

Stanhopea wardii 304, *304*

star orchid (*Huntleya*) 191

stately helmet (*Corybas diemenicus*) 111, *111*

Staurochilus 304

Staurochilus fasciatus 304, *304*

Staurochilus luchuensis 304, *304*

Staurochilus philippinensis see *Trichoglottis philippinensis* 309, *309*

Stauropsis see *Trichoglottis* 308–09

Stauropsis parishii see *Hygrochilus parishii* 191, *191*

Stauropsis philippinensis see *Trichoglottis philippinensis* 309, *309*

Stauropsis undulata see *Vandopsis undulata* 315, *315*

Stauropsis warocqueana see *Vandopsis warocqueana* 314, *315*

Stelis 304–05

Stelis argentata 304

Stelis imraei 304, *305*

Stenoglottis 304–05

Stenoglottis fimbriata 305

Stenoglottis longifolia 305, *305*

Stenorrhynchos 305

Stenorrhynchos lanceolatum 305

Stenorrhynchos orchioides see *Stenorrhynchos lanceolatum* 305

Stenorrhynchos speciosum 305, *305*

stream orchid (*Epipactis gigantea*) 180, 181

sun orchid (*Thelymitra*) 306

swamp orchid (*Phaius*) 255

swamp root orchid (*Epipactis*) 180–81

swan orchid (*Cycnoches*) 112–13

sword-leafed helleborine (*Cephalanthera longifolia*) 103

Symphoglossum 305

Symphoglossum sanguineum 305, *305*

T

tall bird orchid (*Chiloglottis gunnii*) 104, *104*

tangle orchid (*Plectorrhiza*) 267

tangle orchid (*Plectorrhiza tridentata*) 267, *267*

tangleroot orchid (*Plectorrhiza tridentata*) 267, *267*

Telipogon 306

Telipogon octavoi 306, *306*

tessellated rattlesnake-plantain (*Goodyera tesselata*) 187

Thelymitra 306

Thelymitra aristata 306, *306*

Thelymitra grandiflora see *Thelymitra aristata* 306, *306*

Thelymitra ixioides 306, *306*

Thelymitra matthewsii 306

thumbnail orchid (*Dockrillia linguiformis*) 168, *168*

Thunia 306–07

Thunia alba 307

Thunia marshalliana see *Thunia alba* 307

Thunia Veitchiana *306*, 307

tiger orchids (*Rossioglossum*) 288

Tolumnia 307

Tolumnia pulchella 307

Tolumnia pulchella var. *concava* 307

Tolumnia triquetra 307

Tolumnia variegata 307, *307*

tongue orchid (*Dockrillia linguiformis*) 168, *168*

tongue orchid (*Serapias*) 296–97

tongue orchid (*Serapias lingua*) 296, *296*

tongue orchid (*Serapias parviflora*) 296

Trias 307

Trias oblonga 307, *307*

Trias picta 307, *307*

Trichocentrum 308

Trichocentrum ascendens 308, *308*

Trichocentrum cebolleta 308, *308*

Trichocentrum luridum 308

Trichocentrum maculatum see *Trichocentrum pulchrum* 308

Trichocentrum pulchrum 308

Trichocentrum speciosum see *Trichocentrum pulchrum* 308

Trichocentrum splendidum 308, *308*

Trichocentrum tigrinum 308

Trichocentrum verruciferum see *Trichocentrum pulchrum* 308

Trichoglottis 308–09

Trichoglottis atropurpurea 308–09

Trichoglottis brachiata see *Trichoglottis atropurpurea* 308–09

Trichoglottis geminata 309, *309*

Trichoglottis ionosma see *Staurochilus luchuensis* 304, *304*

Trichoglottis philippinensis 309, *309*

Trichoglottis wenzelii see *Trichoglottis geminata* 309, *309*

Trichopilia 309

Trichopilia albida see *Trichopilia fragrans* 309

Trichopilia candida see *Trichopilia fragrans* 309

Trichopilia fragrans 309

Trichopilia kienastiana see *Trichopilia suavis* 309

Trichopilia lehmannii see *Trichopilia fragrans* 309

Trichopilia marginata 309 'Faye' 309, *309*

Trichopilia suavis 309

Trichopilia tortilis 309

Trigonanthe see *Dryadella* 172

Trigonanthe edwallii see *Dryadella edwallii* 172

Trigonidium 309

Trigonidium egertonianum 309, *309*

Trudelia see *Vanda* 310–13

Trudelia alpina see *Vanda alpina* 310

Trudelia cristata see *Vanda cristata* 310, *311*

Trudelia pumila see *Vanda pumila* 310, *311*

tulip orchid (*Anguloa*) 65

Tylochilus see *Cyrtopodium* 132

U

underground orchid (*Rhizanthella*) 285

undertaker orchid (*Pyrorchis nigricans*) 281, *281*

upside-down orchid (*Stanhopea*) 303–04

V

Vanda 310–13

Vanda alpina 310

Vanda Bangkok Pink *312*, 313

Vanda coerulea 310, *311*

Vanda coerulescens 310, *310* 'Magnificent' 310, *310*

Vanda cristata 310, *311*

Vanda denisoniana 310, *311*

Vanda Gordon Dillon *312*, 313
Vanda (Gordon Dillon × Robert Fuchs) *312*
Vanda Happy Smile *312*, 313
Vanda hindsii 310
Vanda hookeriana see *Papilionanthe hookeriana* 253
Vanda Hybrids 312–13
Vanda javierae 310, *311*
Vanda lamellata 310, *311*
Vanda lamellata var. *boxallii* 310
Vanda lowii see *Dimorphorchis lowii* *164*, 165
Vanda Lumpini Red 'AM' *312*
Vanda luzonica 310
Vanda Manisaki *312*, 313
Vanda Marlie Dolera *312*, 313
Vanda Miss Joaquim see *Papilionanthe* Miss Joaquim 253, *253*
Vanda parishii see *Hygrochilus parishii* 191, *191*
Vanda parviflora see *Vanda testacea* 310
Vanda Pat Delight *312*, 313
Vanda pumila 310, *311*
Vanda Reverend Masao Yamada 313, *313*
Vanda Robert's Delight *312*, 313
Vanda Rothschildiana 313
Vanda sanderiana 310, *311*
Vanda Sansai Blue *312*, 313
Vanda Tailor Blue *313*
Vanda teres see *Papilionanthe teres* 253
Vanda testacea 310
Vanda tricolor 310, *311*
Vanda undulata see *Vandopsis undulata* 315, *315*
Vandopsis 314–15
Vandopsis lowii see *Dimorphorchis lowii* *164*, 165
Vandopsis parishii see *Hygrochilus parishii* 191, *191*
Vandopsis undulata 315, *315*
Vandopsis warocqueana 314, 315
Vanilla 315
Vanilla planifolia 315
Vanilla polylepis 315, *315*
Vascostylis 315
Vascostylis Pine Rivers 'Pink' 315, *315*
veined helmet orchid (*Corybas diemenicus*) 111, *111*
violet helleborine (*Epipactis viridiflora*) 181
virgin orchid (*Caularthron bicornutum*) 103
Vuylstekeara 316
Vuylstekeara Cambria 316, *316*
Vuylstekeara Edna 'Stamperland' 316, *316*
Vuylstekeara Ephyra 316, *316*
Vuylstekeara Everglades Promise 316, *316*
Vuylstekeara Hybrids 316
Vuylstekeara Linda Isler 316, *316*
Vuylstekeara Memoria Hanna Lassfolk 316, *316*
Vuylstekeara Memoria Mary Kavanaugh 316, *316*

W
wax-lip orchid (*Glossodia*) 186–87

waxy sarcochilus (*Sarcochilus aequalis*) 289, *289*
white feather orchid (*Dendrobium aemulum*) 136
white helleborine (*Cephalanthera damasonium*) 103
white scorpion orchid (*Arachnis hookeriana*) 67
white spider orchid (*Arachnis hookeriana*) 67
Wilsonara 317
Wilsonara Athol Bell 317, *317*
Wilsonara Blazing Lustre 317, *317*
Wilsonara Dorset Gold 317, *317*
Wilsonara Firecracker 317, *317*
Wilsonara Hybrids 317
Wilsonara Kendrick Williams 'Rosslow' 317, *317*
Wilsonara Russiker Tiger 317, *317*
Woodwardara Adelaide Alive see *Neopabstopetalum* Adelaide Alive 224, *224*
Woodwardara Beverley Lou see *Neopabstopetalum* Beverley Lou 224, *224*

X
Xylobium 318
Xylobium carnosum see *Xylobium variegatum* 318, *318*
Xylobium scabrilingua see *Xylobium variegatum* 318, *318*
Xylobium squalens see *Xylobium variegatum* 318, *318*
Xylobium supinum see *Xylobium variegatum* 318, *318*
Xylobium variegatum 318, *318*

Y
yellow bee orchid (*Ophrys lutea*) 237
yellow lady's-slipper (*Cypripedium parviflorum*) 130

Z
Zelenkoara see *Howeara* 190
Zygocolax see *Zygopabstia* 318
Zygopabstia 318
Zygopabstia Gumeracha 318, *318*
Zygopetalum 318–20
Zygopetalum Alan Greatwood 319, *319*
Zygopetalum Blanchetown 319, *319*
Zygopetalum crinitum 318–19, *318*
Zygopetalum gramineum see *Kefersteinia graminea* 194
Zygopetalum Hybrids 319–20
Zygopetalum Imagination 320, *320*
Zygopetalum intermedium 318, 319
Zygopetalum Kiwi Dusk 320, *320*
Zygopetalum lindeniae see *Zygosepalum lindeniae* 320
Zygopetalum mackayi *318*, 319
Zygopetalum maxillare 319
Zygopetalum meleagris see *Huntleya meleagris* 191
Zygopetalum (106 'Royale Romp' × Redvale 'Heir Apparent') 319, *319*
Zygopetalum Titanic 320, *320*
Zygosepalum 320
Zygosepalum lindeniae 320
Zygostates 320
Zygostates alleniana 320
Zygostates lunata 320

Photography
David Banks, Chris Bell, Rob Blakers, Lorraine Blyth, Greg Bourke, Ken Brass, Geoff Bryant, Derek Butcher, Claver Carroll, Leigh Clapp, Mike Comb, Grant Dixon, Heather Donovan, e-garden Ltd, Bruce Elder, Katie Fallows, Derek Fells, Stuart Owen Fox, Richard Francis, Robert Gibson, William Grant, Denise Greig, Barry Griffith, Barry Grossman, Gil Hanly, Ivy Hansen, Dennis Harding, Jack Hobbs, Neil Holmes, Paul Huntley, Richard I'Anson, Jason Ingram, Steve Johnson, David Keith Jones, Ionas Kaltenbach, Willie Kempen, Colin Kerr, Robert M. Knight, Carol Knoll, Albert Kuhnigk, Stan Lamond, Mike Langford, Gary Lewis, Geoff Longford, Stirling Macoboy, John McCann, David McGonigal, Richard McKenna, Ron Moon, Eberhard Morell, Barry Myers-Rice, Steve Newall, Connall Oosterbrock, Ron Parsons, Luke Pellatt, Larry Pitt, Craig Potton, Janet Price, Geof Prigge, Nick Rains, Christo Reid, Howard Rice, Jamie Robertson, Tony Rodd, Rolf Ulrich Roesler, Luke Saffigna, Don Skirrow, Raoul Slater, Michael Snedic, Peter Solness, Ken Stepnell, Warren Steptoe, Angus Stewart, Oliver Strewe, J. Peter Thoeming, David Titmuss, Wayne Turville, Georg Uebelhart, Sharyn Vanderhorst, Kim Westerskov, Murray White, Vic Widman, Brent Wilson, Geoff Woods, Gary Yong Gee, Grant Young, James Young

Produced by
Global Book Publishing Pty Ltd
1/181 High Street, Willoughby,
NSW 2068, Australia
Phone (612) 9967 3100
Fax (612) 9967 5891
Email rightsmanager@globalpub.com.au
Photographs from the Global Photo Library
© Global Book Publishing Pty Ltd 2005
except for page 27 top right: The Art Archive/ Eileen Tweedy; page 28 top right: The Art Archive
Text © Global Book Publishing Pty Ltd 2005

Global Book Publishing would like to thank the following nurseries:
Dark Star Orchids, Bowraville
Easy Orchids, Woodburn
Hills District Orchids, Seven Hills
P & R Orchids, Port Macquarie
Royale Orchids, Peats Ridge
Smokey Cape Orchids, South West Rocks
Tinonee Orchid Nursery, Tinonee

Photographers
Global Book Publishing would be pleased to hear from photographers interested in supplying photographs.